We fought through hell and fire to give freedom to you.
FRSB give with confidence
Please donate at erskine.org.uk or call 0300 123 1203
ERSKINE
Caring for veterans since 1916
Erskine is the trading name of Erskine Hospital. Scottish Charity No. SC006609

MAKE YOUR MONEY GO FURTHER IN THE FIGHT TO END POVERTY

POVERTY

Christian Aid partners are making a real difference for people living in some of the world's poorest communities. You can support this work by joining the Christian Aid Partnership Scheme, which helps to fund projects in Africa, Asia and Latin America.

By joining the Partnership Scheme, your church can make a connection with the life-changing work of one of our partner organisations overseas. These experienced partners are helping to give some of the world's poorest communities power over their lives and a way out of poverty. If you can raise at least £5,000 over the next two years, for every £1 that you give at least £3 more will go to the project, hugely increasing the impact of your donation.

To find out more, call **Wendy Young** on **0141 241 6137** or email **wyoung@christian-aid.org**

Christian Aid/Karen Lobo-Morell

Stay in touch with Christian Aid Scotland

- Sign up to the Scottish e-zine to receive news and events from across Scotland in your inbox (to register email **scotland@christian-aid.org**)
- Visit our website **christianaid.org.uk/scotland**
- Are you on Facebook? If so, please visit the Christian Aid Scotland page.
- Call us on **0141 221 7475**

Christian Aid, Pentagon Centre, 36 Washington Street, Glasgow G3 8AZ

K2 SPECIALIST SERVICES (UK) LTD
FOR PROJECTS REQUIRING A RANGE OF MASONRY, WOODWORK & ROOFING SKILLS
COST EFFECTIVE SOLUTIONS FOR IDENTIFYING AND DEALING WITH STRUCTURAL FAILURES AT HEIGHT
OUR MODERN APPROACH TO HEALTH & SAFETY, CLEAR COMMUNICATION & ATTENTION TO DETAIL IS YOUR PROFESSIONAL ASSURANCE OF QUALITY
Working with..
HISTORIC SCOTLAND
Maintaining Monuments of National Importance
LIGHTNING PROTECTION SYSTEMS
SCOTTISH LIME CENTRE
K2 SPECIALIST SERVICES (UK) LTD
TEL: 0131 440 9700
FAX: 0131 440 9701
E-MAIL: info:@k2steeplejacks.com
WEB: www.k2steeplejacks.co.uk
K2
SPECIALIST SERVICES (UK) LTD

The Right Reverend A. David K. Arnott MA BD

MODERATOR

The Church of Scotland YEAR BOOK 2011/2012

Editor

Rev. Ronald S. Blakey
MA BD MTh

Published on behalf of
THE CHURCH OF SCOTLAND
by SAINT ANDREW PRESS
121 George Street, Edinburgh EH2 4YN

THE OFFICES OF THE CHURCH

121 George Street
Edinburgh EH2 4YN

Tel: 0131-225 5722
Fax: 0131-220 3113
Website: www.churchofscotland.org.uk/

Office Hours: Monday–Friday 9:00am–5:00pm
Facilities Manager: Carole Tait 0131-240 2214

THE COUNCILS OF THE CHURCH

The following five Councils of the Church operate from the Church Offices, 121 George Street, Edinburgh EH2 4YN (Tel: 0131-225 5722):

- The Council of Assembly
- The Church and Society Council
- The Ministries Council — E-mail: ministries@cofscotland.org.uk
- The Mission and Discipleship Council — E-mail: mandd@cofscotland.org.uk; Website: www.churchofscotland.org.uk
- The World Mission Council — Answerphone: 0131-240 2231; Fax: 0131-226 6121; E-mail: world@cofscotland.org.uk; Website: www.churchofscotland.org.uk/worldmission

The Social Care Council (Crossreach) operates from Charis House, 47 Milton Road East, Edinburgh EH15 2SR
Tel: 0131-657 2000
Fax: 0131-657 5000
E-mail: info@crossreach.org.uk
Website: www.crossreach.org.uk

SCOTTISH CHARITY NUMBERS

The Church of Scotland: unincorporated Councils and Committees	SC011353
The Church of Scotland General Trustees	SC014574
The Church of Scotland Investors Trust	SC022884
The Church of Scotland Trust	SC020269

(For the Scottish Charity Numbers of congregations, see Section 7)

First published in 2011 by SAINT ANDREW PRESS, 121 George Street, Edinburgh EH2 4YN on behalf of THE CHURCH of SCOTLAND

ISBN 978 0 86153 623 8

It is the Publisher's policy to only use papers that are natural and recyclable and that have been manufactured from timber grown in renewable, properly managed forests. All of the manufacturing processes of the papers are expected to conform to the environmental regulations of the country of origin.

British Library Cataloguing in Publication Data
A catalogue record for this book is available from the British Library.

Printed and bound by Bell and Bain Ltd, Glasgow

QUICK DIRECTORY

A.C.T.S. 01259 216980
Bridgeton, St Francis-in-the-East Church House 0141-554 8045
Carberry 0131-665 3135
Christian Aid London 020 7620 4444
Christian Aid Scotland 0141-221 7475
Church of Scotland Insurance Co. Ltd 0131-220 4119
Glasgow Lodging House Mission 0141-552 0285
Media Relations Team (Press Office) 0131-240 2204/2268
Pension Trustees (E-mail: pensions@cofscotland.org.uk) 0131-240 2255
Priority Areas Office 0141-248 2905
Safeguarding Office (item 31 in Assembly Committee list) 0131-240 2256
Scottish Churches Parliamentary Office 0131-558 8137
Scottish Storytelling Centre/John Knox House 0131-556 9579
Trust Housing Association Ltd (formerly Kirk Care) 0131-661 1793
Year Book Editor 01899 229226

Pulpit Supply: Fee and Expenses

Details of the current fee and related expenses in respect of Pulpit Supply will be found as the last item in number 3 (the Ministries Council) on page 10.

Rehoboth Children's Home – Philippines

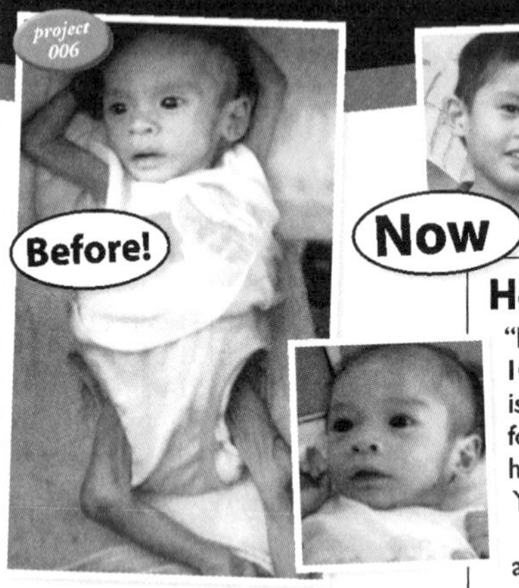

John in the loving arms of his adopted parents at his new home in Michigan.

John Ray Carlo on admission 19th July 2005. Right, after a few weeks of loving care, John responds and slowly gains weight.

Help a wee bairn in the Philippines

"For more than 15 years Siloam has saved more than 100 abandoned babies' lives in the Philippines. Siloam is currently working alongside Rehoboth to rescue forsaken and rejected little ones and find them new homes with loving couples worldwide.
Your gift is needed right now, your love does matter!!
Has your heart been touched? Please write or phone and help Siloam rescue another child today."

free phone 08000-27-79-17
email info@siloam.org.uk
website www.siloam.org.uk
and scroll down to project 006

…and for your visual aids visit website www.decadeministries.co.uk

to find out more please contact Siloam Christian Ministries, PO box No. 4198 Leamington Spa CV31 9BP

Registered under the Charities Act 1960 No. 327396 Registered in the United Kingdom No. 2104165

SILOAM
CHRISTIAN MINISTRIES

J & M SEWING SERVICE LTD

1 Charlotte Square,
Newcastle upon Tyne NE1 4XF

'Quality is not expensive........ it's priceless'

By Appointment to
Her Majesty The Queen
Manufacturers of Clerical Robes

CASSOCKS + SURPLICES
ALBS + COTTAS
CLERICAL BLOUSES
CLERICAL SHIRTS
STOLES
CLOAKS
CHOIR ROBES
VERGERS ROBES
VESTMENTS
BANNERS + FRONTALS

you name it,
we probably make it.

Visit our Website
www.jandmsewing.com
or ask for our free catalogue
Tel. 0191 232 9589 Fax. 0191 230 1215
Email jandmsewing@btconnect.com

OUR MOTTO ... "THERE'S ALWAYS TIME FOR COURTESY!"

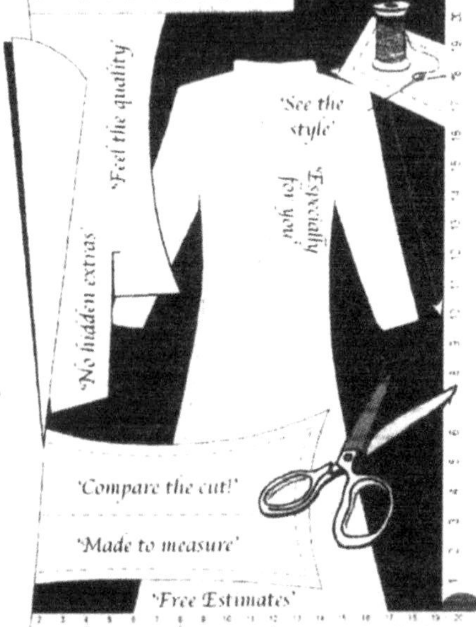

Established by
Joyce Davison & Maureen Waterston in 1980

CONTENTS

All correspondence regarding the *Year Book* should be sent to
The Editor, *Church of Scotland Year Book*,
Saint Andrew Press, 121 George Street, Edinburgh EH2 4YN
Fax: 0131-220 3113
[E-mail: yearbookeditor@cofscotland.org.uk]

GENERAL ASSEMBLY OF 2012
The General Assembly of 2012 will convene on
Saturday, 19th May 2012

FROM THE MODERATOR

It is perhaps an unlikely place to trace the history of the Church of Scotland, but the *Year Book* allows the reader to do just that. For example, if you happen to pick up an old copy, you will find it brings into focus the names of lists of ministers, missionaries, deacons and countless others who have served the Church with such faithfulness in their day. It also reminds us of congregations, and Presbyteries too, whose names are no longer in common usage and therefore are no longer familiar to us. People interpret these changes in many ways. Some look at them wistfully as a reminder of halcyon days. I prefer to think of them as illustrating the changing nature of the Church of Scotland and as a record of how it has adapted to the world it serves.

The Presbytery of Eastern Himalaya, the Presbytery of the Gold Coast and the Presbytery of Punjab and North West Frontier Province speak not just of colonial days now locked firmly in the past. They don't just talk of days now gone. They also serve to remind us of how the Church of Scotland helped to sow the seeds of the Christian faith in these distant lands and then has stood back, proud to see indigenous worshippers taking control of their own Church. Partnership has become the watchword as we now walk together in faith with so many churches around the world that still look to the Church of Scotland as the mother Church. The strength of a church never lies in numbers alone. It lies in its commitment to the gospel of Jesus Christ. It lies in the quality of the service it offers. It lies in the living stones we see around us in Scotland and abroad.

Times have changed, and life has changed, and we have moved on, but the value of the *Year Book* remains a constant. It is so much more than an in-house telephone directory. It is an up-to-date record of who we are and where we are; it is a reminder that, in these changing times, the influence of the Church is still nationwide and far beyond.

That influence is due to some of the names listed. It is due to the continuing witness of the congregations that are named – congregations made up of people who, through their Sunday worship and daily work, bear witness to the Risen Christ. This edition, in other words, is history in the making. It is being written by those whose names you can read for yourself and by countless others.

I have known Ronald Blakey for many years now, and he has always impressed me with his encyclopaedic knowledge of the Church of Scotland and its personnel. There is nobody more suited, nor more able, than Ronald for this meticulously detailed task. The Church is in Ronald's debt, and we remain grateful to him as we write this latest chapter in the history of our Church.

Rev. A. David K. Arnott

ON MHODERATOR

'S dòcha gur e àite neo-àbhaisteach a tha seo airson rannsachadh a dhèanamh air eachdraidh Eaglais na h-Alba, ach tha an *Leabhar Bliadhnail* a' toirt cothrom don leughadair an dearbh rud sin a dhèanamh. Mar eisimpleir, ma thèid agad air seann leth-bhreac a thogail chì thu gu bheil e a' toirt fa chomhair ar n-inntinn nan ainmean a tha air clàir nam ministearan, nam miseanaraidhean, nan diacon agus feadhainn eile nach gabh àireamh a rinn seirbheis don Eaglais gu fìor dhìleas nan latha. Tha e cuideachd a' toirt gu ar cuimhne choitheanalan, agus chlèirean cuideachd, aig an robh ainmean nach eil gan cleachdadh anns a' chumantas an-diugh, agus mar sin air nach eil sinn eòlach. Bidh daoine a' mìneachadh nan atharrachaidhean sin ann an iomadh dòigh eadar-dhealaichte. Bidh cuid a' coimhead orra le ionndrain mar chuimhneachan air linn an àigh. 'S fheàrr leamsa a bhith a' smaoineachadh orra mar shùileachan air mar a tha gnè Eaglais na h-Alba ag atharrachadh agus mar chunntas air an dòigh anns a bheil i ga cumadh fhèin ris an t-saoghal dam bheil i a' dèanamh seirbheis.

Chan ann a-mhàin mu làithean na h-impireachd a tha a' buntainn ri seann eachdraidh a tha Clèir Taobh-siar Himalaya, Clèir a' Chòrsa Oir, Clèir a' Phunjab agus Roinn Crìoch an Ear-thuath. Chan eil iad dìreach a' labhairt mu làithean a dh'aom. Tha iad cuideachd a' cur nar cuimhne mar a chuidich Eaglais na h-Alba ann a bhith a' cur sìol a' chreidimh Chrìosdail ann an tìrean cèine agus a ghabh ceum air ais, moiteil gu robh luchd-adhraidh a bhuineadh don àite a' gabhail seilbh air an Eaglais aca fhèin. 'S e 'co-roinn' ar facal-suaicheantais agus sinn a-nis ag imeachd ann an creideamh ann an caidreachas ri iomadh eaglais air feadh an t-saoghail a tha fhathast a' coimhead air Eaglais na h-Alba mar an Eaglais a thug breith dhaibh. Chan ann a-mhàin ann an àireamhan a tha neart eaglais an co-sheasamh. 'S ann na dìlseachd do shoisgeul Iosa Crìosd a tha a neart an co-sheasamh. Tha e an co-sheasamh anns na clachan beò a chì sinn mun cuairt oirnn ann an Alba agus thall thairis.

Thàinig atharrachadh air na linntean, agus thàinig atharrachadh air ar beatha, agus tha sinn air gluasad air adhart, ach tha an luach a tha anns an *Leabhar Bhliadhnail* gun atharrachadh. 'S e barrachd air clàr-fòn a bhuineas don bhuidhinn againn a tha seo; 's e a tha ann ach iomradh a tha a' buntainn ris an latha an-diugh air cò sinn agus càit a bheil sinn: tha e a' cur nar cuimhne gu bheil buaidh aig an eaglais fhathast air beatha na rìoghachd agus mòran nas fharsainge na sin.

'S ann mar thoradh air cuid de na h-ainmean a tha air an clàradh a tha a' bhuaidh seo. Tha a' bhuaidh mar thoradh air fianais shìor-leantainneach nan coitheanalan tha air an clàradh – coitheanalan anns a bheil daoine a tha tren adhradh aca gach Sàbaid agus nam beatha làitheil a' dèanamh fianais air a' Chrìosd a tha air èirigh. Ga chur ann an dòigh eile, 's e a tha anns an deasachadh seo den leabhar ach eachdraidh ga cruthachadh. Tha an eachdraidh sin ga sgrìobhadh le feadhainn a dh'fhaodas an ainmean a bhith air an leughadh leatsa agus le cuid eile nach gabh àireamh.

'S fhada bho chuir mi eòlas an toiseach air Raghnall Blakey, agus tha e an còmhnaidh a' cur iongnaidh na tha e aige de dh'fhiosrachadh farsaing domhainn mu Eaglais na h-Alba agus mu na daoine a tha ceangailte rithe. Chan eil duine eile ann a tha nas fhreagarraiche, no nas comasaiche, na Raghnall gu bhith a' gabhail os làimh na h-obrach seo a tha cho cùramach agus cho mionaideach. Tha an Eaglais fo fhiachan do Raghnall agus tha sinn fìor thaingeil dha agus sinn a' sgrìobhadh na caibideil ùir seo ann an eachdraidh ar n-Eaglais.

An t-Urr. A. Daibhidh K. Arnott

FROM THE EDITOR

Welcome to the first edition of the *Year Book* published by Hymns Ancient and Modern. This highly esteemed publisher of *Church Times*, with a pedigree stretching back some 150 years, has in the past year added Saint Andrew Press to its already impressive list of imprints which include SCM Press, Canterbury Press and Church House Publishing. In these days of uncertainty for many in the book world, it is reassuring to have the support and encouragement of this very experienced player.

Over the past year, it has been good as always to receive from users of the *Year Book* letters and e-mails written with the aim of ensuring that each succeeding edition is as accurate and up to date as possible. No less interesting of course are those that indicate areas where a lack of information can cause frustration. For example:

- There has been increasing correspondence from vacant congregations' Nominating Committees. Among requests emanating from that source are: the listing, where appropriate, of women ministers' maiden names or previous married names 'so that we can track them'; a requirement that women ministers should indicate with a Mrs or Miss their marital status; and the inclusion for each minister of his/her year of birth.
- There is frustration at the fact that, while parish ministers are expected to list their home addresses and telephone numbers, a number of those in non-parochial appointments 'shelter' behind their business address and number so that out-of-hours contact can be one-way only. Funeral undertakers are not alone in registering disquiet that some manse telephones appear to be diverted permanently to answering machines.
- The inclusion of post-nominal letters continues to be a source of irritation. Some would have them all discontinued; others wish a fairly savage pruning so that only 'relevant' qualifications are shown; and there has been a plea for the *Year Book* to include a dictionary of such abbreviations.

The above points are noted; it is probably neither possible nor politic to do more.

Several correspondents are in touch at least annually. One of those this year felt compelled to return to a concern he had raised previously, namely the Editor's lack of discipline in the use of colons and semicolons. It is entirely likely that this grievous shortcoming would have been kept out of the glare of publicity had attention not been drawn to the fact that, in an English college chapel around 1970, a thought-provoking sermon was delivered on 'the punctuational aspect' of these words in St Matthew's Gospel chapter 25: 'well done, thou good and faithful servant: enter thou into the joy of thy Lord'. The sermon's three points stemmed from the different mid-text punctuation marks found in the Authorised Version, the Revised Standard Version and the New English Bible.

The New English Bible inserts an exclamation mark, implying surprise that even the most saintly of mortals could be worthy of such a divine accolade. The Authorised Version, as quoted above, uses the colon, suggesting that the second half of the text does relate to or depend on the first part and that entry to the Kingdom is, in measure at least, 'reward' for a life well lived. The Revised Standard Version favours a semicolon, indicating that there is a clear break between the two parts of the text and that the gift of eternal life is down to God's all-embracing forgiveness and mercy.

While not doubting that such a sermon was preached in those more grimly grammatical days, the sceptic in us might question whether the anecdote that traditionally accompanies the reporting of it was truly as instantaneous as represented and not a later accretion. For all that, it is worth repeating. It is alleged that, in the vestibule at the close of the service, one of the worshippers offered this advice to the preacher: 'if, when you reach the pearly gates, you hear that verdict passed on your life, ask for it in writing, and then you will know for certain where the truth lies'.

One of the sessions at an in-service course for ministers south of the Border was to be on 'stress in the ministry'. Participants were asked to come prepared to outline a form of relaxation that they enjoyed, the conditions being that it had to be possible to indulge in it without leaving one's favourite armchair, that it would afford gentle mental or intellectual stimulation but without the merest trace of matters theological or ecclesiastical, and that it would not require a mobile phone, a computer or the Internet. (Among the answers given was 'reading one of my curate's sermons'.)

Had this Editor been invited to contribute, he might well have offered the pastime of 'subtitling'. One of the undoubted marvels of modern communication is the ability that television boffins have to render almost instantaneously in subtitles what a television newsreader or reporter has said live and unscripted to camera. It is a quite immeasurable boon to the hard of hearing. It can also provide an intriguing and, yes, a very relaxing game for the viewer who wants peace and quiet together with gentle mental activity. Much of the time, with the sound switched off, the subtitles are clear, intelligible and accurate – but just occasionally the machines find difficulty in identifying at once some unusual word or name, sometimes with challenging and amusing results. During a spell of wintry weather, for example, the subtitles confused time with depth and warned us to 'expect fifteen centuries of snow'. With mounting trouble in Egypt and concerns for the safety of traffic using its famous canal, our Foreign Secretary was seen to warn Britons to 'avoid all non-essential trips to sewers'. From the world of football, two classics stick in the mind. There was the footballer who was making a more rapid recovery from injury than expected: 'it is due', said the subtitle, 'to twice daily fizz yo'. Was this a new high-energy drink? No, it was subtitle speak for the popular abbreviation of 'physiotherapy'. Before a celebrated Rangers striker began to talk Turkey, he was weighing up the relative charms of Birmingham and Florence, where, we read, 'Kenny Miller is wanted by Florrie and Tina'. Discussing the merits of this pastime, a coffee-table companion wondered what the subtitling machinery would make of some of our Church's special words. 'Moderator' seemed a good word to choose for a trial run – and someone who operates that machinery for a living agreed to check it out for us. Back came word that the first-off attempt rendered it as 'mauled or ate her'.

Reflecting on an edition of BBC Television's *Antiques Roadshow* from Saltaire near Bradford, a group of ministers sighed wistfully for the good old days when Health and Safety regulations were not as all-pervasive as they now are. The programme had featured an aged but remarkably resilient rocking horse, able comfortably to accommodate three young riders. Sadly, it was now for show only because of such regulations. Speculation began to run riot about what next might be put off-limits – until one of the group brought matters crashing back down to earth, suggesting ruefully that he would favour a regulation forbidding ministers to engage in public dialogue with children during worship. As was his wont, he had begun his words to the children one Sunday with what he thought was an innocent question: 'what can you tell me about Dennis the Menace?' His expectation had been that one of the youngsters would know that the character of that name had now appeared in *The Beano* for no less than sixty years. Certainly, a hand shot up very speedily – but the voice that accompanied it said: 'That's what my mummy calls you'. (To thwart any would-be Sherlock Holmes and render mute scurrilous gossips in at least a few parishes, it should at once be made clear that the actual name of the minister thus labelled is not 'Dennis'.)

Across a crowded '121' vestibule, a shout rang out: 'Is your new publisher going to give the *Year Book* a new name?' The thought had never crossed the editorial mind – but, if it did or ever had to, what options might there be? A somewhat cursory look at similar publications offered 'Almanac', 'Directory', 'Handbook', 'Vade Mecum' and something incorporating the words 'Who's Who'. On later not-very-serious reflection, the thought occurred that, bearing in mind the extent to which the *Year Book* is an offering of named personnel, the new publisher might understand if the eventual title was 'Church of Scotland Hims and Hers, ancient and modern'.

Ronald S. Blakey
July 2011

SECTION 1

Assembly Councils, Committees, Departments and Agencies

INDEX OF ASSEMBLY COUNCILS, COMMITTEES, DEPARTMENTS AND AGENCIES

[Note: Years, where given, indicate the year of appointment]

1. THE COUNCIL OF ASSEMBLY

The voting members of the Council of Assembly act as the Charity Trustees for the Unincorporated Councils and Committees of the General Assembly: Scottish Charity No. SC011353.

Remit (as amended May 2011)
The Council of Assembly shall be a standing Committee of the General Assembly, to which it shall be directly accountable and to which it shall report through its Convener. The General Assembly has conferred on the Council the powers as described in the following remit and in particular the powers of supervision of its Agencies (said Agencies being as defined in the Appendix) in the matters as detailed therein.

Membership
The Council shall comprise the following:

1. Convener, Vice-Convener and ten members appointed by the General Assembly on the Report of the Nomination Committee.
2. The Conveners of the Councils, namely Church and Society, Ministries, Mission and Discipleship, Social Care and World Mission together with the Convener of the Panel on Review and Reform.
3. The Secretaries of the following Councils, namely Church and Society, Ministries, Mission and Discipleship, Social Care and World Mission, all with a right to speak on matters affecting the interest of their Council, but not to vote or make a motion.
4. The Principal Clerk, the General Treasurer and the Solicitor of the Church without a right to vote or make a motion.
5. The Secretary to the Council of Assembly without a right to vote or make a motion.
6. The Ecumenical Officer, the Head of Communications and the Head of Human Resources and Information Technology to be in attendance without a right to vote or make a motion.

Remit and Powers

1. To advise the General Assembly on matters of reorganisation and structural change, including adjustments to the membership and remits of relevant Agencies of the General Assembly.
2. To keep under review the central administration of the Church, with particular regard to resolving issues of duplication of resources.
3. To monitor, evaluate and co-ordinate the work of the Agencies of the General Assembly, within the context of policy determined by the Assembly.
4. To advise the General Assembly on the relative importance of work being undertaken by its various Agencies.
5. To receive reports from, offer guidance to and issue instructions to Agencies of the General Assembly as required from time to time on matters of management, organisation and administration.
6. To oversee the implementation and development of the Co-ordinated Communication Strategy across the Church.
7. To determine policy in relation to:
   (a) the teaching and promotion of Christian stewardship throughout the Church;
   (b) Ministries and Mission Contributions from congregations, subject to the approval of Regulations by the General Assembly.

8. To determine annually the stipend rate, having regard to the recommendation thereanent of the Ministries Council, said determination to be made by the voting members of the Council of Assembly with the exception of those members in receipt of either a salary or stipend from the Parish Ministries Fund.
9. To bring recommendations to the General Assembly concerning the total amount of the Church's Co-ordinated Budget for the Parish Ministries Fund and the Mission and Renewal Fund for the following financial year, and to determine the allocation of the budget for the Mission and Renewal Fund among the relevant Agencies of the General Assembly and Ecumenical Bodies.
10. To prepare and present to the General Assembly an indicative Rolling Budget for the following five financial years.
11. To receive and distribute unrestricted legacies and donations among the Agencies of the General Assembly with power to specify the use to which the same are to be applied.
12. To approve and submit annually to the General Assembly the audited Report and Financial Statements of the Unincorporated Councils and Committees of the General Assembly.
13. To determine the types and rates of expenses which may be claimed by members serving on Councils, Committees and Statutory Corporations.
14. Through its oversight of the Stewardship and Finance Department, to be responsible for:
    (a) providing support to Presbyteries and congregations in the teaching and promotion of Christian stewardship;
    (b) determining with Presbyteries the Ministries and Mission Contributions required annually from congregations;
    (c) providing assistance to Presbyteries and congregations in adhering to financial standards required by charity law and by Regulations of the General Assembly;
    (d) setting standards of financial management and providing financial services for the Councils and Committees, Statutory Corporations and other Agencies of the General Assembly.
15. To consider and decide on proposals from Agencies of the General Assembly to purchase heritable property or any other asset (except investments) valued in excess of £50,000 or lease any heritable property where the annual rental exceeds £25,000 per annum, declaring that no Agency save those referred to in section 24 hereof shall proceed to purchase or lease such property without prior approval from the Council.
16. To consider and decide on proposals from Agencies of the General Assembly, save those referred to in section 24 hereof, to sell or lease for a period in excess of five years or otherwise dispose of any heritable property, or sell or otherwise dispose of any asset (except investments) valued in excess of £50,000, held by or on behalf of that Agency, with power to allocate all or part of the sale or lease proceeds to another Agency or Agencies in terms of section 18 hereof.
17. To consider and decide on proposals from Agencies of the General Assembly to enter into an agreement or contract (with the exception of contracts of employment or those relating to property transactions) with a total actual or potential financial commitment in excess of £50,000, declaring that no Agency shall proceed to enter into such an agreement or contract without prior approval from the Council.
18. To reallocate, following upon consultation with the Agency or Agencies affected, unrestricted funds held by or on behalf of any of the Agencies of the General Assembly to another Agency or Agencies with power to specify the use to which the same are to be applied.
19. To determine staffing and resourcing requirements of Agencies of the General Assembly, including inter-Departmental sharing or transfer of staff, in accordance with policies drawn

up by the Council of Assembly in line with priorities approved by the General Assembly, it being declared that the term 'staffing' shall not include those appointed or employed to serve in particular Parishes or overseas or by the Social Care Council in service-provision facilities around the country.

20. To consult with the relative Councils and Agencies in their appointment of Council Secretaries to the Church and Society, Ministries, Mission and Discipleship, Social Care and World Mission Councils, to appoint the Ecumenical Officer, the Head of Stewardship, the Head of Communications and the Head of Human Resources and Information Technology and to nominate individuals to the General Assembly for appointment to the offices of Principal Clerk of the General Assembly, Depute Clerk of the General Assembly, Secretary to the Council of Assembly, General Treasurer of the Church and Solicitor of the Church.
21. To attend to the general interests of the Church in matters which are not covered by the remit of any other Agency.
22. To deal with urgent issues arising between meetings of the General Assembly, provided that (a) these do not fall within the jurisdiction of the Commission of Assembly or of any Presbytery or Kirk Session, (b) they are not of a legislative or judicial nature and (c) any action taken in terms of this clause shall be reported to the next General Assembly.
23. To encourage all Agencies of the General Assembly to work ecumenically wherever possible and to have regard to the international, evangelical and catholic nature of the Church.
24. For the avoidance of doubt, sections 15 and 16 shall not apply to the Church of Scotland General Trustees, the Church of Scotland Housing and Loan Fund for Retired Ministers and Widows and Widowers of Ministers and the Ministries Council Emerging Ministries Task Group, all of which may deal with heritable property and other assets without the approval of the Council.

Appendix to Remit

For the purposes only of this remit, the term 'Agencies' shall mean the following bodies being Standing Committees of the General Assembly, namely:

- The following Councils: Church and Society, Ministries, Mission and Discipleship, Social Care, World Mission.
- The following Committees: Assembly Arrangements, Central Services, Chaplains to Her Majesty's Forces, Ecumenical Relations, Legal Questions, Panel on Review and Reform, Parish Development Fund, Safeguarding.

Convener: Rev. Alan Greig BSc BD (2008)
Vice-Convener: Rev. Dr Grant Barclay LLB BD (2011)
Secretary: Mrs Pauline Weibye MA DPA Chartered FCIPD

---

2. THE CHURCH AND SOCIETY COUNCIL

Remit

The remit of the Church and Society Council is to facilitate the Church of Scotland's engagement with, and comment upon, national, political and social issues through:

- the development of theological, ethical and spiritual perspectives in the formulation of policy on such issues;

- the effective representation of the Church of Scotland in offering on its behalf appropriate and informed comment on political and social issues;
- the building, establishing and maintaining of a series of networks and relationships with leaders and influence-shapers in civic society, and engaging long-term in dialogue and the exchange of ideas with them;
- the support of the local church in its mission and engagement by offering professional and accessible resources on contemporary issues;
- the conducting of an annual review of progress made in discharging the remit and the provision of a written report to the Council of Assembly.

Membership
Convener, Vice-Convener, 28 members appointed by the General Assembly, one of whom will also be appointed to the Ecumenical Relations Committee, and one member appointed from and by the Social Care Council and the Guild. The Nomination Committee will ensure that the Council membership contains at least five individuals with specific expertise in each of the areas of Education, Societal/Political, Science and Technology and Social/Ethical. This number may include the Convener and Vice-Convener of the Council.

Convener:	Rev. Ian F. Galloway BA BD (2008)
Vice-Convener:	Rev. Sally Foster-Fulton (2011)
Secretary:	Rev. Ewan R. Aitken BA BD

---

3. THE MINISTRIES COUNCIL

Tel: 0131-225 5722; Fax: 0131-240 2201
E-mail: ministries@cofscotland.org.uk

Ministries Council Remit
The remit of the Ministries Council is the enabling of ministries in every part of Scotland, giving special priority to the poorest and most marginalised, through the recruitment, training and support of recognised ministries of the Church and the assessment and monitoring of patterns of deployment of those ministries.

In the fulfilment of this remit, the Council offers strategic leadership in the development of patterns of collaborative ministry which enable the Church of Scotland to be effective in its missionary calling and faithful in its participation in the one ministry of Jesus Christ, and operates within the following spheres of work:

Priority Areas – following the Gospel imperative of priority to the poor
- Working directly in support of the poorest parishes in Scotland to enable and resource ministries and to build communities of hope;
- Assisting the whole Church in fulfilling its responsibility to the Gospel imperative of giving priority to the poorest and most marginalised in society;
- Enabling and supporting work in partnership with ecumenical, inter-faith and statutory agencies to achieve the goal of alleviating poverty in Scotland.

Education and Support – recruitment, training and support of ministries personnel
- Developing and implementing patterns of enquiry and assessment and vocational guidance which enable the identification of appropriately called and gifted people to train for recognised ministries;

- Developing and implementing training patterns for those accepted into training for the recognised ministries of the Church;
- Enabling the transfer of people from other denominations into the ministries of the Church;
- Delivering pastoral support to those involved in the recognised ministries of the Church through the development and resourcing of local pastoral networks, direct one-to-one engagement and the provision of occupational health support, counselling, mediation and conflict-resolution services;
- Promoting and providing vocational guidance and lifelong learning opportunities for ministries personnel through in-service events, self-appraisal processes and a study-leave programme.

Partnership Development – working with Presbyteries and other partners in planning and resourcing ministries

- Working with Presbyteries for effective deployment of ministries to meet the needs of the parishes of Scotland and charges in the Presbytery of England, including consulting with congregations and other denominations where appropriate;
- Working in partnership with other agencies of the Church and ecumenical partners, to enable the emergence of ministries to meet the needs of the people of Scotland in every part;
- Supporting those engaged in chaplaincy services both directly employed by the Council and employed by other agencies;
- Ensuring best practice in the employment, care and support of staff, including setting appropriate terms and conditions, offering developmental training to staff and those responsible for their management.

Finance – ensuring good management of funds and monitoring budgets

- Planning strategically for the future funding of the recognised ministries of the Church;
- Managing the funds and overseeing the budgeting processes of the Council to ensure that maximum benefit is derived for the Church's ministries through the use of income and capital;
- Preparing recommendations on the level of stipends and salaries and liaising with Pension Trustees on matters relating to the setting of the Standard Annuity and discretionary increases in pension, and negotiating and reaching agreement with Pension Trustees on funding rates.

Membership

Convener, four Vice-Conveners, 36 members appointed by the General Assembly, one of whom will also be appointed to the Ecumenical Relations Committee, and one member appointed from and by the General Trustees, the Housing and Loan Fund, the Committee on Chaplains to Her Majesty's Forces and the Diaconate Council. For the avoidance of doubt, where a representative of these other bodies is a member of staff, he or she will have no right to vote.

Convener:	Rev. Neil J. Dougall BD
Vice-Conveners:	Rev. Neil Glover
	Rev. Anne S. Paton BA BD
	Mr David Stewart
	Rev. Muriel B. Pearson MA BD

Staff

Council Secretary:	Rev. Dr Martin Scott DipMusEd RSAM BD PhD (Tel: ext. 2389; E-mail: mscott@cofscotland.org.uk)
Education and Support Secretary:	Appointment awaited

Partnership Development Secretary:	Rev. Angus R. Mathieson MA BD (Tel: ext. 2312; E-mail: amathieson@cofscotland.org.uk)
Priority Areas Secretary:	Rev. Dr H. Martin J. Johnstone MA BD MTh PhD (Tel: 0141-248 2905; E-mail: mjohnstone@cofscotland.org.uk)
Strategic Projects Manager:	Appointment awaited
Ministries Support Officers:	Mr Ronald Clarke BEng MSc PECE (Tel: ext. 2242; E-mail: rclarke@cofscotland.org.uk) Mrs Dorothy Davidson MA (part-time) (Tel: ext. 2353; E-mail: ddavidson@cofscotland.org.uk) Rev. Jane Denniston MA BD (Tel: ext. 2204; E-mail: jdenniston@cofscotland.org.uk) Rev. Gavin J. Elliott MA BD (Tel: ext. 2255; E-mail: gelliott@cofscotland.org.uk) Miss Carol-Anne Frame BA (Tel: ext. 2348; E-mail: caframe@cofscotland.org.uk) Mrs Anne Law MA (Tel: ext. 2379; E-mail: alaw@cofscotland.org.uk) Mr Noel Mathias BA BTh MA (Tel: 0141-248 2905; E-mail: nmathias@cofscotland.org.uk) Mr John Thomson (Tel: ext. 2248; E-mail: jthomson@cofscotland.org.uk) Mrs Joyce Watkinson CQSW COSCA, Accredited Counsellor (Tel: ext. 2225; E-mail: jwatkinson@cofscotland.org.uk) Mrs Moira Whyte MA (Tel: ext. 2266; E-mail: mwhyte@cofscotland.org.uk)

Ministries Council
Further information about the Council's work and services is obtainable through the Ministries Council at the Church Offices. Information is available on a wide range of matters including the Consolidated Stipend Fund, National Stipend Fund, endowment grants, travelling and other expenses, pulpit supply, study leave, ministries development conferences, pastoral care services (including occupational health), Enquiry and Assessment, Education and Training, Presbytery Planning, Priority Areas, New Charge Development, Area Team Ministry, Interim Ministry, Readership, Chaplaincies, the Diaconate, Presbytery and Parish Workers (PPWs), and all aspects of work connected with ministers and the ministry of word and sacrament.

Committees
The policy development and implementation of the work of the Ministries Council is managed under the following committees:

1. Strategic Planning Group
Convener: Rev. Neil J. Dougall BD
The Strategic Planning Group comprises the Convener, Vice-Conveners and senior staff of all four areas (including Finance) of the Council and is empowered by the Council to engage in broad-ranging thinking regarding the future outlook and plans of the Council. It reports directly to Council and brings forward to it ideas and consultation papers offering options as to the future strategic direction of the Council's work. Though a key part of the Council's work, it is a consultative and advisory group rather than a decision-making one.

2. Priority Areas Committee
Convener: Rev. Muriel B. Pearson MA BD
The Priority Areas Committee implements the policy of the Council in developing, encouraging and overseeing strategy within Priority Area parishes. It is empowered to develop resources to enable congregations to make appropriate responses to the needs of people living in poverty in their parishes, and to raise awareness of the effects of poverty on people's lives in Scotland. It also co-ordinates the strategy of the wider Church in its priority to Scotland's poorest parishes.

3. Education and Support Committee
Convener: Rev. Anne S. Paton BA BD
The Education and Support Committee is responsible for the development and oversight of policy in relation to the enquiry and assessment process for ministers of Word and Sacrament (full-time and ordained local ministry), Deacons and Readers, together with the admission and readmission of ministers. It is further responsible for the supervision of those in training for those recognised ministries of the Church and operates with powers in relation to both of these areas of work to make recommendations on suitability for training and readiness to engage in ministries at the end of a training period. It also implements Council policies on pastoral care for all recognised ministries, the integration of Occupational Health with ministries support services, and the oversight of the working of those Acts relating to long-term illness of ministers in charges. It promotes development opportunities for those engaged in recognised ministries, including study leave and accompanied reviews.

4. Partnership Development Committee
Convener: Mr David Stewart
The Partnership Development Committee is responsible for maintaining and developing relationships with Presbyteries and other agencies and partners in the planning and resourcing of ministries. This includes the overall planning of the deployment of the Church's ministries, primarily through the ongoing monitoring of the development of Presbytery Plans. The Committee also oversees work on emerging ministries (including New Charge Development work). It deals further with the work of Interim Ministry and Area Team Ministry, and with all aspects of chaplaincy work.

5. Finance Committee
Convener: Mr Leslie Purdie
The Finance Committee operates with powers to deal with the Parish Ministries Fund, the National Stipend Scheme, Vacancy Schedules, Maintenance Allowances, Hardship Grants and Bursaries, Stipend Advances, management of investments, writing-off shortfalls and the granting of further endowments. It also maintains an oversight of the budgets for all recognised ministries.

The Council also has several *ad hoc* Task Groups, which report to the Committees and implement specific policies of the Council, as follows:

Recruitment Task Group
Leader: Rev. Andrea E. Price

Assessment Task Group
Leader: Rev. Iain M. Greenshields BD DipRS ACMA MSc MTh

Training Task Group
Leader: Rev. Donald G.B. McCorkindale BD DipMin

Interim Ministries Task Group
Leader: Rev. James Reid BD

Chaplaincies Task Group
Leader: Rev. Hugh O'Brien CSS MTheol

Pastoral and Vocational Care Task Group
Leader: Mrs Sandra Holt

Emerging Ministries Task Group
Leader: Rev. Colin Brough BSc BD

Presbytery Planning Task Group
Leader: Rev. Alison A. Meikle BD

Other Related Bodies:
Chaplains to HM Forces
See separate entry at number 9.

The Church of Scotland Housing and Loan Fund
See separate entry at number 22.

Pulpit Supply: Fee and Expenses
The General Assembly of 1995 approved new regulations governing the amount of Supply Fee and Expenses. These were effective from 1 July 1995 and are as follows:

1. In Charges where there is only one diet of worship, the Pulpit Supply Fee shall be a Standard Fee of £50 (or as from time to time agreed by the Ministries Council).
2. In Charges where there are additional diets of worship on a Sunday, the person fulfilling the Supply shall be paid £10 for each additional Service (or as from time to time agreed by the Ministries Council).
3. Where the person is unwilling to conduct more than one diet of worship on a given Sunday, he or she shall receive a pro-rata payment based on the total available Fee shared on the basis of the number of Services conducted.
4. The Fee thus calculated shall be payable in the case of all persons permitted to conduct Services under Act II 1986.
5. In all cases, Travelling Expenses shall be paid. Where there is no convenient public conveyance, the use of a private car shall be paid for at the Committee rate of Travelling Expenses. In exceptional circumstances, to be approved in advance, the cost of hiring a car may be met.
6. Where weekend board and lodging are agreed as necessary, these may be claimed for the weekend at a maximum rate of that allowed when attending the General Assembly. The Fee and Expenses should be paid to the person providing the Supply before he or she leaves on the Sunday.

4. THE MISSION AND DISCIPLESHIP COUNCIL

Remit

The remit of the Mission and Discipleship Council is:

- to take a lead role in developing and maintaining an overall focus for mission in Scotland, and to highlight its fundamental relationships with worship, service, doctrine, education and nurture;
- to take a lead role in developing strategies, resources and services in Christian education and nurture, recognising these as central to both mission and discipleship;
- to offer appropriate servicing and support nationally, regionally and locally in the promotion of nurturing, worshipping and witnessing communities of faith;
- to introduce policy on behalf of the Church in the following areas: adult education and elder training, church art and architecture, congregational mission and development, doctrine, resourcing youth and children's work and worship;
- to establish and support the Mission Forum with representatives of relevant Councils;
- to encourage appropriate awareness of, and response to, the requirements of people with particular needs including physical, sensory and/or learning disabilities;
- to conduct an annual review of progress made in discharging the remit and provide a written report to the Council of Assembly.

Statement of Purpose

Resourcing Christ's Mission: to enable and empower people to engage in Christ's mission through resourcing worship, witness and discipleship in the context of the changing contemporary culture of Scotland and beyond.

Specifically, we will:

- stimulate critical reflection and development of places and practice of worship = WORSHIP
- communicate Christ's message lovingly, effectively and relevantly = WITNESS
- nurture and develop learning and growth within congregations and communities = DISCIPLESHIP.

Membership

Convener, three Vice-Conveners and 24 members appointed by the General Assembly, one of whom will also be appointed to the Ecumenical Relations Committee, the Director of Stewardship, one member appointed from and by the General Trustees, the Guild and the Scottish Community Trust, and the Convener or Vice-Convener of the Committee on Church Art and Architecture as that Committee shall determine. The Nomination Committee will ensure that the Council membership contains individuals with specific expertise in the areas of Mission, Education, Worship, Doctrine and Publishing.

Convener:	Rev. Mark E. Johnstone MA BD
Vice-Conveners:	Mrs Shirley Billes BEd
	Rev. David C. Cameron BD CertMin

Staff

Council Secretary:	Dr Steven Mallon MSc TQ(SE) BA (E-mail: smallon@cofscotland.org.uk)
Faith Expressions Team Leader:	Rev. Nigel Robb FCP MA BD ThM MTh (E-mail: nrobb@cofscotland.org.uk)
Church Without Walls Team Leader:	Mrs Lesley Hamilton-Messer MA (E-mail: lhamilton-messer@cofscotland.org.uk)

Congregational Learning Team Leader: Ms Fiona Fidgin BEd
(E-mail: ffidgin@cofscotland.org.uk)

Mission Development Workers
Mission Development Workers are tasked with supporting local congregations to help them become more resourceful so that they can engage effectively with their communities. They are:

Mr Steve Aisthorpe BA (E-mail: saisthorpe@cofscotland.org.uk)
Mr Robert Rawson BA (E-mail: rrawson@cofscotland.org.uk)
Mr Iain Campbell BA PGDE (E-mail: icampbell@cofscotland.org.uk)

Specialist Development Workers
The following staff members provide specialist advice and support to congregations on key areas of work:

Mr Graham Fender-Allison BA Worship Development Worker
(E-mail: gfender-allison@cofscotland.org.uk)
Rev. David E.P. Currie BSc BD New Frontiers Development Worker
(E-mail: dcurrie@cofscotland.org.uk)
Mr Iain Stewart BA DipEd Interfaith Development Worker
(E-mail: istewart@cofscotland.org.uk)
Rev. Pauline Steenbergen MA BD Leadership Development Worker
(E-mail: psteenbergen@cofscotland.org.uk)

The Netherbow: Scottish Storytelling Centre: The integrated facilities of the **Netherbow Theatre** and the **John Knox House Museum**, together with the outstanding new conference and reception areas, are an important cultural and visitor centre on the Royal Mile in Edinburgh and provide advice and assistance nationally in the use of the arts in mission, education and worship. 'Story Source', 'Scriptaid' and other resources are available. Contact the Director, The Netherbow: Scottish Storytelling Centre, 43–45 High Street, Edinburgh EH1 1SR (Tel: 0131-556 9579; E-mail; donald@scottishstorytellingcentre.com; Website: www.scottishstorytellingcentre.co.uk). The Centre also houses the **Scottish Churches Parliamentary Office**.

Life and Work
(Tel: 0131-225 5722; Fax: 0131-240 2207; E-mail: magazine@lifeandwork.org)
Life and Work is the Church of Scotland's monthly magazine. Its purpose is to keep the Church informed about events in church life at home and abroad and to provide a forum for Christian opinion and debate on a variety of topics. It has an independent editorial policy. Contributions which are relevant to any aspect of the Christian faith are welcome.

The price of *Life and Work* this year is £1.80. With a circulation of around 32,000, it also offers advertisers a first-class opportunity to reach a discerning readership in all parts of Scotland.

Saint Andrew Press
Saint Andrew Press is now managed on behalf of the Church of Scotland by Hymns Ancient and Modern.

The publishing programme includes the updated series of New Testament commentaries, *The New Daily Study Bible*, by the late Professor William Barclay, which has been read by many millions of people around the world. Best-sellers include *A Glasgow Bible* by Jamie Stuart, *Outside Verdict* by Harry Reid, *Iona* by Kenneth Steven, *My Father: Reith of the BBC* by Marista

Leishman and *Silent Heroes* by John Miller. Other popular titles include *Practical Caring* by Sheilah Steven, *Will You Follow Me?* by Leith Fisher, Beginners' Guides to the Old and New Testaments, *Pray Now* and *Common Order* and *Common Ground* from the Church of Scotland Office for Worship and Doctrine.

Saint Andrew Press is compiling a mailing list for all those who would like to receive regular information on its publications. Up-to-date information on all Saint Andrew Press titles can be found at www.standrewpress.com

All new proposals for publication should be sent to the Senior Commissioning Editor in the form of a two-page description of the book and its readership, together with one sample chapter. The Senior Commissioning Editor (ann@hymnsam.co.uk) is always happy to offer help and advice. For further information, please refer to www.standrewpress.com/topics/10-submission-guidelines

Committee on Church Art and Architecture
Membership
The Committee shall comprise a Convener, Vice-Convener and 15 members appointed by the General Assembly.

Remit
This Committee replaced the Committee on Artistic Matters and will take forward that Committee's remit, which is in the following terms:

The Committee advises congregations and Presbyteries regarding the most appropriate way of carrying out renovations, alterations and reordering of interiors, having regard to the architectural quality of Church buildings. It also advises on the installation of stained glass, tapestries, memorials, furniture and furnishings, and keeps a list of accredited artists and craftsworkers.

Any alteration to the exterior or interior of a Church building which affects its appearance must be referred to the Committee for approval, which is given through the General Trustees. Congregations contemplating alterations are urged to consult the Committee at an early stage.

Members of the Committee are prepared, when necessary, to visit churches and meet office-bearers. The Committee's services are given free.

The Committee seeks the conservation of the nation's heritage as expressed in its Church buildings, while at the same time helping to ensure that these buildings continue to serve the worship and witness of the Church in the present day.

In recent years, the General Assembly has conferred these additional duties on the Committee:

1. preparation of reports on the architectural, historical and aesthetic merit of the buildings of congregations involved in questions of readjustment
2. verification of the propriety of repair and renovation work forming the basis of grant applications to public bodies
3. the offering of advice on the maintenance and installation of organs
4. facilitating the transfer of unwanted furnishings from one church to another through the quarterly *Exchange and Transfer*
5. the processing of applications from congregations for permission to dispose of surplus communion plate, and the carrying out of an inventory of sacramental vessels held by congregations.

Work with Rural Churches
The Council aims to affirm, support and resource rural churches and is responsible for planning for a Church presence at the Royal Highland Show. It seeks to reflect the full extent of rural

experience, encompassing farming, fishing, tourism, forestry and other professions/industries that have a bearing on rural life. This will involve collaboration with ecumenical partners and responding periodically to requests for submissions to government consultations.

---

5. THE SOCIAL CARE COUNCIL

SOCIAL CARE (CrossReach)
Charis House, 47 Milton Road East, Edinburgh EH15 2SR
Tel: 0131-657 2000; Fax: 0131-657 5000
E-mail: info@crossreach.org.uk; Website: www.crossreach.org.uk

The Social Care Council, known as CrossReach, provides social-care services as part of the Christian witness of the Church to the people of Scotland.

Remit

The remit of the Social Care Council is:

- as part of the Church's mission, to offer services in Christ's name to people in need;
- to provide specialist resources to further the caring work of the Church;
- to identify existing and emerging areas of need, to guide the Church in pioneering new approaches to relevant problems and to make responses on issues arising within the area of the Council's concern through appropriate channels such as the Church's Church and Society Council, the Scottish Government and the like;
- to conduct an annual review of progress made in discharging the remit and provide an annual written report to the General Assembly;
- to oversee an appropriate corporate management and support service to deliver the above and be responsible for funding all salaries and related costs;
- to set and review terms and conditions of staff and establish appropriate internal governance systems.

Membership

Convener, two Vice-Conveners and 28 members appointed by the General Assembly, one of whom will also be appointed to the Ecumenical Relations Committee. The Council shall have power to appoint such Committees and Groups as it may from time to time determine to be appropriate to ensure that the Council's Remit is fulfilled.

Convener:	Rev. Sydney S. Graham (2009)
Vice-Conveners:	Dr Sally Bonnar (2008)
	Rev. Ramsay Shields (2009)

Staff

Chief Executive Officer:	Peter Bailey (peter.bailey@crossreach.org.uk)

Management Structure

The management structure is service-based. There are three Operational Directors, each with a specialist area of responsibility. They are supported by Heads of Service, who have lead roles for particular types of service and client groups.

Director of Services to Older People:	Marlene Smith (marlene.smith@crossreach.org.uk)

Heads of Service:	Brenda Fraser (East) Allan Logan (West) Annie McDonald (North)
Director of Adult Care Services:	Calum Murray (calum.murray@crossreach.org.uk)
Heads of Service:	George McNeilly Dave Clark Viv Dickenson
Director of Children's Services:	
General and Strategic Manager:	Chris McNaught (chris.mcnaught@crossreach.org.uk)
Operations Manager:	Paul Gilroy
Director of Finance and Resources:	Ian Wauchope (ian.wauchope@crossreach.org.uk)
Business Partner:	Arthur Akugbo
Director of Human Resources and Organisational Development:	Mari Rennie (mari.rennie@crossreach.org.uk)
Business Partners:	Jane Allan Ronnie Black
Head of Estates and Health and Safety:	David Reid (david.reid@crossreach.org.uk)
Health and Safety Manager:	Richard Park
Business, Compliance and Improvement Manager:	Post vacant
Income Generation Manager:	Pete Cuthbertson (pete.cuthbertson@crossreach.org.uk)

List of Services

CrossReach operates over 80 services across Scotland, and a list of these can be obtained from Charis House on 0131-657 2000, or from the CrossReach website: www.crossreach.org.uk

---

6. THE WORLD MISSION COUNCIL

Tel: 0131-225 5722; Fax: 0131-226 6121
Answerphone: 0131-240 2231
E-mail: world@cofscotland.org.uk
Website: www.churchofscotland.org.uk/worldmission

Remit

The remit of the World Mission Council is:

- to give life to the Church of Scotland's understanding that it is part of Jesus Christ's Universal Church committed to the advance of the Kingdom of God throughout the world;
- to discern priorities and form policies to guide the Church of Scotland's ongoing worldwide participation in God's transforming mission, through the Gospel of Jesus Christ;

- to develop and maintain mutually enriching relationships with the Church of Scotland's partner churches overseas through consultation in the two-way sharing of human and material resources;
- to equip and encourage Church of Scotland members at local, Presbytery and national levels to become engaged in the life of the world Church;
- to help the people of Scotland to appreciate the worldwide nature of the Christian faith;
- to keep informed about the cultural, political, social, economic, religious and ecclesiastical issues of relevance to worldwide mission;
- to recruit, train and support paid staff and volunteers to work overseas;
- to direct the work of the Council's centres in Israel;
- to foster and facilitate local partnerships between congregations and Presbyteries and the partner churches;
- to undertake the responsibilities of the former Board of World Mission in regard to the Presbytery of Europe and its congregations as set out in the relevant Assembly legislation;
- to conduct an annual review of progress made in discharging the remit and provide a written report to the Council of Assembly.

Membership

Convener, two Vice-Conveners, 24 members appointed by the General Assembly, one of whom will also be appointed from the Committee on Ecumenical Relations, and one member appointed by the Presbytery of Europe.

Convener:	Very Rev. Andrew R.C. McLellan MA BD STM DD (2010)
Vice-Conveners:	Mrs Shirley Brown BSc (2009)
	Rev. Iain D. Cunningham MA BD (2011)

Departmental Staff

Council Secretary:	Rev. Ian Alexander
Secretaries:	Mrs Jennie Chinembiri (Africa and Caribbean)
	Carol Finlay (Twinning and Local Development)
	Mr Sandy Sneddon (Asia)
Administration:	Donna Maclean
Finance:	Mr Kenny Roger (Assistant Treasurer)
Human Resources:	Kelly Smith
	Sarah-Jayne McVeigh
	Angela Ocak

Strategic Commitments:
Mission in a New Mode – Local to Local

- **Evangelism** – working with partner churches on new initiatives in evangelism
- **Reconciliation** – working for justice, peace and reconciliation in situations of conflict or threat
- **The Scandal of Poverty** – resourcing the Church to set people free from the oppression of poverty.

Partnership Priorities
With the overarching aim of involving everyone in the Church of Scotland, the priority areas for partnership in mission are:

1. Sharing the Good News
2. The scandal of poverty
3. The ministry of reconciliation.

World Mission and World Resources
Sharing in the mission of God worldwide requires a continuing commitment to sharing the Church of Scotland's resources of people and money for mission in six continents as contemporary evidence that it is 'labouring for the advancement of the Kingdom of God throughout the world' (First Article Declaratory). Such resource-sharing remains an urgent matter because most of our overseas work is in the developing world, or 'South', in nations where the effects of the widening gap between rich and poor is *the* major issue for the Church. Our partner churches in Africa, the Middle East, most of Asia and the Caribbean are desperately short of financial and technical resources, which we can to some extent meet with personnel and grants. However, they are more than willing to share the resources of their Christian faith with us, including things which the Church in the West often lacks: enthusiasm in worship, hospitality and evangelism, and a readiness to suffer and struggle for righteousness, and in many areas a readiness to sink denominational differences. Mutual sharing in the world Church witnesses to its international nature and has much to offer a divided world, not least in Scotland. Much fruit has been borne since the beginning of the twinning programme, and many congregations are experiencing and sharing the challenges and opportunities of their connection with the World Church. Information and support are available from Karen Francis (Twinning Development Officer: E-mail: kfrancis@cofscotland.org.uk).

Vacancies Overseas
The Council welcomes enquiries from men and women interested in serving in the Church overseas. Vacancies for mission partner appointments in the Church's centrally supported partnerships, volunteer programme and opportunities with other organisations can all be considered. Those interested in more information are invited to contact the Human Resources Department at the Church Offices (E-mail: hr@cofscotland.org.uk).

HIV Programme
The Programme aims to raise awareness in congregations about the impact of HIV and AIDS and seeks to channel urgently needed support to partner churches. For further information, contact Marjorie Clark, Co-ordinator, HIV Programme (E-mail: mclark@cofscotland.org.uk).

Christian Aid Scotland
Christian Aid is the official relief and development agency of 41 Churches in Britain and Ireland. Christian Aid's mandate is to challenge and enable us to fulfil our responsibilities to the poor of the world. Half a million volunteers and collectors make this possible, with money given by millions of supporters. The Church of Scotland marks its commitment as a Church to this part of its mission through an annual grant from the Mission and Renewal Fund, transmitted through the World Mission Council, which keeps in close touch with Christian Aid and its work. Up-to-date information about projects and current emergency relief work can be obtained from:

- The Head of Christian Aid Scotland, Rev. Kathy Galloway: Christian Aid Scotland, Pentagon Centre, 36 Washington Street, Glasgow G3 8AZ (Tel: 0141-221 7475)
- The Director: Loretta Minghella, Christian Aid Office, PO Box 100, London SE1 7RT (Tel: 020 7620 4444)

Pilgrimage

The Church of Scotland encourages visitors and pilgrims to visit the Christian Community of Israel and Palestine, to walk with them in fellowship and build relationships to help understand their life, witness and situation. There are two Christian Residential Centres in Israel which provide comfortable accommodation for pilgrims and visitors to the Holy Land. Further information is available from:

(a) St Andrew's Guest House, 1 David Remez Street, PO Box 8619, Jerusalem 91086, Israel (Tel: 00 972 2 6732401; Fax: 00 972 2 6731711; E-mail: standjer@netvision.net.il)

(b) The Scots Hotel, St Andrew's, Galilee: 1 Gdud Barak Street, PO Box 104, Tiberias 14100, Israel (Tel: 00 972 4 671 0710; Fax: 00 972 4 671 0711; E-mail: scottie@netvision.net.il)

A list of Overseas Appointments will be found in List K in Section 6.

A *World Mission Year Book* is available with more details of our partner churches and of people currently serving abroad, including those with ecumenical bodies and para-church bodies.

A list of Retired Missionaries will be found in List L in Section 6.

---

7. Assembly Arrangements Committee

Membership

Convener, Vice-Convener and ten members appointed by the General Assembly on the Report of the Nomination Committee; the Convener and Vice-Convener also to serve as Convener and Vice-Convener of the General Assembly's Business Committee.

The Clerks are non-voting members of the Assembly Arrangements Committee, and the Moderator and Moderator Designate are members of the Committee.

Convener:	Rev. Janet S. Mathieson MA BD
Vice-Convener:	Rev. E. Lorna Hood MA BD
Secretary:	The Principal Clerk

Remit

The Committee's remit is:

- to make all necessary arrangements for the General Assembly;
- to advise the Moderator on his or her official duties if so required;
- to be responsible to the General Assembly for the care and maintenance of the Assembly Hall and the Moderator's flat;
- to be responsible to the General Assembly for all arrangements in connection with the letting of the General Assembly Hall;
- to conduct an annual review of progress made in discharging the remit and provide a written report to the Support and Services Council.

8. Central Services Committee

Membership
(13 members: nine appointed by the General Assembly, and four *ex officiis* and non-voting, namely the Secretary to the Council of Assembly, the Solicitor of the Church, the General Treasurer and the Head of Human Resources and Information Technology)

Convener: Mr Angus Macpherson MA BSc DPSA (2010)
Vice-Conveners: Mr Bill Steele (2010)
Mr Philip Craig MA MEd MSc DipRE (2010)

Staff
Administrative Secretary: Mrs Pauline Wilson
(E-mail: pwilson@cofscotland.org.uk)

Remit

- To be responsible for the proper maintenance and insurance of the Church Offices at 117–123 George Street and 21 Young Street, Edinburgh ('the Church Offices');
- To be responsible for matters relating to Health and Safety within the Church Offices;
- To be responsible for matters relating to Data Protection within the Church Offices and with respect to the General Assembly Councils based elsewhere;
- To be responsible for the allocation of accommodation within the Church Offices and the annual determination of rental charges to the Councils and other parties accommodated therein;
- To oversee the delivery of central services to departments within the Church Offices, to Councils of the General Assembly and, where appropriate, to the Statutory Corporations, Presbyteries and Congregations, namely:
  1. Those facilities directly managed by the Facilities Manager;
  2. Information Technology (including the provision of support services to Presbytery Clerks);
  3. Human Resources;
  4. Legal Services (as delivered by the Law Department and subject to such oversight not infringing principles of 'client/solicitor' confidentiality);
  5. Property Services (as delivered by the Central Properties Department).
- The Committee shall act as one of the employing agencies of the Church and shall, except in so far as specifically herein provided, assume and exercise the whole rights, functions and responsibilities of the former Personnel Committee;
- While the Committee shall *inter alia* have responsibility for determining the terms and conditions of the staff for whom it is the employing agency, any staff who are members of the Committee or who are appointed directly by the General Assembly shall not be present when matters solely relating to their own personal terms and conditions of employment/office are under consideration;
- To conduct an annual review of progress made in discharging this remit and provide a written report to the Council of Assembly.

9. Chaplains to HM Forces

Convener: Rev. Neil N. Gardner MA BD
Vice-Convener: Rev. Jackie G. Petrie
Secretary: Mr John K. Thomson, Ministries Council, 121 George Street, Edinburgh EH2 4YN

Recruitment
The Chaplains' Committee is entrusted with the task of recruitment of Chaplains for the Regular, Reserve and Auxiliary Forces. Vacancies occur periodically, and the Committee is happy to receive enquiries from all interested ministers.

Forces Registers
The Committee maintains a Register of all those who have been baptised and/or admitted to Communicant Membership by Service Chaplains.

Parish Ministers are asked to take advantage of the facilities by applying for Certificates, where appropriate, from the Secretary of the Committee.

Full information may be obtained from the Secretary, Mr John K. Thomson (Tel: 0131-225 5722; E-mail: jthomson@cofscotland.org.uk).

A list of Chaplains will be found in List B in Section 6.

---

10. Church of Scotland Guild

National Office-bearers and Executive Staff
Convener: Mrs Alison Angus BSc
Vice-Convener: Mrs Mary Ford
General Secretary:

Information Officer: Mrs Fiona J. Punton MCIPR
(E-mail: fpunton@cofscotland.org.uk)
(Tel: 0131-225 5722 ext. 2317 or 0131-240 2217)

The Church of Scotland Guild is a movement within the Church of Scotland whose aim is '**to invite and encourage both women and men to commit their lives to Jesus Christ and to enable them to express their faith in worship, prayer and action**'. Membership of the Guild is open to all who subscribe to that aim.

Groups at congregational level are free to organise themselves under the authority of the Kirk Session, as best suits their own local needs and circumstances. Large groups with frequent meetings and activities continue to operate with a committee or leadership team, while other, smaller groups simply share whatever tasks need to be done among the membership as a whole. Similarly, at Presbyterial Council level, frequency and style of meetings vary according to local needs, as do leadership patterns. Each Council may nominate one person to serve at national level, where five committees take forward the work of the Guild in accordance with the stated Aim.

These committees are:

- National Executive

- Finance and General Purposes
- Projects and Topics
- Programmes and Resources
- Marketing and Publicity.

There has always been a close relationship between the Guild and other Departments of the Church, and members welcome the opportunity to contribute to the Church's wider mission through the Project Partnership Scheme and other joint ventures. The Guild is represented on both the Church and Society Council and the Mission and Discipleship Council.

The project scheme affords groups at congregational level the opportunity to select a project, or projects, from a range of up to six, selected from proposals submitted by a wide range of Church Departments and other Church-related bodies. A project partner in each group seeks ways of promoting the project locally, increasing awareness of the issues raised by it, and encouraging support of a financial and practical nature. Support is available from the Project Co-ordinator at Council level and the Information Officer based at the Guild Office.

The Guild is very aware of the importance of good communication in any large organisation, and regularly sends mailings to its groups to pass on information and resources to the members. In addition, the Newsletter, sent to members three times per session, is a useful communication tool, as is the website (www.cos-guild.org.uk). These are a means of sharing experiences and of communicating something of the wider interest and influence of the Guild, which participates in other national bodies such as the Network of Ecumenical Women in Scotland and the Scottish Women's Convention.

Each year, the Guild follows a Theme and produces a resources pack covering worship and study material. There is also a related Discussion Topic with supporting material and background information. The theme, topic and projects all relate to a common three-year strategy which, for 2009–12, is **'What does the Lord require of you?'** Each of the six current projects reflects some aspect of the challenge from Micah chapter 6 to act justly, love mercy and walk humbly with God. The 2011–12 theme is **'Called to walk humbly with God'**, and Guilds are invited to explore this defining characteristic of the faith. The related discussion topic is **'Thanking God for His creation'**, which challenges us to be stewards rather than exploiters of the earth's resources.

Further information is available from the Guild Office (Tel: 0131-225 5722 ext. 2317, or 0131-240 2217) or from the website (www.cos-guild.org.uk).

---

11. Church of Scotland Investors Trust

Membership

(Trustees are appointed by the General Assembly, on the nomination of the Investors Trust)

Chairman:	Mrs I.J. Hunter MA
Vice-Chairman:	Mr A.W.T. Gibb BA
Treasurer:	Mr I.W. Grimmond BAcc CA
Deputy Treasurer:	Mrs A.F. Macintosh BA CA
Secretary:	Mr F.E. Marsh MCIBS

Remit

The Church of Scotland Investors Trust was established by the Church of Scotland (Properties and Investments) Order Confirmation Act 1994 – Scottish Charity Number SC022884 – and offers investment services to the Church of Scotland and to bodies and trusts within or connected with the Church. It offers simple and economical facilities for investment in its three Funds, and investors receive the benefits of professional management, continuous portfolio supervision, spread of investment risk and economies of scale.

The three Funds are:

1. Deposit Fund
The Deposit Fund is intended for short-term investment and seeks to provide a competitive rate of interest while preserving nominal capital value. It is invested mainly in short-term loans to banks and building societies. Interest is calculated quarterly in arrears and paid gross on 15 May and 15 November. Withdrawals are on demand. The Fund is managed by Thomas Miller Investments Limited, Edinburgh and London.

2. Growth Fund
The Growth Fund is a unitised fund, largely equity-based, intended to provide a growing annual income sufficient to meet the Trustees' target distributions and to provide an increase in the value of capital long term. Units can only be purchased or sold on a monthly dealing date, and income is distributed gross on 15 May and 15 November. The Fund is managed by Newton Investment Management Limited, London.

3. Income Fund
The Income Fund is a unitised fund, invested predominantly in fixed-interest securities, intended to provide a high and sustainable income at a level as agreed between the Trustees and the manager from time to time and to protect the long-term nominal value of capital. Units can only be purchased or sold on a monthly dealing date, and income is distributed gross on 15 March and 15 September. The Fund is managed by Baillie Gifford & Co., Edinburgh.

Further information and application forms for investment are available on the Church of Scotland website or by writing to the Secretary, The Church of Scotland Investors Trust, 121 George Street, Edinburgh EH2 4YN (E-mail: fmarsh@cofscotland.org.uk).

---

12. The Church of Scotland Pension Trustees

Chairman:	Mr W.J. McCafferty ACII APFS TEP
Vice-Chairman:	Mr A.J. Priestly FCII
Secretary:	Mr S.D. Kaney BSc MPMI

Staff

Pensions Manager:	Mr S.D. Kaney BSc MPMI
Assistant Pensions Administrators:	Mrs M. Marshall
	Mr M. Hannam
	Miss M. Paterson

Remit
The body acts as Trustees for the Church of Scotland's three Pension Schemes:

1. The Church of Scotland Pension Scheme for Ministers and Overseas Missionaries

2. The Church of Scotland Pension Scheme for Staff
3. The Church of Scotland Pension Scheme for Presbytery and Parish Workers.

The Trustees have wide-ranging duties and powers detailed in the Trust Law, Pension Acts and other regulations, but in short the Trustees are responsible for the administration of the Pension Schemes and for the investment of the Scheme Funds. Six Trustees are appointed by the General Assembly, and members nominate up to three Trustees for each Scheme.

The investment of the Funds is delegated to external Investment Managers under the guidelines and investment principles set by the Trustees: Baillie Gifford & Co., Newton Investment Management Ltd, Aviva, Black Rock, Aegon, Rogge and Legal & General.

The benefits provided by the three Pension Schemes differ in detail, but all provide a pension to the Scheme member and dependants on death of the member, and a lump-sum death benefit on death in service. Scheme members also have the option to improve their benefits by paying additional voluntary contributions (AVCs) to arrangements set up by the Trustees with leading Insurance Companies.

Further information on any of the Church of Scotland Pension Schemes or on individual benefits can be obtained from the Pensions Manager, Church of Scotland Offices, 121 George Street, Edinburgh EH2 4YN (Tel: 0131-240 2255; Fax: 0131-240 2220; E-mail: pensions@cofscotland.org.uk).

---

13. The Church of Scotland Trust

Membership

(Members are appointed by the General Assembly, on the nomination of the Trust)

Chairman:	Mr Robert Brodie CB WS
Vice-Chairman:	Mr Christopher N. Mackay WS
Treasurer:	Mr Iain W. Grimmond BAcc CA
Secretary and Clerk:	Mrs Jennifer M. Hamilton BA

Remit

The Church of Scotland Trust was established by Act of Parliament in 1932 and has Scottish Charity Number SC020269. The Trust's function since 1 January 1995 has been to hold properties outwith Scotland and to act as Trustee in a number of third-party trusts.

Further information can be obtained from the Secretary and Clerk of The Church of Scotland Trust, 121 George Street, Edinburgh EH2 4YN (Tel: 0131-240 2222; E-mail: jhamilton@cofscotland.org.uk).

---

14. Committee on Church Art and Architecture

See entry in full under **The Mission and Discipleship Council** (number 4).

15. Communications Unit

(Details of the responsibilities and work of this Unit formerly appeared under the heading of Media Relations and Communications Unit.)

Communications Department

Head of Communications:	Appointment awaited
Communications Manager:	Post vacant

Media Relations Team

Senior Media Relations Officer:	Gordon Bell
Senior Media Relations Officer:	Nick Jury

Web Team

Web Editor:	Shirley James
Web Developer:	Alan Murray

Design Services

Senior Graphic Designer:	Claire Bewsey
Senior Graphic Designer:	Chris Flexen

The Communications Department has responsibility for providing and promoting effective internal and external communications across the Church of Scotland.

The Media Relations Team services local, regional, national, UK and international media. News releases are issued on a regular basis to a large network of media contacts, and staff provide advice and information on media matters within the Church. Media Relations staff can be contacted on 0131-240 2204/2268 during office hours, or on 07854 783539 after hours, at weekends and on public holidays.

The Web Team is responsible for developing and updating the Church's website (www.churchofscotland.org), and the Design Team creates printed and online material for the Church.

---

16. The Department of the General Assembly

The Department of the General Assembly supports the General Assembly and the Moderator, the Council of Assembly and the Ecumenical Relations Committee. In addition, Departmental staff service the following Committees: Assembly Arrangements, Legal Questions, the Committee to Nominate the Moderator, the Nomination Committee, the Committee on Overtures and Cases, the Committee on Classifying Returns to Overtures and the Central Services Committee. The Clerks of Assembly are available for consultation on matters of Church Law, Practice and Procedure.

Staff

Principal Clerk of the General Assembly:	Rev. John P. Chalmers BD CPS
Depute Clerk of the General Assembly*:	Rev. George J. Whyte BSc BD DMin
Secretary to the Council of Assembly:	Mrs Pauline Weibye MA DPA Chartered FCIPD

Ecumenical Officer:	Very Rev. Sheilagh M. Kesting BA BD DD
Personal Assistant to the Principal Clerk:	Mrs Linda Jamieson
Senior Administration Officer: (Assembly Arrangements and Moderatorial Support)	Mrs Alison Murray MA
Senior Administration Officer: (Council of Assembly, Central Services Committee and Nomination Committee)	Mrs Pauline Wilson
Senior Administrator: (Ecumenical Relations)	Miss Rosalind Milne

Contact Details:

Principal Clerk:	0131-240 2240
Secretary to the Council of Assembly:	0131-240 2229
Ecumenical Officer:	0131-240 2208
Linda Jamieson:	0131-240 2240
Rosalind Milne:	0131-225 5722 ext. 2370
Alison Murray:	0131-225 5722 ext. 2250
Pauline Wilson:	0131-240 2229
Office Fax number:	0131-240 2239
Office E-mail address:	pcoffice@cofscotland.org.uk

** Note: the office of Depute Clerk is part-time, and the office-holder is not based in the Church Offices. Contact should be made through the Principal Clerk.*

---

17. Design Services

For further details, see Communications Unit at number 15.

---

18. Ecumenical Relations Committee

Remit

- to advise the General Assembly on matters of policy affecting ecumenical relations;
- to ensure that the members on the Committee serving on the other Councils are appropriately informed and resourced so as to be able to represent the ecumenical viewpoint on the Council on which they serve;
- to ensure appropriate support for the Ecumenical Officer's representative function in the event of his or her absence, whether through illness, holidays or other commitments;
- to nominate people from across the work of the Church of Scotland to represent the Church in Assemblies and Synods of other churches, ecumenical consultations and delegations to ecumenical assemblies and so on;
- to call for and receive reports from representatives of the Church of Scotland attending

Assemblies and Synods of other churches and those ecumenical conferences and gatherings which are held from time to time;
- to ensure that appropriate parts of such reports are made available to relevant Councils;
- to ensure that information is channelled from and to ecumenical bodies of which the Church of Scotland is a member;
- to ensure that information is channelled from and to other churches in Scotland and beyond;
- to ensure the continued development of ecumenical relations by means of the Web and other publications;
- to ensure personal support for the Ecumenical Officer;
- to approve guidelines for the setting up and oversight of Local Ecumenical Partnerships.

Membership

a) Five members appointed by the General Assembly, each to serve as a member of one of the five Councils of the Church (excluding the Support and Services Council, on which the Convener of the Committee will sit).
b) A Convener who is not a member of any of the other Councils and who will act as a personal support for the Ecumenical Officer, and a Vice-Convener, appointed by the General Assembly.
c) A representative of the United Free Church of Scotland appointed by that Church.
d) A representative of the Roman Catholic Church in Scotland appointed by the Bishops' Conference and one representative from each of three churches drawn from among the member churches of ACTS and the Baptist Union of Scotland, each to serve for a period of four years.
e) The Committee shall co-opt Church of Scotland members elected to the central bodies of Churches Together in Britain and Ireland (CTBI), the Conference of European Churches (CEC), the World Council of Churches (WCC), the World Communion of Reformed Churches (WCRC) and the Community of Protestant Churches in Europe (CPCE, formerly the Leuenberg Fellowship of Churches).
f) The General Secretary of ACTS shall be invited to attend as a corresponding member.
g) For the avoidance of doubt, while, for reasons of corporate governance, only Church of Scotland members of the Committee shall be entitled to vote, before any vote is taken the views of members representing other churches shall be ascertained.

Convener:	Rev. Alan D. Falconer MA BD DLitt (2009)
Vice-Convener:	Rev. Alison P. McDonald MA BD (2011)
Secretary and Ecumenical Officer:	Very Rev. Sheilagh M. Kesting BA BD DD
Senior Administrator:	Miss Rosalind Milne

INTER-CHURCH ORGANISATIONS

World Council of Churches

The Church of Scotland is a founder member of the World Council of Churches, formed in 1948. As its basis declares, it is 'a fellowship of Churches which confess the Lord Jesus Christ as God and Saviour according to the Scriptures, and therefore seek to fulfil their common calling to the glory of the one God, Father, Son and Holy Spirit'. Its member Churches, which number over 300, are drawn from all continents and include all the major traditions – Eastern and Oriental Orthodox, Reformed, Lutheran, Anglican, Baptist, Disciples, Methodist, Moravian, Friends, Pentecostalist and others. Although the Roman Catholic Church is not a member, there is very close co-operation with the departments in the Vatican.

The World Council holds its Assemblies every seven years. The last, held in Porto Alegre, Brazil, in February 2006, had the theme 'God, in your grace, transform the world'. At that Assembly, Mr Graham McGeoch was elected to the new Executive and to the Central Committee of the Council.

The WCC is divided into six programme areas:

- WCC and the Ecumenical Movement in the 21st Century
- Unity, Mission, Evangelism and Spirituality
- Public Witness: Addressing Power, Affirming Peace
- Justice, Diakonia and Responsibility for Creation
- Education and Ecumenical Formation
- Inter-Religious Dialogue and Co-operation.

The General Secretary is Rev. Dr Olav Fykse Tveit, PO Box 2100, 150 route de Ferney, CH-1211 Geneva 2, Switzerland (Tel: 00 41 22 791 61 11; Fax: 00 41 22 791 03 61; E-mail: infowcc@wcc-coe.org; Website: www.oikumene.org).

World Communion of Reformed Churches

The Church of Scotland was a founder member of 'The Alliance of the Reformed Churches Throughout the World Holding the Presbyterian System', which began in 1875. As the World Alliance of Reformed Churches, it included also Churches of the Congregational tradition. In June 2010, WARC merged with the Reformed Ecumenical Council and became the World Communion of Reformed Churches.

The World Communion of Reformed Churches (WCRC) brings together 80 million Reformed Christians in 108 countries around the world – united in their commitment to mission, church unity and justice. WCRC links Presbyterian, Reformed, Congregational, Waldensian, United and Uniting Churches.

The WCRC works in four main areas:

- Communication (fostering church unity and interfaith dialogue)
- Justice (helping churches to act for social and economic rights and care of the environment)
- Mission (facilitating mission renewal and empowerment)
- Partnership (providing funds for church unity, mission and justice projects).

The Uniting General Council was held in Grand Rapids, Michigan, USA from 18–28 June 2010. The theme was 'Unity of the Spirit in the Bond of Peace'.

The General Secretary is Rev. Dr Setri Nyomi, PO Box 2100, 150 route de Ferney, CH-1211 Geneva 2, Switzerland (Tel: 00 41 22 791 62 40; Fax: 00 41 22 791 65 05; E-mail: wcrc@wcrc.ch; Website: www.wcrc.ch).

Conference of European Churches

The Church of Scotland is a founder member of the Conference of European Churches, formed in 1959 and until recently the only body which involved in common membership representatives of every European country (except Albania) from the Atlantic to the Urals. More than 100 Churches, Orthodox and Protestant, are members. Although the Roman Catholic Church is not a member, there is very close co-operation with the Council of European Catholic Bishops' Conferences. With the removal of the long-standing political barriers in Europe, the Conference has now opportunities and responsibilities to assist the Church throughout the continent to offer united witness and service.

CEC held its thirteenth Assembly in Lyons, France from 15–21 July 2009. The theme was 'Called to One Hope in Christ'.

General Secretary, PO Box 2100, 150 route de Ferney, CH-1211 Geneva 2, Switzerland (Tel: 00 41 22 791 61 11; Fax: 00 41 22 791 62 27; E-mail: cec@cec-kek.org; Website: www.ceceurope.org).

CEC: Church and Society Commission

The Church of Scotland was a founder member of the European Ecumenical Commission for Church and Society (EECCS). The Commission owed its origins to the Christian concern and vision of a group of ministers and European civil servants about the future of Europe. It was established in 1973 by Churches recognising the importance of this venture. Membership included Churches and ecumenical bodies from the European Union. The process of integration with CEC was completed in 2000, and the name, Church and Society Commission (CSC), established. In Brussels, CSC monitors Community activity, maintains contact with MEPs and promotes dialogue between the Churches and the institutions. It plays an educational role and encourages the Churches' social and ethical responsibility in European affairs. It has a General Secretary, a study secretary and an executive secretary in Brussels and a small office in Strasbourg.

The Director is Rev. Rüdiger Noll, Ecumenical Centre, 174 rue Joseph II, B-1000 Brussels, Belgium (Tel: 00 32 2 230 17 32; Fax: 00 32 2 231 14 13; E-mail: ved@cec-kek.be).

Community of Protestant Churches in Europe

The Church of Scotland is a founder member of the Community of Protestant Churches in Europe (CPCE), which was formerly known as the Leuenberg Church Fellowship. The Fellowship came into being in 1973 on the basis of the Leuenberg Agreement between the Reformation churches in Europe; the name was changed to the CPCE in 2003. The Leuenberg Agreement stipulates that a common understanding of the Gospel based on the doctrine of Justification by Faith, and interpreted with reference to the proclamation of the Word of God, Baptism and the Lord's Supper, is sufficient to overcome the Lutheran–Reformed church division. The text entitled *The Church of Jesus Christ (1994)* may be regarded as the most significant document produced by the CPCE since its inception.

Over 100 Protestant churches in Europe, and a number of South American churches with European origin, have been signatories to the Leuenberg Agreement, including Lutheran, Reformed, United and Methodist Churches, as well as pre-Reformation Waldensian, Hussite and Czech Brethren, and they grant each other pulpit and table fellowship. Most of the CPCE member churches are minority churches, and this imparts a particular character to their life and witness. A General Assembly is held every six years – the sixth General Assembly was held in Budapest in 2006 – and a thirteen-member Council carries on the work of the CPCE in the intervening period.

The General Secretary of the CPCE is Bishop Professor Dr Michael Bunker, Severin-Schreiber-Gasse 3, A-1180 Vienna, Austria (Tel: 00 43 1 4791523 900; Fax: 00 43 1 4791523 580; E-mail: office@leuenberg.eu; Website: www.leuenberg.eu).

Churches Together in Britain and Ireland (CTBI)

In September 1990, Churches throughout Britain and Ireland solemnly committed themselves to one another, promising to one another to do everything possible together. To provide frameworks for this commitment to joint action, the Churches established CTBI for the United Kingdom and Ireland, and, for Scotland, ACTS, with sister organisations for Wales and for England.

Churches Together in Britain and Ireland works with member churches to co-ordinate responses, share resources and learn from each other's experiences.

There are currently eight subject-based work areas:

- Church and Public Issues
- Theology and Unity
- Mission
- China Desk
- Inter-Religious
- International Students

- Racial Justice
- Action on Asylum and Refugees.

There are also three theme-based work areas:

- Environment and Climate Change
- Culture, Identity and the Public Square
- Migration and Movements of People.

The General Secretary of CTBI is Rev. Bob Fyffe, 39 Eccleston Square, London SW1V IBX (Tel: 0845 680 6851; Fax: 0845 680 6852; E-mail: info@ctbi.org.uk; Website: www.ctbi.org.uk).

Action of Churches Together in Scotland (ACTS)
ACTS is governed by a Board of Trustees which consults with the Members' Meeting. The Members' Meeting is composed of representatives from the nine trustee member Churches. There are four Networks: Church Life, Faith Studies, Mission, and Church and Society. Contributing to the life of the Networks are associated ecumenical groups. Such groups are expressions of the Churches' commitment to work together and to bring together key people in a defined field of interest or expertise. ACTS is an expression of the commitment of the Churches to one another.

ACTS is staffed by a General Secretary, an Assistant General Secretary and two Network Officers. Their offices are based in Alloa.

These structures facilitate regular consultation and intensive co-operation among those who frame the policies and deploy the resources of the Churches in Scotland and throughout Britain and Ireland. At the same time, they afford greater opportunity for a wide range of members of different Churches to meet in common prayer and study.

The General Secretary is Brother Stephen Smyth fms, 7 Forrester Lodge, Inglewood House, Alloa FK10 2HU (Tel: 01259 216980; Fax: 01259 215964; E-mail: ecumenical@acts-scotland.org; Website: www.acts-scotland.org).

---

19. Facilities Management Department

Staff

Facilities Manager: Carole Tait
(Tel: 0131-240 2214)

The responsibilities of the Facilities Manager's Department include:

- management of a maintenance budget for the upkeep of the Church Offices at 121 George Street, Edinburgh;
- responsibility for all aspects of health and safety for staff, visitors and contractors working in the building;
- managing a team of staff providing the Offices with security, reception, mail room, print room, switchboard, day-to-day maintenance services and Committee room bookings;
- overseeing all sub-contracted services to include catering, cleaning, boiler-room maintenance, intruder alarm, fire alarms, lifts and water management;
- maintaining building records in accordance with the requirements of statutory legislation;
- overseeing all alterations to the building and ensuring, where applicable, that they meet DDR, Planning and Building Control regulations.

20. General Treasurer's Department

The General Treasurer's Department and the Stewardship Department have merged to form the Stewardship and Finance Department. See number 30.

---

21. General Trustees

Membership

(New Trustees are appointed, as required, by the General Assembly, on the recommendation of the General Trustees)

Chairman:	Rev. James A.P. Jack BSc BArch BD DMin RIBA ARIAS (2010)
Vice-Chairman:	Mr Iain C. Douglas RD BArch FRIAS RIBA (2010)
Secretary and Clerk:	Mr David D. Robertson LLB NP
Depute Secretary and Clerk:	Mr Keith S. Mason LLB NP

Committees:

Fabric Committee

Convener: Mr Roger G.G. Dodd DipBldgCons(RICS) FRICS (2010)

Chairman's Committee

Convener: Rev. James A.P. Jack BSc BArch BD DMin RIBA ARIAS (2010)

Glebes Committee

Convener: Rev. William Paterson BD (2003)

Finance Committee

Convener: Mr Peter F. King LLB MCIBS (2010)

Audit Committee

Convener: Dr J. Kenneth Macaldowie LLD CA (2005)

Law Committee

Convener: Rev. Alistair G.C. McGregor BA LLB BD QC WS (2008)

Staff

Secretary and Clerk:	Mr David D. Robertson LLB NP
Depute Secretary and Clerk:	Mr Keith S. Mason LLB NP
Assistant Secretaries:	Mr Keith J. Fairweather LLB (Glebes)
	Mrs Morag J. Menneer BSc MRICS (Glebes)
	Mr Brian D. Waller LLB (Ecclesiastical Buildings)
Treasurer:	Mr Iain W. Grimmond BAcc CA
Deputy Treasurer:	Mrs Anne F. Macintosh BA CA
Assistant Treasurer:	Mr Robert A. Allan ACMA CPFA

Remit

The General Trustees are a Property Corporation created and incorporated under the Church of Scotland (General Trustees) Order Confirmation Act 1921. They have Scottish Charity Number SC014574. Their duties, powers and responsibilities were greatly extended by the Church of Scotland (Property & Endowments) Acts and Orders 1925 to 1995, and they are also charged with the administration of the Central Fabric Fund (see below) and the Consolidated Fabric Fund and the Consolidated Stipend Fund in which monies held centrally for the benefit of individual congregations are lodged.

The scope of the work of the Trustees is broad, covering all facets of property administration, but particular reference is made to the following matters:

1. **ECCLESIASTICAL BUILDINGS.** The Trustees' Fabric Committee considers proposals for work at buildings, regardless of how they are vested, and plans of new buildings. Details of all such projects should be submitted to the Committee before work is commenced. The Committee also deals with applications for the release of fabric monies held by the General Trustees for individual congregations, and considers applications for assistance from the Central Fabric Fund from which grants and/or loans may be given to assist congregations faced with expenditure on fabric. Application forms relating to consents for work and possible financial assistance from the Central Fabric Fund are available from the Secretary of the Trustees and require to be submitted through Presbytery with its approval. The Committee normally meets on the first or second Tuesday of each month, apart from July, when it meets on the second last Tuesday, and August, when there is no meeting.

2. **SALE, PURCHASE AND LETTING OF PROPERTIES.** All sales or lets of properties vested in the General Trustees fall to be carried out by them in consultation with the Financial Board of the congregation concerned, and no steps should be taken towards any sale or let without prior consultation with the Secretary of the Trustees. Where property to be purchased is to be vested in the General Trustees, it is essential that contact be made at the earliest possible stage with the Solicitor to the Trustees, who is responsible for the lodging of offers for such properties and all subsequent legal procedure.

3. **GLEBES.** The Trustees are responsible for the administration of Glebes vested in their ownership. All lets fall to be granted by them in consultation with the minister concerned. It should be noted that neither ministers nor Kirk Sessions may grant lets of Glebe land vested in the General Trustees. As part of their Glebe administration, the Trustees review regularly all Glebe rents.

4. **INSURANCE.** Properties vested in the General Trustees must be insured with the Church of Scotland Insurance Co. Ltd, a company wholly owned by the Church of Scotland whose profits are applied for Church purposes. Insurance enquiries should be sent directly to the Company at 67 George Street, Edinburgh EH2 2JG (Tel: 0131-220 4119; Fax: 0131-220 4120; E-mail: enquiries@cosic.co.uk).

22. The Church of Scotland Housing and Loan Fund for Retired Ministers and Widows and Widowers of Ministers

Membership

The Trustees shall be a maximum of 11 in number, being:

1. four appointed by the General Assembly on the nomination of the Trustees, who, having served a term of three years, shall be eligible for reappointment;
2. three ministers and one member appointed by the Ministries Council;
3. three appointed by the Baird Trust.

Chairman:	Mr J.G. Grahame Lees MA LLB NP
Deputy Chairman:	Rev. Ian Taylor BD ThM
Secretary:	Miss Lin J. Macmillan MA

Staff

Property Manager:	Miss Hilary J. Hardy
Property Assistant:	Mr John Lunn

Remit

The Fund, as established by the General Assembly, facilitates the provision of housing accommodation for retired ministers and widows, widowers and separated or divorced spouses of Church of Scotland ministers. When provided, help may take the form of either a house to rent or a house-purchase loan.

The Trustees may grant tenancy of one of their existing houses or they may agree to purchase for rental occupation an appropriate house of an applicant's choosing. Leases are normally on very advantageous terms as regards rental levels. Alternatively, the Trustees may grant a housing loan of up to 70 per cent of a house-purchase price but with an upper limit. Favourable rates of interest are charged.

The Trustees are also prepared to consider assisting those who have managed to house themselves but are seeking to move to more suitable accommodation. Those with a mortgaged home on retirement may be granted a loan to enable them to repay such a mortgage and thereafter to enjoy the favourable rates of interest charged by the Fund.

Ministers making application within five years of retirement, upon their application being approved, will be given a fairly firm commitment that, in due course, either a house will be made available for renting or a house-purchase loan will be offered. Only within nine months of a minister's intended retiral date will the Trustees initiate steps to find a suitable house; only within one year of that date will a loan be advanced. Applications submitted about ten years prior to retirement have the benefit of initial review and, if approved, a place on the preliminary applications list for appropriate decision in due time.

Donations and legacies over the years have been significant in building up this Fund. Congregational contributions have been, and will continue to be, an essential backbone.

The Board of Trustees is a completely independent body answerable to the General Assembly, and enquiries and applications are dealt with in the strictest confidence.

Further information can be obtained from the Secretary, Miss Lin J. Macmillan MA, at the Church of Scotland Offices, 121 George Street, Edinburgh EH2 4YN (Tel: 0131-225 5722 ext. 2310; Fax: 0131-240 2264; E-mail: lmacmillan@cofscotland.org.uk; Website: www.churchofscotland.org.uk).

23. Human Resources Department

Staff

Head of Human Resources and Information Technology: Mike O'Donnell Chartered FCIPD
Human Resources Manager: Karen Tait Chartered CIPO

Remit

The Human Resources Department has responsibility for Recruitment and Selection, Learning and Development, and producing and updating HR Policies and Procedures to ensure that the Central Services Committee, the Ministries Council and the World Mission Council, as employing agencies, are in line with current employment-law legislation. The Department produces contracts of employment and advises on any changes to an individual employee's terms and conditions of employment. It also provides professional Human Resources advice to the organisation on Employee Relations matters, Performance Management and Diversity and Equality.

Our main aim is to work closely with Councils within the organisation to influence strategy so that each Council is making best use of its people and its people opportunities. We take a consultancy role that facilitates and supports each Council's own initiatives and help each other share and work together in consultation with Unite.

---

24. Information Technology Department

Staff

Head of Human Resources and Information Technology: Mike O'Donnell
Information Technology Manager: David Malcolm

The Department provides computer facilities to Councils and Departments within 121 George Street and to Presbytery Clerks and other groups within the Councils. It is also responsible for the telephone service within 121 George Street and the provision of assistance and advice on this to other groups.

The facilities provided include:

- the provision and maintenance of data and voice networks
- the purchase and installation of hardware and software
- support for problems and guidance on the use of hardware and software
- development of in-house software
- maintenance of data within some central systems.

---

25. Law Department

Staff

Solicitor of the Church and of the General Trustees: Mrs Janette S. Wilson LLB NP
Depute Solicitor: Miss Mary E. Macleod LLB NP

Solicitors:	Mrs Jennifer M. Hamilton BA NP
	Mrs Elspeth Annan LLB NP
	Miss Susan Killean LLB NP
	Mrs Anne Steele LLB NP
	Miss Lesa Burns LLB NP
	Miss Jennifer A. Sharp LLB NP

The Law Department of the Church was created in 1937/38. The Department acts in legal matters for the Church and all of its Courts, Councils, Committees, the Church of Scotland General Trustees, the Church of Scotland Trust and the Church of Scotland Investors Trust. It also acts for individual congregations and is available to give advice on any legal matter arising.

The Department is under the charge of the Solicitor of the Church, a post created at the same time as the formation of the Department and a post which is now customarily held along with the traditional posts of Law Agent of the General Assembly and the Custodier of former United Free Church titles (E-mail: lawdept@cofscotland.org.uk).

---

26. Legal Questions Committee

Membership

Convener, Vice-Convener and ten members appointed by the General Assembly on the Report of the Nomination Committee.

Convener:	Rev. Alan J. Hamilton LLB BD
Vice-Convener:	Rev. Sheila M. Kirk BA LLB BD
Secretary:	The Depute Clerk

The Assembly Clerks, Procurator and Solicitor of the Church are non-voting members of the Legal Questions Committee.

Remit

- to advise the General Assembly on questions of Church Law and of Constitutional Law affecting the relationship between Church and State;
- to advise and assist Agencies of the General Assembly in the preparation of proposed legislation and on questions of interpretation, including interpretation of and proposed changes to remits;
- to compile the statistics of the Church, except Youth and Finance; and to supervise on behalf of the General Assembly all arrangements for care of Church Records and for Presbytery visits;
- to conduct an annual review of progress made in discharging the remit and provide a written report to the Council of Assembly.

27. Nomination Committee

Membership
(44 members)

Convener:	Rev. James Dewar MA BD (2011)
Vice-Convener:	Iain McLarty BSc MMus AMusTCL
Secretary:	The Secretary to the Council of Assembly

Remit
To bring before the General Assembly names of persons to serve on the Councils and Standing Committees of the General Assembly.

---

28. Panel on Review and Reform

Membership
(10 members appointed by the General Assembly)

Convener:	Rev. Donald Campbell (2011)
Vice-Convener:	Rev. Jack Holt (2011)

(The Ecumenical Officer attends but without the right to vote or make a motion.)

Staff

Senior Administrator:	Mrs Valerie A. Cox (Tel: 0131-225 5722 ext. 2336; E-mail: vcox@cofscotland.org.uk)

Remit
The remit of the Panel on Review and Reform, as determined by the General Assembly of 2004, is as follows:

- To listen to the voices of congregations, Presbyteries, Agencies and those beyond the Church of Scotland.
- To present a vision of what a Church in need of continual renewal might become and to offer paths by which congregations, Presbyteries and Agencies might travel towards that vision.
- To consider the changing needs, challenges and responsibilities of the Church.
- To have particular regard to the Gospel imperative of priority for the poor, needy and marginalised.

29. Parish Development Fund Committee

This Committee, formerly independent, now operates under the Ministries Council.

Membership
(11 members appointed by the General Assembly. In addition, the Committee has powers to co-opt up to six non-voting advisers with appropriate skills and knowledge.)

Convener:	Rev. Rolf Billes
Vice-Convener:	Rev. Scott Marshall

Staff

Co-ordinator:	Post vacant
Administrator:	Ms Amy Norton
Development Workers:	Mrs Jessie Bruce
	Mrs Fiona Thomson
Contact details:	Tel: 0131-225 5722 ext. 2357
	E-mail: pdf@cofscotland.org.uk

Remit
The aim of the Parish Development Fund is to encourage local churches to work for the benefit of the whole community – and to take risks in living and sharing the Gospel in relevant ways.

The Committee considers applications which are in the spirit of the above aim and the following principles:

- making a positive difference in the lives of people in greatest need in the community
- encouraging partnership work
- helping local people develop their gifts
- encouraging imagination and creativity.

The Committee also administers the Priority Areas Staffing Fund (on behalf of the Ministries Council) to help priority-area congregations to employ extra staff in addition to their Presbytery Plan allocation.

The Committee meets four or five times each year and considers main grant applications twice a year.

Further information on the types of projects supported by the Fund can be found in the Parish Development Fund section of the Church of Scotland website. Please contact the staff for informal discussion about grant-application enquiries and general advice on funding and project development.

---

30. Stewardship and Finance Department

The General Treasurer's Department and the Stewardship Department merged to form the Stewardship and Finance Department on 1 June 2009. This Department is accountable to the Council of Assembly through its Finance Group.

The Departmental e-mail address is: sfadmin@cofscotland.org.uk

Staff based at the Church Offices

General Treasurer:	Mr Iain W. Grimmond BAcc CA
Deputy Treasurer:	Mrs Anne F. Macintosh BA CA
Head of Stewardship:	Rev Gordon D. Jamieson MA BD
Finance Managers:	
Congregational Support	Mr Archie McDowall BA CA
General Trustees	Mr Robert A. Allan ACMA CPFA
Ministries	Miss Catherine E. Robertson BAcc CA
Mission and Discipleship and World Mission	Mr Kenneth C.M. Roger BA CA
Management and Pensions Accountant:	Mrs Kay C. Hastie BSc CA
Payroll Manager:	Mr Ross W. Donaldson

Regional Staff

Stewardship Consultants:

- Mrs Margot R. Robertson (Tel: 01620 893459) for the Presbyteries of: Edinburgh, West Lothian, Lothian, Melrose and Peebles, Duns, Jedburgh, Falkirk
- Mrs Edith Scott (Tel: 01357 520503) for the Presbyteries of: Annandale and Eskdale, Dumfries and Kirkcudbright, Wigtown and Stranraer, Ayr, Irvine and Kilmarnock, Ardrossan, Lanark, Greenock and Paisley, Hamilton
- Mr Stuart G. Sangster (Tel: 01360 622302) for the Presbyteries of: Glasgow, Dumbarton, Argyll, Stirling, Lochaber
- Appointment awaited for the Presbyteries of: Dunfermline, Kirkcaldy, St Andrews, Dunkeld and Meigle, Perth, Dundee, Angus
- Mrs Fiona Penny (Tel: 01771 653442) for the Presbyteries of: Aberdeen, Kincardine and Deeside, Gordon, Buchan, Moray, Abernethy, Inverness

Stewardship requests from congregations in the Presbyteries of Ross, Sutherland, Caithness, Lochcarron – Skye, Uist, Lewis, Orkney, Shetland, England and Europe should be addressed to the Head of Stewardship at the Church Offices in the first instance.

Main Responsibilities of the Stewardship and Finance Department

- Teaching and promoting Christian stewardship throughout the Church;
- Planning and delivery of stewardship programmes in congregations;
- Calculating the annual Ministries and Mission Contribution for each congregation, and processing payments;
- Providing support, training and advice on financial and accounting matters to Congregational Treasurers;
- Providing management and financial accounting support for the Councils, Committees and Statutory Corporations;
- Providing banking arrangements and operating a central banking system for the Councils, Committees and Statutory Corporations;
- Receiving and discharging legacies and bequests on behalf of the Councils, Committees and Statutory Corporations;
- Making VAT returns and tax recoveries on behalf of the Councils, Committees and Statutory Corporations;
- Payroll processing for the Ministries Council, Central Services Committee and the Pension Schemes.

31. Safeguarding Office

Tel: 0131-240 2256; Fax: 0131-220 3113
E-mail: www.churchofscotland.org.uk

Convener:	Ranald Mair (2010)
Vice-Convener:	Rev. Karen Watson (2010)

Staff

Head of Safeguarding	Richard Crosse
Assistant Head of Safeguarding:	Jennifer Milligan

The Church of Scotland Safeguarding Service: What we aim to do and how we provide the service

Introduction

Harm or abuse of children **and** 'adults at risk' can happen anywhere – even in church communities. We have a duty 'to ensure a safe church for all'. The Church of Scotland has a zero-tolerance approach to harm or abuse of people: any type or level is unacceptable.

The possibility of harm or abuse cannot be eliminated, but the safeguarding structures in the Church and the work of the Safeguarding Service seek to minimise the risk of harm occurring or not being responded to appropriately. The Safeguarding Committee, with representation from across the Church, ensures accountability back to the General Assembly, and also provides a forum for shaping policy and direction.

Remit

The Church of Scotland Safeguarding Service aims to:

- ensure best practice in preventing harm or abuse, and
- ensure that the Church makes a timely and appropriate response when harm or abuse is witnessed, suspected or reported.

Preventing harm and abuse

The Safeguarding Service aims to prevent harm or abuse through ensuring that there is good recognition and reporting. It does this by providing:

- information, support and advice on everyday safeguarding matters where there is not an incident of suspected or reported harm or abuse
- advice and support for the **safe recruitment and selection** of all paid staff and volunteers
- the process of applying for membership of the Protection of Vulnerable Groups (Scotland) Act 2007 Scheme for those working with children or 'protected adults'.

Safe recruitment

Safe recruitment is about ensuring that only people suitable to work with children and 'adults at risk' are employed. There is a comprehensive range of safeguarding training programmes to meet the particular learning needs of different groups of people in the Church, including, for example, volunteers, Kirk Sessions, Safeguarding Co-ordinators, Ministries Council, Parish Development Fund and CrossReach services.

Responding to disclosures of harm or abuse or risk of abuse

The Safeguarding Service provides:

- verbal and written advice in situations where harm or abuse is suspected, witnessed or reported to members of the Church. This service is also provided for CrossReach Social Care Council services

- support for Safeguarding Panels working with **convicted sex offenders** to ensure their safe inclusion in worship.

In summary, harm or abuse in the Church is rare, and thankfully the vast majority of people will have no knowledge or experience of it, but even one case is one too many. Our key message is: *'if you suspect or witness harm or abuse, or it is reported to you, you must immediately report it to your Safeguarding Co-ordinator or line manager'.*

Contact can be made with the Safeguarding Office at the address, telephone number, e-mail address and website shown at the head of this article.

---

32. Scottish Churches Parliamentary Office

Tel: 0131-558 8137
E-mail: chloe@actsparl.org

The Scottish Churches Parliamentary Officer is Chloe Clemmons MA MA. The office is within the Scottish Storytelling Centre, 43–45 High Street, Edinburgh EH1 1SR.

The Church of Scotland and the Gaelic Language

Duilleagan Gàidhlig

Ro-ràdh

Ann an 2008, airson a' chiad turais riamh, bha duilleagan air leth againn ann an Gàidhlig anns an *Leabhar Bhliadhnail*, agus a rèir iomraidh rinn mòran toileachadh ris a' ghluasad ùr seo. Tha sinn fo fhiachan am bliadhna a-rithist don Fhear-dheasachaidh airson a bhith cho deònach cuibhreann Ghàidhlig a bhith an lùib na Beurla. An deidh a bhith a' crìonadh fad ghrunn ghinealach, tha a' Ghàidhlig a-nis a' dèanamh adhartais. Tha e cudthromach gum bi Eaglais na h-Alba a' toirt cùl-taic don leasachadh seo, agus gu dearbha tha i aig teis-meadhan a' ghluasaid seo. Ma bheir sinn sùil air eachdraidh, chì sinn nuair a bha a' Ghàidhlig a' fulang làmhachais-làidir anns na linntean a dh'fhalbh, gu robh an Eaglais glè shoirbheachail ann a bhith a' gabhail ceum-tòisich airson an cànan a dhìon.

Eachdraidh

Bha na thachair an dèidh Blàr Chùil Lodair 'na bhuille chruaidh don Ghàidhlig. Cha do chuidich Achd an Fhòghlaim ann an 1872 le cùisean, Achd nach tug fiù 's iomradh air a' Ghàidhlig. Mar thoradh air seo bha a' Ghàidhlig air a fuadach à sgoiltean na h-Alba. Ach bha a' Ghàidhlig air a cleachdadh anns an Eaglais agus bha sin na mheadhan air a cumail o bhith a' dol à sealladh mar chainnt làitheil.

Poileataics

Tha Pàrlamaid na h-Eòrpa a' toirt inbhe don Ghàidhlig mar aon de na mion-chànanan Eòrpach a tha i a' smaoineachadh a bu chòir a cuideachadh agus a h-altram. Beagan bhliadhnachan air ais chuir iad lagh an gnìomh a bha a' cur mar dhleasdanas air Pàrlamaid Bhreatainn àite a thoirt don Ghàidhlig. Ann an 2005, thug Pàrlamaid na h-Alba Achd Gàidhlig na h-Alba air adhart a' cur na Gàidhlig air stèidh mar chainnt nàiseanta, leis an aon spèis ris a' Bheurla.

Cultar

Tha An Comunn Gàidhealach agus buidhnean eile air obair ionmholta a dhèanamh bho chionn fada ann a bhith a' cur na Gàidhlig air adhart mar nì cudthromach nar cultar. Bho chionn ghoirid chuir An Comunn air bhonn co-chruinneachadh de riochdairean o na h-Eaglaisean airson dòighean a lorg air a bhith a' cleachdadh na Gàidhlig ann an adhradh follaiseach. Fad còrr is fichead bliadhna chaidh adhartas mòr a dhèanamh ann am fòghlam tro mheadhan na Gàidhlig, an toiseach tro chròileagain, bun-sgoiltean, agus a-nis ann an àrd-sgoiltean. Thàinig seo gu ìre nuair a stèidhicheadh Sabhal Mòr Ostaig ann am fòghlam àrd-ìre. Bidh an Sabhal Mòr mar phàirt chudthromach de dh'Oilthigh ùr na Gàidhealtachd agus nan Eilean nuair a gheibh an Oilthigh còraichean sgrìobhte. Tha Comann Albannach a' Bhìobaill glè dhealasach ann a bhith a' sìor thoirt taic don Ghàidhlig le bhith a' foillseachadh nan Sgriobtar anns a' chànan. Rinn Gàidheil toileachadh mòr ris an eadar-theangachadh ùr de Shoigeul Eòin ann an Gàidhlig an latha an-diugh a thàinig a-mach bho chaidh an *Leabhar Bliadhnail* mu dheireadh fhoillseachadh.

Eaglais na h-Alba

1. Air feadh na dùthcha, tha adhradh air a chumail ann an Gàidhlig, air Ghàidhealtachd agus air Ghalldachd. (Mar eisimpleir, anns na bailtean mòra tha seirbheis Ghàidhlig air a cumail gach Sàbaid ann an Eaglais Ghàidhealach nam Manach Liatha ann an Dùn Eideann, agus ann an Eaglais Chaluim Chille agus Eaglais Sràid a' Ghàradair ann an Glaschu.) Tha còir gum biodh fios aig Clèireach na Clèire air eaglaisean far a bheil seirbheisean Gàidhlig air an cumail. Thug an t-Àrd-sheanadh ann an 2008 misneachadh do Chlèirean coitheanalan freagarrach ainmeachadh far am bu chòir a' Ghàidhlig a bhith air a cleachdadh ann an adhradh nuair a bha iad a' cur phlànaichean-clèire air bhonn. A bharrachd air sin, tha goireasan ann a bheir cuideachadh don fheadhainn a tha airson Gàidhlig a chleachdadh ann an adhradh.
2. Cha mhòr bho stèidhicheadh *Life and Work* tha *Na Duilleagan Gàidhlig* air a bhith rim faotainn as-asgaidh do neach sam bith a tha gan iarraidh.
3. Tha Eaglais na h-Alba, mar phàirt de dh'Iomairt Chonaltraidh na h-Eaglais, airson a bhith a' brosnachadh cleachdadh na Gàidhlig. Tha duilleagan Gàidhlig air leth air an làraich-lìn.
4. Bho chionn beagan bhliadhnachan tha an t-Àrd-sheanadh air na nithean cudthromach seo a mholadh co-cheangailte ris a' Ghàidhlig.
   (i) Tha an t-Àrd-sheanadh a' cur mealadh-naidheachd air Pàrlamaid na h-Alba airson Achd a' Chànain Ghàidhlig (Alba) a stèidheachadh; tha e a' brosnachadh a' BhBC ach an toir iad cùl-taic do OFCOM a tha ag iarraidh craoladh na Gàidhlig a leudachadh; tha e duilich gu bheil chleachdadh na Gàidhlig a' dol an lughad anns an Eaglais, agus tha e a' toirt cuiridh do Chomhairlean na h-Eaglais, far a bheil sin freagarrach, rannsachadh a dhèanamh air dòighean a lorg a bheir don Ghàidhlig an t-àite sònraichte a chleachd a bhith aice ann am beatha spioradail na h-Alba.
   (ii) Tha an t-Àrd-sheanadh a' cur ìmpidh air Comhairle a' Mhisein agus na Deisciobalachd, ann an co-bhoinn ri Comhairle na Ministrealachd, rannsachadh a dhèanamh air inbhe na Gàidhlig ann an Eaglais na h-Alba ann an dùil ri aithisg a thoirt air beulaibh an Àrd-sheanaidh ann an 2008 air mar a ghabhas leasachadh a dhèanamh air cleachdadh na Gàidhlig anns an Eaglais.
   (iii) Tha an t-Àrd-sheanadh a' gabhail beachd air àireamh nan sgìrean Gàidhlig, agus tha e a' cur ìmpidh Comhairle na Ministrealachd slatan-tomhais a thoirt chun an Ard-sheanaidh ann an 2008 airson gun tèid na sgìrean seo a chomharrachadh anns na bliadhnachan air thoiseach.
   (iv) Tha an t-Àrd-sheanadh a' cur ìmpidh air Comhairle an Àrd-sheanaidh cumail romhpa a bhith a' toirt cùl-taic don Ghàidhlig an taobh a-staigh na h-Eaglais, am measg rudan eile a bhith a' còmhradh ri buidhnean maoineachaidh freagarrach.
   (v) Tha an t-Àrd-sheanadh a' dèanamh toileachaidh ris an Aithisg air Leasachadh ann an

Cleachdadh na Gàidhlig, agus tha e a' brosnachadh Comhairle a' Mhisein agus na Deisciobalachd na plànaichean a tha aca airson an ama air thoiseach a chur an gnìomh.

(vi) Tha an t-Àrd-sheanadh a' dèanamh toileachaidh ris an naidheachd gu bheil Seanal Digiteach Gàidhlig ga chur air bhog, agus tha e a' cur ìmpidh air Comhaire na h-Eaglais agus na Coimhearsnachd, ann an co-bhoinn ri Comhairle an Àrd-sheanaidh, a bhith a' còmhradh ri Comhairle nam Meadhanan Gàidhlig mun àite shònraichte a bu chòir a bhith aig prògraman spioradail anns na prògraman a bhios iad a' cur a-mach.

'S e àm air leth inntinneach a tha seo don Ghàidhlig, agus tha an Eaglais airson a bhith a' gabhail a h-àite anns an iomairt as leth ar cànain. 'S iad na duilleagan seo aon de na dòighean anns a bheil sinn a' dèanamh sin.

An t-Àrd-sheanadh 2011

Aig seirbheis Ghàidhlig an Àrd-sheanaidh ann an Eaglais nam Manach Liath thug an t-Oll. Urr. Ruairidh MacLeòid seachad an searmon, co-cheangailte ri *Bliadhna nan Eilean*. A' togail an fhuinn bha Iain MacLeòid, leugh Seumas Mac an Tàilleir na Sgriobtaran, agus bha an t-Urr. Dòmhnall Iain Moireasdan air ceann na h-ùrnaigh. Sheinn Còisir Lodainn aig toiseach agus aig crìch na seirbheis. Rinn am Moderàtor am Beannachadh ann an deagh Ghàidhlig.

Bha grunnan math an-làthair aig Coinneamh Ghàidhealach an Ard-sheanaidh. A' labhairt am bliadhna bha Iain Moireasdan, seinneadair à Leòdhas a tha air cliù a chosnadh mar fhear-ciùil.

Anns an dealachadh

Tha *Na Duilleagan Gàidhlig* aig *Life and Work* air an leughadh le Gàidheil agus luchd-ionnsachaidh air feadh an t-saoghail. Gheibhear iad an-asgaidh an lùib na h-iris Beurla ma chuirear sibh fios gu oifis *Life and Work*.

Anns an Og-mhìos chaidh a' Bhuidheann Ghàidhlig aig Comhairle an Ard-sheanaidh ath-bheothachadh anns an Og-mhìos, agus tha sùil gum bi pàipearan agus beachdan air an cur air adhart gu dealasach anns na mìosan air thoiseach.

Introduction

The *Year Book 2008/2009*, for the first time ever, featured dedicated pages in Gaelic; and this innovation was very well received. Again, appreciation is expressed to the Editor for his willing co-operation. After many generations of decline, Gaelic is once more moving forward. It is important that the Church of Scotland is seen to be encouraging this progress and indeed is part of it. History teaches that, in the past, when the Gaelic language has been under political oppression, the Church has stood successfully in the vanguard of the defence of the language.

History

The events of Culloden in 1746, as part of the Jacobite rebellion, dealt a cruel blow to the Gaelic language. This was compounded by the Education (Scotland) Act of 1872, which made no mention of the Gaelic language and, indeed, resulted in the outlawing of Gaelic in Scottish schools. The continued use of Gaelic in the Church proved to be the only formal antidote to the disappearance of Gaelic as a viable language.

Politics

The European Parliament recognises Gaelic as one of the minority European languages it sees as important to support and nurture. Some years ago, it passed appropriate legislation laying some responsibility on the United Kingdom Parliament. In 2005, the Scottish Parliament delivered the Gaelic (Scotland) Act, establishing Gaelic as a national language given the same respect as English.

Culture

Traditionally, An Comunn Gaidhealach has done an excellent job in promoting the cultural importance of Gaelic. In recent years, it convened a gathering of representatives from Churches to research how they could help promote the use of Gaelic in public worship. For over twenty years now, there has been substantial growth in Gaelic-medium education, first of all through nurseries, then primary schools and now secondary schools. This has moved on to the establishing of Sabhal Mòr Ostaig in the tertiary sector. The latter, all being well, will become a vital part of the new University of the Highlands and Islands when its charter is granted. The Scottish Bible Society is also eager to continue its support of Gaelic through the provision of Scriptures. Since the last *Year Book* appeared, Gaelic-speakers and learners have warmly welcomed the publication of John's Gospel in modern Gaelic.

The Church of Scotland and its ongoing support for Gaelic

1. Across the nation, public worship continues to be conducted in Gaelic. The General Assembly of 2008 encouraged Presbyteries, as part of their planning, to identify appropriate congregations in which Gaelic must be used regularly in public worship. Furthermore, resources are available to encourage the use of Gaelic in worship in all congregations.
2. Almost since its inception, *Na Duilleagan Gàidhlig*, as part of *Life and Work*, has been available free of charge to any who request it with their *Life and Work* subscription. This is still very much alive.
3. The Church of Scotland, as part of its Communication Strategy, is concerned to promote the use of Gaelic. There are dedicated Gaelic pages on the website.
4. Recent years have seen the General Assembly approve a number of important Deliverances relating to Gaelic. For example:
   (i) The General Assembly congratulate the Scottish Parliament on its passing of the Gaelic Language (Scotland) Bill, encourage the BBC to support OFCOM in its desire for the extension of Gaelic broadcasting, express regret at the substantial decrease in the use of Gaelic in the Church and invite Councils of the Church, where appropriate, to explore ways in which Gaelic can resume its distinctive place within the religious life of Scotland.
   (ii) The General Assembly instructed the Mission and Discipleship Council, in collaboration with the Ministries Council, to undertake an investigation into the present status of Gaelic in the Church of Scotland with a view to reporting to the 2008 General Assembly on the strategic development of the use of the language in the Kirk.
   (iii) The General Assembly note the statistics regarding Gaelic-speaking charges and instructed the Ministries Council to bring to the General Assembly of 2008 an agreed set of criteria for future determination of such designations.
   (iv) The General Assembly instruct the Council of Assembly to continue to support the development of Gaelic within the Church, including discussions with appropriate funding bodies.
   (v) The General Assembly welcome the Report on the Strategic Development of the Use of Gaelic and encourage the Mission and Discipleship Council to develop its future plans.
   (vi) The General Assembly welcome the launch of the Gaelic Digital Broadcasting channel and instruct the Church and Society Council, in co-operation with the Council of Assembly, to discuss with the Gaelic Media Council the significant place of religious programmes in its output.

These are exciting times for the Gaelic language, and the Church is responding to the challenge of our day.

The General Assembly 2011

The preacher at the General Assembly Gaelic service was Rev. Dr Roderick MacLeod, the theme of the service recognising that this is *The Year of Islands*. John MacLeod was the precentor; a Reader, Hamish Taylor, read the Scriptures; and prayers were led by auxiliary minister Rev. Donald John Morrison. Lothian Gaelic choir sang at the beginning and end of the service. The Moderator pronounced the Benediction in excellent Gaelic.

The speaker at the Highland Meeting was Iain Morrison from Lewis, who is gaining fame as a musician.

In conclusion

The Gaelic Supplement of *Life and Work* is read by Gaels and learners of Gaelic all over the world. The monthly Supplement is available on request free of charge along with the main *Life and Work*.

The Gaelic Group within the Council of Assembly was revamped in June 2011, and we look forward to this group making practical suggestions on the use and status of Gaelic within Church and nation.

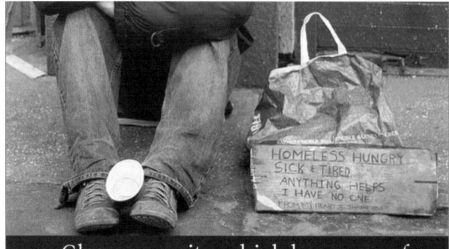

SECTION 2

General Information

(1) OTHER CHURCHES IN THE UNITED KINGDOM

ASSOCIATED PRESBYTERIAN CHURCHES
Clerk of Presbytery: Rev. Archibald N. McPhail, APC Manse, Polvinister Road, Oban PA34 5TN (Tel: 01631 567076; E-mail: archibald.mcphail@virgin.net).

THE REFORMED PRESBYTERIAN CHURCH OF SCOTLAND
Clerk of Presbytery: Rev. Andrew Quigley, Church Offices, 48 North Bridge Street, Airdrie ML6 6NE (Tel: 01236 753971; E-mail: sandrewq@aol.com).

THE FREE CHURCH OF SCOTLAND
Principal Clerk: Rev. James MacIver, 15 North Bank Street, The Mound, Edinburgh EH1 2LS (Tel: 0131-226 5286; E-mail: principal.clerk@freechurch.org).

THE FREE PRESBYTERIAN CHURCH OF SCOTLAND
Clerk of Synod: Rev. John MacLeod, 6 Church Avenue, Sidcup, Kent DA14 6BU (E-mail: jmacl265@aol.com).

THE UNITED FREE CHURCH OF SCOTLAND
General Secretary: Rev. John Fulton BSc BD, United Free Church Offices, 11 Newton Place, Glasgow G3 7PR (Tel: 0141-332 3435; E-mail: office@ufcos.org.uk).

THE PRESBYTERIAN CHURCH IN IRELAND
Clerk of the General Assembly and General Secretary: Rev. Dr Donald J. Watts, Church House, Fisherwick Place, Belfast BT1 6DW (Tel: 02890 322284; E-mail: clerk@presbyterianireland.org).

THE PRESBYTERIAN CHURCH OF WALES
General Secretary: Rev. W. Bryn Williams, Tabernacle Chapel, 81 Merthyr Road, Whitchurch, Cardiff CF14 1DD (Tel: 02920 627465; Fax: 02920 616188; E-mail: swyddfa.office@ebcpcw.org.uk).

THE UNITED REFORMED CHURCH
General Secretary: Rev. Roberta Rominger, 86 Tavistock Place, London WC1H 9RT (Tel: 020 7916 8646; Fax: 020 7916 2021; E-mail: roberta.rominger@urc.org.uk).

UNITED REFORMED CHURCH SYNOD OF SCOTLAND
Synod Clerk: Dr James Merrilees, Church House, 340 Cathedral Street, Glasgow G1 2BQ (Tel: 0141-332 7667; E-mail: jmerrilees@urcscotland.org.uk).

BAPTIST UNION OF SCOTLAND
General Director: Rev. Alan Donaldson, 14 Aytoun Road, Glasgow G41 5RT (Tel: 0141-423 6169; E-mail: director@scottishbaptist.org.uk).

CONGREGATIONAL FEDERATION IN SCOTLAND
Chair: Rev. Malcolm Muir LTh, The Manse, 67 Hinkar Way, Eyemouth, Berwickshire TD14 5EH (Tel: 01890 751506; E-mail: mmuir@cfscotland.org.uk).

RELIGIOUS SOCIETY OF FRIENDS (QUAKERS)
Robin Waterston, Clerk to the General Meeting for Scotland, 128 North Street, St Andrews KY16 9AF (Tel: 01334 474129; E-mail: robin.waterston128@gmail.com).

ROMAN CATHOLIC CHURCH
Rev. Paul Conroy, General Secretary, Bishops' Conference of Scotland, 64 Aitken Street, Airdrie ML6 6LT (Tel: 01236 764061; Fax: 01236 762489; E-mail: gensec@bpsconfscot.com).

THE SALVATION ARMY
Lt-Col. Alan Burns, Divisional Commander and Scotland Secretary, Headquarters and Scotland Secretariat, 12A Dryden Road, Loanhead EH20 9LZ (Tel: 0131-440 9101; E-mail: alan.burns@salvationarmy.org.uk).

SCOTTISH EPISCOPAL CHURCH
General Secretary: Mr John F. Stuart, 21 Grosvenor Crescent, Edinburgh EH12 5EL (Tel: 0131-225 6357; E-mail: secgen@scotland.anglican.org).

THE SYNOD OF THE METHODIST CHURCH IN SCOTLAND
District Administrator: Mrs Fiona Inglis, Methodist Church Office, Scottish Churches House, Kirk Street, Dunblane FK15 0AJ (Tel/Fax: 01786 820295; E-mail: meth@scottishchurcheshouse.org).

GENERAL SYNOD OF THE CHURCH OF ENGLAND
Secretary General: Mr William Fittall, Church House, Great Smith Street, London SW1P 3NZ (Tel: 020 7898 1000; E-mail: william.fittall@churchofengland.org).

---

(2) OVERSEAS CHURCHES

PRESBYTERIAN CHURCH IN CANADA
Clerk of Assembly: 50 Wynford Drive, Toronto, Ontario M3C 1J7, Canada (E-mail: pccadmin@presbycan.ca; Website: www.presbycan.ca).

UNITED CHURCH OF CANADA
General Secretary: Suite 300, 3250 Bloor Street West, Toronto, Ontario M8X 2Y4, Canada (E-mail: info@united-church.ca; Website: www.united-church.ca).

PRESBYTERIAN CHURCH (USA)
Stated Clerk: 100 Witherspoon Street, Louisville, KY 40202-1396, USA (E-mail: presbytel@pcusa.org; Website: www.pcusa.org).

UNITING CHURCH IN AUSTRALIA
General Secretary: PO Box A2266, Sydney South, New South Wales 1235, Australia (E-mail: enquiries@nat.uca.org.au; Website: www.uca.org.au).

PRESBYTERIAN CHURCH OF AUSTRALIA
Clerk of Assembly: PO Box 2196, Strawberry Hills, NSW 2012; 168 Chalmers Street, Surry Hills, NSW 2010, Australia (E-mail: general@pcnsw.org.au; Website: www.presbyterian.org.au).

PRESBYTERIAN CHURCH OF AOTEAROA, NEW ZEALAND
Executive Secretary: PO Box 9049, Wellington, New Zealand (E-mail: aes@presbyterian.org.nz; Website: www.presbyterian.org.nz).

EVANGELICAL PRESBYTERIAN CHURCH, GHANA
Synod Clerk: PO Box 18, Ho, Volta Region, Ghana.

PRESBYTERIAN CHURCH OF GHANA
Director of Ecumenical and Social Relations: PO Box 1800, Accra, Ghana.

PRESBYTERIAN CHURCH OF EAST AFRICA
Secretary General: PO Box 27573, 00506 Nairobi, Kenya.

CHURCH OF CENTRAL AFRICA PRESBYTERIAN
Secretary General, General Assembly: PO Box 30398, Lilongwe 3, Malawi.
General Secretary, Blantyre Synod: PO Box 413, Blantyre, Malawi.
General Secretary, Livingstonia Synod: PO Box 112, Mzuzu, Malawi.
General Secretary, Nkhoma Synod: PO Box 45, Nkhoma, Malawi.

IGREJA EVANGELICA DE CRISTO EM MOÇAMBIQUE (EVANGELICAL CHURCH OF CHRIST IN MOZAMBIQUE)
(Nampula) General Secretary: Cx. Postale 284, Nampula 70100, Mozambique.

PRESBYTERIAN CHURCH OF NIGERIA
Principal Clerk: 26–29 Ehere Road, Ogbor Hill, PO Box 2635, Aba, Abia State, Nigeria.

UNITING PRESBYTERIAN CHURCH IN SOUTHERN AFRICA (SOUTH AFRICA)
General Secretary: PO Box 96188, Brixton 2019, South Africa (postal address); 28 Rhodes Avenue, Parktown 2193, South Africa (street address).

UNITING PRESBYTERIAN CHURCH IN SOUTHERN AFRICA (ZIMBABWE)
Presbytery Clerk: PO Box CY224, Causeway, Harare, Zimbabwe.

PRESBYTERIAN CHURCH OF SUDAN
Head Office: PO Box 40, Malakal, Sudan.

UNITED CHURCH OF ZAMBIA
General Secretary: Nationalist Road at Burma Road, PO Box 50122, 15101 Ridgeway, Lusaka, Zambia.

CHURCH OF BANGLADESH
Moderator: Synod Office, Church of Bangladesh, 54/1 Barobag, Mirpur-2, Dhaka 1216, Bangladesh.

CHURCH OF NORTH INDIA
General Secretary: Synod Office, 16 Pandit Pant Marg, New Delhi 110 001, India.

CHURCH OF SOUTH INDIA
General Secretary: Synod Office, 5 White's Road, Royapettah, Chennai 600 114, India.

PRESBYTERIAN CHURCH OF KOREA
General Secretary: CPO Box 1125, Seoul 110 611, Korea.

PRESBYTERIAN CHURCH IN THE REPUBLIC OF KOREA
General Secretary: 1501 The Korean Ecumenical Building, 136–156 Yunchi-Dong, Chongno-Ku, Seoul, Korea.

THE UNITED MISSION TO NEPAL
Executive Director: PO Box 126, Kathmandu, Nepal.

CHURCH OF PAKISTAN
Moderator: Bishop Sammy Azariah, Diocese of Raiwind, 17 Warris Road, Lahore 54000, Pakistan.

PRESBYTERY OF LANKA
Moderator: 127/1 D S Senanayake Veedyan, Kandy, Sri Lanka.

PRESBYTERIAN CHURCH IN TAIWAN
General Secretary: 3 Lane 269 Roosevelt Road, Sec. 3, Taipei, Taiwan 10763, ROC.

CHURCH OF CHRIST IN THAILAND
General Secretary: 109 CCT (13th Floor), Surawong Road, Khet Bangrak, Bangkok 10500, Thailand.

UNITED CHURCH IN JAMAICA AND THE CAYMAN ISLANDS
General Secretary: 12 Carlton Crescent, PO Box 359, Kingston 10, Jamaica (E-mail: generalsecretary@ucjci.com).

PRESBYTERIAN CHURCH IN TRINIDAD AND TOBAGO
General Secretary: Box 187, Paradise Hill, San Fernando, Trinidad (E-mail: pctt@tstt.net.tt).

PRESBYTERIAN REFORMED CHURCH IN CUBA
General Secretary: Evangelical Theological Seminary of Matanzas, Apartada 149, Dos de Mayofinal, Matanzas, Cuba.

EVANGELICAL CHURCH OF THE CZECH BRETHREN
Moderator: Jungmannova 9, PO Box 466, CZ-11121 Praha 1, Czech Republic (E-mail: ekumena@srcce.cz; Website: www.srcce.cz).

HUNGARIAN REFORMED CHURCH
General Secretary: PF Box 5, H-1440 Budapest, Hungary (E-mail: tz@zsinatiiroda.hu; Website: www.reformatus.hu).

WALDENSIAN CHURCH
Moderator: Via Firenze 38, 00184 Rome, Italy (E-mail: moderatore@chiesavaldese.org; Website: www.chiesavaldese.org).

PROTESTANT CHURCH IN THE NETHERLANDS
Joseph Haydnlaan 2A, Postbus 8504, NL-3503 RM Utrecht. Landelijk Dienstcentrum Samen op Weg-Kerken, Postbus 8504, NL-3503 RM Utrecht (Tel/Fax: +31 30 880 1880; Website: www.protestantchurch.nl).

SYNOD OF THE NILE OF THE EVANGELICAL CHURCH
General Secretary: Synod of the Nile of the Evangelical Church, PO Box 1248, Cairo, Egypt (E-mail: epcegypt@yahoo.com).

DIOCESE OF THE EPISCOPAL CHURCH IN JERUSALEM AND THE MIDDLE EAST
Bishop's Office: PO Box 19122, Jerusalem 91191, via Israel (E-mail: development@j-diocese.org; Website: www.j.diocese.org).

NATIONAL EVANGELICAL SYNOD OF SYRIA AND LEBANON
General Secretary: PO Box 70890, Antelias, Lebanon (E-mail: nessl@synod-sl.org).

[Full information on Churches overseas may be obtained from the World Mission Council.]

---

(3) SCOTTISH DIVINITY FACULTIES

[* denotes a Minister of the Church of Scotland]
[(R) Reader (SL) Senior Lecturer (L) Lecturer]

ABERDEEN

(School of Divinity, History and Philosophy)
King's College, Old Aberdeen AB24 3UB
(Tel: 01224 272380; Fax: 01224 273750;
E-mail: divinity@abdn.ac.uk)

Master of Christ's College: Rev. J.H.A. Dick* MA MSc BD
(E-mail: christs-college@abdn.ac.uk)

Head of School: Rev. Philip Ziegler BA MA MDiv ThD

Deputy Head of School: Rev. Christopher Brittain BA MDiv PhD

Professors:
Tom Greggs MA(Oxon) PhD(Cantab) (Historical and Doctrinal Theology)
Steve Mason BA MA PhD (New Testament Exegesis)
Robert Segal BA MA PhD (Religious Studies)
Rev. Joachim Schaper DipTheol PhD (Old Testament)
Rev. John Swinton* BD PhD RNM RNMD (Practical Theology and Pastoral Care)
Rev. Bernd Wannenwetsch MA DrTheol DrTheolHabil (Theological Ethics)
John Webster MA PhD DD (Systematic Theology)

Senior Lecturers:
Andrew Clarke BA MA PhD (New Testament)
Martin Mills MA PhD (Religious Studies)
Rev. Philip Ziegler BA MA MDiv ThD (Systematic Theology)

Lecturers:

Kenneth Aitken BD PhD (Hebrew Bible)
Thomas Bokedal ThD MTh (New Testament)
Rev. Christopher Brittain BA MDiv PhD (Practical Theology)
Brian Brock BS MA DipTheol DPhil (Moral and Practical Theology)
Marie-Luise Ehrenschwendtner DrTheol PhD (Church History)
Jane Heath BA PhD (New Testament)
Jutta Leonhardt-Balzer DipTheol PhD (New Testament)
Lukas Pokorny MA PhD (Religious Studies)
Lena-Sofia Tiemeyer BA MA MPhil (Old Testament/Hebrew Bible)
Will Tuladhar-Douglas BA MA MPhil DPhil (Religious Studies)
Donald Wood BA MA MPhil DPhil (Systematic Theology)

ST ANDREWS

(University College of St Mary)
St Mary's College, St Andrews, Fife KY16 9JU
(Tel: 01334 462850/1; Fax: 01334 462852)

Principal, Dean and Head of School: I.J. Davidson MA PhD MTh

Chairs:

M.I. Aguilar BA MA STB PhD (Religion and Politics)
D.W. Brown MA PhD DPhil FBA (Theology, Aesthetics and Culture and Wardlaw Professor)
J.R. Davila BA MA PhD (Early Jewish Studies)
I.J. Davidson MA PhD MTh (Systematic and Historical Theology)
K. de Troyer STB MA STL PhD (Old Testament/Hebrew Bible)
T.A. Hart BA PhD (Divinity)
R.A. Piper BA BD PhD (Christian Origins)
A.J. Torrance* MA BD DrTheol (Systematic Theology)
N.T. Wright MA DPhil DD (New Testament and Early Christianity)

Readerships, Senior Lectureships, Lectureships:

I.C. Bradley* BA MA BD DPhil (R) (Practical Theology)
M.W. Elliott BA BD PhD (Church History)
S.R. Holmes BA MA MTh PGDip PhD (Theology)
G.R. Hopps BA MPhil PhD (Literature and Theology)
K.R. Iverson BS ThM PhD (New Testament)
G. Macaskill BSc DipTh PhD (New Testament)

N. MacDonald MA MPhil PhD (R) (Old Testament and Hebrew)
E. Stoddart BD PhD (Practical Theology)
W.A. Tooman BA MA MA PhD (Old Testament/Hebrew Bible)

EDINBURGH

(School of Divinity and New College)
New College, Mound Place, Edinburgh EH1 2LX
(Tel: 0131-650 8900; Fax: 0131-650 7952; E-mail: divinity.faculty@ed.ac.uk)

Head of School:	Professor Stewart J. Brown BA MA PhD FRHistS FRSE
Principal of New College:	Rev. Professor David A.S. Fergusson* MA BD DPhil FRSE
Assistant Principal of New College:	Rev. Frances M. Henderson* BA BD PhD
Chairs:	Professor Hans Barstad DrTheol (Hebrew and Old Testament)
	Professor Stewart J. Brown BA MA PhD FRHistS FRSE (Ecclesiastical History)
	Professor Jane E.A. Dawson BA PhD DipEd (John Laing Professor of Reformation History)
	Rev. Professor David A.S. Fergusson* MA BD DPhil FRSE (Divinity)
	Professor Timothy Lim BA MPhil DPhil (Biblical Studies)
	Professor Michael S. Northcott MA PhD (Ethics)
	Rev. Professor Oliver O'Donovan BA MA DPhil FRSE (Christian Ethics and Practical Theology)
	Professor Brian Stanley MA PhD (World Christianity)

Readers, Senior Lecturers and Lecturers:

Biblical Studies:	David J. Reimer BTh BA MA DPhil (SL)
	Graham Paul Foster PhD MSt BD (SL)
	Helen K. Bond MTheol PhD (SL)
Theology and Ethics:	Nicholas Adams MA PhD (SL)
	Jolyon Mitchell BA MA PhD (SL)
	Cecelia Clegg BD MSc PhD (SL)
	Rev. Ewan Kelly* MB ChB BD PhD (SL) (part-time)
	Paul Nimmo MA BD DipIA ThM PhD (L)
	Michael Purcell MA PhD PhL PhB (SL)
	Sara Parvis BA PhD (L)
Ecclesiastical History:	Susan Hardman Moore MA PhD (SL)
Religious Studies:	Elizabeth Koepping MA PhD (SL)
	Steven Sutcliffe BA MPhil PhD (SL)
	Hannah Holtschneider MPhil PhD (SL)
	Afeosemime U. Adogame BA MA PhD (SL)

Fulton Lecturer in Speech and Communication:
Richard Ellis BSc MEd LGSM

GLASGOW

School of Critical Studies
Theology and Religious Studies Subject Area
4 The Square, University of Glasgow, Glasgow G12 8QQ
(Tel: 0141-330 6526; Fax: 0141-330 4943; E-mail: divinity@arts.gla.ac.uk;
Website: www.gla.ac.uk/departments/theology)

Head of Subject: Dr Heather Walton

Trinity College
Principal of Trinity College: Rev. Dr Doug Gay
Clerk to Trinity College: Rev. Dr Akma Adam

Chairs:
Prof. Werner Jeanrond (Divinity)
Rev. Prof. David Jasper (Theology and Literature)
Prof. Richard King (Religious Studies)
Prof. Mona Siddiqui (Public Understanding of Islam)
Prof. Yvonne Sherwood (Biblical Studies)

Readers, Senior Lecturers, Lecturers and Fellows etc.

Biblical Studies:
Rev. Dr Akma Adam (L)
Dr Ward Blanton (L)
Mrs Linda Knox (Language Tutor)
Dr Sarah Nicholson (L)

Church History: Rev. Canon Dr Charlotte Methven

Catholic Theology: Ms Julie Clague (L)

Practical Theology:
Rev. Dr Doug Gay (L)
Dr Heather Walton

Islamic Studies: Dr Lloyd Ridgeon (SL)

Associate Staff (Free Church of Scotland College, Edinburgh)
Rev. Donald M. MacDonald
Rev. Prof. John R. McIntosh
Rev. Prof. John L. Mackay
Rev. Alasdair I. MacLeod
Rev. Prof. Donald Macleod
Rev. John A. MacLeod
Rev. Neil MacMillan
Rev. Duncan Peters

HIGHLAND THEOLOGICAL COLLEGE UHI

High Street, Dingwall IV15 9HA
(Tel: 01349 780000; Fax: 01349 780201;
E-mail: htc@uhi.ac.uk)

Principal of HTC: Rev. Hector Morrison* BSc BD MTh
Vice-Principal of HTC: Jamie Grant PhD MA LLB

Lecturers:
Hector Morrison* BSc BD MTh (Old Testament and Hebrew)
Jamie Grant PhD MA LLB (Biblical Studies)
Jason Maston BA MA PhD (New Testament)
Innes Visagie MA BTh BA PhD (Pastoral Theology)
Nick Needham BD PhD (Church History)
Robert Shillaker BSc BA PhD (Systematic Theology)

---

(4) SOCIETIES AND ASSOCIATIONS

The undernoted list shows the name of the Association, along with the name and address of the Secretary.

INTER-CHURCH ASSOCIATIONS

THE FELLOWSHIP OF ST ANDREW: The fellowship promotes dialogue between Churches of the east and the west in Scotland. Further information available from the Secretary, Rev. John G. Pickles, 1 Annerley Road, Annan DG12 6HE (Tel: 01461 202626; E-mail: jgpickles@hotmail.com).

THE FELLOWSHIP OF ST THOMAS: An ecumenical association formed to promote informed interest in and to learn from the experience of Churches in South Asia (India, Pakistan, Bangladesh, Nepal, Sri Lanka and Burma (Myanmar)). Secretary: Rev. Murdoch MacKenzie, 'Torridon', 4 Ferryfield Road, Connel, Oban PA37 1SR (Tel: 01631 710550; E-mail: mackenziema@ymail.com).

FRONTIER YOUTH TRUST: Encourages and resources those engaged in youth work, particularly with disadvantaged young people. Co-ordinator: Matt Hall, 8 Dalswinton Street, Glasgow G34 0PS (Tel: 0141-771 9151).

IONA COMMUNITY: Leader: Rev. Peter J. Macdonald, Fourth Floor, Savoy House, 140 Sauchiehall Street, Glasgow G2 3DH (Tel: 0141-332 6343; Fax: 0141-332 1090; E-mail: admin@iona.org.uk; Website: www.iona.org.uk); Warden: Iona Abbey, Isle of Iona, Argyll PA76 6SN (Tel: 01681 700404).

SCOTTISH CHURCHES HOUSING ACTION: Unites the Scottish Churches in tackling homelessness; advises on using property for affordable housing. Chief Executive: Alastair Cameron, 44 Hanover Street, Edinburgh EH2 2DR (Tel: 0131-477 4500; Fax: 0131-477 2710; E-mail: info@churches-housing.org; Website: www.churches-housing.org).

SCOTTISH JOINT COMMITTEE ON RELIGIOUS AND MORAL EDUCATION: This is an interfaith body that began as a joint partnership between the Educational Institute of Scotland and the Church of Scotland to provide resources, training and support for the work of religious and moral education in schools. Rev. Ewan R. Aitken, 121 George Street, Edinburgh EH2 4YN (Tel: 0131-225 5722), and Mr Lachlan Bradley, 6 Clairmont Gardens, Glasgow G3 7LW (Tel: 0141-353 3595).

YMCA SCOTLAND: Offers support, training and guidance to churches seeking to reach out to love and serve community needs. National General Secretary: Mr Peter Crory, James Love House, 11 Rutland Street, Edinburgh EH1 2DQ (Tel: 0131-228 1464; E-mail: info@ymcascotland.org; Website: www.ymcascotland.org).

INTERSERVE SCOTLAND: We are part of Interserve, an international, evangelical and interdenominational organisation with over 150 years of Christian service. The purpose of Interserve is 'to make Jesus Christ known through *wholistic* ministry in partnership with the global church, among the neediest peoples of Asia and the Arab world', and our vision is 'Lives and communities transformed through encounter with Jesus Christ'. Interserve supports over 800 people in cross-cultural ministry in a wide range of work including children and youth, the environment, evangelism, Bible training, engineering, agriculture, business development and health. We rely on supporters in Scotland and throughout the UK to join us. Director: Grace Penney, 4 Blairtummock Place, Panorama Business Village, Queenslie, Glasgow G33 4EN (Tel: 0141-781 1982; Fax: 0141-781 1572; E-mail: info@isscot.org; Website: www.interservescotland.org.uk).

SCRIPTURE UNION SCOTLAND: 70 Milton Street, Glasgow G4 0HR (Tel: 0141-332 1162; Fax: 0141-352 7600; E-mail: info@suscotland.org.uk; Website: www.suscotland.org.uk). Scripture Union Scotland's vision is to see all the children and young people in Scotland exploring the Bible and responding to the significance of Jesus. SU Scotland works in schools running Christian Focus Weeks, taking part in assemblies and supporting extra-curricular groups. It also offers 'Classroom Outdoors', an outdoor education programme for school groups that is based around Curriculum for Excellence. These events take place at its two activity centres, Lendrick Muir (near Kinross) and Altnacriche (near Aviemore), which also cater for church or school groups throughout the year. During the school holidays and at weekends, it runs an extensive programme of events for school-age children – including residential holidays (some focused on disadvantaged children and young people), missions and church-based holiday clubs. In addition, it runs discipleship and training programmes for young people and is committed to promoting prayer for, and by, the young people of Scotland through a range of national prayer events and the *Pray for Schools Scotland* initiative. *Ignite* is SU Scotland's online discipleship website for young people, providing a safe space for them to delve deeper into the Bible and the Christian faith, ask questions and join online discussions.

STUDENT CHRISTIAN MOVEMENT: National Co-ordinator: Hilary Topp, SCM, 308F, The Big Peg, 120 Vyse Street, Hockley, Birmingham B18 6ND (Tel: 0121-200 3355; E-mail: scm@movement.org.uk; Website: www.movement.org.uk). The Student Christian Movement (SCM) is a student-led community passionate about living out our faith in the real world. We have a network of groups around the country and organise national events.

UNIVERSITIES AND COLLEGES CHRISTIAN FELLOWSHIP: Pod Bhogal, 38 De Montfort Street, Leicester LE1 7GP (Tel: 0116-255 1700; E-mail: pbhogal@uccf.org.uk).

WORLD DAY OF PRAYER: SCOTTISH COMMITTEE: Convener: Christian Williams, 61 McCallum Gardens, Strathview Estate, Bellshill ML4 2SR. Secretary: Marjorie Paton, 'Lindisfarne', 19 Links Road, Lundin Links, Leven KY8 6AS (Tel: 01333 329830; E-mail: marjoriepaton.wdp@btinternet.com; Website: www.wdpscotland.org.uk).

CHURCH OF SCOTLAND SOCIETIES

CHURCH OF SCOTLAND ABSTAINER'S ASSOCIATION: Recognising that alcohol is a major – indeed a growing – problem within Scotland, the aim of the Church of Scotland Abstainer's Association, with its motto 'Abstinence makes sense', is to encourage more people to choose a healthy alcohol-free lifestyle. Further details are available from 'Blochairn', 17A Culduthel Road, Inverness IV24 4AG (Website: www.kirkabstainers.org.uk).

CHURCH OF SCOTLAND WORLD MISSION COUNCIL OVERSEAS ASSOCIATION: (previously AROS): Secretary: Mr Walter Dunlop, 50 Oxgangs Road North, Edinburgh EH13 9DR (Tel: 0131-477 9586).

FORUM OF GENERAL ASSEMBLY AND PRESBYTERY CLERKS: Rev. Rosemary Frew, 83 Milton Road, Kirkcaldy KY1 1TP (Tel: 01592 260315; E-mail: kirkcaldy@cofscotland.org.uk).

FORWARD TOGETHER: An organisation for evangelicals within the Church of Scotland. Chairman: Rev. Steven Reid BAcc CA BD, 74 Lanark Road, Crossford, Carluke ML8 5RE (Tel: 01555 860415; Website: www.forwardtogether.org.uk).

SCOTTISH CHURCH SOCIETY: Secretary: Rev. W. Gerald Jones MA BD MTh, The Manse, Patna Road, Kirkmichael, Maybole KA19 7PJ (Tel: 01655 750286; Website: www.scottishchurchsociety.org.uk).

SCOTTISH CHURCH THEOLOGY SOCIETY: Rev. Mary M. Cranfield MA BD DMin, The Manse, Daviot, Inverurie AB51 0HY (Tel: 01467 671241; E-mail: marymc@ukgateway.net). The Society encourages theological exploration and discussion of the main issues confronting the Church in the twenty-first century.

SOCIETY OF FRIENDS OF ST ANDREW'S JERUSALEM: Hon. Secretary: Major J.M.K. Erskine MBE, World Mission Council, 121 George Street, Edinburgh EH2 4YN. Hon. Treasurer: Mrs Anne Macintosh BA CA, Assistant Treasurer, The Church of Scotland, 121 George Street, Edinburgh EH2 4YN (Tel: 0131-225 5722).

THE FRIENDS OF TABEETHA SCHOOL, JAFFA: President: Miss Eileen Robertson. Hon. Secretary: Rev. Iain F. Paton, 'Lindisfarne', 19 Links Road, Lundin Links, Leven KY8 6AS (Tel: 01333 320765).

THE CHURCH OF SCOTLAND CHAPLAINS' ASSOCIATION: Hon. Secretary: Rev. Neil N. Gardner MA BD, The Manse of Canongate, Edinburgh EH8 8BR (Tel: 0131-556 3515).

THE CHURCH OF SCOTLAND RETIRED MINISTERS' ASSOCIATION: Hon. Secretary: Rev. Murray Chalmers, 8 Easter Warriston, Edinburgh EH7 4QX (Tel: 0131-552 4211).

THE CHURCH SERVICE SOCIETY: Secretary: Rev. Dr Douglas Galbraith, 34 Balbirnie Street, Markinch, Glenrothes KY7 6DA (E-mail: dgalbraith@hotmail.com).

THE IRISH MINISTERS' FRATERNAL: Secretary: Rev. Eric G. McKimmon BA BD MTh, The Manse, St Andrews Road, Ceres, Cupar KY15 5NQ (Tel: 01334 829466).

BIBLE SOCIETIES

THE SCOTTISH BIBLE SOCIETY: Chief Executive: Elaine Duncan, 7 Hampton Terrace, Edinburgh EH12 5XU (Tel: 0131-347 9813).

WEST OF SCOTLAND BIBLE SOCIETY: Secretary: Rev. Finlay MacKenzie, 51 Rowallan Gardens, Glasgow G11 7LH (Tel: 0141-563 5276; E-mail: f.c.mack51@ntlworld.com).

GENERAL

THE BOYS' BRIGADE: Scottish Headquarters, Carronvale House, Carronvale Road, Larbert FK5 3LH (Tel: 01324 562008; Fax: 01324 552323; E-mail: scottishhq@boys-brigade.org.uk).

THE GIRLS' BRIGADE IN SCOTLAND: 11A Woodside Crescent, Glasgow G3 7UL (Tel: 0141-332 1765; E-mail: enquiries@girls-brigade-scotland.org.uk; Website: www.girls-brigade-scotland.org.uk).

GIRLGUIDING SCOTLAND: 16 Coates Crescent, Edinburgh EH3 7AH (Tel: 0131-226 4511; Fax: 0131-220 4828; E-mail: administrator@girlguiding-scot.org.uk).

THE SCOUT ASSOCIATION: Scottish Headquarters, Fordell Firs, Hillend, Dunfermline KY11 7HQ (Tel: 01383 419073; E-mail: shq@scouts-scotland.org.uk; Website: www.scouts-scotland.org.uk).

YOUTH SCOTLAND: Balfour House, 19 Bonnington Grove, Edinburgh EH6 4BL (Tel: 0131-554 2561; Fax: 0131-454 3438; E-mail: office@youthscotland.org.uk).

CHRISTIAN AID SCOTLAND: Kathy Galloway, Head of Christian Aid Scotland, The Pentagon Centre, 36 Washington Street, Glasgow G3 8AZ (Tel: 0141-221 7475; Fax: 0141-241 6145; E-mail: glasgow@christian-aid.org). Edinburgh Office: Tel: 0131-220 1254. Perth Office: Tel: 01738 643982.

ECO-CONGREGATION SCOTLAND: 121 George Street, Edinburgh EH2 4YN (Tel: 0131-240 2274; E-mail: manager@econgregation.org; Website: www.econgregation.org/scotland). Eco-Congregation Scotland is the largest movement of community-based environment groups in Scotland. We offer a programme to help congregations reduce their impact on climate change and live sustainably in a world of limited resources.

FEED THE MINDS: Park Place, 12 Lawn Lane, London SW8 1UD (Tel: 08451 212102).

LADIES' GAELIC SCHOOLS AND HIGHLAND BURSARY ASSOCIATION: Mr Donald J. Macdonald, 35 Durham Avenue, Edinburgh EH15 1RZ.

RELATIONSHIPS SCOTLAND: Chief Executive: Mr Stuart Valentine, 18 York Place, Edinburgh EH1 3EP (Tel: 0845 119 2020; Fax: 0845 119 6089; E-mail: enquiries@relationships-scotland.org.uk; Website: www.relationships-scotland.org.uk).

BROKEN RITES: Support group for divorced and separated clergy spouses (Tel: 01309 641526 or 01257 423893; Website: www.brokenrites.org).

SCOTTISH CHURCH HISTORY SOCIETY: Hon. Secretary: Miss Christine Lumsden BA MA, 80/3 Slateford Road, Edinburgh EH11 1QU (Tel: 0131-337 3644; E-mail: christinalumsden@btinternet.com).

SCOTTISH EVANGELICAL THEOLOGY SOCIETY: Secretary: Rosemary Dowsett, 4 Borden Road, Glasgow G13 1QX (Tel: 0141-959 4976; E-mail: dickandrosedowsett@googlemail.com).

CHRISTIAN ENDEAVOUR IN SCOTLAND: Winning, Teaching and Training Youngsters for Christ and the Church: 16 Queen Street, Alloa FK10 2AR (Tel: 01259 215101; E-mail: admin@cescotland.org; Website: www.cescotland.org).

TEARFUND: 100 Church Road, Teddington TW11 8QE (Tel: 0845 355 8355). Director: Lynne Paterson, Tearfund Scotland, Challenge House, 29 Canal Street, Glasgow G4 0AD (Tel: 0141-332 3621; E-mail: scotland@tearfund.org; Website: www.tearfund.org).

THE LEPROSY MISSION SCOTLAND: Suite 2, Earlsgate Lodge, Livilands Lane, Stirling FK8 2BG (Tel: 01786 449266; Fax: 01786 449766). National Director: Miss Linda Todd. Communications Manager (including Area Co-ordinator, Central and South): Mr Stuart McAra. Area Co-ordinator, North and Islands: Mr Jim Clark (Tel: 01343 843837; E-mail: contactus@tlmscotland.org.uk or meetings@tlmscotland.org.uk; Website: www.tlmscotland.org.uk).

DAYONE CHRISTIAN MINISTRIES (THE LORD'S DAY OBSERVANCE SOCIETY): Ryelands Road, Leominster, Herefordshire HR6 8NZ. Contact Mark Roberts for further information (Tel: 01568 613740; E-mail: sales@dayone.co.uk).

THE SCOTTISH REFORMATION SOCIETY: Chairman: Rev. Dr S. James Millar. Vice-Chairman: Mr John Smart. Hon. Treasurer and Secretary: Mr James A. Dickson, The Magdalen Chapel, 41 Cowgate, Edinburgh EH1 1JR (Tel: 0131-220 1450; E-mail: info@scottishreformationsociety.org.uk; Website: www.scottishreformationsociety.org.uk).

THE SOCIETY IN SCOTLAND FOR PROPAGATING CHRISTIAN KNOWLEDGE: Chairman: Rev. Andrew Anderson; Honorary Secretary: Philip Halford-MacLeod. Address: SSPCK, c/o Tods Murray LLP, Edinburgh Quay, 133 Fountainbridge, Edinburgh EH3 9AG (Tel: 0131-656 2000; Website: www.sspck.co.uk; E-mail: philip_h@madasafish.com).

THE WALDENSIAN MISSIONS AID SOCIETY FOR WORK IN ITALY: David A. Lamb SSC, 36 Liberton Drive, Edinburgh EH16 6NN (Tel: 0131-664 3059; E-mail: david@dlamb.co.uk).

YWCA SCOTLAND: National Co-ordinator: Kim Smith, 4B Gayfield Place, Edinburgh EH7 4AB (Tel: 0131-558 8000; E-mail: reception@ywcascotland.org; Website: www.ywcascotland.org).

---

(5) TRUSTS AND FUNDS

THE SOCIETY FOR THE BENEFIT OF THE SONS AND DAUGHTERS OF THE CLERGY OF THE CHURCH OF SCOTLAND

Secretary and Treasurer: Mrs Fiona M.M. Watson CA
Exchange Place 3,
Semple Street,
Edinburgh EH3 8BL (Tel: 0131-473 3500;
E-mail: charity@scott-moncrieff.com)

Annual grants are made to assist in the education of the children (normally between the ages of 12 and 25 years) of ministers of the Church of Scotland. The Society also gives grants to aged and infirm daughters of ministers and ministers' unmarried daughters and sisters who are in need. Applications are to be lodged by 31 May in each year.

THE GLASGOW SOCIETY OF THE SONS AND DAUGHTERS OF MINISTERS OF THE CHURCH OF SCOTLAND

Secretary and Treasurer: Mrs Fiona M.M. Watson CA
Exchange Place 3,
Semple Street,
Edinburgh EH3 8BL (Tel: 0131-473 3500;
E-mail: charity@scott-moncrieff.com)

The Society's primary purpose is to grant financial assistance to children (no matter what age) of deceased ministers of the Church of Scotland. Applications are to be submitted by 1 February in each year. To the extent that funds are available, grants are also given for the children of ministers or retired ministers, although such grants are normally restricted to university and college students. These latter grants are considered in conjunction with the Edinburgh-based Society. Limited funds are also available for individual application for special needs or projects. Applications are to be submitted by 31 May in each year. Emergency applications can be dealt with at any time when need arises. Application forms may be obtained from the Secretary.

ESDAILE TRUST:

Clerk and Treasurer: Mrs Fiona M.M. Watson CA
Exchange Place 3,
Semple Street,
Edinburgh EH3 8BL (Tel: 0131-473 3500;
E-mail: charity@scott-moncrieff.com)

Assists education and advancement of daughters of ministers, missionaries and widowed deaconesses of the Church of Scotland between 12 and 25 years of age. Applications are to be lodged by 31 May in each year.

HOLIDAYS FOR MINISTERS

The undernoted hotels provide special terms for ministers and their families. Fuller information may be obtained from the establishments:

CRIEFF HYDRO Ltd and MURRAYPARK HOTEL: The William Meikle Trust Fund and Paton Fund make provision whereby active ministers and their spouses, members of the Diaconate and other full-time employees of the Church of Scotland may enjoy hotel and self-catering accommodation at certain times of the year. BIG Country provides supervised childcare for children aged 2 to 12 years. (Free supervised childcare is not available for guests staying at the Murraypark Hotel.) For all our guests, Crieff Hydro offers a wide range of leisure facilities such as the Leisure Pool, gym, in-house cinema, entertainment and many outdoor activities. To make a reservation, please contact Accommodation Sales on 01764 651670, quoting your employee reference number; they are available to take your call from 8am to 9pm daily. Alternatively, you can e-mail your enquiry to enquiries@crieffhydro.com or post it to Accommodation Sales Team, Crieff Hydro, Ferntower Road, Crieff PH7 3LQ. If you are unable to quote your employee reference number at the time of making your reservation, you must ask the Church of Scotland's Human Resources Department to e-mail us to verify your eligibility. Only e-mails originated from the Church of Scotland will be accepted.

THE CINTRA BEQUEST: The Trust provides financial assistance towards the cost of accommodation in Scotland for missionaries on leave, or for ministers on temporary holiday, or on rest. In addition, due to additional funds generously donated by the Tod Endowment Trust, grants can be given to defray the cost of obtaining rest and recuperation in Scotland. In appropriate cases, therefore, the cost of travel within Scotland may also be met. Applications should be made to Mrs J.S. Wilson, Solicitor, 121 George Street, Edinburgh EH2 4YN.

TOD ENDOWMENT TRUST: CINTRA BEQUEST: MINISTRY BENEVOLENT FUND: The Trustees of the Cintra Bequest and of the Church of Scotland Ministry Benevolent Fund can consider an application for a grant from the Tod Endowment funds from any ordained or commissioned minister or deacon in Scotland of at least two years' standing before the date of application, to assist with the cost of the beneficiary and his or her spouse or partner and dependants obtaining rest and recuperation in Scotland. The Trustees of the Church of Scotland Ministry Benevolent Fund can also consider an application from an ordained or commissioned minister or deacon who has retired. Application forms are available from Mrs J.S. Wilson, Solicitor (for the Cintra Bequest), and from Mrs C. Robertson, Assistant Treasurer (Ministries) (for the Ministry Benevolent Fund). The address in both cases is 121 George Street, Edinburgh EH2 4YN (Tel: 0131-225 5722). (Attention is drawn to separate individual entries for both the Cintra Bequest and the Church of Scotland Ministry Benevolent Fund.)

THE LYALL BEQUEST: Scottish Charity Number SC005542. Makes available the following benefits to ministers of the Church of Scotland:

1. A grant towards the cost of holiday accommodation in or close to the town of St Andrews may be paid to any minister and to his or her spouse at the rate of £100 per week each for a stay of one week or longer. Grants for a stay of less than one week may also be paid, at the rate of £14 per day each. Due to the number of applications which the Trustees now receive, an applicant will not be considered to be eligible if he or she has received a grant from the Bequest during the three years prior to the holiday for which the application is made. Applications prior to the holiday should be made to the Secretaries. Retired ministers are not eligible for grants.

2. Grants towards costs of sickness and convalescence so far as not covered by the National Health Service or otherwise may be available to applicants, who should apply to the Secretaries giving relevant details.

All communications should be addressed to Pagan Osborne, Solicitors, Secretaries to the Lyall Bequest, 106 South Street, St Andrews KY16 9QD (Tel: 01334 475001; E-mail: elcalderwood@pagan.co.uk).

MARGARET AND JOHN ROSS TRAVELLING FUND: Offers grants to ministers and their spouses for travelling and other expenses for trips to the Holy Land where the purpose is recuperation or relaxation. Applications should be made to the Secretary and Clerk, The Church of Scotland Trust, 121 George Street, Edinburgh EH2 4YN (Tel: 0131-240 2222; E-mail: jhamilton@cofscotland.org.uk).

The undernoted represents a list of the more important trusts available for ministers, students and congregations. A brief indication is given of the trust purposes, but application should be made in each case to the person named for full particulars and forms of application.

THE ABERNETHY TRUST: Offers residential accommodation and outdoor activities for Youth Fellowships, Church family weekends and Bible Classes at four outdoor centres in Scotland. Further details from the Executive Director, Abernethy Trust, Nethy Bridge PH25 3ED (Tel: 01479 821279; Website: www.abernethy.org.uk).

THE ARROL TRUST: The Arrol Trust gives small grants to young people between the ages of 16 and 25 for the purposes of travel which will provide education or work experience. Potential recipients would be young people with disabilities or who would for financial reasons be otherwise unable to undertake projects. It is expected that projects would be beneficial not only to applicants but also to the wider community. Application forms are available from Callum S. Kennedy WS, Lindsays WS, Caledonian Exchange, 19A Canning Street, Edinburgh EH3 8HE (Tel: 0131-229 1212).

THE BAIRD TRUST: Assists in the building and repair of churches and halls, and generally assists the work of the Church of Scotland. Apply to Iain A.T. Mowat CA, 182 Bath Street, Glasgow G2 4HG (Tel: 0141-332 0476; Fax: 0141-331 0874; E-mail: info@bairdtrust.org.uk; Website: www.bairdtrust.org.uk).

THE REV. ALEXANDER BARCLAY BEQUEST: Assists mother, daughter, sister or niece of deceased minister of the Church of Scotland who at the time of his death was acting as his housekeeper and who is in needy circumstances. Apply to Robert Hugh Allan LLB DipLP NP, Pomphreys, 79 Quarry Street, Hamilton ML3 7AG (Tel: 01698 891616).

BELLAHOUSTON BEQUEST FUND: Gives grants to Protestant evangelical denominations in the City of Glasgow and certain areas within five miles of the city boundary for building and repairing churches and halls and the promotion of religion. Apply to Mr Donald B. Reid, Mitchells Roberton, 36 North Hanover Street, Glasgow G1 2AD.

BEQUEST FUND FOR MINISTERS: Assists ministers in outlying districts with manse furnishings, pastoral efficiency aids, and their own and family medical or educational costs, including university. Apply to A. Linda Parkhill CA, 60 Wellington Street, Glasgow G2 6HJ (Tel: 0141-226 4994; E-mail: mail@parkhillmackie.co.uk).

CARNEGIE TRUST FOR THE UNIVERSITIES OF SCOTLAND: In cases of hardship, the Carnegie Trust is prepared to consider applications by students of Scottish birth or extraction (at least one parent born in Scotland), or who have had at least two years' education at a secondary school in Scotland, for financial assistance with the payment of their fees for a first degree at a Scottish university. For further details, students should apply to the Secretary, Carnegie Trust for the Universities of Scotland, Andrew Carnegie House, Pittencrieff Street, Dunfermline KY12 8AW (Tel: 01383 724990; Fax: 01383 749799; E-mail: jgray@carnegie-trust.org; Website: www.carnegie-trust.org).

CHURCH OF SCOTLAND INSURANCE CO. LTD: Undertakes insurance of Church property and pays surplus profits to Church schemes. It is authorised and regulated by the Financial Services Authority. The company can also arrange household insurance for members and adherents of the Church of Scotland. At 67 George Street, Edinburgh EH2 2JG (Tel: 0131-220 4119; Fax: 0131-220 4120; E-mail: enquiries@cosic.co.uk).

CHURCH OF SCOTLAND MINISTRY BENEVOLENT FUND: Makes grants to retired men and women who have been ordained or commissioned for the ministry of the Church of Scotland and to widows, widowers, orphans, spouses or children of such, who are in need. Apply to the Assistant Treasurer (Ministries), 121 George Street, Edinburgh EH2 4YN (Tel: 0131-225 5722).

CLARK BURSARY: Awarded to accepted candidate(s) for the ministry of the Church of Scotland whose studies for the ministry are pursued at the University of Aberdeen. Applications or recommendations for the Bursary to the Clerk to the Presbytery of Aberdeen, Mastrick Church, Greenfern Road, Aberdeen AB16 6TR by 16 October annually.

CRAIGCROOK MORTIFICATION:

Clerk and Factor:	Mrs Fiona M.M. Watson CA Exchange Place 3, Semple Street, Edinburgh EH3 8BL (Tel: 0131-473 3500; E-mail: charity@scott-moncrieff.com)

Pensions are paid to poor men and women over 60 years old, born in Scotland or who have resided in Scotland for not less than ten years. At present, pensions amount to £1,000–£1,500 p.a.

Ministers are invited to notify the Clerk and Factor of deserving persons and should be prepared to act as a referee on the application form.

CROMBIE SCHOLARSHIP: Provides grants annually on the nomination of the Deans of Faculty of Divinity of the Universities of St Andrews, Glasgow, Aberdeen and Edinburgh, who each nominate one matriculated student who has taken a University course in Greek (Classical or Hellenistic) and Hebrew. Award by recommendation only.

THE DRUMMOND TRUST: Makes grants towards the cost of publication of books of 'sound Christian doctrine and outreach'. The Trustees are also willing to receive grant requests towards the cost of audio-visual programme material, but not equipment. Requests for application forms should be made to the Secretaries, Hill and Robb, 3 Pitt Terrace, Stirling FK8 2EY (Tel: 01786 450985; E-mail: douglaswhyte@hillandrobb.co.uk). Manuscripts should *not* be sent.

THE DUNCAN TRUST: Makes grants annually to students for the ministry in the Faculties of Arts and Divinity. Preference is given to those born or educated within the bounds of the former Presbytery of Arbroath. Applications not later than 31 October to Thorntons Law LLP, Brothockbank House, Arbroath DD11 1NE (reference: G.J.M. Dunlop; Tel: 01241 872683; E-mail: gdunlop@thorntons-law.co.uk).

FERGUSON BEQUEST FUND: Assists with the building and repair of churches and halls and, more generally, with the work of the Church of Scotland. Priority is given to the Counties of Ayr, Kirkcudbright, Wigtown, Lanark, Dunbarton and Renfrew, and to Greenock, Glasgow, Falkirk and Ardrossan; applications are, however, accepted from across Scotland. Apply to Iain A.T. Mowat CA, 182 Bath Street, Glasgow G2 4HG (Tel: 0141-332 0476; Fax: 0141-331 0874; E-mail: info@fergusonbequestfund.org.uk; Website: www.fergusonbequestfund.org.uk).

GEIKIE BEQUEST: Makes small grants to students for the ministry, including students studying for entry to the University, preference being given to those not eligible for SAAS awards. Apply to the Assistant Treasurer (Ministries), 121 George Street, Edinburgh EH2 4YN by September for distribution in November each year.

JAMES GILLAN'S BURSARY FUND: Bursaries are available for male students for the ministry who were born or whose parents or parent have resided and had their home for not less than three years continually in the old counties (not Districts) of Moray or Nairn. Apply to R. and R. Urquhart LLP, 117–121 High Street, Forres IV36 1AB.

HAMILTON BURSARY TRUST: Awarded, subject to the intention to serve overseas under the Church of Scotland World Mission Council or to serve with some other Overseas Mission Agency approved by the Council, to a student at the University of Aberdeen. Preference is given to a student born or residing in (1) Parish of Skene, (2) Parish of Echt, (3) the Presbytery of Aberdeen, Kincardine and Deeside, or Gordon; failing which to Accepted Candidate(s) for the Ministry of the Church of Scotland whose studies for the Ministry are pursued at Aberdeen University. Applications or recommendations for the Bursary to the Clerk to the Presbytery of Aberdeen by 16 October annually.

MARTIN HARCUS BEQUEST: Makes annual grants to candidates for the ministry resident within the City of Edinburgh. Applications to the Clerk to the Presbytery of Edinburgh, 10/1 Palmerston Place, Edinburgh EH12 5AA by 15 October (E-mail: edinburgh@cofscotland.org.uk).

THE HOPE TRUST: Gives some support to organisations involved in combating drink and drugs, and has as its main purpose the promotion of the Reformed tradition throughout the world. There is also a Scholarship programme for Postgraduate Theology Study in Scotland. Apply to Robert P. Miller SSC LLB, 31 Moray Place, Edinburgh EH3 6BY (Tel: 0131-226 5151).

KEAY THOM TRUST: The principal purposes of the Keay Thom Trust are:

1. To benefit the widows, daughters or other dependent female relatives of deceased ministers, or wives of ministers who are now divorced or separated, all of whom have supported the minister in the fulfilment of his duties and who, by reason of death, divorce or separation, have been required to leave the manse. The Trust can assist them in the purchase of a house or by providing financial or material assistance whether it be for the provision of accommodation or not.

2. To assist in the education or training of the above female relatives or any other children of deceased ministers.

Further information and application forms are available from Miller Hendry, Solicitors, 10 Blackfriars Street, Perth PH1 5NS (Tel: 01738 637311).

GILLIAN MACLAINE BURSARY FUND: Open to candidates for the ministry of the Church of Scotland of Scottish or Canadian nationality. Preference is given to Gaelic-speakers. Information and terms of award from Rev. George G. Cringles BD, Depute Clerk of the Presbytery of Argyll, St Oran's Manse, Connel, Oban PA37 1PJ.

THE E. McLAREN FUND: The persons intended to be benefited are widows and unmarried ladies, preference being given to ladies above 40 years of age in the following order:

(a) Widows and daughters of Officers in the Highland Regiment, and

(b) Widows and daughters of Scotsmen.

Further details from the Secretary, The E. McLaren Fund, Messrs BMK Wilson, Solicitors, 90 St Vincent Street, Glasgow G2 5UB (Tel: 0141-221 8004; Fax: 0141-221 8088; E-mail: rrs@bmkwilson.co.uk).

THE MISSES ANN AND MARGARET McMILLAN'S BEQUEST: Makes grants to ministers of the Free and United Free Churches, and of the Church of Scotland, in charges within the Synod of Argyll, with income not exceeding the minimum stipend of the Church of Scotland. Apply by 30 June in each year to Rev. Samuel McC. Harris, 36 Adam Wood Court, Troon KA10 6BP.

MORGAN BURSARY FUND: Makes grants to candidates for the Church of Scotland ministry studying at the University of Glasgow. Apply to Rev. Dr Angus Kerr, 260 Bath Street, Glasgow G2 4JP (Tel: 0141-332 6606).

NOVUM TRUST: Provides small short-term grants – typically between £200 and £2,500 – to initiate projects in Christian action and research which cannot readily be financed from other sources. Trustees welcome applications from projects that are essentially Scottish, are distinctively new, and are focused on the welfare of young people, on the training of lay people or on new ways of communicating the Christian faith. The Trust cannot support large building projects, staff salaries or individuals applying for maintenance during courses or training. Application forms and guidance notes from novumt@cofscotland.org.uk or Mrs Susan Masterton, Blair Cadell WS, The Bond House, 5 Breadalbane Street, Edinburgh EH6 5JH (Tel: 0131-555 5800).

PARK MEMORIAL BURSARY FUND: Provides grants for the benefit of candidates for the ministry of the Church of Scotland from the Presbytery of Glasgow under full-time training. Apply to Rev. Dr Angus Kerr, Presbytery of Glasgow, 260 Bath Street, Glasgow G2 4JP (Tel: 0141-332 6606).

PATON TRUST: Assists ministers in ill health to have a recuperative holiday outwith, and free from the cares of, their parishes. Apply to Alan S. Cunningham CA, Alexander Sloan, Chartered Accountants, 38 Cadogan Street, Glasgow G2 7HF (Tel: 0141-204 8989; Fax: 0141-248 9931; E-mail: alan.cunningham@alexandersloan.co.uk).

SCOTTISH CHURCHES ARCHITECTURAL HERITAGE TRUST: Assists congregations of any denomination in the preservation of the fabric of buildings in regular use for public worship. Application form from the Grants Administrator, Scottish Churches Architectural Heritage Trust, 15 North Bank Street, The Mound, Edinburgh EH1 2LP (Tel: 0131-225 8644; E-mail: info@scaht.org.uk).

MISS M.E. SWINTON PATERSON'S CHARITABLE TRUST: The Trust can give modest grants to support smaller congregations in urban or rural areas who require to fund essential maintenance or improvement works at their buildings. Apply to Mr Callum S. Kennedy WS, Messrs Lindsays WS, Caledonian Exchange, 19A Canning Street, Edinburgh EH3 8HE (Tel: 0131-229 1212).

SMIETON FUND: Makes small holiday grants to ministers. Administered at the discretion of the pastoral staff, who will give priority in cases of need. Applications to the Associate Secretary (Support and Development), Ministries Council, 121 George Street, Edinburgh EH2 4YN.

MARY DAVIDSON SMITH CLERICAL AND EDUCATIONAL FUND FOR ABERDEENSHIRE: Assists ministers who have been ordained for five years or over and are in full charge of a congregation in Aberdeen, Aberdeenshire and the north, to purchase books, or to travel for educational purposes, and assists their children with scholarships for further education or vocational training. Apply to Alan J. Innes MA LLB, 100 Union Street, Aberdeen AB10 1QR.

THE NAN STEVENSON CHARITABLE TRUST FOR RETIRED MINISTERS: Provides houses, or loans to purchase houses, for retired ministers or missionaries on similar terms to the Housing and Loan Fund, with preference given to those with a North Ayrshire connection. Secretary and Treasurer: Mrs Ann Turner, 62 Caledonia Road, Saltcoats KA21 5AP.

PRESBYTERY OF ARGYLL BURSARY FUND: Open to students who have been accepted as candidates for the ministry and the readership of the Church of Scotland. Preference is given to applicants who are natives of the bounds of the Presbytery, or are resident within the bounds of the Presbytery, or who have a strong connection with the bounds of the Presbytery. Information and terms of award from Rev. George G. Cringles BD, Depute Clerk of the Presbytery of Argyll, St Oran's Manse, Connel, Oban PA37 1PJ.

SYNOD OF GRAMPIAN CHILDREN OF THE CLERGY FUND: Makes annual grants to children of deceased ministers. Apply to Rev. Iain U. Thomson, Clerk and Treasurer, 4 Keirhill Gardens, Westhill AB32 6AZ.

SYNOD OF GRAMPIAN WIDOWS FUND: Makes annual grants (currently £225 p.a.) to widows or widowers of deceased ministers who have served in a charge in the former Synod. Apply to Rev. Iain U. Thomson, Clerk and Treasurer, 4 Keirhill Gardens, Westhill AB32 6AZ.

YOUNG MINISTERS' FURNISHING LOAN FUND: Makes loans (of £1,000) to ministers in their first charge to assist with furnishing the manse. Apply to the Assistant Treasurer (Ministries), 121 George Street, Edinburgh EH2 4YN.

(6) RECENT LORD HIGH COMMISSIONERS TO THE GENERAL ASSEMBLY

1967/68	The Rt Hon. Lord Reith of Stonehaven GCVO GBE CB TD
1969	Her Majesty the Queen attended in person
1970	The Rt Hon. Margaret Herbison PC
1971/72	The Rt Hon. Lord Clydesmuir of Braidwood CB MBE TD
1973/74	The Rt Hon. Lord Ballantrae of Auchairne and the Bay of Islands GCMG GCVO DSO OBE
1975/76	Sir Hector MacLennan Kt FRCPGLAS FRCOG
1977	Francis David Charteris, Earl of Wemyss and March KT LLD
1978/79	The Rt Hon. William Ross MBE LLD
1980/81	Andrew Douglas Alexander Thomas Bruce, Earl of Elgin and Kincardine KT DL JP
1982/83	Colonel Sir John Edward Gilmour BT DSO TD
1984/85	Charles Hector Fitzroy Maclean, Baron Maclean of Duart and Morvern KT GCVO KBE
1986/87	John Campbell Arbuthnott, Viscount of Arbuthnott KT CBE DSC FRSE FRSA
1988/89	Sir Iain Mark Tennant KT FRSA
1990/91	The Rt Hon. Donald MacArthur Ross FRSE
1992/93	The Rt Hon. Lord Macfarlane of Bearsden KT FRSE
1994/95	Lady Marion Fraser LT
1996	Her Royal Highness the Princess Royal LT LG GCVO
1997	The Rt Hon. Lord Macfarlane of Bearsden KT FRSE
1998/99	The Rt Hon. Lord Hogg of Cumbernauld
2000	His Royal Highness the Prince Charles, Duke of Rothesay KG KT GCB OM
2001/02	The Rt Hon. Viscount Younger of Leckie
	Her Majesty the Queen attended the opening of the General Assembly of 2002
2003/04	The Rt Hon. Lord Steel of Aikwood KT KBE
2005/06	The Rt Hon. Lord Mackay of Clashfern KT
2007	His Royal Highness the Prince Andrew, Duke of York KG KCVO
2008/09	The Rt Hon. George Reid MA
2010/11	Lord Wilson of Tillyorn KT GCMG PRSE

(7) RECENT MODERATORS OF THE GENERAL ASSEMBLY

1967	W. Roy Sanderson DD, Stenton with Whittingehame
1968	J.B. Longmuir TD DD, Principal Clerk of Assembly
1969	T.M. Murchison MA DD, Glasgow: St Columba Summertown
1970	Hugh O. Douglas CBE LLD DD, Dundee: St Mary's
1971	Andrew Herron MA BD LLB LLD DD, Clerk to the Presbytery of Glasgow
1972	R.W.V. Selby Wright CVO TD DD FRSE JP, Edinburgh: Canongate
1973	George T.H. Reid MC MA BD DD, Aberdeen: Langstane
1974	David Steel MA BD LLD DD, Linlithgow: St Michael's
1975	James G. Matheson MA BD DD, Portree

1976 Thomas F. Torrance MBE DLitt DD FRSE, University of Edinburgh
1977 John R. Gray VRD MA BD ThM DD, Dunblane: Cathedral
1978 Peter P. Brodie MA BD LLB DD, Alloa: St Mungo's
1979 Robert A.S. Barbour KCVO MC MA BD STM DD, University of Aberdeen
1980 William B. Johnston MA BD DLitt DD, Edinburgh: Colinton
1981 Andrew B. Doig BD STM DD, National Bible Society of Scotland
1982 John McIntyre CVO DLitt DD FRSE, University of Edinburgh
1983 J. Fraser McLuskey MC DD, London: St Columba's
1984 John M.K. Paterson MA BD DD ACII, Milngavie: St Paul's
1985 David M.B.A. Smith MA BD DUniv, Logie
1986 Robert Craig CBE DLitt LLD DD, Emeritus of Jerusalem
1987 Duncan Shaw of Chapelverna *Bundesverdienstkreuz* PhD ThDr Drhc, Edinburgh: Craigentinny St Christopher's
1988 James A. Whyte MA LLD DD DUniv, University of St Andrews
1989 William J.G. McDonald MA BD DD, Edinburgh: Mayfield
1990 Robert Davidson MA BD DD FRSE, University of Glasgow
1991 William B.R. Macmillan MA BD LLD DD, Dundee: St Mary's
1992 Hugh R. Wyllie MA DD FCIBS, Hamilton: Old Parish Church
1993 James L. Weatherhead CBE MA LLB DD, Principal Clerk of Assembly
1994 James A. Simpson BSc BD STM DD, Dornoch Cathedral
1995 James Harkness KCVO CB OBE MA DD, Chaplain General (Emeritus)
1996 John H. McIndoe MA BD STM DD, London: St Columba's linked with Newcastle: St Andrew's
1997 Alexander McDonald BA DUniv CMIWSc, General Secretary, Department of Ministry
1998 Alan Main TD MA BD STM PhD DD, Professor of Practical Theology at Christ's College, University of Aberdeen
1999 John B. Cairns LTh LLB LLD DD, Dumbarton: Riverside
2000 Andrew R.C. McLellan MA BD STM DD, Edinburgh: St Andrew's and St George's
2001 John D. Miller BA BD DD, Glasgow: Castlemilk East
2002 Finlay A.J. Macdonald MA BD PhD DD, Principal Clerk of Assembly
2003 Iain R. Torrance TD DPhil DD DTheol LHD CorrFRSE, University of Aberdeen
2004 Alison Elliot OBE MA MSc PhD LLD DD FRSE, Associate Director CTPI
2005 David W. Lacy BA BD DLitt, Kilmarnock: Henderson
2006 Alan D. McDonald LLB BD MTh DLitt DD, Cameron linked with St Andrews: St Leonard's
2007 Sheilagh M. Kesting BA BD DD, Secretary of Ecumenical Relations Committee
2008 David W. Lunan MA BD, Clerk to the Presbytery of Glasgow
2009 William C. Hewitt BD DipPS, Greenock: Westburn
2010 John C. Christie BSc BD MSB CBiol, Interim Minister
2011 A. David K. Arnott MA BD, St Andrews: Hope Park with Strathkinness

MATTER OF PRECEDENCE

The Lord High Commissioner to the General Assembly of the Church of Scotland (while the Assembly is sitting) ranks next to the Sovereign and the Duke of Edinburgh and before the rest of the Royal Family.

The Moderator of the General Assembly of the Church of Scotland ranks next to the Lord Chancellor of Great Britain and before the Keeper of the Great Seal of Scotland (the First Minister) and the Dukes.

(8) HER MAJESTY'S HOUSEHOLD IN SCOTLAND
ECCLESIASTICAL

Dean of the Chapel Royal: Very Rev. John B. Cairns LTh LLB LLD DD
Dean of the Order of the Thistle: Very Rev. Gilleasbuig Macmillan CVO MA BD Drhc DD

Domestic Chaplains:
Rev. Kenneth I. Mackenzie BD CPS
Rev. Neil N. Gardner MA BD

Chaplains in Ordinary:
Very Rev. Gilleasbuig Macmillan CVO MA BD Drhc DD
Rev. Norman W. Drummond MA BD
Rev. Alastair H. Symington MA BD
Very Rev. Prof. Iain R. Torrance TD DPhil DD DTheol LHD CorrFRSE
Very Rev. Finlay A.J. Macdonald MA BD PhD DD
Rev. James M. Gibson TD LTh LRAM
Rev. Angus Morrison MA BD PhD
Rev. E. Lorna Hood MA BD
Rev. Alistair G. Bennett BSc BD
Rev. Susan M. Brown BD DipMin

Extra Chaplains:
Rev. Kenneth MacVicar MBE DFC TD MA
Very Rev. Prof. Robert A.S. Barbour KCVO MC BD STM DD
Rev. Alwyn Macfarlane MA
Rev. Mary I. Levison BA BD DD
Very Rev. William J. Morris KCVO PhD LLD DD JP
Rev. John MacLeod MA
Very Rev. James L. Weatherhead CBE MA LLB DD
Very Rev. James A. Simpson BSc BD STM DD
Very Rev. James Harkness KCVO CB OBE MA DD
Rev. John L. Paterson MA BD STM
Rev. Charles Robertson LVO MA JP

(9) LONG SERVICE CERTIFICATES

Long Service Certificates, signed by the Moderator, are available for presentation to elders and others in respect of not less than thirty years of service. It should be noted that the period is years of *service*, not (for example) years of ordination in the case of an elder.

In the case of Sunday School teachers and Bible Class leaders, the qualifying period is twenty-one years of service.

Certificates are not issued posthumously, nor is it possible to make exceptions to the rules, for example by recognising quality of service in order to reduce the qualifying period, or by reducing the qualifying period on compassionate grounds, such as serious illness.

A Certificate will be issued only once to any particular individual.

Applications for Long Service Certificates should be made in writing to the Principal Clerk at 121 George Street, Edinburgh EH2 4YN by the parish minister, or by the session clerk on behalf of the Kirk Session. Certificates are not issued from this office to the individual recipients, nor should individuals make application themselves.

---

(10) LIBRARIES OF THE CHURCH

GENERAL ASSEMBLY LIBRARY AND RECORD ROOM
Most of the books contained in the General Assembly Library have been transferred to the New College Library. Records of the General Assembly, Synods, Presbyteries and Kirk Sessions are now in HM Register House, Edinburgh.

CHURCH MUSIC
The Library of New College contains a selection of works on Church music.

---

(11) RECORDS OF THE CHURCH OF SCOTLAND

Church records more than fifty years old, unless still in use, should be sent or delivered to the Principal Clerk for onward transmission to the National Archives of Scotland. Where ministers or session clerks are approached by a local repository seeking a transfer of their records, they should inform the Principal Clerk, who will take the matter up with the National Archives of Scotland.

Where a temporary retransmission of records is sought, it is extremely helpful if notice can be given three months in advance so that appropriate procedures can be carried out satisfactorily.

SECTION 3

Church Procedure

(1) THE MINISTER AND BAPTISM

The administration of Baptism to infants is governed by Act V 2000 as amended by Act IX 2003. A Statement and Exposition of the Doctrine of Baptism may be found at page 13/8 in the published volume of Reports to the General Assembly of 2003.

The Act itself is as follows:

3. Baptism signifies the action and love of God in Christ, through the Holy Spirit, and is a seal upon the gift of grace and the response of faith.
   (a) Baptism shall be administered in the name of the Father and of the Son and of the Holy Spirit, with water, by sprinkling, pouring, or immersion.
   (b) Baptism shall be administered to a person only once.
4. Baptism may be administered to a person upon profession of faith.
   (a) The minister and Kirk Session shall judge whether the person is of sufficient maturity to make personal profession of faith, where necessary in consultation with the parent(s) or legal guardian(s).
   (b) Baptism may be administered only after the person has received such instruction in its meaning as the minister and Kirk Session consider necessary, according to such basis of instruction as may be authorised by the General Assembly.
   (c) In cases of uncertainty as to whether a person has been baptised or validly baptised, baptism shall be administered conditionally.
5. Baptism may be administered to a person with learning difficulties who makes an appropriate profession of faith, where the minister and Kirk Session are satisfied that the person shall be nurtured within the life and worship of the Church.
6. Baptism may be administered to a child:
   (a) where at least one parent, or other family member (with parental consent), having been baptised and being on the communion roll of the congregation, will undertake the Christian upbringing of the child;
   (b) where at least one parent, or other family member (with parental consent), having been baptised but not on the communion roll of the congregation, satisfies the minister and Kirk Session that he or she is an adherent of the congregation and will undertake the Christian upbringing of the child;
   (c) where at least one parent, or other family member (with parental consent), having been baptised, professes the Christian faith, undertakes to ensure that the child grows up in the life and worship of the Church and expresses the desire to seek admission to the communion roll of the congregation;
   (d) where the child is under legal guardianship, and the minister and Kirk Session are satisfied that the child shall be nurtured within the life and worship of the congregation;

   and, in each of the above cases, only after the parent(s), or other family member, has received such instruction in its meaning as the minister and Kirk Session consider necessary, according to such basis of instruction as may be authorised by the General Assembly.
7. Baptism shall normally be administered during the public worship of the congregation in which the person makes profession of faith, or of which the parent or other family member is on the communion roll, or is an adherent. In exceptional circumstances, baptism may be administered elsewhere (e.g. at home or in hospital). Further, a minister may administer baptism to a person resident outwith the minister's parish, and who is not otherwise

connected with the congregation, only with the consent of the minister of the parish in which the person would normally reside, or of the Presbytery.

8. In all cases, an entry shall be made in the Kirk Session's Baptismal Register and a Certificate of Baptism given by the minister. Where baptism is administered in a chaplaincy context, it shall be recorded in the Baptismal Register there, and, where possible, reported to the minister of the parish in which the person resides.
9. Baptism shall normally be administered by an ordained minister. In situations of emergency,
   (a) a minister may, exceptionally, notwithstanding the preceding provisions of the Act, respond to a request for baptism in accordance with his or her pastoral judgement, and
   (b) baptism may be validly administered by a person who is not ordained, always providing that it is administered in the name of the Father and of the Son and of the Holy Spirit, with water.

   In every occurrence of the latter case, of which a minister or chaplain becomes aware, an entry shall be made in the appropriate Baptismal Register and where possible reported to the Clerk of the Presbytery within which the baptism was administered.
10. Each Presbytery shall form, or designate, a committee to which reference may be made in cases where there is a dispute as to the interpretation of this Act. Without the consent of the Presbytery, no minister may administer baptism in a case where to his or her knowledge another minister has declined to do so.
11. The Church of Scotland, as part of the Universal Church, affirms the validity of the sacrament of baptism administered in the name of the Father and of the Son and of the Holy Spirit, with water, in accordance with the discipline of other members of the Universal Church.

---

(2) THE MINISTER AND MARRIAGE

1. BACKGROUND

Prior to 1939, every marriage in Scotland fell into one or other of two classes: regular or irregular. The former was marriage by a minister of religion after due notice of intention had been given; the latter could be effected in one of three ways: (1) declaration *de presenti*, (2) by promise *subsequente copula*, or (3) by co-habitation with habit and repute.

The Marriage (Scotland) Act of 1939 put an end to (1) and (2) and provided for a new classification of marriage as either religious or civil. Marriage by co-habitation with habit and repute was abolished by the Family Law (Scotland) Act 2006.

The law of marriage as it was thus established in 1939 had two important limitations to the celebration of marriage: (1) certain preliminaries had to be observed; and (2) in respect of religious marriage, the service had to be conducted according to the forms of either the Christian or the Jewish faith.

2. THE MARRIAGE (SCOTLAND) ACT 1977

These two conditions were radically altered by the Marriage (Scotland) Act 1977.

Since 1 January 1978, in conformity with the demands of a multi-racial society, the benefits of religious marriage have been extended to adherents of other faiths, the only requirements being the observance of monogamy and the satisfaction of the authorities with the forms of the vows imposed.

Since 1978, the calling of banns has also been discontinued. The couple themselves must each complete a Marriage Notice form and return this to the District Registrar for the area in which they are to be married, irrespective of where they live, at least fifteen days before the ceremony is due to take place. The form details the documents which require to be produced with it.

If everything is in order, the District Registrar will issue, not more than seven days before the date of the ceremony, a Marriage Schedule. This must be in the hands of the minister officiating at the marriage ceremony before the service begins. Under no circumstances must the minister deviate from this rule. To do so is an offence under the Act.

Ministers should note the advice given by the Procurator of the Church in 1962, that they should not officiate at any marriage until at least one day after the 16th birthday of the younger party.

Furthermore, a marriage involving someone who is not an EU citizen involves extra registration requirements, and initial contact should be made with the local Registrar several months before the intended date of marriage.

3. THE MARRIAGE (SCOTLAND) ACT 2002

Although there have never been any limitations as to the place where a religious marriage can be celebrated, civil marriage originally could take place only in the Office of a Registrar. The Marriage (Scotland) Act 2002 permits the solemnisation of civil marriages at places approved by Local Authorities. Regulations have been made to specify the kinds of place which may be 'approved' with a view to ensuring that the places approved will not compromise the solemnity and dignity of civil marriage and will have no recent or continuing connection with any religion so as to undermine the distinction between religious and civil ceremonies.

4. PROCLAMATION OF BANNS

Proclamation of banns is no longer required in Scotland; but, in the Church of England, marriage is governed by the provisions of the Marriage Act 1949, which requires that the parties' intention to marry has to have been proclaimed and which provides that in the case of a party residing in Scotland a Certificate of Proclamation given according to the law or custom prevailing in Scotland shall be sufficient for the purpose. In the event that a minister is asked to call banns for a person resident within the registration district where his or her church is situated, the proclamation needs only to be made on one Sunday if the parties are known to the minister. If they are not, it should be made on two Sundays. In all cases, the Minister should, of course, have no reason to believe that there is any impediment to the marriage.

Proclamation should be made at the principal service of worship in this form:

> There is a purpose of marriage between AB (Bachelor/Widower/Divorced), residing at .... in this Registration District, and CD (Spinster/Widow/Divorced), residing at .... in the Registration District of ...., of which proclamation is hereby made for the first and only (second and last) time.

Immediately after the second reading, or not less than forty-eight hours after the first and only reading, a Certificate of Proclamation signed by either the minister or the Session Clerk should be issued in the following terms:

> At .... the ...... day of ...... 20 ....
> It is hereby certified that AB, residing at ...., and CD, residing at ...., have been duly proclaimed in order to marriage in the Church of .... according to the custom of the Church of Scotland, and that no objections have been offered.
> Signed .... minister or
> Signed .... Session Clerk

5. MARRIAGE OF FOREIGNERS

Marriages in Scotland of foreigners, or of foreigners with British subjects, are, if they satisfy the requirements of Scots Law, valid within the United Kingdom and the various British overseas territories; but they will not necessarily be valid in the country to which the foreigner belongs. This will be so only if the requirements of the law of his or her country have also been complied with. It is therefore most important that, before the marriage, steps should be taken to obtain from the Consul, or other diplomatic representative of the country concerned, a satisfactory assurance that the marriage will be accepted as valid in the country concerned.

6. REMARRIAGE OF DIVORCED PERSONS

By virtue of Act XXVI 1959, a minister of the Church of Scotland may lawfully solemnise the marriage of a person whose former marriage has been dissolved by divorce and whose former spouse is still alive. The minister, however, must carefully adhere to the requirements of the Act which, as slightly altered in 1985, are briefly as follows:

1. The minister should not accede as a matter of routine to a request to solemnise such a marriage. To enable a decision to be made, he or she should take all reasonable steps to obtain relevant information, which should normally include the following:
   (a) Adequate information concerning the life and character of the parties. The Act enjoins the greatest caution in cases where no pastoral relationship exists between the minister and either or both of the parties concerned.
   (b) The grounds and circumstances of the divorce case.
   (c) Facts bearing upon the future well-being of any children concerned.
   (d) Whether any other minister has declined to solemnise the proposed marriage.
   (e) The denomination to which the parties belong. The Act enjoins that special care should be taken where one or more parties belong to a denomination whose discipline in this matter may differ from that of the Church of Scotland.
2. The minister should consider whether there is danger of scandal arising if he or she should solemnise the remarriage, at the same time taking into careful consideration before refusing to do so the moral and spiritual effect of a refusal on the parties concerned.
3. As a determinative factor, the minister should do all he or she can to be assured that there has been sincere repentance where guilt has existed on the part of any divorced person seeking remarriage. He or she should also give instruction, where needed, in the nature and requirements of a Christian marriage.
4. A minister is not required to solemnise a remarriage against his or her conscience. Every Presbytery is required to appoint certain individuals with one of whom ministers in doubt as to the correct course of action may consult if they so desire. The final decision, however, rests with the minister who has been asked to officiate.

---

(3) CONDUCT OF MARRIAGE SERVICES
(CODE OF GOOD PRACTICE)

The code which follows was submitted to the General Assembly in 1997. It appears, on page 1/10, in the Volume of Assembly Reports for that year within the Report of the Board of Practice and Procedure.

1. *Marriage in the Church of Scotland is solemnised by an ordained minister in a religious ceremony wherein, before God, and in the presence of the minister and at least two competent witnesses, the parties covenant together to take each other as husband and wife as long as they both shall live, and the minister declares the parties to be husband and wife. Before solemnising a marriage, a minister must be assured that the necessary legal requirements are being complied with and that the parties know of no legal impediment to their marriage, and he or she must afterwards ensure that the Marriage Schedule is duly completed.* (Act I 1977)
2. Any ordained minister of the Church of Scotland who is a member of Presbytery or who holds a current Ministerial Certificate may officiate at a marriage service (see Act II 1987).
3. While the marriage service should normally take place in church, a minister may, at his or her discretion, officiate at a marriage service outwith church premises. Wherever conducted, the ceremony will be such as to reflect appropriately both the joy and the solemnity of the occasion. In particular, a minister shall ensure that nothing is done which would bring the Church and its teaching into disrepute.
4. A minister agreeing to conduct a wedding should endeavour to establish a pastoral relationship with the couple within which adequate pre-marriage preparation and subsequent pastoral care may be given.
5. 'A minister should not refuse to perform ministerial functions for a person who is resident in his or her parish without sufficient reason' (Cox, *Practice and Procedure in the Church of Scotland*, sixth edition, page 55). Where either party to the proposed marriage has been divorced and the former spouse is still alive, the minister invited to officiate may solemnise such a marriage, having regard to the guidelines in the Act anent the Remarriage of Divorced Persons (Act XXVI 1959 as amended by Act II 1985).
6. A minister is acting as an agent of the National Church which is committed to bringing the ordinances of religion to the people of Scotland through a territorial ministry. As such, he or she shall not be entitled to charge a fee or allow a fee to be charged for conducting a marriage service. When a gift is spontaneously offered to a minister as a token of appreciation, the above consideration should not be taken to mean that he or she should not accept such an unsolicited gift. The Financial Board of a congregation is at liberty to set fees to cover such costs as heat and light, and in addition Organists and Church Officers are entitled to a fee in respect of their services at weddings.
7. A minister should not allow his or her name to be associated with any commercial enterprise that provides facilities for weddings.
8. A minister is not at liberty to enter the bounds of another minister's parish to perform ministerial functions without the previous consent of the minister of that parish. In terms of Act VIII 1933, a minister may 'officiate at a marriage or funeral by private invitation', but, for the avoidance of doubt, an invitation conveyed through a commercial enterprise shall not be regarded as a 'private invitation' within the meaning of that Act.
9. A minister invited to officiate at a Marriage Service where neither party is a member of his or her congregation or is resident within his or her own parish or has any connection with the parish within which the service is to take place should observe the following courtesies:
   (a) he or she should ascertain from the parties whether either of them has a Church of Scotland connection or has approached the appropriate parish minister(s);
   (b) if it transpires that a ministerial colleague has declined to officiate, then he or she (the invited minister) should ascertain the reasons therefor and shall take these and all other relevant factors into account in deciding whether or not to officiate.

(4) CONDUCT OF FUNERAL SERVICES: FEES

The General Assembly of 2007 received the Report of the Legal Questions Committee which included a statement regarding fees for funerals. That statement had been prepared in the light of approaches from two Presbyteries seeking guidance on the question of the charging of fees (on behalf of ministers) for the conduct of funerals. It had seemed to the Presbyteries that expectations and practice were unacceptably varied across the country, and that the question was complicated by the fact that, quite naturally and legitimately, ministers other than parish ministers occasionally conduct funeral services.

The full text of that statement was engrossed in the Minutes of the General Assembly, and it was felt that it would be helpful to include it also in the *Year Book*.

The statement

The (Legal Questions) Committee believes that the question is two-fold, relating firstly to parish ministers (including associate and assistant ministers, deacons and the like) within their regular ministry, and secondly to ministers and others taking an occasional funeral, for instance by private invitation or in the course of pastoral cover of another parish.

Ministers in receipt of a living

The Committee believes that the position of the minister of a parish, and of other paid staff on the ministry team of a parish, is clear. The Third Declaratory Article affirms the responsibility of the Church of Scotland to provide the ordinances of religion through its territorial ministry, while the stipend system (and, for other staff members, the salary) provides a living that enables that ministry to be exercised without charging fees for services conducted. The implication of this principle is that no family in Scotland should ever be charged for the services of a Church of Scotland minister at the time of bereavement. Clearly, therefore, no minister in receipt of a living should be charging separately (effectively being paid doubly) for any such service. The Committee is conscious that the position of congregations outside Scotland may be different, and is aware that the relevant Presbyteries will offer appropriate superintendence of these matters.

A related question is raised about the highly varied culture of gift-giving in different parts of the country. The Committee believes it would be unwise to seek to regulate this. In some places, an attempt to quash a universal and long-established practice would seem ungracious, while in other places there is no such practice, and encouragement in that direction would seem indelicate.

A second related question was raised about Funeral Directors charging for the services of the minister. The Committee believes that Presbyteries should make it clear to Funeral Directors that, in the case of Church of Scotland funerals, such a charge should not be made.

Ministers conducting occasional services

Turning to the position of ministers who do not receive a living that enables them to conduct funerals without charge, the Committee's starting point is the principle articulated above that no bereaved person should have to pay for the services of a minister. The territorial ministry and the parish system of this Church mean that a bereaved family should not find itself being contingently charged because the parish minister happens to be unavailable, or because the parish is vacant.

Where a funeral is being conducted as part of the ministry of the local parish, but where for any reason another minister is taking it and not otherwise being paid, it is the responsibility of the congregation (through its financial body) to ensure that appropriate fees and expenses are met.

Where that imposes a financial burden upon a congregation because of the weight of pastoral need, the need should be taken into account in calculating the resource-needs of that parish in the course of updating the Presbytery Plan.

It is beyond the remit of the Legal Questions Committee to make judgements about the appropriate level of payment. The Committee suggests that the Ministries Council should give the relevant advice on this aspect of the issue.

The Committee believes that these principles could be applied to the conduct of weddings and are perfectly compatible with the Guidelines on that subject which are reproduced in the *Year Book* at item 3 of section 3 dealing with Church Procedure.

---

(5) THE MINISTER AND WILLS

The Requirements of Writing (Scotland) Act 1995, which came into force on 1 August 1995, has removed the power of a minister to execute wills notarially. Further clarification, if required, may be obtained from the Solicitor of the Church.

---

(6) PROCEDURE IN A VACANCY

Procedure in a vacancy is regulated by Act VIII 2003 as amended by Acts IX and X 2004, II 2005, V 2006, I, IV and VI 2008 and II and V 2009. The text of the most immediately relevant sections is given here for general information. Schedules of Intimation referred to are also included. The full text of the Act and subsequent amendments can be obtained from the Principal Clerk.

1. Vacancy Procedure Committee

(1) Each Presbytery shall appoint a number of its members to be available to serve on Vacancy Procedure Committees and shall provide information and training as required for those so appointed.

(2) As soon as the Presbytery Clerk is aware that a vacancy has arisen or is anticipated, he or she shall consult the Moderator of the Presbytery and they shall appoint a Vacancy Procedure Committee of five persons from among those appointed in terms of subsection (1), which Committee shall (a) include at least one minister and at least one elder and (b) exclude any communicant member or former minister of the vacant charge or of any constituent congregation thereof. The Vacancy Procedure Committee shall include a Convener and Clerk, the latter of whom need not be a member of the Committee but may be the Presbytery Clerk. The same Vacancy Procedure Committee may serve for more than one vacancy at a time.

(3) The Vacancy Procedure Committee shall have a quorum of three for its meetings.

(4) The Convener of the Vacancy Procedure Committee may, where he or she reasonably believes a matter to be non-contentious, consult members individually, provided that reasonable efforts are made to consult all members of the Committee. A meeting shall be held at the request of any member of the Committee.

(5) Every decision made by the Vacancy Procedure Committee shall be reported to the next meeting of Presbytery, but may not be recalled by Presbytery where the decision was subject to the provisions of section 2 below.

2. Request for Consideration by Presbytery

Where in this Act any decision by the Vacancy Procedure Committee is subject to the provisions of this section, the following rules shall apply:

(1) The Presbytery Clerk shall intimate to all members of the Presbytery by mailing or at a Presbytery meeting the course of action or permission proposed, and shall arrange for one Sunday's pulpit intimation of the same to be made to the congregation or congregations concerned, in terms of Schedule A. The intimation having been made, it shall be displayed as prominently as possible at the church building for seven days.

(2) Any four individuals, being communicant members of the congregation or full members of the Presbytery, may give written notice requesting that action be taken in terms of subsection (3) below, giving reasons for the request, within seven days after the pulpit intimation.

(3) Upon receiving notice in terms of subsection (2), the Presbytery Clerk shall sist the process or permission referred to in subsection (1), which shall then require the approval of the Presbytery.

(4) The Moderator of the Presbytery shall in such circumstances consider whether a meeting *pro re nata* of the Presbytery should be called in order to avoid prejudicial delay in the vacancy process.

(5) The Presbytery Clerk shall cause to have served upon the congregation or congregations an edict in terms of Schedule B citing them to attend the meeting of Presbytery for their interest.

(6) The consideration by Presbytery of any matter under this section shall not constitute an appeal or a Petition, and the decision of Presbytery shall be deemed to be a decision at first instance subject to the normal rights of appeal or dissent-and-complaint.

3. Causes of Vacancy

The causes of vacancy shall normally include:

(a) the death of the minister of the charge;

(b) the removal of status of the minister of the charge or the suspension of the minister in terms of section 20(2) of Act III 2001;

(c) the dissolution of the pastoral tie in terms of Act I 1988 or Act XV 2002;

(d) the demission of the charge and/or status of the minister of the charge;

(e) the translation of the minister of the charge to another charge;

(f) the termination of the tenure of the minister of the charge in terms of Act VI 1984.

4. Release of Departing Minister

The Presbytery Clerk shall be informed as soon as circumstances have occurred that cause a vacancy to arise or make it likely that a vacancy shall arise. Where the circumstances pertain to section 3(d) or (e) above, the Vacancy Procedure Committee shall

(1) except in cases governed by subsection (2) below, decide whether to release the minister from his or her charge and, in any case involving translation to another charge or introduction to an appointment, instruct him or her to await the instructions of the Presbytery or another Presbytery;

(2) in the case of a minister in the first five years of his or her first charge, decide whether there are exceptional circumstances to justify releasing him or her from his or her charge and proceeding in terms of subsection (1) above;

(3) determine whether a vacancy has arisen or is anticipated and, as soon as possible, determine the date upon which the charge becomes actually vacant, and
(4) inform the congregation or congregations by one Sunday's pulpit intimation as soon as convenient.
(5) The provisions of section 2 above shall apply to the decisions of the Vacancy Procedure Committee in terms of subsections (1) and (2) above.

5. Demission of Charge

(1) Subject to the provisions of subsection (2) below, when a vacancy has occurred in terms of section 3(c), (d) or (f) above, the Presbytery shall determine whether the minister is, in the circumstances, entitled to a seat in the Presbytery in terms of section 16 of Act III 2000 (as amended).
(2) In the case where it is a condition of any basis of adjustment that a minister shall demit his or her charge to facilitate union or linking, and the minister has agreed in writing in terms of the appropriate regulations governing adjustments, formal application shall not be made to the Presbytery for permission to demit. The minister concerned shall be regarded as retiring in the interest of adjustment, and he or she shall retain a seat in Presbytery unless in terms of Act III 2000 (as amended) he or she elects to resign it.
(3) A minister who demits his or her charge without retaining a seat in the Presbytery shall, if he or she retains status as a minister, be subject to the provisions of sections 5 to 15 of Act II 2000 (as amended).

6. Appointment of Interim Moderator

(1) At the same time as the Vacancy Procedure Committee makes a decision in terms of section 4 above, or where circumstances pertain to section 3(a), (b), (c) or (f) above, the Vacancy Procedure Committee shall appoint an Interim Moderator for the charge and make intimation thereof to the congregation subject to the provisions of section 2 above. The Interim Moderator shall be either a ministerial member of the Presbytery in terms of Act III 2000 or Act V 2001 or a member of the Presbytery selected from a list of those who have received such preparation for the task as the Ministries Council shall from time to time recommend or provide, and he or she shall not be a member in the vacant charge nor a member of the Vacancy Procedure Committee. The name of the Interim Moderator shall be forwarded to the Ministries Council.
(2) If the Interim Moderator appointed is a ministerial member of Presbytery, it is understood that, in accepting the appointment, he or she is thereby disqualified from becoming an applicant or accepting an invitation to be considered in the current vacancy.

7. Duties of Interim Moderator

(1) It shall be the duty of the Interim Moderator to preside at all meetings of the Kirk Session (or of the Kirk Sessions in the case of a linked charge) and to preside at all congregational meetings in connection with the vacancy, or at which the minister would have presided had the charge been full. In the case of a congregational meeting called by the Presbytery in connection with adjustment, the Interim Moderator, having constituted the meeting, shall relinquish the chair in favour of the representative of the Presbytery, but he or she shall be at liberty to speak at such a meeting. In consultation with the Kirk Session and the Financial Court, he or she shall make arrangements for the supply of the vacant pulpit.
(2) The Interim Moderator appointed in a prospective vacancy may call and preside at meetings of the Kirk Session and of the congregation for the transaction of business relating to the

said prospective vacancy. He or she shall be associated with the minister until the date of the actual vacancy; after that date, he or she shall take full charge.

(3) The Interim Moderator shall act as an assessor to the Nominating Committee, being available to offer guidance and advice. If the Committee so desire, he or she may act as their Convener, but in no case shall he or she have a vote.

(4) In the event of the absence of the Interim Moderator, the Vacancy Procedure Committee shall appoint a member of the Presbytery who is not a member of the vacant congregation to fulfil any of the rights and duties of the Interim Moderator.

(5) The Interim Moderator shall have the same duties and responsibilities towards all members of ministry teams referred to in section 16 of Act VII 2003 as if he or she were the parish minister, both in terms of this Act and in respect of the terms and conditions of such individuals.

8. Permission to Call

When the decision to release the minister from the charge has been made and the Interim Moderator appointed, the Vacancy Procedure Committee shall consider whether it may give permission to call a minister in terms of Act VII 2003, and may proceed subject to the provisions of section 2 above. The Vacancy Procedure Committee must refer the question of permission to call to the Presbytery if:

(a) shortfalls exist which in the opinion of the Committee require consideration in terms of section 9 hereunder;

(b) the Committee has reason to believe that the vacancy schedule referred to in section 10 below will not be approved;

(c) the Committee has reason to believe that the Presbytery will, in terms of section 11 below, instruct work to be carried out on the manse before a call can be sustained, and judges that the likely extent of such work warrants a delay in the granting of permission to call, or

(d) the Committee has reason to believe that the Presbytery may wish to delay or refuse the granting of permission for any reason.

Any decision by Presbytery to refuse permission to call shall be subject to appeal or dissent-and-complaint.

9. Shortfalls

(1) As soon as possible after intimation of a vacancy or anticipated vacancy reaches the Presbytery Clerk, the Presbytery shall ascertain whether the charge has current or accumulated shortfalls in contributions to central funds, and shall determine whether and to what extent any shortfalls that exist are justified.

(2) If the vacancy is in a charge in which the Presbytery has determined that shortfalls are to any extent unjustified, it shall not resolve to allow a call of any kind until:

(a) the shortfalls have been met to the extent to which the Presbytery determined that they were unjustified, or

(b) a scheme for the payment of the unjustified shortfall has been agreed between the congregation and the Presbytery and receives the concurrence of the Ministries Council and/or the Stewardship and Finance Committee for their respective interests, or

(c) a fresh appraisal of the charge in terms of Act VII 2003 has been carried out, regardless of the status of the charge in the current Presbytery plan:

(i) During such appraisal, no further steps may be taken in respect of filling the vacancy, and the Presbytery shall make final determination of what constitutes such steps.

(ii) Following such appraisal and any consequent adjustment or deferred adjustment, the shortfalls shall be met or declared justifiable or a scheme shall be agreed in terms of subsection (b) above; the Presbytery shall inform the Ministries Council and the Stewardship and Finance Committee of its decisions in terms of this section; and the Presbytery shall remove the suspension-of-vacancy process referred to in sub-paragraph (i).

10. Vacancy Schedule

(1) When in terms of sections 4 and 6 above the decision to release the minister from the charge has been made and the Interim Moderator appointed, there shall be issued by the Ministries Council a Schedule or Schedules for completion by the responsible Financial Board(s) of the vacant congregation(s) in consultation with representatives of the Presbytery, setting forth the proposed arrangements for payment of ministerial expenses and for provision of a manse, showing the ministry requirements and details of any endowment income. The Schedule, along with an Extract Minute from each relevant Kirk Session containing a commitment fully and adequately to support the ministry, shall be forwarded to the Presbytery Clerk.

(2) The Schedule shall be considered by the Vacancy Procedure Committee and, if approved, transmitted to the Ministries Council by the Presbytery Clerk. The Vacancy Procedure Committee or Presbytery must not sustain an appointment and call until the Schedule has been approved by them and by the Ministries Council, which shall intimate its decision within six weeks of receiving the schedule from the Presbytery.

(3) The accuracy of the Vacancy Schedule shall be kept under review by the Vacancy Procedure Committee.

(4) The provisions of section 2 above shall apply to the decisions of the Vacancy Procedure Committee.

11. Manse

As soon as possible after the manse becomes vacant, the Presbytery Property Committee shall inspect the manse and come to a view on what work, if any, must be carried out to render it suitable for a new incumbent. The views of the Property Committee should then be communicated to the Presbytery, which should, subject to any modifications which might be agreed by that Court, instruct the Financial Board of the congregation to have the work carried out. No induction date shall be fixed until the Presbytery Property Committee has again inspected the manse and confirmed that the work has been undertaken satisfactorily.

12. Advisory Committee

(1) As soon as possible after intimation of a vacancy or anticipated vacancy reaches the Presbytery Clerk, the Vacancy Procedure Committee shall appoint an Advisory Committee of three, subject to the following conditions:

(a) at least one member shall be an elder and at least one shall be a minister;

(b) the Advisory Committee may comprise members of the Vacancy Procedure Committee and act as a support committee to congregations in a vacancy;

(c) the Advisory Committee may contain individuals who are not members of the Presbytery;

(d) the appointment shall be subject to section 2 above.

(2) The Advisory Committee shall meet:

(a) before the election of the Nominating Committee, with the Kirk Session (or Kirk Sessions both separately and together) of the vacant charge, to consider together in the light of the whole circumstances of the parish or parishes (i) what kind of ministry would be best suited to their needs and (ii) which system of election of the Nominating Committee described in paragraph 14(2)(d) hereunder shall be used;

(b) with the Nominating Committee before it has taken any steps to fill the vacancy, to consider how it should proceed;

(c) with the Nominating Committee before it reports to the Kirk Session and Presbytery the identity of the nominee, to review the process followed and give any further advice it deems necessary;

(d) with the Kirk Session(s) as soon as an application is made for permission to proceed in terms of section 25A of this Act, to ensure that the requirements of that section are fulfilled;

(e) with the Nominating Committee at any other time by request of either the Nominating Committee or the Advisory Committee.

In the case of charges which are in the opinion of the Presbytery remote, it will be adequate if the Interim Moderator (accompanied if possible by a member of the Nominating Committee) meets with the Advisory Committee for the purposes listed in paragraphs (a) to (c) above.

13. Electoral Register

(1) It shall be the duty of the Kirk Session of a vacant congregation to proceed to make up the Electoral Register of the congregation. This shall contain (1) as communicants the names of those persons (a) whose names are on the communion roll of the congregation as at the date on which it is made up and who are not under Church discipline, (b) whose names have been added or restored to the communion roll on revision by the Kirk Session subsequently to the occurrence of the vacancy, and (c) who have given in valid Certificates of Transference by the date specified in terms of Schedule C hereto; and (2) as adherents the names of those persons who, being parishioners or regular worshippers in the congregation at the date when the vacancy occurred, and not being members of any other congregation, have claimed (in writing in the form prescribed in Schedule D and within the time specified in Schedule C) to be placed on the Electoral Register, the Kirk Session being satisfied that they desire to be permanently connected with the congregation and knowing of no adequate reasons why they should not be admitted as communicants should they so apply.

(2) At a meeting to be held not later than fourteen days after intimation has been made in terms of Schedule C hereto, the Kirk Session shall decide on the claims of persons to be placed on the Electoral Register, such claims to be sent to the Session Clerk before the meeting. At this meeting, the Kirk Session may hear parties claiming to have an interest. The Kirk Session shall thereupon prepare the lists of names and addresses of communicants and of adherents which it is proposed shall be the Electoral Register of the congregation, the names being arranged in alphabetical order and numbered consecutively throughout. The decision of the Kirk Session in respect of any matter affecting the preparation of the Electoral Register shall be final.

(3) The proposed Electoral Register having been prepared, the Interim Moderator shall cause intimation to be made on the first convenient Sunday in terms of Schedule E hereto that on that day an opportunity will be given for inspecting the Register after service, and that it will lie for inspection at such times and such places as the Kirk Session shall have determined; and further shall specify a day when the Kirk Session will meet to hear parties claiming an interest and will finally revise and adjust the Register. At this meeting, the list, having been revised, numbered and adjusted, shall on the authority of the court be attested by the Interim Moderator and the Clerk as the Electoral Register of the congregation.

(4) This Register, along with a duplicate copy, shall without delay be transmitted to the Presbytery Clerk, who, in name of the Presbytery, shall attest and return the principal copy, retaining the duplicate copy in his or her own possession. For all purposes connected with this Act, the congregation shall be deemed to be those persons whose names are on the Electoral Register, and no other.

(5) If after the attestation of the Register any communicant is given a Certificate of Transference, the Session Clerk shall delete that person's name from the Register and initial the deletion. Such a Certificate shall be granted only when application for it has been made in writing, and the said written application shall be retained until the vacancy is ended.

(6) When a period of more than six months has elapsed between the Electoral Register being attested and the congregation being given permission to call, the Kirk Session shall have power, if it so desires, to revise and update the Electoral Register. Intimation of this intention shall be given in terms of Schedule F hereto. Additional names shall be added to the Register in the form of an Addendum which shall also contain authority for the deletions which have been made; two copies of this Addendum, duly attested, shall be lodged with the Presbytery Clerk, who, in name of the Presbytery, shall attest and return the principal copy, retaining the duplicate copy in his or her own possession.

14. Appointment of Nominating Committee

(1) When permission to call has been given and the Electoral Register has been attested, intimation in terms of Schedule G shall be made that a meeting of the congregation is to be held to appoint a Committee of its own number for the purpose of nominating one person to the congregation with a view to the appointment of a minister.

(2) (a) The Interim Moderator shall preside at this meeting, and the Session Clerk, or in his or her absence a person appointed by the meeting, shall act as Clerk.

(b) The Interim Moderator shall remind the congregation of the number of members it is required to appoint in terms of this section and shall call for Nominations. To constitute a valid Nomination, the name of a person on the Electoral Register has to be proposed and seconded, and assurance given by the proposer that the person is prepared to act on the Committee. The Clerk shall take a note of all Nominations in the order in which they are made.

(c) When it appears to the Interim Moderator that the Nominations are complete, they shall be read to the congregation and an opportunity given for any withdrawals. If the number of persons nominated does not exceed the maximum fixed in terms of subsection (4) below, there is no need for a vote, and the Interim Moderator shall declare that these persons constitute a Nominating Committee.

(d) If the number exceeds the maximum, the election shall proceed by one of the following means, chosen in advance by the Kirk Session, and being either (i) the submission of the names by the Interim Moderator, one by one as they appear on the list, to the vote of the congregation, each member having the right to vote for up to the maximum number fixed for the Committee, and voting being by standing up, or (ii) a system of written ballot devised by the Kirk Session to suit the size of the congregation and approved by the Vacancy Procedure Committee or the Presbytery. In either case, in the event of a tie for the last place, a further vote shall be taken between or among those tying.

(e) The Interim Moderator shall, at the same meeting or as soon thereafter as the result of any ballot has been determined, announce the names of those thus elected to serve on the Nominating Committee, and intimate to them the time and place of their first meeting, which may be immediately after the congregational meeting provided that has been intimated along with the intimation of the congregational meeting.

(3) Where there is an agreement between the Presbytery and the congregation or congregations that the minister to be inducted shall serve either in a team ministry involving another congregation or congregations, or in a designated post such as a chaplaincy, it shall be competent for the agreement to specify that the Presbytery shall appoint up to two representatives to serve on the Nominating Committee.

(4) The Vacancy Procedure Committee shall, subject to the provisions of section 2 above, determine the number who will act on the Nominating Committee, being an odd number up to a maximum of thirteen.

(5) When the vacancy is in a linked charge, or when a union or linking of congregations has been agreed but not yet effected, or when there is agreement to a deferred union or a deferred linking, or where the appointment is to more than one post, the Vacancy Procedure Committee shall, subject to the provisions of section 2 above, determine how the number who will act on the Nominating Committee will be allocated among the congregations involved, unless provision for this has already been made in the Basis of Union or Basis of Linking as the case may be.

(6) The Nominating Committee shall not have power to co-opt additional members, but the relevant Kirk Session shall have power when necessary to appoint a replacement for any of its appointees who ceases, by death or resignation, to be a member of the Nominating Committee, or who, by falling ill or by moving away from the area, is unable to serve as a member of it.

15. Constitution of the Nominating Committee

It shall be the duty of the Interim Moderator to summon and preside at the first meeting of the Nominating Committee, which may be held at the close of the congregational meeting at which it is appointed and at which the Committee shall appoint a Convener and a Clerk. The Clerk, who need not be a member of the Committee, shall keep regular minutes of all proceedings. The Convener shall have a deliberative vote (if he or she is not the Interim Moderator) but shall in no case have a casting vote. If the Clerk is not a member of the Committee, he or she shall have no vote. At all meetings of the Committee, only those present shall be entitled to vote.

16. Task of the Nominating Committee

(1) The Nominating Committee shall have the duty of nominating one person to the congregation with a view to the election and appointment of a minister. It shall proceed by a process of announcement in a monthly vacancy list, application and interview, and may also advertise, receive recommendations and pursue enquiries in other ways.

(2) The Committee shall give due weight to any guidelines which may from time to time be issued by the Ministries Council or the General Assembly.

(3) The Committee shall make themselves aware of the roles of the other members of any ministry team as described in section 16 of Act VII 2003 and may meet with them for this purpose, but shall not acquire responsibility or authority for the negotiation or alteration of their terms and conditions.

17. Eligibility for Election

The following categories of persons, and no others, are eligible to be nominated, elected and called as ministers of parishes in the Church of Scotland, but always subject, where appropriate, to the provisions of Act IX 2002:

(1) A minister of a parish of the Church, a minister holding some other appointment that entitles him or her to a seat in Presbytery or a minister holding a current Practising Certificate in terms of Section 5 of Act II 2000 (as amended).
(2) A minister of the Church of Scotland who has retired from a parish or appointment as above, provided he or she has not reached his or her 65th birthday (or, subject to the provisions of Regulations II 2004, his or her 70th birthday).
(3) (a) A licentiate of the Church of Scotland who has satisfactorily completed, or has been granted exemption from, his or her period of probationary service.
(b) A graduate candidate in terms of section 22 of Act X 2004.
(4) A minister, licentiate or graduate candidate of the Church of Scotland who, with the approval of the World Mission Council, has entered the courts of an overseas Church as a full member, provided he or she has ceased to be such a member.
(5) A minister, licentiate or graduate candidate of the Church of Scotland who has neither relinquished nor been judicially deprived of the status he or she possessed and who has served, or is serving, furth of Scotland in any Church which is a member of the World Alliance of Reformed Churches.
(6) The holder of a Certificate of Eligibility in terms of Act IX 2002. The holder of a Certificate of Eligibility who is a national outside the European Economic Area and Switzerland shall be eligible to apply for charges only in terms of section 25A of this Act.
(7) For the avoidance of doubt, anyone who has served as an Interim Moderator in the current vacancy shall not be eligible to apply or to be considered as an applicant.

18. Ministers of a Team
Ministers occupying positions within a team ministry in the charge, or larger area including the charge, and former holders of such positions, shall be eligible to apply and shall not by virtue of office be deemed to have exercised undue influence in securing the call. A *locum tenens* in the vacant charge shall not by virtue of office be deemed to have exercised undue influence in securing the call. Any Interim Moderator in the current vacancy shall not be eligible to apply.

19. Ministers of Other Churches
(1) Where a minister of a church furth of Scotland, who holds a certificate of eligibility in terms of Act IX 2002, is nominated, the nominee, Kirk Session and Presbytery may agree that he or she shall be inducted for a period of three years only and shall retain status as a minister of his or her denomination of origin.
(2) Upon induction, such a minister shall be accountable to the Presbytery for the exercise of his or her ministry and to his or her own church for matters of life and doctrine. He or she shall be awarded corresponding membership of the Presbytery.
(3) With the concurrence of the Presbytery and the Ministries Council, and at the request of the congregation, the period may be extended for one further period of not more than three years.
(4) The provisions of this section shall apply in the case of an appointment as a member of a ministry team as defined in section 16(2)(a) of Act VII 2003 (as amended), provided that the appointment is one which the Presbytery deems must be held by a Ministry of Word and Sacrament.

20. Nomination
(1) Before the candidate is asked to accept Nomination, the Interim Moderator shall ensure that the candidate is given an adequate opportunity to see the whole ecclesiastical buildings (including the manse) pertaining to the congregation, and to meet privately with all members of staff of the charge or of any wider ministry team, and shall be provided with a copy of the constitution of the congregation, a copy of the current Presbytery Plan and of any

current Basis of Adjustment or Basis of Reviewable Tenure, and the most recent audited accounts and statement of funds, and the candidate shall acknowledge receipt in writing to the Interim Moderator.

(2) Before any Nomination is intimated to the Kirk Session and Presbytery Clerk, the Clerk to the Nominating Committee shall secure the written consent thereto of the nominee.

(3) Before reporting the Nomination to the Vacancy Procedure Committee, the Presbytery Clerk shall obtain from the nominee or Interim Moderator evidence of the eligibility of the nominee to be appointed to the charge.

(a) In the case of a minister not being a member of any Presbytery of the Church of Scotland, this shall normally constitute an Exit Certificate in terms of Act X 2004, or evidence of status from the Ministries Council, or a current practising certificate, or certification from the Ministries Council of eligibility in terms of Act IX 2002.

(b) In the case of a minister in the first five years of his or her first charge, this shall consist of an extract minute either from the Vacancy Procedure Committee of his or her current Presbytery, or from that Presbytery, exceptionally releasing the minister.

21. Preaching by Nominee

(1) The Interim Moderator, on receiving notice of the Committee's Nomination, shall arrange that the nominee conduct public worship in the vacant church or churches, normally within four Sundays, and that the ballot take place immediately after each such service.

(2) The Interim Moderator shall thereupon cause intimation to be made on two Sundays regarding the arrangements made in connection with the preaching by the nominee and the ballot thereafter, all in terms of Schedule H hereto.

22. Election of Minister

(1) The Interim Moderator shall normally preside at all congregational meetings connected with the election which shall be in all cases by ballot and shall normally be in charge of the ballot.

(2) The Interim Moderator may invite one or more persons (not being persons whose names are on the Electoral Register of the vacant congregation) to assist him or her in the conduct of a ballot vote when he or she judges this desirable.

(3) When a linking or a deferred union or deferred linking is involved, the Interim Moderator shall consult and reach agreement with the minister or Interim Moderator of the other congregation regarding the arrangements for the conduct of public worship in these congregations by the nominee as in section 21(1) above. The Interim Moderator shall in writing appoint a member of Presbytery to take full charge of the ballot vote for the other congregation. In the case of a deferred union or deferred linking, the minister already inducted shall not be so appointed, nor shall he or she be in any way involved in the conduct of the election.

23. Ballot Procedure

(1) The Kirk Session shall arrange to have available at the time of election a sufficient supply of voting-papers printed in the form of Schedule I hereto, and these shall be put into the custody of the Interim Moderator who shall preside at the election, assisted as in section 22 above. He or she shall issue on request to any person whose name is on the Electoral Register a voting-paper, noting on the Register that this has been done. Facilities shall be provided whereby the voter may mark the paper in secrecy, and a ballot-box shall be available wherein the paper is to be deposited when marked. The Interim Moderator may assist any person who asks for help in respect of completing the voting-paper, but no other person whatever shall communicate with the voter at this stage. The Interim Moderator, or

the deputy appointed by him or her, shall be responsible for the safe custody of ballot-box, papers and Electoral Register.

(2) As soon as practicable, and at latest within twenty-four hours after the close of the voting, the Interim Moderator shall constitute the Kirk Session, or the joint Kirk Sessions when more than one congregation is involved, and in presence of the Kirk Session shall proceed with the counting of the votes, in which he or she may be assisted as provided in section 22 above. When more than one ballot-box has been used and when the votes of more than one congregation are involved, all ballot-boxes shall be emptied and the voting-papers shall be mixed together before counting begins so that the preponderance of votes in one area or in one congregation shall not be disclosed.

(3) A voting-paper shall only be considered as spoilt and the vote not counted where the intention of the voter is unclear, and in no other circumstances. It shall be for the Kirk Session, on the recommendation of the Interim Moderator, to determine whether the intention of the voter is clear.

(4) If the number voting For exceeds the number voting Against, the nominee shall be declared elected and the Nominating Committee shall be deemed to be discharged.

(5) If the number voting For is equal to or less than the number voting Against, the Interim Moderator shall declare that there has been failure to elect and that the Nominating Committee is deemed to have been discharged. He or she shall proceed in terms of section 26(b) without further reference to the Presbytery.

(6) After the counting has been completed, the Interim Moderator shall sign a declaration in one of the forms of Schedule J hereto, and this shall be recorded in the minute of the Kirk Session or of the Kirk Sessions. An extract shall be affixed to the notice-board of the church, or of each of the churches, concerned. In presence of the Kirk Session, the Interim Moderator shall then seal up the voting-papers along with the marked copy of the Electoral Register, and these shall be transmitted to the Presbytery Clerk in due course along with the other documents specified in section 27 below.

24. Withdrawal of Nominee

(1) Should a nominee intimate withdrawal before he or she has preached as nominee, the Nominating Committee shall continue its task and seek to nominate another nominee.

(2) Should a nominee intimate withdrawal after he or she has been elected, the Interim Moderator shall proceed in terms of sections 23(4) above and 26(b) below without further reference to the Presbytery.

25. The Call

(1) The Interim Moderator shall, along with the intimation regarding the result of the voting, intimate the arrangements made for members of the congregation over a period of not less than eight days to subscribe the Call (Schedule K). Intimation shall be in the form of Schedule L hereto.

(2) The Call may be subscribed on behalf of a member not present to sign in person, provided a mandate authorising such subscription is produced as in Schedule M. All such entries shall be initialled by the Interim Moderator or by the member of the Kirk Session appending them.

(3) Those eligible to sign the call shall be all those whose names appear on the Electoral Register. A paper of concurrence in the Call may be signed by regular worshippers in the congregation and by adherents whose names have not been entered on the Electoral Register.

25A. Ministers from Non-EEA Countries excluding Switzerland

(1) Six months after the vacancy has first appeared in a monthly vacancy list, and provided there

are no applications currently under the consideration of the Nominating Committee, the Kirk Session (or in the case of a linkage the Kirk Sessions in agreement) may apply to the Presbytery to have the charge listed for the purposes of this section.

(2) Such applications shall be considered by the whole Presbytery, and shall not form part of the remit of the Vacancy Procedure Committee.

(3) The Presbytery must be satisfied that there are no outstanding issues of superintendence, or other factors that would make such listing inappropriate, and must consult with the Ministries Council before deciding whether to permit the listing. The Presbytery Clerk shall within seven days send an extract minute of the decision to the Ministries Council.

(4) Upon receiving notification of the listing from the Presbytery, the Nominating Committee shall proceed again from section 16 of this Act, and holders of Certificates of Eligibility who are nationals of countries outwith the EEA and Switzerland shall now be eligible to apply.

(5) For the avoidance of doubt, the Nominating Committee (a) must always dispose of any competent applications received in terms of section 17 of this Act before considering those made in terms of this section, but (b) shall not be obliged to make a nomination from any particular group of applicants.

(6) When a Presbytery withdraws permission to call, or the permission lapses in terms of section 26 of this Act, the Presbytery shall decide whether permission to proceed in terms of this section remains in force during the ensuing process to make a nomination.

26. Failure to Nominate

The exercise by a congregation of its right to call a minister shall be subject to a time-limit of one year; this period shall be calculated from the date when intimation is given of the agreement to grant leave to call. If it appears that an appointment is not to be made within the allotted time (allowing one further calendar month for intimation to the Presbytery), the congregation may make application to the Presbytery for an extension, which will normally be for a further six months. For clear cause shown, a further extension of six months may be granted. If no election has been made and intimated to the Presbytery by the expiry of that time, the permission to call shall be regarded as having lapsed. The Presbytery may thereupon look afresh at the question of adjustment. If the Presbytery is still satisfied that a minister should be appointed, it shall itself take steps to make such an appointment, proceeding in one of the following ways:

(a) (i) The Presbytery may discharge the Nominating Committee, strengthen the Advisory Committee which had been involved in the case by the appointment of an additional minister and elder, instruct that Committee to bring forward to a subsequent meeting the name of an eligible individual for appointment to the charge and intimate this instruction to the congregation. If satisfied with the recommendation brought by the Advisory Committee, the Presbytery shall thereupon make the appointment.

(ii) The Presbytery Clerk shall thereupon intimate to the person concerned the fact of his or her appointment, shall request him or her to forward a letter of acceptance along with appropriate Certificates if these are required in terms of section 27 below, and shall arrange with him or her to conduct public worship in the vacant church or churches on an early Sunday.

(iii) The Presbytery Clerk shall cause intimation to be made in the form of Schedule N that the person appointed will conduct public worship on the day specified and that a Call in the usual form will lie with the Session Clerk or other suitable person for not less than eight free days to receive the signatures of the congregation. The conditions governing the signing of the Call shall be as in section 25 above.

(iv) At the expiry of the time allowed, the Call shall be transmitted by the Session Clerk to the Presbytery Clerk who shall lay it, along with the documents referred to in sub-paragraph (ii) above, before the Presbytery at its first ordinary meeting or at a meeting *in hunc effectum*.

(b) Otherwise, the Presbytery shall instruct that a fresh Nominating Committee be elected in terms of section 14 above. The process shall then be followed in terms of this Act from the point of the election of the Nominating Committee.

27. Transmission of Documents

(1) After an election has been made, the Interim Moderator shall secure from the person appointed a letter of acceptance of the appointment.

(2) The Interim Moderator shall then without delay transmit the relevant documents to the Presbytery Clerk. These are: the minute of Nomination by the Nominating Committee, all intimations made to the congregation thereafter, the declaration of the election and appointment, the voting-papers, the marked copy of the Register and the letter of acceptance. He or she shall also inform the Clerk of the steps taken in connection with the signing of the Call, and shall arrange that, at the expiry of the period allowed for subscription, the Call shall be transmitted by the Session Clerk to the Presbytery Clerk.

(3) After the person elected has been inducted to the charge, the Presbytery Clerk shall:

(a) deliver to him or her the approved copy of the Vacancy Schedule referred to in section 10(2) above, and

(b) destroy the intimations and voting-papers lodged with him or her in terms of subsection (2) above and ensure that confidential documents and correspondence held locally are destroyed.

28. Sustaining the Call

(1) All of the documents listed in section 27 above shall be laid before the Vacancy Procedure Committee, which may resolve to sustain the call and determine arrangements for the induction of the new minister, subject to (a) a request for the release, if appropriate, of the minister from his or her current charge in terms of this Act and (b) the provisions of section 2 above. The Moderator of the Presbytery shall, if no ordinary meeting of the Presbytery falls before the proposed induction date, call a meeting *pro re nata* for the induction.

(2) In the event that the matter comes before the Presbytery in terms of section 2 above, the procedure shall be as follows:

(a) The Call and other relevant documents having been laid on the table, the Presbytery shall hear any person whom it considers to have an interest. In particular, the Advisory Committee shall be entitled to be heard if it so desires, or the Presbytery may ask for a report from it. The Presbytery shall then decide whether to sustain the appointment in terms of subsection (1) above, and in doing so shall give consideration to the number of signatures on the Call. It may delay reaching a decision and return the Call to the Kirk Session to give further opportunity for it to be subscribed.

(b) If the Presbytery sustain an appointment and Call to a Graduate Candidate, and there be no appeal tendered in due form against its judgement, it shall appoint the day and hour and place at which the ordination and induction will take place.

(c) If the Presbytery sustain an appointment and Call to a minister of the Church of Scotland not being a minister of a parish, or to a minister of another denomination, and there be no ecclesiastical impediment, the Presbytery shall appoint the day and hour and place at which the induction will take place.

(3) In the event that the Call is not sustained, the Presbytery shall determine either (a) to give

more time for it to be signed in terms of section 25 above or (b) to proceed in terms of subsection (a) or (b) of section 26 above.

29. Admission to a Charge

(1) When the Presbytery has appointed a day for the ordination and induction of a Graduate Candidate, or for the induction of a minister already ordained, the Clerk shall arrange for an edict in the form of Schedule O to be read to the congregation on the two Sundays preceding the day appointed.

(2) At the time and place named in the edict, the Presbytery having been constituted, the Moderator shall call for the return of the edict attested as having been duly served. If the minister is being translated from another Presbytery, the relevant minute of that Presbytery or of its Vacancy Procedure Committee agreeing to translation shall also be laid on the table. Any objection, to be valid at this stage, must have been intimated to the Presbytery Clerk at the objector's earliest opportunity, must be strictly directed to life or doctrine and must be substantiated immediately to the satisfaction of the Presbytery, in which case procedure shall be sisted and the Presbytery shall take appropriate steps to deal with the situation that has arisen. Otherwise, the Presbytery shall proceed with the ordination and induction, or with the induction, as hereunder.

(3) The Presbytery shall proceed to the church where public worship shall be conducted by those appointed for the purpose. The Clerk shall read a brief narrative of the cause of the vacancy and of the steps taken for the settlement. The Moderator, having read the Preamble, shall, addressing him or her by name, put to the person to be inducted the questions prescribed (*see the Ordinal of the Church as authorised from time to time by the General Assembly*). Satisfactory answers having been given, the person to be inducted shall sign the Formula. If he or she has not already been ordained, the person to be inducted shall then kneel, and the Moderator by prayer and the imposition of hands, in which members of the Presbytery, appointed by the Presbytery for the purpose, and other ordained persons associated with it, if invited to share in such imposition of hands, shall join, shall ordain him or her to the office of the Holy Ministry. Prayer being ended, the Moderator shall say: 'I now declare you to have been ordained to the office of the Holy Ministry, and in name of the Lord Jesus Christ, the King and Head of the Church, and by authority of this Presbytery, I induct you to this charge, and in token thereof we give you the right hand of fellowship'. The Moderator with all other members of Presbytery present and those associated with it shall then give the right hand of fellowship. The Moderator shall then put the prescribed question to the members of the congregation. Suitable charges to the new minister and to the congregation shall then be given by the Moderator or by a minister appointed for the purpose.

(4) *[This subsection is to be construed in conformity with Act III 2004.]* When an ordained minister is being inducted to a charge, the act of ordination shall not be repeated, and the relevant words shall be omitted from the declaration. In other respects, the procedure shall be as in subsection (3) above.

(5) When the appointment is for a limited or potentially limited period (including Reviewable Tenure, or an appointment in terms of section 19 above), the service shall proceed as in subsections (3) or (4) above, except that in the declaration the Moderator shall say: 'I induct you to this charge on the Basis of [specific Act and Section] and in terms of Minute of Presbytery of date . . .'.

(6) After the service, the Presbytery shall resume its session, when the name of the new minister shall be added to the Roll of Presbytery, and the Clerk shall be instructed to send certified intimation of the induction to the Session Clerk to be engrossed in the minutes of

the first meeting of Kirk Session thereafter, and, in the case of a translation from another Presbytery or where the minister was prior to the induction subject to the supervision of another Presbytery, to the Clerk of that Presbytery.

30. Service of Introduction

(1) When a minister has been appointed to a linked charge, the Presbytery shall determine in which of the churches of the linking the induction is to take place. This shall be a service of induction to the charge, in consequence of which the person inducted shall become minister of each of the congregations embraced in the linking. The edict regarding the induction, which shall be in terms of Schedule O, shall be read in all of the churches concerned. There shall be no other service of induction; but, if the churches are far distant from one another, or for other good reason, the Presbytery may appoint a service of introduction to be held in the other church or churches. Intimation shall be given of such service, but not in edictal form.

(2) In any case of deferred union or deferred linking, the minister elected and appointed shall be inducted 'to the vacant congregation of A in deferred union (or linking) with the congregation of B' and there shall be no need for any further act to establish his or her position as minister of the united congregation or of the linked congregation as the case may be. The Presbytery, however, shall in such a case arrange a service of introduction to the newly united congregation of AB or the newly linked congregation of B. Intimation shall be given of such service, but not in edictal form.

(3) When an appointment has been made to an extra-parochial office wholly or mainly under control of the Church (community ministry, full-time chaplaincy in hospital, industry, prison or university, full-time clerkship and so on), the Presbytery may deem it appropriate to arrange a service of introduction to take place in a church or chapel suitable to the occasion.

(4) When an appointment has been made to a parochial appointment other than that of an inducted minister, the Presbytery may arrange a service of introduction to take place within the parish. If ordination is involved, suitable arrangements shall be made and edictal intimation shall be given in terms of Schedule P.

(5) A service of introduction not involving ordination shall follow the lines of an induction except that, instead of putting the normal questions to the minister, the Moderator shall ask him or her to affirm the vows taken at his or her ordination. Where the service, in terms of subsection (3) or (4) above, includes the ordination of the minister, the vows shall be put in full. In either case, in the declaration, the Moderator in place of 'I induct you to . . .' shall say: 'I welcome you as . . .'.

31. Demission of Status

If a minister seeks to demit his or her status as a minister of the Church of Scotland, any accompanying demission of a charge will be dealt with by the Vacancy Procedure Committee in terms of section 4 of this Act without further delay, but the question of demission of status shall be considered by the Presbytery itself. The Moderator of Presbytery, or a deputy appointed by him or her, shall first confer with the minister regarding his or her reasons and shall report to the Presbytery if there appears to be any reason not to grant permission to demit status. Any decision to grant permission to demit status shall be immediately reported to the Ministries Council.

32. Miscellaneous

For the purposes of this Act, intimations to congregations may be made (a) verbally during every act of worship or (b) in written intimations distributed to the whole congregation provided that the congregation's attention is specifically drawn to the presence of an intimation there in terms of this Act.

For the purposes of this Act, attestation of all intimations to congregations shall consist of certification thereof by the Session Clerk as follows:

(a) Certification that all intimations received have been duly made on the correct number of Sundays shall be sent to the Presbytery Clerk before the service of induction or introduction.

(b) Certification that any particular intimation received has been duly made on the correct number of Sundays shall be furnished on demand to the Vacancy Procedure Committee or the Presbytery Clerk.

(c) Intimation shall be made immediately to the Presbytery Clerk in the event that intimation has not been duly made on the appropriate Sunday.

33. Repeals and Amendments

(1) Act V 1984 (as amended) is hereby repealed; it is hereby provided that all other legislation prior to this Act shall be construed in conformity with this Act.

(2) Earlier Acts and Regulations are amended as follows:

(a) In sections 2 and 7 of Act XVIII 1932, delete the latter sentence of section 2 and all of subsection 7(b).

(b) In Act IV 1999, delete 'Act V 1984 section 25(3)' and substitute 'section 29(3) of Act VIII 2003'.

(c) In section 19(2) of Act II 2000, delete 'section 2(3) of Act V 1984' and substitute 'section 7 of Act VIII 2003'.

(d) In section 9 of Act XV 2002, delete 'in terms of section 27 of Act V 1984'.

(e) In section 12(i) of Act XIII 2000 and in section 2(i) of Regulations V 2000, delete 'sections 6-8 of Act V 1984' and substitute section 13 of Act VIII 2003'.

(f) In section 2(2) of Act IV 2001, delete 'in terms of Act V 1984 section 27' and 'in terms of the said Act V 1984'.

(g) In paragraph 1 of Schedule 3 to Act V 2002, delete 'section 13 of Act V 1984' and substitute 'section 17 of Act VIII 2003'.

(h) In paragraph 2(ii) of Schedule 3 to Act V 2002, delete 'Sections 6 to 8 of Act V 1984' and substitute 'section 13 of Act VIII 2003'.

(i) In section 2 of Act VII 2002, delete 'Act V 1984 section 25' and substitute 'section 29 of Act VIII 2003'.

(j) In section 9 of Act XV 2002, delete 'in terms of section 27 of Act V 1984'.

(k) In Regulations II 1996, delete reference to Act V 1984 (as amended) and substitute Act VIII 2003.

(3) Notwithstanding subsection (1) above, the repeal of Act V 1984 as amended shall not affect the operation of the said Act (or Deliverances of the General Assembly in pursuance thereof) prior to the repeal of the said Act, or anything done or suffered under the said Act or Deliverances; and any rights or obligations acquired or incurred thereunder shall have effect as if the said Act had not been repealed.

34. Interpretation

For the purposes of this Act, the Interpretation section (section 1) of Act VII 2003 will apply.

SCHEDULES

A INTIMATION OF ACTION OR DECISION OF VACANCY PROCEDURE COMMITTEE – Section 2(1)

To be read on one Sunday

The Vacancy Procedure Committee of the Presbytery of ……… proposes [here insert action or permission proposed]……. Any communicant member of the congregation(s) of A [and B] may submit to the Presbytery Clerk a request for this proposal to be considered at the next meeting of the Presbytery: where such requests are received from four individuals, being communicant members of the congregation(s) or full members of the Presbytery, the request shall be met. Such request should be submitted in writing to [name and postal address of Presbytery Clerk] by [date seven days after intimation].

A ………. B ………. Presbytery Clerk

B EDICT CITING A CONGREGATION TO ATTEND – Section 2(5)

To be read on one Sunday

Intimation is hereby given that, in connection with the [anticipated] vacancy in this congregation, a valid request has been made for the matter of [here insert action or permission which had been proposed] to be considered by the Presbytery. [The proposed course of action] is in the meantime sisted.

Intimation is hereby further given that the Presbytery will meet to consider this matter at ……… on ………. the ………. day of ………. at ………. o'clock and that the congregation are hereby cited to attend for their interests.

A ………. B ………. Presbytery Clerk

C PREPARATION OF ELECTORAL REGISTER – Section 13(1) and (2)

To be read on two Sundays

Intimation is hereby given that in view of the [1]anticipated vacancy, the Kirk Session is about to make up an Electoral Register of this congregation. Any communicant whose name is not already on the Communion Roll as a member should hand in to the Session Clerk a Certificate of Transference, and anyone wishing his or her name added to the Register as an adherent should obtain from the Session Clerk, and complete and return to him or her, a Form of Adherent's Claim. All such papers should be in the hands of the Session Clerk not later than ………. . The Kirk Session will meet in ………. on ………. at ………. to make up the Electoral Register, when anyone wishing to support his or her claim in person should attend.

C ………. D ………. Interim Moderator

[1] This word to be included where appropriate – otherwise to be deleted

D FORM OF ADHERENT'S CLAIM – Section 13(1)

I, [1] .... of [2] ...., being a parishioner or regular worshipper in the Church of .... and not being a member of any other congregation in Scotland, claim to have my name put on the Electoral Register of the parish of .... as an adherent.

Date .... (Signed)......................

[1] Here enter full name in block capitals
[2] Here enter address in full

E INSPECTION OF ELECTORAL REGISTER – Section 13(3)

To be read on one Sunday

Intimation is hereby given that the proposed Electoral Register of this congregation has now been prepared and that an opportunity of inspecting it will be given today in .... at the close of this service, and that it will be open for inspection at .... on .... between the hours of .... and .... each day. Any questions regarding entries in the Register should be brought to the notice of the Kirk Session which is to meet in .... on .... at .... o'clock, when it will finally make up the Electoral Register.

C .... D .... Interim Moderator

F REVISION OF ELECTORAL REGISTER – Section 13(6)

To be read on two Sundays

Intimation is hereby given that, more than six months having elapsed since the Electoral Register of this congregation was finally made up, it is now proposed that it should be revised. An opportunity of inspecting the Register will be given in .... at the close of this service, and also at .... on .... between the hours of .... and .... each day. Anyone wishing his or her name added to the Electoral Register as a member should give in a Transference Certificate, or as an adherent should give in a Form of Adherent's Claim (copies of which may be had from the Session Clerk) not later than .... The Kirk Session will meet in .... on .... at .... o'clock, when it will finally make up the Revised Register.

C .... D .... Interim Moderator

G INTIMATION OF ELECTION OF NOMINATING COMMITTEE – Section 14(1)

To be read on two Sundays

Intimation is hereby given that a meeting of this congregation will be held in the Church [or other arrangement may be given here] on Sunday .... at the close of morning worship for the purpose of appointing a Nominating Committee which will nominate one person to the congregation with a view to the appointment of a minister.

C .... D .... Interim Moderator

H MINUTE OF NOMINATION BY NOMINATING COMMITTEE – Section 21

To be read on two Sundays

(1) The Committee chosen by this congregation to nominate a person with a view to the election and appointment of a minister, at a meeting held at .... on ...., resolved to name and propose [1] ...., and they accordingly do name and propose the said ....

Date ....

E .... F .... Convener of Committee

[1] The name and designation of the person should at this point be entered in full

(2) Intimation is therefore hereby given that the Nominating Committee having, as by minute now read, named and proposed [*Name*], arrangements have been made whereby public worship will be conducted in this Church by him or her on Sunday the .... day of .... at .... o'clock; and that a vote will be taken by voting-papers immediately thereafter; and that electors may vote For or Against electing and appointing the said [*Name*] as minister of this vacant charge.

C .... D .... Interim Moderator

I VOTING-PAPER – Section 23

FOR Electing [*Name*]	
AGAINST Electing [*Name*]	

Directions to Voters: If you are in favour of electing [*Name*], put a cross (x) on the upper right-hand space. If you are not in favour of electing [*Name*], put a cross (x) in the lower right-hand space. Mark your voting-paper in this way with a cross and put no other mark on your voting-paper, or your vote may not be counted.

Note: The Directions to Voters must be printed prominently on the face of the voting-paper.

J DECLARATION OF ELECTION RESULT – Section 23(5)

First Form (Successful Election)

I hereby declare that the following are the results of the voting for the election and appointment of a minister to the vacant charge of [1] .... and that the said [*Name*] has accordingly been elected and appointed subject to the judgement of the courts of the Church.

Date .... C .... D .... Interim Moderator

[1] Here enter details

FOR Electing [*Name*]
AGAINST Electing [*Name*]

Second Form (Failure to Elect)

I hereby declare that the following are the results of the voting for the election and appointment of a minister to the vacant charge of [1] .... and that in consequence of this vote there has been a failure to elect, and the Nominating Committee is deemed to have been discharged. [Continue in terms of Schedule G if appropriate.]

Date .... C .... D .... Interim Moderator

[1] Here enter details

FOR Electing [*Name*]
AGAINST Electing [*Name*]

K THE CALL – Section 25(1)

Form of Call

We, members of the Church of Scotland and of the congregation known as ...., being without a minister, address this Call to be our minister to you, ..., of whose gifts and qualities we have been assured, and we warmly invite you to accept this Call, promising that we shall devote ourselves with you to worship, witness, mission and service in this parish, and also to the furtherance of these in the world, to the glory of God and for the advancement of His Kingdom.

Paper of Concurrence

We, regular worshippers in the congregation of the Church of Scotland known as ...., concur in the Call addressed by that congregation to .... to be their minister.

Note: The Call and Paper of Concurrence should be dated and attested by the Interim Moderator before they are transmitted to the Clerk of the Presbytery.

L SUBSCRIBING THE CALL – Section 25(1)

To be read on at least one Sunday

Intimation is hereby given that this congregation having elected [*Name*] to be their minister, a Call to the said [*Name*] has been prepared and will lie in .... on .... the .... day of .... between the hours of .... and ...., when those whose names are on the Electoral Register of the congregation may sign in person or by means of mandates. Forms of mandate may be obtained from the Session Clerk.

A Paper of Concurrence will also be available for signature by persons who are connected with the congregation but whose names are not on the Electoral Register of the congregation.

C .... D .... Interim Moderator

M MANDATE TO SIGN CALL – Section 25(2)

I, ... of ...., being a person whose name is on the Electoral Register of the congregation, hereby authorise the Session Clerk, or other member of Session, to add my name to the Call addressed to [*Name*] to be our minister.

(Signed) ....

N CITATION IN CASE OF NOMINATION BY PRESBYTERY – Section 26(a)(iii)

To be read on one Sunday

Intimation is hereby given that [*Name*], whom the Presbytery has appointed to be minister of this congregation, will conduct public worship in the Church on Sunday the .... day of .... at .... o'clock.

Intimation is hereby further given that a Call addressed to the said [*Name*] will lie in .... on .... the .... day of .... between the hours of .... and .... during the day and between the hours of .... and .... in the evening, when members may sign in person or by means of mandates, forms of which may be had from the Session Clerk.

Intimation is hereby further given that the Presbytery will meet to deal with the appointment and Call at .... on .... the .... day of .... at .... o'clock and that the congregation are hereby cited to attend for their interests.

A .... B .... Presbytery Clerk

O EDICTAL INTIMATION OF ADMISSION – Section 29

To be read on two Sundays

- The Presbytery of .... has received a Call from this congregation addressed to [*Name*] to be their minister, and the Call has been sustained as a regular Call, and has been accepted by him/her[1];
- The Presbytery, having judged the said [*Name*] qualified[2] for the ministry of the Gospel and for this charge, has resolved to proceed to his or her[3] ordination and induction on .... the .... day of .... at .... o'clock unless something occur which may reasonably impede it:

Notice is hereby given to all concerned that if they, or any of them, have anything to object to in the life or doctrine of the said [*Name*], they should intimate their objection at their earliest opportunity to the Presbytery Clerk, with evidence of substantiation of the objection.

The Presbytery is to meet at [*time*] on [*date as above*]. In accordance with section 29 of Act VIII 2003, an objection first brought at that time must be immediately substantiated, and the objector must satisfy the Presbytery that there was no earlier opportunity to bring the objection to the attention of the Presbytery Clerk. Otherwise the Presbytery shall proceed without further delay.

By order of the Presbytery

A .... B .... Presbytery Clerk

[1] add, where appropriate, 'and his or her translation has been agreed to by the Presbytery of ....'
[2] omit 'for the ministry of the Gospel and' if the minister to be inducted has been ordained previously
[3] omit, where appropriate, 'ordination and'

P EDICTAL INTIMATION OF ORDINATION IN CASE OF INTRODUCTION – Section 30(1)

To be read on two Sundays

- Whereas [narrate circumstances requiring service of introduction]
- And whereas the Presbytery, having found the said [*Name*] to have been regularly appointed and to be qualified for the ministry of the Gospel and for the said appointment, has resolved to proceed to his or her ordination to the Holy Ministry and to his or her introduction as [specify appointment] on .... the .... day of .... at .... o'clock unless something occur which may reasonably impede it:

Notice is hereby given to all concerned that if they, or any of them, have anything to object to in the life or doctrine of the said [*Name*], they may appear at the Presbytery which is to meet at .... on .... the .... day of .... at .... o'clock; with certification that if no relevant objection be then made and immediately substantiated, the Presbytery will proceed without further delay.

By order of the Presbytery

A .... B .... Presbytery Clerk

SECTION 4

The General Assembly of 2011

(1) THE GENERAL ASSEMBLY

The Lord High Commissioner:	Lord Wilson of Tillyorn KT GCMG PRSE
Moderator:	Right Rev. A. David K. Arnott MA BD
Chaplains to the Moderator:	Rev. Joanne C. Hood MA BD Rev. Donald G.B. McCorkindale BD DipMin
Principal Clerk:	Rev. John P. Chalmers BD
Depute Clerk:	Rev. George J. Whyte BSc BD DMin PhD
Procurator:	Ms Laura Dunlop QC
Law Agent:	Mrs Janette S. Wilson LLB NP
Convener of the Business Committee:	Rev. Janet S. Mathieson MA BD
Vice-Convener of the Business Committee:	Rev. E. Lorna Hood MA BD
Precentor:	Rev. Douglas Galbraith MA BD BMus MPhil ARSCM PhD
Assembly Officer:	Mr David McColl
Assistant Assembly Officer:	Mr Craig Marshall

---

(2) THE MODERATOR

The Right Reverend A. David K. Arnott MA BD

At the end of the General Assembly of 2010, the retiring Business Convener assured his 'playpen' colleagues of his thoughts and prayers for the General Assembly of 2011 while he would be enjoying retirement living in Peebles. Little did he know that retirement would not remove him from the Assembly limelight and onto the 'back benches' of the public gallery but would lead him instead straight into the Moderator's chair.

David has served the Church in three parishes and in several roles nationally, regionally and locally over the years of his influential ministry. His wide-ranging experience of the Church and its work will undoubtedly enable him to bring valuable insight to the office of Moderator during this year.

David was born and brought up in Fife along with his brother Robin, now an elder and Reader. David was educated at Burntisland Primary, at Lochgelly West Primary and at George Watson's College in Edinburgh. This was followed by a scholarship year at Hamilton College, Clinton, New York, USA. He attended the Universities of St Andrews and Edinburgh, graduating MA (French and Spanish) and BD (with Honours in New Testament).

In 1971, David was ordained and inducted to Stobhill Parish Church in Gorebridge, Midlothian, where his ministry spanned the period of time during which three congregations united to form Gorebridge Parish Church. David moved in 1977 to Netherlee Parish Church, Glasgow, where a nineteen-year ministry benefited both the local congregation and the community. In 1996, David accepted the call to Hope Park Church in St Andrews, which, in 2005, linked with Strathkinness. It was from this linked charge that David 'retired' in the summer of 2010. His parish ministries were all marked with a great love for his people; dignified, meaningful and engaging worship; and involvement in the wider community at home and abroad.

Beyond parish ministry, David has been involved in many areas of the Church's work, at Presbytery level and nationally. In the three Presbyteries in which he has served, he has been active in committee work and has held several convenerships, including Business Convener of Glasgow Presbytery, and Ministry Convener and Superintendence Convener of St Andrews Presbytery. David was Moderator of St Andrews Presbytery in 2007.

In Glasgow, David worked briefly as a part-time prison chaplain at Barlinnie; in St Andrews, he was a part-time hospital chaplain and honorary Church of Scotland university chaplain. David has been a regular broadcaster on BBC Radio Scotland's *Thought for the Day* for more than thirty-five years, and his leading of worship has been broadcast on a fairly regular basis. He has also contributed to Radio 4's *Prayer for the Day* and has appeared on both Scottish and Grampian Television.

David convened the Assembly's former Education for the Ministry Committee, and for a time was Joint Convener of the Board of Ministry. His involvement in the assessment and training of candidates for the ministry has continued more recently in leading sessions with them on many topics including preaching, and in his role as Senior Director of Assessment Conferences, within the current Ministries Council, during 2006–9.

David brings to his Moderatorial year a wealth of knowledge and experience of how the Church, and its General Assembly in particular, operates. He has served on and convened the Assembly Arrangements Committee, a Committee that among other things has the remit to make arrangements for the General Assembly and to advise the Moderator on his or her official duties! Until last year, David was Assembly Business Convener, a role which also brought opportunities to support, guide and assist his predecessors in the Moderatorial chair!

David loves the Church and its courts from Kirk Session to General Assembly. He also loves being a husband, grandpa, golfer and photographer, and watching rugby on a Saturday afternoon! David's wife Rosemary and their children Jenny, Dougie, Kenny and their families are rightly proud of David's achievements and the high regard in which he is held within the Kirk.

It is a great honour and privilege for us, David's Chaplains, to share a little bit of this year with him. To us, he has been parish minister, supervising 'bishop' during probation, a good friend and a trusted colleague. He has shaped and influenced our ministries; and both of us can acknowledge the 'Arnottisms' that feature in us! We know him to be a man of great faith, integrity and gentle good humour, whose leadership abilities are well proven and fit for the task. We join with the whole Church in wishing David and Rosemary well in this year not only during General Assembly week but also as they travel at home and abroad as ambassadors for Christ and for the Church of Scotland.

Joanne Hood
Donald McCorkindale
Chaplains

(3) DIGEST OF ASSEMBLY DECISIONS

Continuing the practice of recent years, this section of the *Year Book* contains the Editor's personal selection of the decisions of the most recent General Assembly which, in his view at the time of writing, seemed likely to be of most immediate or practical interest to those who will read it.

With the brief headline approach that the constraints of space dictate, full justice cannot be done to every important topic that was raised – and so, as before, there may be some surprise that this or that decision has been included or omitted. By the same token, important Deliverances of the Assembly are on occasion framed with reference to some particular Act of Assembly to the extent that the Act in question would require to be quoted at some length to enable the full significance of one year's changes to be appreciated. It has never been and surely should never be the practice in this section to venture either comment or commentary, to express either approval or apprehension in regard to what the Assembly decided.

Those who wish to explore more fully the Assembly's Reports and Deliverances can obtain from the office of the Principal Clerk the relevant volumes and papers. In addition, individual Departments and those who were Commissioners to the Assembly are often happy to make this material available on loan.

Assembly Arrangements Committee

The Assembly warmly welcomed the celebration of our Church life in the event 'Roll away the stone' and invited the Committee to consider other ways in which future General Assemblies might spend less time on formal business and more time focused on seeking the will of the Lord for our Church and our nation through prayer and listening to God's Word.

Central Services Committee

The Assembly:

- noted with thanks those congregations that had responded to the 2010 instruction to provide a Church and Society contact and encouraged those congregations that had not yet responded to do so;
- instructed the Church and Society Council to explore with the Priority Areas Committee and the General Trustees opportunities for installing in church buildings renewable energy devices such as solar panels to help congregations reduce their carbon footprints and energy bills: it was noted that this might generate an income from feed-in tariffs;
- urged every Presbytery, national Council and Committee to appoint a named person, working in a partnership with the National Youth Assembly elected representatives, to champion young people's involvement in their decision-making, whose role would be to work with the established structures and develop new and appropriate ways for young people to be involved;
- instructed the Church and Society Council:
    1. to work with the Legal Questions Committee, the Assembly Arrangements Committee, the Mission and Discipleship Council and the National Youth Assembly to bring to the General Assembly of 2014 a report fully exploring the possibility of allowing Youth Representatives the right to vote at the General Assembly;
    2. to consider, jointly with the Assembly Arrangements Committee and as an interim measure, the possibility of bringing to the Assembly of 2012 proposals for granting an indicative vote to Youth Representatives;
- noted the capacity of the Internet to shape as well as reflect society;
- commended to Kirk Sessions for their prayerful consideration and actions a particular booklet on the issue of Suicide Among Young Men;

- noted with concern the recent reported escalation in sectarianism in Scotland and expressed thanks to those in the Church working hard to engage with this complex issue.

Church of Scotland Guild
The Assembly:
- urged ministers and Kirk Sessions to encourage local guilds, particularly those which need support in identifying and developing leaders;
- supported the Guild's involvement in the Interfaith Group on domestic violence;
- recognised the Guild's contribution to the Decade to Overcome Violence;
- encouraged and warmly commended the Guild in its commitment to awareness-raising and advocacy on the issue of human trafficking.

Church of Scotland Pension Trustees
The Assembly encouraged the Pension Trustees to put more information on the Pension Funds on to the Church of Scotland website.

Committee on Chaplains to HM Forces
The Assembly reaffirmed the support of the Church for all who serve in Her Majesty's Forces as Chaplains, and acknowledged with particular gratitude the dedicated service of Chaplains on operations in Afghanistan and the immeasurable support shown by their own families.

Committee on Ecumenical Relations
The Assembly noted with regret the decision to close Scottish Churches House, Dunblane, on 15 July 2011, gave thanks for the work of the House since 1960 and held in prayer the staff affected by the closure.

Council of Assembly
The Assembly, welcoming proposals for a national stewardship programme,
- agreed that the programme should include a letter from the Moderator to every member of the Church;
- agreed that there should be national publicity for the programme;
- instructed Presbyteries to instruct their congregations to participate in this programme.

General Trustees
The Assembly instructed Presbyteries and congregations to fulfil their responsibilities with regard to the care of ecclesiastical properties, including quinquennial property inspections, and noted with appreciation the significant progress made in completing the re-valuation for insurance purposes of ecclesiastical buildings throughout Scotland.

Iona Community Board
The Assembly expressed appreciation for the contribution of the Iona Community, through its members and associate members, to the life of the churches and in local communities, and encouraged it in its work to counter sectarianism.

Legal Questions Committee
In respect of the Acts and Regulations of the General Assembly, the Assembly:
- authorised the Clerks of Assembly to correct inconsistencies of style and language and to update references to courts and agencies of the Church within these Acts and Regulations, all without changing the meaning or legal force of any of them;

- declared that the text of these Acts and Regulations as so updated and published on the Church of Scotland website would prevail over the current text as from 1 January 2012;
- instructed the Committee to bring to the General Assembly of 2012 more significant amendments or repeals required to make these Acts and Regulations clearer and more accessible;
- instructed the Committee, in collaboration with the Assembly Arrangements Committee, to undertake a review of Regulations V 1962 governing the duties of the Moderator of the General Assembly and Regulations 1 1999 anent the Nomination of the Moderator of the General Assembly and to bring to the General Assembly of 2012 an interim report, highlighting the main issues to be considered.

Ministries Council

The Assembly:

- reaffirmed the commitment of the Church of Scotland to a variety of ministries within which the parish ministry is the pivotal expression of the ministry of Word and Sacrament in the fulfilment of the Church's role as a national Church charged with the responsibility of a territorial ministry to every part of Scotland;
- approved the introduction of an Ordained Local Ministry as outlined in the Council's Report and instructed the Council to bring to the General Assembly of 2012 further details both of the training process and of appropriate legislation;
- undertook to appoint through its Selection Committee nine members to an independent Special Commission anent Ministerial Tenure and the Leadership of the local congregation. (The Assembly subsequently appointed the Very Rev. William C. Hewitt to serve as Convener of the Commission.) The remit of the Commission is as detailed in the Council's Report, and the Commission is instructed to report to the General Assembly of 2013;
- confirmed:
    1. the commitment of the whole Church of Scotland to the equality of women and men in the ministries and courts of the Church;
    2. the need for Presbyteries to ensure that congregations and Kirk Sessions within their bounds are acting within the provisions of Church Law with respect to gender equality;
- welcomed the establishing of Work Place Chaplaincy Scotland and the appointment of its National Director, and instructed the Ministries Council to ensure that appropriate financial support is forthcoming from the Church of Scotland;
- noted what has been done thus far in integrating the work of the Parish Development Committee into the wider work of the Ministries Council, and instructed the Council to complete this work and report on it by May 2012.

Mission and Discipleship Council

The Assembly instructed:

- Presbyteries and Kirk Sessions to provide parish and Presbytery boundary information as requested by the Statistics for Mission Group;
- the Council, in consultation with the Council of Assembly, to seek ways of strengthening doctrinal work within the structures of the General Assembly;
- the Council to collate the outputs from the day's conference session, to present them in a discussion document about mission in the Church of Scotland today and to distribute copies to Presbyteries and congregations for their consideration.

Panel on Review and Reform
When the Panel on Review and Reform was formed in 2004, one of its remits was to present a vision of what the Church might become and offer paths by which the Church might travel towards that vision. The General Assembly of 2008 instructed the Panel to focus that vision on the role of Presbyteries, the relevant Deliverance being as follows: 'Instruct the Panel on Review and Reform to bring to the Assembly proposals for an alternative presbytery structure, including size, devolved powers, staffing and appropriate budgets, along with the resources necessary to facilitate and sustain such changes'.

In response to that instruction, the Panel's Report to the 2011 Assembly included a number of proposed Deliverances which, if accepted and implemented, would certainly have led to very significant changes in these areas with, for example, a reduced number of better-resourced Presbyteries operating through and with Local Area Groupings, Presbytery Assemblies and Presbytery Councils. As the Panel itself said, 'Presbyteries would become the primary levers of change for their own re-formation'.

The Panel's proposals, however, did not in the main find favour with the Assembly. In their place, the Assembly affirmed the three key functions of Presbytery as being:

- proclamation of the Gospel of Jesus Christ through worship, witness, nurture and service;
- encouraging, strengthening and supporting the people of God;
- supervision of the work of the Church within its bounds, including appropriate oversight of congregations and ministries.

The Assembly did encourage Presbyteries to engage imaginatively with their neighbours to develop and strengthen the life and work of Presbytery, supported by the Councils of the Church.

Safeguarding Committee
The Assembly:

- Reminded all Kirk Sessions who have not already done so of the need to establish a Safeguarding Panel, as instructed by the General Assembly of 2010, and of their duty to support the work of Safeguarding Panels, recognising the confidential nature of their work;
- instructed all Kirk Sessions to observe all the requirements of the Protection of Vulnerable Groups (Scotland) Act 2007 as now implemented;
- noted the arrangements made for the production and distribution of a new Safeguarding Handbook to replace the previous Handbook and commended its use across the Church.

Social Care Council
While appreciating the tight financial constraints, the Assembly urged the Convention of Scottish Local Authorities, central government and Health Boards to maintain their investment in the services provided by CrossReach.

Noting the comments of the Moderator, the Cabinet Secretary for Justice and the Chief Inspector of Prisons, the Assembly:

- urged the Scottish Prison Service to resource the Perth Prison Visitors Centre;
- instructed the Principal Clerk to communicate to the Cabinet Secretary for Justice the feelings of the General Assembly that the Scottish Government should adopt the principle that such productive facilities should be established in all Scottish prisons.

Special Commission on Same-Sex Relationships and the Ministry
In the light of the experience of the Special Commission and, in particular, the need for a sustained theological addressing of the matters before the Church, the Assembly:

- agreed to establish a Theological Commission of seven persons representative of the breadth of the Church's theological understanding, with the task of addressing the theological issues raised in the course of the Special Commission's work;

- instructed the Selection Committee to bring names to a future session of the Assembly. (The Assembly subsequently appointed Rev. Dr John L. McPake, minister of East Kilbride: Mossneuk and a former Convener of the General Assembly's Panel on Doctrine, to serve as Convener of the Commission.)

The Assembly resolved to consider further the lifting of the moratorium on the acceptance for training and ordination of persons in a same-sex relationship, and to that end instructed the Theological Commission to prepare a report for the General Assembly of 2013 containing:

1. a theological discussion of issues around same-sex relationships, civil partnerships and marriage;
2. an examination of whether, if the Church were to allow its ministers and deacons freedom of conscience in deciding whether to bless same-sex relationships involving life-long commitments, the recognition of such life-long relationships should take the form of a blessing of a civil partnership or should involve a liturgy to recognise and celebrate commitments which the parties enter into in a Church service in addition to the civil partnership, and if so to recommend liturgy therefor;
3. an examination of whether persons, who have entered into a civil partnership and have made life-long commitments in a Church ceremony, should be eligible for admission for training, ordination and induction as ministers of Word and Sacrament or deacons in the context that no member of Presbytery will be required to take part in such ordination or induction against his or her conscience.

The Assembly:

- agreed to allow the induction into pastoral charges of ministers and deacons ordained before 31 May 2009 who are in a same-sex relationship;
- subject to the above provision, instructed all Courts, Councils and Committees of the Church not to make decisions in relation to contentious matters of same-sex relationships, or to accept for training, allow to transfer from another denomination, ordain or induct any person in a same-sex relationship until the General Assembly of 2013 has heard the report of the Theological Commission.

World Mission Council

The Assembly approved a number of Deliverances urging members of the Church of Scotland to pray for and to support Presbyterian and other Christian Churches and communities in the Middle East generally, with Egypt, Lebanon, Syria, Israel and Palestine receiving particular mention.

The Assembly gave thanks for:

- Jewish, Christian and Muslim co-operation in upholding the rights of the poor and oppressed in the Middle East and beyond;
- the renewed co-operation that there is between the Church of Scotland (through its congregations and its World Mission Council) and Christian Aid: members of the Church of Scotland were urged to support Christian Aid in expressing solidarity with the world Church;
- the HIV Programme and the work of our Church's partners at home and overseas, and recommitted the Church of Scotland to playing its part in response to the pandemic.

SECTION 5

Presbytery Lists

SECTION 5 – PRESBYTERY LISTS

In each Presbytery list, the congregations are listed in alphabetical order. In a linked charge, the names appear under the first named congregation. Under the name of the congregation will be found the name of the minister and, where applicable, that of an associate minister, auxiliary minister and member of the Diaconate. The years indicated after a minister's name in the congregational section of each Presbytery list are the year of ordination (column 1) and the year of current appointment (column 2). Where only one date is given, it is both the year of ordination and the year of appointment.

In the second part of each Presbytery list, those named are listed alphabetically. The first date is the year of ordination, and the following date is the year of appointment or retirement. If the person concerned is retired, then the appointment last held will be shown in brackets.

KEY TO ABBREVIATIONS

(E) Indicates a Church Extension charge. New Charge Developments are separately indicated.
(GD) Indicates a charge where it is desirable that the minister should have a knowledge of Gaelic.
(GE) Indicates a charge where public worship must be regularly conducted in Gaelic.
(H) Indicates that a Hearing Aid Loop system has been installed. In Linked charges, the (H) is placed beside the appropriate building as far as possible.
(L) Indicates that a Chair Lift has been installed.
(T) Indicates that the minister has been appointed on the basis of Terminable Tenure.

PRESBYTERY NUMBERS

1 Edinburgh
2 West Lothian
3 Lothian
4 Melrose and Peebles
5 Duns
6 Jedburgh
7 Annandale and Eskdale
8 Dumfries and Kirkcudbright
9 Wigtown and Stranraer
10 Ayr
11 Irvine and Kilmarnock
12 Ardrossan
13 Lanark
14 Greenock and Paisley
15
16 Glasgow
17 Hamilton
18 Dumbarton
19 Argyll
20
21
22 Falkirk
23 Stirling
24 Dunfermline
25 Kirkcaldy
26 St Andrews
27 Dunkeld and Meigle
28 Perth
29 Dundee
30 Angus
31 Aberdeen
32 Kincardine and Deeside
33 Gordon
34 Buchan
35 Moray
36 Abernethy
37 Inverness
38 Lochaber
39 Ross
40 Sutherland
41 Caithness
42 Lochcarron – Skye
43 Uist
44 Lewis
45 Orkney
46 Shetland
47 England
48 Europe
49 Jerusalem

(1) EDINBURGH

The Presbytery meets:

- **at Palmerston Place Church, Edinburgh, on 11 October and 6 December 2011, and on 7 February, 20 March, 8 May and 26 June 2012;**
- **in the church of the Moderator on 6 September 2011.**

Clerk:	REV. GEORGE J. WHYTE BSc BD DMin PhD	10/1 Palmerston Place, Edinburgh EH12 5AA [E-mail: edinburgh@cofscotland.org.uk]	0131-225 9137

1	**Edinburgh: Albany Deaf Church of Edinburgh (H) (0131-444 2054)**				
	Alistair F. Kelly BL (Locum)	1961		19 Avon Place, Edinburgh EH4 6RE [E-mail: alistair.kelly@tiscali.co.uk]	0131-317 9877
2	**Edinburgh: Balerno (H)**				
	Louise J. Duncan (Mrs) BD	2005	2010	3 Johnsburn Road, Balerno EH14 7DN [E-mail: bpc-minister@btconnect.com]	0131-449 3830
3	**Edinburgh: Barclay Viewforth (0131-229 6810) (E-mail: admin@barclaychurch.org.uk)**				
	Samuel A.R. Torrens BD	1995	2005	113 Meadowspot, Edinburgh EH10 5UY [E-mail: barclayminister@btinternet.com]	0131-478 2376
	Howard Espie (Mission Facilitator and Enabler)	2011		Barclay Viewforth Parish Church, 1 Barclay Place, Edinburgh EH10 4HW	0131-229 6810
4	**Edinburgh: Blackhall St Columba's (0131-332 4431) (E-mail: secretary@blackhallstcolumba.org.uk)**				
	Alexander B. Douglas BD	1979	1991	5 Blinkbonny Crescent, Edinburgh EH4 3NB [E-mail: alexandjill@douglas.net]	0131-343 3708
5	**Edinburgh: Bristo Memorial Craigmillar**				
	James Patterson BSc BD	2003	2006	72 Blackchapel Close, Edinburgh EH15 3SL [E-mail: patterson@jimandmegan.force9.co.uk]	0131-657 3266
	Agnes M. Rennie (Miss) DCS			3/1 Craigmillar Court, Edinburgh EH16 4AD	0131-661 8475
6	**Edinburgh: Broughton St Mary's (H) (0131-556 4786)**				
	Joanne C. Hood (Miss) MA BD	2003		103 East Claremont Street, Edinburgh EH7 4JA [E-mail: hood137@btinternet.com]	0131-556 7313
7	**Edinburgh: Canongate (H)**				
	Neil N. Gardner MA BD	1991	2006	The Manse of Canongate, Edinburgh EH8 8BR [E-mail: nng22@btinternet.com]	0131-556 3515

8 Edinburgh: Carrick Knowe (H) (0131-334 1505) (E-mail: ckchurch@talktalk.net)

Fiona M. Mathieson (Mrs) BEd BD PGCommEd MTh	1988	2001	21 Traquair Park West, Edinburgh EH12 7AN [E-mail: fiona.mathieson@ukgateway.net]	0131-334 9774

9 Edinburgh: Colinton (H) (0131-441 2232) (E-mail: church.office@colinton-parish.com)

Rolf H. Billes BD	1996	2009	The Manse, Colinton, Edinburgh EH13 0JR [E-mail: rolf.billes@colinton-parish.com]	0131-466 8384
Gayle J.A. Taylor (Mrs) MA BD (Assoc)	1999	2009	Colinton Parish Church, Dell Road, Edinburgh EH13 0JR [E-mail: gayle.taylor@colinton-parish.com]	0131-441 2232

10 Edinburgh: Colinton Mains (H)

Ian A. McQuarrie BD	1993		17 Swanston Green, Edinburgh EH10 7EW [E-mail: ian.mcquarrie1@btinternet.com]	0131-445 3451

11 Edinburgh: Corstorphine Craigsbank (H) (0131-334 6365)

Stewart M. McPherson BD CertMin	1991	2003	17 Craigs Bank, Edinburgh EH12 8HD [E-mail: smcpherson@blueyonder.co.uk]	0131-467 6826 07814 901429 (Mbl)
Stephen Manners MA BD (Assoc)	1989	2009	124 Fernieside Crescent, Edinburgh EH17 7DH [E-mail: sk.manners@blueyonder.co.uk]	0131-620 0589

12 Edinburgh: Corstorphine Old (H) (0131-334 7864) (E-mail: corold@aol.com)

Moira McDonald MA BD	1997	2005	23 Manse Road, Edinburgh EH12 7SW [E-mail: moira.mc@tesco.net]	0131-476 5893

13 Edinburgh: Corstorphine St Anne's (0131-316 4740) (E-mail: office@stannes.corstorphine.org.uk)

MaryAnn R. Rennie (Mrs) BD MTh	1998	2002	23 Belgrave Road, Edinburgh EH12 6NG [E-mail: maryann.rennie@blueyonder.co.uk]	0131-334 3188

14 Edinburgh: Corstorphine St Ninian's (H) (0131-539 6204) (E-mail: office@st-ninians.co.uk)

Alexander T. Stewart MA BD FSAScot	1975	1995	17 Templeland Road, Edinburgh EH12 8RZ [E-mail: alextstewart@blueyonder.co.uk]	0131-334 2978

15 Edinburgh: Craigentinny St Christopher's (0131-258 2759)

Caroline R. Lockerbie BA MDiv DMin	2007		61 Milton Crescent, Edinburgh EH15 3PQ [E-mail: carolinelockerbie@blueyonder.co.uk]	0131-258 2759

16 Edinburgh: Craiglockhart (H) (E-mail: office@craiglockhartchurch.org.uk)

Andrew Ritchie BD DipMin DMin	1984	1991	202 Colinton Road, Edinburgh EH14 1BP [E-mail: andrewritchie@talk21.com]	0131-443 2020

17 Edinburgh: Craigmillar Park (H) (0131-667 5862) (E-mail: cpkirk@btinternet.com)

John C.C. Urquhart MA MA BD — 2010 — 14 Hallhead Road, Edinburgh EH16 5QJ — 0131-667 1623
[E-mail: jccurquhart@gmail.com]

18 Edinburgh: Cramond (H) (E-mail: cramond.kirk@blueyonder.co.uk)

G. Russell Barr BA BD MTh DMin — 1979 1993 — Manse of Cramond, Edinburgh EH4 6NS — 0131-336 2036
[E-mail: rev.r.barr@blueyonder.co.uk]

19 Edinburgh: Currie (H) (0131-451 5141) (E-mail: currie_kirk@btconnect.com)

Lezley J. Stewart BD ThM MTh — 2000 2008 — 43 Lanark Road West, Currie EH14 5JX — 0131-449 4719
[E-mail: lezleystewart@btinternet.com]

Margaret Gordon (Mrs) DCS — 92 Lanark Road West, Currie EH14 5LA — 0131-449 2554

20 Edinburgh: Dalmeny linked with Edinburgh: Queensferry

David C. Cameron BD CertMin — 1993 2009 — 1 Station Road, South Queensferry EH30 9HY — 0131-331 1100
[E-mail: qpcminister@btconnect.com]

21 Edinburgh: Davidson's Mains (H) (0131-312 6282) (E-mail: life@dmainschurch.plus.com)

Jeremy R.H. Middleton LLB BD — 1981 1988 — 1 Hillpark Terrace, Edinburgh EH4 7SX — 0131-336 3078
[E-mail: life@dmainschurch.plus.com]

22 Edinburgh: Dean (H)

Mark M. Foster BSc BD — 1998 — 1 Ravelston Terrace, Edinburgh EH4 3EF — 0131-332 5736
[E-mail: markmfoster@mac.com]

23 Edinburgh: Drylaw (0131-343 6643)

Patricia Watson (Mrs) BD — 2005 — 15 House o' Hill Gardens, Edinburgh EH4 2AR — 0131-343 1441
[E-mail: p.g.watson@blueyonder.co.uk] — 07969 942627 (Mbl)

24 Edinburgh: Duddingston (H) (E-mail: dodinskirk@aol.com)

James A.P. Jack BSc BArch BD DMin RIBA ARIAS — 1989 2001 — Manse of Duddingston, Old Church Lane, Edinburgh EH15 3PX — 0131-661 4240
[E-mail: jamesAPJACK@aol.com]

25 Edinburgh: Fairmilehead (H) (0131-445 2374) (E-mail: fairmilehead.p.c@btconnect.com)

John R. Munro BD — 1976 1992 — 6 Braid Crescent, Edinburgh EH10 6AU — 0131-446 9363
[E-mail: revjohnmunro@hotmail.com]

Hayley O'Connor MDiv (Assist) — 2009 — c/o 6 Braid Crescent, Edinburgh EH10 6AU — 0131-623 6661
[E-mail: oconnorhe@gmail.com]

26 Edinburgh: Gorgie Dalry (H) (0131-337 7936)
Peter I. Barber MA BD 1984 1995 90 Myreside Road, Edinburgh EH10 5BZ 0131-337 2284
[E-mail: pibarber@toucansurf.com]
(New charge formed by the union of Edinburgh: Gorgie and Edinburgh: St Colm's)

27 Edinburgh: Granton (H) (0131-552 3033)
Norman A. Smith MA BD 1997 2005 8 Wardie Crescent, Edinburgh EH5 1AG 0131-551 2159
[E-mail: norm@familysmith.biz]
Marilynn Steele (Mrs) DCS 2 Northfield Gardens, Prestonpans EH32 9LQ 01875 811497
[E-mail: marilynnsteele@aol.com]

28 Edinburgh: Greenbank (H) (0131-447 9969) (E-mail: greenbankchurch@btconnect.com)
Alison J. Swindells (Mrs) LLB BD 1998 2007 112 Greenbank Crescent, Edinburgh EH10 5SZ 0131-447 4032
[E-mail: alisonswindells@blueyonder.co.uk]

29 Edinburgh: Greenside (H) (0131-556 5588)
Andrew F. Anderson MA BD 1981 80 Pilrig Street, Edinburgh EH6 5AS 0131-554 3277 (Tel/Fax)
[E-mail: andrew@pilrig.fsnet.co.uk]

30 Edinburgh: Greyfriars Tolbooth and Highland Kirk (GE) (H) (0131-225 1900) (E-mail: enquiries@greyfriarskirk.com)
Richard E. Frazer BA BD DMin 1986 2003 12 Tantallon Place, Edinburgh EH9 1NZ 0131-667 6610
[E-mail: tantallon@ukonline.co.uk]

31 Edinburgh: High (St Giles') (0131-225 4363) (E-mail: info@stgilescathedral.org.uk)
Gilleasbuig Macmillan CVO MA BD Drhc DD 1969 1973 St Giles' Cathedral, Edinburgh EH1 1RE 0131-225 4363
[E-mail: minister@stgilescathedral.org.uk]

32 Edinburgh: Holyrood Abbey (H) (0131-661 6002)
Philip R. Hair BD 1980 1998 100 Willowbrae Avenue, Edinburgh EH8 7HU 0131-652 0640
[E-mail: phil@holyroodabbey.f2s.com]

33 Edinburgh: Holy Trinity (H) (0131-442 3304)
Kenneth S. Borthwick MA BD 1983 2005 16 Thorburn Road, Edinburgh EH13 0BQ 0131-441 1403
[E-mail: kennysamuel@aol.com]
Ian MacDonald (Assoc) 2005 12 Sighthill Crescent, Edinburgh EH11 4QE 0131-453 6279
Oliver M.H. Clegg BD (Youth Minister) 2003 256/5 Lanark Road, Edinburgh EH14 2LR 0131-443 0825

34 Edinburgh: Inverleith (H)
Vacant 43 Inverleith Gardens, Edinburgh EH3 5PR 0131-552 3874

35 Edinburgh: Juniper Green (H)

James S. Dewar MA BD	1983	2000	476 Lanark Road, Juniper Green, Edinburgh EH14 5BQ [E-mail: jim.dewar@blueyonder.co.uk]	0131-453 3494

36 Edinburgh: Kaimes Lockhart Memorial linked with Edinburgh: Liberton

John N. Young MA BD PhD	1996		7 Kirk Park, Edinburgh EH16 6HZ [E-mail: LLLjyoung@btinternet.com]	0131-664 3067
David Rankin (Assoc)	2009		4/16 Elliot Street, Edinburgh EH7 5LU [E-mail: dave@indigoice.f2s.com]	0131-553 5337

37 Edinburgh: Kirkliston

Margaret R. Lane (Mrs) BA BD MTh	2009		43 Main Street, Kirkliston EH29 9AF [E-mail: margaretlane@btinternet.com]	0131-333 3298 07795 481441 (Mbl)

38 Edinburgh: Kirk o' Field (T) (H)

Ian D. Maxwell MA BD PhD	1977	1996	31 Hatton Place, Edinburgh EH9 1UA [E-mail: i.d.maxwell@quista.net]	0131-667 7954

39 Edinburgh: Leith North (H) (0131-553 7378) (E-mail: nlpc-office@btinternet.com)

Alexander T. McAspurren BD MTh	2002	2011	6 Craighall Gardens, Edinburgh EH6 4RJ [E-mail: alexander.mcaspurren@btinternet.com]	0131-551 5252

40 Edinburgh: Leith St Andrew's (H)

Elizabeth J.B. Youngson BD	1996	2006	30 Lochend Road, Edinburgh EH6 8BS [E-mail: elizabeth.youngson@btinternet.com]	0131-554 7695

41 Edinburgh: Leith St Serf's (T) (H)

Vacant			20 Wilton Road, Edinburgh EH16 5NX	0131-478 1624

42 Edinburgh: Leith South (H) (0131-554 2578) (E-mail: slpc@dial.pipex.com)

Vacant			37 Claremont Road, Edinburgh EH6 7NN	0131-554 3062

43 Edinburgh: Leith Wardie (H) (0131-551 3847) (E-mail: churchoffice@wardie.org.uk)

Brian C. Hilsley LLB BD	1990		35 Lomond Road, Edinburgh EH5 3JN [E-mail: minister@wardie.org.uk]	0131-552 3328

44 Edinburgh: Liberton (H) See Edinburgh: Kaimes Lockhart Memorial

45 Edinburgh: Liberton Northfield (H) (0131-551 3847)

John M. McPake LTh	2000		9 Claverhouse Drive, Edinburgh EH16 6BR [E-mail: john_mcpake9@yahoo.co.uk]	0131-658 1754

46 Edinburgh: London Road (H) (0131-661 1149)
Sigrid Marten | 1997 | 2006 | 26 Inchview Terrace, Edinburgh EH7 6TQ [E-mail: minister.lrpc@phonecoop.coop] | 0131-669 5311

47 Edinburgh: Marchmont St Giles' (H) (0131-447 4359)
Karen K. Watson BD MTh | 1997 | 2002 | 19 Hope Terrace, Edinburgh EH9 2AP [E-mail: karen@marchmontstgiles.org.uk] | 0131-447 2834

48 Edinburgh: Mayfield Salisbury (0131-667 1522)
Scott S. McKenna BA BD MTh | 1994 | 2000 | 26 Seton Place, Edinburgh EH9 2JT [E-mail: ScottSMcKenna@aol.com] | 0131-667 1286
Sheila Wallace (Mrs) DCS BA BD | 2009 | | 18 West Mayfield, Edinburgh EH9 1TQ [E-mail: sheilad.wallace@virgin.net] | 0131-667 1522

49 Edinburgh: Morningside (H) (0131-447 6745) (E-mail: office@morningsideparishchurch.org.uk)
Derek Browning MA BD DMin PhD | 1987 | 2001 | 20 Braidburn Crescent, Edinburgh EH10 6EN [E-mail: derek.browning@btinternet.com] | 0131-447 1617; 07050 133876 (Mbl)

50 Edinburgh: Morningside United (H) (0131-447 3152)
John R. Smith MA BD | 1973 | 1998 | 1 Midmar Avenue, Edinburgh EH10 6BS [E-mail: office@jrsmith.eu] | 0131-447 8724

51 Edinburgh: Muirhouse St Andrew's (E) (Website: www.stampc.co.uk)
Linda J. Dunbar BSc BA BD PhD FRHS (Full-time Locum) | 2000 | 2011 | 35 Silverknowes Road, Edinburgh EH4 5LL [E-mail: lindatheleither@googlemail.com] | 0131-447 5335; 07801 969995 (Mbl)

52 Edinburgh: Murrayfield (H) (0131-337 1091) (E-mail: mpchurch@btconnect.com)
William D. Brown BD CQSW | 1987 | 2001 | 45 Murrayfield Gardens, Edinburgh EH12 6DH [E-mail: wdb@talktalk.net] | 0131-337 5431

53 Edinburgh: Newhaven (H)
Peter Bluett | 2007 | | 158 Granton Road, Edinburgh EH5 3RF [E-mail: peterbluett@sky.com] | 0131-476 5212

54 Edinburgh: New Restalrig (H) (0131-661 5676)
David L. Court BSc BD | 1989 | 2000 | 19 Abercorn Road, Edinburgh EH8 7DP [E-mail: david@dlc.org.uk] | 0131-661 4045

55 Edinburgh: Old Kirk (H) (0131-332 4354) (E-mail: minister.oldkirk@btinternet.com)
Tony McLean-Foreman 1987 2007 24 Pennywell Road, Edinburgh EH4 4HD 0131-332 4354
[E-mail: tony@foreman.org.uk]

56 Edinburgh: Palmerston Place (H) (0131-220 1690) (E-mail: admin@palmerstonplacechurch.com)
Colin A.M. Sinclair BA BD 1981 1996 30B Cluny Gardens, Edinburgh EH10 6BJ 0131-447 9598
[E-mail: colins.ppc@virgin.net] 0131-225 3312 (Fax)

57 Edinburgh: Pilrig St Paul's (0131-553 1876)
John M. Tait BSc BD 1985 1999 78 Pilrig Street, Edinburgh EH6 5AS 0131-554 1842
[E-mail: j.m.tait@blueyonder.co.uk]

58 Edinburgh: Polwarth (H) (0131-346 2711) (E-mail: polwarthchurch@tiscali.co.uk)
Jack Holt BSc BD MTh 1985 2011 88 Craiglockhart Road, Edinburgh EH14 1EP 0131-441 6105
[E-mail: jack9holt@gmail.com]

59 Edinburgh: Portobello Old (H)
Andrew R.M. Patterson MA BD 1985 2006 6 Hamilton Terrace, Edinburgh EH15 1NB 0131-657 5545
[E-mail: apatt@tiscali.co.uk]

60 Edinburgh: Portobello St James' (H)
Peter Webster BD 1977 2002 34 Brighton Place, Edinburgh EH15 1LT 0131-669 1767
[E-mail: peterwebster101@hotmail.com]

61 Edinburgh: Portobello St Philip's Joppa (H) (0131-669 3641)
Stewart G. Weaver BA BD PhD 2003 6 St Mary's Place, Edinburgh EH15 2QF 0131-669 2410
[E-mail: stewartweaver@btinternet.com]

62 Edinburgh: Priestfield (H) (0131-667 5644)
Jared W. Hay BA MTh DipMin DMin 1987 2009 13 Lady Road, Edinburgh EH16 5PA 0131-468 1254
[E-mail: jared.hay@blueyonder.co.uk]

63 Edinburgh: Queensferry (H) See Edinburgh: Dalmeny

64 Edinburgh: Ratho
Ian J. Wells BD 1999 2 Freelands Road, Ratho, Newbridge EH28 8NP 0131-333 1346
[E-mail: ianjwells@btinternet.com]

65 Edinburgh: Reid Memorial (H) (0131-662 1203) (E-mail: reid.memorial@btinternet.com)
Brian M. Embleton BD 1976 1985 20 Wilton Road, Edinburgh EH16 5NX 0131-667 3981
[E-mail: brianembleton@btinternet.com]

66 Edinburgh: Richmond Craigmillar (H) (0131-661 6561)
Elizabeth M. Henderson (Mrs) MA BD MTh | 1985 | 1997 | Manse of Duddingston, Old Church Lane, Edinburgh EH15 3PX [E-mail: lizhende@aol.com] | 0131-661 4240

67 Edinburgh: St Andrew's and St George's West (H) (0131-225 3847) (E-mail: info@standrewsandstgeorges.org.uk)
Ian Y. Gilmour BD | 1985 | 2011 | 25 Comely Bank, Edinburgh EH4 1AJ [E-mail: IanYG@blueyonder.co.uk] | 0131-332 5848

68 Edinburgh: St Andrew's Clermiston
Alistair H. Keil BD DipMin | 1989 | | 87 Drum Brae South, Edinburgh EH12 8TD [E-mail: ahkeil@blueyonder.co.uk] | 0131-339 4149

69 Edinburgh: St Catherine's Argyle (H) (0131-667 7220)
Robin S. Sydserff PhD | | | 5 Palmerston Road, Edinburgh EH9 1TL [E-mail: robin@sydserff.co.uk] | 0131-667 9344

70 Edinburgh: St Cuthbert's (H) (0131-229 1142) (E-mail: office@stcuthberts.net)
David W. Denniston BD DipMin | 1981 | 2008 | 34A Murrayfield Road, Edinburgh EH12 6ER [E-mail: denniston.david@googlemail.com] | 0131-337 6637; 07903 926727 (Mbl)

71 Edinburgh: St David's Broomhouse (H) (0131-443 9851)
Robert A. Mackenzie LLB BD | 1993 | 2005 | 33 Traquair Park West, Edinburgh EH12 7AN [E-mail: rob.anne@blueyonder.co.uk] | 0131-334 1730
Liz Crocker (Mrs) DipComEd DCS | | | 77C Craigcrook Road, Edinburgh EH4 3PH | 0131-332 0227

72 Edinburgh: St John's Oxgangs
Vacant | | | 2 Caiystane Terrace, Edinburgh EH10 6SR | 0131-445 1688

73 Edinburgh: St Margaret's (H) (0131-554 7400) (E-mail: stm.parish@virgin.net)
Carol H.M. Ford DSD RSAMD BD | 2003 | | 43 Moira Terrace, Edinburgh EH7 6TD [E-mail: revcford@btinternet.com] | 0131-669 7329
Pauline Rycroft-Sadi (Mrs) DCS | 2006 | | 6 Ashville Terrace, Edinburgh EH6 8DD | 0131-554 6564

74 Edinburgh: St Martin's
Russel Moffat BD MTh PhD | 1986 | 2008 | 5 Duddingston Crescent, Edinburgh EH15 3AS [E-mail: rbmoffat@tiscali.co.uk] | 0131-657 9894

75 Edinburgh: St Michael's (H) (E-mail: office@stmichaels-kirk.co.uk)
James D. Aitken BD | 2002 | 2005 | 9 Merchiston Gardens, Edinburgh EH10 5DD [E-mail: james.aitken2@btinternet.com] | 0131-346 1970

76 Edinburgh: St Nicholas' Sighthill				
Alan R. Cobain BD	2000	2008	122 Sighthill Loan, Edinburgh EH11 4NT [E-mail: erinbro@hotmail.co.uk]	0131-442 2510
77 Edinburgh: St Stephen's Comely Bank (0131-315 4616)				
Jonathan de Groot BD MTh CPS	2007		8 Blinkbonny Crescent, Edinburgh EH4 3NB [E-mail: minister@st-stephenschurch.org.uk]	0131-332 3364
78 Edinburgh: Slateford Longstone				
Michael W. Frew BSc BD	1978	2005	50 Kingsknowe Road South, Edinburgh EH14 2JW [E-mail: mwfrew@blueyonder.co.uk]	0131-466 5308
79 Edinburgh: Stenhouse St Aidan's				
Keith Edwin Graham MA PGDip BD	2008		65 Balgreen Road, Edinburgh EH12 5UA [E-mail: keithedwingraham@gmail.com]	0131-337 7711
80 Edinburgh: Stockbridge (H) (0131-552 8738) (E-mail: stockbridgechurch@btconnect.com)				
Anne T. Logan (Mrs) MA BD MTh DMin	1981	1993	19 Eildon Street, Edinburgh EH3 5JU [E-mail: annetlogan@blueyonder.co.uk]	0131-557 6052
81 Edinburgh: The Tron Kirk (Gilmerton and Moredun)				
Cameron Mackenzie BD	1997	2010	467 Gilmerton Road, Edinburgh EH17 7JG [E-mail: mackenz550@aol.com]	0131-664 7538

(New charge formed by the union of Edinburgh: Tron Moredun and Edinburgh: Gilmerton New Charge Development)

Aitken, Alexander R. MA	1965	1997	(Newhaven)	36 King's Meadow, Edinburgh EH16 5JW	0131-667 1404
Aitken, Ewan R. BA BD	1992	2002	Church and Society Council	159 Restalrig Avenue, Edinburgh EH7 6PJ	0131-467 1660
Alexander, Ian W. BA BD STM	1990	2010	General Secretary: World Mission Council	World Mission Council, 121 George Street, Edinburgh EH2 4YN [E-mail: iwalexander@gmail.com]	0131-225 5722
Anderson, Robert S. BD	1988	1997	Scottish Churches World Exchange	St Colm's International House, 23 Inverleith Terrace, Edinburgh EH3 5NS	0131-315 4444
Armitage, William L. BSc BD	1976	2006	(Edinburgh: London Road)	75 Toll House Grove, Tranent EH33 2QR [E-mail: bill@billarm.plus.com]	01875 612047
Baird, Kenneth S. MSc PhD BD MIMarEST	1998	2009	(Edinburgh: Leith North)	3 Maule Terrace, Gullane EH31 2DB	01620 843447
Barrington, Charles W.H. MA BD	1997	2007	(Associate: Edinburgh: Balerno)	502 Lanark Road, Edinburgh EH14 5DH	0131-453 4826
Beckett, David M. BA BD	1964	2002	(Greyfriars, Tolbooth and Highland Kirk)	1F1, 31 Sciennes Road, Edinburgh EH9 1NT [E-mail: davidbeckett3@aol.com]	0131-667 2672
Blakey, Ronald S. MA BD MTh	1962	2000	Editor: *The Year Book*	5 Moss Side Road, Biggar ML12 6GF	01899 229226
Booth, Jennifer (Mrs) BD	1996	2004	(Associate: Leith South)	39 Lilyhill Terrace, Edinburgh EH8 7DR	0131-661 3813
Boyd, Kenneth M. MA BD PhD FRCPE	1970	1996	University of Edinburgh: Medical Ethics	1 Doune Terrace, Edinburgh EH3 6DY	0131-225 6485

Name	Ord.	Ret.	Charge	Address	Tel.
Brady, Ian D. BSc ARCST BD	1967	2001	(Edinburgh: Corstorphine Old)	28 Frankfield Crescent, Dalgety Bay, Dunfermline KY11 9LW [E-mail: pidb@dbay28.fsnet.co.uk]	01383 825104
Brown, William D. MA	1963	1989	(Wishaw: Thornlie)	9/3 Craigend Park, Edinburgh EH16 5XY [E-mail: wdbrown@surefish.co.uk]	0131-672 2936
Cameron, G. Gordon MA BD STM	1957	1997	(Juniper Green)	4 Ladywell Grove, Clackmannan FK10 4JQ	01259 723769
Cameron, John W.M. MA BD	1957	1996	(Liberton)	10 Plewlands Gardens, Edinburgh EH10 5JP	0131-447 1277
Chalmers, Murray MA	1965	2006	(Hospital Chaplain)	8 Easter Warriston, Edinburgh EH7 4QX	0131-552 4211
Clinkenbeard, William W. BSc BD STM	1966	2000	(Edinburgh: Carrick Knowe)	4 Aline Court, Dalgety Bay, Dunfermline KY11 9TU [E-mail: bjclinks@compuserve.com]	01383 824011
Cook, John MA BD	1967	2005	(Edinburgh: Leith St Andrew's)	26 Silverknowes Court, Edinburgh EH4 5NR	0131-312 8447
Cook, John Weir MA BD	1962	2002	(Edinburgh: Portobello St Philip's Joppa)	74 Pinkie Road, Musselburgh EH21 7QT [E-mail: johnweircook@hotmail.com]	0131-653 0992
Crichton, Thomas JP ChStJ MA	1965	2004	(Hospital Chaplain)	18 Carlton Terrace, Edinburgh EH7 5DD	0131-557 0009
Curran, Elizabeth M. (Miss) BD	1995	2008	(Aberlour)	27 Captain's Road, Edinburgh EH17 8HR [E-mail: ecurran8@aol.com]	0131-664 1358
Cuthell, Tom C. MA BD MTh	1965	2007	(Edinburgh: St Cuthbert's)	Flat 10, 2 Kingsburgh Crescent, Waterfront, Edinburgh EH5 1JS	0131-476 3864
Davidson, D. Hugh MA	1965	2009	(Edinburgh: Inverleith)	Flat 1/2, 22 Summerside Place, Edinburgh EH6 4NZ [E-mail: dhd39@btinternet.com]	0131-554 8420
Davidson, Ian M.P. MBE MA BD	1957	1994	(Stirling: Allan Park South with Church of the Holy Rude)	13/8 Craigend Park, Edinburgh EH16 5XX	0131-664 0074
Dawson, Michael S. BTech BD	1979	2005	(Associate: Edinburgh: Holy Trinity)	9 The Broich, Alva FK12 5NR [E-mail: mixpen.dawson@btinternet.com]	01259 769309
Denniston, Jane M. MA BD	2002		Ministries Council	34A Murrayfield Road, Edinburgh EH12 6ER	0131-337 6637
Dilbey, Mary D. (Miss) BD	1997	2002	(West Kirk of Calder)	41 Bonaly Rise, Edinburgh EH13 0QU	0131-441 9092
Donald, Alistair P. MA PhD BD	1999	2009	Chaplain: Heriot-Watt University	The Chaplaincy, Heriot-Watt University, Edinburgh EH14 4AS [E-mail: a.p.donald@hw.ac.uk]	0131-451 4508
Dougall, Elspeth G. (Mrs) MA BD	1989	2001	(Edinburgh: Marchmont St Giles')	60B Craigmillar Park, Edinburgh EH16 5PU	0131-668 1342
Douglas, Colin R. MA BD STM	1969	2007	(Livingston Ecumenical Parish)	34 West Pilton Gardens, Edinburgh EH4 4EQ [E-mail: colinrdouglas@btinternet.com]	0131-551 3808
Doyle, Ian B. MA BD PhD	1946	1991	(Department of National Mission)	21 Lygon Road, Edinburgh EH16 5QD	0131-667 2697
Drummond, Rhoda (Miss) DCS			(Deaconess)	Flat K, 23 Grange Loan, Edinburgh EH9 2ER	0131-668 3631
Dunn, W. Iain C. DA LTh	1983	1998	(Pilrig and Dalmeny Street)	10 Fox Covert Avenue, Edinburgh EH12 6UQ	0131-334 1665
Elliott, Gavin J. MA BD	1976	2004	Ministries Council	c/o 121 George Street, Edinburgh EH2 4YN	0131-225 5722
Embleton, Sara R. (Mrs) BA BD MTh	1987	2010	(Edinburgh: Leith St Serf's)	20 Wilton Road, Edinburgh EH16 5NX [E-mail: sara.embleton@blueyonder.co.uk]	0131-478 1624
Farquharson, Gordon MA BD DipEd	1998	2007	(Stonehaven: Dunnottar)	26 Learmonth Court, Edinburgh EH4 1PB [E-mail: gfarqu@talktalk.net]	0131-343 1047
Faulds, Norman L. MA BD FSAScot	1968	2000	(Aberlady with Gullane)	10 West Fenton Court, West Fenton, North Berwick EH39 5AE	01620 842331
Fergusson, David A.S. MA BD DPhil FRSE	1984	2000	University of Edinburgh	23 Riselaw Crescent, Edinburgh EH10 6HN	0131-447 4022
Foggitt, Eric W. MA BSc BD	1991	2009	(Dunbar)	49/3 Falcon Avenue, Edinburgh EH10 4AN [E-mail: ericleric3@btinternet.com]	0131-447 7712

Name	Ord.	Ret.	Charge	Address		Telephone
Forrester, Duncan B. MA BD DPhil DD FRSE	1962	1978	(University of Edinburgh)	25 Kingsburgh Road, Edinburgh EH12 6DZ [E-mail: dbforrester@dsl.pipex.com]		0131-337 5646
Forrester, Margaret R. (Mrs) MA BD	1974	2003	(Edinburgh: St Michael's)	25 Kingsburgh Road, Edinburgh EH12 6DZ [E-mail: margaretforrester@dsl.pipex.com]		0131-337 5646
Fraser, Shirley A. (Miss) MA BD	1992	2008	(Scottish Field Director: Friends International)	30 Parkhead Avenue, Edinburgh EH11 4SG		0131-443 7268
Gardner, John V.	1997	2003	(Glamis, Inverarity and Kinnettles)	75/1 Lockharton Avenue, Edinburgh EH14 1BD [E-mail: jvg66@hotmail.com]		0131-443 7126
Gordon, Margaret (Mrs) DCS			(Edinburgh: Corstorphine St Ninian's)	92 Lanark Road West, Currie EH14 5LA		0131-449 2554
Gordon, Tom MA BD	1974	2009	(Chaplain: Marie Curie Hospice, Edinburgh)	22 Gosford Road, Port Seton, Prestonpans EH32 0HF		01875 812262
Graham, W. Peter MA BD	1967	2008	(Presbytery Clerk)	23/6 East Comiston, Edinburgh EH10 6RZ		0131-445 5763
Harkness, James CB OBE QHC MA DD	1961	1995	(Chaplain General: Army)	13 Saxe Coburg Place, Edinburgh EH3 5BR		0131-343 1297
Hill, J. William BA BD	1967	2001	(Edinburgh: Corstorphine St Anne's)	33/9 Murrayfield Road, Edinburgh EH12 6EP		
Irving, William D. LTh	1985	2005	(Golspie)	122 Swanston Muir, Edinburgh EH10 7HY		0131-441 3384
Jamieson, Gordon D. MA BD	1974	2000	Head of Stewardship	41 Goldpark Place, Livingston EH54 6LW		01506 412020
Jeffrey, Eric W.S. JP MA	1954	1994	(Edinburgh: Bristo Memorial)	18 Gillespie Crescent, Edinburgh EH10 4HT		0131-229 7815
Kant, Everard FVCM MTh	1953	1988	(Kinghorn)	10/1 Maxwell Street, Edinburgh EH10 5GZ		0131-466 2607
Kelly, Ewan R. MB ChB BD PhD	1994	2006	NHS Education for Scotland	15 Boswall Road, Edinburgh EH5 3RW [E-mail: ewan.kelly@nes.scot.nhs.uk]		0131-551 7706
Lawson, Kenneth C. MA BD	1963	1999	(Adviser in Adult Education)	56 Easter Drylaw View, Edinburgh EH4 2QP		0131-539 3311
McCaskill, George I.L. MA BD	1953	1990	(Religious Education)	19 Tyler's Acre Road, Edinburgh EH12 7HY		0131-334 7451
Macdonald, Finlay A.J. MA BD PhD DD	1971	2010	(Principal Clerk)	59 Auchingane, Edinburgh EH10 7HU [E-mail: finlay_macdonald@btinternet.com]		0131-441 7906
Macdonald, Peter J. BD	1986	2009	Leader of the Iona Community	63 Jim Bush Drive, Prestonpans EH32 9GB [E-mail: petermacdonald@iona.org.uk] [E-mail: petermacdonald166@btinternet.com]	(Office) (Mbl)	0141-332 6343 07946 715166 01875 819655
Macdonald, William J. BD	1976	2002	(Board of National Mission: New Charge Development)	1/13 North Werber Park, Edinburgh EH4 1SY		0131-332 0254
MacGregor, Margaret S. (Miss) MA BD DipEd	1985	1994	(Calcutta)	16 Learmonth Court, Edinburgh EH4 1PB		0131-332 1089
McGregor, Alistair G.C. QC BD	1987	2002	(Edinburgh: Leith North)	22 Primrose Bank Road, Edinburgh EH5 3JG		0131-551 2802
McGregor, T. Stewart MBE MA BD	1957	1998	(Chaplain: Edinburgh Royal Infirmary)	19 Lonsdale Terrace, Edinburgh EH3 9HL [E-mail: cetsm@waitrose.com]		0131-229 5332
MacKay, Stewart A.	2009		Army Chaplain	5 Scots, Howe Barracks, Canterbury, Kent CT1 1JU		
McLarty, R. Russell MA BD	1985	2011	*A Chance to Thrive* – Project Co-ordinator	9 Sanderson's Wynd, Tranent EH33 1DA		01875 614496
Maclean, Ailsa G. (Mrs) BD DipCE	1979	1988	Chaplain: George Heriot's School	28 Swan Spring Avenue, Edinburgh EH10 6NJ		0131-445 1320
McMahon, John K.S. MA BD	1998	2006	Lead Chaplain: NHS Lothian Primary Care and Mental Health	Department of Spiritual Care, Royal Edinburgh Hospital, Morningside Terrace, Edinburgh EH10 5HF [E-mail: john.mcmahon@lpct.scot.nhs.uk]	 (Mbl)	0131-537 6734 07971 339571
MacMurchie, F. Lynne LLB BD	1998	2003	Health Care Chaplain	Edinburgh Community Mental Health Chaplaincy, 41 George IV Bridge, Edinburgh EH1 1EL		0131-220 5150
McPheat, Elspeth DCS			Deaconess: CrossReach	11/5 New Orchardfield, Edinburgh EH6 5ET		0131-554 4143
McPhee, Duncan C. MA BD	1953	1993	(Department of National Mission)	8 Belvedere Park, Edinburgh EH6 4LR		0131-552 6784

Name			Appointment	Address	Telephone
Macpherson, Allan S. MA	1967	1993	Merchiston Castle School	36 Craigmillar Castle Road, Edinburgh EH16 4AR	
Macpherson, Colin C.R. MA BD	1958	1996	(Dunfermline St Margaret's)	7 Eva Place, Edinburgh EH9 3ET	0131-667 1456
Mathieson, Angus R. MA BD	1988	1998	Ministries Council	21 Traquair Park West, Edinburgh EH12 7AN	0131-334 9774
Moir, Ian A. MA BD	1962	2000	(Adviser for Urban Priority Areas)	28/6 Comely Bank Avenue, Edinburgh EH4 1EL	0131-332 2748
Monteith, W. Graham BD PhD	1974	1994	(Flotta and Fara with Hoy and Walls)	20/3 Grandfield, Edinburgh EH6 4TL	0131-552 2564
Morrice, William G. MA BD STM PhD	1957	1991	(St John's College Durham)	Flat 37, The Cedars, 2 Manse Road, Edinburgh EH12 7SN [E-mail: w.g.morrice@btinternet.com]	0131-316 4845
Morrison, Mary B. (Mrs) MA BD DipEd	1978	2000	(Edinburgh: Stenhouse St Aidan's)	14 Eildon Terrace, Edinburgh EH3 5LU	0131-556 1962
Morton, Andrew R. MA BD DD	1956	1994	(Board of World Mission and Unity)	7A Laverockbank Terrace, Edinburgh EH5 3DJ	0131-538 7049
Moyes, Sheila A. (Miss) DCS			(Deaconess)	158 Pilton Avenue, Edinburgh EH5 2JZ	0131-551 1731
Mulligan, Anne MA DCS			Deaconess: Hospital Chaplain	27A Craigour Avenue, Edinburgh EH17 1NH	0131-664 3426
Munro, George A.M.	1968	2000	(Edinburgh: Cluny)	108 Caiyside, Edinburgh EH10 7HR	0131-445 5829
Murrie, John BD	1953	1996	(Kirkliston)	31 Nicol Road, The Whins, Broxburn EH52 6JJ	01506 852464
Musgrave, Clarence W. BA BD ThM	1966	2006	(Jerusalem: St Andrew's)	4 Ravelston Heights, Edinburgh EH4 3LX [E-mail: clarencejoan@talktalk.net]	0131-332 6337
Page, Ruth MA BD DPhil	1976	2000	(University of Edinburgh)	22/5 West Mill Bank, West Mill Road, Edinburgh EH13 0QT	0131-441 3740
Paterson, Douglas S. MA BD	1976	2010	(Edinburgh: St Colm's)	4 Ards Place, High Street, Aberlady EH32 0DB	01875 870192
Plate, Maria A.G. (Miss) LTh BA	1983	2000	(South Ronaldsay and Burray)	Flat 29, 77 Barnton Park View, Edinburgh EH4 6EL	0131-339 8539
Ridland, Alistair K. MA BD	1982	2000	Chaplain: Western General Hospital	13 Stewart Place, Kirkliston EH29 0BQ	0131-333 2711
Robertson, Charles LVO MA	1965	2005	(Edinburgh: Canongate)	3 Ross Gardens, Edinburgh EH9 3BS	0131-662 9025
Robertson, Norma P. (Miss) BD DMin MTh	1993	2002	(Kincardine O'Neil with Lumphanan)	Flat 5, 2 Burnbrae Drive, Grovewood Hill, Edinburgh EH12 8AS	0131-339 6701
Robson, Brenda PhD	2005		Auxiliary Minister	2 Baird Road, Ratho, Newbridge EH28 8RA	0131-333 2746
Ronald, Norma A. (Miss) MBE DCS			(Deaconess)	2B Saughton Road North, Edinburgh EH12 7HG	0131-334 8736
Schofield, Melville F. MA	1960	2000	(Chaplain: Western General Hospitals)	25 Rowantree Grove, Currie EH14 5AT	0131-449 4745
Scott, Ian G. BSc BD STM	1965	2006	(Edinburgh: Greenbank)	50 Forthview Walk, Tranent EH33 1FE [E-mail: iandascott@tiscali.co.uk]	01875 612907
Scott, Martin DipMusEd RSAM BD PhD	1986	2000	Ministries Council	The Manse, Culross, Dunfermline KY12 8JD	01383 880231
Shewan, Frederick D. MA BD	1970	2005	(Edinburgh: Muirhouse St Andrew's)	38 Tremayne Place, Dunfermline KY12 9YH	01383 734354
Slorach, Alexander CA BD	1970	2002	(Kirk of Lammermuir with Langton and Polwarth)	61 Inverleith Row, Edinburgh EH3 5PX	
Smith, Angus MA LTh	1965	2006	(Chaplain to the Oil Industry)	3/7 West Powburn, West Savile Gait, Edinburgh EH9 3EW	0131-667 1761
Stephen, Donald M. TD MA BD ThM	1962	2001	(Edinburgh: Marchmont St Giles')	10 Hawkhead Crescent, Edinburgh EH16 6LR	0131-658 1216
Stevenson, John MA BD PhD	1963	2001	(Department of Education)	12 Swanston Gardens, Edinburgh EH10 7DL	0131-445 3960
Stirling, A. Douglas BSc	1956	1994	(Rhu and Shandon)	162 Avontoun Park, Linlithgow EH49 6QH	01506 845021
Taylor, Howard G. BSc BD MTh	1971	1998	(Chaplain: Heriot Watt University)	Westerlea, Pittenweem Road, Anstruther KY10 3DT [E-mail: HowardTaylor1944@live.co.uk]	
Taylor, William R. MA BD	1983	2003	Chaplaincy Co-ordinator: Scottish Prison Service	33 Kingsknowe Drive, Edinburgh EH14 2JY	
Teague, Yvonne (Mrs) DCS			(Board of Ministry)	46 Craigcrook Avenue, Edinburgh EH4 3PX	0131-336 3113
Telfer, Iain J.M. BD DPS	1978	2001	Chaplain: Royal Infirmary	Royal Infirmary of Edinburgh, 51 Little France Crescent, Edinburgh EH16 4SA	0131-242 1997
Thom, Helen (Miss) DCS			(Deaconess)	84 Great King Street, Edinburgh EH3 6QU	0131-556 5687

Whyte, George J. BSc BD DMin PhD	1981 2008	Presbytery Clerk	4 Baberton Mains Lea, Edinburgh EH14 3HB [E-mail: edinburgh@cofscotland.org.uk]	0131-466 1674
Whyte, Iain A. BA BD STM PhD	1968 2001	Community Mental Health Chaplain	14 Carlingnose Point, North Queensferry, Inverkeithing KY11 1ER [E-mail: iainisabel@whytes28.fsnet.co.uk]	01383 410732
Wigglesworth, J. Christopher MBE BSc PhD BD	1968 1999	(St Andrew's College, Selly Oak)	12 Leven Terrace, Edinburgh EH3 9LW	0131-228 6335
Wilkie, James L. MA BD	1959 1998	(Board of World Mission)	7 Comely Bank Avenue, Edinburgh EH4 1EW [E-mail: jl.wilkie@btinternet.com]	0131-343 1552
Wilkinson, John BD MD FRCP DTM&H	1946 1975	(Kikuyu)	70 Craigleith Hill Gardens, Edinburgh EH4 2JH	0131-332 2994
Williams, Jenny M. (Miss) BSc CQSW BD	1996 1997	Christian Fellowship of Healing	16 Blantyre Terrace, Edinburgh EH10 5AE	0131-447 0050
Wilson, John M. MA	1964 1995	(Adviser in Religious Education)	27 Bellfield Street, Edinburgh EH15 2BR	0131-669 5257
Young, Alexander W. BD DipMin	1988 1999	Chaplain: Royal Infirmary	32 Lindsay Circus, The Hawthorns, Rosewell EH24 9EP	(Work) 0131-242 1997

EDINBURGH ADDRESSES

Albany	At Greenside
Balerno	Johnsburn Road, Balerno
Barclay Viewforth	Barclay Place
Blackhall St Columba's	Queensferry Road
Bristo Memorial	Peffermill Road, Craigmillar
Broughton St Mary's	Bellevue Crescent
Canongate	Canongate
Carrick Knowe	North Saughton Road
Colinton	Dell Road
Colinton Mains	Oxgangs Road North
Corstorphine	
Craigsbank	Craig's Crescent
Old	Kirk Loan
St Anne's	Kaimes Road
St Ninian's	St John's Road
Craigentinny St Christopher's	Craigentinny Road
Craiglockhart	Craiglockhart Avenue
Craigmillar Park	Craigmillar Park
Cramond	Cramond Glebe Road
Currie	Kirkgate, Currie
Davidson's Mains	Quality Street
Dean	Dean Path
Drylaw	Groathill Road North
Duddingston	Old Church Lane, Duddingston
Fairmilehead	Frogston Road West, Fairmilehead
Gorgie Dalry	Gorgie Road
Granton	Boswall Parkway
Greenbank	Braidburn Terrace
Greenside	Royal Terrace
Greyfriars Tolbooth and Highland Kirk	Greyfriars Place
High (St Giles')	High Street
Holyrood Abbey	Dalziel Place x London Road
Holy Trinity	Hailesland Place, Wester Hailes
Inverleith	Inverleith Gardens
Juniper Green	Lanark Road, Juniper Green
Kaimes Lockhart Memorial	Gracemount Drive
Kirkliston	The Square, Kirkliston
Kirk o' Field	Pleasance
Leith	
North	Madeira Street off Ferry Road
St Andrew's	Easter Road
St Serf's	Ferry Road
South	Kirkgate, Leith
Wardie	Primrosebank Road
Liberton	Kirkgate, Liberton
Northfield	Gilmerton Road, Liberton
London Road	London Road
Marchmont St Giles'	Kilgraston Road
Mayfield Salisbury	Mayfield Road x West Mayfield
Morningside	Cluny Gardens
Morningside United	Bruntsfield Place x Chamberlain Road
Muirhouse St Andrew's	Pennywell Gardens
Murrayfield	Abinger Gardens
Newhaven	Craighall Road
New Restalrig	Willowbrae Road
Old Kirk	Pennywell Road
Palmerston Place	Palmerston Place
Pilrig St Paul's	Pilrig Street
Polwarth	Polwarth Terrace x Harrison Road
Portobello	
Old	Bellfield Street
St James'	Rosefield Place
St Philip's Joppa	Abercorn Terrace
Priestfield	Dalkeith Road x Marchhall Place
Queensferry	The Loan, South Queensferry
Ratho	Baird Road, Ratho
Reid Memorial	West Savile Terrace
Richmond Craigmillar	Niddrie Mains Road
St Andrew's and St George's West	George Street and Shandwick Place
St Andrew's Clermiston	Clermiston View
St Catherine's Argyle	Grange Road x Chalmers Crescent
St Cuthbert's	Lothian Road
St David's Broomhouse	Broomhouse Crescent
St John's Oxgangs	Oxgangs Road
St Margaret's	Restalrig Road South
St Martin's	Magdalene Drive
St Michael's	Slateford Road
St Nicholas' Sighthill	Calder Road
St Stephen's Comely Bank	Comely Bank
Slateford Longstone	Kingsknowe Road North
Stenhouse St Aidan's	Chesser Avenue
Stockbridge	Saxe Coburg Street
The Tron Kirk (Gilmerton and Moredun)	Craigour Gardens and Ravenscroft Street

(2) WEST LOTHIAN

Meets in the church of the incoming Moderator on the first Tuesday of September and in St John's Church Hall, Bathgate, on the first Tuesday of every other month, except December, when the meeting is on the second Tuesday, and January, July and August, when there is no meeting.

Clerk: REV. DUNCAN SHAW BD MTh — **St John's Manse, Mid Street, Bathgate EH48 1QD** — **01506 653146**
[E-mail: westlothian@cofscotland.org.uk]

Abercorn (H) linked with Pardovan, Kingscavil (H) and Winchburgh (H)

A. Scott Marshall DipComm BD | 1984 | 1998 | The Manse, Winchburgh, Broxburn EH52 6TT [E-mail: pkwla@aol.com] | 01506 890919

Armadale (H)

Julia C. Wiley (Ms) MA(CE) MDiv | 1998 | 2010 | 70 Mount Pleasant, Armadale, Bathgate EH48 3HB [E-mail: preachergrace@gmail.com] | 01501 730358

Avonbridge (H) linked with Torphichen (H)

Vacant | | | Manse Road, Torphichen, Bathgate EH48 4LT | 01506 652794

Bathgate: Boghall (H)

Vacant | | | 1 Manse Place, Ash Grove, Bathgate EH48 1NJ | 01506 652940

Bathgate: High (H)

Murdo C. Macdonald MA BD | 2002 | 2011 | 19 Hunter Grove, Bathgate EH48 1NN [E-mail: murdocmacdonald@gmail.com] | 01506 652654

Bathgate: St John's (H)

Duncan Shaw BD MTh | 1975 | 1978 | St John's Manse, Mid Street, Bathgate EH48 1QD [E-mail: westlothian@cofscotland.org.uk] | 01506 653146

Blackburn and Seafield (H)

Robert A. Anderson MA BD DPhil | 1980 | 1998 | The Manse, 5 MacDonald Gardens, Blackburn, Bathgate EH47 7RE [E-mail: robertanderson307@btinternet.com] | 01506 652825

Blackridge (H) linked with Harthill: St Andrew's (H)

Robert B. Gehrke BSc BD CEng MIEE | 1994 | 2006 | East Main Street, Harthill, Shotts ML7 5QW [E-mail: bob.gehrke@gmail.com] | 01501 751239

Breich Valley (H)				
Vacant			Stoneyburn, Bathgate EH47 8AU	01501 762018
Broxburn (H)				
Terry Taylor BA MTh	2005		2 Church Street, Broxburn EH52 5EL [E-mail: terry@broxburn.plus.com]	01506 852825
Fauldhouse: St Andrew's (H)				
Robert Sloan BD	1997	2011	7 Glebe Court, Fauldhouse, Bathgate EH47 9DX [E-mail: robertsloan@scotnet.co.uk]	01501 771190
Harthill: St Andrew's See Blackridge				
Kirknewton (H) and East Calder (H)				
Andre Groenewald BA BD MDiv DD	1995	2009	8 Manse Court, East Calder, Livingston EH53 0HF [E-mail: groenstes@yahoo.com]	01506 884585 07588 845814 (Mbl)
Kirk of Calder (H)				
John M. Povey MA BD	1981		19 Maryfield Park, Mid Calder, Livingston EH53 0SB [E-mail: revjpovey@aol.com]	01506 882495
Linlithgow: St Michael's (H) (E-mail: info@stmichaels-parish.org.uk)				
D. Stewart Gillan BSc MDiv PhD	1985	2004	St Michael's Manse, Kirkgate, Linlithgow EH49 7AL [E-mail: stewart@stmichaels-parish.org.uk]	01506 842195
John H. Paton BSc BD (Assoc)	1983	2008	Cross House, The Cross, Linlithgow EH49 7AL [E-mail: jonymar@globalnet.co.uk [E-mail: johnny@stmichaels-parish.org.uk]	01506 842665
Thomas S. Riddell BSc CEng FIChemE (Aux)	1993	1994	4 The Maltings, Linlithgow EH49 6DS [E-mail: tsriddell@blueyonder.co.uk]	01506 843251
Linlithgow: St Ninian's Craigmailen (H)				
W. Richard Houston BSc BD	1998	2004	29 Philip Avenue, Linlithgow EH49 7BH [E-mail: wrichardhouston@blueyonder.co.uk]	01506 202246
Livingston Ecumenical Parish				
*Incorporating the **Worship Centres** at:*				
Carmondean (H) and Knightsridge				
Helen Jenkins BSc MRES PhD BA MA (*The Methodist Church*)			13 Eastcroft Court, Livingston EH54 7ET [E-mail: revhelen@chjenkins.plus.com]	01506 464567
Craigshill (St Columba's) and Ladywell (St Paul's)				
Ronald G. Greig MA BD	1987	2008	2 Eastcroft Court, Livingston EH54 7ET [E-mail: rongreig@bethere.co.uk]	01506 467426

Dedridge and Murieston				
Eileen Thompson BD MTh (*Scottish Episcopal Church*) Team Leader			53 Garry Walk, Craigshill, Livingston EH54 5AS [E-mail: ectlepc@googlemail.com]	01506 433451
Robin R. Hine MA (*The United Reformed Church*)			21 Bankton Gardens, Livingston EH54 9DZ [E-mail: robin@hiner.com]	01506 207360
Livingston: Old (H)				
Graham W. Smith BA BD FSAScot	1995		Manse of Livingston, Charlesfield Lane, Livingston EH54 7AJ [E-mail: info@gwsmith.abel.co.uk]	01506 420227
Pardovan, Kingscavil and Winchburgh See Abercorn				
Polbeth Harwood linked with West Kirk of Calder (H)				
Vacant			27 Learmonth Crescent, West Calder EH55 8AF	01506 870460
Strathbrock (H)				
Marc B. Kenton BTh MTh	1997	2009	1 Manse Park, Uphall, Broxburn EH52 6NX [E-mail: marc@kentonfamily.co.uk]	01506 852550
Torphichen See Avonbridge				
Uphall: South (H)				
Margaret Steele (Miss) BSc BD	2000		8 Fernlea, Uphall, Broxburn EH52 6DF [E-mail: mdsteele@tiscali.co.uk]	01506 852788
West Kirk of Calder (H) See Polbeth Harwood				
Whitburn: Brucefield (H)				
Vacant				
Whitburn: South (H)				
Vacant			5 Mansewood Crescent, Whitburn, Bathgate EH47 8HA	01501 740333

Black, David W. BSc BD	1968 2008	(Strathbrock)	66 Bridge Street, Newbridge EH28 8SH [E-mail: alexandra.black@btopenworld.com]	0131-333 2609
Cameron, Ian MA BD	1953 1981	(Kilbrandon and Kilchattan)	Craigellen, West George Street, Blairgowrie PH10 6DZ	01250 872087
Darroch, Richard J.G. BD MTh MA(CMS)	1993 2010	(Whitburn: Brucefield)	23 Barnes Green, Livingston EH54 8PP [E-mail: richdarr@aol.com]	01506 436648
Dundas, Thomas B.S. LTh	1969 1996	(West Kirk of Calder)	35 Coolkill, Sandyford, Dublin 18, Republic of Ireland	00353 12953061

Kelly, Isobel J.M. (Miss) MA BD DipEd	1974	2010	(Greenock: St Margaret's)	76 Bankton Park East, Livingston EH54 9BN	01506 438511
Mackay, Kenneth J. MA BD	1971	2007	(Edinburgh: St Nicholas' Sighthill)	46 Chuckethall Road, Livingston EH54 8FB [E-mail: knnth_mackay@yahoo.co.uk]	01506 410884
MacRae, Norman I. LTh	1966	2003	(Inverness: Trinity)	144 Hope Park Gardens, Bathgate EH48 2QX [E-mail: normanmacrae@talktalk.com]	01506 635254
Merrilees, Ann (Miss) DCS			(Deaconess)	23 Cuthill Brae, West Calder EH55 8QE [E-mail: ann@merrilees.freeserve.co.uk]	01501 762909
Morrison, Iain C. BA BD	1990	2003	(Linlithgow: St Ninian's Craigmailen)	Whaligoe, 53 Eastcroft Drive, Polmont, Falkirk FK2 0SU [E-mail: iain@kirkweb.org]	01324 713249
Nelson, Georgina (Mrs) MA BD PhD DipEd	1990	1995	Hospital Chaplain	63 Hawthorn Bank, Seafield, Bathgate EH47 7EB	
Nicol, Robert M.	1984	1996	(Jersey: St Columba's)	59 Kinloch View, Blackness Road, Linlithgow EH49 7HT [E-mail: revrob.nicol@tiscali.co.uk]	01506 670391
Thomson, Phyllis (Miss) DCS	2003	2010	(Deaconess)	63 Caroline Park, Mid Calder, Livingston EH53 0SJ	01506 883207
Trimble, Robert DCS			(Deacon)	5 Templar Rise, Dedridge, Livingston EH54 6PJ	01506 412504
Walker, Ian BD MEd DipMS	1973	2007	(Rutherglen: Wardlawhill)	92 Carseknowe, Linlithgow EH49 7LG [E-mail: walk102822@aol.com]	01506 844412
Whitson, William S. MA	1959	1999	(Cumbernauld: St Mungo's)	2 Chapman's Brae, Bathgate EH48 4LH [E-mail: william_whitson@tiscali.co.uk]	01506 650027

(3) LOTHIAN

Meets at Musselburgh: St Andrew's High Parish Church at 7pm on the last Thursday in April, June and November, and in a different church on the last Thursday in September; meets also in another different church at 10am on the last Saturday in February.

Clerk:	**MR JOHN D. McCULLOCH DL**			**20 Tipperwell Way, Howgate, Penicuik EH26 8QP [E-mail: lothian@cofscotland.org.uk]**	**01968 676300**
Aberlady (H) linked with Gullane (H)					
Christine M. Clark (Mrs) BA BD MTh		2006	2009	The Manse, Hummel Road, Gullane EH31 2BG [E-mail: gcclark20@aol.com]	01620 843192
Athelstaneford linked with Whitekirk and Tyninghame					
Joanne H.G. Evans-Boiten BD		2004	2009	The Manse, Athelstaneford, North Berwick EH39 5BE [E-mail: joanne.evansboiten@gmail.com]	01620 880378
Belhaven (H) linked with Spott					
Laurence H. Twaddle MA BD MTh		1977	1978	The Manse, Belhaven Road, Dunbar EH42 1NH [E-mail: revtwaddle@aol.com]	01368 863098

Bilston linked with Glencorse (H) linked with Roslin (H)
John R. Wells BD DipMin 1991 2005 31A Manse Road, Roslin EH25 9LG 0131-440 2012
[E-mail: wellsjr3@aol.com]

Bolton and Saltoun linked with Humbie linked with Yester (H)
Malcolm Lyon BD 2007 The Manse, Tweeddale Avenue, Gifford, Haddington EH41 4QN 01620 810515
[E-mail: malcolmlyon2@hotmail.com]

Bonnyrigg (H)
John Mitchell LTh CMin 1991 9 Viewbank View, Bonnyrigg EH19 2HU 0131-663 8287 (Tel/Fax)
[E-mail: jmitchell241@tiscali.co.uk]

Cockenzie and Port Seton: Chalmers Memorial (H)
Kristina M. Herbold Ross (Mrs) 2008 2011 Braemar Villa, 2 Links Road, Port Seton, Prestonpans EH32 0HA 01875 819254
[E-mail: khross@btinternet.com]

Cockenzie and Port Seton: Old (H)
Continued Vacancy 1 Links Road, Port Seton, Prestonpans EH32 0HA 01875 812310

Cockpen and Carrington (H) linked with Lasswade (H) and Rosewell (H)
Matthew Z. Ross LLB BD MTh FSAScot 1998 2009 Braemar Villa, 2 Links Road, Port Seton, Prestonpans EH32 0HA 01875 819544
[E-mail: mzross@btinternet.com] 07711 706950 (Mbl)

Dalkeith: St John's and King's Park (H)
Keith L. Mack BD MTh DPS 2002 13 Weir Crescent, Dalkeith EH22 3JN 0131-454 0206
[E-mail: kthmacker@aol.com]

Dalkeith: St Nicholas' Buccleuch (H)
Alexander G. Horsburgh MA BD 1995 2004 116 Bonnyrigg Road, Dalkeith EH22 3HZ 0131-663 3036
[E-mail: alexanderhorsburgh@googlemail.com]

Dirleton (H) linked with North Berwick: Abbey (H) (01620 892800) (E-mail: abbeychurch@hotmail.com)
David J. Graham BSc BD PhD 1982 1998 Sydserff, Old Abbey Road, North Berwick EH39 4BP 01620 840878
[E-mail: dirletonkirk@btinternet.com]

Dunbar (H)
Gordon Stevenson BSc BD 2010 The Manse, 10 Bayswell Road, Dunbar EH42 1AB 01368 865482
[E-mail: gstev@btinternet.com]

Dunglass
Suzanne G. Fletcher (Mrs) BA MDiv MA | 2001 | 2011 | The Manse, Cockburnspath TD13 5XZ | 01368 830713

Garvald and Morham linked with Haddington: West (H)
John Vischer | 1993 | 2011 | 15 West Road, Haddington EH41 3RD [E-mail: j_vischer@yahoo.co.uk] | 01620 822213

Gladsmuir linked with Longniddry (H)
Robin E. Hill LLB BD PhD | 2004 | The Manse, Elcho Road, Longniddry EH32 0LB [E-mail: robinailsa@btinternet.com] | 01875 853195

Glencorse (H) See Bilston

Gorebridge (H)
Mark S. Nicholas MA BD | 1999 | 100 Hunterfield Road, Gorebridge EH23 4TT [E-mail: mark@nicholasfamily.wanadoo.co.uk] | 01875 820387

Gullane See Aberlady

Haddington: St Mary's (H)
Jennifer Macrae (Mrs) MA BD | 1998 | 2007 | 1 Nungate Gardens, Haddington EH41 4EE [E-mail: minister@stmaryskirk.com] | 01620 823109

Haddington: West See Garvald and Morham

Howgate (H) linked with Penicuik: South (H)
Ian A. Cathcart BSc BD | 1994 | 2007 | 15 Stevenson Road, Penicuik EH26 0LU [E-mail: reviac@yahoo.co.uk] | 01968 674692

Humbie See Bolton and Saltoun
Lasswade and Rosewell See Cockpen and Carrington

Loanhead
Graham L. Duffin BSc BD DipEd | 1989 | 2001 | 120 The Loan, Loanhead EH20 9AJ [E-mail: gduffin@talktalk.net] | 0131-448 2459

Longniddry See Gladsmuir

Musselburgh: Northesk (H)
Alison P. McDonald MA BD 1991 1998 16 New Street, Musselburgh EH21 6JP 0131-665 2128
[E-mail: alisonpmcdonald@btinternet.com]

Musselburgh: St Andrew's High (H) (0131-665 7239)
Yvonne E.S. Atkins (Mrs) BD 1997 2004 8 Ferguson Drive, Musselburgh EH21 6XA 0131-665 1124
[E-mail: yesatkins@yahoo.co.uk]

Musselburgh: St Clement's and St Ninian's
Vacant The Manse, Wallyford Loan Road, Wallyford, Musselburgh EH21 8BU 0131-653 6588

Musselburgh: St Michael's Inveresk
Andrew B. Dick BD DipMin 1986 1999 8 Hope Place, Musselburgh EH21 7QE 0131-665 0545
[E-mail: dixbit@aol.com]

Newbattle (H) (Website: http://freespace.virgin.net/newbattle.focus)
Sean Swindells BD DipMin MTh 1996 2011 112 Greenbank Crescent, Edinburgh EH10 5SZ 0131-663 3245
[E-mail: sswindells@blueyonder.co.uk] 07791 755976 (Mbl)
Gordon R. Steven BD DCS 2004 51 Nantwich Drive, Edinburgh EH7 6RB 0131-669 2054
[E-mail: grsteven@btinternet.com] 07904 385256 (Mbl)

Newton
Vacant The Manse, Newton, Dalkeith EH22 1SR 0131-663 3845

North Berwick: Abbey See Dirleton

North Berwick: St Andrew Blackadder (H) (E-mail: admin@standrewblackadder.org.uk) (Website: www.standrewblackadder.org.uk)
Neil J. Dougall BD 1991 2003 7 Marine Parade, North Berwick EH39 4LD 01620 892132
[E-mail: neil@neildougall.co.uk]

Ormiston linked with Pencaitland
David J. Torrance BD DipMin 1993 2009 The Manse, Pencaitland, Tranent EH34 5DL 01875 340963
[E-mail: torrance@talktalk.net]

Pencaitland See Ormiston

Penicuik: North (H)
Vacant 93 John Street, Penicuik EH26 8AG 01968 672213

Penicuik: St Mungo's (H)				
Geoff T. Berry BD BSc	2009		31A Kirkhill Road, Penicuik EH26 8JB [E-mail: geofftalk@yahoo.co.uk]	01968 677040
Penicuik: South See Howgate				
Prestonpans: Prestongrange				
Vacant			The Manse, East Loan, Prestonpans EH32 9ED	01875 810308
Roslin See Bilston				
Spott See Belhaven				
Tranent				
Jan Gillies BD	1998	2008	1 Toll House Gardens, Tranent EH33 2QQ [E-mail: jan@tranentparishchurch.co.uk]	01875 824604
Traprain				
David D. Scott BSc BD	1981	2010	The Manse, Preston Road, East Linton EH40 3DS [E-mail: revdd.scott@gmail.com]	01620 860227 (Tel/Fax)
Tyne Valley Parish (H)				
D. Graham Leitch MA BD	1974	2003	Cranstoun Cottage, Ford, Pathhead EH37 5RE [E-mail: leitch@cranscott.fsnet.co.uk]	01875 320314
Andrew Don MBA (Aux)	2006		5 Eskvale Court, Penicuik EH26 8HT [E-mail: a.a.don@btinternet.com]	01968 675766
Whitekirk and Tyninghame See Athelstaneford				
Yester See Bolton and Saltoun				

Andrews, J. Edward MA BD DipCG	1985 2005	(Armadale)	Dunnichen, 1B Cameron Road, Nairn IV12 5NS [E-mail: edward.andrews@btinternet.com]	(Mbl) 07808 720708
Bayne, Angus L. LTh BEd MTh	1969 2005	(Edinburgh: Bristo Memorial Craigmillar)	14 Myredale, Bonnyrigg EH19 3NW [E-mail: angus@mccookies.com]	0131-663 6871
Black, A. Graham MA	1964 2003	(Gladsmuir with Longniddry)	26 Hamilton Crescent, Gullane EH31 2HR [E-mail: grablack@aol.com]	01620 843899
Brown, Ronald H.	1974 1998	(Musselburgh: Northesk)	6 Monktonhall Farm Cottages, Musselburgh EH21 6RZ	0131-653 2531
Brown, William BD	1972 1997	(Edinburgh: Polwarth)	13 Thornyhall, Dalkeith EH22 2ND	0131-654 0929
Cairns, John B. LTh LLB LLD DD	1974 2009	(Aberlady with Gullane)	Bell House, Roxburghe Park, Dunbar EH42 1LR [E-mail: johncairns@mail.com]	01368 862501
Forbes, Iain M. BSc BD	1964 2005	(Aberdeen: Beechgrove)	69 Dobbie's Road, Bonnyrigg EH19 2AY [E-mail: panama.forbes@tiscali.co.uk]	0131-454 0717
Fraser, John W. MA BD	1974 2011	(Penicuik: North)	66 Camus Avenue, Edinburgh EH10 6QX	

Gilfillan, James LTh	1968	1997	(East Kilbride: Old)	15 Long Cram, Haddington EH41 4NS	01620 824843
Glover, Robert L. BMus BD MTh ARCO	1971	2010	(Cockenzie and Port Seton: Chalmers Memorial)	27 Winton Park, Cockenzie, Prestonpans EH32 0JN [E-mail: rlglover@btinternet.com]	
Haslett, Howard J. BA BD	1972	2010	(Traprain)	48 The Maltings, Haddington EH41 4EF [E-mail: howard.haslett@btinternet.com]	01620 820292
Hutchison, Alan E.W.			(Deacon)	132 Lochbridge Road, North Berwick EH39 4DR	01620 894077
Jones, Anne M. (Mrs) BD	1998	2002	Hospital Chaplain	7 North Elphinstone Farm, Tranent EH33 2ND [E-mail: revamjones@aol.com]	01875 614442
Levison, L. David MA BD	1943	1982	(Ormiston with Pencaitland)	Westdene Conservatory Flat, 506 Perth Road, Dundee DD2 1LS	01382 630460
Lithgow, Anne R. (Mrs) MA BD	1992	2009	(Dunglass)	14 Thorntonloch Holdings, Dunbar EH42 1QT [E-mail: anne.lithgow@btinternet.com]	
Macdonell, Alasdair W. MA BD	1955	1992	(Haddington: St Mary's)	St Andrews Cottage, Duns Road, Gifford, Haddington EH41 4QW [E-mail: alasdair.macdonell@btinternet.com]	01620 810341
Macrae, Norman C. MA DipEd	1942	1985	(Loanhead)	49 Lixmount Avenue, Edinburgh EH5 3EW [E-mail: nandcmacrae@onetel.com]	0131-552 2428
Manson, James A. LTh	1981	2004	(Glencorse with Roslin)	31 Nursery Gardens, Kilmarnock KA1 3JA [E-mail: james.manson@virgin.net]	01563 535430
Pirie, Donald LTh	1975	2006	(Bolton and Saltoun with Humbie with Yester)	46 Caiystane Avenue, Edinburgh EH10 6SH	0131-445 2654
Ritchie, James McL. MA BD MPhil	1950	1985	(Coalsnaughton)	Flat 2/25, Croft-an-Righ, Edinburgh EH8 8EG [E-mail: jasritch_77@msn.com]	0131-557 1084
Robertson, James LTh	1970	2000	(Newton)	11 Southfield Square, Edinburgh EH15 1QS	0131-657 5661
Stein, Jock MA BD	1973	2008	(Tulliallan and Kincardine)	35 Dunbar Road, Haddington EH41 3PJ [E-mail: jstein@handselpress.org.uk]	01620 824896
Stein, Margaret E. (Mrs) DA BD DipRE	1984	2008	(Tulliallan and Kincardine)	35 Dunbar Road, Haddington EH41 3PJ [E-mail: margaretestein@hotmail.com]	01620 824896
Swan, Andrew F. BD	1983	2000	(Loanhead)	3 Mackenzie Gardens, Dolphinton, West Linton EH46 7HS	01968 682247
Torrance, David W. MA BD	1955	1991	(Earlston)	38 Forth Street, North Berwick EH39 4JQ [E-mail: torrance103@btinternet.com]	(Tel/Fax) 01620 895109
Underwood, Florence A. (Mrs) BD	1992	2006	(Assistant: Gladsmuir with Longniddry)	18 Covenanters Rise, Pitreavie Castle, Dunfermline KY11 8SQ [E-mail: geoffrey.underwood@homecall.co.uk]	01383 740745
Underwood, Geoffrey H. BD DipTh FPhS	1964	1992	(Cockenzie and Port Seton: Chalmers Memorial)	18 Covenanters Rise, Pitreavie Castle, Dunfermline KY11 8SQ [E-mail: geoffrey.underwood@homecall.co.uk]	01383 740745

(4) MELROSE AND PEEBLES

Meets at Innerleithen on the first Tuesday of February, March, May, October, November and December, and on the fourth Tuesday of June, and in places to be appointed on the first Tuesday of September.

Clerk:	**MR JACK STEWART**	**3 St Cuthbert's Drive, St Boswells, Melrose TD6 0DF [E-mail: melrosepeebles@cofscotland.org.uk]**	**01835 822600**

Ashkirk linked with Selkirk (H)
Vacant 1 Loanside, Selkirk TD7 4DJ 01750 22833

Bowden (H) and Melrose (H)
Alistair G. Bennett BSc BD 1978 1984 Tweedmount Road, Melrose TD6 9ST 01896 822217
[E-mail: agbennettmelrose@aol.com]

Broughton, Glenholm and Kilbucho (H) linked with Skirling linked with Stobo and Drumelzier linked with Tweedsmuir (H)
Robert B. Milne BTh 1999 2009 The Manse, Broughton, Biggar ML12 6HQ 01899 830331
[E-mail: rbmilne@aol.com]

Caddonfoot (H) linked with Galashiels: Trinity (H)
Morag A. Dawson BD MTh 1999 2005 8 Mossilee Road, Galashiels TD1 1NF 01896 752420
[E-mail: moragdawson@yahoo.co.uk]

Carlops linked with Kirkurd and Newlands (H) linked with West Linton: St Andrew's (H)
Thomas W. Burt BD 1982 1985 The Manse, West Linton EH46 7EN 01968 660221
[E-mail: tomburt@westlinton.com]

Channelkirk and Lauder
Vacant The Manse, Brownsmuir Park, Lauder TD2 6QD 01578 722320

Earlston
Julie M. Woods (Ms) BTh 2005 2011 The Manse, High Street, Earlston TD4 6DE 01896 849236
[E-mail: missjulie@btinternet.com]

Eddleston (H) linked with Peebles: Old (H)
Malcolm M. Macdougall BD MTh DipCE 1981 2001 The Old Manse, Innerleithen Road, Peebles EH45 8BD 01721 720568
[E-mail: calum.macdougall@btopenworld.com]

Ettrick and Yarrow
Samuel Siroky BA MTh 2003 Yarrow Manse, Yarrow, Selkirk TD7 5LA 01750 82336
[E-mail: sesiroky@tiscali.co.uk]

Galashiels: Old and St Paul's (H) (Website: www.oldparishandstpauls.org.uk)
Leslie M. Steele MA BD 1973 1988 Woodlea, Abbotsview Drive, Galashiels TD1 3SL 01896 752320
[E-mail: leslie@oldparishandstpauls.org.uk]

Galashiels: St John's (H)
Jane M. Howitt (Miss) MA BD 1996 2006 St John's Manse, Hawthorn Road, Galashiels TD1 2JZ 01896 752573
[E-mail: jane@stjohnsgalashiels.co.uk]

Galashiels: Trinity (H) See Caddonfoot

Innerleithen (H), Traquair and Walkerburn

Janice M. Faris (Mrs) BSc BD	1991	2001	The Manse, 1 Millwell Park, Innerleithen, Peebles EH44 6JF [E-mail: revjfaris@hotmail.com]	01896 830309

Kirkurd and Newlands See Carlops

Lyne and Manor

Nancy M. Norman (Miss) BA MDiv MTh	1988	1998	25 March Street, Peebles EH45 8EP [E-mail: nancy.norman1@btinternet.com]	01721 721699

Maxton and Mertoun linked with Newtown linked with St Boswells

Sheila W. Moir (Ms) MTheol	2008		7 Strae Brigs, St Boswells, Melrose TD6 0DH [E-mail: sheila377@btinternet.com]	01835 822255

Newtown See Maxton and Mertoun
Peebles: Old See Eddleston

Peebles: St Andrew's Leckie (H) (01721 723121)

Vacant			Mansefield, Innerleithen Road, Peebles EH45 8BE	01721 721749

St Boswells See Maxton and Mertoun
Selkirk See Ashkirk
Skirling See Broughton, Glenholm and Kilbucho
Stobo and Drumelzier See Broughton, Glenholm and Kilbucho

Stow: St Mary of Wedale and Heriot

Victoria J. Linford (Mrs) LLB BD	2010		The Manse, 209 Galashiels Road, Stow, Galashiels TD1 2RE [E-mail: victorialinford@yahoo.co.uk]	01578 730237

Tweedsmuir See Broughton, Glenholm and Kilbucho
West Linton: St Andrew's See Carlops

Arnott, A. David K. MA BD	1971	2010	(St Andrews: Hope Park with Strathkinness)	53 Whitehaugh Park, Peebles EH45 9DB [E-mail: adka53@btinternet.com]	01721 725979 (Mbl) 07759 709205
Bowie, Adam McC.	1976	1996	(Cavers and Kirkton with Hobkirk and Southdean)	Glenbield, Redpath, Earlston TD4 6AD	01896 848173

Name	Ord.	Ret.	Charge	Address	Tel.
Brown, Robert BSc	1962	1997	(Kilbrandon and Kilchattan)	11 Thornfield Terrace, Selkirk TD7 4DU [E-mail: ruwcb@tiscali.co.uk]	01750 20311
Cashman, P. Hamilton BSc	1985	1998	(Dirleton with North Berwick: Abbey)	38 Abbotsford Road, Galashiels TD1 3HR [E-mail: mcashman@tiscali.co.uk]	01896 752711
Devenny, Robert P.	2002		Borders Health Board	Blakeburn Cottage, Wester Housebyres, Melrose TD6 9BW	01896 822350
Dick, J. Ronald BD	1973	1996	Hospital Chaplain	5 Georgefield Farm Cottages, Earlston TD4 6BH	01896 848956
Dobie, Rachel J.W. (Mrs) LTh	1991	2008	(Broughton, Glenholm and Kilbucho with Skirling with Stobo and Drumelzier with Tweedsmuir)	20 Moss Side Crescent, Biggar ML12 6GE [E-mail: revracheldobie@talktalk.net]	01899 229244
Duncan, Charles A. MA	1956	1992	(Heriot with Stow: St Mary of Wedale)	10 Elm Grove, Galashiels TD1 3JA	01896 753261
Hardie, H. Warner BD	1979	2005	(Blackridge with Harthill: St Andrew's)	Keswick Cottage, Kingsmuir Drive, Peebles EH45 9AA [E-mail: hardies@bigfoot.com]	01721 724003
Hogg, Thomas M. BD	1986	2007	(Tranent)	22 Douglas Place, Galashiels TD1 3BT	01896 759381
Kellet, John M. MA	1962	1995	(Leith: South)	4 High Cottages, Walkerburn EH43 6AZ	01896 870351
Kennon, Stanley BA BD	1992	2000	Chaplain: Navy	The Chaplaincy, HMS *Drake*, HMMB Devonport, Plymouth PL2 2BG	
Laing, William F. DSC VRD MA	1952	1986	(Selkirk: St Mary's West)	10 The Glebe, Selkirk TD7 5AB	01750 21210
MacFarlane, David C. MA	1957	1997	(Eddleston with Peebles: Old)	11 Station Bank, Peebles EH45 8EJ	01721 720639
Moore, W. Haisley MA	1966	1996	(Secretary: The Boys' Brigade)	26 Tweedbank Avenue, Tweedbank, Galashiels TD1 3SP	01896 668577
Munson, Winnie (Ms) BD	1996	2006	(Delting with Northmavine)	6 St Cuthbert's Drive, St Boswells, Melrose TD6 0DF	01835 823375
Rae, Andrew W.	1951	1987	(Annan: St Andrew's Greenknowe Erskine)	Roseneuk, Tweedside Road, Newtown St Boswells TD6 0PQ	01835 823783
Rennie, John D. MA	1962	1996	(Broughton, Glenholm and Kilbucho with Skirling with Stobo and Drumelzier with Tweedsmuir)	29/1 Rosetta Road, Peebles EH45 8HJ [E-mail: tworennies@talktalk.net]	01721 720963
Riddell, John A. MA BD	1967	2006	(Jedburgh: Trinity)	Orchid Cottage, Gingham Row, Earlston TD4 6ET	01896 848784
Taverner, Glyn R. MA BD	1957	1995	(Maxton and Mertoun with St Boswells)	Woodcot Cottage, Waverley Road, Innerleithen EH44 6QW	01896 830156
Wallace, James H. MA BD	1973	2011	(Peebles: St Andrew's Leckie)	52 Waverley Mills, Innerleithen EH44 6RH [E-mail: jimwallace121@btinternet.com]	01896 831637

(5) DUNS

Meets at Duns, in the Old Parish Church Hall, normally on the first Tuesday of February, March, April, May, October, November and December, on the last Tuesday in June, and in places to be appointed on the first Tuesday of September.

Clerk: MRS HELEN LONGMUIR — **Viewfield, South Street, Gavinton, Duns TD11 3QT** **[E-mail: duns@cofscotland.org.uk]** — **01361 882728**

Ayton (H) and Burnmouth linked with Foulden and Mordington linked with Grantshouse and Houndwood and Reston

Norman R. Whyte BD MTh DipMin — 1982 — 2006 — The Manse, Beanburn, Ayton, Eyemouth TD14 5QY [E-mail: burraman@msn.com] — 01890 781333

Berwick-upon-Tweed: St Andrew's Wallace Green (H) and Lowick
Vacant — 3 Meadow Grange, Berwick-upon-Tweed TD15 1NW — 01289 303304

Bonkyl and Preston linked with Chirnside (H) linked with Edrom: Allanton (H)
Duncan E. Murray BA BD — 1970 — 2005 — Parish Church Manse, The Glebe, Chirnside, Duns TD11 3XL — 01890 819109
[E-mail: duncanemurray@tiscali.co.uk]

Chirnside See Bonkyl and Preston

Coldingham and St Abb's linked with Eyemouth
Daniel G. Lindsay BD — 1978 — 1979 — Victoria Road, Eyemouth TD14 5JD — 01890 750327

Coldstream (H) linked with Eccles
David J. Taverner MCIBS ACIS BD — 1996 — 2011 — 36 Bennecourt Drive, Coldstream TD12 4BY — 01890 883887
[E-mail: rahereuk@hotmail.com]

Duns (H)
Vacant — The Manse, Duns TD11 3DG — 01361 883755

Eccles See Coldstream
Edrom: Allanton See Bonkyl and Preston
Eyemouth See Coldingham and St Abb's

Fogo and Swinton linked with Ladykirk linked with Leitholm linked with Whitsome (H)
Alan C.D. Cartwright BSc BD — 1976 — Swinton, Duns TD11 3JJ — 01890 860228
[E-mail: alan@cartwright-family.co.uk]

Foulden and Mordington See Ayton and Burnmouth

Gordon: St Michael's linked with Greenlaw (H) linked with Legerwood linked with Westruther
Thomas S. Nicholson BD DPS — 1982 — 1995 — The Manse, Todholes, Greenlaw, Duns TD10 6XD — 01361 810316
[E-mail: nst54@hotmail.com]

Grantshouse and Houndwood and Reston See Ayton and Burnmouth
Greenlaw See Gordon: St Michael's

Hutton and Fishwick and Paxton
Continuing Vacancy

Ladykirk See Fogo and Swinton

Langton and Lammermuir Kirk
Ann Inglis (Mrs) LLB BD 1986 2003 The Manse, Cranshaws, Duns TD11 3SJ 01361 890289
[E-mail: revainglis@btinternet.com]

Legerwood See Gordon: St Michael's
Leitholm See Fogo and Swinton
Westruther See Gordon: St Michael's
Whitsome See Fogo and Swinton

Gaddes, Donald R.	1961	1994	(Kelso: North and Ednam)	35 Winterfield Gardens, Duns TD11 3EZ [E-mail: doruga@winterfield.fslife.co.uk]	01361 883172
Gale, Ronald A.A. LTh	1982	1995	(Dunoon: Old and St Cuthbert's)	55 Lennel Mount, Coldstream TD12 4NS	01890 883699
Hay, Bruce J.L.	1957	1997	(Makerstoun and Smailholm with Stichill, Hume and Nenthorn)	Assynt, 1 East Ord Gardens, Berwick-upon-Tweed TD15 2LS	01289 303171
Higham, Robert D. BD	1985	2002	(Tiree)	36 Low Greens, Berwick-upon-Tweed TD15 1LZ	01289 302392
Hope, Geraldine H. (Mrs) MA BD	1986	2007	(Foulden and Mordington with Hutton and Fishwick and Paxton)	4 Well Court, Chirnside, Duns TD11 3UD [E-mail: geraldine.hope@virgin.net]	01890 818134
Kerr, Andrew MA BLitt	1948	1991	(Kilbarchan: West)	4 Lairds Gate, Port Glasgow Road, Kilmacolm PA13 4EX	01507 874852
Landale, William S.	2005		Auxiliary Minister	Green Hope Guest House, Green Hope, Duns TD11 3SG	01361 890242
Ledgard, J. Christopher BA	1969	2004	(Ayton and Burnmouth with Grantshouse and Houndwood and Reston)	Streonshalh, 8 David Hume View, Chirnside, Duns TD11 3SX	01890 817105
Neill, Bruce F. MA BD	1966	2007	(Maxton and Mertoun with St Boswells)	18 Brierydean, St Abbs, Eyemouth TD14 5PQ	01890 771569
Paterson, William BD	1977	2001	(Bonkyl and Preston with Chirnside with Edrom: Allanton)	Benachie, Gavinton, Duns TD11 3QT	01361 882727
Walker, Kenneth D.F. MA BD PhD	1976	2008	(Athelstaneford with Whitekirk and Tyninghame)	Allanbank Kothi, Allanton, Duns TD11 3PY [E-mail: kenver.walker@btinternet.com]	01890 817102
Watson, James B. BSc	1968	2009	(Coldstream with Eccles)	49 Lennel Mount, Coldstream TD12 4NS	01890 883149

(6) JEDBURGH

Meets at various venues on the first Wednesday of February, March, May, September, October, November and December and on the last Wednesday of June.

Clerk REV. FRANK CAMPBELL 22 The Glebe, Ancrum, Jedburgh TD8 6UX 01835 830318
[E-mail: jedburgh@cofscotland.org.uk] 01835 830262 (Fax)

Ale and Teviot United (H) (Website: www.aleandteviot.org.uk)
Frank Campbell 1989 1991 22 The Glebe, Ancrum, Jedburgh TD8 6UX 01835 830318 (Tel)
[E-mail: jedburgh@cofscotland.org.uk] 01835 830262 (Fax)

Cavers and Kirkton linked with Hawick: Trinity
Michael D. Scouler MBE BSc BD 1988 2009 Kerrscroft, Howdenburn, Hawick TD9 8PH 01450 378248
[E-mail: michaelscouler@hotmail.co.uk]

Hawick: Burnfoot (Website: www.burnfootparishchurch.org.uk)
Charles J. Finnie LTh DPS 1991 1997 29 Wilton Hill, Hawick TD9 8BA 01450 373181
[E-mail: charles.finnie@gmail.com]

Hawick: St Mary's and Old (H)
Marina D. Brown (Mrs) MA BD MTh 2000 2007 The Manse of St Mary's and Old, Braid Road, Hawick TD9 9LZ 01450 378163
[E-mail: smop07@btinternet.com]

Hawick: Teviot (H) and Roberton
Neil R. Combe BSc MSc BD 1984 Teviot Manse, Buccleuch Road, Hawick TD9 0EL 01450 372150
[E-mail: neil.combe@btinternet.com]

Hawick: Trinity (H) See Cavers and Kirkton

Hawick: Wilton linked with Teviothead
Lisa-Jane Rankin (Miss) BD CPS 2003 4 Wilton Hill Terrace, Hawick TD9 8BE 01450 370744 (Tel/Fax)
[E-mail: revlj@talktalk.net]

Hobkirk and Southdean (Website: www.hobkirkruberslaw.org) linked with Ruberslaw (Website: www.hobkirkruberslaw.org)
Douglas A.O. Nicol MA BD 1974 2009 The Manse, Denholm, Hawick TD9 8NB 01450 870268
[E-mail: daon@lineone.net]

Jedburgh: Old and Trinity (Website: www.jedburgh-parish.org.uk)
Graham D. Astles BD MSc 2007 The Manse, Honeyfield Drive, Jedburgh TD8 6LQ 01835 863417
[E-mail: minister@jedburgh-parish.org.uk] 07906 290568 (Mbl)

Kelso Country Churches (Website: www.kelsolinkedchurchescofs.org) linked with Kelso: Old and Sprouston (Website: www.kelsolinkedchurchescofs.org)
Jenny Earl MA BD 2007 The Manse, 1 The Meadow, Stichill, Kelso TD5 7TG 01573 470607
[E-mail: jennyearl@btinternet.com]

Kelso: North (H) and Ednam (H) (01573 224154) (E-mail: office@kelsonorthandednam.org.uk) (Website: www.kelsonorthandednam.org.uk)
Tom McDonald BD 1994 20 Forestfield, Kelso TD5 7BX 01573 224677
[E-mail: revtom@20thepearlygates.co.uk]

Kelso: Old (H) and Sprouston See Kelso Country Churches

Linton, Morebattle, Hownam and Yetholm (H) (Website: www.cheviotchurches.org)
Robin D. McHaffie BD 1979 1991 The Manse, Main Street, Kirk Yetholm, Kelso TD5 8PF 01573 420308
[E-mail: robinmchaffie@f2s.com]

Oxnam (Website: www.oxnamkirk.co.uk)
Continued Vacancy

Ruberslaw See Hobkirk and Southdean
Teviothead See Hawick: Wilton

Auld, A. Graeme MA BD PhD DLitt FSAScot FRSE	1973		(University of Edinburgh)	Nether Swanshiel, Hobkirk, Bonchester Bridge, Hawick TD9 8JU [E-mail: a.g.auld@ed.ac.uk]	01450 860636
Dodd, Marion E. (Miss) MA BD LRAM	1988	2010	(Kelso: Old and Sprouston)	Esdaile, Tweedmount Road, Melrose TD6 9ST [E-mail: mariondodd@btinternet.com]	01896 822446
Finlay, Quintin BA BD	1975	1996	(North Bute)	Ivy Cottage, Greenlees Farm, Kelso TD5 8BT	(Mbl) 07901 981171
McNicol, Bruce	1967	2006	(Jedburgh: Old and Edgerston)	42 Dounehill, Jedburgh TD8 6LJ [E-mail: mcnicol95@btinternet.com]	01835 862991
Rodwell, Anna S. (Mrs) BD DipMin	1998	2003	(Langbank)	The Old Mill House, Hownam Howgate, Kelso TD5 8AJ [E-mail: anna.rodwell@gmail.com]	01573 440761
Shields, John M. MBE LTh	1972	2007	(Channelkirk and Lauder)	12 Eden Park, Ednam, Kelso TD5 7RG	01573 229015
Thomson, E.P. Lindsay MA	1964	2008	(Cavers and Kirkton with Hawick: Trinity	4 Bourtree Bank, Hawick TD9 9HP [E-mail: eplindsay@btinternet.com]	01450 374318

HAWICK ADDRESSES

		St Mary's and Old	Kirk Wynd	Wilton	Princes Street
		Teviot	off Buccleuch Road		
Burnfoot	Fraser Avenue	Trinity	Central Square		

(7) ANNANDALE AND ESKDALE

Meets on the first Tuesday of February, May, September and December, and the third Tuesday of March, June and October. The September meeting is held in the Moderator's charge. The other meetings are held in St Andrew's Parish Church, Gretna.

Clerk: REV. C. BRYAN HASTON LTh **The Manse, Gretna Green, Gretna DG16 5DU** **01461 338313**
[E-mail: annandaleeskdale@cofscotland.org.uk]
[E-mail: cbhaston@cofs.demon.co.uk]

Annan: Old (H) linked with Dornock
Hugh D. Steele LTh DipMin 1994 2004 12 Plumdon Park Avenue, Annan DG12 6EY 01461 201405
[E-mail: hugdebra@aol.com]

Annan: St Andrew's (H) linked with Brydekirk
John G. Pickles BD MTh MSc 2011 1 Annerley Road, Annan DG12 6HE 01461 202626
[E-mail: jgpickles@hotmail.com]

Applegarth, Sibbaldbie (H) and Johnstone linked with Lochmaben (H)
Jack M. Brown BSc BD 1977 2002 The Manse, Barrashead, Lochmaben, Lockerbie DG11 1QF 01387 810066
[E-mail: jackm.brown@tiscali.co.uk]

Brydekirk See Annan: St Andrew's

Canonbie United (H) linked with Liddesdale (H)
Stephen Fulcher BA MA 1993 2009 23 Langholm Street, Newcastleton TD9 0QX 01387 375242
[E-mail: steve@pcmanse.plus.com]

Dalton linked with Hightae linked with St Mungo
Vacant The Manse, Hightae, Lockerbie DG11 1JL 01387 811499

Dornock See Annan: Old

Gretna: Old (H), Gretna: St Andrew's (H) Half Morton and Kirkpatrick Fleming
C. Bryan Haston LTh 1975 The Manse, Gretna Green, Gretna DG16 5DU 01461 338313
[E-mail: cbhaston@cofs.demon.co.uk]

Hightae See Dalton

Hoddom, Kirtle-Eaglesfield and Middlebie
Vacant

Kirkpatrick Juxta linked with Moffat: St Andrew's (H) linked with Wamphray
Adam J. Dillon BD ThM 2003 2008 The Manse, 1 Meadowbank, Moffat DG10 9LR 01683 220128
[E-mail: adamdillon@btinternet.com]

Kirtle-Eaglesfield See Hoddom

Langholm Eskdalemuir Ewes and Westerkirk
I. Scott McCarthy BD 2010 The Manse, Langholm DG13 0BL 01387 380252
[E-mail: iscottmccarthy@googlemail.com]

Liddesdale (H) See Canonbie United
Lochmaben See Applegarth, Sibbaldbie and Johnstone

Lockerbie: Dryfesdale, Hutton and Corrie
Alexander C. Stoddart BD 2001 2008 The Manse, 5 Carlisle Road, Lockerbie DG11 2DW 01576 202361
[E-mail: sandystoddart@supanet.com]

Middlebie See Hoddom
Moffat: St Andrew's (H) See Kirkpatrick Juxta
St Mungo See Dalton

The Border Kirk (Church office: Chapel Street, Carlisle CA1 1JA; Tel: 01228 591757)
David G. Pitkeathly LLB BD 1996 2007 95 Pinecroft, Carlisle CA3 0DB 01228 593243 (Tel/Fax)
[E-mail: david.pitkeathly@btinternet.com]

Tundergarth
Continued Vacancy

Wamphray See Kirkpatrick Juxta

Annand, James M. MA BD	1955	1995	(Lockerbie: Dryfesdale)	48 Main Street, Newstead, Melrose TD6 9DX	
Beveridge, S. Edwin P. BA	1959	2004	(Brydekirk with Hoddom)	19 Rothesay Terrace, Edinburgh EH3 7RY	0131-225 3393
Byers, Alan J.	1959	1992	(Gamrie with King Edward)	Meadowbank, Plumdon Road, Annan DG12 6SJ	01461 206512
Byers, Mairi (Mrs) BTh CPS	1992	1998	(Jura)	Meadowbank, Plumdon Road, Annan DG12 6SJ	01461 206512
Gibb, James Daniel MacGhee BA LTh	1994	2006	(Aberfoyle with Port of Menteith)	21 Victoria Gardens, Eastriggs, Dumfries DG12 6TW [E-mail: dannygibb@hotmail.co.uk]	01461 40560
Harvey, P. Ruth (Ms)	2009	2007	Congregational Facilitator	Croslands, Beacon Street, Penrith CA11 7TL [E-mail: facilitator@phonecoop.coop]	01768 840749 (Mbl) 07882 259631
MacMillan, William M. LTh	1980	1998	(Kilmory with Lamlash)	Balskia, 61 Queen Street, Lochmaben DG11 1PP	01387 811528
Macpherson, Duncan J. BSc BD	1993	2002	Chaplain: Army	Household Cavalry Regiment, Combermere Barracks, Windsor, Berkshire SL4 3DN	
Ross, Alan C. CA BD	1988	2007	(Eskdalemuir with Hutton and Corrie with Tundergarth)	Yarra, Ettrickbridge, Selkirk TD7 5JN [E-mail: alkaross@aol.com]	01750 52324
Seaman, Ronald S. MA	1967	2007	(Dornock)	1 Springfield Farm Court, Springfield, Gretna DG16 5EH	01461 337228
Steenbergen, Pauline (Ms) MA BD	1996	2007	Congregational Facilitator	95 Pinecroft, Carlisle CA3 0DB [E-mail: psteenbergen@cofscotland.org.uk]	(Tel/Fax) 01228 593243 (Mbl) 07854 711988
Swinburne, Norman BA	1960	1993	(Sauchie)	Damerosehay, Birch Hill Lane, Kirkbride, Wigton CA7 5HZ	01697 351497

Vivers, Katherine A.	2004	Auxiliary Minister	Blacket House, Eaglesfield, Lockerbie DG11 3AA [E-mail: katevivers@yahoo.co.uk]	01461 500412
Williams, Trevor C. LTh	1990 2007	(Hoddom with Kirtle-Eaglesfield with Middlebie with Waterbeck)		

(8) DUMFRIES AND KIRKCUDBRIGHT

Meets at Dumfries on the last Wednesday of February, June, September and November.

Clerk:	**REV. GORDON M.A. SAVAGE MA BD**	**11 Laurieknowe, Dumfries DG2 7AH** **[E-mail: dumfrieskirkcudbright@cofscotland.org.uk]**	**01387 252929**
Depute Clerk:	**REV. WILLIAM T. HOGG MA BD**	**The Manse, Glasgow Road, Sanquhar DG4 6BZ** **[E-mail: wthogg@yahoo.com]**	**01659 50247**

Auchencairn (H) and Rerrick linked with Buittle (H) and Kelton (H)

Vacant			Auchencairn, Castle Douglas DG7 1QS	01556 640041

Balmaclellan and Kells (H) linked with Carsphairn (H) linked with Dalry (H)

David S. Bartholomew BSc MSc PhD BD	1994		The Manse, Dalry, Castle Douglas DG7 3PJ [E-mail: dhbart@care4free.net]	01644 430380

Balmaghie linked with Tarff and Twynholm (H)

Christopher Wallace BD DipMin	1988		Manse Road, Twynholm, Kirkcudbright DG6 4NY [E-mail: minister@twynholm.org.uk]	01557 860381

Borgue linked with Gatehouse of Fleet

Valerie J. Ott (Mrs) BA BD	2002		The Manse, Planetree Park, Gatehouse of Fleet, Castle Douglas DG7 2EQ [E-mail: dandvott@aol.com]	01557 814233

Buittle and Kelton See Auchencairn and Rerrick

Caerlaverock linked with Dumfries: St Mary's-Greyfriars

Gordon A. McCracken BD CertMin DMin	1988	2010	4 Georgetown Crescent, Dumfries DG1 4EQ [E-mail: gordonangus@btopenworld.com]	01387 253877

Carsphairn See Balmaclellan and Kells

Castle Douglas (H)
Robert J. Malloch BD 1987 2001 1 Castle View, Castle Douglas DG7 1BG 01556 502171
[E-mail: rojama@live.com]

Closeburn
Continued Vacancy

Colvend, Southwick and Kirkbean
James F. Gatherer BD 1984 2003 The Manse, Colvend, Dalbeattie DG5 4QN 01556 630255
[E-mail: james@gatherer.net]

Corsock and Kirkpatrick Durham linked with Crossmichael and Parton
Sally Russell BTh MTh 2006 Knockdrocket, Clarebrand, Castle Douglas DG7 3AH 01556 503645
[E-mail: rev.sal@btinternet.com]

Crossmichael and Parton See Corsock and Kirkpatrick Durham

Cummertrees, Mouswald and Ruthwell (H)
Vacant The Manse, Ruthwell, Dumfries DG1 4NP 01387 870217
(New charge formed by the union of Cummertrees, Mouswald and Ruthwell)

Dalbeattie (H) linked with Urr (H)
Norman M. Hutcheson MA BD 1973 1988 36 Mill Street, Dalbeattie DG5 4HE 01556 610029
[E-mail: norman.hutcheson@virgin.net]

Dalry See Balmaclellan and Kells

Dumfries: Maxwelltown West (H)
Gordon M.A. Savage MA BD 1977 1984 Maxwelltown West Manse, 11 Laurieknowe, Dumfries DG2 7AH 01387 252929
[E-mail: gordon.savage@cdsmail.co.uk]

Dumfries: Northwest
Neil G. Campbell BA BD 1988 2006 27 St Anne's Road, Dumfries DG2 9HZ 01387 249964
[E-mail: mail@neilgcampbell.co.uk]

Dumfries: St George's (H)
Donald Campbell BD 1997 9 Nunholm Park, Dumfries DG1 1JP 01387 252965
[E-mail: saint-georges@ukonline.co.uk]

Dumfries: St Mary's-Greyfriars (H) See Caerlaverock

Dumfries: St Michael's and South
Maurice S. Bond MTh BA DipEd PhD 1981 1999 39 Cardoness Street, Dumfries DG1 3AL 01387 253849
[E-mail: mauricebond399@btinternet.com]

Dumfries: Troqueer (H)
William W. Kelly BSc BD 1994 Troqueer Manse, Troqueer Road, Dumfries DG2 7DF 01387 253043
[E-mail: wwkelly@yahoo.com]

Dunscore linked with Glencairn and Moniaive
Christine Sime (Miss) BSc BD 1994 Wallaceton, Auldgirth, Dumfries DG2 0TJ 01387 820245
[E-mail: revsime@btinternet.com]

Durisdeer linked with Penpont, Keir and Tynron linked with Thornhill (H)
Vacant The Manse, Manse Park, Thornhill DG3 5ER 01848 331191

Gatehouse of Fleet See Borgue
Glencairn and Moniaive See Dunscore

Irongray, Lochrutton and Terregles
Vacant Shawhead Road, Dumfries DG2 9SJ 01387 730287

Kirkconnel (H)
Alistair J. MacKichan MA BD 1984 2009 The Manse, 31 Kingsway, Kirkconnel, Sanquhar DG4 6PN 01659 67241

Kirkcudbright (H)
Douglas R. Irving LLB BD WS 1984 1998 6 Bourtree Avenue, Kirkcudbright DG6 4AU 01557 330489
[E-mail: douglasirving05@tiscali.co.uk]

Kirkgunzeon linked with Lochend and New Abbey
Vacant The Manse, 28 Main Street, New Abbey, Dumfries DG2 8BY 01387 850232

Kirkmahoe
David M. Almond BD 1996 2008 The Manse, Kirkmahoe, Dumfries DG1 1ST 01387 710572
[E-mail: almond.david138@googlemail.com]

Kirkmichael, Tinwald and Torthorwald
Willem J. Bezuidenhout BA BD MHEd MEd 1977 2010 Manse of Tinwald, Tinwald, Dumfries DG1 3PL 01387 710246
[E-mail: willembezuidenhout@btinternet.com]

Lochend and New Abbey See Kirkgunzeon
Penpont, Keir and Tynron See Durisdeer

Sanquhar: St Bride's (H)
William T. Hogg MA BD 1979 2000 St Bride's Manse, Glasgow Road, Sanquhar DG6 6BZ 01659 50247
[E-mail: wthogg@yahoo.com]

Tarff and Twynholm See Balmaghie
Thornhill (H) See Durisdeer
Urr See Dalbeattie

Bennett, David K.P. BA	1974	2000	(Kirkpatrick Irongray with Lochrutton with Terregles)	53 Anne Arundel Court, Heathhall, Dumfries DG1 3SL	01387 257755
Duncan, Maureen M. (Mrs) BD	1996	2008	(Dunlop)	Dunedin, Whitepark, Castle Douglas DG7 1QA [E-mail: revmo@talktalk.net]	01556 502867
Geddes, Alexander J. MA BD	1960	1998	(Stewarton: St Columba's)	166 Georgetown Road, Dumfries DG1 4DT [E-mail: sandy.elizabeth@tiscali.co.uk]	01387 252287
Greer, A. David C. LLB DMin DipAdultEd	1956	1996	(Barra)	17 Duthac Wynd, Tain IV19 1LP [E-mail: kandadc@greer10.fsnet.co.uk]	01862 892065
Hamill, Robert BA	1956	1989	(Castle Douglas: St Ringan's)	11 St Andrew Drive, Castle Douglas DG7 1EW	01556 502962
Hammond, Richard J. BA BD	1993	2007	(Kirkmahoe)	3 Marchfield Mount, Marchfield, Dumfries DG1 1SE [E-mail: libby.hammond@virgin.net]	(Mbl) 07764 465783
Henig, Gordon BSc BD	1997	2003	(Bellie with Speymouth)	4 Galla Crescent, Dalbeattie DG5 4JY	01556 611183
Holland, William MA	1967	2009	(Lochend and New Abbey)	Ardshean, 55 Georgetown Road, Dumfries DG1 4DD [E-mail: billholland55@btinternet.com]	01387 256131 (Mbl) 07766 531732
Kirk, W. Logan MA BD MTh	1988	2000	(Dalton with Hightae with St Mungo)	2 Raecroft Avenue, Collin, Dumfries DG1 4LP	01387 750489
Leishman, James S. LTh BD MA(Div)	1969	1999	(Kirkmichael with Tinwald with Torthorwald)	11 Hunter Avenue, Heathhall, Dumfries DG1 3UX	01387 249241
Mack, Elizabeth A. (Miss) DipEd	1994	2011	(Auxiliary Minister)	24 Roberts Crescent, Dumfries DG2 7RS [E-mail: mackliz@btinternet.com]	01387 264847
McKay, David M. MA BD	1979	2007	(Kirkpatrick Juxta with Moffat: St Andrew's with Wamphray)	20 Auld Brig View, Auldgirth, Dumfries DG2 0XE [E-mail: davidmckay20@tiscali.co.uk]	01387 740013
McKenzie, William M. DA	1958	1993	(Dumfries: Troqueer)	41 Kingholm Road, Dumfries DG1 4SR [E-mail: mckenzie.dumfries@virgin.net]	01387 253688
Miller, John G. BEd BD MTh	1983	2005	(Port Glasgow: St Martin's)	22 Lime Grove, Georgetown, Dumfries DG1 4SQ [E-mail: johnmiller22@hotmail.co.uk]	01387 252502
Miller, John R. MA BD	1958	1992	(Carsphairn with Dalry)	4 Fairgreen Court, Rhonehouse, Castle Douglas DG7 1SA	01556 680428

Owen, John J.C. LTh	1967	2001	(Applegarth and Sibbaldbie with Lochmaben)	5 Galla Avenue, Dalbeattie DG5 4JZ [E-mail: jj.owen@onetel.net]	01556 612125
Robertson, Ian W. MA BD	1956	1995	(Colvend, Southwick and Kirkbean)	10 Marjoriebanks, Lochmaben, Lockerbie DG11 1QH	01387 810541
Smith, Richmond OBE MA BD	1952	1983	(World Alliance of Reformed Churches)	Aignish, Merse Way, Kippford, Dalbeattie DG5 4LH	01556 620624
Strachan, Alexander E. MA BD	1974	1999	Dumfries Health Care Chaplain	2 Leafield Road, Dumfries DG1 2DS [E-mail: aestrachan@aol.com]	01387 279460
Sutherland, Colin A. LTh	1995	2007	(Blantyre: Livingstone Memorial)	71 Caulstran Road, Dumfries DG2 9FJ [E-mail: colin.csutherland@btinternet.com]	01387 279954
Vincent, C. Raymond MA FSAScot	1952	1992	(Stonehouse)	Rosebank, Newton Stewart Road, New Galloway, Castle Douglas DG7 3RT	01644 420451
Wilkie, James R. MA MTh	1957	1993	(Penpont, Keir and Tynron)	31 West Morton Street, Thornhill DG3 5NF	01848 331028
Williamson, James BA BD	1986	2009	(Cummertrees with Mouswald with Ruthwell)	12 Mulberry Drive, Dunfermline KY11 8BZ [E-mail: jimwill@rcmkirk.fsnet.co.uk]	01383 734872
Wotherspoon, Robert C. LTh	1976	1998	(Corsock and Kirkpatrick Durham with Crossmichael and Parton)	7 Hillowton Drive, Castle Douglas DG7 1LL [E-mail: robert.wotherspoon@tiscali.co.uk]	01556 502267
Young, John MTh DipMin	1963	1999	(Airdrie: Broomknoll)	Craigview, North Street, Moniaive, Thornhill DG3 4HR	01848 200318

DUMFRIES ADDRESSES

		Northwest	Lochside Road	St Michael's and South	St Michael's Street
		St George's	George Street	Troqueer	Troqueer Road
Maxwelltown West	Laurieknowe	St Mary's-Greyfriars	St Mary's Street		

(9) WIGTOWN AND STRANRAER

Meets at Glenluce, in the church hall, on the first Tuesday of March, October and December for ordinary business; on the first Tuesday of September for formal business followed by meetings of committees; on the first Tuesday of November, February and May for worship followed by meetings of committees; and at a church designated by the Moderator on the first Tuesday of June for Holy Communion followed by ordinary business.

Clerk:	**MRS NICOLA STEEL**	**Auchengallie Farm, Port William, Newton Stewart DG8 9RQ [E-mail: wigtownstranraer@cofscotland.org.uk]**	**01988 700534**

Ervie Kirkcolm linked with Leswalt

Michael J. Sheppard BD	1997	Ervie Manse, Stranraer DG9 0QZ [E-mail: mjs@uwclub.net]	01776 854225

Glasserton and Isle of Whithorn linked with Whithorn: St Ninian's Priory				
Alexander I. Currie BD CPS	1990		The Manse, Whithorn, Newton Stewart DG8 8PT	01988 500267
Inch linked with Stranraer: Town Kirk (H)				
John H. Burns BSc BD	1985	1988	Bayview Road, Stranraer DG9 8BE	01776 702383
Kirkcowan (H) linked with Wigtown (H)				
Eric Boyle BA MTh	2006		Seaview Manse, Church Lane, Wigtown, Newton Stewart DG8 9HT [E-mail: ecthered@aol.com]	01988 402314
Kirkinner linked with Sorbie (H)				
Jeffrey M. Mead BD	1978	1986	The Manse, Kirkinner, Newton Stewart DG8 9AL	01988 840643
Kirkmabreck linked with Monigaff (H)				
Peter W.I. Aiken	1996	2005	Creebridge, Newton Stewart DG8 6NR [E-mail: aikenp@btinternet.com]	01671 403361
Kirkmaiden (H) linked with Stoneykirk				
Melvyn J. Griffiths BTh DipTheol DMin	1978	2011	Church Road, Sandhead, Stranraer DG9 9JJ [E-mail: mel@thehavyn.wanadoo.co.uk]	01776 830548
Leswalt See Ervie Kirkcolm				
Mochrum (H)				
Mary C. McLauchlan (Mrs) LTh	1997	2010	Manse of Mochrum, Port William, Newton Stewart DG8 9QP [E-mail: mary@revmother.co.uk]	01988 700871
Monigaff (H) See Kirkmabreck				
New Luce (H) linked with Old Luce (H)				
Thomas M. McWhirter MA MSc BD	1992	1997	Glenluce, Newton Stewart DG8 0PU	01581 300319
Old Luce See New Luce				
Penninghame (H)				
Edward D. Lyons BD MTh	2007		The Manse, 1A Corvisel Road, Newton Stewart DG8 6LW [E-mail: edwardlyons@hotmail.com]	01671 404425

Portpatrick linked with Stranraer: St Ninian's (H)

Gordon Kennedy BSc BD MTh	1993	2000	2 Albert Terrace, London Road, Stranraer DG9 8AB [E-mail: gordon.k1@btinternet.com]	01776 702443

Sorbie See Kirkinner
Stoneykirk See Kirkmaiden

Stranraer: High Kirk (H)

Ian McIlroy BSS BD	1996	2009	Stoneleigh, Whitehouse Road, Stranraer DG9 0JB	01776 700616

Stranraer: St Ninian's See Portpatrick
Stranraer: Town Kirk See Inch
Whithorn: St Ninian's Priory See Glasserton and Isle of Whithorn
Wigtown See Kirkcowan

Binks, Mike	2007 2009	Auxiliary Minister	5 Maxwell Drive, Newton Stewart DG8 6EL [E-mail: mike@hollybank.net]	01671 402201 (Mbl) 07590 507917
Crawford, Joseph F. BA	1970 2006	(Bowden with Newtown)	21 South Street, Port William, Newton Stewart DG8 9SH	01988 700761
Dean, Roger A.F. LTh	1983 2004	(Mochrum)	Albion Cottage, 59 Main Street, Kirkinner, Newton Stewart DG8 9AN [E-mail: roger.dean4@btopenworld.com]	01988 840621
Dutton, David W. BA	1973 2008	(Stranraer: High Kirk)	13 Acredales, Haddington EH41 4NT	
McGill, Thomas W.	1972 1990	(Portpatrick with Stranraer: St Ninian's)	Westfell, Monreith, Newton Stewart DG8 9LT	01988 700449
Munro, Mary (Mrs) BA	1993 2004	(Auxiliary Minister)	14 Auchneel Crescent, Stranraer DG9 0JH	01776 702305
Munro, Sheila BD	1995 2003	Chaplain: RAF	RAF Halton, Aylesbury, Bucks HP22 5PG	
Ogilvy, Oliver M.	1959 1985	(Leswalt)	8 Dale Crescent, Stranraer DG9 0HG	01776 706285

(10) AYR

Meets on the first Tuesday of every month from September to May, excluding January, and on the fourth Tuesday of June. The June meeting will be held in the Moderator's church. One meeting will be held in a venue to be determined by the Business Committee. Other meetings will be held in Alloway Church Hall.

Clerk:	**REV. KENNETH C. ELLIOTT BD BA CertMin**	**68 St Quivox Road, Prestwick KA9 1JF** **[E-mail: ayr@cofscotland.org.uk]**	**01292 478788**
Presbytery Office:		**Prestwick South Parish Church, 50 Main Street, Prestwick KA9 1NX** **[E-mail: ayroffice@cofscotland.org.uk]**	**01292 678556**

Alloway (H)				
Neil A. McNaught BD MA	1987	1999	1A Parkview, Alloway, Ayr KA7 4QG [E-mail: neil@mcnaught3427.freeserve.co.uk]	01292 441252
Annbank (H) linked with Tarbolton				
Alexander Shuttleworth MA BD	2004		1 Kirkport, Tarbolton, Mauchline KA5 5QJ [E-mail: revshuttleworth@aol.com]	01292 541236
Auchinleck (H) linked with Catrine				
Stephen F. Clipston MA BD	1982	2006	28 Mauchline Road, Auchinleck KA18 2BN [E-mail: steveclipston@btinternet.com]	01290 424776
Ayr: Auld Kirk of Ayr (St John the Baptist) (H)				
David R. Gemmell MA BD	1991	1999	58 Monument Road, Ayr KA7 2UB [E-mail: drgemmell@hotmail.com]	01292 262580 (Tel/Fax)
Ayr: Castlehill (H)				
Elizabeth A. Crumlish (Mrs) BD	1995	2008	3 Old Hillfoot Road, Ayr KA7 3LW [E-mail: lizcrumlish@aol.com]	01292 263001
Douglas T. Moore (Aux)	2003	2009	9 Midton Avenue, Prestwick KA9 1PU [E-mail: douglastmoore@hotmail.com]	01292 671352
Ayr: Newton Wallacetown (H)				
G. Stewart Birse CA BD BSc	1980	1989	9 Nursery Grove, Ayr KA7 3PH [E-mail: axhp44@dsl.pipex.com]	01292 264251

Ayr: St Andrew's (H)
Harry B. Mealyea BArch BD | 1984 | 2000 | 31 Bellevue Crescent, Ayr KA7 2DP [E-mail: mealyea@tiscali.co.uk] | 01292 261126

Ayr: St Columba (H)
Fraser R. Aitken MA BD | 1978 | 1991 | 3 Upper Crofts, Alloway, Ayr KA7 4QX [E-mail: frasercolumba@msn.com] | 01292 443747

Ayr: St James' (H)
Robert McCrum BSc BD | 1982 | 2005 | 1 Prestwick Road, Ayr KA8 8LD [E-mail: robert@stjamesayr.org.uk] | 01292 262420

Ayr: St Leonard's (H) linked with Dalrymple
Vacant

Ayr: St Quivox (H)
Rona M. Young (Mrs) BD DipEd | 1991 | 2009 | 11 Springfield Avenue, Prestwick KA9 2HA [E-mail: revronyoung@hotmail.com] | 01292 478306

Ballantrae (H) linked with St Colmon (Arnsheen Barrhill and Colmonell)
Stephen Ogston MPhys MSc BD | 2009 | The Manse, 1 The Vennel, Ballantrae, Girvan KA26 0NH [E-mail: ogston@macfish.com] | 01465 831252

Barr linked with Dailly linked with Girvan South
Ian K. McLachlan MA BD | 1999 | 30 Henrietta Street, Girvan KA26 9AL [E-mail: iankmclachlan@yetiville.freeserve.co.uk] | 01465 713370

Catrine See Auchinleck

Coylton linked with Drongan: The Schaw Kirk
David Whiteman BD | 1998 | 2008 | 4 Hamilton Place, Coylton, Ayr KA6 6JQ [E-mail: davesoo@sky.com] | 01292 571442

Craigie linked with Symington
Glenda J. Keating (Mrs) MTh | 1996 | 2008 | 16 Kerrix Road, Symington, Kilmarnock KA1 5QD [E-mail: kirkglen@btinternet.com] | 01563 830205

Crosshill (H) linked with Maybole
Brian Hendrie BD 1992 2010 The Manse, 3 Barns Terrace, Maybole KA19 7EP 01655 883710
[E-mail: hendrie962@btinternet.com]

Dailly See Barr

Dalmellington linked with Patna: Waterside
Vacant 4 Carsphairn Road, Dalmellington, Ayr KA6 7RE 01292 550353
Muriel Wilson (Ms) DCS BD 28 Bellevue Crescent, Ayr KA7 2DR 01292 264939
[E-mail: muriel.wilson4@btinternet.com]

Dalrymple See Ayr: St Leonard's
Drongan: The Schaw Kirk See Coylton

Dundonald (H)
Robert Mayes BD 1982 1988 64 Main Street, Dundonald, Kilmarnock KA2 9HG 01563 850243
[E-mail: bobmayes@fsmail.net]

Fisherton (H) linked with Kirkoswald
Arrick D. Wilkinson BSc BD 2000 2003 The Manse, Kirkoswald, Maybole KA19 8HZ 01655 760210
[E-mail: arrick@clergy.net]

Girvan: North (Old and St Andrew's) (H)
Vacant 38 The Avenue, Girvan KA26 9DS 01465 713203

Girvan: South See Barr

Kirkmichael linked with Straiton: St Cuthbert's
W. Gerald Jones MA BD MTh 1984 1985 Patna Road, Kirkmichael, Maybole KA19 7PJ 01655 750286
[E-mail: revgerald@jonesg99.freeserve.co.uk]

Kirkoswald (H) See Fisherton

Lugar linked with Old Cumnock: Old (H)
John W. Paterson BSc BD DipEd 1994 33 Barrhill Road, Cumnock KA18 1PJ 01290 420769
[E-mail: ocochurchwow@hotmail.com]
Nancy Jackson (Aux) 2009 Cygnet House, Holmfarm Road, Catrine, Mauchline KA5 6TA 01290 550511

Mauchline (H) linked with Sorn				
David A. Albon BA MCS	1991	2011	4 Westside Gardens, Mauchline KA5 5DJ [E-mail: albon@onetel.com]	01290 518528
Maybole See Crosshill				
Monkton and Prestwick: North (H)				
David Clarkson BSc BA MTh	2010		40 Monkton Road, Prestwick KA9 1AR [E-mail: revdavidclarkson@gmail.com]	01292 471379
Muirkirk (H) linked with Old Cumnock: Trinity				
Scott M. Rae MBE BD CPS	1976	2008	46 Ayr Road, Cumnock KA18 1DW [E-mail: scottrae1@btopenworld.com]	01290 422145
New Cumnock (H)				
Helen E. Cuthbert MA MSc BD	2009		37 Castle, New Cumnock, Cumnock KA18 4AG [E-mail: helencuthbert@mypostoffice.co.uk]	01290 338296
Ochiltree linked with Stair				
William R. Johnston BD	1998	2009	10 Mauchline Road, Ochiltree, Cumnock KA18 2PZ	01290 700365
Old Cumnock: Old See Lugar **Old Cumnock: Trinity** See Muirkirk **Patna: Waterside** See Dalmellington				
Prestwick: Kingcase (H) (E-mail: office@kingcase.freeserve.co.uk)				
T. David Watson BSc BD	1988	1997	15 Bellrock Avenue, Prestwick KA9 1SQ [E-mail: tdavidwatson@btinternet.com]	01292 479571
Prestwick: St Nicholas' (H)				
George R. Fiddes BD	1979	1985	3 Bellevue Road, Prestwick KA9 1NW [E-mail: gfiddes@stnicholasprestwick.org.uk]	01292 477613
Prestwick: South (H)				
Kenneth C. Elliott BD BA CertMin	1989		68 St Quivox Road, Prestwick KA9 1JF [E-mail: kcelliott@tiscali.co.uk]	01292 478788

St Colmon (Arnsheen Barrhill and Colmonell) See Ballantrae
Sorn See Mauchline
Stair See Ochiltree
Straiton: St Cuthbert's See Kirkmichael
Symington See Craigie
Tarbolton See Annbank

Troon: Old (H)				
Alastair H. Symington MA BD	1972	1998	85 Bentinck Drive, Troon KA10 6HZ [E-mail: revdahs@talktalk.net]	01292 313644
Troon: Portland (H)				
Vacant			89 South Beach, Troon KA10 6EQ	01292 313285
Troon: St Meddan's (H) (E-mail: st.meddan@virgin.net)				
David L. Harper BSc BD	1972	1979	27 Bentinck Drive, Troon KA10 6HX [E-mail: d.l.harper@btinternet.com]	01292 311784

Baker, Carolyn M. (Mrs) BD	1997	2008	(Ochiltree with Stair)	Clanary, 1 Maxwell Drive, Newton Stewart DG8 6EL [E-mail: cncbaker@btinternet.com]	
Blyth, James G.S. BSc BD	1963	1986	(Glenmuick)	40 Robsland Avenue, Ayr KA7 2RW	01292 261276
Bogle, Thomas C. BD	1983	2003	(Fisherton with Maybole: West)	38 McEwan Crescent, Mossblown, Ayr KA6 5DR	01292 521215
Boyd, Ronald M.H. BD DipTh	1995	2010	Chaplain and Teacher of RMPS: Queen Victoria School, Dunblane	6 Victoria Green, Queen Victoria School, Dunblane FK15 0JY	01786 822288
Cranston, George BD	1976	2001	(Rutherglen: Wardlawhill)	20 Capperview, Prestwick KA9 1BH	01292 476627
Crichton, James MA BD MTh	1969	2010	(Crosshill with Dalrymple)	4B Garden Court, Ayr KA8 0AT [E-mail: crichton.james@btinternet.com]	01292 288978
Dickie, Michael M. BSc	1955	1994	(Ayr: Castlehill)	8 Noltmire Road, Ayr KA8 9ES	01292 618512
Glencross, William M. LTh	1968	1999	(Bellshill: Macdonald Memorial)	1 Lochay Place, Troon KA10 7HH	01292 317097
Grant, J. Gordon MA BD PhD	1957	1997	(Edinburgh: Dean)	33 Fullarton Drive, Troon KA10 6LE	01292 311852
Guthrie, James A.	1969	2005	(Corsock and Kirkpatrick Durham with Crossmichael and Parton)	2 Barrhill Road, Pinwherry, Girvan KA26 0QE [E-mail: p.h.m.guthrie@btinternet.com]	01465 841236
Hannah, William BD MCAM MIPR	1987	2001	(Muirkirk)	8 Dovecote View, Kirkintilloch, Glasgow G66 3HY [E-mail: revbillnews@btinternet.com]	0141-776 1337
Harris, Samuel McC. OStJ BA BD	1974	2010	(Rothesay: Trinity)	36 Adam Wood Court, Troon KA10 6BP	01292 319603
Helon, George G. BA BD	1984	2000	(Barr linked with Dailly)	9 Park Road, Maxwelltown, Dumfries DG2 7PW	01387 259255
Johnston, Kenneth L. BA LTh	1969	2001	(Annbank)	2 Rylands, Prestwick KA9 2DX [E-mail: ken@kenston.co.uk]	01292 471980
Kent, Arthur F.S.	1966	1999	(Monkton and Prestwick: North)	17 St David's Drive, Evesham, Worcs WR11 6AS [E-mail: afskent@onetel.com]	01386 421562

Name	Ord.	Ret.	Charge	Address	Tel.
King, Chris (Mrs) MA BD DCS			Deaconess	28 Kilnford Drive, Dundonald, Kilmarnock KA2 9ET	01563 851197
Laing, Iain A. MA BD	1971	2009	(Bishopbriggs: Kenmuir)	9 Annfield Road, Prestwick KA9 1PP [E-mail: iandrlaing@yahoo.co.uk]	01292 471732
Lennox, Lawrie I. MA BD DipEd	1991	2006	(Cromar)	7 Carwinshoch View, Ayr KA7 4AY [E-mail: lawrie@lennox.myzen.co.uk]	
Lochrie, John S. BSc BD MTh PhD	1967	2008	(St Colmon)	Cosyglen, Kilkerran, Maybole KA19 8LS	01465 811262
Lynn, Robert MA BD	1984	2011	(Ayr: St Leonard's with Dalrymple)	8 Kirkbrae, Maybole KA19 7ER	(Mbl) 07771 481698
McCrorie, William	1965	1999	(Free Church Chaplain: Royal Brompton Hospital)	12 Shieling Park, Ayr KA7 2UR [E-mail: billevemccrorie@btinternet.com]	01292 288854
Macdonald, Ian U.	1960	1997	(Tarbolton)	18 Belmont Road, Ayr KA7 2PF	01292 283085
McNidder, Roderick H. BD	1987	1997	Chaplain: NHS Ayrshire and Arran Trust	6 Hollow Park, Alloway, Ayr KA7 4SR	01292 442554
McPhail, Andrew M. BA	1968	2002	(Ayr: Wallacetown)	25 Maybole Road, Ayr KA7 2QA	01292 282108
Mitchell, Sheila M. (Miss) BD MTh	1995	2002	Chaplain: NHS Ayrshire and Arran Trust	Ailsa Hospital, Ayr KA6 6BQ	01292 610556
Morrison, Alistair H. BTh DipYCS	1985	2004	(Paisley: St Mark's Oldhall)	92 St Leonard's Road, Ayr KA7 2PU [E-mail: alistairmorrison@supanet.com]	01292 266021
Ness, David T. LTh	1972	2008	(Ayr: St Quivox)	17 Winston Avenue, Prestwick KA9 2EZ [E-mail: dtness@tiscali.co.uk]	
Russell, Paul R. MA BD	1984	2006	Chaplain: NHS Ayrshire and Arran Trust	23 Nursery Wynd, Ayr KA7 3NZ	01292 618020
Sanderson, Alastair M. BA LTh	1971	2007	(Craigie with Symington)	26 Main Street, Monkton, Prestwick KA9 2QL [E-mail: alel@sanderson29.fsnet.co.uk]	01292 475819
Saunders, Campbell M. MA BD	1952	1989	(Ayr: St Leonard's)	27 St Vincent Crescent, Alloway, Ayr KA7 4QW	01292 441673
Simpson, Edward V. BSc BD	1972	2009	(Glasgow: Giffnock South)	8 Paddock View, Thorntoun, Crosshouse, Kilmarnock KA2 0BH [E-mail: eddie.simpson3@talktalk.net]	01563 522841
Smith, Elizabeth (Mrs) BD	1996	2009	(Fauldhouse: St Andrew's)	16 McIntyre Road, Prestwick KA9 1BE [E-mail: smithrevb@btinternet.com]	01292 471588
Stirling, Ian R. BSc BD	1990	2002	Chaplain: The Ayrshire Hospice	Ayrshire Hospice, 35–37 Racecourse Road, Ayr KA7 2TG	01292 269200
Yorke, Kenneth B.	1982	2009	(Dalmellington with Patna: Waterside)	13 Annfield Terrace, Prestwick KA9 1PS [E-mail: kenneth.yorke@googlemail.com]	(Mbl) 07766 320525

AYR ADDRESSES

Ayr

Auld Kirk	Kirkport (116 High Street)
Castlehill	Castlehill Road x Hillfoot Road
Newton Wallacetown	Main Street
St Andrew's	Park Circus
St Columba	Midton Road x Carrick Park
St James'	Prestwick Road x Falkland Park Road
St Leonard's	St Leonard's Road x Monument Road

Girvan

North	Montgomerie Street
South	Stair Park

Prestwick

Kingcase	Waterloo Road
Monkton and Prestwick North	Monkton Road
St Nicholas	Main Street
South	Main Street

Troon

Old	Ayr Street
Portland	St Meddan's Street
St Meddan's	St Meddan's Street

(11) IRVINE AND KILMARNOCK

The Presbytery meets ordinarily at 6:30pm in the Hall of Howard St Andrew's Church, Kilmarnock, on the first Tuesday of each month from September to May (except January and April), and on the fourth Tuesday in June. The September meeting begins with the celebration of Holy Communion.

Clerk: REV. COLIN G.F. BROCKIE BSc(Eng) BD SOSc — 36 Braehead Court, Kilmarnock KA3 7AB — 01563 526295
[E-mail: irvinekilmarnock@cofscotland.org.uk]

Mr Brockie will retire as Clerk on 31 December 2011. His successor will be Mr I. Steuart Dey, the current Depute Clerk, whose details are as follows:
Depute Clerk: I. STEUART DEY LLB NP — 72 Dundonald Road, Kilmarnock KA1 1RZ — 01563 521686
[E-mail: steuart.dey@btinternet.com]

The Depute Clerk from 31 December 2011 will be Rev. S. Grant Barclay LLB BD, Minister of Kilmarnock: St Kentigern's.
Treasurer: JAMES McINTOSH BA CA — 15 Dundonald Road, Kilmarnock KA1 1RU — 01563 523552

The Presbytery office is manned each Tuesday, Wednesday and Thursday from 9am until 12:45pm. The office telephone number is 01563 526295.

Caldwell linked with Dunlop				
David Donaldson MA BD DMin	1969	2010	4 Dampark, Dunlop, Kilmarnock KA3 4BZ [E-mail: jd.donaldson@talktalk.net]	01560 483268
Crosshouse				
T. Edward Marshall BD	1987	2007	27 Kilmarnock Road, Crosshouse, Kilmarnock KA2 0EZ [E-mail: marshall862@btinternet.com]	01563 524089
Darvel (01560 322924)				
Charles Lines BA	2010		46 West Main Street, Darvel KA17 0AQ [E-mail: cmdlines@tiscali.co.uk]	01560 322924
Dreghorn and Springside				
Gary E. Horsburgh BA	1976	1983	96A Townfoot, Dreghorn, Irvine KA11 4EZ [E-mail: garyhorsburgh@hotmail.co.uk]	01294 217770
Dunlop See Caldwell				
Fenwick (H)				
Geoffrey Redmayne BSc BD MPhil	2000		2 Kirkton Place, Fenwick, Kilmarnock KA3 6DW [E-mail: gnredmayne@googlemail.com]	01560 600217

Galston (H) (01563 820136)

Graeme R. Wilson MCIBS BD ThM	2006		60 Brewland Street, Galston KA4 8DX [E-mail: graeme.wilson@gmail.com]	01563 820246
John H.B. Taylor MA BD DipEd FEIS (Assoc)	1952	1990	62 Woodlands Grove, Kilmarnock KA3 1TZ	01563 526698

Hurlford (H)

James D. McCulloch BD MIOP MIP3	1996		12 Main Road, Crookedholm, Kilmarnock KA3 6JT [E-mail: mccullochmanse1@btinternet.com]	01563 535673

Irvine: Fullarton (H) (Website: www.fullartonchurch.co.uk)

Neil Urquhart BD DipMin	1989		48 Waterside, Irvine KA12 8QJ [E-mail: neilurquhart@f2s.com]	01294 279909

Irvine: Girdle Toll (E) (H) (Website: www.girdletoll.fsbusiness.co.uk)

Vacant			2 Littlestane Rise, Irvine KA11 2BJ	01294 213565

Irvine: Mure (H)

Hugh M. Adamson BD	1976		West Road, Irvine KA12 8RE [E-mail: hmadamson768@btinternet.com]	01294 279916

Irvine: Old (H) (01294 273503)

Robert Travers BA BD	1993	1999	22 Kirk Vennel, Irvine KA12 0DQ [E-mail: robert.travers@tesco.net]	01294 279265

Irvine: Relief Bourtreehill (H)

Andrew R. Black BD	1987	2003	4 Kames Court, Irvine KA11 1RT [E-mail: andrewblack@tiscali.co.uk]	01294 216939

Irvine: St Andrew's (H) (01294 276051)

Ian W. Benzie BD	1999	2008	1 Lime Place, Kilmarnock KA1 2ES [E-mail: revian@btopenworld.com]	01563 524807
Fiona Blair (Miss) DCS (Pastoral Assistant)	2010		33 Calder Street, Lochwinnoch PA12 4DD	

Kilmarnock: Henderson (H) (01563 541302) (Website: www.hendersonchurch.org.uk)

David W. Lacy BA BD DLitt	1976	1989	52 London Road, Kilmarnock KA3 7AJ [E-mail: thelacys@tinyworld.co.uk]	01563 523113 (Tel/Fax)

Kilmarnock: New Laigh Kirk (H)

David S. Cameron BD	2001		1 Holmes Farm Road, Kilmarnock KA1 1TP [E-mail: dvdcam5@msn.com]	01563 525416
Barbara Urquhart (Mrs) DCS			9 Standalane, Kilmaurs, Kilmarnock KA3 2NB [E-mail: barbaraurquhart@uko2.co.uk]	01563 538289

Kilmarnock: Old High Kirk (H)

Vacant			107 Dundonald Road, Kilmarnock KA1 1UP	01563 525608

Kilmarnock: Riccarton (H)

Colin A. Strong BSc BD	1989	2007	2 Jasmine Road, Kilmarnock KA1 2HD [E-mail: colinastrong@aol.com]	01563 549490

Kilmarnock: St Andrew's and St Marnock's

James McNaughtan BD DipMin	1983	1989	35 South Gargieston Drive, Kilmarnock KA1 1TB [E-mail: jim@mcnaughtan.demon.co.uk]	01563 521665
Jamie Milliken BD (Assoc)	2005	2009	The Howard Centre, 5 Portland Road, Kilmarnock KA1 2BT [E-mail: jamie@howardcentre.org]	01563 541337 07929 349045 (Mbl)

Kilmarnock: St John's Onthank (H)

Susan M. Anderson (Mrs)	1997		84 Wardneuk Drive, Kilmarnock KA3 2EX [E-mail: stjohnthank@talktalk.net]	01563 521815

Kilmarnock: St Kentigern's (Website: www.stkentigern.org.uk)

S. Grant Barclay LLB BD	1995		1 Thirdpart Place, Kilmarnock KA1 1UL [E-mail: minister@stkentigern.org.uk]	01563 571280

Kilmarnock: St Ninian's Bellfield (01563 524705) linked with Kilmarnock: Shortlees

H. Taylor Brown BD CertMin	1997	2002	14 McLelland Drive, Kilmarnock KA1 1SF [E-mail: htaylorbrown@hotmail.com]	01563 529920

Kilmarnock: Shortlees See Kilmarnock: St Ninian's Bellfield

Kilmaurs: St Maur's Glencairn (H) (Website: www.jimcorbett.freeserve.co.uk/page2.html)

John A. Urquhart BD	1993		9 Standalane, Kilmaurs, Kilmarnock KA3 2NB [E-mail: john.urquhart@talktalk.net]	01563 538289

Newmilns: Loudoun (H)

David S. Randall BA BD	2003	2009	Loudoun Manse, 116A Loudoun Road, Newmilns KA16 9HH [E-mail: dsrandall@sky.com]	01560 320174

Stewarton: John Knox				
Gavin A. Niven BSc MSc BD	2010		27 Avenue Street, Stewarton, Kilmarnock KA3 5AP [E-mail: minister@johnknox.org.uk]	01560 482418
Stewarton: St Columba's (H)				
George K. Lind BD MCIBS	1998	2010	1 Kirk Glebe, Stewarton, Kilmarnock KA3 5BJ [E-mail: gklind@talktalk.net]	01560 482453
Ayrshire Mission to the Deaf				
Graeme R. Wilson BD ThM MCIBS (Chaplain)	2006		60 Brewland Street, Galston KA4 8DX [E-mail: graeme.wilson@gmail.com]	01563 820246

Brockie, Colin G.F. BSc(Eng) BD SOSc	1967 2007	Presbytery Clerk	36 Braehead Court, Kilmarnock KA3 7AB [E-mail: revcol@revcol.demon.co.uk]	
Campbell, George H.	1957 1992	(Stewarton: John Knox)	20 Woodlands Grove, Kilmarnock KA3 1TZ [E-mail: george.campbell13@hotmail.co.uk]	01563 536365
Campbell, John A. JP FIEM	1984 1998	(Irvine: St Andrew's)	Flowerdale, Balmoral Lane, Blairgowrie PH10 7AF [E-mail: exrevjack@aol.com]	01250 872795
Cant, Thomas M. MA BD	1964 2004	(Paisley: Laigh Kirk)	3 Meikle Cutstraw Farm, Stewarton, Kilmarnock KA3 5HU [E-mail: revtmcant@aol.com]	01560 480566
Christie, Robert S. MA BD ThM	1964 2001	(Kilmarnock: West High)	24 Homeroyal House, 2 Chalmers Crescent, Edinburgh EH9 1TP	
Davidson, James BD DipAFH	1989 2002	(Wishaw: Old)	13 Redburn Place, Irvine KA12 9BQ	01294 312515
Davidson Kelly, Thomas A. MA BD FSAScot	1975 2002	(Glasgow: Govan Old)	2 Springhill Stables, Portland Road, Kilmarnock KA1 2EJ [E-mail: dks@springhillstables.freeserve.co.uk]	01563 573994
Gillon, C. Blair BD	1980 2007	(Glasgow: Ibrox)	East Muirshield Farmhouse, by Dunlop, Kilmarnock KA3 4EJ [E-mail: blair.gillon2@btinternet.com]	01560 483778
Hall, William M. BD	1972 2010	(Kilmarnock: Old High Kirk)	33 Cairns Terrace, Kilmarnock KA1 1JG [E-mail: revwillie@talktalk.net]	
Hare, Malcolm M.W. BA BD	1956 1994	(Kilmarnock: St Kentigern's)	21 Raith Road, Fenwick, Kilmarnock KA3 6DB	01560 600388
Hay, W.J.R. MA BD	1959 1995	(Buchanan with Drymen)	18 Jamieson Place, Stewarton, Kilmarnock KA3 3AY	01560 482799
Huggett, Judith A. (Miss) BA BD	1990 1998	Hospital Chaplain	4 Westmoor Crescent, Kilmarnock KA1 1TX [E-mail: judith.huggett@aaaht.scotnhs.uk]	
Lamarti, Samuel H. BD MTh PhD	1979 2006	(Stewarton: John Knox)	7 Dalwhinnie Crescent, Kilmarnock KA3 1QS [E-mail: samuel.h2@ukonline.co.uk]	01563 529632
McAlpine, Richard H.M. BA FSAScot	1968 2000	(Lochgoilhead and Kilmorich)	7 Kingsford Place, Kilmarnock KA3 6FG	01563 572075
MacDonald, James M.	1964 1987	(Kilmarnock: St John's Onthank)	29 Carmel Place, Kilmaurs, Kilmarnock KA3 2QU	01563 525254
Roy, James BA	1967 1982	(Irvine: Girdle Toll)	23 Bowes Rigg, Stewarton, Kilmarnock KA3 5EL [E-mail: rev.j.roy@btinternet.com]	01560 482185
Scott, Thomas T.	1968 1989	(Kilmarnock: St Marnock's)	6 North Hamilton Place, Kilmarnock KA1 2QN [E-mail: tomtscott@btinternet.com]	01563 531415

Shaw, Catherine A.M. MA	1998 2006	(Auxiliary Minister)	40 Merrygreen Place, Stewarton, Kilmarnock KA3 5EP [E-mail: catherine.shaw@tesco.net]	01560 483352
Sutcliffe, Clare B. BSc BD	2000 2009	(Irvine: Girdle Toll)	4 Dalmailing Avenue, Dreghorn, Irvine KA11 4HX [E-mail: revclare@tesco.net]	
Welsh, Alex M. MA BD	1979 2007	Hospital Chaplain	8 Greenside Avenue, Prestwick KA9 2HB [E-mail: alexanderevelyn@hotmail.com]	01292 475341

IRVINE and KILMARNOCK ADDRESSES

Irvine

Dreghorn and Springside	Townfoot x Station Brae
Fullarton	Marress Road x Church Street
Girdle Toll	Bryce Knox Court
Mure	West Road
Old	Kirkgate
Relief Bourtreehill	Crofthead, Bourtreehill
St Andrew's	Caldon Road x Oaklands Ave

Kilmarnock

Ayrshire Mission to the Deaf	10 Clark Street
Henderson	London Road
New Laigh Kirk	John Dickie Street
Old High Kirk	Church Street x Soulis Street
Riccarton	Old Street
St Andrew's and St Marnock's	St Marnock Street
St John's Onthank	84 Wardneuk Street
St Ninian's Bellfield	Whatriggs Road
Shortlees	Central Avenue

(12) ARDROSSAN

Meets at Saltcoats, New Trinity, on the first Tuesday of February, March, April, May, September, October, November and December, and on the second Tuesday of June.

Clerk:	**MR ALAN K. SAUNDERSON**	**17 Union Street, Largs KA30 8DG** **[E-mail: ak.dj.saunderson@hotmail.co.uk]**	**01475 687217** **07866 034355 (Mbl)**

Ardrossan: Barony St John's (H) (01294 465009) (E-mail: www.baronystjohns.co.uk)

Dorothy A. Granger BA BD	2009	10 Seafield Drive, Ardrossan KA22 8NU [E-mail: dorothygranger61@gmail.com]	01294 463571 07918 077877 (Mbl)

Ardrossan: Park (01294 463711)

Tanya Webster BCom DipAcc BD	2011	35 Ardneil Court, Ardrossan KA22 7NQ [E-mail: tanya.webster@talktalk.net]	01294 538903

Beith (H) (01505 502686)				
Roderick I.T. MacDonald BD CertMin	1992	2005	2 Glebe Court, Beith KA15 1ET [E-mail: rodannmac@btinternet.com]	01505 503858
Valerie G.C. Watson MA BD STM (Assoc)	1987	2007	16 Spiers Avenue, Beith KA15 1JD [E-mail: vgcwatson@tiscali.co.uk]	01505 228362
(New charge formed by the union of Beith: High and Beith: Trinity)				
Brodick linked with Corrie linked with Lochranza and Pirnmill linked with Shiskine (H)				
Angus Adamson BD	2006		4 Manse Crescent, Brodick, Isle of Arran KA27 8AS [E-mail: s-adamson@corriecraviehome.fsnet.co.uk]	01770 302334
Corrie See Brodick				
Cumbrae				
Vacant			Marine Parade, Millport, Isle of Cumbrae KA28 0ED	01475 530416
Dalry: St Margaret's				
James R. Teasdale BA BD	2009		33 Templand Crescent, Dalry KA24 5EZ [E-mail: st.margaret@talktalk.net]	01294 832234
Dalry: Trinity (H)				
Martin Thomson BSc DipEd BD	1988	2004	Trinity Manse, West Kilbride Road, Dalry KA24 5DX [E-mail: martin.thomson40@btinternet.com]	01294 832363
Fairlie (H)				
Vacant			14 Fairlieburne Gardens, Fairlie, Largs KA29 0ER	01475 568342
Kilbirnie: Auld Kirk (H)				
Vacant			49 Holmhead, Kilbirnie KA25 6BS	01505 682348
Kilbirnie: St Columba's (H) (01505 685239)				
Fiona C. Ross (Miss) BD DipMin	1996	2004	Manse of St Columba's, Dipple Road, Kilbirnie KA25 7JU [E-mail: fionaross@calvin78.freeserve.co.uk]	01505 683342
Kilmory linked with Lamlash				
Gillean P. Maclean (Mrs) BD	1994	2008	Lamlash, Isle of Arran KA27 8LE [E-mail: gillean.maclean@hotmail.co.uk]	01770 600318
Kilwinning: Mansefield Trinity (E) (01294 550746)				
Vacant			21 Foundry Wynd, Kilwinning KA13 6UG	01294 550084

Kilwinning: Old				
Jeanette Whitecross BD	2002	2011	54 Dalry Road, Kilwinning KA13 7HE [E-mail: jwx@hotmail.co.uk]	01294 552606
Lamlash See Kilmory				
Largs: Clark Memorial (H) (01475 675186)				
Stephen J. Smith BSc BD	1993	1998	31 Douglas Street, Largs KA30 8PT [E-mail: stephenrevsteve@aol.com]	01475 672370
Largs: St Columba's (01475 686212)				
Vacant			17 Beachway, Largs KA30 8QH	
Largs: St John's (H) (01475 674468)				
Andrew F. McGurk BD	1983	1993	1 Newhaven Grove, Largs KA30 8NS [E-mail: afmcg.largs@talk21.com]	01475 676123
Lochranza and Pirnmill See Brodick				
Saltcoats: New Trinity (H) (01294 472001)				
Vacant			1 Montgomerie Crescent, Saltcoats KA21 5BX	01294 461143
Saltcoats: North (01294 464679)				
Alexander B. Noble MA BD ThM	1982	2003	25 Longfield Avenue, Saltcoats KA21 6DR	01294 604923
Saltcoats: St Cuthbert's (H)				
Vacant			10 Kennedy Road, Saltcoats KA21 5SF	
Shiskine (H) See Brodick				
Stevenston: Ardeer linked with Stevenston: Livingstone (H)				
John M.M. Lafferty BD	1999		32 High Road, Stevenston KA20 3DR	01294 464180
Stevenston: High (H) (Website: www.highkirk.com)				
M. Scott Cameron MA BD	2002		Glencairn Street, Stevenston KA20 3DL [E-mail: revhighkirk@btinternet.com]	01294 463356
Stevenston: Livingstone (H) See Stevenston: Ardeer				

West Kilbride (H)

James J. McNay MA BD	2008		The Manse, Goldenberry Avenue, West Kilbride KA23 9LJ [E-mail: j.mcnay@lycos.com]	01294 823186

Whiting Bay and Kildonan

Elizabeth R.L. Watson (Miss) BA BD	1981	1982	Whiting Bay, Brodick, Isle of Arran KA27 8RE [E-mail: revewatson@btinternet.com]	01770 700289

Cruickshank, Norman BA BD	1983 2006	(West Kilbride: Overton)	24D Faulds Wynd, Seamill, West Kilbride KA23 9FA	01294 822239
Currie, Ian S. MBE BD	1975 2010	(The United Church of Bute)	15 Northfield Park, Largs KA30 8NZ [E-mail: ianscurrie@tiscali.co.uk]	(Mbl) 07764 254300
Dailly, J.R. BD DipPS	1979 1979	(DACG)	2 Curtis Close, Pound Street, Warminster, Wiltshire BA12 9NN	
Downie, Alexander S.	1975 1997	(Ardrossan: Park)	12 Loanhead Road, Ardrossan KA22 8AW	01294 464097
Drysdale, James H. LTh	1987 2006	(Blackbraes and Shieldhill)	10 John Clark Street, Largs KA30 9AH	01475 674870
Forsyth, D. Stuart MA	1948 1992	(Belhelvie)	39 Homemount House, Gogoside Road, Largs KA30 9LS	01475 673379
Gordon, David C.	1953 1988	(Gigha and Cara)	South Beach House, South Crescent Road, Ardrossan KA22 8DU	
Harbison, David J.H.	1958 1998	(Beith: High with Beith: Trinity)	42 Mill Park, Dalry KA24 5BB [E-mail: djh@harbi.fsnet.co.uk]	01294 834092
Hebenton, David J. MA BD	1958 2002	(Ayton and Burnmouth linked with Grantshouse and Houndwood and Reston)	22B Faulds Wynd, Seamill, West Kilbride KA23 9FA	01294 829228
Howie, Marion L.K. (Mrs) MA ACRS	1992	Auxiliary Minister	51 High Road, Stevenston KA20 3DY [E-mail: marion@howiefamily.net]	01294 466571
Leask, Rebecca M. (Mrs)	1977 1985	(Callander: St Bride's)	20 Strathclyde House, 31 Shore Road, Skelmorlie PA17 5AN [E-mail: rmleask@hotmail.com]	01475 520765
McCallum, Alexander D. BD	1987 2005	(Saltcoats: New Trinity)	59 Woodcroft Avenue, Largs KA30 9EW [E-mail: sandyandjose@madasafish.com]	01475 670133
McCance, Andrew M. BSc	1986 1995	(Coatbridge: Middle)	6A Douglas Place, Largs KA30 8PU	01475 673303
Mackay, Marjory H. (Mrs) BD DipEd CCE	1998 2008	(Cumbrae)	4 Golf Road, Millport, Isle of Cumbrae KA28 0HB [E-mail: mhmackay@tiscali.co.uk]	01475 530388
McKay, Johnston R. MA BA PhD	1969 1987	(Religious Broadcasting: BBC)	15 Montgomerie Avenue, Fairlie, Largs KA29 0EE [E-mail: johnston.mckay@btopenworld.com]	01475 568802
MacLeod, Ian LTh BA MTh PhD	1969 2006	(Brodick with Corrie)	Cromla Cottage, Corrie, Isle of Arran KA27 8JB [E-mail: i.macleod829@btinternet.com]	01770 810237
Mitchell, D. Ross BA BD	1972 2007	(West Kilbride: St Andrew's)	11 Dunbar Gardens, Saltcoats KA21 6GJ [E-mail: ross.mitchell@virgin.net]	
Paterson, John H. BD	1977 2000	(Kirkintilloch: St David's Memorial Park)	Creag Bhan, Golf Course Road, Whiting Bay, Isle of Arran KA27 8QT	01770 700569
Roy, Iain M. MA BD	1960 1997	(Stevenston: Livingstone)	2 The Fieldings, Dunlop, Kilmarnock KA3 4AU	01560 483072
Taylor, Andrew S. BTh FPhS	1959 1992	(Greenock Union)	9 Raillies Avenue, Largs KA30 8QY [E-mail: andrew.taylor123@tiscali.co.uk]	01475 674709
Thomson, Margaret (Mrs)	1988 1993	(Saltcoats: Erskine)	7 Glen Farg, St Leonards, East Kilbride, Glasgow G74 2JW	

(13) LANARK

Meets on the first Tuesday of February, March, April, May, September, October, November and December, and on the third Tuesday of June.

Clerk:	**REV. MRS HELEN E. JAMIESON BD DipEd**	**120 Clyde Street, Carluke ML8 5BG** **[E-mail: lanark@cofscotland.org.uk]**	**01555 771218**
Depute Clerk:	**REV. BRYAN KERR BA BD**	**Greyfriars Manse, 3 Bellefield Way, Lanark ML11 7NW**	**01555 663363**

Biggar (H)
Vacant

Black Mount linked with Culter (H) linked with Libberton and Quothquan (H)

James S.H. Cutler BD CEng MIStructE	1986	2004	12 Kittlegairy Place, Peebles EH45 9LW [E-mail: revjimcutler@btinternet.com]	

(Mr Cutler will retire to the above address in mid-October 2011 and become a member of Melrose and Peebles Presbytery.)

Cairngryffe linked with Symington

Vacant			16 Abington Road, Symington, Biggar ML12 6JX	01899 308838

Carluke: Kirkton (H) (01555 750778) (E-mail: iaindc@btconnect.com)

Iain D. Cunningham MA BD	1979	1987	9 Station Road, Carluke ML8 5AA [E-mail: iaindc@btconnect.com]	01555 771262

Carluke: St Andrew's (H)

Helen E. Jamieson (Mrs) BD DipEd	1989		120 Clyde Street, Carluke ML8 5BG [E-mail: helenejamieson@o2.co.uk]	01555 771218

Carluke: St John's (H) (Website: www.carluke-stjohns.org.uk)

Roy J. Cowieson BD	1979	2007	18 Old Bridgend, Carluke ML8 4HN [E-mail: roy.cowieson@btinternet.com]	01555 752519

Carnwath (H)
Vacant

Carstairs and Carstairs Junction, The United Church of

Alan W. Gibson BA BD	2001	2008	11 Range View, Kames, Carstairs, Lanark ML11 8TF [E-mail: awgibson82@hotmail.com]	01555 871123

Coalburn (H) linked with Lesmahagow: Old (H) (Church office: 01555 892425)
Aileen Robson BD 2003 9 Elm Bank, Lesmahagow, Lanark ML11 0EA 01555 895325
[E-mail: a.robson@lanarkpresbytery.org]

Crossford (H) linked with Kirkfieldbank (E-mail: s.reid@lanarkpresbytery.org)
Steven Reid BAcc CA BD 1989 1997 74 Lanark Road, Crossford, Carluke ML8 5RE 01555 860415
[E-mail: steven.reid@sky.com]

Culter (H) See Black Mount

Forth: St Paul's (H) (Website: www.forthstpauls.com)
Sarah L. Ross (Mrs) BD MTh PGDip 2004 22 Lea Rig, Forth, Lanark ML11 8EA 01555 812832
[E-mail: minister@forthstpauls.com]

Glencaple linked with Lowther
Margaret A. Muir (Miss) MA LLB BD 1989 2001 66 Carlisle Road, Crawford, Biggar ML12 6TW 01864 502625

Kirkfieldbank See Crossford

Kirkmuirhill (H)
Ian M. Watson LLB DipLP BD 1998 2003 The Manse, 2 Lanark Road, Kirkmuirhill, Lanark ML11 9RB 01555 892409
[E-mail: ian.watson21@btopenworld.com]

Lanark: Greyfriars (Church office: 01555 661510) (E-mail: b.kerr@lanarkpresbytery.org) (Website: www.lanarkgreyfriars.com)
Bryan Kerr BA BD 2002 2007 Greyfriars Manse, 3 Bellefield Way, Lanark ML11 7NW 01555 663363
[E-mail: bryan@lanarkgreyfriars.com]

Lanark: St Nicholas' (H)
Alison A. Meikle (Mrs) BD 1999 2002 2 Kaimhill Court, Lanark ML11 9HU 01555 662600
[E-mail: alison-meikle@sky.com]

Law
Una B. Stewart (Ms) BD DipEd 1995 2009 3 Shawgill Court, Law, Carluke ML8 5SJ 01698 373180
[E-mail: rev.ubs@virgin.net]

Lesmahagow: Abbeygreen
David S. Carmichael 1982 Abbeygreen Manse, Lesmahagow, Lanark ML11 0DB 01555 893384
[E-mail: david.carmichael@abbeygreen.org.uk]

Lesmahagow: Old (H) See Coalburn
Libberton and Quothquan (H) See Black Mount
Lowther See Glencaple
Symington See Cairngryffe

The Douglas Valley Church (Church office: Tel/Fax: 01555 850000) (Website: www.douglasvalleychurch.org)
Robert Cleland 1997 2009 The Manse, Douglas, Lanark ML11 0RB 01555 851213
[E-mail: cleland810@btinternet.com]

Cowell, Susan G. (Miss) BA BD	1986	1998	(Budapest)	3 Gavel Lane, Regency Gardens, Lanark ML11 9FB	01555 665509
Craig, William BA LTh	1974	1997	(Cambusbarron: The Bruce Memorial)	31 Heathfield Drive, Blackwood, Lanark ML11 9SR	01555 893710
Easton, David J.C. MA BD	1965	2005	(Glasgow: Burnside-Blairbeth)	Rowanbank, Cormiston Road, Quothquan, Biggar ML12 6ND [E-mail: deaston@btinternet.com]	01899 308459
Findlay, Henry J.W. MA BD	1965	2005	(Wishaw: St Mark's)	2 Alba Gardens, Carluke ML8 5US	01555 759995
Fox, George H.	1959	1977	(Coalsnaughton)	Braehead House, Crossford, Carluke ML8 5NQ	01555 860716
Francis, James BD PhD	2002	2009	Chaplain: Army	Bachstrasse 18, D-29223 Celle, Germany	
Gauld, Beverly G.D.D. MA BD	1972	2009	(Carnwath)	7 Rowan View, Lanark ML11 9FQ	01555 665765
Houston, Graham R. BSc BD MTh PhD	1978	2011	(Cairngryffe with Symington)	3 Alder Lane, Beechtrees, Lanark ML11 9FT [E-mail: gandih6156@btinternet.com]	01555 678004
Lyall, Ann (Miss) DCS	1980	2011	The Biggar Area	17 Mercat Loan, Biggar ML12 6DG [E-mail: ann.lyall@btinternet.com]	01899 220625
Pacitti, Stephen A. MA	1963	2003	(Black Mount with Culter with Libberton and Quothquan)	157 Nithsdale Road, Glasgow G41 5RD	0141-423 5792
Seath, Thomas J.G.	1980	1992	(Motherwell: Manse Road)	Flat 11, Wallace Court, South Vennel, Lanark ML11 7LL	01555 665399
Stewart, John M. MA BD	1964	2001	(Johnstone with Kirkpatrick Juxta)	5 Rathmor Road, Biggar ML12 6QG	01899 220398
Turnbull, John LTh	1994	2006	(Balfron with Fintry)	4 Rathmor Road, Biggar ML12 6QG	01899 221502
Young, David A.	1972	2003	(Kirkmuirhill)	15 Mannachie Rise, Forres IV36 2US [E-mail: youngdavid@aol.com]	01309 672849

(14) GREENOCK AND PAISLEY

Meets on the second Tuesday of September, October, November, December, February, March, April and May, and on the third Tuesday of June.

Clerk: **REV. ALASTAIR J. CHERRY BA BD FPLD** **The Presbytery Office as detailed below**
[E-mail: greenockpaisley@cofscotland.org.uk]

Presbytery Office: **'Homelea', Faith Avenue, Quarrier's Village, Bridge of Weir PA11 3SX** **01505 615033 (Tel)**
01505 615088 (Fax)

Barrhead: Arthurlie (H) (0141-881 8442)				
James S.A. Cowan BD DipMin	1986	1998	10 Arthurlie Avenue, Barrhead, Glasgow G78 2BU [E-mail: jim_cowan@ntlworld.com]	0141-881 3457
Barrhead: Bourock (H) (0141-881 9813)				
Vacant			14 Maxton Avenue, Barrhead, Glasgow G78 1DY	0141-881 1462
Barrhead: South and Levern (H) (0141-881 7825)				
Morris M. Dutch BD BA	1998	2002	3 Colinbar Circle, Barrhead, Glasgow G78 2BE [E-mail: mnmdutch@yahoo.co.uk]	0141-571 4059
Bishopton (H) (Office: 01505 862583)				
Daniel Manastireanu BA MTh	2010		The Manse, Newton Road, Bishopton PA7 5JP [E-mail: daniel@bishoptonkirk.org.uk]	01505 862161
Bridge of Weir: Freeland (H) (01505 612610)				
Kenneth N. Gray BA BD	1988		15 Lawmarnock Crescent, Bridge of Weir PA11 3AS [E-mail: aandkgray@btinternet.com]	01505 690918
Bridge of Weir: St Machar's Ranfurly (01505 614364)				
Suzanne Dunleavy (Miss) BD DipEd	1990	1992	9 Glen Brae, Bridge of Weir PA11 3BH [E-mail: suzanne.dunleavy@btinternet.com]	01505 612975
Elderslie Kirk (H) (01505 323348)				
Robin N. Allison BD DipMin	1994	2005	282 Main Road, Elderslie, Johnstone PA5 9EF [E-mail: revrobin@sky.com]	01505 321767
Erskine (0141-812 4620)				
Vacant			The Manse, 7 Leven Place, Linburn, Erskine PA8 6AS	0141-581 0955
Gourock: Old Gourock and Ashton (H)				
David T. Young BA BD	2007		331 Eldon Street, Gourock PA16 7QN [E-mail: minister@ogachurch.org.uk]	01475 635578
Gourock: St John's (H)				
Glenn A. Chestnutt BA DASE MDiv ThM PhD	2009		6 Barrhill Road, Gourock PA19 1JX [E-mail: glenn.chestnutt@gmail.com]	01475 632143

Greenock: East End				
David J. McCarthy BSc BD	1985	2003	29 Denholm Street, Greenock PA16 8RH [E-mail: greenockeastendparish@googlemail.com]	01475 722111
Eileen Manson (Mrs) DipCE (Aux)	1994	2005	1 Cambridge Avenue, Gourock PA19 1XT [E-mail: rev.eileen@ntlworld.com]	01475 632401
Greenock: Lyle Community Kirk				
C. Ian W. Johnson MA BD	1997		39 Fox Street, Greenock PA16 8PD [E-mail: ian.ciw.johnson@btinternet.com]	01475 888277
(New charge formed by the union of Greenock: Ardgowan, Greenock: Finnart St Paul's and Greenock: Old West Kirk)				
Greenock: Mount Kirk				
Francis E. Murphy BEng DipDSE BD	2006		76 Finnart Street, Greenock PA16 8HJ [E-mail: francis_e_murphy@hotmail.com]	01475 722338
Greenock: St Margaret's (01475 781953)				
Vacant			105 Finnart Street, Greenock PA16 8HN	01475 786590
Greenock: St Ninian's				
Allan G. McIntyre BD	1985		5 Auchmead Road, Greenock PA16 0PY [E-mail: agmcintyre@lineone.net]	01475 631878
Greenock: Wellpark Mid Kirk				
Alan K. Sorensen BD MTh DipMin FSAScot	1983	2000	101 Brisbane Street, Greenock PA16 8PA [E-mail: alan.sorensen@ntlworld.com]	01475 721741
Greenock: Westburn				
William C. Hewitt BD DipPS	1977	1994	50 Ardgowan Street, Greenock PA16 8EP [E-mail: william.hewitt@ntlworld.com]	01475 721048
Houston and Killellan (H)				
Donald Campbell BD	1998	2007	The Manse of Houston, Main Street, Houston, Johnstone PA6 7EL [E-mail: houstonmanse@btinternet.com]	01505 612569
Howwood				
David Stewart MA DipEd BD MTh	1977	2001	The Manse, Beith Road, Howwood, Johnstone PA9 1AS [E-mail: revdavidst@aol.com]	01505 703678

Inchinnan (H) (0141-812 1263)				
Alison McBrier MA BD	2011		The Manse, Inchinnan, Renfrew PA4 9PH	0141-812 1688
Inverkip (H)				
Vacant			The Manse, Langhouse Road, Inverkip, Greenock PA16 0BJ	01475 521207
Johnstone: High (H) (01505 336303)				
Ann C. McCool (Mrs) BD DSD IPA ALCM	1989	2001	76 North Road, Johnstone PA5 8NF [E-mail: ann.mccool@ntlworld.com]	01505 320006
Johnstone: St Andrew's Trinity				
May Bell (Mrs) LTh	1998	2002	The Manse, 7 Leven Place, Linburn, Erskine PA8 6AS [E-mail: may.bell@ntlbusiness.com]	0141-581 7352
Johnstone: St Paul's (H) (01505 321632)				
Alistair N. Shaw MA BD MTh	1982	2003	9 Stanley Drive, Brookfield, Johnstone PA5 8UF [E-mail: ans2006@talktalk.net]	01505 320060
Kilbarchan: East				
Vacant			East Manse, Church Street, Kilbarchan, Johnstone PA10 2JQ	01505 702621
Kilbarchan: West				
Arthur Sherratt BD	1994		West Manse, Shuttle Street, Kilbarchan, Johnstone PA10 2JR [E-mail: arthur.sherratt@ntlworld.com]	01505 342930
Kilmacolm: Old (H) (01505 873911)				
Peter McEnhill BD PhD	1992	2007	The Old Kirk Manse, Glencairn Road, Kilmacolm PA13 4NJ [E-mail: petermcenhill@btinternet.com]	01505 873174
Kilmacolm: St Columba (H)				
R. Douglas Cranston MA BD	1986	1992	6 Churchill Road, Kilmacolm PA13 4LH [E-mail: robert.cranston@sccmanse.plus.com]	01505 873271
Langbank (T)				
Vacant			The Manse, Main Road, Langbank, Port Glasgow PA14 6XP	01475 540252

Linwood (H) (01505 328802)
Eileen M. Ross (Mrs) BD MTh 2005 2008 28 Fulbar Crescent, Paisley PA2 9AS 01505 812304
[E-mail: eileenmross@btinternet.com]

Lochwinnoch (T)
Christine Murdoch 1999 2007 1 Station Rise, Lochwinnoch PA12 4NA 01505 843484
[E-mail: rev.christine@btinternet.com]

Neilston (0141-881 9445)
Vacant The Manse, Neilston Road, Neilston, Glasgow G78 3NP 0141-881 1958

Paisley: Abbey (H) (Tel: 0141-889 7654; Fax: 0141-887 3929)
Alan D. Birss MA BD 1979 1988 15 Main Road, Castlehead, Paisley PA2 6AJ 0141-889 3587
[E-mail: alan.birss@paisleyabbey.com]

Paisley: Glenburn (0141-884 2602)
Graham Nash MA BD 2006 10 Hawick Avenue, Paisley PA2 9LD 0141-884 4903
[E-mail: gpnash@btopenworld.com]

Paisley: Lylesland (H) (0141-561 7139)
Alistair W. Cook BSc CA BD 2008 36 Potterhill Avenue, Paisley PA2 8BA 0141-561 9277
[E-mail: alistaircook@ntlworld.com]
Greta Gray (Miss) DCS 67 Crags Avenue, Paisley PA3 6SG 0141-884 6178

Paisley: Martyrs' Sandyford (0141-889 6603)
Kenneth A.L. Mayne BA MSc CertEd 1976 2007 21 John Neilson Avenue, Paisley PA1 2SX 0141-889 2182

Paisley: Oakshaw Trinity (H) (Tel: 0141-889 4010; Fax: 0141-848 5139)
Vacant 16 Golf Drive, Paisley PA1 3LA 0141-887 0884

Paisley: St Columba Foxbar (H) (01505 812377)
Drausio Goncalves 2008 13 Corsebar Drive, Paisley PA2 9QD 0141-848 5826
[E-mail: drausiopg@gmail.com]

Paisley: St James' (0141-889 2422)
Vacant 38 Woodland Avenue, Paisley PA2 8BH 0141-884 3246

Paisley: St Luke's (H)
D. Ritchie M. Gillon BD DipMin 1994 31 Southfield Avenue, Paisley PA2 8BX 0141-884 6215
[E-mail: revgillon@hotmail.com]

Paisley: St Mark's Oldhall (H) (0141-882 2755)
Robert G. McFarlane BD 2001 2005 36 Newtyle Road, Paisley PA1 3JX 0141-889 4279
[E-mail: robertmcf@hotmail.com]

Paisley: St Ninian's Ferguslie (E) (0141-887 9436) (New Charge Development)
William Wishart DCS 10 Stanely Drive, Paisley PA2 6HE 0141-884 4177
[E-mail: bill@saintninians.co.uk]

Paisley: Sherwood Greenlaw (H) (0141-889 7060)
Alasdair F. Cameron BD CA 1986 1993 5 Greenlaw Drive, Paisley PA1 3RX 0141-889 3057
[E-mail: alcamron@lineone.net]

Paisley: Stow Brae Kirk
Vacant 25 John Neilson Avenue, Paisley PA1 2SX 0141-887 5434
(New charge formed by the union of Paisley: Castlehead and Paisley: Laigh Kirk)

Paisley: Wallneuk North (0141-889 9265)
Peter G. Gill MA BA 2008 5 Glenville Crescent, Paisley PA2 8TW 0141-884 4429
[E-mail: petergill18@hotmail.com]

Port Glasgow: Hamilton Bardrainney
James A. Munro BA BD DMS 1979 2002 80 Bardrainney Avenue, Port Glasgow PA14 6HD 01475 701213
[E-mail: james@jmunro33.wanadoo.co.uk]

Port Glasgow: St Andrew's (H)
Andrew T. MacLean BA BD 1980 1993 St Andrew's Manse, Barr's Brae, Port Glasgow PA14 5QA 01475 741486
[E-mail: standrews.pg@me.com]

Port Glasgow: St Martin's
Archibald Speirs BD 1995 2006 Clunebraehead, Clune Brae, Port Glasgow PA14 5SL 01475 704115
[E-mail: archiespeirs1@aol.com]

Renfrew: North (0141-885 2154)				
E. Lorna Hood (Mrs) MA BD	1978	1979	1 Alexandra Drive, Renfrew PA4 8UB [E-mail: lorna.hood@ntlworld.com]	0141-886 2074
Renfrew: Old				
Lilly C. Easton (Mrs)	1999	2009	31 Gibson Road, Renfrew PA4 0RH [E-mail: revlillyeaston@hotmail.co.uk]	0141-886 2005
Renfrew: Trinity (H) (0141-885 2129)				
Stuart C. Steell BD CertMin	1992		25 Paisley Road, Renfrew PA4 8JH [E-mail: ssren@tiscali.co.uk]	0141-886 2131
Skelmorlie and Wemyss Bay				
Vacant			3A Montgomerie Terrace, Skelmorlie PA17 5TD	01475 520703

Alexander, Douglas N. MA BD	1961 1999	(Bishopton)	West Morningside, Main Road, Langbank, Port Glasgow PA4 6XP	01475 540249
Armstrong, Gordon B. BD FIAB BRC	2010	West of Scotland Industrial Chaplain	52 Balgonie Avenue, Paisley PA2 9LP [E-mail: revgordon@ntlworld.com]	0141-587 3124
Armstrong, William R. BD	1979 2008	(Skelmorlie and Wemyss Bay)	25A The Lane, Skelmorlie PA17 5AR [E-mail: warmstrong17@tiscali.co.uk]	01475 520891
Bell, Ian W. LTh	1990 2011	(Erskine)	1 Swallow Brae, Inverkip, Greenock PA16 0LF [E-mail: rviwbepc@ntlworld.com]	01475 529312
Black, Janette M.K. (Mrs) BD	1993 2006	(Assistant: Paisley: Oakshaw Trinity)	5 Craigiehall Avenue, Erskine PA8 7DB	0141-812 0794
Cameron, Margaret (Miss) DCS		(Deaconess)	2 Rowans Gate, Paisley PA2 6RD	0141-840 2479
Campbell, John MA BA BSc	1973 2009	(Caldwell)	96 Boghead Road, Lenzie, Glasgow G66 4EN [E-mail: johncampbell.lenzie@gmail.com]	0141-776 0874
Cherry, Alastair J. BA BD FPLD	1982 2009	Presbytery Clerk (and Glasgow: Penilee St Andrew's)	8 Coruisk Drive, Clarkston, Glasgow G76 7NG [E-mail: alastair.j.cherry@btinternet.com]	0141-620 3852
Chestnut, Alexander MBE BA	1948 1987	(Greenock: St Mark's Greenbank)	5 Douglas Street, Largs KA30 8PS	01475 674168
Christie, John C. BSc BD MSB CBiol	1990 2004	Interim Minister	10 Cumberland Avenue, Helensburgh G84 8QG [E-mail: rev.jcc@btinternet.com]	01436 674078 (Mbl) 07711 336392
Copland, Agnes M. (Mrs) MBE DCS		(Deacon)	3 Craigmuschat Road, Gourock PA19 1SE	01475 631870
Coull, Morris C. BD	1974 2011	(Skelmorlie and Wemyss Bay)	Flat 0/1 Toward, The Lighthouses, Greenock Road, Wemyss Bay PA18 6DT	01475 522677
Cubie, John P. MA BD	1961 1999	(Caldwell)	36 Winram Place, St Andrews KY16 8XH	01334 474708
Erskine, Morag (Miss) DCS	1979	(Deacon)	111 Mains Drive, Park Mains, Erskine PA8 7JJ [E-mail: morag.erskine@ntlworld.com]	0141-812 6096
Forrest, Kenneth P. CBE BSc PhD	2006	Auxiliary Minister	5 Carruth Road, Bridge of Weir PA11 3HQ [E-mail: kenpforrest@hotmail.com]	01505 612651
Fraser, Ian C. BA BD	1983 2008	(Glasgow: St Luke's and St Andrew's)	62 Kingston Avenue, Neilston, Glasgow G78 3JG [E-mail: ianandlindafraser@gmail.com]	0141-563 6794

Name	Ord.	Ret.	Former charge	Address	Telephone
Gardner, Frank J. MA	1966	2007	(Gourock: Old Gourock and Ashton)	1 Levanne Place, Gourock PA16 1AX [E-mail: fjg@clyde-mail.co.uk]	(Tel/Fax) 01475 630187
Hamilton, W. Douglas BD	1975	2009	(Greenock: Westburn)	5 Corse Road, Penilee, Glasgow G52 4DG [E-mail: douglas.hamilton44@hotmail.co.uk]	0141-810 1194
Hetherington, Robert M. MA BD	1966	2002	(Barrhead South and Levern)	31 Brodie Park Crescent, Paisley PA2 6EU [E-mail: r-hetherington@sky.com]	0141-848 6560
Irvine, Euphemia H.C. (Mrs) BD	1972	1988	(Milton of Campsie)	32 Baird Drive, Bargarran, Erskine PA8 6BB	0141-812 2777
Johnston, Mary (Miss) DCS			(Deaconess)	19 Lounsdale Drive, Paisley PA2 9ED	0141-849 1615
Kay, David BA BD MTh	1974	2008	(Paisley: Sandyford: Thread Street)	36 Donaldswood Park, Paisley PA2 8RS [E-mail: david.kay500@o2.co.uk]	0141-884 2080
Leitch, Maureen (Mrs) BA BD	1995	2011	(Barrhead: Bourock)	Rockfield, 92 Paisley Road, Barrhead G78 1NW [E-mail: maureen.leitch@ntlworld.com]	0141-580 2927
Lodge, Bernard P. BD	1967	2004	(Glasgow: Govanhill Trinity)	6 Darluith Park, Brookfield, Johnstone PA5 8DD [E-mail: bernardlodge@yahoo.co.uk]	01505 320378
McBain, Margaret (Miss) DCS				33 Quarry Road, Paisley PA2 7RD	0141-884 2920
MacColl, James C. BSc BD	1966	2002	(Johnstone: St Andrew's Trinity)	Greenways, Winton, Kirkby Stephen, Cumbria CA17 4HL	01768 372290
MacColl, John BD DipMin	1989	2001	Teacher: Religious Education	1 Birch Avenue, Johnstone PA5 0DD	01505 326506
McCully, M. Isobel (Miss) DCS			(Deacon)	10 Broadstone Avenue, Port Glasgow PA14 5BB [E-mail: mi.mccully@btinternet.com]	01475 742240
Macdonald, Alexander MA BD	1966	2006	(Neilston)	35 Lochore Avenue, Paisley PA3 4BY [E-mail: alexmacdonald42@aol.com]	0141-889 0066
McDonald, Alexander BA CMIWSC DUniv	1968	1988	Department of Ministry	36 Alloway Grove, Paisley PA2 7DQ [E-mail: amcdonald1@ntlworld.com]	0141-560 1937
Macfarlane, Thomas G. BSc PhD BD	1956	1992	(Glasgow: South Shawlands)	12 Elphinstone Court, Lochwinnoch Road, Kilmacolm PA13 4DW	01505 874962
McKaig, William G. BD	1979	2011	(Langbank)	54 Brisbane Street, Greenock PA16 8NT [E-mail: bill.mckaig@virgin.net]	
MacLaine, Marilyn (Mrs) LTh	1995	2009	(Inchinnan)	37 Bankton Brae, Livingston EH54 9LA	01506 400619
MacMahon, Janet P.H. (Mrs) MSc BD	1992	2010	Chaplain: Erskine	14 Hillfoot Drive, Bearsden, Glasgow G61 3QQ [E-mail: janetmacmahon@yahoo.co.uk]	0141-942 8611
Nicol, Joyce M. (Mrs) BA DCS			(Deacon)	93 Brisbane Street, Greenock PA16 8NY [E-mail: joycenicol@hotmail.co.uk]	01475 723235
Page, John R. BD DipMin	1988	2003	(Gibraltar)	1 The Walton Building, North Street, Mere, Warminster, Wiltshire BA12 6HU	
Palmer, S.W. BD	1980	1991	(Kilbarchan: East)	4 Bream Place, Houston PA6 7ZJ	01505 615280
Prentice, George BA BTh	1964	1997	(Paisley: Martyrs)	46 Victoria Gardens, Corsebar Road, Paisley PA2 9AQ [E-mail: g.prentice04@talktalk.net]	0141-842 1585
Scott, Ernest M. MA	1957	1992	(Port Glasgow: St Andrew's)	17 Brueacre Road, Wemyss Bay PA18 6ER [E-mail: ernie.scott@ernest70.fsnet.co.uk]	01475 522267
Simpson, James H. BD LLB	1964	2004	(Greenock: Mount Kirk)	82 Harbourside, Inverkip, Greenock PA16 0BF [E-mail: jameshsimpson@yahoo.co.uk]	01475 520582
Smillie, Andrew M. LTh	1990	2005	(Langbank)	7 Turnbull Avenue, West Freeland, Erskine PA8 7DL [E-mail: andrewsmillie@talktalk.net]	0141-812 7030

Stone, W. Vernon MA BD	1949 1985	(Langbank)	36 Woodrow Court, Port Glasgow Road, Kilmacolm KA13 4QA [E-mail: stone@kilmacolm.fsnet.co.uk]	01505 872644
Whyte, John H. MA	1946 1986	(Gourock: Ashton)	6 Castle Levan Manor, Cloch Road, Gourock PA19 1AY	01475 636788
Whyte, Margaret A. (Mrs) BA BD	1988 2011	(Glasgow: Pollokshaws)	4 Springhill Road, Barrhead G78 2AA [E-mail: tdpwhyte@tiscali.co.uk]	0141-881 4942

GREENOCK ADDRESSES

Gourock

Old Gourock and Ashton	41 Royal Street
St John's	Bath Street x St John's Road

Greenock

Lyle Community Kirk	31 Union Street; Newark Street x Bentinck Street; Esplanade x Campbell Street

(Lyle Community Kirk is continuing meantime to retain all three buildings)

Mount Kirk	Dempster Street at Murdieston Park
St Margaret's	Finch Road x Kestrel Crescent
St Ninian's	Warwick Road, Larkfield
Wellpark Mid Kirk	Cathcart Square
Westburn	9 Nelson Street

Port Glasgow

Hamilton Bardrainney	Bardrainney Avenue x Auchenbothie Road
St Andrew's	Princes Street
St Martin's	Mansion Avenue

PAISLEY ADDRESSES

Abbey	Town Centre
Glenburn	Nethercraigs Drive off Glenburn Road
Lylesland	Rowan Street off Neilston Road
Martyrs'	King Street
Oakshaw Trinity	Churchill
St Columba Foxbar	Amochrie Road, Foxbar
St James'	Underwood Road
St Luke's	Neilston Road
St Mark's Oldhall	Glasgow Road, Ralston
St Ninian's Ferguslie	Blackstoun Road
Sandyford (Thread St)	Montgomery Road
Sherwood Greenlaw	Glasgow Road
Stow Brae Kirk	Causeyside Street
Wallneuk North	off Renfrew Road

(16) GLASGOW

Meets at Govan and Linthouse Parish Church, Govan Cross, Glasgow, on the following Tuesdays: 2011: 13 September, 11 October, 8 November, 13 December; 2012: 14 February, 13 March, 17 April, 8 May, 19 June.

Clerk:	**REV. DR ANGUS KERR BD CertMin ThM DMin**	**260 Bath Street, Glasgow G2 4JP** **[E-mail: glasgow@cofscotland.org.uk]** **[Website: www.presbyteryofglasgow.org.uk]**	**0141-332 6606** **0141-352 6646** (Fax)
Treasurer:	**DOUGLAS BLANEY**	**[E-mail: treasurer@presbyteryofglasgow.org.uk]**	

1	**Banton linked with Twechar**				
	Vacant			Manse of Banton and Twechar, Banton, Glasgow G65 0QL	01236 826129
2	**Bishopbriggs: Kenmure**				
	James Gemmell BD MTh	1999	2010	5 Marchfield, Bishopbriggs, Glasgow G64 3PP [E-mail: revgemmell@hotmail.com]	0141-772 1468
3	**Bishopbriggs: Springfield Cambridge (0141-772 1596)**				
	Ian Taylor BD ThM	1995	2006	64 Miller Drive, Bishopbriggs, Glasgow G64 1FB [E-mail: taylorian@btinternet.com]	0141-772 1540
4	**Broom (0141-639 3528)**				
	James A.S. Boag BD CertMin	1992	2007	3 Laigh Road, Newton Mearns, Glasgow G77 5EX [E-mail: office@broomchurch.org.uk]	0141-639 2916 (Tel) 0141-639 3528 (Fax)
	Margaret McLellan (Mrs) DCS			18 Broom Road East, Newton Mearns, Glasgow G77 5SD [E-mail: office@broomchurch.org.uk]	0141-639 6853
5	**Burnside Blairbeth (0141-634 4130)**				
	William T.S. Wilson BSc BD	1999	2006	59 Blairbeth Road, Burnside, Glasgow G73 4JD [E-mail: william.wilson@burnsideblairbethchurch.org.uk]	0141-583 6470
	Colin Ogilvie DCS			32 Upper Bourtree Court, Glasgow G73 4HT [E-mail: colin.ogilvie@burnsideblairbethchurch.org.uk]	0141-569 2725
6	**Busby (0141-644 2073)**				
	Jeremy C. Eve BSc BD	1998		17A Carmunnock Road, Busby, Glasgow G76 8SZ [E-mail: j-eve@sky.com]	0141-644 3670

7	**Cadder (0141-772 7436)**				
	Graham S. Finch MA BD	1977	1999	231 Kirkintilloch Road, Bishopbriggs, Glasgow G64 2JB [E-mail: gsf1957@ntlworld.com]	0141-772 1363
8	**Cambuslang: Flemington Hallside**				
	Neil Glover	2005		103 Overton Road, Halfway, Cambuslang, Glasgow G72 7XA [E-mail: neil@naglover.plus.com]	0141-641 1049 07779 280074 (Mbl)
9	**Cambuslang Parish Church**				
	A. Leslie Milton MA BD PhD	1996	2008	74 Stewarton Drive, Cambuslang, Glasgow G72 8DG [E-mail: lesliemilton@btconnect.com]	0141-641 2028
	Hilary N. McDougall (Mrs) MA BD (Assoc)	2002	2009	86 Stewarton Drive, Cambuslang, Glasgow G72 8DG [E-mail: hilary.mcdougall@ntlworld.com]	0141-586 4301
10	**Campsie (01360 310939)**				
	Alexandra Farrington LTh	2003	2011	19 Redhills View, Lennoxtown, Glasgow G66 7BL [E-mail: sandra.farrington@virgin.net]	01360 238126
11	**Chryston (H) (0141-779 4188)**				
	Mark Malcolm MA BD	1999	2008	The Manse, 109 Main Street, Chryston, Glasgow G69 9LA [E-mail: mark.minister@btinternet.com]	0141-779 1436 07731 737377 (Mbl)
	David J. McAdam BSc BD (Assoc)	1990	2000	12 Dunellan Crescent, Moodiesburn, Glasgow G69 0GA [E-mail: dmca29@hotmail.co.uk]	01236 870472
12	**Eaglesham (01355 302047)**				
	Lynn M. McChlery BA BD	2005		The Manse, Cheapside Street, Eaglesham, Glasgow G76 0NS [E-mail: lsmcchlery@btinternet.com]	01355 303495
13	**Fernhill and Cathkin**				
	Margaret McArthur BD DipMin	1995	2002	82 Blairbeth Road, Rutherglen, Glasgow G73 4JA [E-mail: revmaggiemac@hotmail.co.uk]	0141-634 1508
14	**Gartcosh (H) (01236 873770) linked with Glenboig**				
	David G. Slater BSc BA DipThRS	2011		26 Inchnock Avenue, Gartcosh, Glasgow G69 8EA [E-mail: minister@gartcoshchurch.co.uk] [E-mail: minister@glenboigchurch.co.uk] [E-mail: slater_david5@sky.com]	01236 870331 01236 872274 (Office)
15	**Giffnock: Orchardhill (0141-638 3604)**				
	Chris Vermeulen DipLT BTh MA	1986	2005	23 Huntly Avenue, Giffnock, Glasgow G46 6LW [E-mail: chris@orchardhill.org.uk]	0141-620 3734

16	**Giffnock: South (0141-638 2599)**				
	Catherine J. Beattie (Mrs) BD	2008	2011	19 Westerlands Gardens, Glasgow G77 6YJ [E-mail: catherinejbeat@aol.com]	0141-616 3451
17	**Giffnock: The Park (0141-620 2204)**				
	Calum D. Macdonald BD	1993	2001	41 Rouken Glen Road, Thornliebank, Glasgow G46 7JD [E-mail: parkhoose@msn.com]	0141-638 3023
18	**Glenboig** See Gartcosh				
19	**Greenbank (H) (0141-644 1841)**				
	Jeanne Roddick BD	2003		Greenbank Manse, 38 Eaglesham Road, Clarkston, Glasgow G76 7DJ [E-mail: jeanne.roddick@ntlworld.com]	0141-644 1395
20	**Kilsyth: Anderson**				
	Vacant			Anderson Manse, Kingston Road, Kilsyth, Glasgow G65 0HR	01236 822345
21	**Kilsyth: Burns and Old**				
	Vacant			The Grange, 17 Glasgow Road, Kilsyth, Glasgow G65 9AE	01236 823116
22	**Kirkintilloch: Hillhead**				
	Vacant				
23	**Kirkintilloch: St Columba's (H) (0141-578 0016)**				
	David M. White BA BD DMin	1988	1992	14 Crossdykes, Kirkintilloch, Glasgow G66 3EU [E-mail: write.to.me@ntlworld.com]	0141-578 4357
24	**Kirkintilloch: St David's Memorial Park (H) (0141-776 4989)**				
	Bryce Calder MA BD	1995	2001	2 Roman Road, Kirkintilloch, Glasgow G66 1EA [E-mail: ministry100@aol.com]	0141-776 1434 07986 144834 (Mbl)
	Sandy Forsyth LLB BD DipLP (Assoc)	2009		48 Kerr Street, Kirkintilloch, Glasgow G66 1JZ [E-mail: sandyforsyth67@hotmail.co.uk]	0141-777 8194 07739 639037 (Mbl)
25	**Kirkintilloch: St Mary's (0141-775 1166)**				
	Mark E. Johnstone MA BD	1993	2001	St Mary's Manse, 60 Union Street, Kirkintilloch, Glasgow G66 1DH [E-mail: markjohnstone@me.com]	0141-776 1252
26	**Lenzie: Old (H)**				
	Douglas W. Clark LTh	1993	2000	41 Kirkintilloch Road, Lenzie, Glasgow G66 4LB [E-mail: douglaswclark@hotmail.com]	0141-776 2184

27	**Lenzie: Union (H) (0141-776 1046)**				
	Daniel J.M. Carmichael MA BD	1994	2003	1 Larch Avenue, Lenzie, Glasgow G66 4HX [E-mail: minister@lupc.org]	0141-776 3831
28	**Maxwell Mearns Castle (Tel/Fax: 0141-639 5169)**				
	Scott R.McL. Kirkland BD MAR	1996	2011	122 Broomfield Avenue, Newton Mearns, Glasgow G77 5JR [E-mail: scottkirkland@maxwellmearns.org.uk]	0141-616 0642
29	**Mearns (H) (0141-639 6555)**				
	Joseph A. Kavanagh BD DipPTh MTh	1992	1998	Manse of Mearns, Mearns Road, Newton Mearns, Glasgow G77 5DE [E-mail: revjoe@hotmail.co.uk]	0141-616 2410 (Tel/Fax)
30	**Milton of Campsie (H)**				
	Julie H.C. Wilson BA BD PGCE	2006		Dunkeld, 33 Birdston Road, Milton of Campsie, Glasgow G66 8BX [E-mail: jhcwilson@msn.com]	01360 310548 07787 184800 (Mbl)
31	**Netherlee (H) (0141-637 2503)**				
	Thomas Nelson BSc BD	1992	2002	25 Ormonde Avenue, Netherlee, Glasgow G44 3QY [E-mail: tomnelson@ntlworld.com]	0141-585 7502 (Tel/Fax)
32	**Newton Mearns (H) (0141-639 7373)**				
	Esther J. Ninian (Miss) MA BD	1993	2009	28 Waterside Avenue, Newton Mearns, Glasgow G77 6TJ [E-mail: estherninian5194@btinternet.com]	0141-616 2079
33	**Rutherglen: Old (H)**				
	Alexander Thomson BSc BD MPhil PhD	1973	1985	31 Highburgh Drive, Rutherglen, Glasgow G73 3RR [E-mail: alexander.thomson6@btopenworld.com]	0141-647 6178
34	**Rutherglen: Stonelaw (0141-647 5113)**				
	Alistair S. May LLB BD PhD	2002		80 Blairbeth Road, Rutherglen, Glasgow G73 4JA [E-mail: alistair.may@ntlworld.com]	0141-583 0157
35	**Rutherglen: West and Wardlawhill (0844 736 1470)**				
	Vacant			12 Albert Drive, Rutherglen, Glasgow G73 3RT	0141-569 8547
36	**Stamperland (0141-637 4999) (H)**				
	George C. MacKay BD CertMin CertEd DipPc	1994	2004	109 Ormonde Avenue, Netherlee, Glasgow G44 3SN [E-mail: g.mackay3@btinternet.com]	0141-637 4976 (Tel/Fax)

37	**Stepps (H)**				
	Vacant				
	Linda Walker (Aux)	2008		18 Valeview Terrace, Glasgow G42 9LA [E-mail: walkerlinda@hotmail.com]	0141-649 1340
38	**Thornliebank (H)**				
	Vacant			19 Arthurlie Drive, Giffnock, Glasgow G46 6UR	
39	**Torrance (T) (01360 620970)**				
	Nigel L. Barge BSc BD	1991		1 Atholl Avenue, Torrance, Glasgow G64 4JA [E-mail: nigel.barge@sky.com]	01360 622379
40	**Twechar** See Banton				
41	**Williamwood (0141-638 2091)**				
	Iain M.A. Reid MA BD	1990	2007	125 Greenwood Road, Clarkston, Glasgow G76 7LL [E-mail: reviain.reid@ntlworld.com]	0141-571 7949
42	**Glasgow: Anderston Kelvingrove (0141-221 9408)**				
	Vacant			16 Royal Terrace, Glasgow G3 7NY	0141-332 7704
43	**Glasgow: Baillieston Mure Memorial (0141-773 1216)**				
	Malcolm Cuthbertson BA BD	1984	2010	28 Beech Avenue, Baillieston, Glasgow G69 6LF [E-mail: malcuth@aol.com]	0141-771 1217
44	**Glasgow: Baillieston St Andrew's (0141-771 6629)**				
	Alisdair T. MacLeod-Mair MEd DipTheol	2001	2007	55 Station Park, Baillieston, Glasgow G69 7XY [E-mail: revalisdair@hotmail.com]	0141-771 1791
45	**Glasgow: Balshagray Victoria Park**				
	Campbell Mackinnon BSc BD	1982	2001	20 St Kilda Drive, Glasgow G14 9JN [E-mail: campbell54@btinternet.com]	0141-954 9780
46	**Glasgow: Barlanark Greyfriars (0141-771 6477)**				
	Vacant			4 Rhindmuir Grove, Glasgow G69 6NE	0141-771 1240
47	**Glasgow: Blawarthill**				
	G. Melvyn Wood MA BD	1982	2009	46 Earlbank Avenue, Glasgow G14 9HL [E-mail: gmelvynwood@gmail.com]	0141-579 6521

48	**Glasgow: Bridgeton St Francis in the East (H) (L) (0141-556 2830) (Church House: Tel: 0141-554 8045)**				
	Howard R. Hudson MA BD	1982	1984	10 Albany Drive, Rutherglen, Glasgow G73 3QN [E-mail: howard.hudson@ntlworld.com]	0141-587 8667
	Margaret S. Beaton (Miss) DCS			64 Gardenside Grove, Fernlee Meadows, Carmyle, Glasgow G32 8EZ [E-mail: margaret@churchhouse.plus.com]	0141-646 2297
49	**Glasgow: Broomhill (0141-334 2540)**				
	William B. Ferguson BA BD	1971	1987	27 St Kilda Drive, Glasgow G14 9LN [E-mail: revferg@aol.com]	0141-959 3204
50	**Glasgow: Calton Parkhead (0141-554 3866)**				
	Alison Davidge MA BD	1990	2008	98 Drumover Drive, Glasgow G31 5RP [E-mail: adavidge@sky.com]	07843 625059 (Mbl)
51	**Glasgow: Cardonald (0141-882 6264)**				
	Calum MacLeod BA BD	1979	2007	133 Newtyle Road, Paisley PA1 3LB [E-mail: pangur@sky.com]	0141-887 2726
52	**Glasgow: Carmunnock (0141-644 0655)**				
	G. Gray Fletcher BSc BD	1989	2001	The Manse, 161 Waterside Road, Carmunnock, Glasgow G76 9AJ [E-mail: gray.fletcher@virgin.net]	0141-644 1578 (Tel/Fax)
53	**Glasgow: Carmyle linked with Kenmuir Mount Vernon**				
	Murdo Maclean BD CertMin	1997	1999	3 Meryon Road, Glasgow G32 9NW [E-mail: murdo.maclean@ntlworld.com]	0141-778 2625
54	**Glasgow: Carnwadric (E)**				
	Graeme K. Bell BA BD	1983		62 Loganswell Road, Thornliebank, Glasgow G46 8AX [E-mail: graemekbell@googlemail.com]	0141-638 5884
	Mary Gargrave (Mrs) DCS	1989		90 Mount Annan Drive, Glasgow G44 4RZ [E-mail: mary.gargrave@btinternet.com]	0141-561 4681
55	**Glasgow: Castlemilk East (H) (0141-634 2444) linked with Castlemilk West**				
	Vacant			156 Old Castle Road, Glasgow G44 5TW	0141-637 5451
	Karen Hamilton (Mrs) DCS	1995	2009	6 Beckfield Gate, Glasgow G33 1SW [E-mail: k.hamilton6@btinternet.com]	0141-558 3195 07970 872859 (Mbl)
56	**Glasgow: Castlemilk West (H) (0141-634 1480)** See Castlemilk East				

57	**Glasgow: Cathcart Old (0141-637 4168)**				
	Neil W. Galbraith BD CertMin	1987	1996	21 Courthill Avenue, Cathcart, Glasgow G44 5AA [E-mail: revneilgalbraith@hotmail.com]	0141-633 5248 (Tel/Fax)
58	**Glasgow: Cathcart Trinity (H) (0141-637 6658)**				
	Iain Morrison BD	1991	2003	82 Merrylee Road, Glasgow G43 2QZ [E-mail: iain77@tiscali.co.uk]	0141-633 3744
	Wilma Pearson (Mrs) BD (Assoc)	2004		90 Newlands Road, Glasgow G43 2JR [E-mail: wilma.pearson@ntlworld.com]	0141-632 2491
59	**Glasgow: Cathedral (High or St Mungo's) (0141-552 6891)**				
	Laurence A.B. Whitley MA BD PhD	1975	2007	41 Springfield Road, Bishopbriggs, Glasgow G64 1PL [E-mail: labwhitley@btinternet.com]	0141-762 2719
60	**Glasgow: Clincarthill (H) (0141-632 4206)**				
	Mike R. Gargrave BD	2008	2010	90 Mount Annan Drive, Glasgow G44 4RZ [E-mail: mike.gargrave@btinternet.com]	0141-561 4681
61	**Glasgow: Colston Milton (0141-772 1922)**				
	Christopher J. Rowe BA BD	2008		118 Birsay Road, Milton, Glasgow G22 7QP [E-mail: ministercolstonmilton@yahoo.co.uk]	0141-564 1138
62	**Glasgow: Colston Wellpark (H)**				
	Vacant			16 Bishopsgate Gardens, Colston, Glasgow G21 1XS	0141-589 8866
63	**Glasgow: Cranhill (H) (0141-774 3344)**				
	Muriel B. Pearson (Ms) MA BD PGCE	2004		31 Lethamhill Crescent, Glasgow G33 2SH [E-mail: murielpearson@btinternet.com]	0141-770 6873 07951 888860 (Mbl)
64	**Glasgow: Croftfoot (H) (0141-637 3913)**				
	Robert M. Silver BA BD	1995	2011	4 Inchmurrin Gardens, High Burnside, Rutherglen, Glasgow G73 5RU [E-mail: rob.silver@tiscali.co.uk]	
65	**Glasgow: Dennistoun New (H) (0141-550 2825)**				
	Ian M.S. McInnes BD DipMin	1995	2008	31 Pencaitland Drive, Glasgow G32 8RL [E-mail: ian.liz1@ntlworld.com]	0141-564 6498

66	**Glasgow: Drumchapel Drumry St Mary's (0141-944 1998)** **This charge will be dissolved in September 2011**				
67	**Glasgow: Drumchapel St Andrew's (0141-944 3758)**				
	John S. Purves LLB BD	1983	1984	6 Firdon Crescent, Old Drumchapel, Glasgow G15 6QQ [E-mail: john.s.purves@talk21.com]	0141-944 4566
68	**Glasgow: Drumchapel St Mark's**				
	Audrey Jamieson BD MTh	2004	2007	146 Garscadden Road, Glasgow G15 6PR [E-mail: audrey.jamieson2@btinternet.com]	0141-944 5440
69	**Glasgow: Easterhouse St George's and St Peter's (E) (0141-771 8810)**				
	Vacant			3 Barony Gardens, Baillieston, Glasgow G69 6TS	0141-573 8200
70	**Glasgow: Eastwood**				
	Graham R.G. Cartlidge MA BD STM	1977	2010	54 Mansewood Road, Eastwood, Glasgow G43 1TL [E-mail: g.cartlidge@ntlworld.com]	0141-649 0463
71	**Glasgow: Gairbraid (H)**				
	Donald Michael MacInnes BD	2002	2011	8 Fruin Road, Glasgow G15 6SQ [E-mail: revdmmi@googlemail.com]	0141-258 8683
72	**Glasgow: Gallowgate**				
	Peter L.V. Davidge BD MTh	2003	2009	98 Drumover Drive, Glasgow G31 5RP	07765 096599 (Mbl)
73	**Glasgow: Garthamlock and Craigend East (E)**				
	Valerie J. Duff (Miss) DMin	1993	1996	9 Craigievar Court, Glasgow G33 5DJ [E-mail: valduff@tiscali.co.uk]	0141-774 6364
	Marion Buchanan (Mrs) MA DCS			16 Almond Drive, East Kilbride, Glasgow G74 2HX [E-mail: marion.buchanan@btinternet.com]	01355 228776
74	**Glasgow: Gorbals**				
	Ian F. Galloway BA BD	1976	1996	44 Riverside Road, Glasgow G43 2EF [E-mail: ianfgalloway@msn.com]	0141-649 5250
75	**Glasgow: Govan and Linthouse**				
	Moyna McGlynn (Mrs) BD PhD	1999	2008	19 Dumbreck Road, Glasgow G41 5LJ [E-mail: moyna_mcglynn@hotmail.com]	0141-419 0308
	Judith Breakey (Ms) LizTheol MTh DipEd (Assoc)	2010		Flat 3/2, 8 Mingarry Street, Glasgow G20 8NT [E-mail: judith.breakey@gmail.com]	07858 507282 (Mbl)
	Paul Cathcart DCS			9 Glen More, East Kilbride, Glasgow G74 2AP	01355 243970

76 Glasgow: Govanhill Trinity
Lily F. McKinnon MA BD PGCE 1993 2006 12 Carlton Gate, Giffnock, Glasgow G46 6NU 0141-637 8399
[E-mail: lily.mckinnon@yahoo.co.uk]

77 Glasgow: High Carntyne (0141-778 4186)
Joan Ross (Miss) BSc BD PhD 1999 2005 163 Lethamhill Road, Glasgow G33 2SQ 0141-770 9247
[E-mail: joan@highcarntyne.plus.com]

78 Glasgow: Hillington Park (H)
John B. MacGregor BD 1999 2004 61 Ralston Avenue, Glasgow G52 3NB 0141-882 7000
[E-mail: johnmacgregor61@hotmail.co.uk]

79 Glasgow: Househillwood St Christopher's
May M. Allison (Mrs) BD 1988 2001 12 Leverndale Court, Crookston, Glasgow G53 7SJ 0141-810 5953
[E-mail: revmayallison@hotmail.com]

80 Glasgow: Hyndland (H) (Website: www.hyndlandparishchurch.org)
Vacant 24 Hughenden Gardens, Glasgow G12 9YH 0141-334 1002

81 Glasgow: Ibrox (H) (0141-427 0896)
Elisabeth G.B. Spence (Miss) BD DipEd 1995 2008 59 Langhaul Road, Glasgow G53 7SE 0141-883 7744
[E-mail: revelisabeth@spenceweb.net]

82 Glasgow: John Ross Memorial Church for Deaf People
(Voice Text: 0141-420 1391; Fax: 0141-420 3778)
Richard C. Durno DSW CQSW 1989 1998 31 Springfield Road, Bishopbriggs, (Voice/Text/Fax) 0141-772 1052
Glasgow G64 1PJ (Voice/Text/Voicemail) (Mbl) 07748 607721
[E-mail: richard.durno@btinternet.com]

83 Glasgow: Jordanhill (Tel: 0141-959 2496)
Colin C. Renwick BMus BD 1989 1996 96 Southbrae Drive, Glasgow G13 1TZ 0141-959 1310
[E-mail: jordchurch@btconnect.com]

84 Glasgow: Kelvin Stevenson Memorial (0141-339 1750)
Gordon Kirkwood BSc BD PGCE MTh 1987 2003 Flat 2/2, 94 Hyndland Road, Glasgow G12 9PZ 0141-334 5352
[E-mail: gordonkirkwood@tiscali.co.uk]

85	**Glasgow: Kelvinside Hillhead (0141-334 2788)**				
	Vacant			39 Athole Gardens, Glasgow G12 9BQ	0141-339 2865
86	**Glasgow: Kenmuir Mount Vernon** See Carmyle				
87	**Glasgow: King's Park (H) (0141-636 8688)**				
	Sandra Boyd (Mrs) BEd BD	2007		1101 Aikenhead Road, Glasgow G44 5SL [E-mail: sandraboyd.bofa@btopenworld.com]	0141-637 2803
88	**Glasgow: Kinning Park (0141-427 3063)**				
	Margaret H. Johnston BD	1988	2000	168 Arbroath Avenue, Cardonald, Glasgow G52 3HH [E-mail: marniejohnston7@aol.com]	0141-810 3782
89	**Glasgow: Knightswood St Margaret's (H)**				
	Alexander M. Fraser BD DipMin	1985	2009	26 Airthrey Avenue, Glasgow G14 9LJ [E-mail: sandyfraser2@hotmail.com]	0141-959 7075
	Marion Perry (Mrs) (Aux)	2009		0/2, 75 Earl Street, Glasgow G14 0DG [E-mail: perryask@hotmail.com]	0141-434 1280 07563 180662 (Mbl)
90	**Glasgow: Langside (0141-632 7520)**				
	David N. McLachlan BD	1985	2004	36 Madison Avenue, Glasgow G44 5AQ [E-mail: dmclachlan77@hotmail.com]	0141-637 0797
91	**Glasgow: Lansdowne**				
	Roy J.M. Henderson MA BD DipMin	1987	1992	18 Woodlands Drive, Glasgow G4 9EH [E-mail: roy.henderson7@ntlworld.com]	0141-339 2794
92	**Glasgow: Lochwood (H) (0141-771 2649)**				
	Stuart M. Duff BA	1997		42 Rhindmuir Road, Swinton, Glasgow G69 6AZ [E-mail: stuart.duff@gmail.com]	0141-773 2756
93	**Glasgow: Martyrs', The**				
	Vacant			30 Louden Hill Road, Robroyston, Glasgow G33 1GA	0141-558 7451
94	**Glasgow: Maryhill (H) (0141-946 3512)**				
	Stuart C. Matthews BD MA	2006		251 Milngavie Road, Bearsden, Glasgow G61 3DQ [E-mail: stuartandlindsay@gmail.com]	0141-942 0804
	James Hamilton DCS	1997	2000	6 Beckfield Gate, Robroyston, Glasgow G33 1SW [E-mail: j.hamilton111@btinternet.com]	0141-558 3195

95 Glasgow: Merrylea (0141-637 2009)
David P. Hood BD CertMin DipIOB(Scot) 1997 2001 4 Pilmuir Avenue, Glasgow G44 3HX 0141-637 6700
[E-mail: dphood3@ntlworld.com]

96 Glasgow: Mosspark (H) (0141-882 2240)
Vacant 396 Kilmarnock Road, Glasgow G43 2DJ 0141-632 1247

97 Glasgow: Newlands South (H) (0141-632 3055)
John D. Whiteford MA BD 1989 1997 24 Monreith Road, Glasgow G43 2NY 0141-632 2588
[E-mail: jwhiteford@hotmail.com]

98 Glasgow: Partick South (H)
James Andrew McIntyre BD 2010 3 Branklyn Crescent, Glasgow G13 1GJ 0141-959 3732
[E-mail: revparticksouth@hotmail.co.uk]

99 Glasgow: Partick Trinity (H)
Stuart J. Smith BEng BD MTh 1994 99 Balshagray Avenue, Glasgow G11 7EQ 0141-576 7149
[E-mail: ssmith99@ntlworld.com]

100 Glasgow: Penilee St Andrew (H) (0141-882 2691)
Lyn Peden (Mrs) BD 2010 80 Tweedsmuir Road, Glasgow G52 2RX 0141-883 9873
[E-mail: lynpeden@yahoo.com]

101 Glasgow: Pollokshaws (0141-649 1879)
Vacant 33 Mannering Road, Glasgow G41 3SW 0141-649 0458

102 Glasgow: Pollokshields (H)
David R. Black MA BD 1986 1997 36 Glencairn Drive, Glasgow G41 4PW 0141-423 4000
[E-mail: minister@pollokshieldschurch.org.uk]

103 Glasgow: Possilpark (0141-336 8028)
Vacant 108 Erradale Street, Lambhill, Glasgow G22 6PT 0141-336 6909

104 Glasgow: Priesthill and Nitshill (0141-881 6541)
Douglas M. Nicol BD CA 1987 1996 36 Springkell Drive, Glasgow G41 4EZ 0141-427 7877
[E-mail: dougiemnicol@aol.com]

105 Glasgow: Queen's Park (0141-423 3654)

David S.M. Malcolm BD	2011		17 Linndale Drive, Carmunnock Grange, Glasgow G45 0QE [E-mail: DavidSMMalcolm@aol.com]	0141-634 1097

106 Glasgow: Renfield St Stephen's (Tel: 0141-332 4293; Fax: 0141-332 8482)

Peter M. Gardner MA BD	1988	2002	101 Hill Street, Glasgow G3 6TY [E-mail: peter@rsschurch.net]	0141-353 0349

107 Glasgow: Robroyston (New Charge Development) (0141-558 8414)

Jonathan A. Keefe BSc BD	2009		7 Beckfield Drive, Glasgow G33 1SR [E-mail: jonathanakeefe@aol.com]	0141-558 2952

108 Glasgow: Ruchazie (0141-774 2759)

William F. Hunter MA BD	1986	1999	18 Borthwick Street, Glasgow G33 3UU [E-mail: mail@billhunter.plus.com]	0141-774 6860

109 Glasgow: Ruchill Kelvinside (0141-946 0466)

Vacant			9 Kirklee Road, Glasgow G12 0RQ	0141-357 3249

110 Glasgow: St Andrew's East (0141-554 1485)

Barbara D. Quigley (Mrs) MTheol ThM DPS	1979	2011	43 Broompark Drive, Glasgow G31 2JB [E-mail: bdquigley@aol.com]	0141-237 7982

111 Glasgow: St Columba (GE) (0141-221 3305)

Vacant			1 Reelick Avenue, Peterson Park, Glasgow G13 4NF	0141-952 0948

112 Glasgow: St David's Knightswood (0141-954 1081)

Graham M. Thain LLB BD	1988	1999	60 Southbrae Drive, Glasgow G13 1QD [E-mail: graham_thain@btopenworld.com]	0141-959 2904

113 Glasgow: St Enoch's Hogganfield (H) (Tel: 0141-770 5694; Fax: 0870 284 0084) (E-mail: church@st-enoch.org.uk) (Website: www.stenochshogganfield.org.uk)

Graham K. Blount LLB BD PhD	1976	2010	43 Smithycroft Road, Glasgow G33 2RH [E-mail: graham.blount@yahoo.co.uk]	0141-770 7593

114 Glasgow: St George's Tron (0141-221 2141)

William J.U. Philip MB ChB MRCP BD	2004		12 Dargarvel Avenue, Glasgow G41 5LU [E-mail: wp@wphilip.com]	0141-427 1402
Robert S. Fyall MA BD PhD (Assoc)	1986	2009	7 Queen's Gate, Glasgow G76 7HE	0141-638 9077

115 Glasgow: St James' (Pollok) (0141-882 4984)
John W. Mann BSc MDiv DMin | 2004 | | 30 Ralston Avenue, Glasgow G52 3NA [E-mail: drjohnmann@hotmail.com] | 0141-883 7405

116 Glasgow: St John's Renfield (0141-339 7021) (Website: www.stjohns-renfield.org.uk)
Fiona L. Lillie (Mrs) BA BD MLitt | 1995 | 2009 | 26 Leicester Avenue, Glasgow G12 0LU [E-mail: fionalillie@btinternet.com] | 0141-339 4637

117 Glasgow: St Margaret's Tollcross Park
Vacant | | | 31 Kenmuir Avenue, Sandyhills, Glasgow G32 9LE | 0141-778 5060

118 Glasgow: St Nicholas' Cardonald
Sandi McGill (Ms) BD | 2002 | 2007 | 104 Lamington Road, Glasgow G52 2SE [E-mail: smcgillbox-mail@yahoo.co.uk] | 0141-882 2065

119 Glasgow: St Paul's (0141-770 8559)
Martin R. Forrest BA MA BD | 1988 | 2009 | 38 Lochview Drive, Glasgow G33 1QF [E-mail: jmr.forrest@btopenworld.com] | 0141-770 1505

120 Glasgow: St Rollox (0141-558 1809)
James K. Torrens MB ChB BD | 2005 | | 42 Melville Gardens, Bishopbriggs, Glasgow G64 3DE [E-mail: james.torrens@ntlworld.com] | 0141-562 6296

121 Glasgow: Sandyford Henderson Memorial (H) (L)
Vacant | | | 66 Woodend Drive, Glasgow G13 1TG | 0141-954 9013

122 Glasgow: Sandyhills (0141-778 3415)
Graham T. Atkinson MA BD MTh | 2006 | | 60 Wester Road, Glasgow G32 9JJ [E-mail: gtatkinson@o2.co.uk] | 0141-778 2174

123 Glasgow: Scotstoun (T)
Richard Cameron BD DipMin | 2000 | | 15 Northland Drive, Glasgow G14 9BE [E-mail: rev.rickycam@live.co.uk] | 0141-959 4637

124 Glasgow: Shawlands (0141-649 1773)
Stephen A. Blakey BSc BD | 1977 | 2005 | 29 St Ronan's Drive, Glasgow G41 3SQ [E-mail: shawlandskirk@aol.com] | 0141-649 2034

125 Glasgow: Sherbrooke St Gilbert's (H) (0141-427 1968)

Thomas L. Pollock BA BD MTh FSAScot JP	1982	2003	114 Springkell Avenue, Glasgow G41 4EW [E-mail: tompollock06@aol.com]	0141-427 2094

126 Glasgow: Shettleston New (0141-778 0857)

Ronald A.S. Craig BAcc BD	1983	2007	211 Sandyhills Road, Glasgow G32 9NB [E-mail: rascraig@ntlworld.com]	0141-778 1286
Dot Getliffe (Mrs) DCS	2008		3 Woodview Terrace, Hamilton ML3 9DP [E-mail: dgetliffe@aol.com]	01698 423504

127 Glasgow: Shettleston Old (T) (H) (0141-778 2484)

Vacant			57 Mansionhouse Road, Mount Vernon, Glasgow G32 0RP	0141-778 8904

128 Glasgow: South Carntyne (H) (0141-778 1343)

Vacant			47 Broompark Drive, Glasgow G31 2JB	0141-554 3275

129 Glasgow: South Shawlands (T) (0141-649 4656)

Vacant			391 Kilmarnock Road, Glasgow G43 2NU	0141-632 0013

130 Glasgow: Springburn (H) (0141-557 2345)

Alan A. Ford BD	1977	2000	3 Tofthill Avenue, Bishopbriggs, Glasgow G64 3PA [E-mail: springburnchurch@fordsall.com]	0141-762 1844 07710 455737 (Mbl)

131 Glasgow: Temple Anniesland (0141-959 1814)

Fiona Gardner (Mrs) BD MA MLitt	1997	2011	76 Victoria Park Drive North, Glasgow G14 9PJ [E-mail: fionaandcolin@hotmail.com]	0141-959 5835
Marion Perry (Mrs) (Aux)	2009		0/2, 75 Earl Street, Glasgow G14 0DG [E-mail: perryask@hotmail.com]	0141-434 1280 07563 180662 (Mbl)

132 Glasgow: Toryglen (H)

Sandra Black (Mrs) BSc BD	1988	2003	36 Glencairn Drive, Glasgow G41 4PW [E-mail: revsblack@btinternet.com]	0141-423 0867

133 Glasgow: Trinity Possil and Henry Drummond

Richard G. Buckley BD MTh	1990	1995	50 Highfield Drive, Glasgow G12 0HL [E-mail: richardbuckleyis@hotmail.com]	0141-339 2870

134 Glasgow: Tron St Mary's (0141-558 1011)				
P. Jill Clancy (Mrs) BD DipMin	2000	2008	Tron St Mary's Church, 128 Red Road, Balornock, Glasgow G21 4PJ [E-mail: jgibson@totalise.co.uk]	0141-558 1011
135 Glasgow: Victoria Tollcross				
Monica Michelin Salomon BD	1999	2007	228 Hamilton Road, Glasgow G32 9QU [E-mail: monica@michelin-salomon.freeserve.co.uk]	0141-778 2413
136 Glasgow: Wallacewell (New Charge Development)				
Daniel Frank BA MDiv DMin	1984	2011	8 Streamfield Gate, Glasgow G33 1SJ [E-mail: daniellouis106@gmail.com]	0141-558 5653
137 Glasgow: Wellington (H) (0141-339 0454)				
David I. Sinclair BSc BD PhD DipSW	1990	2008	31 Hughenden Gardens, Glasgow G12 9YH [E-mail: davidsinclair@btinternet.com]	0141-334 2343
138 Glasgow: Whiteinch (Website: www.whiteinchcofs.co.uk)				
Alan McWilliam BD MTh	1993	2000	65 Victoria Park Drive South, Glasgow G14 9NX [E-mail: alan@whiteinchchurch.org]	0141-576 9020
Alex W. Smeed MA BD (Assoc)	2008		3/1, 24 Thornwood Road, Glasgow G11 7RB [E-mail: alex@whiteinchchurch.org]	0141-337 3878 07709 756495 (Mbl)
139 Glasgow: Yoker (T)				
Karen E. Hendry BSc BD	2005		15 Coldingham Avenue, Glasgow G14 0PX [E-mail: karen@hendry-k.fsnet.co.uk]	0141-952 3620

Alexander, Eric J. MA BD	1958 1997	(Glasgow: St George's Tron)	77 Norwood Park, Bearsden, Glasgow G61 2RZ	0141-942 4404
Allen, Martin A.W. MA BD ThM	1977 2007	(Chryston)	Lealenge, 85 High Barrwood Road, Kilsyth, Glasgow G65 0EE	01236 826616
Alston, William G.	1961 2009	(Glasgow: North Kelvinside)	Flat 0/2, 5 Knightswood Court, Glasgow G13 2XN [E-mail: williamalston@hotmail.com]	0141-959 3113
Barr, Alexander C. MA BD	1950 1992	(Glasgow: St Nicholas' Cardonald)	25 Fisher Drive, Phoenix Park, Paisley PA1 2TP	0141-848 5941
Barr, John BSc PhD BD	1958 1979	(Kilmacolm: Old)	31 Kelvin Court, Glasgow G12 0AD	0141-357 4338
Bayes, Muriel C. DCS	1963	(Deaconess)	Flat 6, Carlton Court, 10 Fenwick Road, Glasgow G46 6AN	0141-633 0865
Bell, John L. MA BD FRSCM DUniv	1978 1988	Iona Community	Flat 2/1, 31 Lansdowne Crescent, Glasgow G20 6NH	0141-334 0688
Bell, Sandra (Mrs) DCS		Chaplain: Royal Infirmary	62 Loganswell Road, Glasgow G42 8AX	0141-638 5884
Birch, James PgDip FRSA FIOC	2001 2007	(Auxiliary Minister)	1 Kirkhill Grove, Cambuslang, Glasgow G72 8EH	0141-583 1722
Black, William B. MA BD	1972 2011	(Stornoway: High)	33 Tankerland Road, Glasgow G44 4EN [E-mail: revwillieblack@gmail.com]	0141-637 4717

Blount, A. Sheila (Mrs) BD BA	1978	2010	(Cupar: St John's and Dairsie United)	43 Smithycroft Road, Glasgow G33 2RH [E-mail: asblount@orange.net]	0141-770 7593
Bradley, Andrew W. BD	1975	2007	(Paisley: Lylesland)	Flat 1/1, 38 Cairnhill View, Bearsden, Glasgow G61 1RP	0141-931 5344
Brain, Isobel J. (Mrs) MA	1987	1997	(Ballantrae)	14 Chesterfield Court, 1240 Great Western Road, Glasgow G12 0BJ	0141-357 2249
Brice, Dennis G. BSc BD	1981		(Taiwan)	18 Hermitage Avenue, Benfleet, Essex SS7 1TQ	01702 555333
Brough, Robin BA	1968	2002	(Whitburn: Brucefield)	'Kildavanan', 10 Printers Lea, Lennoxtown, Glasgow G66 7GF	01360 310223
Bryden, William A. BD	1977	1984	(Yoker: Old with St Matthew's)	145 Bearsden Road, Glasgow G13 1BS	0141-959 5213
Bull, Alister W. BD DipMin	1994	2001	Head of Chaplaincy Service	Chaplaincy Centre Office, First Floor, Queen Mother's Hospital, Yorkhill Division, Dalnair Street, Glasgow G3 8SJ [E-mail: alister.bull@yorkhill.scot.nhs.uk]	0141-201 0000
Campbell, A. Iain MA DipEd	1961	1997	(Busby)	430 Clarkston Road, Glasgow G44 3QF [E-mail: bellmac@sagainternet.co.uk]	0141-637 7460
Campbell-Jack, W.C. BD MTh PhD	1979	2011	(Glasgow: Possilpark)	c/o The Presbytery of Glasgow, 260 Bath Street, Glasgow G2 4JP [E-mail: c.c-j@homecall.co.uk]	0141-332 6606
Collard, John K. MA BD	1986	2003	Presbytery Congregational Facilitator	1 Nelson Terrace, East Kilbride, Glasgow G74 2EY	01355 520093
Cunningham, Alexander MA BD	1961	2002	(Presbytery Clerk)	The Glen, 103 Glenmavis Road, Airdrie ML6 0PQ	01236 763012
Cunningham, James S.A. MA BD BLitt PhD	1992	2000	(Glasgow: Barlanark Greyfriars)	'Kirkland', 5 Inveresk Place, Coatbridge ML5 2DA	01236 421541
Currie, Robert MA	1955	1990	(Community Minister)	Flat 3/2, 13 Redlands Road, Glasgow G12 0SJ	0141-334 5111
Drummond, John W. MA BD	1971	2011	(Rutherglen: West and Wardlawhill)	25 Kingsburn Drive, Rutherglen, Glasgow G73 2AN	0141-647 6507
Duff, T. Malcolm F. MA BD	1985	2009	(Glasgow: Queen's Park)	54 Hawkhead Road, Paisley PA1 3NB	0141-570 0614 (Mbl) 07846 926584
Ferguson, James B. LTh	1972	2002	(Lenzie: Union)	3 Bridgeway Place, Kirkintilloch, Glasgow G66 3HW	0141-588 5868
Finlay, William P. MA BD	1969	2000	(Glasgow: Townhead Blochairn)	High Corrie, Brodick, Isle of Arran KA27 8JB	01770 810689
Fleming, Alexander F. MA BD	1966	1995	(Strathblane)	11 Bankwood Drive, Kilsyth, Glasgow G65 0GZ	01236 821461
Galloway, Kathy (Mrs) BD	1977	2002	(Leader: Iona Community)	20 Hamilton Park Avenue, Glasgow G12 8UU	0141-357 4079
Gay, Douglas C. MA BD PhD	1998	2005	University of Glasgow	23 Clouston Street, Glasgow G20 8QP [E-mail: doug.gay@glasgow.ac.uk]	0141-330 2073 (Mbl) 07971 321452
Gibson, H. Marshall MA BD	1957	1996	(Glasgow: St Thomas' Gallowgate)	39 Burntbroom Drive, Glasgow G69 7XG	0141-771 0749
Gibson, Michael BD STM	1974	2001	(Giffnock: The Park)	12 Mile End Park, Pocklington, York YO42 2TH	
Grant, David I.M. MA BD	1969	2003	(Dalry: Trinity)	8 Mossbank Drive, Glasgow G33 1LS	0141-770 7186
Gray, Christine M. (Mrs)			(Deaconess)	11 Woodside Avenue, Thornliebank, Glasgow G46 7HR	0141-571 1008
Green, Alex H. MA BD	1986	2010	(Strathblane)	44 Laburnum Drive, Milton of Campsie, Glasgow G66 8HY [E-mail: lesvert@btinternet.com]	01360 313001
Gregson, Elizabeth M. (Mrs) BD	1996	2001	(Drumchapel: St Andrew's)	17 Westfields, Bishopbriggs, Glasgow G64 3PL	0141-563 1918
Grimstone, A. Frank MA	1949	1986	(Glasgow: Calton Parkhead)	144C Howth Drive, Glasgow G13 1RL [E-mail: doreen@dodistone.plus.com]	0141-954 1009
Haley, Derek BD DPS	1960	1999	(Chaplain: Gartnavel Royal)	9 Kinnaird Crescent, Bearsden, Glasgow G61 2BN	0141-942 9281
Harper, Anne J.M. (Miss) BD STM MTh CertSocPsych	1979	1990	(Hospital Chaplain)	122 Greenock Road, Bishopton PA7 5AS	01505 862466
Harvey, W. John BA BD	1965	2002	(Edinburgh: Corstorphine Craigsbank)	501 Shields Road, Glasgow G41 2RF	0141-429 3774
Haughton, Frank MA BD	1942	2000	(Kirkintilloch: St Mary's)	64 Regent Street, Kirkintilloch, Glasgow G66 1JF	0141-777 6802
Hope, Evelyn P. (Miss) BA BD	1990	1998	(Wishaw: Thornlie)	Flat 0/1, 48 Moss Side Road, Glasgow G41 3UA	0141-649 1522
Houston, Thomas C. BA	1975	2004	(Glasgow: Priesthill and Nitshill)	63 Broomhouse Crescent, Uddingston, Glasgow G71 7RE	0141-771 0577

Name	Ord.	Ret.	Position	Address		Telephone
Hughes, Helen (Miss) DCS			Deacon	2/2, 43 Burnbank Terrace, Glasgow G20 6UQ		0141-333 9459
Hunter, Alastair G. MSc BD	1976	1980	(University of Glasgow)	487 Shields Road, Glasgow G41 2RG		0141-429 1687
Johnston, Robert W.M. MA BD STM	1964	1999	(Glasgow: Temple Anniesland)	13 Kilmardinny Crescent, Bearsden, Glasgow G61 3NP		0141-931 5862
Johnstone, H. Martin J. MA BD MTh PhD	1989	2000	Urban Priority Areas Adviser	3/1, 952 Pollokshaws Road, Glasgow G41 2ET [E-mail: mjohnstone@cofscotland.org.uk]		0141-636 5819
Keddie, David A. MA BD	1966	2005	(Glasgow: Linthouse St Kenneth's)	21 Ilay Road, Bearsden, Glasgow G61 1QG [E-mail: revked@hotmail.com]		0141-942 5173
Kerr, Angus BD CertMin ThM DMin	1983	2008	Presbytery Clerk	27 Pelham Court, Thornton Grange, Jackton, East Kilbride, Glasgow G74 5PZ		0141-332 6606
Lancaster, Craig MA BD	2004	2011	Chaplain: RAF	c/o The Ministries Council, 121 George Street, Edinburgh EH2 4YN		0131-225 5722
Lang, I. Pat (Miss) BSc	1996	2003	(Dunoon: The High Kirk)	37 Crawford Drive, Glasgow G15 6TW		0141-944 2240
Levison, C.L. MA BD	1972	1998	(Health Care Chaplaincy Training and Development Officer)	5 Deaconsbank Avenue, Stewarton Road, Glasgow G46 7UN		0141-620 3492
Lewis, E.M.H. MA	1962	1993	(Glasgow: Drumchapel St Andrew's)	c/o Mr Kelvin McAlister, 30 Ardbeg Road, Carfin, Motherwell ML1 4FE		
Lloyd, John M. BD CertMin	1984	2009	(Glasgow: Croftfoot)	17 Acacia Way, Cambuslang, Glasgow G72 7ZY	(Mbl)	07879 812816
Locke, David I.W. MA MSc BD	2000	2009	(Glasgow: Barlanark Greyfriars)	Flat 15, 65 Partickhill Road, Glasgow G11 5AD [E-mail: davidlockerev@yahoo.co.uk]	(Mbl)	07776 448301
Lunan, David W. MA BD DUniv	1970	2002	(Presbytery Clerk)	30 Mill Road, Banton, Glasgow G65 0RD		01236 824110
Macaskill, Marjory (Mrs) LLB BD	1990	1998	Chaplain: University of Strathclyde	1/3, 2 Wyndham Court, Glasgow G12 0TY [E-mail: marjory.macaskill@strath.ac.uk]	(Home) (Work)	0141-337 6196 0141-548 2727
MacBain, Ian W. BD	1971	1993	(Coatbridge: Coatdyke)	24 Thornyburn Drive, Baillieston, Glasgow G69 7ER		0141-771 7030
MacDonald, Anne (Miss) BA DCS			Healthcare Chaplain: Leverndale Hospital	c/o Leverndale Hospital, Glasgow G53 7TU		0141-211 6695
MacDonald, Kenneth MA BA	2001	2006	(Auxiliary Minister)	5 Henderland Road, Bearsden, Glasgow G61 1AH		0141-943 1103
MacFadyen, Anne M. (Mrs) BSc BD FSAScot	1995		(Auxiliary Minister)	295 Mearns Road, Glasgow G77 5LT		0141-639 3605
MacKay, Alan H. BD	1974	2010	(Glasgow: Mosspark)	Flat 1/1, 18 Newburgh Street, Glasgow G43 2XR [E-mail: alanhmackay@aol.com]		0141-632 0527
MacKinnon, Charles M. BD	1989	2009	(Kilsyth: Anderson)	36 Hilton Terrace, Bishopbriggs, Glasgow G64 3HB [E-mail: cm.ccmackinnon@tiscali.co.uk]		0141-772 3811
McLachlan, Eric BD MTh	1978	2005	(Glasgow: Cardonald)	268 Dyke Road, Knightswood, Glasgow G13 4QX [E-mail: eric.mclachlan@ntlworld.com]		0141-954 1574
McLachlan, Fergus C. BD	1982	2009	(Hospital Chaplain)	46 Queen Square, Glasgow G41 2AZ		0141-423 3830
McLachlan, T. Alastair BSc	1972	2009	(Craignish with Kilbrandon and Kilchattan with Kilninver and Kilmelford)	9 Alder Road, Milton of Campsie, Glasgow G66 8HH [E-mail: talastair@btinternet.com]		01360 319861
McLaren, D. Muir MA BD MTh PhD	1971	2001	(Glasgow: Mosspark)	House 44, 145 Shawhill Road, Glasgow G43 1SX [E-mail: muir44@yahoo.co.uk]	(Mbl)	07931 155779
McLay, Alastair D. BSc BD	1989	2004	(Glasgow: Shawlands)	183 King's Park Avenue, Glasgow G44 4HZ		0141-569 5503
Macleod, Donald BD LRAM DRSAM	1987	2008	(Blairgowrie)	9 Millersneuk Avenue, Lenzie G66 5HJ		0141-776 6235
Macnaughton, J.A. MA BD	1949	1989	(Glasgow: Hyndland)	62 Lauderdale Gardens, Glasgow G12 9QW		0141-339 1294
MacPherson, James B. DCS			(Deacon)	0/1, 104 Cartside Street, Glasgow G42 9TQ		0141-616 6468
MacQuarrie, Stuart JP BD BSc MBA	1984	2001	Chaplain: Glasgow University	The Chaplaincy Centre, University of Glasgow, Glasgow G12 8QQ		0141-330 5419
MacQuien, Duncan DCS	1988		(Deacon)	35 Criffel Road, Mount Vernon, Glasgow G32 9JE		0141-575 1137

Name	Ord.	Ret.	Former charge	Address	Tel.
Martindale, John P.F. BD	1994	2005	(Glasgow: Sandyhills)	Flat 3/2, 25 Albert Avenue, Glasgow G42 8RB	0141-433 4367
Matthews, John C. MA BD OBE	1992	2010	(Glasgow: Ruchill Kelvinside)	9 Kirklee Road, Glasgow G12 0RQ	0141-357 3249
Miller, John D. BA BD DD	1971	2007	(Glasgow: Castlemilk East)	98 Kirkcaldy Road, Glasgow G41 4LD [E-mail: rev.john.miller@zol.co.zw]	0141-423 0221
Moffat, Thomas BSc BD	1976	2008	(Culross and Torryburn)	Flat 8/1, 8 Cranston Street, Glasgow G3 8GG [E-mail: tom@gallus.org.uk]	0141-248 1886
Moore, William B.			(Prison Chaplain: Low Moss)	10 South Dumbreck Road, Kilsyth, Glasgow G65 9LX	01236 821918
Morrice, Alastair M. MA BD	1968	2002	(Rutherglen: Stonelaw)	5 Brechin Road, Kirriemuir DD8 4BX	
Morris, William J. KCVO PhD LLD DD JP	1951	2005	(Glasgow: Cathedral)	1 Whitehill Grove, Newton Mearns, Glasgow G77 5DH	0141-639 6327
Morrison, Roderick MA BD	1974	2008	(Glasgow: Gardner Street)	Flat 2/1, 73 Lumsden Street, Glasgow G3 8RH	
Morton, Thomas MA BD LGSM	1945	1986	(Rutherglen: Stonelaw)	54 Greystone Avenue, Burnside, Rutherglen, Glasgow G73 3SW	0141-647 2682
Muir, Fred C. MA BD ThM ARCM	1961	1997	(Stepps)	20 Alexandra Avenue, Stepps, Glasgow G33 6BP	0141-779 2504
Murray, George M. LTh	1995	2011	(Glasgow: St Margaret's Tollcross Park)	31 Kenmuir Avenue, Sandyhills, Glasgow G32 9LE [E-mail: george.murray7@gmail.com]	0141-778 5060
Newlands, George M. MA BD PhD DLitt FRSA FRSE	1970	1986	(University of Glasgow)	12 Jamaica Street North Lane, Edinburgh EH3 6HQ	
Philip, George M. MA	1953	1996	(Glasgow: Sandyford Henderson Memorial)	44 Beech Avenue, Bearsden, Glasgow G61 3EX	0141-942 1327
Raeburn, Alan C. MA BD	1971	2010	(Glasgow: Battlefield East)	3 Orchard Gardens, Strathaven ML10 6UN [E-mail: acraeburn@hotmail.com]	(Mbl) 07709 552161
Ramsay, W.G.	1967	1999	(Glasgow: Springburn)	53 Kelvinvale, Kirkintilloch, Glasgow G66 1RD [E-mail: billram@btopenworld.com]	0141-776 2915
Robertson, Archibald MA BD	1957	1999	(Glasgow: Eastwood)	19 Canberra Court, Braidpark Drive, Glasgow G46 6NS	0141-637 7572
Robertson, Blair MA BD ThM	1990	1998	Chaplain: Southern General Hospital	c/o Chaplain's Office, Southern General Hospital, 1345 Govan Road, Glasgow G51 4TF	0141-201 2357
Ross, Donald M. MA	1953	1994	(Industrial Mission Organiser)	14 Cartsbridge Road, Busby, Glasgow G76 8DH	0141-644 2220
Ross, James MA BD	1968	1998	(Kilsyth: Anderson)	53 Turnberry Gardens, Westerwood, Cumbernauld, Glasgow G68 0AY	01236 730501
Saunders, Keith BD	1983	1999	Hospital Chaplain	Western Infirmary, Dumbarton Road, Glasgow G11 6NT	0141-211 2000
Shackleton, William	1960	1996	(Greenock: Wellpark West)	3 Tynwald Avenue, Burnside, Glasgow G73 4RN	0141-569 9407
Shanks, Norman J. MA BD DD	1983	2007	(Glasgow: Govan Old)	1 Marchmont Terrace, Glasgow G12 9LT [E-mail: rufuski@btinternet.com]	0141-339 4421
Simpson, Neil A. BA BD PhD	1992	2001	(Glasgow: Yoker Old with Yoker St Matthew's)	c/o Glasgow Presbytery Office	
Smith, G. Stewart MA BD STM	1966	2006	(Glasgow: King's Park)	33 Brent Road, Stewartfield, East Kilbride, Glasgow G74 4RA [E-mail: stewartandmary@googlemail.com]	(Tel/Fax) 01355 226718
Smith, James S.A.	1956	1991	(Drongan: The Schaw Kirk)	146 Aros Drive, Glasgow G52 1TJ	0141-883 9666
Spencer, John MA BD	1962	2001	(Dumfries: Lincluden with Holywood)	10 Kinkell Gardens, Kirkintilloch, Glasgow G66 2HJ	0141-777 8935
Spiers, John M. LTh MTh	1972	2004	(Giffnock: Orchardhill)	58 Woodlands Road, Thornliebank, Glasgow G46 7JQ	(Tel/Fax) 0141-638 0632
Stewart, Diane E. BD	1988	2006	(Milton of Campsie)	4 Miller Gardens, Bishopbriggs, Glasgow G64 1FG [E-mail: destewart@givemail.co.uk]	0141-762 1358
Stewart, Norma D. (Miss) MA MEd BD MTh	1977	2000	(Glasgow: Strathbungo Queen's Park)	127 Nether Auldhouse Road, Glasgow G43 2YS	0141-637 6956
Sutherland, Denis I.	1963	1995	(Glasgow: Hutchesontown)	56 Lime Crescent, Cumbernauld, Glasgow G67 3PQ	01236 731723

Sutherland, Elizabeth W. (Miss) BD	1972 1996	(Balornock North with Barmulloch)	20 Kirkland Avenue, Blanefield, Glasgow G63 9BZ [E-mail: ewsutherland@aol.com]	01360 770154
Thomson, Andrew BA	1976 2007	(Airdrie: Broomknoll)	3 Laurel Wynd, Drumfargard Village, Cambuslang, Glasgow G72 7BH [E-mail: andrewthomson@hotmail.com]	0141-641 2936
Turner, Angus BD	1976 1998	(Industrial Chaplain)	46 Keir Street, Pollokshields, Glasgow G41 2LA	0141-424 0493
Tuton, Robert M. MA	1957 1995	(Glasgow: Shettleston Old)	6 Holmwood Gardens, Uddingston, Glasgow G71 7BH	01698 321108
Walker, A.L.	1955 1988	(Glasgow: Trinity Possil and Henry Drummond)	11 Dundas Avenue, Torrance, Glasgow G64 4BD	01360 622281
Walton, Ainslie MA MEd	1954 1995	(University of Aberdeen)	501 Shields Road, Glasgow G41 2RF [E-mail: revainslie@aol.com]	0141-420 3327
White, C. Peter BVMS BD MRCVS	1974 2011	(Glasgow: Sandyford Henderson Memorial)	2 Hawthorn Place, Torrance, Glasgow G64 4EA [E-mail: revcpw@gmail.com]	01360 622680
Whyte, James BD	1981 2011	(Fairlie)	32 Torburn Avenue, Giffnock, Glasgow G46 7RB [E-mail: jameswhyte89@btinternet.com]	
Wilson, John BD	1985 2010	(Glasgow: Temple Anniesland)	4 Carron Crescent, Bearsden, Glasgow G61 1HJ [E-mail: revjwilson@btinternet.com]	0141-931 5609
Younger, Adah (Mrs) BD	1978 2004	(Glasgow: Dennistoun Central)	Flat 0/1, 101 Greenhead Street, Glasgow G40 1HR	0141-550 0878

GLASGOW ADDRESSES

Banton	Kelvinhead Road, Banton
Bishopbriggs	
Kenmure	Viewfield Road, Bishopbriggs
Springfield Cambridge	The Leys, off Springfield Road
Broom	Mearns Road, Newton Mearns
Burnside Blairbeth	Church Avenue, Burnside Kirkriggs Avenue, Blairbeth
Busby	Church Road, Busby
Cadder	Cadder Road, Bishopbriggs
Cambuslang	
Flemington Hallside	Hutchinson Place
Parish	Cairns Road
Campsie	Main Street, Lennoxtown
Chryston	Main Street, Chryston
Eaglesham	Montgomery Street, Eaglesham
Fernhill and Cathkin	Neilvaig Drive
Gartcosh	113 Lochend Road, Gartcosh
Giffnock	
Orchardhill	Church Road
South	Eastwood Toll
The Park	Ravenscliffe Drive
Glenboig	138 Main Street, Glenboig
Greenbank	Eaglesham Road, Clarkston
Kilsyth	
Anderson	Kingston Road, Kilsyth
Burns and Old	Church Street, Kilsyth
Kirkintilloch	
Hillhead	Newdyke Road, Kirkintilloch
St Columba's	Waterside Road nr Auld Aisle Road
St David's Mem Pk	Alexandra Street
St Mary's	Cowgate
Lenzie	
Old	Kirkintilloch Road x Garngaber Ave
Union	65 Kirkintilloch Road
Maxwell	
Mearns Castle	Waterfoot Road
Mearns	Mearns Road, Newton Mearns
Milton of Campsie	Antermony Road, Milton of Campsie
Netherlee	Ormonde Drive x Ormonde Avenue
Newton Mearns	Ayr Road, Newton Mearns
Rutherglen	
Old	Main Street at Queen Street
Stonelaw	Stonelaw Road x Dryburgh Avenue
West and Wardlawhill	3 Western Avenue
Stamperland	Stamperland Gardens, Clarkston
Stepps	Whitehill Avenue
Thornliebank	61 Spiersbridge Road
Torrance	School Road, Torrance
Twechar	Main Street, Twechar
Williamwood	4 Vardar Avenue, Clarkston

Glasgow

Anderston Kelvingrove	759 Argyle St x Elderslie St
Baillieston	
Mure Memorial	Maxwell Drive, Garrowhill
St Andrew's	Bredisholm Road

Balshagray Victoria Pk	218–230 Broomhill Drive
Barlanark Greyfriars	Edinburgh Rd x Hallhill Rd (365)
Blawarthill	Millbrix Avenue
Bridgeton St Francis in the East	26 Queen Mary Street
Broomhill	64–66 Randolph Rd (x Marlborough Ave)
Calton Parkhead	122 Helenvale Street
Cardonald	2155 Paisley Road West
Carmunnock	Kirk Road, Carmunnock
Carmyle	155 Carmyle Avenue
Carnwadric	556 Boydstone Road, Thornliebank
Castlemilk	
East	Barlia Terrace
West	Carmunnock Road
Cathcart	
Old	119 Carmunnock Road
Trinity	90 Clarkston Road
Cathedral	Cathedral Square, 2 Castle Street
Clincarthill	1216 Cathcart Road
Colston Milton	Egilsay Crescent
Colston Wellpark	1378 Springburn Road
Cranhill	109 Bellrock St (at Bellrock Cr)
Croftfoot	Croftpark Ave x Crofthill Road
Dennistoun New	9 Armadale Street
Drumchapel	
Drumry St Mary's	217 Drumry Road East
St Andrew's	153 Garscadden Road
St Mark's	281 Kinfauns Drive
Easterhouse St George's and St Peter's	Boyndie Street
Eastwood	Mansewood Road
Gairbraid	1517 Maryhill Road
Gallowgate	David Street and Bain Square (two buildings)
Garthamlock and Craigend East	46 Porchester Street
Govan and Linthouse	Govan Cross
Govanhill Trinity	28 Daisy Street nr Allison Street
High Carntyne	358 Carntynehall Road
Hillington Park	24 Berryknowes Road
Househillwood St Christopher's	Meikle Road
Hyndland	79 Hyndland Rd, opp Novar Dr
Ibrox	Carillon Road x Clifford Street
John Ross Memorial	100 Norfolk Street
Jordanhill	28 Woodend Drive (x Munro Road)
Kelvin Stevenson Mem	Belmont Street at Belmont Bridge
Kelvinside Hillhead	Observatory Road
Kenmuir Mount Vernon	2405 London Road, Mount Vernon
King's Park	242 Castlemilk Road
Kinning Park	Eaglesham Place
Knightswood St Margaret's	2000 Great Western Road
Langside	167–169 Ledard Road (x Lochleven Road)
Lansdowne	416 Gt Western Rd at Kelvin Bridge
Lochwood	2A Liff Place, Easterhouse
Martyrs', The	St Mungo Avenue
Maryhill	1990 Maryhill Road
Merrylea	78 Merrylee Road
Mosspark	167 Ashkirk Drive
Newlands South	Riverside Road x Langside Drive
Partick	
South	259 Dumbarton Road
Trinity	20 Lawrence Street
Penilee St Andrew's	Bowfield Cres x Bowfield Avenue
Pollokshaws	223 Shawbridge Street
Pollokshields	Albert Drive x Shields Road
Possilpark	124 Saracen Street
Priesthill and Nitshill	100 Priesthill Rd (x Muirshiel Cr) Dove Street
Queen's Park	170 Queen's Drive
Renfield St Stephen's	260 Bath Street
Robroyston	34 Saughs Road
Ruchazie	4 Elibank Street (x Milncroft Road)
Ruchill Kelvinside	Shakespeare Street nr Maryhill Rd and 10 Kelbourne Street (two buildings)
St Andrew's East	681 Alexandra Parade
St Columba	300 St Vincent Street
St David's Knightswood	66 Boreland Drive (nr Lincoln Avenue)
St Enoch's Hogganfield	860 Cumbernauld Road
St George's Tron	163 Buchanan Street
St James' (Pollok)	Lyoncross Road x Byrebush Road
St John's Renfield	22 Beaconsfield Road
St Margaret's Tollcross Pk	179 Braidfauld Street
St Nicholas' Cardonald	Hartlaw Crescent nr Gladsmuir Road
St Paul's	30 Langdale St (x Greenrig St)
St Rollox	9 Fountainwell Road
Sandyford Henderson Memorial	Kelvinhaugh Street at Argyle Street
Sandyhills	28 Baillieston Rd nr Sandyhills Rd
Scotstoun	Earlbank Avenue x Ormiston Avenue
Shawlands	Shawlands Cross (1114 Pollokshaws Road)
Sherbrooke St Gilbert's	Nithsdale Rd x Sherbrooke Avenue
Shettleston New	679 Old Shettleston Road
Shettleston Old	99–111 Killin Street
South Carntyne	538 Carntyne Road
South Shawlands	Regwood Street x Deanston Drive
Springburn	180 Springburn Way
Temple Anniesland	869 Crow Road
Toryglen	Glenmore Ave nr Prospecthill Road
Trinity Possil and Henry Drummond	2 Crowhill Street (x Broadholm Street)
Tron St Mary's	128 Red Road
Victoria Tollcross	1134 Tollcross Road
Wallacewell New Charge Development	no building yet obtained
Wellington	University Ave x Southpark Avenue
Whiteinch	35 Inchlee Street
Yoker	10 Hawick Street

(17) HAMILTON

Meets at Motherwell: Dalziel St Andrew's Parish Church Halls, on the first Tuesday of February, March, May, September, October, November and December, and on the third Tuesday of June.

Presbytery Office:		**353 Orbiston Street, Motherwell ML1 1QW** **[E-mail: hamilton@cofscotland.org.uk]** **[E-mail: clerk@presbyteryofhamilton.co.uk]**	**01698 259135**
Clerk:	**REV. SHAW J. PATERSON BSc BD MSc**	**c/o The Presbytery Office**	
Depute Clerk:	**Appointment awaited**	**c/o The Presbytery Office**	
Presbytery Treasurer:	**MR ROBERT A. ALLAN**	**7 Graham Place, Ashgill, Larkhall ML9 3BA** **[E-mail: Fallan3246@aol.com]**	**01698 883246**

---

1 **Airdrie: Broomknoll (H) (01236 762101) (E-mail: airdrie-broomknoll@presbyteryofhamilton.co.uk)**
linked with Calderbank (E-mail: calderbank@presbyteryofhamilton.co.uk)
Isobel Birrell (Mrs) BD 1994 2009 38 Commonhead Street, Airdrie ML6 6NS 01236 609584
[E-mail: isobel.birrell@peacenik.co.uk] 07540 797945 (Mbl)

2 **Airdrie: Clarkston (E-mail: airdrie-clarkston@presbyteryofhamilton.co.uk)**
F. Derek Gunn BD 1986 2009 Clarkston Manse, Forrest Street, Airdrie ML6 7BE 01236 769676

3 **Airdrie: Flowerhill (H) (E-mail: airdrie-flowerhill@presbyteryofhamilton.co.uk)**
Gary J. Caldwell BSc BD 2007 31 Victoria Place, Airdrie ML6 9BU 01236 754430
[E-mail: garyjcaldwell@btinternet.com]

4 **Airdrie: High (E-mail: airdrie-high@presbyteryofhamilton.co.uk)**
Ian R.W. McDonald BSc BD PhD 2007 17 Etive Drive, Airdrie ML6 9QL 01236 760023
[E-mail: ian@spingetastic.freeserve.co.uk]

5 **Airdrie: Jackson (E-mail: airdrie-jackson@presbyteryofhamilton.co.uk)**
Kay Gilchrist (Miss) BD 1996 2008 48 Dunrobin Road, Airdrie ML6 8LR 01236 760154
[E-mail: gilky61@yahoo.co.uk]

6 **Airdrie: New Monkland (H) (E-mail: airdrie-newmonkland@presbyteryofhamilton.co.uk)**
linked with Greengairs (E-mail: greengairs@presbyteryofhamilton.co.uk)
William Jackson BD CertMin 1994 2008 3 Dykehead Crescent, Airdrie ML6 6PU 01236 763554

7 Airdrie: St Columba's (E-mail: airdrie-stcolumbas@presbyteryofhamilton.co.uk)
Margaret F. Currie BEd BD 1980 1987 52 Kennedy Drive, Airdrie ML6 9AW 01236 763173
[E-mail: margaretfcurrie@btinternet.com]

8 Airdrie: The New Wellwynd (E-mail: airdrie-newwellwynd@presbyteryofhamilton.co.uk)
Robert A. Hamilton BA BD 1995 2001 20 Arthur Avenue, Airdrie ML6 9EZ 01236 763022
[E-mail: revrob13@blueyonder.co.uk]

9 Bargeddie (H) (E-mail: bargeddie@presbyteryofhamilton.co.uk)
John Fairful BD 1994 2001 The Manse, Manse Road, Bargeddie, Baillieston, Glasgow G69 6UB 0141-771 1322

10 Bellshill: Macdonald Memorial (E-mail: bellshill-macdonald@presbyteryofhamilton.co.uk) linked with Bellshill: Orbiston
Alan McKenzie BSc BD 1988 2001 32 Adamson Street, Bellshill ML4 1DT 01698 849114
[E-mail: rev.a.mckenzie@btopenworld.com]

11 Bellshill: Orbiston (E-mail: bellshill-orbiston@presbyteryofhamilton.co.uk) See Bellshill: Macdonald Memorial

12 Bellshill: West (H) (01698 747581) (E-mail: bellshill-west@presbyteryofhamilton.co.uk)
Agnes A. Moore (Miss) BD 1987 2001 16 Croftpark Street, Bellshill ML4 1EY 01698 842877
[E-mail: revamoore2@tiscali.co.uk]

13 Blantyre: Livingstone Memorial (E-mail: blantyre-livingstone@presbyteryofhamilton.co.uk)
Fiona A. Wilson (Mrs) BD 2008 286 Glasgow Road, Blantyre, Glasgow G72 9DB 01698 823794
[E-mail: weefi12b@hotmail.co.uk]

14 Blantyre: Old (H) (E-mail: blantyre-old@presbyteryofhamilton.co.uk)
Vacant The Manse, Craigmuir Road, High Blantyre, Glasgow G72 9UA 01698 823130

15 Blantyre: St Andrew's (E-mail: blantyre-standrews@presbyteryofhamilton.co.uk)
J. Peter N. Johnston BSc BD 2001 332 Glasgow Road, Blantyre, Glasgow G72 9LQ 01698 828633
[E-mail: peter.johnston@standrewsblantyre.com]

16 Bothwell (H) (E-mail: bothwell@presbyteryofhamilton.co.uk)
James M. Gibson TD LTh LRAM 1978 1989 Manse Avenue, Bothwell, Glasgow G71 8PQ 01698 853189 (Tel)
[E-mail: jamesmgibson@msn.com] 01698 854903 (Fax)

17 Calderbank See Airdrie: Broomknoll

18	**Caldercruix and Longriggend (H) (E-mail: caldercruix@presbyteryofhamilton.co.uk)**				
	George M. Donaldson MA BD	1984	2005	Main Street, Caldercruix, Airdrie ML6 7RF [E-mail: gmdonaldson@gmdonaldson.force9.co.uk]	01236 842279
19	**Carfin (E-mail: carfin@presbyteryofhamilton.co.uk) linked with Newarthill (E-mail: newarthill@presbyteryofhamilton.co.uk)**				
	Vacant			Church Street, Newarthill, Motherwell ML1 5HS	01698 860316
20	**Chapelhall (H) (E-mail: chapelhall@presbyteryofhamilton.co.uk)**				
	Gordon R. Mackenzie BScAgr BD	1977	2009	The Manse, Russell Street, Chapelhall, Airdrie ML6 8SG [E-mail: rev.g.mackenzie@btopenworld.com]	01236 763439
21	**Chapelton (E-mail: chapelton@presbyteryofhamilton.co.uk) linked with Strathaven: Rankin (H) (E-mail: strathaven-rankin@presbyteryofhamilton.co.uk)**				
	Shaw J. Paterson BSc BD MSc	1991		15 Lethame Road, Strathaven ML10 6AD [E-mail: s.paterson195@btinternet.com]	01357 520019 (Tel) 01357 529316 (Fax)
	Maxine Buck (Aux)	2007		Brownlee House, Mauldslie Road, Carluke ML8 5HW	01555 759063
22	**Cleland (H) (E-mail: cleland@presbyteryofhamilton.co.uk)**				
	John A. Jackson BD	1997		The Manse, Bellside Road, Cleland, Motherwell ML1 5NP [E-mail: johnajackson932@btinternet.com]	01698 860260
23	**Coatbridge: Blairhill Dundyvan (H) (E-mail: coatbridge-blairhill@presbyteryofhamilton.co.uk)**				
	Patricia A. Carruth (Mrs) BD	1998	2004	18 Blairhill Street, Coatbridge ML5 1PG	01236 432304
24	**Coatbridge: Calder (H) (E-mail: coatbridge-calder@presbyteryofhamilton.co.uk)**				
	Vacant			26 Bute Street, Coatbridge ML5 4HF	01236 421516
	Roddy S. Dick (Aux)	2010		27 Easter Crescent, Wishaw ML2 8XB [E-mail: roddy.dick@btopenworld.com]	01698 383453
25	**Coatbridge: Middle (E-mail: coatbridge-middle@presbyteryofhamilton.co.uk)**				
	Alexander M. Roger BD PhD	1982	2009	47 Blair Road, Coatbridge ML5 1JQ [E-mail: s.roger@btinternet.com]	01236 432427
26	**Coatbridge: New St Andrew's (E-mail: coatbridge-standrews@presbyteryofhamilton.co.uk)**				
	Fiona Nicolson BA BD	1996	2005	77 Eglinton Street, Coatbridge ML5 3JF	01236 437271

27	**Coatbridge: Old Monkland (E-mail: coatbridge-oldmonkland@presbyteryofhamilton.co.uk)**				
	Vacant			2 Brandon Way, Coatbridge ML5 5QT	01236 423788
28	**Coatbridge: Townhead (H) (E-mail: coatbridge-townhead@presbyteryofhamilton.co.uk)**				
	Ecilo Selemani LTh MTh	1993	2004	Crinan Crescent, Coatbridge ML5 2LH [E-mail: eciloselemani@msn.com]	01236 702914
29	**Dalserf (E-mail: dalserf@presbyteryofhamilton.co.uk)**				
	D. Cameron McPherson BSc BD DMin	1982		Manse Brae, Dalserf, Larkhall ML9 3BN [E-mail: dCameronMc@aol.com]	01698 882195
30	**East Kilbride: Claremont (H) (01355 238088) (E-mail: ek-claremont@presbyteryofhamilton.co.uk)**				
	Gordon R. Palmer MA BD STM	1986	2003	17 Deveron Road, East Kilbride, Glasgow G74 2HR [E-mail: gkrspalmer@blueyonder.co.uk]	01355 248526
	Paul Cathcart DCS			59 Glen Isla, St Leonards, East Kilbride, Glasgow G74 3TG [E-mail: paulcathcart@msn.com]	0141-569 6865
31	**East Kilbride: Greenhills (E) (01355 221746) (E-mail: ek-greenhills@presbyteryofhamilton.co.uk)**				
	John Brewster MA BD DipEd	1988		21 Turnberry Place, East Kilbride, Glasgow G75 8TB [E-mail: johnbrewster@blueyonder.co.uk]	01355 242564
32	**East Kilbride: Moncreiff (H) (01355 223328) (E-mail: ek-moncreiff@presbyteryofhamilton.co.uk)**				
	Neil Buchanan BD	1991	2011	16 Almond Drive, East Kilbride, Glasgow G74 2HX [E-mail: neil.buchanan@talk21.com]	01355 238639
33	**East Kilbride: Mossneuk (E) (01355 260954) (E-mail: ek-mossneuk@presbyteryofhamilton.co.uk)**				
	John L. McPake BA BD PhD	1987	2000	30 Eden Grove, Mossneuk, East Kilbride, Glasgow G75 8XU	01355 234196
34	**East Kilbride: Old (H) (E-mail: ek-old@presbyteryofhamilton.co.uk)**				
	Anne S. Paton BA BD	2001		40 Maxwell Drive, East Kilbride, Glasgow G74 4HJ [E-mail: annepaton@fsmail.net]	01355 220732
	Nigel G. Watson MA (Assoc)	1998	2009	15 Macrae Gardens, East Kilbride, Glasgow G74 4TP [E-mail: nigel.g.watson@gmail.com]	01355 276502
35	**East Kilbride: South (H) (E-mail: ek-south@presbyteryofhamilton.co.uk)**				
	Vacant			7 Clamps Wood, East Kilbride, Glasgow G74 2HB	01355 247993

36 East Kilbride: Stewartfield (New Charge Development)

Douglas W. Wallace MA BD	1981	2001	8 Thistle Place, Stewartfield, East Kilbride, Glasgow G74 4RH	01355 260879
Nigel G. Watson MA (Assoc)	1998	2009	15 Macrae Gardens, East Kilbride, Glasgow G74 4TP [E-mail: nigel.g.watson@gmail.com]	01355 276502

37 East Kilbride: West (H) (E-mail: ek-west@presbyteryofhamilton.co.uk)

Mahboob Masih BA MDiv MTh	1999	2008	4 East Milton Grove, East Kilbride, Glasgow G75 8FN [E-mail: m_masih@sky.com]	01355 224469
Nigel G. Watson MA (Assoc)	1998	2009	15 Macrae Gardens, East Kilbride, Glasgow G74 4TP [E-mail: nigel.g.watson@gmail.com]	01355 276502

38 East Kilbride: Westwood (H) (01355 245657) (E-mail: ek-westwood@presbyteryofhamilton.co.uk)

Kevin Mackenzie BD DPS	1989	1996	16 Inglewood Crescent, East Kilbride, Glasgow G75 8QD [E-mail: kevin@westwoodmanse.freeserve.co.uk]	01355 223992

39 Glasford (E-mail: glassford@presbyteryofhamilton.co.uk) linked with Strathaven: East (E-mail: strathaven-east@presbyteryofhamilton.co.uk)

William T. Stewart BD	1980		68 Townhead Street, Strathaven ML10 6DJ	01357 521138

40 Greengairs See Airdrie: New Monkland

**41 Hamilton: Burnbank (E-mail: hamilton-burnbank@presbyteryofhamilton.co.uk)
linked with Hamilton: North (H) (E-mail: hamilton-north@presbyteryofhamilton.co.uk)**

Raymond D. McKenzie BD	1978	1987	9 South Park Road, Hamilton ML3 6PJ	01698 424609

42 Hamilton: Cadzow (H) (01698 428695) (E-mail: hamilton-cadzow@presbyteryofhamilton.co.uk)

John Carswell BS MDiv	1996	2009	3 Carlisle Road, Hamilton ML3 7BZ	01698 426682

43 Hamilton: Gilmour and Whitehill (H) (E-mail: hamilton-gilmourwhitehill@presbyteryofhamilton.co.uk)

Ronald J. Maxwell Stitt LTh BA ThM BREd DMin FSAScot	1977	2000	86 Burnbank Centre, Burnbank, Hamilton ML3 0NA	01698 284201

44 Hamilton: Hillhouse (E-mail: hamilton-hillhouse@presbyteryofhamilton.co.uk)

David W.G. Burt BD DipMin	1989	1998	66 Wellhall Road, Hamilton ML3 9BY [E-mail: dwgburt@blueyonder.co.uk]	01698 422300

45 Hamilton: North See Hamilton: Burnbank

46 Hamilton: Old (H) (01698 281905) (E-mail: hamilton-old@presbyteryofhamilton.co.uk)
John M.A. Thomson TD JP BD ThM 1978 2001 1 Chateau Grove, Hamilton ML3 7DS 01698 422511
[E-mail: jt@john1949.plus.com]

47 Hamilton: St Andrew's (T) (E-mail: hamilton-standrews@presbyteryofhamilton.co.uk)
Norman MacLeod BTh 1999 2005 15 Bent Road, Hamilton ML3 6QB 01698 283264
[E-mail: normanmacleod@btopenworld.com]

48 Hamilton: St John's (H) (01698 283492) (E-mail: hamilton-stjohns@presbyteryofhamilton.co.uk)
Vacant 12 Castlehill Crescent, Hamilton ML3 7DG 01698 425002

49 Hamilton: South (H) (01698 281014) (E-mail: hamilton-south@presbyteryofhamilton.co.uk)
linked with Quarter (E-mail: quarter@presbyteryofhamilton.co.uk)
Vacant The Manse, Limekilnburn Road, Quarter, Hamilton ML3 7XA 01698 424511

50 Hamilton: Trinity (01698 284254) (E-mail: hamilton-trinity@presbyteryofhamilton.co.uk)
Karen E. Harbison (Mrs) MA BD 1991 69 Buchan Street, Hamilton ML3 8JY 01698 425326

51 Hamilton: West (H) (01698 284670) (E-mail: hamilton-west@presbyteryofhamilton.co.uk)
Elizabeth A. Waddell (Mrs) BD 1999 2005 43 Bothwell Road, Hamilton ML3 0BB 01698 458770

52 Holytown (E-mail: holytown@presbyteryofhamilton.co.uk) linked with New Stevenston: Wrangholm Kirk
Caryl A.E. Kyle (Mrs) BD DipEd 2008 The Manse, 260 Edinburgh Road, Holytown, Motherwell ML1 5RU 01698 832622
[E-mail: caryl_kyle@hotmail.com]

53 Kirk o' Shotts (H) (E-mail: kirk-o-shotts@presbyteryofhamilton.co.uk)
Vacant The Manse, Kirk o' Shotts, Salsburgh, Shotts ML7 4NS 01698 870208

54 Larkhall: Chalmers (H) (E-mail: larkhall-chalmers@presbyteryofhamilton.co.uk)
Vacant Quarry Road, Larkhall ML9 1HH 01698 882238

55 Larkhall: St Machan's (H) (E-mail: larkhall-stmachans@presbyteryofhamilton.co.uk)
Alastair McKillop BD DipMin 1995 2004 2 Orchard Gate, Larkhall ML9 1HG 01698 321976

56 Larkhall: Trinity (E-mail: larkhall-trinity@presbyteryofhamilton.co.uk)
Lindsay Schluter (Miss) ThE CertMin 1995 13 Machan Avenue, Larkhall ML9 2HE 01698 881401

57 **Motherwell: Crosshill (H) (E-mail: mwell-crosshill@presbyteryofhamilton.co.uk)**
Gavin W.G. Black BD 2006 15 Orchard Street, Motherwell ML1 3JE 01698 263410
[E-mail: gavin.black12@blueyonder.co.uk]

58 **Motherwell: Dalziel St Andrew's (H) (01698 264097) (E-mail: mwell-dalzielstandrews@presbyteryofhamilton.co.uk)**
Derek W. Hughes BSc BD DipEd 1990 1996 4 Pollock Street, Motherwell ML1 1LP 01698 263414
[E-mail: derekthecleric@btinternet.com]

59 **Motherwell: North (E-mail: mwell-north@presbyteryofhamilton.co.uk)**
Derek H.N. Pope BD 1987 1995 35 Birrens Road, Motherwell ML1 3NS 01698 266716
[E-mail: derekpopemotherwell@hotmail.com]

60 **Motherwell: St Margaret's (E-mail: mwell-stmargarets@presbyteryofhamilton.co.uk)**
Vacant 70 Baron's Road, Motherwell ML1 2NB 01698 263803

61 **Motherwell: St Mary's (H) (E-mail: mwell-stmarys@presbyteryofhamilton.co.uk)**
David W. Doyle MA BD 1977 1987 19 Orchard Street, Motherwell ML1 3JE 01698 263472

62 **Motherwell: South (H)**
Georgina M. Baxendale (Mrs) BD 1981 2009 62 Manse Road, Motherwell ML1 2PT 01698 263054
[E-mail: georgiebaxendale6@tiscali.co.uk]

63 **Newarthill** See Carfin

64 **Newmains: Bonkle (H) (E-mail: bonkle@presbyteryofhamilton.co.uk)**
linked with Newmains: Coltness Memorial (H) (E-mail: coltness@presbyteryofhamilton.co.uk)
Graham Raeburn MTh 2004 5 Kirkgate, Newmains, Wishaw ML2 9BT 01698 383858
[E-mail: grahamraeburn@tiscali.co.uk]

65 **Newmains: Coltness Memorial** See Newmains: Bonkle
66 **New Stevenston: Wrangholm Kirk (E-mail: wrangholm@presbyteryofhamilton.co.uk)** See Holytown

67 **Overtown (E-mail: overtown@presbyteryofhamilton.co.uk)**
Bruce H. Sinclair BA BD 2009 The Manse, 146 Main Street, Overtown, Wishaw ML2 0QP 01698 352090
[E-mail: brucehsinclair@btinternet.com]

68 **Quarter** See Hamilton: South

69 **Shotts: Calderhead Erskine (E-mail: calderhead-erskine@presbyteryofhamilton.co.uk)**
Allan B. Brown BD MTh 1995 2010 The Manse, 9 Kirk Road, Shotts ML7 5ET 01501 820042
07578 448655 (Mbl)

70 **Stonehouse: St Ninian's (H) (E-mail: stonehouse@presbyteryofhamilton.co.uk)**
Paul G.R. Grant BD MTh 2003 4 Hamilton Way, Stonehouse, Larkhall ML9 3PU 01698 792947
[E-mail: minister@st-ninians-stonehouse.org.uk]

71 **Strathaven: Avendale Old and Drumclog (H) (01357 529748) (E-mail: strathaven-avendaleold@presbyteryofhamilton.co.uk and E-mail: drumclog@presbyteryofhamilton.co.uk)**
Alan B. Telfer BA BD 1983 2010 4 Fortrose Gardens, Strathaven ML10 6SH 01357 523031
(This congregation has united with the congregation of Strathaven: West)

72 **Strathaven: East** See Glasford
73 **Strathaven: Rankin** See Chapelton

74 **Uddingston: Burnhead (H) (E-mail: uddingston-burnhead@presbyteryofhamilton.co.uk)**
Les Brunger BD 2010 90 Laburnum Road, Uddingston, Glasgow G71 5DB 01698 813716
[E-mail: lesbrunger@hotmail.co.uk]

75 **Uddingston: Old (H) (01698 814015) (E-mail: uddingston-old@presbyteryofhamilton.co.uk)**
Fiona L.J. McKibbin (Mrs) MA BD 2011 1 Belmont Avenue, Uddingston, Glasgow G71 7AX 01698 814757
[E-mail: fionamckibbin@sky.com]

76 **Uddingston: Viewpark (H) (E-mail: uddingston-viewpark@presbyteryofhamilton.co.uk)**
Michael G. Lyall BD 1993 2001 14 Holmbrae Road, Uddingston, Glasgow G71 6AP 01698 813113
[E-mail: michaellyall@blueyonder.co.uk]

77 **Wishaw: Cambusnethan North (H) (E-mail: wishaw-cambusnethannorth@presbyteryofhamilton.co.uk)**
Mhorag Macdonald (Ms) MA BD 1989 350 Kirk Road, Wishaw ML2 8LH 01698 381305
[E-mail: mhorag@mhorag.force9.co.uk]

78 **Wishaw: Cambusnethan Old (E-mail: wishaw-cambusnethanold@presbyteryofhamilton.co.uk) and Morningside (E-mail: wishaw-morningside@presbyteryofhamilton.co.uk)**
Iain C. Murdoch MA LLB DipEd BD 1995 22 Coronation Street, Wishaw ML2 8LF 01698 384235
[E-mail: iaincmurdoch@btopenworld.com]

79 **Wishaw: Craigneuk and Belhaven (H) (E-mail: wishaw-craigneukbelhaven@presbyteryofhamilton.co.uk) linked with Wishaw: Old**
Robert Craig BA BD 2008 130 Glen Road, Wishaw ML2 7NP 01698 375134
[E-mail: rab-craig@tiscali.co.uk]

80 Wishaw: Old (H) (01698 376080) (E-mail: wishaw-old@presbyteryofhamilton.co.uk) See Wishaw: Craigneuk and Belhaven

81 Wishaw: St Mark's (E-mail: wishaw-stmarks@presbyteryofhamilton.co.uk)

Graham Austin BD	1997	2008	The Manse, 302 Coltness Road, Wishaw ML2 7EY	01698 384596

82 Wishaw: South Wishaw (H)

Klaus O.F. Buwert LLB BD DMin	1984	1999	3 Walter Street, Wishaw ML2 8LQ [E-mail: klaus@buwert.co.uk]	01698 387292

Barrie, Arthur P. LTh	1973 2007	(Hamilton: Cadzow)	30 Airbles Crescent, Motherwell ML1 3AR [E-mail: elizabethbarrie@ymail.com]	01698 261147
Campbell, Andrew M. BD CertMin	1984 2009	(Motherwell: St Margaret's)	17 Clyde View, Ashgill, Larkhall ML9 3DS [E-mail: drewdorca@hotmail.com]	01698 887974
Colvin, Sharon E.F. (Mrs) BD LRAM LTCL	1985 2007	(Airdrie: Jackson)	25 Balblair Road, Airdrie ML6 6GQ	
Cook, J. Stanley BD Dip PSS	1974 2001	(Hamilton: West)	Mansend, 137A Old Manse Road, Netherton, Wishaw ML2 0EW [E-mail: stancook@blueyonder.co.uk]	01698 299600
Cullen, William T. BA LTh	1984 1996	(Kilmarnock: St John's Onthank)	6 Laurel Wynd, Cambuslang, Glasgow G72 7BA	0141-641 4337
Currie, David E.P. BSc BD	1983 2000	Congregational Development Consultant	21 Rosa Burn Avenue, Lindsayfield, East Kilbride, Glasgow G75 9DE	01355 248510
Currie, R. David BSc BD	1984 2004	(Cambuslang: Flemington Hallside)	69 Kethers Street, Motherwell ML1 3HN	01698 323424
Davidson, Amelia (Mrs) BD	2004 2011	(Coatbridge: Calder)	c/o Presbytery of Hamilton, 353 Orbiston Street, Motherwell ML1 1QW	
Dunn, W. Stuart LTh	1970 2006	(Motherwell: Crosshill)	10 Macrostie Gardens, Crieff PH7 4LP	01764 655178
Fraser, James P.	1951 1988	(Strathaven: Avendale Old and Drumclog)	26 Hamilton Road, Strathaven ML10 6JA	01357 522758
Grier, James BD	1991 2005	(Coatbridge: Middle)	14 Love Drive, Bellshill ML4 1BY	01698 742545
Hastie, James S.G. CA BD	1990 2009	(Larkhall: Chalmers)	29 Mornington Grove, Blackwood, Kirkmuirhill, Lanark ML11 9GQ [E-mail: jim@jimandros.co.uk]	01555 896965
Hunter, James E. LTh	1974 1997	(Blantyre: Livingstone Memorial)	57 Dalwhinnie Avenue, Blantyre, Glasgow G72 9NQ	01698 826177
Kent, Robert M. MA BD	1973 2011	(Hamilton: St John's)	48 Fyne Crescent, Larkhall ML9 2UX [E-mail: robertmkent@talktalk.net]	01698 769244
Lusk, Alastair S. BD	1974 2010	(East Kilbride: Moncreiff)	9 MacFie Place, Stewartfield, East Kilbride, Glasgow G74 4TY	
McAlpine, John BSc	1988 2004	(Auxiliary Minister)	Braeside, 201 Bonkle Road, Newmains, Wishaw ML2 9AA	01698 384610
McCabe, George	1963 1996	(Airdrie: High)	Flat 8, Park Court, 2 Craighouse Park, Edinburgh EH10 5LD	0131-447 9522
McDonald, John A. MA BD	1978 1997	(Cumbernauld: Condorrat)	17 Thomson Drive, Bellshill ML4 3ND	
McKee, Norman B. BD	1987 2010	(Uddingston: Old)	148 Station Road, Blantyre, Glasgow G72 9BW [E-mail: n.mckee1@btinternet.com]	01698 827358
MacKenzie, Ian C. MA BD	1970 2011	(Interim Minister)	21 Wilson Street, Motherwell ML1 1NP [E-mail: iancmac@blueyonder.co.uk]	01698 301230
Mackenzie, James G. BA BD	1980 2005	(Jersey: St Columba's)	10 Sandpiper Crescent, Carnbroe, Coatbridge ML5 4UW	
Martin, James MA BD DD	1946 1987	(Glasgow: High Carntyne)	9 Magnolia Street, Wishaw ML2 7EQ	01698 385825

Melrose, J.H. Loudon MA BD MEd	1955	1996	(Gourock: Old Gourock and Ashton [Assoc])	1 Laverock Avenue, Hamilton ML3 7DD	01698 427958
Munton, James G. BA	1969	2002	(Coatbridge: Old Monkland)	2 Moorcroft Drive, Airdrie ML6 8ES [E-mail: jacjim@supanet.com]	01236 754848
Price, Peter O. CBE QHC BA FPhS	1960	1996	(Blantyre: Old)	22 Old Bothwell Road, Bothwell, Glasgow G71 8AW [E-mail: peteroprice@aol.com]	01698 854032
Rogerson, Stuart D. BSc BD	1980	2001	(Strathaven: West)	17 Westfield Park, Strathaven ML10 6XH [E-mail: srogerson@cnetwork.co.uk]	01357 523321
Ross, Keith W.	1984	2007	Congregational Development Officer for the Presbytery of Hamilton	Easter Bavelaw House, Pentland Hills Regional Park, Balerno EH14 7JS	(Mbl) 07855 163449
Salmond, James S. BA BD MTh ThD	1979	2003	(Holytown)	165 Torbothie Road, Shotts ML7 5NE	
Sharp, John C. BSc BD PhD	1980	2011	(East Kilbride: South)	10 Rogerhill Gait, Kirkmuirhill, Lanark ML11 9XR	01555 892742
Spence, Sheila M. (Mrs) MA BD	1979	2010	(Kirk o' Shotts)	6 Drumbowie Crescent, Salsburgh, Shotts ML7 4NP	01698 870598
Stevenson, John LTh	1998	2006	(Cambuslang: St Andrew's)	20 Knowehead Gardens, Uddingston, Glasgow G71 7PY [E-mail therev20@sky.com]	01698 817582
Thorne, Leslie W. BA LTh	1987	2001	(Coatbridge: Clifton)	'Hatherleigh', 9 Chatton Walk, Coatbridge ML5 4FH [E-mail: lesthorne@tiscali.co.uk]	01236 432241 (Mbl) 07963 199921
Wilson, James H. LTh	1970	1996	(Cleland)	21 Austine Drive, Hamilton ML3 7YE [E-mail: wilsonjh@blueyonder.co.uk]	01698 457042
Wyllie, Hugh R. MA DD FCIBS	1962	2000	(Hamilton: Old)	18 Chantinghall Road, Hamilton ML3 8NP	01698 420002
Zambonini, James LIADip	1997		Auxiliary Minister	100 Old Manse Road, Wishaw ML2 0EP	01698 350889

HAMILTON ADDRESSES

Airdrie	
Broomknoll	Broomknoll Street
Clarkston	Forrest Street
Flowerhill	89 Graham Street
High	North Bridge Street
Jackson	Glen Road
New Monkland	Glenmavis
St Columba's	Thrashbush Road
The New Wellwynd	Wellwynd
Coatbridge	
Blairhill Dundyvan	Blairhill Street
Calder	Calder Street
Middle	Bank Street
New St Andrew's	Church Street
Old Monkland	Woodside Street
Townhead	Crinan Crescent
East Kilbride	
Claremont	High Common Road, St Leonard's
Greenhills	Greenhills Centre
Moncreiff	Calderwood Road
Mossneuk	Eden Drive
Old	Montgomery Street
South	Baird Hill, Murray
West	Kittoch Street
Westwood	Belmont Drive, Westwood
Hamilton	
Burnbank	High Blantyre Road
Cadzow	Woodside Walk
Gilmour and	Glasgow Road, Burnbank
Whitehill	Abbotsford Road, Whitehill
Hillhouse	Clerkwell Road
North	Windmill Road
Old	Leechlee Road
St Andrew's	Avon Street
St John's	Duke Street
South	Strathaven Road
Trinity	Neilsland Square off North Road
West	Burnbank Road
Motherwell	
Crosshill	Windmillhill Street x Airbles Street
Dalziel St Andrew's	Merry Street and Muir Street
North	Chesters Crescent
St Margaret's	Shields Road
St Mary's	Avon Street
South	Gavin Street
Uddingston	
Burnhead	Laburnum Road
Old	Old Glasgow Road
Viewpark	Old Edinburgh Road
Wishaw	
Cambusnethan	
North	Kirk Road
Old	Kirk Road
Craigneuk and Belhaven	Craigneuk Street
Old	Main Street
St Mark's	Coltness Road
South Wishaw	East Academy Street

(18) DUMBARTON

Meets at Dumbarton, in Riverside Church Halls, on the first Tuesday of February, March, April, May, October, November and December, on the second Tuesday of June and September (and April when the first Tuesday falls in Holy Week), and at the incoming Moderator's church on the first Tuesday of June for the installation of the Moderator.

Clerk:	**REV. J. COLIN CASKIE BA BD**		**11 Ardenconnel Way, Rhu, Helensburgh G84 8LX** **[E-mail: dumbarton@cofscotland.org.uk]**	**01436 820213**

Alexandria				
Elizabeth W. Houston MA BD DipEd	1985	1995	32 Ledrish Avenue, Balloch, Alexandria G83 8JB	01389 751933
Arrochar linked with Luss				
H. Dane Sherrard BD DMin	1971	1998	The Manse, Luss, Alexandria G83 8NZ [E-mail: dane@cadder.demon.co.uk]	01436 860240 07801 939138 (Mbl)
Baldernock (H)				
Andrew P. Lees BD	1984	2002	The Manse, Bardowie, Milngavie, Glasgow G62 6ES [E-mail: andrew.lees@yahoo.co.uk]	01360 620471
Bearsden: Baljaffray (H)				
Ian McEwan BSc PhD BD FRSE	2008		5 Fintry Gardens, Bearsden, Glasgow G61 4RJ [E-mail: mcewan7@btinternet.com]	0141-942 0366
Bearsden: Cross (H)				
John W.F. Harris MA	1967	2006	61 Drymen Road, Bearsden, Glasgow G61 2SU [E-mail: jwfh@bearsdencross.org]	0141-942 0507 07740 982079 (Mbl)
Bearsden: Killermont (H)				
Alan J. Hamilton LLB BD	2003		8 Clathic Avenue, Bearsden, Glasgow G61 2HF [E-mail: ajh63@o2.co.uk]	0141-942 0021
Bearsden: New Kilpatrick (H) (0141-942 8827) (E-mail: mail@nkchurch.org.uk)				
Roderick G. Hamilton MA BD	1992	2011	51 Manse Road, Bearsden, Glasgow G61 3PN [E-mail: rghamilton@ntlworld.com]	0141-942 0035

Bearsden: Westerton Fairlie Memorial (H) (0141-942 6960)
Christine M. Goldie LLB BD MTh DMin 1984 2008 3 Canniesburn Road, Bearsden, Glasgow G61 1PW 0141-942 2672
[E-mail: christinegoldie@talktalk.net]

Bonhill (H) (01389 756516)
Ian H. Miller BA BD 1975 1 Glebe Gardens, Bonhill, Alexandria G83 9NZ 01389 753039
[E-mail: ianmiller@bonhillchurch.freeserve.co.uk]

Cardross (H) (01389 841322)
Vacant The Manse, Main Road, Cardross, Dumbarton G82 5LB 01389 841289

Clydebank: Abbotsford (E-mail: abbotsford@lineone.net) (Website: www.abbotsford.org.uk)
Vacant 35 Montrose Street, Clydebank G81 2PA 0141-952 5151

Clydebank: Faifley
Gregor McIntyre BSc BD 1991 Kirklea, Cochno Road, Hardgate, Clydebank G81 6PT 01389 876836
[E-mail: mail@gregormcintyre.com]

Clydebank: Kilbowie St Andrew's
Vacant 5 Melfort Avenue, Clydebank G81 2HX 0141-951 2455

Clydebank: Radnor Park (H)
Margaret J.B. Yule BD 1992 11 Tiree Gardens, Old Kilpatrick, Glasgow G60 5AT 01389 875599
[E-mail: mjbyule@yahoo.co.uk]

Clydebank: St Cuthbert's (T) linked with Duntocher (H)
Vacant The Manse, Roman Road, Duntocher, Clydebank G81 6BT 01389 873471

Craigrownie linked with Rosneath: St Modan's (H)
Richard B. West 1994 2008 Edenkiln, Argyll Road, Kilcreggan, Helensburgh G84 0JW 01436 842274
[E-mail: rickangelawest@yahoo.co.uk]

Dalmuir: Barclay (0141-941 3988)
Fiona E. Maxwell BA BD 2004 16 Parkhall Road, Dalmuir, Clydebank G81 3RJ 0141-941 3317
[E-mail: fionamaxi@btinternet.com]

Dumbarton: Riverside (H) (01389 742551)
Eleanor J. McMahon BEd BD 1994 2010 81 Moorpark Square, Renfrew PA4 8DB 0141-886 1351
[E-mail: e.mcmahon212@btinternet.com]

Dumbarton: St Andrew's (H)				
Charles M. Cameron BA BD PhD	1980	2009	17 Mansewood Drive, Dumbarton G82 3EU [E-mail: minister@standrewsdumbarton.co.uk]	01389 726715
Dumbarton: West Kirk (H)				
Elaine W. McKinnon MA BD	1988	2010	3 Havoc Road, Dumbarton G82 4JW	01389 604840
Duntocher (H) See Clydebank: St Cuthbert's				
Garelochhead (01436 810589)				
Alastair S. Duncan MA BD	1989		Old School Road, Garelochhead, Helensburgh G84 0AT [E-mail: gpc@churchuk.fsnet.co.uk]	01436 810022
Helensburgh: Park (H) (01436 674825)				
Gavin McFadyen BEng BD	2006		Park Manse, 35 East Argyle Street, Helensburgh G84 7EL [E-mail: parkchurchminister@tiscali.co.uk]	01436 679970
Helensburgh: St Columba (H)				
George Vidits BD MTh	2000	2006	46 Suffolk Street, Helensburgh G84 9QZ [E-mail: george.vidits@btinternet.com]	01436 672054
Helensburgh: The West Kirk (H) (01436 676880)				
David W. Clark MA BD	1975	1986	37 Campbell Street, Helensburgh G84 9NH [E-mail: clarkdw@talktalk.net]	01436 674063
Jamestown (H)				
Norma Moore MA BD	1995	2004	26 Kessog's Gardens, Balloch, Alexandria G83 8QJ [E-mail: norma.moore5@btinternet.com]	01389 756447
Kilmaronock Gartocharn linked with Renton: Trinity (H)				
Vacant			Kilmaronock Manse, Alexandria G83 8SB	01360 660295
Luss See Arrochar				
Milngavie: Cairns (H) (0141-956 4868)				
Andrew Frater BA BD MTh	1987	1994	4 Cairns Drive, Milngavie, Glasgow G62 8AJ [E-mail: office@cairnschurch.org.uk]	0141-956 1717

Milngavie: St Luke's (0141-956 4226)				
Ramsay B. Shields BA BD	1990	1997	70 Hunter Road, Milngavie, Glasgow G62 7BY [E-mail: rbs@minister.com]	0141-577 9171 (Tel) 0141-577 9181 (Fax)
Milngavie: St Paul's (H) (0141-956 4405)				
Fergus C. Buchanan MA BD MTh	1982	1988	8 Buchanan Street, Milngavie, Glasgow G62 8DD [E-mail: f.c.buchanan@ntlworld.com]	0141-956 1043
Old Kilpatrick Bowling				
Vacant			The Manse, 175 Dumbarton Road, Old Kilpatrick, Glasgow G60 5JQ	01389 873130
Renton: Trinity (H) See Kilmaronock Gartocharn				
Vacant			38 Main Street, Renton, Dumbarton G82 4PU	01389 752017
Rhu and Shandon (H)				
J. Colin Caskie BA BD	1977	2002	11 Ardenconnel Way, Rhu, Helensburgh G84 8LX [E-mail: colin@jcaskie.eclipse.co.uk]	01436 820213
Rosneath: St Modan's See Craigrownie				

Booth, Frederick M. LTh	1970	2005	(Helensburgh: St Columba)	Achnashie Coach House, Clynder, Helensburgh G84 0QD	01436 831858
Crombie, William D. MA BD	1947	1987	(Calton New with St Andrew's)	32 Westbourne Drive, Bearsden, Glasgow G61 4BH	0141-943 0235
Davidson, Professor Robert MA BD DD FRSE	1956	1991	(University of Glasgow)	30 Dumgoyne Drive, Bearsden, Glasgow G61 3AP	0141-942 1810
Donaghy, Leslie G. BD DipMin PGCE FSAScot	1990	2004	(Dumbarton: St Andrew's)	130 Dumbuck Road, Dumbarton G82 3LZ	01389 604251
Easton, I.A.G. MA FIPM	1945	1988	(Lecturer)	6 Edgehill Road, Bearsden, Glasgow G61 3AD	0141-942 4214
Ferguson, Archibald M. MSc PhD CEng FRINA	1989	2004	(Auxiliary Minister)	The Whins, 2 Barrowfield, Station Road, Cardross, Dumbarton G82 5NL [E-mail: archieferguson@supanet.com]	01389 841517
Hamilton, David G. MA BD	1971	2004	(Braes of Rannoch with Foss and Rannoch)	79 Finlay Rise, Milngavie, Glasgow G62 6QL [E-mail: davidhamilton@onetel.com]	0141-956 4202
Hudson, Eric V. LTh	1971	2007	(Bearsden: Westerton Fairlie Memorial)	2 Murrayfield Drive, Bearsden, Glasgow G61 1JE	0141-942 6110
Kemp, Tina MA		2005	Auxiliary Minister	12 Oaktree Gardens, Dumbarton G82 1EU	01389 730477
Lawson, Alexander H. ThM ThD FPhS	1950	1988	(Clydebank: Kilbowie)	Erskine Park Nursing Home, Bishopton PA7	
McIntyre, J. Ainslie MA BD	1963	1984	(University of Glasgow)	60 Bonnaughton Road, Bearsden, Glasgow G61 4DB [E-mail: jamcintyre@hotmail.com]	0141-942 5143 (Mbl) 07050 295103
Munro, David P. MA BD STM	1953	1996	(Bearsden: North)	14 Birch Road, Killearn, Glasgow G63 9SQ	01360 550098
O'Donnell, Barbara	2007		Auxiliary Minister	Ashbank, 258 Main Street, Alexandria G83 0NU	01389 752356

Ramage, Alistair E. MA BA ADB CertEd	1996	2004	Auxiliary Minister	16 Claremont Gardens, Milngavie, Glasgow G62 6PG [E-mail: ara3@waitrose.com]	0141-956 2897
Stewart, Charles E. BSc BD MTh PhD	1976	2010	(Chaplain of the Fleet)	105 Sinclair Street, Helensburgh G84 9HY [E-mail: c.e.stewart@btinternet.com]	01436 678113
Steven, Harold A.M. MStJ LTh FSA Scot	1970	2001	(Baldernock)	9 Cairnhill Road, Bearsden, Glasgow G61 1AT	0141-942 1598
Wright, Malcolm LTh	1970	2003	(Craigrownie with Rosneath: St Modan's)	30 Clairinsh, Drumkinnon Gate, Balloch, Alexandria G83 8SE	01389 720338

DUMBARTON ADDRESSES

Clydebank		**Dumbarton**		**Helensburgh**	
Abbotsford	Town Centre	Riverside	High Street	Park	Charlotte Street
Faifley	Faifley Road	St Andrew's	Aitkenbar Circle	St Columba	Sinclair Street
Kilbowie St Andrew's	Kilbowie Road	West Kirk	West Bridgend	The West Kirk	Colquhoun Square
Radnor Park	Radnor Street				
St Cuthbert's	Linnvale				

(19) ARGYLL

Meets in the Village Hall, Tarbert, Loch Fyne, Argyll on the first Tuesday or Wednesday of March, June, September and December. For details, contact the Presbytery Clerk.

Clerk:	**MR IAN MACLAGAN LLB FSAScot**	**Carmonadh, Eastlands Road, Rothesay, Isle of Bute PA20 9JZ [E-mail: argyll@cofscotland.org.uk]**	**01700 503015**
Depute Clerk:	**REV. GEORGE G. CRINGLES BD**	**St Oran's Manse, Connel, Oban PA37 1PJ [E-mail: george.cringles@btinternet.com]**	**01631 710242**
Treasurer:	**MRS PAMELA A. GIBSON**	**Allt Ban, Portsonachan, Dalmally PA33 1BJ [E-mail: justpam1@tesco.net]**	**01866 833344**

Appin linked with Lismore

Roderick D.M. Campbell TD BD DMin FSAScot	1975	2008	The Manse, Appin PA38 4DD [E-mail: rdmcampbell@aol.com]	01631 730143

Ardchattan (H)

Jeffrey A. McCormick BD	1984		Ardchattan Manse, North Connel, Oban PA37 1RG [E-mail: jeff.mcc@virgin.net]	01631 710364

Ardrishaig (H) linked with South Knapdale

David Carruthers BD	1998		The Manse, Park Road, Ardrishaig, Lochgilphead PA30 8HE	01546 603269

Campbeltown: Highland (H)

Michael J. Lind LLB BD	1984	1997	Highland Church Manse, Kirk Street, Campbeltown PA28 6BN [E-mail: mijylind@btinternet.com]	01586 551146

Campbeltown: Lorne and Lowland (H)

Philip D. Burroughs BSc BTh DTS	1998	2004	Lorne and Lowland Manse, Castlehill, Campbeltown PA28 6AN [E-mail: burroughs@btinternet.com]	01586 552468
Kirsty-Ann Burroughs (Mrs) BA BD CertTheol DRM PhD (Aux)	2007		Lorne and Lowland Manse, Castlehill, Campbeltown PA28 6AN [E-mail: burroughs@btinternet.com]	01586 552468

Coll linked with Connel

George G. Cringles BD	1981	2002	St Oran's Manse, Connel, Oban PA37 1PJ [E-mail: george.cringles@btinternet.com]	(Connel) 01631 710242 (Coll) 01879 230366

Colonsay and Oronsay (Website: www.islandchurches.org.uk)
Vacant

Connel See Coll

Craignish linked with Kilbrandon and Kilchattan linked with Kilninver and Kilmelford

Kenneth R. Ross BA BD PhD	1982	2010	The Manse, Kilmelford, Oban PA34 4XA [E-mail: kennethr.ross@btinternet.com]	01852 200565

Cumlodden, Lochfyneside and Lochgair linked with Glenaray and Inveraray

Louis C. Bezuidenhout BA MA BD DD	1978	2009	The Manse, Inveraray PA32 8XT [E-mail: macbez@btinternet.com]	01499 302060

Dunoon: St John's linked with Kirn (H) linked with Sandbank (H)

Sarah E.C. Nicol (Mrs) BSc BD	1985	2009	The Manse, 13 Dhailling Park, Hunter Street, Kirn, Dunoon PA23 8FB [E-mail: kirnkirk@btinternet.com]	01369 702256
Glenda M. Wilson (Mrs) DCS	1990	2006	Glenmorven, 74 Alexander Street, Dunoon PA23 6BB [E-mail: GlendaMWilson@aol.com]	01369 700848

Dunoon: The High Kirk (H) linked with Innellan linked with Toward

Vacant			7A Mathieson Lane, Innellan, Dunoon PA23 7SH	01369 830276
Ruth I. Griffiths (Mrs) (Aux)	2004		Kirkwood, Mathieson Lane, Innellan, Dunoon PA23 7TA [E-mail: ruthigriffiths@googlemail.com]	01369 830145

Gigha and Cara (H) (GD)

Anne McIvor (Miss) SRD BD	1996	2008	The Manse, Isle of Gigha PA41 7AA [E-mail: annemcivor@btinternet.com]	01583 505245

Glassary, Kilmartin and Ford linked with North Knapdale

Clifford R. Acklam BD MTh	1997	2010	The Manse, Kilmichael Glassary, Lochgilphead PA31 8QA [E-mail: clifford.acklam@btinternet.com]	01546 606926

Glenaray and Inveraray See Cumlodden, Lochfyneside and Lochgair

Glenorchy and Innishael linked with Strathfillan

Elizabeth A. Gibson (Mrs) MA MLitt BD	2003	2008	The Manse, Dalmally PA33 1AA [E-mail: lizgibson@phonecoop.coop]	01838 200207

Innellan (H) See Dunoon: The High Kirk

Iona linked with Kilfinichen and Kilvickeon and the Ross of Mull

Linda E. Pollock BD ThM ThM	2001	2010	The Manse, Bunessan, Isle of Mull PA67 6DW [E-mail: fantazomi@yahoo.co.uk]	01681 700227

Jura (GD)

Vacant			Church of Scotland Manse, Craighouse, Isle of Jura PA60 7XG	01496 820384

Kilarrow (H) linked with Kildalton and Oa (GD) (H)

Robert D. Barlow BA BSc MSc PhD CChem MRSC	2010		The Manse, Bowmore, Isle of Islay PA43 7LH [E-mail: rob@miragemedia.co.uk]	01496 810271

Kilberry linked with Tarbert (Loch Fyne) (H)
Vacant — The Manse, Tarbert, Argyll PA29

Kilbrandon and Kilchattan See Craignish

Kilcalmonell linked with Killean and Kilchenzie (H)
Vacant — The Manse, Muasdale, Tarbert, Argyll PA29 6XD — 01583 421249

Kilchoman (GD) linked with Kilmeny linked with Portnahaven (GD)
Vacant — The Manse, Port Charlotte, Isle of Islay PA48 7TW — 01496 850241

Kilchrenan and Dalavich linked with Muckairn
Robert E. Brookes BD — 2009 — Muckairn Manse, Taynuilt PA35 1HW — 01866 822204
[E-mail: eilanview@uwclub.net]

Kildalton and Oa (GD) (H) See Kilarrow

Kilfinan linked with Kilmodan and Colintraive linked with Kyles (H)
David Mitchell BD DipPTheol MSc — 1988 — 2006 — West Cowal Manse, Kames, Tighnabruaich PA21 2AD — 01700 811045
[E-mail: revdmitchell@yahoo.co.uk]

Kilfinichen and Kilvickeon and the Ross of Mull See Iona
Killean and Kilchenzie (H) See Kilcalmonell
Kilmeny See Kilchoman
Kilmodan and Colintraive See Kilfinan

Kilmore (GD) and Oban (E-mail: obancofs@btinternet.com) (Website: www.obanchurch.com)
Dugald J.R. Cameron BD DipMin MTh — 1990 — 2007 — Kilmore and Oban Manse, Ganavan Road, Oban PA34 5TU — 01631 566253

Kilmun (St Munn's) (H) linked with Strone (H) and Ardentinny
David Mill KJSJ MA BD — 1978 — 2010 — The Manse, Blairmore, Dunoon PA23 8TE — 01369 840313
[E-mail: revandevmill@aol.com]

Kilninver and Kilmelford See Craignish
Kirn (H) See Dunoon: St John's
Kyles See Kilfinan
Lismore See Appin

Lochgilphead
Hilda C. Smith (Miss) MA BD MSc — 1992 — 2005 — Parish Church Manse, Manse Brae, Lochgilphead PA31 8QZ — 01546 602238
[E-mail: hilda.smith2@btinternet.com]

Lochgoilhead (H) and Kilmorich

James Macfarlane PhD	1991	2000	The Manse, Lochgoilhead, Cairndow PA24 8AA [E-mail: jmacfarlane@stmac.demon.co.uk]	01301 703059

Muckairn See Kilchrenan

Mull, Isle of, Kilninian and Kilmore linked with Salen (H) and Ulva linked with Tobermory (GD) (H) linked with Torosay (H) and Kinlochspelvie

Vacant			The Manse, Gruline Road, Salen, Aros, Isle of Mull PA72 6JF	01680 300001

North Knapdale See Glassary, Kilmartin and Ford
Portnahaven See Kilchoman

Rothesay: Trinity (H)

Andrew Barrie BSc BD	1984	2010	12 Crichton Road, Rothesay, Isle of Bute PA20 9JR [E-mail: andrew.barrie@blueyonder.co.uk]	01700 503010

Saddell and Carradale (H) linked with Skipness

Vacant			The Manse, Carradale, Campbeltown PA28 6QG	01583 431253

Salen and Ulva See Mull
Sandbank (H) See Dunoon: St John's
Skipness See Saddell and Carradale
South Knapdale See Ardrishaig

Southend (H)

Vacant			St Blaan's Manse, Southend, Campbeltown PA28 6RQ	01586 830274

Strachur and Strathlachlan

Robert K. Mackenzie MA BD PhD	1976	1998	The Manse, Strachur, Cairndow PA27 8DG [E-mail: rkmackenzie@strachurmanse.fsnet.co.uk]	01369 860246

Strathfillan See Glenorchy
Strone (H) and Ardentinny See Kilmun
Tarbert (Loch Fyne) See Kilberry

The United Church of Bute

John Owain Jones MA BD FSAScot	1981	2011	10 Bishop Terrace, Rothesay, Isle of Bute PA20 9HF [E-mail: johnowainjones@ntlworld.com]	01700 504502
Raymond Deans DCS	1994	2003	60 Ardmory Road, Rothesay, Isle of Bute PA20 0PG [E-mail: deans@fish.co.uk]	01700 504893

Tiree (GD) Elspeth MacLean BVMS BD	2011	The Manse, Scarinish, Isle of Tiree PA77 6TN [E-mail: ejmaclean@yahoo.co.uk]	01879 220377

Tobermory See Mull
Torosay and Kinlochspelvie See Mull
Toward (H) See Dunoon: The High Kirk

Anderson, David P.	2002 2007	Chaplain: Army	3 Bn The Royal Regiment of Scotland (Black Watch), BFPO 806	
Beautyman, Paul H. MA BD	1993 2009	Team Leader: Youth Education Ministries	59 Alexander Street, Dunoon PA23 7BB [E-mail: paul.beautyman@dunoongrammar.argyll-bute.sch.uk]	
Bell, Douglas W. MA LLB BD	1975 1993	(Alexandria: North)	3 Cairnbaan Lea, Cairnbaan, Lochgilphead PA31 8BA	01546 606815
Bristow, W.H.G. BEd HDipRE DipSpecEd	1951 2002	(Chaplain: Army)	Laith Cottage, Southend, Campbeltown PA28 6RU	01586 830667
Dunlop, Alistair J. MA	1965 2004	(Saddell and Carradale)	8 Pipers Road, Cairnbaan, Lochgilphead PA31 8UF [E-mail: dunrevn@btinternet.com]	01546 600316
Forrest, Alan B. MA	1956 1993	(Uphall: South)	126 Shore Road, Innellan, Dunoon PA23 7SX	01369 830424
Gibson, Frank S. BL BD STM DSWA DD	1963 1995	(Kilarrow with Kilmeny)	163 Gilbertstoun, Edinburgh EH15 2RG	0131-657 5208
Goss, Alister J. BD	1975 2009	(Industrial Chaplain)	24 Albert Place, Ardnadam, Sandbank, Dunoon PA23 8QF [E-mail: scimwest@hotmail.com]	01369 704495
Gray, William LTh	1971 2006	(Kilberry with Tarbert)	Lochnagar, Longsdale Road, Oban PA34 5DZ [E-mail: gray98@hotmail.com]	01631 567471
Henderson, Charles M.	1952 1989	(Campbeltown: Highland)	Springbank House, Askomill Walk, Campbeltown PA28 6EP	01586 552759
Henderson, Grahame McL. BD	1974 2008	(Kirn)	6 Gerhallow, Bullwood Road, Dunoon PA23 7QB [E-mail: ghende5884@aol.com]	01369 702433
Hood, Catriona A.	2006	Auxiliary Minister	'Elyside', Dalintober, Campbeltown PA28 6EB	01586 551490
Hood, H. Stanley C. MA BD	1966 2000	(London: Crown Court)	10 Dalriada Place, Kilmichael Glassary, Lochgilphead PA31 8QA	01546 606168
Inglis, Donald B.C. MA MEd BD	1975 2000	(Turriff: St Andrew's)	'Lindores', 11 Bullwood Road, Dunoon PA23 7QJ	01369 701334
Lamont, Archibald	1952 1994	(Kilcalmonell with Skipness)	8 Achlonan, Taynuilt PA35 1JJ	01866 822385
MacLeod, Roderick MA BD PhD(Edin) PhD(Open)	1966 2011	(Cumlodden, Lochfyneside and Lochgair)	Creag-nam-Barnach, Furnace, Inveraray PA32 8XU [E-mail: revroddy@btinternet.com]	01499 500629
Marshall, Freda (Mrs) BD FCII	1993 2005	(Colonsay and Oronsay with Kilbrandon and Kilchattan)	Allt Mhaluidh, Glenview, Dalmally PA33 1BE [E-mail: mail@freda.org.uk]	01838 200693
Millar, Margaret R.M. (Miss) BTh	1977 2008	(Kilchrenan and Dalavich with Muckairn)	Fearnoch Cottage, Fearnoch, Taynuilt PA35 1JB [E-mail: macoje@aol.com]	01866 822416
Morrison, Angus W. MA BD	1959 1999	(Kildalton and Oa)	1 Livingstone Way, Port Ellen, Isle of Islay PA42 7EP	01496 300043
Pollock, William MA BD PhD	1987 2002	(Isle of Mull Parishes)	Correay, Salen, Aros, Isle of Mull PA72 6JF	01680 300507
Risby, Lesley P. (Mrs) BD	1994 2011	(Irvine: Girdle Toll)	Tigh an Achaidh, 21 Fernoch Crescent, Lochgilphead PA31 8AE [E-mail: mrsrisby@hotmail.com]	
Ritchie, Walter M.	1973 1999	(Uphall: South)	Hazel Cottage, Barr Mor View, Kilmartin, Lochgilphead PA31 8UN	01546 510343

Shedden, John CBE BD DipPSS	1971	2008	(Fuengirola)	Orchy Cottage, Dalmally PA33 1AX [E-mail: shedden7@googlemail.com]	01838 200535
Stewart, Jean E. (Mrs)	1983	1989	(Kildalton and Oa)	Chamberlain Nursing Home, 7–9 Chamberlain Road, Edinburgh EH10 4DJ	
Stewart, Joseph LTh	1979	2011	(Dunoon: St John's with Sandbank)	7 Glenmorag Avenue, Dunoon PA23 7LG	
Taylor, Alan T. BD	1980	2005	(Isle of Mull Parishes)	Erray Road, Tobermory, Isle of Mull PA75 6PS	01688 302496
Watson, James LTh	1968	1994	(Bowden with Lilliesleaf)	7 Lochan Avenue, Kirn, Dunoon PA23 8HT	01369 702851
Wilkinson, W. Brian MA BD	1968	2007	(Glenaray and Inveraray)	3 Achlonan, Taynuilt PA35 1JJ [E-mail: brianwilkinson@f2s.com]	01866 822036

Communion Sundays

Ardrishaig	4th Apr, 1st Nov	Kilarrow	1st Mar, Jun, Sep, Dec	Lochgoilhead and Kilmorich	2nd Mar, Jun, Sep, Nov
Campbeltown		Kilberry with Tarbert	1st May, Oct		1st Aug, Easter
Highland	1st May, Nov	Kilcalmonell	1st Jul, 3rd Nov	North Knapdale	3rd Oct, 2nd May
Lorne and Lowland	1st May, Nov	Kilchoman	1st Jul, 2nd Dec, Easter	Portnahaven	3rd Jul
Craignish	1st Jun, Nov	Kildalton	Last Jan, Jun, Oct, Easter	Rothesay Trinity	1st Feb, Jun, Nov
Cumlodden, Lochfyneside		Kilfinan	Last Apr, Oct	Saddell and Carradale	2nd May, 1st Nov
and Lochgair	1st May, 3rd Nov	Killean and Kilchenzie	1st Mar, Jul, Oct	Sandbank	1st Jan, May, Nov
Dunoon		Kilmeny	2nd May, 3rd Nov	Skipness	2nd May, Nov
St John's	1st Mar, Jun, Nov	Kilmodan and	1st Apr, Sep	Southend	1st Jun, Dec
The High Kirk	1st Feb, Jun, Oct	Colintraive	Last Jun, Nov	South Knapdale	4th Apr, 1st Nov
Gigha and Cara	1st May, Nov	Kilmun	Last Feb, Jun, Oct	Strachur and Strathlachlan	1st Mar, Jun, Nov
Glassary, Kilmartin and Ford	1st Apr, Sep	Kilninver and Kilmelford	2nd Jun, Oct	Strone and Ardentinny	Last Feb, Jun, Oct
Glenaray and Inveraray	1st Apr, Jul, Oct, Dec	Kirn	1st May, Nov	Tayvallich	2nd May, Nov
Innellan	1st Mar, Jun, Sep, Dec	Kyles	Last Apr, Oct	The United Church of Bute	1st Feb, Jun, Nov
Inverlussa and Bellanoch	2nd May, Nov	Lochgair	2nd Oct (Gaelic)	Toward	Last Feb, May, Aug, Nov
Jura	Passion Sun., 2nd Jul, 3rd Nov	Lochgilphead	1st Apr, Nov		

(22) FALKIRK

Meets at Falkirk Old and St Modan's Parish Church on the first Tuesday of September, December, March and May, on the fourth Tuesday of October and January and on the third Tuesday of June.

Clerk:	**REV. ROBERT S.T. ALLAN LLB DipLP BD**	**9 Major's Loan, Falkirk FK1 5QF** **[E-mail: falkirk@cofscotland.org.uk]**	**01324 625124**
Treasurer:	**MR IAN MACDONALD**	**1 Jones Avenue, Larbert FK5 3ER** **[E-mail: ian_macdonald1938@hotmail.com]**	**01324 553603**

Airth (H)				
Vacant			The Manse, Airth, Falkirk FK2 8LS	01324 831474
Blackbraes and Shieldhill linked with Muiravonside				
Louise J.E. McClements RGN BD	2008		81 Stevenson Avenue, Polmont, Falkirk FK2 0GU [E-mail: louise.mcclements@virgin.net]	01324 717757
Bo'ness: Old (H)				
Douglas I. Campbell BD DPS	2004	2009	10 Dundas Street, Bo'ness EH51 0DG [E-mail: douglas@bokonline.org.uk]	01506 204585
Bo'ness: St Andrew's (Website: www.standonline.org.uk) (01506 825803)				
Albert O. Bogle BD MTh	1981		St Andrew's Manse, 11 Erngath Road, Bo'ness EH51 9DP [E-mail: albertbogle@mac.com]	01506 822195
Bonnybridge: St Helen's (H) (Website: www.bbshnc.com)				
George MacDonald BTh	2004	2009	The Manse, 32 Reilly Gardens, High Bonnybridge FK4 2BB [E-mail: georgemacdonald1@virginmedia.com]	01324 874807
Bothkennar and Carronshore				
Andrew J. Moore BSc BD	2007		11 Hunter Place, Greenmount Park, Carronshore, Falkirk FK2 8QS [E-mail: theminister@themoores.me.uk]	01324 570525
Brightons (H)				
Murdo M. Campbell BD DipMin	1997	2007	The Manse, Maddiston Road, Brightons, Falkirk FK2 0JP [E-mail: murdocampbell@hotmail.com]	01324 712062
Carriden (H)				
Vacant			The Spires, Foredale Terrace, Carriden, Bo'ness EH51 9LW	01506 822141
David Wandrum (Aux)	1993	2009	5 Cawder View, Carrickstone Meadows, Cumbernauld, Glasgow G68 0BN	01236 723288
Cumbernauld: Abronhill (H)				
Joyce A. Keyes (Mrs) BD	1996	2003	26 Ash Road, Cumbernauld, Glasgow G67 3ED	01236 723833
Linda Black (Miss) BSc DCS			148 Rowan Road, Cumbernauld, Glasgow G67 3DA	01236 786265
Cumbernauld: Condorrat (H)				
Grace Saunders BSc BTh	2007	2011	11 Rosehill Drive, Cumbernauld, Glasgow G67 4EQ [E-mail: rev.grace.saunders@btinternet.com]	01236 452090

Cumbernauld: Kildrum (H)				
Elinor J. Gordon (Miss) BD	1988	2004	64 Southfield Road, Balloch, Cumbernauld, Glasgow G68 9DZ [E-mail: elinorgordon@aol.com]	01236 723204
David Nicholson DCS			2D Doon Side, Kildrum, Cumbernauld, Glasgow G67 2HX [E-mail: deacdave@btinternet.com]	01236 732260
Cumbernauld: Old (H) (Website: cumbernauldold.org.uk)				
Catriona Ogilvie (Mrs) MA BD	1999		The Manse, 23 Baronhill, Cumbernauld, Glasgow G67 2SD	01236 721912
Valerie Cuthbertson (Miss) DCS			105 Bellshill Road, Motherwell ML1 3SJ	01698 259001
Cumbernauld: St Mungo's				
Vacant			18 Fergusson Road, Cumbernauld, Glasgow G67 1LS	01236 721513
Ronald M. Mackinnon DCS			12 Mossywood Court, Airdrie ML6 7DY	01236 763389
Denny: Dunipace (H)				
Jean W. Gallacher (Miss) BD CMin CTheol DMin	1989		Dunipace Manse, Denny FK6 6QJ	01324 824540
Denny: Old				
John Murning BD	1988	2002	31 Duke Street, Denny FK6 6NR [E-mail: bridgebuilder@supanet.com]	01324 824508
Denny: Westpark (H) (Website: www.westparkchurch.org.uk)				
Vacant			13 Baxter Crescent, Denny FK6 5EZ	01324 876224
Falkirk: Bainsford				
Michael R. Philip BD	1978	2001	1 Valleyview Place, Newcarron Village, Falkirk FK2 7JB [E-mail: mrphilip@btinternet.com]	01324 621087
Falkirk: Camelon (Church office: 01324 870011)				
Stuart Sharp MTheol DipPA	2001		30 Cotland Drive, Falkirk FK2 7GE	01324 623631
Margaret Corrie (Miss) DCS			44 Sunnyside Street, Falkirk FK1 4BH	01324 670656
Falkirk: Erskine (H)				
Glendon Macaulay BD	1999		Burnbrae Road, Falkirk FK1 5SD [E-mail: gd.macaulay@blueyonder.co.uk]	01324 623701

Falkirk: Grahamston United (H)				
Ian Wilkie BD PGCE	2001	2007	16 Cromwell Road, Falkirk FK1 1SF [E-mail: yanbluejeans@aol.com]	01324 624461 07877 803280 (Mbl)
Falkirk: Laurieston linked with Redding and Westquarter				
J. Mary Henderson MA BD DipEd PhD	1990	2009	11 Polmont Road, Laurieston, Falkirk FK2 9QQ [E-mail: jmary.henderson@tiscali.co.uk]	01324 621196
Falkirk: Old and St Modan's (H)				
Robert S.T. Allan LLB DipLP BD	1991	2003	9 Major's Loan, Falkirk FK1 5QF	01324 625124
Falkirk: St Andrew's West (H)				
Alastair M. Horne BSc BD	1989	1997	1 Maggiewood's Loan, Falkirk FK1 5SJ	01324 623308
Falkirk: St James'				
Vacant			13 Wallace Place, Falkirk FK2 7EN	01324 632501
Grangemouth: Abbotsgrange				
Aftab Gohar MA MDiv PgDip	1995	2010	8 Naismith Court, Grangemouth FK3 9BQ [E-mail: abbotsgrange@aol.com]	01324 482109 07528 143784 (Mbl)
Grangemouth: Kirk of the Holy Rood				
David J. Smith BD DipMin	1992	2003	The Manse, Bowhouse Road, Grangemouth FK3 0EX [E-mail: davidkhrood@tiscali.co.uk]	01324 471595
Grangemouth: Zetland (H)				
Ian W. Black MA BD	1976	1991	Ronaldshay Crescent, Grangemouth FK3 9JH [E-mail: iwblack@hotmail.com]	01324 472868
Lorna A. MacDougall (Miss) MA (Aux)	2003		34 Millar Place, Carron, Falkirk FK2 8QB	01324 552739
Haggs (H)				
Helen F. Christie (Mrs) BD	1998		5 Watson Place, Dennyloanhead, Bonnybridge FK4 2BG	01324 813786
Larbert: East				
Melville D. Crosthwaite BD DipEd DipMin	1984	1995	1 Cortachy Avenue, Carron, Falkirk FK2 8DH	01324 562402
Larbert: Old (H)				
Andrew M. Randall LLB DipLP BD	2009		The Manse, 38 South Broomage Avenue, Larbert FK5 3ED [E-mail: aandk.randall@hotmail.com]	01324 872760

Larbert: West (H)				
Gavin Boswell BTheol	1993	1999	11 Carronvale Road, Larbert FK5 3LZ	01324 562878
Muiravonside See Blackbraes and Shieldhill				
Polmont: Old				
Jerome O'Brien BA LLB MTh	2001	2005	3 Orchard Grove, Polmont, Falkirk FK2 0XE	01324 718677
Redding and Westquarter See Falkirk: Laurieston				
Slamannan				
Raymond Thomson BD DipMin	1992		Slamannan, Falkirk FK1 3EN	01324 851307
Stenhouse and Carron (H)				
William Thomson BD	2001	2007	The Manse, 21 Tipperary Place, Stenhousemuir, Larbert FK5 4SX	01324 416628

Blair, Douglas B. LTh	1969	2004	(Grangemouth: Dundas)	Flat 6, Hanover Grange, Forth Street, Grangemouth FK3 8LF	01324 484414
Brown, James BA BD DipHSW DipPsychol	1973	2001	(Abercorn with Dalmeny)	6 Salmon Court, Schoolbrae, Bo'ness EH51 9HF	01506 822454
Brown, T. John MA BD	1995	2006	(Tullibody: St Serf's)	1 Callendar Park Walk, Callendar Grange, Falkirk FK1 1TA [E-mail: johnbrown1cpw@talktalk.net]	01324 617352
Chalmers, George A. MA BD MLitt	1962	2002	(Catrine with Sorn)	3 Cricket Place, Brightons, Falkirk FK2 0HZ	01324 712030
Hardie, Robert K. MA BD	1968	2005	(Stenhouse and Carron)	33 Palace Street, Berwick-upon-Tweed TD15 1HN	
Heriot, Charles R. JP BA	1962	1996	(Brightons)	20 Eastcroft Drive, Polmont, Falkirk FK2 0SU	01324 711352
Hill, Stanley LTh	1967	1998	(Muiravonside)	28 Creteil Court, Falkirk FK1 1UL	01324 634483
Holland, John C.	1976	1985	(Strone and Ardentinny)	7 Polmont Park, Polmont, Falkirk FK2 0XT	01324 880109
Job, Anne J. BSc BD	1993	2010	(Kirkcaldy: Viewforth with Thornton)	5 Carse View, Airth, Falkirk FK2 8NY [E-mail: aj@ajjob.co.uk]	01324 832094
Kesting, Sheilagh M. (Miss) BA BD	1980	1993	Ecumenical Relations	12 Glenview Drive, Falkirk FK1 5JU	01324 671489
McCallum, John	1962	1998	(Falkirk: Irving Camelon)	11 Burnbrae Gardens, Falkirk FK1 5SB	01324 619766
McDonald, William G. MA BD	1959	1975	(Falkirk: Grahamston United)	24 Kinkell Terrace, St Andrews KY16 8DS	01334 470481
McDowall, Ronald J. BD	1980	2001	(Falkirk: Laurieston with Redding and Westquarter)	'Kailas', Windsor Road, Falkirk FK1 5EJ	01324 871947
Mathers, Daniel L. BD	1982	2001	(Grangemouth: Charing Cross and West)	10 Ercall Road, Brightons, Falkirk FK2 0RS	01324 872253
Maxton, Ronald M. MA	1955	1995	(Dollar: Associate)	5 Rulley View, Denny FK6 6QQ	01324 825441
Miller, Elsie M. (Miss) DCS			(Deaconess)	30 Swinton Avenue, Rowansbank, Baillieston, Glasgow G69 6JR	0141-771 0857
Munroe, Henry BA LTh LTI	1971	1988	(Denny: Dunipace North with Old)	Viewforth, High Road, Maddiston, Falkirk FK2 0BL	01324 712446
Paul, Iain BSc PhD BD PhD	1976	1991	(Wishaw: Craigneuk and Belhaven)	11 Hope Park Terrace, Larbert Road, Bonnybridge FK4 1DY	
Ross, Evan J. LTh	1986	1998	(Cowdenbeath: West with Mossgreen and Crossgates)	5 Arneil Place, Brightons, Falkirk FK2 0NJ	01324 719936

Scott, Donald H. BA BD	1983 2002	Chaplain: HMYOI Polmont	14 Gibsongray Street, Falkirk FK2 0AB [E-mail: donaldhscott@hotmail.com]	01324 722241
Smith, Richard BD	1976 2002	(Denny: Old)	Easter Wayside, 46 Kennedy Way, Airth, Falkirk FK2 8GB [E-mail: richards@uklinux.net]	01324 831386
Smith, Ronald W. BA BEd BD	1979 2011	(Falkirk: St James')	1F1, 2 Middlefield, Edinburgh EH7 4PF	0131-553 1174 (Mbl) 07900 896954
Whiteford, Robert S. MA	1945 1986	(Shapinsay)	3 Wellside Court, Wellside Place, Falkirk FK1 5RG	01324 610562
Wilson, Phyllis M. (Mrs) DipCom DipRE	1985 2006	(Motherwell: South Dalziel)	'Landemer', 17 Sneddon Place, Airth, Falkirk FK2 8GH [E-mail: thomas.wilson38@btinternet.com]	01324 832257

FALKIRK ADDRESSES

Blackbraes and Shieldhill	Main Street x Anderson Crescent
Bo'ness: Old	Panbrae Road
St Andrew's	Grahamsdyke Avenue
Carriden	Carriden Brae
Cumbernauld: Abronhill	Larch Road
Condorrat	Main Road
Kildrum	Clouden Road
Old	Baronhill
St Mungo's	St Mungo's Road
Denny: Dunipace	Stirling Street
Old	Denny Cross
Westpark	Duke Street
Falkirk: Bainsford	Hendry Street, Bainsford
Camelon	Dorrator Road
Erskine	Cockburn Street x Hodge Street
Grahamston	Bute Street
Laurieston	Main Falkirk Road
Old and St Modan's	Kirk Wynd
St Andrew's West	Newmarket Street
St James'	Thornhill Road x Firs Street
Grangemouth: Abbotsgrange	Abbot's Road
Kirk of the Holy Rood	Bowhouse Road
Zetland	Ronaldshay Crescent
Haggs	Glasgow Road
Larbert: East	Kirk Avenue
Old	Denny Road x Stirling Road
West	Main Street
Muiravonside	off Vellore Road
Polmont: Old	Kirk Entry/Bo'ness Road
Redding and Westquarter	Main Street
Slamannan	Manse Place
Stenhouse and Carron	Church Street

(23) STIRLING

Meets at the Moderator's church on the second Thursday of September, and at Stirling: Allan Park South Church on the second Thursday of February, March, April, May, June, October, November and December.

Clerk:	**MISS DOROTHY KINLOCH OBE DL**	**3 Julia Cottages, Bridgend, Callander FK17 8AE** **Presbytery Office, Bridge of Allan Parish Church, 12 Keir Street, Bridge of Allan FK9 4NW** **[E-mail: stirling@cofscotland.org.uk]**	**01877 330238** **07597 931941 (Mbl)**
Treasurer:	**MR GILMOUR CUTHBERTSON**	**'Denovan', 1 Doune Road, Dunblane FK15 9AR**	**01786 823487**

Aberfoyle (H) linked with Port of Menteith (H)

Linda Stewart (Mrs) BD	1996	2008	The Manse, Loch Ard Road, Aberfoyle, Stirling FK8 3SZ [E-mail: lindacstewart@tiscali.co.uk]	01877 382391

Alloa: Ludgate

Elizabeth Clelland (Mrs) BD	2002		30 Claremont, Alloa FK10 2DF [E-mail: liz_clelland@yahoo.co.uk]	01259 210403
Muriel F. Willoughby (Mrs) MA BD (Assoc)	2006	2010	53 Mary Stevenson Drive, Alloa FK10 2BQ [E-mail: muriel.willoughby@btinternet.com]	01259 727927

Alloa: St Mungo's (H)

Sang Y. Cha BD	2011		37A Claremont, Alloa FK10 2DG [E-mail: syc@cantab.com]	01259 213872

Alva

James N.R. McNeil BSc BD	1990	1997	The Manse, 34 Ochil Road, Alva FK12 5JT	01259 760262

Balfron linked with Fintry (H)

Iain M. Goring BSc BD (Interim Minister)	1976	2011	7 Station Road, Balfron, Glasgow G63 0SX [E-mail: imgoring@tiscali.co.uk]	01360 440285

Balquhidder linked with Killin and Ardeonaig (H)

John Lincoln MPhil BD	1986	1997	The Manse, Killin FK21 8TN [E-mail: eoin22@gmail.com]	01567 820247

Bannockburn: Allan (H) (Website: www.allanchurch.org.uk)

Jim Landels BD CertMin	1990		The Manse, Bogend Road, Bannockburn, Stirling FK7 8NP [E-mail: revjimlandels@btinternet.com]	01786 814692

Bannockburn: Ladywell (H)

Elizabeth M.D. Robertson (Miss) BD CertMin	1997		57 The Firs, Bannockburn FK7 0EG [E-mail: lizrob@talktalk.net]	01786 812467

Bridge of Allan (H) (01786 834155)

Gillian Weighton (Mrs) BD STM	1992	2004	29 Keir Street, Bridge of Allan, Stirling FK9 4QJ [E-mail: gillweighton@aol.com]	01786 832753

Buchanan linked with Drymen

Alexander J. MacPherson BD	1986	1997	Buchanan Manse, Drymen, Glasgow G63 0AQ [E-mail: revalex1@gmail.com]	01360 870212

Buchlyvie (H) linked with Gartmore (H)
Elaine H. MacRae (Mrs) BD | 1985 | 2004 | The Manse, Kippen, Stirling FK8 3DN [E-mail: ge.macrae@btopenworld.com] | 01786 871170

Callander (H) (Tel/Fax: 01877 331409)
Robert R. Simpson BA BD | 1994 | 2010 | 3 Aveland Park Road, Callander FK17 8FD [E-mail: robert@pansmanse.co.uk] | 01877 330097

Cambusbarron: The Bruce Memorial (H)
Brian G. Webster BSc BD | 1998 | | 14 Woodside Court, Cambusbarron, Stirling FK7 9PH [E-mail: Revwebby@aol.com] | 01786 450579

Clackmannan (H)
Scott Raby LTh | 1991 | 2007 | The Manse, Port Street, Clackmannan FK10 4JH [E-mail: s.raby@hotmail.co.uk] | 01259 211255

Cowie (H) and Plean linked with Fallin (Website: www.cowiepleanandfallinchurch.com)
Alan L. Dunnett LLB BD | 1994 | 2008 | 5 Fincastle Place, Cowie, Stirling FK7 7DS [E-mail: alan.dunnett@sky.com] | 01786 818413
Linda Dunnett (Mrs) BA DCS | | | 5 Fincastle Place, Cowie, Stirling FK7 7DS [E-mail: lindadunnett@sky.com] | 01786 818413

Dollar (H) linked with Glendevon linked with Muckhart (Website: www.dollarparishchurch.org.uk)
Alan H. Ward MA BD (Interim Minister) | 1978 | 2010 | Glebe House, Muckhart, Dollar FK14 7JN [E-mail: revalanward@dollarparishchurch.org.uk] | 01259 781638

Drymen See Buchanan

Dunblane: Cathedral (H)
Colin G. McIntosh BSc BD | 1976 | 1988 | Cathedral Manse, The Cross, Dunblane FK15 0AQ [E-mail: revcolcath4@netscape.net] | 01786 822205
Sally Foster-Fulton (Mrs) BA BD (Assoc) | 1999 | 2007 | 21 Craiglea, Causewayhead, Stirling FK9 5EE [E-mail: sallyfulton01@gmail.com] | 01786 463060

Dunblane: St Blane's (H)
Alexander B. Mitchell BD | 1981 | 2003 | 49 Roman Way, Dunblane FK15 9DJ [E-mail: alex.mitchell6@btopenworld.com] | 01786 822268

Fallin See Cowie and Plean
Fintry See Balfron

Gargunnock linked with Kilmadock linked with Kincardine-in-Menteith

Andrew B. Campbell BD DPS MTh	1979	2011	The Manse, Manse Brae, Gargunnock, Stirling FK8 3BQ [E-mail: andycampbell53@btinternet.com]	01786 860678

Gartmore See Buchlyvie
Glendevon See Dollar

Killearn (H)

Lee Messeder BD PgDipMin	2003	2010	2 The Oaks, Killearn, Glasgow G63 9SF [E-mail: lee.messeder@gmail.com]	01360 550045

Killin and Ardeonaig (H) See Balquhidder
Kilmadock See Gargunnock
Kincardine-in-Menteith See Gargunnock

Kippen (H) linked with Norrieston

Gordon MacRae BD MTh	1985	1998	The Manse, Kippen, Stirling FK8 3DN [E-mail: ge.macrae@btopenworld.com]	01786 870229

Lecropt (H)

Alison E.P. Britchfield (Mrs) MA BD	1987	2009	Braehead, 5 Henderson Street, Bridge of Allan, Stirling FK9 4NA [E-mail: lecroptminister@btinternet.com]	01786 832382

Logie (H)

R. Stuart M. Fulton BA BD	1991	2006	21 Craiglea, Causewayhead, Stirling FK9 5EE [E-mail: stuart.fulton@btinternet.com]	01786 463060
Anne Shearer BA DipEd (Aux)	2010		10 Colsnaur, Menstrie FK11 7HG [E-mail: anne.f.shearer@btinternet.com]	01259 769176

Menstrie (H)

Mairi F. Lovett (Miss) BSc BA DipPS MTh	2005		The Manse, 7 Long Row, Menstrie FK11 7BA [E-mail: mairi@kanyo.co.uk]	01259 761461

Muckhart See Dollar
Norrieston See Kippen
Port of Menteith See Aberfoyle

Sauchie and Coalsnaughton
Vacant | | | 19 Graygoran, Sauchie, Alloa FK10 3ET | 01259 212037

Stirling: Allan Park South (H)
Alistair Cowper BD BSc | 2011 | | 22 Laurelhill Place, Stirling FK8 2JH [E-mail: alistaircowper@talktalk.net] | 01786 471998 (Office tel/fax) 07791 524504 (Mbl)

Stirling: Church of the Holy Rude (H) linked with Stirling: Viewfield Erskine
Alan Miller BA MA BD | 2000 | 2010 | 7 Windsor Place, Stirling FK8 2HY [E-mail: revafmiller@gmail.com] | 01786 465166

Stirling: North (H) (01786 463376) (Website: www.northparishchurch.com)
Calum Jack BSc BD | 2004 | | 18 Shirra's Brae Road, Stirling FK7 0BA [E-mail: info@northparishchurch.com] | 01786 475378

Stirling: St Columba's (H) (01786 449516)
Alexander M. Millar MA BD MBA | 1980 | 2010 | 5 Clifford Road, Stirling FK8 2AQ [E-mail: alexmillar0406@gmail.com] | 01786 469979

Stirling: St Mark's (Website: www.stmarksstirling.org.uk)
Stuart Davidson BD | 2008 | | 176 Drip Road, Stirling FK8 1RR [E-mail: info@stmarksstirling.org.uk] | 01786 473716
Jean Porter (Mrs) BD DCS | 2006 | 2008 | 3 Cochrie Road, Tullibody, Alloa FK10 2RR [E-mail: JayteePorter@aol.com] | 07729 316321 (Mbl)

Stirling: St Ninians Old (H)
Gary J. McIntyre BD DipMin | 1993 | 1998 | 7 Randolph Road, Stirling FK8 2AJ [E-mail: gary.mcintyre7@btinternet.com] | 01786 474421

Stirling: Viewfield Erskine (T) (H) See Stirling: Church of the Holy Rude

Strathblane (H)
Richard Begg MA BD | 2008 | 2011 | The Manse, Strathblane, Glasgow G63 9AB [E-mail: RBEGG711@aol.com] | 01360 770226

Tillicoultry (H)
James Cochrane LTh | 1994 | 2000 | The Manse, Dollar Road, Tillicoultry FK13 6PD [E-mail: jcochrane1@tiscali.co.uk] | 01259 750340 01259 752951 (Fax)

Tullibody: St Serf's (H)

Donald M. Thomson BD	1975	2007	16 Menstrie Road, Tullibody, Alloa FK10 2RG [E-mail: donniethomson@tiscali.co.uk]	01259 729804

Aitken, E. Douglas MA	1961 1998	(Clackmannan)	1 Dolan Grove, Saline, Dunfermline KY12 9UP [E-mail: douglasaitken14@btinternet.com]	01383 852730
Blackley, Jean R.M. (Mrs) BD	1989 2001	(Banton with Twechar)	8 Rodders Grove, Alva FK12 5RR	01259 760198
Brown, James H. BD	1977 2005	(Helensburgh: Park)	14 Gullipen View, Callander FK17 8HN [E-mail: revjimhbrown@yahoo.co.uk]	01877 339425
Campbell, Richard S. LTh	1993 2010	(Gargunnock with Kilmadock with Kincardine-in-Menteith)	3 River Wynd, Strathallan Park, Stirling FK9 5GN [E-mail: revrichards@btinternet.com]	01786 469622
Cloggie, June (Mrs)	1997 2006	(Auxiliary Minister)	11A Tulipan Crescent, Callander FK17 8AR	01877 331021
Cruickshank, Alistair A.B. MA	1991 2004	(Auxiliary Minister)	Thistle Cottage, 2A Chapel Place, Dollar FK14 7DW	01259 742549
Gaston, A. Ray C. MA BD	1969 2002	(Leuchars: St Athernase)	'Hamewith', 13 Manse Road, Dollar FK14 7AL [E-mail: raygaston@onetel.com]	01259 743202
Gillespie, Irene C. (Mrs) BD	1991 2007	(Tiree)	39 King O'Muirs Drive, Tullibody, Alloa FK10 3AY [E-mail: revicg@btinternet.com]	01259 723937
Gilmour, William M. MA BD	1969 2008	(Lecropt)	14 Pine Court, Doune FK16 6JE [E-mail: heleng_fk9@firefly.uk.net]	01786 842928
Herkes, Moira BD	1985 2007	(Brechin: Gardner Memorial)	38 King O'Muirs Drive, Tullibody, Alloa FK10 3AY [E-mail: mossherkes@btinternet.com]	01259 725533
Izett, William A.F.	1968 2000	(Law)	1 Duke Street, Clackmannan FK10 4EF	01259 724203
Jack, Alison M. (Mrs) MA BD PhD	1998 2001	Assistant Principal, New College	5 Murdoch Terrace, Dunblane FK15 9JE	01786 825116
MacCormick, Moira G. BA LTh	1986 2003	(Buchlyvie with Gartmore)	12 Rankine Wynd, Tullibody, Alloa FK10 2UW [E-mail: mmaccormick@compuserve.com]	01259 724619
McCreadie, David W.	1961 1995	(Kirkmabreck)	23 Willoughby Place, Callander PH17 8DG	01877 330785
McIntosh, Hamish N.M. MA	1949 1987	(Fintry)	1 Forth Crescent, Stirling FK8 1LE	01786 470453
Malloch, Philip R.M. LLB BD	1970 2009	(Killearn)	8 Michael McParland Drive, Torrance, Glasgow G64 4EE	01360 620089
Millar, Jennifer M. (Mrs) BD DipMin	1986 1995	Teacher: Religious and Moral Education	5 Clifford Road, Stirling FK8 2AQ	01786 469979
Murray, Douglas R. MA BD	1965 2004	(Lausanne)	32 Forth Park, Bridge of Allan, Stirling FK9 5NT [E-mail: d-smurray@supanet.com]	01786 831081
Nicol, John C. MA BD	1965 2002	(Bridge of Allan: Holy Trinity)	37 King O'Muirs Drive, Tullibody, Alloa FK10 3AY [E-mail: jchalmersnicol@aol.com]	01259 212305
Ovens, Samuel B. BD	1982 1993	(Slamannan)	21 Bevan Drive, Alva FK12 5PD	01259 222723
Paterson, John L. MA BD STM	1964 2003	(Linlithgow: St Michael's)	'Kirkmichael', 22 Waterfront Way, Stirling FK9 5GH [E-mail: lornandian.paterson@virgin.net]	01786 447165
Pryce, Stuart F.A.	1963 1997	(Dumfries: St George's)	36 Forth Park, Bridge of Allan, Stirling FK9 5NT	01786 831026
Russell, Kenneth G. BD CCE	1986 2010	NHS Chaplain: Forth Valley	10 Abbeymill, Stirling FK8 1QS	01786 475802
Sangster, Ernest G. BD ThM	1958 1997	(Alva)	6 Law Hill Road, Dollar FK14 7BG	
Scott, James F.	1957 1997	(Dyce)	5 Gullipen View, Callander FK17 8HN	01877 330565
Scoular, J. Marshall	1954 1996	(Kippen)	6 Buccleuch Court, Dunblane FK15 0AH	01786 825976
Sewell, Paul M.N. MA BD	1970 2010	(Berwick-upon-Tweed: St Andrew's Wallace Green and Lowick)	7 Bohum Court, Stirling FK7 7UT	

Sherry, George T. LTh	1977 2004	(Menstrie)	37 Moubray Gardens, Silver Meadows, Cambus, Alloa FK10 2NQ [E-mail: georgetaylorsherry@tiscali.co.uk]	01259 220665
Silcox, John R. BD DipPhilEd CPP CF TD	1976 1984	School Chaplain	Queen Victoria School, Dunblane FK15 0JY	01786 824944
Sinclair, James H. MA BD	1966 2004	(Auchencairn and Rerrick with Buittle and Kelton)	16 Delaney Court, Alloa FK10 1RB	01259 729001
Watson, Jean S. (Miss) MA	1993 2004	(Auxiliary Minister)	29 Strachan Crescent, Dollar FK14 7HL	01259 742872
Wright, John P. BD	1977 2000	(Glasgow: New Govan)	Plane Castle, Airth, Falkirk FK2 8SF	01786 480840

STIRLING ADDRESSES

Allan Park South	Dumbarton Road	St Columba's	Park Terrace	Viewfield Erskine	Barnton Street
Holy Rude	St John Street	St Mark's	Drip Road		
North	Springfield Road	St Ninians Old	Kirk Wynd, St Ninians		

(24) DUNFERMLINE

Meets at Dunfermline in St Andrew's Erskine Church, Robertson Road, on the first Thursday of each month, except January, July and August when there is no meeting, and June when it meets on the last Thursday.

Clerk:	**REV. ELIZABETH S.S. KENNY BD RGN SCM**	**5 Cobden Court, Crossgates, Cowdenbeath KY4 8AU** **[E-mail: dunfermline@cofscotland.org.uk]**	**01383 741495 (Office)** **07831 763494 (Mbl)**

Aberdour: St Fillan's (H) (Website: www.stfillans.presbytery.org)

Peter S. Gerbrandy-Baird MA BD MSc FRSA FRGS	2004	St Fillan's Manse, 36 Bellhouse Road, Aberdour, Fife KY3 0TL	01383 861522

Beath and Cowdenbeath: North (H)

David W. Redmayne BSc BD	2001	10 Stuart Place, Cowdenbeath KY4 9BN [E-mail: beathandnorth@dunfermlinepresbytery.org.uk]	01383 511033

Cairneyhill (H) (01383 882352) linked with Limekilns (H) (01383 873337)

Norman M. Grant BD	1990	The Manse, 10 Church Street, Limekilns, Dunfermline KY11 3HT [E-mail: nmg57@live.com]	01383 872341

Carnock and Oakley (H)				
Maggie R. Roderick BA BD FRSA FTSI	2010		The Manse, Main Street, Carnock, Dunfermline KY12 9JG [E-mail: maggierroderick@yahoo.co.uk]	01383 850327
Cowdenbeath: Trinity (H)				
Vacant			66 Barclay Street, Cowdenbeath KY4 9LD	01383 515089
John Wyllie (Pastoral Assistant)			51 Seafar Street, Kelty KY4 0JX	01383 839200
Culross and Torryburn (H)				
Jayne E. Scott (Mrs) BA MEd MBA	1988	2009	The Manse, Culross, Dunfermline KY12 8JD [E-mail: jayne.scott5@btinternet.com]	01383 880231
Dalgety (H) (01383 824092) (E-mail: office@dalgety-church.co.uk) (Website: www.dalgety-church.co.uk)				
Vacant			9 St Colme Drive, Dalgety Bay, Dunfermline KY11 9LQ	01383 822316
Dunfermline: Abbey (H) (Website: www.dunfabbey.freeserve.co.uk)				
Vacant			12 Garvock Hill, Dunfermline KY12 7UU	01383 721022
Dunfermline: Gillespie Memorial (H) (01383 621253) (E-mail: gillespie.church@btopenworld.com)				
Iain A. Sutherland BSc BD	1996	2009	4 Killin Court, Dunfermline KY12 7XF [E-mail: RevISutherland@aol.com]	01383 723329
Dunfermline: North				
Ian G. Thom BSc PhD BD	1990	2007	13 Barbour Grove, Dunfermline KY12 9YB [E-mail: ianthom58@btinternet.com]	01383 733471
Dunfermline: St Andrew's Erskine (01383 841660)				
Ann Allison BSc PhD BD	2000		71A Townhill Road, Dunfermline KY12 0BN [E-mail: revann@sky.com]	01383 734657
Dunfermline: St Leonard's (01383 620106) (E-mail: office@stleonardsparishchurch.org.uk) (Website: www.stleonardsparishchurch.org.uk)				
Andrew J. Philip BSc BD	1996	2004	12 Torvean Place, Dunfermline KY11 4YY [E-mail: andrewphilip@minister.com]	01383 721054
Dunfermline: St Margaret's				
Iain M. Greenshields BD DipRS ACMA MSc MTh	1985	2007	38 Garvock Hill, Dunfermline KY12 7UU [E-mail: revimaclg@hotmail.co.uk]	01383 723955

Dunfermline: St Ninian's				
Elizabeth A. Fisk (Mrs) BD	1996		51 St John's Drive, Dunfermline KY12 7TL	01383 722256
Dunfermline: St Paul's East (New Charge Development)				
Andrew A. Morrice MA BD	1999	2010	9 Dover Drive, Dunfermline KY11 8HQ [E-mail: andrew@morrice5.wanadoo.co.uk]	01383 620704
Elizabeth Philip (Mrs) DCS MA BA PGCSE			12 Torvean Place, Dunfermline KY11 4YY	01383 721054
Dunfermline: Townhill and Kingseat (H)				
Rosemary A. Smith BD	1997	2010	7 Lochwood Park, Kingseat, Dunfermline KY12 0UX [E-mail: revrosieann@gmail.com]	01383 626181
Inverkeithing linked with North Queensferry (T)				
Vacant			1 Dover Way, Dunfermline KY11 8HR	01383 432158
Kelty (Website: www.keltykirk.org.uk)				
Vacant			15 Arlick Road, Kelty KY4 0BH	01383 830291
Limekilns See Cairneyhill				
Lochgelly and Benarty: St Serf's				
Elisabeth M. Stenhouse (Ms) BD	2006		82 Main Street, Lochgelly KY5 9AA [E-mail: lissten@sky.com]	01592 780435
Patricia Munro (Ms) BSc DCS	1986	2007	82 Balbedie Avenue, Lochore, Lochgelly KY5 8HP [E-mail: pat_munro@btinternet.com]	01592 869240 07814 836314 (Mbl)
North Queensferry See Inverkeithing				
Rosyth				
Violet C.C. McKay (Mrs) BD	1988	2002	42 Woodside Avenue, Rosyth KY11 2LA [E-mail: v.mckay@btinternet.com]	01383 412776
Morag Crawford (Miss) MSc DCS			118 Wester Drylaw Place, Edinburgh EH4 2TG [E-mail: morag.crawford.dcs@blueyonder.co.uk]	0131-332 2253
Saline and Blairingone				
Vacant			8 The Glebe, Saline, Dunfermline KY12 9UT	01383 853062
Tulliallan and Kincardine				
Kenneth W. Donald BA BD	1982	2009	62 Toll Road, Kincardine, Alloa FK10 4QZ [E-mail: kenneth@kdonald.freeserve.co.uk]	01259 730538

Name	Ord.	Ret.	Former charge / post	Address		Phone
Adams, David G. BD	1991	2011	(Cowdenbeath: Trinity)	13 Fernhill Gardens, Windygates, Leven KY8 5DZ [E-mail: adams69@sky.com]		
Boyle, Robert P. LTh	1990	2010	(Saline and Blairingone)	43 Dunipace Crescent, Dunfermline KY12 7JE [E-mail: boab.boyle@btinternet.com]		01383 740980
Brown, Peter MA BD FRAScot	1953	1987	(Holm)	24 Inchmickery Avenue, Dalgety Bay, Dunfermline KY11 5NF		01383 822456
Chalmers, John P. BD	1979	1995	Principal Clerk	10 Liggars Place, Dunfermline KY12 7XZ		01383 739130
Evans, Mark DCS	2006		Chaplain: Queen Margaret Hospital, Dunfermline	13 Easter Drylaw Drive, Edinburgh EH4 2QA	(Home) (Office)	0131-343 3089 01383 674136
Farquhar, William E. BA BD	1987	2006	(Dunfermline: Townhill and Kingseat)	29 Queens Drive, Middlewich, Cheshire CW10 0DG		01606 835097
Jenkins, Gordon F.C. MA BD PhD	1968	2006	(Dunfermline: North)	20 Lumsden Park, Cupar KY15 5YL [E-mail: jenkinsgordon1@sky.com]		01334 652548
Jessamine, Alistair L. MA BD	1979	2011	(Dunfermline: Abbey)	11 Gallowhill Farm Cottages, Strathaven ML10 6BZ [E-mail: chatty.1@talktalk.net]		01357 520934
Johnston, Thomas N. LTh	1972	2008	(Edinburgh: Priestfield)	71 Main Street, Newmills, Dunfermline KY12 8ST [E-mail: tomjohnston@blueyonder.co.uk]		01383 889240
Kenny, Elizabeth S.S. BD RGN SCM	1989	2010	(Carnock and Oakley)	5 Cobden Court, Crossgates, Cowdenbeath KY4 8AU [E-mail: esskenny@homecall.co.uk]	(Mbl)	07831 763494
Laidlaw, Victor W.N. BD	1975	2008	(Edinburgh: St Catherine's Argyle)	9 Tern Road, Dunfermline KY11 8GA		01383 620134
McLellan, Andrew R.C. MA BD STM DD	1970	2002	HM Inspector of Prisons	4 Liggars Place, Dunfermline KY12 7XZ		01383 725959
Melville, David D. BD	1989	2008	(Kirkconnel)	28 Porterfield, Comrie, Dunfermline KY12 9HJ		01383 850075
Orr, J. McMichael MA BD PhD	1949	1986	(Aberfoyle with Port of Menteith)	9 Overhaven, Limekilns, Dunfermline KY11 3JH		01383 872245
Park, Christopher BSc BD	1977	2010	(Inverkeithing with North Queensferry)	65 Moubray Road, Dalgety Bay, Dunfermline KY11 9JP [E-mail: chrispark8649@hotmail.com]		01383 821111
Paterson, Andrew E. JP	1994		Auxiliary Minister	6 The Willows, Kelty KY4 0FQ		01383 830998
Reid, A. Gordon BSc BD	1982	2008	(Dunfermline: Gillespie Memorial)	7 Arkleston Crescent, Paisley PA3 4TG [E-mail: reid501@fsmail.net]	 (Mbl)	0141-842 1542 07773 300989
Reid, David MSc LTh FSAScot	1961	1992	(St Monans with Largoward)	North Lethans, Saline, Dunfermline KY12 9TE		01383 733144
Shewan, Frederick D.F. MA BD	1970	2005	(Edinburgh: Muirhouse St Andrew's)	38 Tremayne Place, Dunfermline KY12 9YH		01383 734354
Stuart, Anne (Miss) DCS			(Deaconess)	19 St Colme Crescent, Aberdour, Burntisland KY3 0ST		01383 860049
Vint, Allan S. BSc BD MTh	1989	2008	Mission Development Officer	St Ninian's Church, Allan Crescent, Dunfermline KY11 4HE [E-mail: allan@vint.co.uk]	(Mbl)	07795 483070
Watt, Robert J. BD	1994	2009	(Dumbarton: Riverside)	101 Birrell Drive, Dunfermline KY11 8FA [E-mail: robertjwatt@blueyonder.co.uk]	(Mbl)	07753 683717
Whyte, Isabel H. (Mrs) BD	1993		(Chaplain: Queen Margaret Hospital, Dunfermline)	14 Carlingnose Point, North Queensferry, Inverkeithing KY11 1ER [E-mail: iainisabel@whytes28.fsnet.co.uk]		01383 410732

(25) KIRKCALDY

Meets at Kirkcaldy, in the St Bryce Kirk Centre, on the first Tuesday of February, March, April (when necessary), May, September, October, November and December, and on the fourth Tuesday of June.

Clerk:	**REV. ROSEMARY FREW** (Mrs) **MA BD**	**83 Milton Road, Kirkcaldy KY1 1TP** **[E-mail: kirkcaldy@cofscotland.org.uk]**	**01592 260315**
Depute Clerk:	**MR DOUGLAS G. HAMILL BEM**	**41 Abbots Mill, Kirkcaldy KY2 5PE** **[E-mail: hamilldg@tiscali.co.uk]**	**01592 267500**

Auchterderran: St Fothad's linked with Kinglassie				
Ben Pieterse BA BTh LTh	2001	2010	7 Woodend Road, Cardenden, Lochgelly KY5 0NE	01592 720202
Auchtertool linked with Kirkcaldy: Linktown (H) (01592 641080)				
Catriona M. Morrison (Mrs) MA BD	1995	2000	16 Raith Crescent, Kirkcaldy KY2 5NN [E-mail: catriona@linktown.org.uk]	01592 265536
Marc Prowe			16 Raith Crescent, Kirkcaldy KY2 5NN [E-mail: marc@linktown.org.uk]	01592 265536
Buckhaven (01592 715577) and Wemyss				
Wilma Cairns (Miss) BD	1999	2004	33 Main Road, East Wemyss, Kirkcaldy KY1 4RE [E-mail: wilcairns@blueyonder.co.uk]	01592 712870
Jacqueline Thomson (Mrs) MTh DCS	2004	2008	1 Barron Terrace, Leven KY8 4DL [E-mail: churchdeacon@blueyonder.co.uk]	01333 301115
Burntisland (H)				
Alan Sharp BSc BD	1980	2001	21 Ramsay Crescent, Burntisland KY3 9JL [E-mail: alansharp03@aol.com]	01592 874303
Dysart (H)				
Tilly Wilson (Miss) MTh	1990	1998	1 School Brae, Dysart, Kirkcaldy KY1 2XB [E-mail: tillywilson@blueyonder.co.uk]	01592 655887
Glenrothes: Christ's Kirk (H)				
Alexandra M. Rosener (Mrs)	2007	2010	12 The Limekilns, Glenrothes KY6 3QJ [E-mail: alexandrarosener@gmx.de]	01592 620536
Glenrothes: St Columba's (01592 752539)				
Vacant			40 Liberton Drive, Glenrothes KY6 3PB	01592 741215

Glenrothes: St Margaret's (H) (01592 328162)
John P. McLean BSc BPhil BD 1994 8 Alburne Park, Glenrothes KY7 5RB 01592 752241
[E-mail: john@mcleanmail.me.uk]

Glenrothes: St Ninian's (H) (01592 610560) (E-mail: office@stninians.co.uk)
Allistair Roy BD DipSW PGDip 2007 1 Cawdor Drive, Glenrothes KY6 2HN 01592 611963
[E-mail: alli@stninians.co.uk]

Innerleven: East (H)
James L. Templeton BSc BD 1975 77 McDonald Street, Methil, Leven KY8 3AJ 01333 426310
[E-mail: jamestempleton@btinternet.com]

Kennoway, Windygates and Balgonie: St Kenneth's (01333 351372) (E-mail: administration@st-kenneths.freeserve.co.uk)
Richard Baxter MA BD 1997 2 Fernhill Gardens, Windygates, Leven KY8 5DZ 01333 352329
[E-mail: richard-baxter@msn.com]

Kinghorn
James Reid BD 1985 1997 17 Myre Crescent, Kinghorn, Burntisland KY3 9UB 01592 890269
[E-mail: jim17reid@aol.com]

Kinglassie See Auchterderran: St Fothad's

Kirkcaldy: Abbotshall (H)
Rosemary Frew (Mrs) MA BD 1988 2005 83 Milton Road, Kirkcaldy KY1 1TP 01592 260315
[E-mail: rosiefrew@blueyonder.co.uk]

Kirkcaldy: Bennochy
Robin J. McAlpine BDS BD MTh 1988 2011 25 Bennochy Avenue, Kirkcaldy KY2 5QE 01592 263821
[E-mail: robinmcalpine@blueyonder.co.uk]

Kirkcaldy: Linktown (01592 641080) See Auchtertool

Kirkcaldy: Pathhead (H) (Tel/Fax: 01592 204635) (E-mail: pathhead@btinternet.com) (Website: www.pathheadparishchurch.co.uk)
Andrew C. Donald BD DPS 1992 2005 73 Loughborough Road, Kirkcaldy KY1 3DD 01592 652215
[E-mail: andrewcdonald@blueyonder.co.uk]

Kirkcaldy: St Bryce Kirk (H) (01592 640016) (E-mail: office@stbrycekirk.org.uk)

Ken Froude MA BD	1979		6 East Fergus Place, Kirkcaldy KY1 1XT [E-mail: kenfroude@blueyonder.co.uk]	01592 264480

Kirkcaldy: Templehall (H)

Anthony J.R. Fowler BSc BD	1982	2004	35 Appin Crescent, Kirkcaldy KY2 6EJ [E-mail: ajrf@btinternet.com]	01592 260156

Kirkcaldy: Torbain

Ian Elston BD MTh	1999		91 Sauchenbush Road, Kirkcaldy KY2 5RN [E-mail: elston667@btinternet.com]	01592 263015

Kirkcaldy: Viewforth (H) linked with Thornton

Vacant			66 Viewforth Street, Kirkcaldy KY1 3DJ	01592 652502

Leslie: Trinity

Vacant			4 Valley Drive, Leslie, Glenrothes KY6 3BQ	01592 745601

Leven

Gilbert C. Nisbet CA BD	1993	2007	5 Forman Road, Leven KY8 4HH [E-mail: gcn-leven@blueyonder.co.uk]	01333 303339

Markinch

Alexander R. Forsyth TD BA MTh	1973	2002	7 Guthrie Crescent, Markinch, Glenrothes KY7 6AY [E-mail: forsythar@aol.com]	01592 758264

Methil (H)

Gillian Paterson (Mrs) BD	2010		10 Vettriano Vale, Leven KY8 4GD [E-mail: gillianpatersonpatolq@supanet.com]	01333 423147

Methilhill and Denbeath

Elisabeth F. Cranfield (Miss) MA BD	1988		9 Chemiss Road, Methilhill, Leven KY8 2BS [E-mail: ecranfield@btinternet.com]	01592 713142

Thornton See Kirkcaldy: Viewforth

Collins, Mitchell BD CPS	1996 2005	(Creich, Flisk and Kilmany with Monimail)	6 Netherby Park, Glenrothes KY6 3PL [E-mail: collinsmit@aol.com]
Connolly, Daniel BD DipTheol DipMin	1983	Army Chaplain	2 CS Reg, RLC, BFPO 47

Dick, James S. MA BTh	1988	1997	(Glasgow: Ruchazie)	20 Church Street, Kirkcaldy KY1 2AD [E-mail: jim.s.dick@googlemail.com]	01592 260289
Elston, Peter K.	1963	2000	(Dalgety)	6 Cairngorm Crescent, Kirkcaldy KY2 5RF [E-mail: peterkelston@btinternet.com]	01592 205622
Ferguson, David J.	1966	2001	(Bellie with Speymouth)	4 Russell Gardens, Ladybank, Cupar KY15 7LT	01337 831406
Forrester, Ian L. MA	1964	1996	(Friockheim, Kinnell with Inverkeilor and Lunan)	8 Bennochy Avenue, Kirkcaldy KY2 5QE	01592 260251
Galbraith, Douglas MA BD BMus MPhil ARSCM PhD	1965	2005	(Office for Worship, Doctrine and Artistic Matters)	34 Balbirnie Street, Markinch, Glenrothes KY7 6DA [E-mail: dgalbraith@hotmail.com]	
Gatt, David W.	1981	1995	(Thornton)	15 Beech Avenue, Thornton, Kirkcaldy KY1 4AT	01592 774328
Gibson, Ivor MA	1957	1993	(Abercorn with Dalmeny)	15 McInnes Road, Glenrothes KY7 6BA	01592 759982
Gisbey, John E. MA BD MSc DipEd	1964	2002	(Thornhill)	Whitemyre House, 28 St Andrews Road, Largoward, Leven KY9 1HZ	01334 840540
Gordon, Ian D. LTh	1972	2001	(Markinch)	2 Somerville Way, Glenrothes KY7 5GE	01592 742487
Houghton, Christine (Mrs) BD	1997	2010	(Whitburn: South)	39 Cedar Crescent, Thornton, Kirkcaldy KY1 4BE [E-mail: c.houghton1@btinternet.com]	01592 772823
McLeod, Alistair G.	1988	2005	(Glenrothes: St Columba's)	13 Greenmantle Way, Glenrothes KY6 3QG [E-mail: aagm@btinternet.com]	01592 744558
McNaught, Samuel M. MA BD MTh	1968	2002	(Kirkcaldy: St John's)	6 Munro Court, Glenrothes KY7 5GD [E-mail: sjmcnaught@btinternet.com]	01592 742352
Munro, Andrew MA BD PhD	1972	2000	(Glencaple with Lowther)	7 Dunvegan Avenue, Kirkcaldy KY2 5SG [E-mail: am.smm@blueyonder.co.uk]	01592 566129
Paterson, Maureen (Mrs) BSc	1992	2010	(Auxiliary Minister)	91 Dalmahoy Crescent, Kirkcaldy KY2 6TA [E-mail: m.e.paterson@blueyonder.co.uk]	01592 262300
Thomson, John D. BD	1985	2005	(Kirkcaldy: Pathhead)	3 Tottenham Court, Hill Street, Dysart, Kirkcaldy KY1 2XY [E-mail: j.thomson10@sky.com]	01592 655313
Tomlinson, Bryan L. TD	1969	2003	(Kirkcaldy: Abbotshall)	2 Duddingston Drive, Kirkcaldy KY2 6JP [E-mail: abbkirk@blueyonder.co.uk]	01592 564843
Webster, Elspeth H. (Miss) DCS			(Deaconess)	82 Broomhill Avenue, Burntisland KY3 0BP	01592 873616
Wynne, Alistair T.E. BA BD	1982	2009	(Nicosia Community Church, Cyprus)	10 Limekilns, Glenrothes KY6 3QJ [E-mail: awynne2@googlemail.com]	01592 571148

KIRKCALDY ADDRESSES

		Linktown	Nicol Street x High Street	Torbain	Lindores Drive
		Pathhead	Harriet Street x Church Street	Viewforth	Viewforth Street x Viewforth Terrace
Abbotshall	Abbotshall Road	St Bryce Kirk	St Brycedale Avenue x Kirk Wynd		
Bennochy	Elgin Street	Templehall	Beauly Place		

(26) ST ANDREWS

Meets at Cupar, in St John's Church Hall, on the second Wednesday of February, March, April, May, September, October, November and December, and on the last Wednesday of June.

Clerk:	**REV. JAMES G. REDPATH BD DipPTh**	**The Manse, Kirk Wynd, Strathmiglo, Cupar KY14 7QS** **[E-mail: standrews@cofscotland.org.uk]**	**01337 860256**
		Presbytery Office	**01337 858442**

Abdie and Dunbog (H) linked with Newburgh (H)

Lynn Brady (Miss) BD DipMin	1996	2002	2 Guthrie Court, Cupar Road, Newburgh, Cupar KY14 6HA [E-mail: lynn@revbrady.freeserve.co.uk]	01337 842228

Anstruther linked with Cellardyke linked with Kilrenny

Arthur A. Christie BD	1997	2009	16 Taeping Close, Cellardyke, Anstruther KY10 3YL [E-mail: revaac@btinternet.com]	01333 313917

Auchtermuchty (H) linked with Edenshead and Strathmiglo

James G. Redpath BD DipPTh	1988	2006	The Manse, Kirk Wynd, Strathmiglo, Cupar KY14 7QS [E-mail: james.redpath2@btopenworld.com]	01337 860256

Balmerino (H) linked with Wormit (H)

James Connolly DipTh CertMin MA(Theol)	1982	2004	5 Westwater Place, Newport-on-Tay DD6 8NS [E-mail: revconnolly@btinternet.com]	01382 542626

Boarhills and Dunino
Continued vacancy (in deferred linking with St Andrews: Holy Trinity)

Cameron linked with St Andrews: St Leonard's (01334 478702) (E-mail: stlencam@btconnect.com)

Alan D. McDonald LLB BD MTh DLitt DD	1979	1998	1 Cairnhill Gardens, St Andrews KY16 8QY [E-mail: alan.d.mcdonald@talk21.com]	01334 472793

Carnbee linked with Pittenweem

Margaret E.S. Rose BD	2007		29 Milton Road, Pittenweem, Anstruther KY10 2LN [E-mail: mgt.r@btopenworld.com]	01333 312838

Cellardyke (H) See Anstruther

Ceres, Kemback and Springfield
James W. Campbell BD 1995 2010 The Manse, St Andrews Road, Ceres, Cupar KY15 5NQ 01334 829350
[E-mail: revjimashkirk@aol.com]

Crail linked with Kingsbarns (H)
Vacant The Manse, St Andrews Road, Crail, Anstruther KY10 3UH 01333 450358

Creich, Flisk and Kilmany linked with Monimail
Neil McLay BA BD 2006 Creich Manse, Brunton, Cupar KY15 4PA 01337 870332
[E-mail: neilmclay@gmail.com]

Cupar: Old (H) and St Michael of Tarvit
Kenneth S. Jeffrey BA BD PhD 2002 76 Hogarth Drive, Cupar KY15 5YH 01334 653196
[E-mail: ksjeffrey@btopenworld.com]

Cupar: St John's and Dairsie United
Vacant 23 Hogarth Drive, Cupar KY15 5YH 01334 656408

Edenshead and Strathmiglo See Auchtermuchty

Elie (H) Kilconquhar and Colinsburgh (H)
Brian McDowell BA BD 1999 2007 30 Bank Street, Elie, Leven KY9 1BW 01333 330685
[E-mail: bmcdowell@btinternet.com]

Falkland linked with Freuchie (H)
George G. Nicol BD DPhil 1982 2006 1 Newton Road, Falkland, Cupar KY15 7AQ 01337 858557
[E-mail: ggnicol@totalise.co.uk]

Freuchie (H) See Falkland

Howe of Fife
Vacant 83 Church Street, Ladybank, Cupar KY15 7ND 01337 830513

Kilrenny See Anstruther
Kingsbarns See Crail

Largo and Newburn (H) linked with Largo: St David's
John A.H. Murdoch BA BD DPSS 1979 2006 The Manse, Church Place, Upper Largo, Leven KY8 6EH 01333 360286
[E-mail: jm.largo@btinternet.com]

Largo: St David's See Largo and Newburn

Largoward (H) linked with St Monans (H)
Donald G. MacEwan MA BD PhD 2001 The Manse, St Monans, Anstruther KY10 2DD 01333 730258
[E-mail: maiadona@tiscali.co.uk]

Leuchars: St Athernase
Caroline Taylor (Mrs) MA BD 1995 2003 7 David Wilson Park, Balmullo, St Andrews KY16 0NP 01334 870038
[E-mail: caro234@btinternet.com]

Monimail See Creich, Flisk and Kilmany
Newburgh See Abdie and Dunbog

Newport-on-Tay (H)
Stanley A. Brook BD MTh 1977 2009 57 Cupar Road, Newport-on-Tay DD6 8DF 01382 543165
[E-mail: stan_brook@hotmail.com]

Pittenweem See Carnbee

St Andrews: Holy Trinity
Rory MacLeod BA MBA BD 1994 2004 19 Priory Gardens, St Andrews KY16 8XX 01334 461098
[E-mail: annicerory@gmail.com]

St Andrews: Hope Park and Martyrs' (H) linked with Strathkinness
Allan McCafferty BSc BD 1993 2011 20 Priory Gardens, St Andrews KY16 8XX 01334 478287 (Tel/Fax)
[E-mail: amcc@grad.com]

St Andrews: St Leonard's (H) See Cameron
St Monans See Largoward
Strathkinness See St Andrews: Hope Park and Martyrs'

Tayport
Brian H. Oxburgh BSc BD 1980 2011 27 Bell Street, Tayport DD6 9AP 01382 553879
[E-mail: b.oxburgh@btinternet.com]

Wormit See Balmerino

Name	Ord.	Ret.	Charge	Address		Phone
Alexander, James S. MA BD BA PhD	1966	1973	University of St Andrews	5 Strathkinness High Road, St Andrews KY16 9RP		01334 472680
Bennett, G. Alestair A. TD MA	1938	1976	(Strathkinness)	7 Bonfield Park, Strathkinness, St Andrews KY16 9SY		01334 850249
Bews, James MA	1942	1981	(Dundee: Craigiebank)	21 Balrymonth Court, St Andrews KY16 8XT		01334 476087
Bradley, Ian MA BD DPhil	1990	1990	University of St Andrews	4 Donaldson Gardens, St Andrews KY16 9DN		01334 475389
Brown, Harry J. LTh	1991	2009	(Dundee: Menzieshill)	6 Hall Street, Kettlebridge, Cupar KY15 7QF		01337 830088
				[E-mail: harrybrown@aol.com]		
Brown, Lawson R. MA	1960	1997	(Cameron with St Andrew's: St Leonard's)	10 Park Street, St Andrews KY16 8AQ		01334 473413
Cameron, James K. MA BD PhD FRHistS	1953	1989	(University of St Andrews)	Priorscroft, 71 Hepburn Gardens, St Andrews KY16 9LS		01334 473996
Cameron, John U. BA BSc PhD BD ThD	1974	2008	(Dundee: Broughty Ferry St Stephen's and West)	10 Howard Place, St Andrews KY16 9HL		01334 474474
Casebow, Brian C. MA BD	1959	1993	(Edinburgh: Salisbury)	'The Rowans', 67 St Michael's Drive, Cupar KY15 5BP		01334 656385
Douglas, Peter C. JP	1966	1993	(Boarhills linked with Dunino)	The Old Schoolhouse, Flisk, Newburgh, Cupar KY14 6HN		01337 870218
Earnshaw, Philip BA BSc BD	1986	1996	(Glasgow: Pollokshields)	22 Castle Street, St Monans, Anstruther KY10 2AP		01333 730640
Edington, George L.	1952	1989	(Tayport)	64B Burghmuir Road, Perth PH1 1LH		
Fairlie, George BD BVMS MRCVS	1971	2002	(Crail with Kingsbarns)	41 Warrack Street, St Andrews KY16 8DR		01334 475868
Fraser, Ann G. BD CertMin	1990	2007	(Auchtermuchty)	24 Irvine Crescent, St Andrews KY16 8LG	(Tel/Fax)	01334 461329
				[E-mail: anngilfraser@btinternet.com]		
Galloway, Robert W.C. LTh	1970	1998	(Cromarty)	22 Haughgate, Leven KY8 4SG		01333 426223
Gibson, Henry M. MA BD PhD	1960	1999	(Dundee: The High Kirk)	4 Comerton Place, Drumoig, Leuchars, St Andrews KY16 0NQ		01382 542199
Gordon, Peter M. MA BD	1958	1995	(Airdrie: West)	3 Cupar Road, Cuparmuir, Cupar KY15 5RH		01334 652341
				[E-mail: machrie@madasafish.com]		
Harrison, Cameron	2006		(Auxiliary Minister)	Woodfield House, Priormuir, St Andrews KY16 8LP		01334 478067
Hegarty, John D. LTh ABSC	1988	2004	(Buckie: South and West with Enzie)	26 Montgomery Way, Kinross KY13 8FD		01577 863829
				[E-mail: john.hegarty@tesco.net]		
Hill, Roy MA	1962	1997	(Lisbon)	Forgan Cottage, Kinnessburn Road, St Andrews KY16 8AD		01334 472121
Learmonth, Walter LTh	1968	1997	(Ceres with Springfield)	14 Marionfield Place, Cupar KY15 5JN		01334 656290
McGregor, Duncan J. MIFM	1982	1996	(Channelkirk with Lauder: Old)	14 Mount Melville, St Andrews KY16 8NG		01334 478314
Macintyre, William J. MA BD DD	1951	1989	(Crail with Kingsbarns)	Tigh a' Ghobhainn, Lochton, Crail, Anstruther KY10 3XE		01333 450327
Mackenzie, A. Cameron MA	1955	1995	(Biggar)	Hedgerow, 5 Shiels Avenue, Freuchie, Cupar KY15 7JD		01337 857763
McKimmon, Eric G. BA BD MTh	1983	2008	(Ceres, Kemback and Springfield)	1F1, 279 Easter Road, Edinburgh EH6 8LQ		0131-554 9317
				[E-mail: mckimmonceres@aol.com]		
Meager, Peter MA BD CertMgmt(Open)	1971	1998	(Elie with Kilconquhar and Colinsburgh)	7 Lorraine Drive, Cupar KY15 5DY		01334 656991
Neilson, Peter MA BD MTh	1975	2006	Mission Consultant	Linne Bheag, 2 School Green, Anstruther KY10 3HF		01333 310477
				[E-mail: neilson.peter@btinternet.com]	(Mbl)	07818 418608
Paton, Iain F. BD FCIS	1980	2006	(Elie with Kilconquhar and Colinsburgh)	Lindisfarne, 19 Links Road, Lundin Links, Leven KY8 6AS		01333 320765
Petrie, Ian D. MA BD	1970	2008	(Dundee: St Andrew's)	27 High Street East, Anstruther KY10 3DQ		01333 310181
				[E-mail: idp-77@hotmail.com]		
Reid, Alan A.S. MA BD STM	1962	1995	(Bridge of Allan: Chalmers)	Wayside Cottage, Bridgend, Ceres, Cupar KY15 5LS		01334 828509
Robb, Nigel J. FCP MA BD ThM MTh	1981	1998	Associate Secretary: Mission and Discipleship Council	c/o 121 George Street, Edinburgh EH2 4YN		0131-225 5722
				[E-mail: nrobb@cofscotland.org.uk]		

Name			Charge	Address	Phone
Roy, Alan J. BSc BD	1960	1999	(Aberuthven with Dunning)	14 Comerton Place, Drumoig, Leuchars, St Andrews KY16 0NQ [E-mail: a.roy225@btinternet.com]	01382 542225
Salters, Robert B. MA BD PhD	1966	1971	(University of St Andrews)	Vine Cottage, 119 South Street, St Andrews KY16 9UH	01334 473198
Stevenson, A.L. LLB MLitt DPA FPEA	1984	1993	(Balmerino linked with Wormit)	41 Main Street, Dairsie, Cupar KY15 4SR	01334 870582
Strong, Clifford LTh	1983	1995	(Creich, Flisk and Kilmany with Monimail)	60 Maryknowe, Gauldry, Newport-on-Tay DD6 8SL	01382 330445
Taylor, Ian BSc MA LTh DipEd	1983	1997	(Abdie and Dunbog with Newburgh)	Lundie Cottage, Arncroach, Anstruther KY10 2RN	01333 720222
Thrower, Charles G. BSc	1965	2002	(Carnbee with Pittenweem)	Grange House, Wester Grangemuir, Pittenweem, Anstruther KY10 2RB [E-mail: c--thrower@pittenweem2.freeserve.co.uk]	01333 312631
Torrance, Alan J. MA BD DrTheol	1984	1999	University of St Andrews	Kincaple House, Kincaple, St Andrews KY16 9SH	(Home) 01334 850755 (Office) 01334 462843
Turnbull, James J. MA	1940	1981	(Arbirlot with Colliston)	Woodlands, Beech Avenue, Ladybank, Cupar KY15 7NG	01337 830279
Tyre, Robert	1960	1998	(Aberdeen: St Ninian's with Stockethill)	44 Doocot Road, St Andrews KY16 8QP [E-mail: robert@roberttyre.wanadoo.co.uk]	01334 473093
Walker, James B. MA BD DPhil	1975	1993	Chaplain: University of St Andrews	1 Gillespie Terrace, The Scores, St Andrews KY16 9AT [E-mail: james.walker@st-andrews.ac.uk]	(Tel) 01334 462866 (Fax) 01334 462868
Wotherspoon, Ian G. BA LTh	1967	2004	(Coatbridge: St Andrew's)	12 Cherry Lane, Cupar KY15 5DA [E-mail: wotherspoonrig@aol.com]	01334 650710
Wright, Lynda (Miss) BEd DCS			Deacon: Retreat Leader, Key House	6 Key Cottage, High Street, Falkland, Cupar KY15 7BD	01337 857705
Young, Evelyn M. (Mrs) BSc BD	1984	2003	(Kilmun (St Munn's) with Strone and Ardentinny)	2 Priestden Place, St Andrews KY16 8DP	01334 479662

(27) DUNKELD AND MEIGLE

Meets at Pitlochry on the first Tuesday of September and December, on the third Tuesday of February, April and October, and at the Moderator's church on the third Tuesday of June.

Clerk: REV. JOHN RUSSELL MA — **Kilblaan, Gladstone Terrace, Birnam, Dunkeld PH8 0DP** — **01350 728896**
[E-mail: dunkeldmeigle@cofscotland.org.uk]

Aberfeldy (H) linked with Amulree (H) and Strathbraan linked with Dull and Weem (H)
Mark Drane BD — 2007 — The Manse, Taybridge Terrace, Aberfeldy PH15 2BS — 01887 820656
[E-mail: mark_drane@hotmail.co.uk]

Alyth (H)
Vacant — The Manse, Cambridge Street, Alyth, Blairgowrie PH11 8AW — 01828 632104

Amulree and Strathbraan See Aberfeldy

Ardler, Kettins and Meigle				
Nicola Frail BLE MBA MDiv	2000	2009	The Manse, Dundee Road, Meigle, Blairgowrie PH12 8SB [E-mail: nrfscot@hotmail.com]	01828 640074
Bendochy linked with Coupar Angus: Abbey				
Bruce Dempsey BD	1997		Caddam Road, Coupar Angus, Blairgowrie PH13 9EF [E-mail: revbruce.dempsey@btopenworld.com]	01828 627331
Blair Atholl and Struan linked with Tenandry				
Vacant			Blair Atholl, Pitlochry PH18 5SX	01796 481213
Blairgowrie				
Harry Mowbray BD CA	2003	2008	The Manse, Upper David Street, Blairgowrie PH10 6HB [E-mail: hmowbray@viewlands.plus.com]	01250 872146
Braes of Rannoch linked with Foss and Rannoch (H)				
Christine A.Y. Ritchie (Mrs) BD DipMin	2002	2005	The Manse, Kinloch Rannoch, Pitlochry PH16 5QA [E-mail: critchie@4afairworld.co.uk]	01882 632381
Caputh and Clunie (H) linked with Kinclaven (H)				
Peggy Roberts BA BD	2003	2011	Caputh Manse, Caputh, Perth PH1 4JH [E-mail: peggy.r@ntlworld.com]	01738 710520
Coupar Angus: Abbey See Bendochy				
Dull and Weem See Aberfeldy				
Dunkeld (H)				
R. Fraser Penny BA BD	1984	2001	Cathedral Manse, Dunkeld PH8 0AW [E-mail: fraserpenn@aol.com]	01350 727249 01350 727102 (Fax)
Fortingall and Glenlyon linked with Kenmore and Lawers				
Anne J. Brennan BSc BD MTh	1999		The Manse, Balnaskeag, Kenmore, Aberfeldy PH15 2HB [E-mail: annebrennan@yahoo.co.uk]	01887 830218
Foss and Rannoch See Braes of Rannoch				

Grantully, Logierait and Strathtay
Vacant — The Manse, Strathtay, Pitlochry PH9 0PG — 01887 840251

Kenmore and Lawers (H) See Fortingall and Glenlyon
Kinclaven See Caputh and Clunie

Kirkmichael, Straloch and Glenshee linked with Rattray (H)
Vacant — The Manse, Alyth Road, Rattray, Blairgowrie PH10 7HF — 01250 872462

Pitlochry (H) (01796 472160)
Vacant — Manse Road, Moulin, Pitlochry PH16 5EP — 01796 472774

Rattray See Kirkmichael, Straloch and Glenshee
Tenandry See Blair Atholl and Struan

Cassells, Alexander K. MA BD	1961	1997	(Leuchars: St Athernase and Guardbridge)	Balloch Cottage, Keltneyburn, Aberfeldy PH15 2LS	01887 830758
Creegan, Christine M. (Mrs) MTh	1993	2005	(Grantully, Logierait and Strathtay)	Lonaig, 28 Lettoch Terrace, Pitlochry PH16 5BA	01796 472422
Dick, Thomas MA	1951	1990	(Dunkeld)	Mo Dhachaidh, Callybrae, Dunkeld PH8 0EP	01350 727338
Duncan, James BTh FSAScot	1980	1995	(Blair Atholl and Struan)	25 Knockard Avenue, Pitlochry PH16 5JE	01796 474096
Ewart, William BSc BD	1972	2010	(Caputh and Clunie with Kinclaven)	Cara Beag, Essendy Road, Blairgowrie PH10 6QU [E-mail: ewe1@btinternet.com]	01250 876897
Henderson, John D. MA BD	1953	1992	(Cluny with Monymusk)	Aldersyde, George Street, Blairgowrie PH10 6HP	01250 875181
Knox, John W. MTheol	1992	1997	(Lochgelly: Macainsh)	Heatherlea, Main Street, Ardler, Blairgowrie PH12 8SR	01828 640731
McAlister, D.J.B. MA BD PhD	1951	1989	(North Berwick: Blackadder)	2 Duff Avenue, Moulin, Pitlochry PH16 5EN	01796 473591
MacRae, Malcolm H. MA PhD	1971	2010	(Kirkmichael, Straloch and Glenshee with Rattray)	10B Victoria Place, Stirling FK8 2QU [E-mail: malcolm.macrae1@btopenworld.com]	01786 465547
MacVicar, Kenneth MBE DFC TD MA	1950	1990	(Kenmore with Lawers with Fortingall and Glenlyon)	Illeray, Kenmore, Aberfeldy PH15 2HE	01887 830514
Nelson, Robert C. BA BD	1980	2010	(Isle of Mull, Kilninian and Kilmore with Salen and Ulva with Tobermory with Torosay and Kinlochspelvie)	St Colme's, Perth Road, Birnam, Dunkeld PH8 0BH [E-mail: robertnelson@onetel.net]	01350 727455
Ormiston, Hugh C. BSc BD MPhil PhD	1969	2004	(Kirkmichael, Straloch and Glenshee with Rattray)	Cedar Lea, Main Road, Woodside, Blairgowrie PH13 9NP	01828 670539
Oswald, John BSc PhD BD	1997	2011	(Muthill with Trinity Gask and Kinkell)	1 Woodlands Meadow, Rosemount, Blairgowrie PH10 6GZ [E-mail: revdocoz@bigfoot.com]	01250 872598
Ramsay, Malcolm BA LLB DipMin	1986	2011	Overseas service in Nepal	c/o World Mission Council, 121 George Street, Edinburgh EH2 4YN	0131-225 5722
Robertson, Matthew LTh	1968	2002	(Cawdor with Croy and Dalcross)	Inver, Strathtay, Pitlochry PH9 0PG	01887 840780
Russell, John MA	1959	2000	(Tillicoultry)	Kilblaan, Gladstone Terrace, Birnam, Dunkeld PH8 0DP	01350 728896
Shannon, W.G. MA BD	1955	1998	(Pitlochry)	19 Knockard Road, Pitlochry PH16 5HJ	01796 473533
Tait, Thomas W. BD	1972	1997	(Rattray)	3 Rosemount Park, Blairgowrie PH10 6TZ	01250 874833
White, Brock A. LTh	1971	2001	(Kirkcaldy: Templehall)	1 Littlewood Gardens, Blairgowrie PH10 6XZ	01250 870399
Whyte, William B. BD	1973	2003	(Nairn: St Ninian's)	The Old Inn, Park Hill Road, Rattray, Blairgowrie PH10 7DS	01250 874401
Wilson, John M. MA BD	1965	2004	(Altnaharra and Farr)	Berbice, The Terrace, Blair Atholl, Pitlochry PH18 5SZ	01796 481619

Wilson, Mary D. (Mrs) RGN SCM DTM	1990	2004	(Auxiliary Minister)	Berbice, The Terrace, Blair Atholl, Pitlochry PH18 5SZ	01796 481619
Young, G. Stuart	1961	1996	(Blairgowrie: St Andrew's)	7 James Place, Stanley, Perth PH1 4PD	01738 828473

(28) PERTH

Meets at Scone: Old, at 7:00pm, in the Elizabeth Ashton Hall, on the second Tuesday of February, March, June, September, November and December in each year.

Clerk: **REV. ALAN D. REID MA BD**
Presbytery Office: **209 High Street, Perth PH1 5PB** **01738 451177**
[E-mail: perth@cofscotland.org.uk]

Abernethy and Dron and Arngask
Alexander C. Wark MA BD STM 1982 2008 3 Manse Road, Abernethy, Perth PH2 9JP 01738 850607
[E-mail: alecwark@yahoo.co.uk]

Almondbank Tibbermore linked with Methven and Logiealmond
Philip W. Patterson BMus BD 1999 2008 The Manse, Pitcairngreen, Perth PH1 3EA 01738 583217
[E-mail: philip.patterson@btinternet.com]

Ardoch (H) linked with Blackford (H)
Stuart D.B. Picken MA BD PhD 1966 2005 3 Millhill Crescent, Greenloaning, Dunblane FK15 0LH 01786 880217
[E-mail: picken@eikoku.demon.co.uk]

Auchterarder (H)
Vacant 24 High Street, Auchterarder, Perth PH3 1DF 01764 662210

Auchtergaven and Moneydie linked with Redgorton and Stanley
Vacant Bankfoot, Perth PH1 4BS 01738 787235

Blackford See Ardoch

Cargill Burrelton linked with Collace
Vacant Manse Road, Woodside, Blairgowrie PH13 9NQ 01828 670352

Cleish (H) linked with Fossoway: St Serf's and Devonside
Joanne G. Finlay (Mrs) DipTMus BD AdvDipCouns 1996 2005 The Manse, Cleish, Kinross KY13 7LR 01577 850231
[E-mail: joanne.finlay196@btinternet.com]

Collace See Cargill Burrelton

Comrie (H) linked with Dundurn (H)
Graham McWilliams BSc BD 2005 The Manse, Strowan Road, Comrie, Crieff PH6 2ES 01764 671045 (Tel/Fax)
[E-mail: Themansefamily@aol.com]

Crieff (H)
James W. MacDonald BD 1976 2002 8 Strathearn Terrace, Crieff PH7 3AQ 01764 653907
[E-mail: rev_up@btinternet.com]

Dunbarney (H) and Forgandenny
Allan J. Wilson BSc MEd BD 2007 Dunbarney Manse, Manse Road, Bridge of Earn, Perth PH2 9DY 01738 812463
[E-mail: allanjwilson@dfpchurch.org.uk]

Dundurn See Comrie

Errol (H) linked with Kilspindie and Rait
Douglas M. Main BD 1986 2005 South Bank, Errol, Perth PH2 7PZ 01821 642279
[E-mail: revdmain@btinternet.com]

Fossoway: St Serf's and Devonside See Cleish

Fowlis Wester, Madderty and Monzie linked with Gask
Eleanor D. Muir (Miss) MTheol DipPTheol 1986 2008 Beechview, Abercairney, Crieff PH7 3NF 01764 652116
[E-mail: eleanordmuir@tiscali.co.uk]

Gask (H) See Fowlis Wester, Madderty and Monzie
Kilspindie and Rait See Errol

Kinross (H)
Alan D. Reid MA BD 1989 2009 15 Station Road, Kinross KY13 8TG 01577 862952
[E-mail: kinrossmanse@tiscali.co.uk]

Methven and Logiealmond See Almondbank Tibbermore

Muthill (H) linked with Trinity Gask and Kinkell
Vacant The Manse, Station Road, Muthill, Crieff PH5 2AR 01764 681205

Orwell (H) and Portmoak (H)				
Vacant			41 Auld Mart Road, Milnathort, Kinross KY13 9FR	01577 863461
Perth: Craigie and Moncreiffe				
Carolann Erskine BD	2009		The Manse, 46 Abbot Street, Perth PH2 0EE [E-mail: erskine21@blueyonder.co.uk]	01738 623748
Perth: Kinnoull (H)				
David I. Souter BD	1996	2001	1 Mount Tabor Avenue, Perth PH2 7BT [E-mail: d.souter@blueyonder.co.uk]	01738 626046
Perth: Letham St Mark's (H) (Office: 01738 446377)				
James C. Stewart BD DipMin	1997		35 Rose Crescent, Perth PH1 1NT [E-mail: diamondboy09@yahoo.com]	01738 624167
Kenneth McKay DCS			11F Balgowan Road, Perth PH1 2JG [E-mail: kennydandcs@hotmail.com]	01738 621169
Perth: North (01738 622298)				
Hugh O'Brien CSS MTheol	2001	2009	127 Glasgow Road, Perth PH2 0LU [E-mail: the.manse@btinternet.com]	01738 625728
Perth: Riverside (New Charge Development)				
Grant MacLaughlan BA BD	1998	2007	44 Hay Street, Perth PH1 5HS [E-mail: revgrm@btconnect.com]	01738 631148
Perth: St John's Kirk of Perth (H) (01738 626159) linked with Perth: St Leonard's-in-the-Fields				
James K. Wallace	1988	2009	5 Strathearn Terrace, Perth PH2 0LS [E-mail: revjwspc@hotmail.com]	01738 621709
Perth: St Leonard's-in-the-Fields (H) (01738 632238) See Perth: St John's Kirk of Perth				
Perth: St Matthew's (Office: 01738 636757; Vestry: 01738 630725)				
Scott Burton BD DipMin	1999	2007	23 Kincarrathie Crescent, Perth PH2 7HH [E-mail: sburton@supanet.com]	01738 626828
Robert Wilkie (Aux)	2011		24 Huntingtower Road, Perth PH1 2JS [E-mail: rwew25879@blueyonder.co.uk]	01738 628301
Redgorton and Stanley See Auchtergaven and Moneydie				

St Madoes and Kinfauns
Marc F. Bircham BD MTh 2000 Glencarse, Perth PH2 7NF 01738 860837
[E-mail: mark.bircham@btinternet.com]

St Martin's linked with Scone: New (H) (01738 553900)
Vacant 24 Victoria Road, Scone, Perth PH2 6JW 01738 551467

Scone: New See St Martin's

Scone: Old (H)
Vacant Burnside, Scone, Perth PH2 6LP 01738 552030

The Stewartry of Strathearn (H) (01738 621674) (E-mail: office@stewartryofstrathearn.org.uk)
Vacant 1 Woodlands Meadow, Rosemount, Blairgowrie PH10 6GZ 01250 872598

Trinity Gask and Kinkell See Muthill

Ballentine, Ann M. (Miss) MA BD	1981	2007	(Kirknewton and East Calder)	17 Nellfield Road, Crieff PH7 3DU [E-mail: annballentine@hotmail.com]	01764 652567
Barr, George K. ARIBA BD PhD	1967	1993	(Uddingston: Viewpark)	7 Tay Avenue, Comrie, Crieff PH6 2PE [E-mail: gbarr2@compuserve.com]	01764 670454
Barr, T. Leslie LTh	1969	1997	(Kinross)	8 Fairfield Road, Kelty KY4 0BY	01383 839330
Bertram, Thomas A.	1972	1995	(Patna: Waterside)	3 Scrimgeours Corner, 29 West High Street, Crieff PH7 4AP	01764 652066
Brown, Elizabeth (Mrs) JP RGN	1996	2007	(Auxiliary Minister)	8 Viewlands Place, Perth PH1 1BS [E-mail: liz.brown@blueyonder.co.uk]	01738 552391
Buchan, William DipTheol BD	1987	2001	(Kilwinning: Abbey)	34 Bridgewater Avenue, Auchterarder PH3 1DQ [E-mail: wbuchan3@aol.com]	01764 660306
Cairns, Evelyn BD	2004		Chaplain: Rachel House	15 Tala Park, Kinross KY13 8AB [E-mail: revelyn@chas.org.uk]	01577 863990
Coleman, Sidney H. BA BD MTh	1961	2001	(Glasgow: Merrylea)	'Blaven', 11 Clyde Place, Perth PH2 0EZ [E-mail: sidney.coleman@blueyonder.co.uk]	01738 565072
Craig, Joan H. (Miss) MTheol	1986	2005	(Orkney: East Mainland)	7 Jedburgh Place, Perth PH1 1SJ [E-mail: joanhcraig@bigfoot.com]	01738 580180
Donaldson, Robert B. BSocSc	1953	1997	(Kilchoman with Portnahaven)	11 Strathearn Court, Crieff PH7 3DS	01764 654976
Drummond, Alfred G. BD DMin	1991	2006	Scottish General Secretary: Evangelical Alliance	10 Errochty Court, Perth PH1 2SU [E-mail: frddrmmnd@aol.com]	01738 621305
Fleming, Hamish K. MA	1966	2001	(Banchory Ternan: East)	36 Earnmuir Road, Comrie, Crieff PH6 2EY	01764 679178
Galbraith, W. James L. BSc BD MICE	1973	1996	(Kilchrenan and Dalavich with Muckairn)	19 Mayfield Gardens, Milnathort, Kinross KY13 9GD	01577 863887
Graham, Sydney S. DipYL MPhil BD	1987	2009	(Iona with Kilfinichen and Kilvickeon and the Ross of Mull)	'Aspen', Milton Road, Luncarty, Perth PH1 3ES [E-mail: sydgraham@btinternet.com]	01738 829350

Gregory, J.C. LTh	1968	1992	(Blantyre: St Andrew's)	2 Southlands Road, Auchterarder PH3 1BA	01764 664594
Gunn, Alexander M. MA BD	1967	2006	(Aberfeldy with Amulree and Strathbraan with Dull and Weem)	'Navarone', 12 Cornhill Road, Perth PH1 1LR [E-mail: sandygunn@btinternet.com]	01738 443216
Halliday, Archibald R. BD MTh	1964	1999	(Duffus, Spynie and Hopeman)	8 Turretbank Drive, Crieff PH7 4LW [E-mail halliday@pittenzie.wanadoo.co.uk]	01764 656464
Henry, Malcolm N. MA BD	1951	1987	(Perth: Craigie)	Kelton, Castle Douglas DG7 1RU	01556 504144
Houston, Alexander McR.	1939	1977	(Tibbermore)	120 Glasgow Road, Perth PH2 0LU	01738 628056
Hughes, Clifford E. MA BD	1993	2001	(Haddington: St Mary's)	Pavilion Cottage, Briglands, Rumbling Bridge, Kinross KY13 0PS	01577 840506
Kelly, T. Clifford	1973	1995	(Ferintosh)	20 Whinfield Drive, Kinross KY13 8UB	01577 864946
Lawson, James B. MA BD	1961	2002	(South Uist)	4 Cowden Way, Comrie, Crieff PH6 2NW [E-mail: james.lawson7@btopenworld.com]	01764 679180
Lawson, Ronald G. MA BD	1964	1999	(Greenock: Wellpark Mid Kirk)	6 East Brougham Street, Stanley, Perth PH1 4NJ	01738 828871
Low, J.E. Stewart MA	1957	1997	(Tarbat)	15 Stormont Place, Scone, Perth PH2 6SR	01738 552023
McCormick, Alastair F.	1962	1998	(Creich with Rosehall)	14 Balmanno Park, Bridge of Earn, Perth PH2 9RJ	01738 813588
McFadzean, Iain MA BD	1989	2010	National Director: Industrial Chaplaincy	c/o 121 George Street, Edinburgh EH2 4YN	0131-225 5722
McGregor, William LTh	1987	2003	(Auchtergaven and Moneydie)	'Ard Choille', 7 Taypark Road, Luncarty, Perth PH1 3FE [E-mail: bill.mcgregor7@btinternet.com]	01738 827866
MacKenzie, Donald W. MA	1941	1983	(Auchterarder: The Barony)	81 Kingswell Terrace, Perth PH1 2DA	01738 633716
MacMillan, Riada M. (Mrs) BD	1991	1998	(Perth: Craigend Moncreiffe with Rhynd)	73 Muirend Gardens, Perth PH1 1JR	01738 628867
McNaughton, David J.H. BA CA	1976	1995	(Killin and Ardeonaig)	30 Hollybush Road, Crieff PH7 3HB	01764 653028
McQuilken, John E. MA BD	1969	1992	(Glenaray and Inveraray)	18 Clark Terrace, Crieff PH7 3QE	01764 655764
Millar, Archibald E. DipTh	1965	1991	(Perth: St Stephen's)	7 Maple Place, Perth PH1 1RT	01738 621813
Munro, Gillian (Miss) BSc BD	1989	2003	Head of Department of Spiritual Care, NHS Tayside	Royal Dundee Liff Hospital, Liff, Dundee DD2 5NF	01382 423116
Pattison, Kenneth J. MA BD STM	1967	2004	(Kilmuir and Logie Easter)	2 Castle Way, St Madoes, Glencarse, Perth PH2 7NY [E-mail: k_pattison@btinternet.com]	01738 860340
Reid, David T. BA BD	1954	1993	(Cleish with Fossoway: St Serf's and Devonside	Benarty, Wester Balgedie, Kinross KY13 9HE	01592 840214
Ritchie, James BD MTh	2000	2008	(Bridge of Don Oldmachar)	11 Levenbridge Place, Kinross KY13 8FL [E-mail: jim.ritchie1@btopenworld.com]	01577 865912
Robertson, Thomas G.M. LTh	1971	2004	(Edenshead and Strathmiglo)	23 Muirend Avenue, Perth PH1 1JL	01738 624432
Ross, William B. LTh CPS	1988	2011	(Muthill with Trinity Gask and Kinkell)	The Manse, Station Road, Muthill, Crieff PH5 2AR [E-mail: williamross278@btinternet.com]	01764 681205
Shirra, James MA	1945	1987	(St Martin's with Scone: New)	17 Dunbarney Avenue, Bridge of Earn, Perth PH2 9BP	01738 812610
Simpson, James A. BSc BD STM DD	1960	2000	(Dornoch Cathedral)	'Dornoch', Perth Road, Bankfoot, Perth PH1 4ED [E-mail: dr.j.simpson@btinternet.com]	01738 787710
Sloan, Robert P. MA BD	1968	2007	(Braemar and Crathie)	1 Broomhill Avenue, Perth PH1 1EN [E-mail: sloans1@btinternet.com]	01738 443904
Stenhouse, W. Duncan MA BD	1989	2006	(Dunbarney and Forgandenny)	32 Sandport Gait, Kinross KY13 8FB [E-mail: duncan.stenhouse@btinternet.com]	01577 866992
Stewart, Anne E. (Mrs) BD CertMin	1998		Prison Chaplain	35 Rose Crescent, Perth PH1 1NT [E-mail: revanne@hotmail.co.uk]	01738 624167

Stewart, Gordon G. MA	1961	2000	(Perth: St Leonard's-in-the-Fields and Trinity)	'Balnoe', South Street, Rattray, Blairgowrie PH10 7BZ	01250 870626
Stewart, Robin J. MA BD STM	1959	1995	(Orwell with Portmoak)	'Oakbrae', Perth Road, Murthly, Perth PH1 4HF	01738 710220
Tait, Henry A.G. MA BD	1966	1997	(Crieff: South and Monzievaird)	14 Shieling Hill Place, Crieff PH7 4ER	01764 652325
Thomson, J. Bruce MA BD	1972	2009	(Scone: Old)	47 Elm Street, Errol, Perth PH2 7SQ [E-mail: RevBruceThomson@aol.com]	01821 641039 (Mbl) 07850 846404
Thomson, Peter D. MA BD	1968	2004	(Comrie with Dundurn)	34 Queen Street, Perth PH2 0EJ [E-mail: rev.pdt@blueyonder.co.uk]	01738 622418

PERTH ADDRESSES

Craigie	Abbot Street	Letham St Mark's	Rannoch Road	St John's	St John's Street		
Kinnoull	Dundee Rd near Queen's Bridge	Moncreiffe	Glenbruar Crescent	St Leonard's-in-the-Fields	Marshall Place		
		North	Mill Street near Kinnoull Street	St Matthew's	Tay Street		
		Riverside	Bute Drive				

(29) DUNDEE

Meets at Dundee, Meadowside St Paul's Church Halls, Nethergate, on the second Wednesday of February, March, May, September, November and December, and on the fourth Wednesday of June.

Clerk:	**REV. JAMES L. WILSON BD CPS**	**[E-mail: dundee@cofscotland.org.uk]** **[E-mail: r3vjw@aol.com]**	**01382 459249 (Home)** **07885 618659 (Mobile)**
Presbytery Office:		**Whitfield Parish Church, Haddington Crescent, Dundee DD4 0NA**	**01382 503012**

Abernyte linked with Inchture and Kinnaird linked with Longforgan (H)

Marjory A. MacLean (Miss) LLB BD PhD	1991	2011	The Manse, Longforgan, Dundee DD2 5EU [E-mail: mrjymcln@aol.com]	01382 360238

Auchterhouse (H) linked with Monikie and Newbigging and Murroes and Tealing (H)

David A. Collins BSc BD	1993	2006	New Kirk Manse, 25 Ballinard Gardens, Broughty Ferry, Dundee DD5 1BZ [E-mail: david.collins@dundeepresbytery.org.uk]	01382 778874

Dundee: Balgay (H)

Vacant			150 City Road, Dundee DD2 2PW	01382 668806

Dundee: Barnhill St Margaret's (H) (01382 737294) (E-mail: church.office@btconnect.com)
Susan Sutherland (Mrs) BD | 2009 | | 2 St Margaret's Lane, Barnhill, Dundee DD5 2PQ [E-mail: susan.sutherland@dundeepresbytery.org.uk] | 01382 779278

Dundee: Broughty Ferry New Kirk (H)
Catherine E.E. Collins (Mrs) MA BD | 1993 | 2006 | New Kirk Manse, 25 Ballinard Gardens, Broughty Ferry, Dundee DD5 1BZ [E-mail: catherine.collins@dundeepresbytery.org.uk] | 01382 778874

Dundee: Broughty Ferry St James' (H)
Alberto A. de Paula BD MTh | 1991 | 2005 | 2 Ferry Road, Monifieth, Dundee DD5 4NT [E-mail: alberto.depaula@dundeepresbytery.org.uk] | 01382 534468

Dundee: Broughty Ferry St Luke's and Queen Street (01382 770329)
C. Graham Taylor BSc BD FIAB | 2001 | | 22 Albert Road, Broughty Ferry, Dundee DD5 1AZ [E-mail: graham.taylor@dundeepresbytery.org.uk] | 01382 779212

Dundee: Broughty Ferry St Stephen's and West (H)
Vacant

Dundee: Camperdown (H) (01382 623958)
Vacant | | | Camperdown Manse, Myrekirk Road, Dundee DD2 4SF | 01382 621383

Dundee: Chalmers Ardler (H)
Kenneth D. Stott MA BD | 1989 | 1997 | The Manse, Turnberry Avenue, Dundee DD2 3TP [E-mail: arkstotts@aol.com] | 01382 827439

Dundee: Coldside
Anthony P. Thornthwaite MTh | 1995 | 2011 | 9 Abercorn Street, Dundee DD4 7HY [E-mail: tony.thornthwaite@sky.com] | 01382 458314

(Dundee: Coldside is the new name for this charge, which was formerly known as Dundee: Clepington and Fairmuir)

Dundee: Craigiebank (H) (01382 731173) linked with Dundee: Douglas and Mid Craigie
Edith F. McMillan (Mrs) MA BD | 1981 | 1999 | 19 Americanmuir Road, Dundee DD3 9AA | 01382 812423

Dundee: Douglas and Mid Craigie See Dundee: Craigiebank

Dundee: Downfield South (H) (01382 810624)				
Vacant			15 Elgin Street, Dundee DD3 8NL	01382 889498
Dundee: Dundee (St Mary's) (H) (01382 226271)				
Keith F. Hall MA BD	1980	1994	33 Strathern Road, West Ferry, Dundee DD5 1PP	01382 778808
Dundee: Fintry Parish Church (01382 508191)				
Colin M. Brough BSc BD	1998	2002	4 Clive Street, Dundee DD4 7AW [E-mail: colin.brough@dundeepresbytery.org.uk]	01382 458629
Dundee: Lochee (H)				
Hazel Wilson (Ms) MA BD DipEd DMS	1991	2006	32 Clayhills Drive, Dundee DD2 1SX [E-mail: hazel.wilson@dundeepresbytery.org.uk]	01382 561989
Dundee: Logie and St John's Cross (H) (01382 668514)				
David S. Scott MA BD	1987	1999	7 Hyndford Street, Dundee DD2 1HQ [E-mail: david.scott@dundeepresbytery.org.uk]	01382 641572
Dundee: Mains (H) (01382 812166)				
Vacant			9 Elgin Street, Dundee DD3 8NL	01382 827207
Dundee: Meadowside St Paul's (H) (01382 202255)				
Maudeen I. MacDougall (Miss) BA BD	1978	1984	36 Blackness Avenue, Dundee DD2 1HH	01382 668828
Dundee: Menzieshill				
Robert Mallinson BD	2010		The Manse, Charleston Drive, Dundee DD2 4ED [E-mail: bobmalli1975@hotmail.co.uk]	01382 667446 07595 249089 (Mbl)
Dundee: St Andrew's (H) (01382 224860)				
Janet P. Foggie MA BD PhD	2003	2009	39 Tullideph Road, Dundee DD2 2JD [E-mail: janet.foggie@dundeepresbytery.org.uk]	01382 660152
Dundee: St David's High Kirk (H)				
Marion J. Paton (Miss) MA BMus BD	1991	2007	6 Adelaide Place, Dundee DD3 6LF [E-mail: marion.paton@dundeepresbytery.org.uk]	01382 322955
Dundee: Steeple (H) (01382 200031)				
David M. Clark MA BD	1989	2000	128 Arbroath Road, Dundee DD4 7HR [E-mail: david.clark@dundeepresbytery.org.uk]	01382 455411

Dundee: Stobswell (H) (01382 461397)
William McLaren MA BD 1990 2007 23 Shamrock Street, Dundee DD4 7AH 01382 459119
[E-mail: william.mclaren@dundeepresbytery.org.uk]

Dundee: Strathmartine (H) (01382 825817)
Stewart McMillan BD 1983 1990 19 Americanmuir Road, Dundee DD3 9AA 01382 812423

Dundee: Trinity (H) (01382 459997)
David J.H. Laing BD DPS 1976 2008 5 Castlewood Avenue, Emmock Woods, The Barns of Claverhouse, Dundee DD4 9FP 01382 506151
[E-mail: edlaing@tiscali.co.uk]

Dundee: West
Andrew T. Greaves BD 1985 2000 Manse of Dundee West Church, Wards of Keithock, by Brechin DD9 7PZ 01356 624479
[E-mail: andrew.greaves@dundeepresbytery.org.uk]

Dundee: Whitfield (H) (01382 503012) (New Charge Development)
James L. Wilson BD CPS 1986 2001 53 Old Craigie Road, Dundee DD4 7JD 01382 459249
[E-mail: r3vjw@aol.com]

Fowlis and Liff linked with Lundie and Muirhead (H)
Donna M. Hays (Mrs) MTheol DipEd DipTMHA 2004 149 Coupar Angus Road, Muirhead of Liff, Dundee DD2 5QN 01382 580210
[E-mail: dmhays32@aol.com]

Inchture and Kinnaird See Abernyte

Invergowrie (H)
Robert J. Ramsay LLB NP BD 1986 1997 2 Boniface Place, Invergowrie, Dundee DD2 5DW 01382 561118
[E-mail: robert.ramsay@dundeepresbytery.org.uk]

Longforgan See Abernyte
Lundie and Muirhead See Fowlis and Liff

Monifieth (H)
Dorothy U. Anderson (Mrs) LLB DipLP BD 2006 2009 8 Church Street, Monifieth, Dundee DD5 4JP 01382 532607
[E-mail: dorothy@gist.org.uk]

Monikie and Newbigging and Murroes and Tealing See Auchterhouse

Name	Ord.	Ret.	Former charge	Address	Tel.
Barrett, Leslie M. BD FRICS	1991	2001	Chaplain: University of Abertay, Dundee	Dunelm Cottage, Logie, Cupar KY15 4SJ [E-mail: l.barrett@abertay.ac.uk]	01334 870396
Campbell, Gordon MA BD CDipAF DipHSM MCMI MIHM AFRIN ARSGS FRGS FSAScot	2001		Auxiliary Minister: Chaplain: University of Dundee	2 Falkland Place, Kingoodie, Invergowrie, Dundee DD2 5DY [E-mail: gordon.campbell@dundeepresbytery.org.uk]	01382 561383
Clarkson, Robert G.	1950	1989	(Dundee: Strathmartine)	320 Strathmartine Road, Dundee DD3 8QG [E-mail: rob.gov@virgin.net]	01382 825380
Craik, Sheila (Mrs) BD	1989	2001	(Dundee: Camperdown)	35 Haldane Terrace, Dundee DD3 0HT	01382 802078
Cramb, Erik M. LTh	1973	1989	(Industrial Mission Organiser)	Flat 35, Braehead, Methven Walk, Dundee DD2 3FJ [E-mail: erikcramb@aol.com]	01382 526196
Donald, Robert M. LTh BA	1969	2005	(Kilmodan and Colintraive)	2 Blacklaw Drive, Birkhill, Dundee DD2 5RJ [E-mail: robbie.donald@dundeepresbytery.org.uk]	01382 581337
Douglas, Fiona C. (Ms) MBE MA BD PhD	1989	1997	Chaplain: University of Dundee	10 Springfield, Dundee DD1 4JE	01382 384157
Ferguson, John F. MA BD	1987	2001	(Perth: Kinnoull)	10 Glamis Crescent, Inchture, Perth PH14 9QU	01828 687881
Fraser, Donald W. MA	1958	2010	(Monifieth)	1 Blake Avenue, Broughty Ferry, Dundee DD5 3LH [E-mail: fraserdonald37@yahoo.co.uk]	01382 477491 (Mbl) 07531 863316
Gammack, George BD	1985	1999	(Dundee: Whitfield)	13A Hill Street, Broughty Ferry, Dundee DD5 2JP	01382 778636
Hawdon, John E. BA MTh AICS	1961	1995	(Dundee: Clepington)	53 Hillside Road, Dundee DD2 1QT [E-mail: john.hawdon@dundeepresbytery.org.uk]	01382 646212
Hudson, J. Harrison DipTh MA BD	1961	1999	(Dundee: St Peter's McCheyne)	22 Hamilton Avenue, Tayport DD6 9BW	01382 552052
Ingram, J.R.	1954	1978	(Chaplain: RAF)	48 Marlee Road, Broughty Ferry, Dundee DD5 3EX	01382 736400
Jamieson, David B. MA BD STM	1974	2011	(Monifieth)	8A Albert Street, Monifieth, Dundee DD5 4JS	01382 532772
Kay, Elizabeth (Miss) DipYCS	1993	2007	(Auxiliary Minister)	1 Kintail Walk, Inchture, Perth PH14 9RY [E-mail: liz.kay@dundeepresbytery.org.uk]	01828 686029
Laidlaw, John J. MA	1964	1973	(Adviser in Religious Education)	14 Dalhousie Road, Barnhill, Dundee DD5 2SQ	01382 477458
McLeod, David C. BSc MEng BD	1969	2001	(Dundee: Fairmuir)	6 Carseview Gardens, Dundee DD2 1NE	01382 641371
McMillan, Charles D. LTh	1979	2004	(Elgin: High)	11 Troon Terrace, The Orchard, Ardler, Dundee DD2 3FX	01382 831358
Mair, Michael V.A. MA BD	1967	2007	(Craigiebank with Dundee: Douglas and Mid Craigie)	6 Emmockwoods Drive, Dundee DD4 9FD [E-mail: mike.mair@dundeepresbytery.org.uk]	01382 502114
Martin, Jane (Miss) DCS			(Deaconess)	16 Wentworth Road, Ardler, Dundee DD2 8SD	01382 813786
Miller, Charles W. MA	1953	1994	(Fowlis and Liff)	Abbey Lodge Care Home, Westwood Hill, East Kilbride, Glasgow G75 8QA	
Milroy, Tom	1960	1992	(Monifieth: St Rule's)	9 Long Row, Westhaven, Carnoustie DD7 6BE	01241 856654
Mitchell, Jack MA BD CTh	1987	1996	(Dundee: Menzieshill)	10 Invergowrie Drive, Dundee DD2 1RF	01382 642301
Mowat, Gilbert M. MA	1948	1986	(Dundee: Albany-Butterburn)	Abbeyfield House, 16 Grange Road, Bearsden, Glasgow G61 3PL	
Pickering, John M. BSc BD DipEd	1997	2010	(Dundee: Mains)	Oriole House, Ardbroilach Road, Kingussie PH21 1JY	
Powrie, James E. LTh	1969	1995	(Dundee: Chalmers Ardler)	3 Kirktonhill Road, Kirriemuir DD8 4HU	01575 572503
Rae, Robert LTh	1968	1983	(Chaplain: Dundee Acute Hospitals)	14 Neddertoun View, Liff, Dundee DD3 5RU	01382 581790

Name	Ord.	Ret.	Charge	Address	Tel.
Randall, David J. MA BD ThM	1971	2010	(Macduff)	5 Applehill Gardens, Wellbank, Broughty Ferry, Dundee DD5 3UG [E-mail: djrandall479@btinternet.com]	01382 351812
Reid, R. Gordon BSc BD MIET	1993	2010	(Carriden)	6 Bayview Place, Monifieth, Dundee DD5 4TN [E-mail: GordonReid@aol.com]	01382 520519 (Mbl) 07952 349884
Robson, George K. LTh DPS BA	1983	2011	(Dundee: Balgay)	11 Ceres Crescent, Broughty Ferry, Dundee DD5 3JN [E-mail: gkrobson@tiscali.co.uk]	01382 901212
Rogers, James M. BA DB DCult	1955	1996	(Gibraltar)	24 Mansion Drive, Dalclaverhouse, Dundee DD4 9DD	01382 506162
Roy, James A. MA BD	1965	2006	(Dundee: Lochee West)	'Beechwood', 7 Northview Terrace, Wormit, Newport-on-Tay DD6 8PP [E-mail: jim.roy@dundeepresbytery.org.uk]	01382 543578
Scott, James MA BD	1973	2010	(Drumoak-Durris)	3 Blake Place, Broughty Ferry, Dundee DD5 3LQ [E-mail: jimscott73@yahoo.co.uk]	01382 739595
Scroggie, John C.	1951	1985	(Mains)	23 Cliffburn Gardens, Broughty Ferry, Dundee DD5 3NB	01382 739354
Scoular, Stanley	1963	2000	(Rosyth)	31 Duns Crescent, Dundee DD4 0RY	01382 501653
Strickland, Alexander LTh	1971	2005	(Dairsie with Kemback with Strathkinness)	12 Ballumbie Braes, Dundee DD5 0UN	01382 685539
Sutherland, David A.	2001		Auxiliary Minister	6 Cromarty Drive, Dundee DD2 2UQ [E-mail: revdavesutherland@virginmedia.com]	01382 621473
Webster, Allan F. MA BD	1978	2008	Workplace Chaplain: Tayside and North Fife	65 Clepington Road, Dundee DD4 7BQ [E-mail: allanfwebster@aol.com]	01382 458764

DUNDEE ADDRESSES

Balgay	200 Lochee Road
Barnhill St Margaret's	10 Invermark Terrace
Broughty Ferry	
New Kirk	370 Queen Street
St James'	5 Fort Street
St Luke's and Queen Street	5 West Queen Street
St Stephen's and West	96 Dundee Road
Camperdown	22 Brownhill Road
Chalmers Ardler	Turnberry Avenue
Coldside	Isla Street
Craigiebank	Craigie Avenue at Greendykes Road
Douglas and Mid Craigie	Balbeggie Place/ Longtown Terrace
Downfield South	Haldane Street off Strathmartine Road
Dundee (St Mary's)	Nethergate
Fintry	Fintry Road x Fintry Drive
Lochee	191 High Street, Lochee
Logie and St John's Cross	Shaftesbury Rd x Blackness Ave
Mains	Foot of Old Glamis Road
Meadowside St Paul's	114 Nethergate
Menzieshill	Charleston Drive, Menzieshill
St Andrew's	2 King Street
St David's High Kirk	119A Kinghorne Road and 273 Strathmore Avenue
Steeple	Nethergate
Stobswell	170 Albert Street
Strathmartine	507 Strathmartine Road
Trinity	73 Crescent Street
West	130 Perth Road
Whitfield	Haddington Crescent

(30) ANGUS

Meets at Forfar in St Margaret's Church Hall, on the first Tuesday of each month, except June when it meets on the last Tuesday, and January, July and August when there is no meeting.

Clerk:	**REV. MICHAEL S. GOSS BD DPS**	**[E-mail: michaelgoss@blueyonder.co.uk]**	
Depute Clerk:	**REV. ALBERT B. REID BSc BD**	**[E-mail: abreid@btinternet.com]**	
Presbytery Office:		**St Margaret's Church, West High Street, Forfar DD8 1BJ** **[E-mail: angus@cofscotland.org.uk]**	**01307 464224**

Aberlemno (H) linked with Guthrie and Rescobie

Brian Ramsay BD DPS MLitt	1980	1984	The Manse, Guthrie, Forfar DD8 2TP	01241 828243

Arbirlot linked with Carmyllie

Stewart J. Lamont BSc BD	1972	2011	The Manse, Arbirlot, Arbroath DD11 2NX	01241 434479

Arbroath: Knox's (H) linked with Arbroath: St Vigeans (H)

Nelu I. Balaj BD MA ThD	2010		The Manse, St Vigeans, Arbroath DD11 4RF [E-mail: nelu@gmx.co.uk]	01241 873206 07954 436879 (Mbl)

Arbroath: Old and Abbey (H) (Church office: 01241 877068)

Valerie L. Allen (Ms) BMus MDiv DMin	1990	1996	51 Cliffburn Road, Arbroath DD11 5BA [E-mail: VL2allen@aol.com]	01241 872196 (Tel/Fax)

Arbroath: St Andrew's (H) (E-mail: st_andrews_arbroath@lineone.net)

W. Martin Fair BA BD DMin	1992		92 Grampian Gardens, Arbroath DD11 4AQ [E-mail: martin.fair@sky.com]	01241 873238 (Tel/Fax)

Arbroath: St Vigeans See Arbroath: Knox's

Arbroath: West Kirk (H)

Alasdair G. Graham BD DipMin	1981	1986	1 Charles Avenue, Arbroath DD11 2EY [E-mail: alasdair.graham@tiscali.co.uk]	01241 872244

Barry linked with Carnoustie

Michael S. Goss BD DPS	1991	2003	44 Terrace Road, Carnoustie DD7 7AR [E-mail: michaelgoss@blueyonder.co.uk]	01241 410194 (Tel/Fax) 07787 141567 (Mbl)

Brechin: Cathedral (H) (Cathedral office: 01356 629360) (Website: www.brechincathedral.org.uk)
Roderick J. Grahame BD CPS 1991 2010 Chanonry Wynd, Brechin DD9 6JS 01356 624980
[E-mail: rjgrahame@talktalk.net]

Brechin: Gardner Memorial (H) linked with Farnell
Jane M. Blackley MA BD 2009 15 Caldhame Gardens, Brechin DD9 7JJ 01356 622789
[E-mail: jmblackley6@aol.com]

Carmyllie See Arbirlot
Carnoustie See Barry

Carnoustie: Panbride (H)
Matthew S. Bicket BD 1989 8 Arbroath Road, Carnoustie DD7 6BL 01241 854478 (Tel)
[E-mail: matthew@bicket.freeserve.co.uk] 01241 855088 (Fax)

Colliston linked with Friockheim Kinnell linked with Inverkeilor and Lunan (H)
Peter A. Phillips BA 1995 2004 The Manse, Inverkeilor, Arbroath DD11 5SA 01241 830464
[E-mail: peter@peterphillips6.orangehome.co.uk]

Dun and Hillside
Linda J. Broadley (Mrs) LTh DipEd 1996 2004 4 Manse Road, Hillside, Montrose DD10 9FB 01674 830288
[E-mail: lindabroadley@btinternet.com]

Dunnichen, Letham and Kirkden
James M. Davies BSc BD (Interim Minister) 1982 2010 7 Braehead Road, Letham, Forfar DD8 2PG 07921 023144 (Mbl)
[E-mail: daviesjim@btinternet.com]

Eassie and Nevay linked with Newtyle
Carleen Robertson (Miss) BD 1992 2 Kirkton Road, Newtyle, Blairgowrie PH12 8TS 01828 650461
[E-mail: carleen.robertson120@btinternet.com]

Edzell Lethnot Glenesk (H) linked with Fern Careston Menmuir
David T. Gray BArch BD 2010 19 Lethnot Road, Edzell, Brechin DD9 7TG 01356 647846
[E-mail: davidgray64@sky.com] 07789 718622 (Mbl)

Farnell See Brechin: Gardner Memorial
Fern Careston Menmuir See Edzell Lethnot Glenesk

Forfar: East and Old (H)
Barbara Ann Sweetin BD 2011 The Manse, Lour Road, Forfar DD8 2BB 01307 248228
[E-mail: barbara.ann17@talktalk.net]

Forfar: Lowson Memorial (H)
Karen Fenwick PhD MPhil BSc BD 2006 1 Jamieson Street, Forfar DD8 2HY 01307 468585
[E-mail: kmfenwick@talktalk.net]

Forfar: St Margaret's (H) (Church office: 01307 464224)
David Logan BD MA FRSA 2009 St Margaret's Manse, 15 Potters Park Crescent, Forfar DD8 1HH 01307 462044
[E-mail: minister@castleroy.org]

Friockheim Kinnell See Colliston

Glamis (H), Inverarity and Kinnettles
Vacant 12 Turfbeg Road, Forfar DD8 3LT 01307 466038

Guthrie and Rescobie See Aberlemno

Inchbrayock linked with Montrose: Melville South
David S. Dixon MA BD 1976 1994 The Manse, Ferryden, Montrose DD10 9SD 01674 672108
[E-mail: david@inchbrayock.wanadoo.co.uk]

Inverkeilor and Lunan See Colliston

Kirriemuir: St Andrew's (H) linked with Oathlaw Tannadice
Vacant 26 Quarry Park, Kirriemuir DD8 4DR 01575 575561

Montrose: Melville South See Inchbrayock

Montrose: Old and St Andrew's
Ian A. McLean BSc BD DMin 1981 2008 2 Rosehill Road, Montrose DD10 8ST 01674 672447
[E-mail: iamclean@lineone.net]

Newtyle See Eassie and Nevay
Oathlaw Tannadice See Kirriemuir: St Andrew's

The Glens and Kirriemuir: Old (H) (Church office: 01575 572819) (Website: www.gkopc.co.uk)

Malcolm I.G. Rooney DPE BEd BD	1993	1999	20 Strathmore Avenue, Kirriemuir DD8 4DJ [E-mail: malcolm@gkopc.co.uk]	01575 573724 07909 993233 (Mbl)
Linda Stevens (Mrs) BSc BD PgDip (Team Minister)	2006		17 North Latch Road, Brechin DD9 6LE [E-mail: linda@gkopc.co.uk]	01356 623415 07701 052552 (Mbl)

The Isla Parishes

Brian Ian Murray BD	2002	2010	Balduff House, Kilry, Blairgowrie PH11 8HS [E-mail: bentleymurray@googlemail.com]	01575 560268

Anderson, John F. MA BD FSAScot	1966	2006	(Aberdeen: Mannofield)	8 Eider Close, Montrose DD10 9NE [E-mail: jfa941@aol.com]	01674 672029
Brodie, James BEM MA BD STM	1955	1974	(Hurlford)	25A Keptie Road, Arbroath DD11 3ED	01241 873298
Butters, David	1964	1998	(Turriff: St Ninian's and Forglen)	68A Millgate, Friockheim, Arbroath DD11 4TN	01241 828030
Douglas, Iain M. MA BD MPhil DipEd	1960	2002	(Farnell with Montrose: St Andrew's)	Old School House, Kinnell, Friockheim, Arbroath DD11 4UL	01241 828717
Drysdale James P.R.	1967	1999	(Brechin: Gardner Memorial)	51 Airlie Street, Brechin DD9 6JX	01356 625201
Duncan, Robert F. MTheol	1986	2001	(Lochgelly: St Andrew's)	25 Rowan Avenue, Kirriemuir DD8 4TB	01575 573973
Gough, Ian G. MA BD MTh DMin	1974	2009	(Arbroath: Knox's with Arbroath: St Vigeans)	23 Keptie Road, Arbroath DD11 3ED [E-mail: ianggough@btinternet.com]	(Mbl) 07891 838379
Hastie, George I. MA BD	1971	2009	(Mearns Coastal)	23 Borrowfield Crescent, Montrose DD10 9BR	01674 672290
Hodge, William N.T.	1966	1995	(Longside)	19 Craigengar Park, Craigshill, Livingston EH54 5NY	01506 435813
London, Dale BTh FSAScot	2011		Chaplain: Army	39 Morrison Street, Kirriemuir DD8 5DB	01575 573518
Milton, Eric G. RD	1963	1994	(Blairdaff)	16 Bruce Court, Links Parade, Carnoustie DD7 7JE	01241 854928
Morrice, Alastair M. MA BD	1968	2002	(Rutherglen: Stonelaw)	5 Brechin Road, Kirriemuir DD8 4BX [E-mail: ambishkek@swissmail.org]	01575 574102
Norrie, Graham MA BD	1967	2007	(Forfar: East and Old)	'Novar', 14A Wyllie Street, Forfar DD8 3DN [E-mail: grahamnorrie@hotmail.com]	01307 468152
Perry, Joseph B.	1955	1989	(Farnell)	19 Guthrie Street, Letham, Forfar DD8 2PS	01307 818741
Reid, Albert B. BD BSc	1996	2001	(Ardler, Kettins and Meigle)	1 Dundee Street, Letham, Forfar DD8 2PQ [E-mail: abreid@btinternet.com]	01307 818416
Robertson, George R. LTh	1985	2004	(Udny and Pitmedden)	3 Slateford Gardens, Edzell, Brechin DD9 7SX [E-mail: geomag.robertson@btinternet.com]	01356 647322
Searle, David C. MA DipTh	1965	2003	(Warden: Rutherford House)	12 Cairnie Road, Arbroath DD11 3DY [E-mail: dcs@davidsearle.plus.com]	01241 872794
Shackleton, Scott J.S. BA BD PhD	1993	2010	Chaplain: Royal Navy	45 Commando Group Royal Marines, RM *Condor*, Arbroath DD11 3SJ [E-mail: shackletonscott@hotmail.com]	
Smith, Hamish G.	1965	1993	(Auchterless with Rothienorman)	11A Guthrie Street, Letham, Forfar DD8 2PS	01307 818973
Thomas, Martyn R.H. CEng MIStructE	1987	2002	(Fowlis and Liff with Lundie and Muirhead of Liff)	14 Kirkgait, Letham, Forfar DD8 2XQ [E-mail: martyn.thomas@mypostoffice.co.uk]	01307 818084
Thomas, Shirley A. (Mrs) DipSocSci AMIA (Aux)	2000	2006	(Auxiliary Minister)	14 Kirkgait, Letham, Forfar DD8 2XQ [E-mail: martyn.thomas@mypostoffice.co.uk]	01307 818084

Warnock, Denis MA	1952	1990	(Kirkcaldy: Torbain)	19 Keptie Road, Arbroath DD11 3ED	01241 872740
Watt, Alan G.N. MTh CQSW DipCommEd	1996	2009	(Edzell Lethnot Glenesk with Fern Careston Menmuir)	128 Restenneth Drive, Forfar DD8 2DH [E-mail: watt455@btinternet.com]	01307 461686
Youngson, Peter	1961	1996	(Kirriemuir: St Andrew's)	'Coreen', Woodside, Northmuir, Kirriemuir DD8 4PG	01575 572832

ANGUS ADDRESSES

Arbroath
Knox's — Howard Street
Old and Abbey — West Abbey Street
St Andrew's — Hamilton Green
West Kirk — Keptie Street

Brechin
Cathedral — Bishops Close
Gardner Memorial — South Esk Street

Carnoustie
Panbride — Dundee Street
Arbroath Road

Forfar
East and Old — East High Street
Lowson Memorial — Jamieson Street
St Margaret's — West High Street

Kirriemuir
Old — High Street
St Andrew's — Glamis Road

Montrose
Melville South — Castle Street
Old and St Andrew's — High Street

(31) ABERDEEN

Meets at Queen's Cross Church, Albyn Place, Aberdeen AB10 1UN, on the first Tuesday of February, March, May, September, October, November and December, and on the fourth Tuesday of June.

Joint Clerks: **REV. GEORGE S. COWIE BSc BD**
REV. JOHN A. FERGUSON BD DipMin DMin

Administrator and Depute Clerk: **MRS MOYRA CAMERON**

Presbytery Office: **Mastrick Church, Greenfern Road, Aberdeen AB16 6TR** **01224 698119**
[E-mail: aberdeen@cofscotland.org.uk]

Aberdeen: Bridge of Don Oldmachar (01224 709299) (Website: www.oldmacharchurch.org)

Bruce K. Gardner MA BD PhD	1988	2010	60 Newburgh Circle, Aberdeen AB22 8QZ [E-mail: drbrucekgardner@aol.com]	01224 701365

Aberdeen: Cove (E)
David Swan BVMS BD | 2005 | | 4 Charleston Way, Cove, Aberdeen AB12 3FA [E-mail: david@covechurch.org.uk] | 01224 899933

Aberdeen: Craigiebuckler (H) (01224 315649)
Kenneth L. Petrie MA BD | 1984 | 1999 | 185 Springfield Road, Aberdeen AB15 8AA [E-mail: patandkenneth@aol.com] | 01224 315125

Aberdeen: Ferryhill (H) (01224 213093)
John H.A. Dick MA MSc BD | 1982 | | 54 Polmuir Road, Aberdeen AB11 7RT [E-mail: jhadick01@talktalk.net] | 01224 586933

Aberdeen: Garthdee (H) linked with Aberdeen: Ruthrieston West (H)
Benjamin D.W. Byun BS MDiv MTh PhD | 2008 | | 53 Springfield Avenue, Aberdeen AB15 8JJ [E-mail: benjamin@byun1.fsnet.co.uk] | 01224 312706

Aberdeen: Gilcomston South (H) (01224 647144)
D. Dominic Smart BSc BD MTh | 1988 | 1998 | 37 Richmondhill Road, Aberdeen AB15 5EQ [E-mail: dominic.smart@gilcomston.org] | 01224 314326

Aberdeen: High Hilton (H) (01224 494717)
A. Peter Dickson BSc BD | 1996 | | 24 Rosehill Drive, Aberdeen AB24 4JJ [E-mail: peter@highhilton.com] | 01224 484155

Aberdeen: Holburn West (H) (01224 571120)
Duncan C. Eddie MA BD | 1992 | 1999 | 31 Cranford Road, Aberdeen AB10 7NJ [E-mail: dceddies@tiscali.co.uk] | 01224 325873

Aberdeen: Mannofield (H) (01224 310087) (E-mail: office@mannofieldchurch.org.uk)
Keith T. Blackwood BD DipMin | 1997 | 2007 | 21 Forest Avenue, Aberdeen AB15 4TU [E-mail: minister@mannofieldchurch.org.uk] | 01224 315748

Aberdeen: Mastrick (H) (01224 694121)
Vacant | | | 8 Corse Wynd, Kingswells, Aberdeen AB15 8TP | 01224 749346

Aberdeen: Middlefield (H)
Anita van der Wal | 2008 | | 25 Kirk Place, Cults, Aberdeen AB15 9RD [E-mail: vanderwal@btinternet.com] | 01224 865195

Aberdeen: Midstocket
Marian Cowie MA BD MTh 1990 2006 54 Woodstock Road, Aberdeen AB15 5JF 01224 208001
[E-mail: mcowieou@aol.com]

Aberdeen: New Stockethill (New Charge Development)
Ian M. Aitken MA BD 1999 52 Ashgrove Road West, Aberdeen AB16 5EE 01224 686929
[E-mail: ncdstockethill@uk.uumail.com]

Aberdeen: Northfield
Scott C. Guy BD 1989 1999 28 Byron Crescent, Aberdeen AB16 7EX 01224 692332
[E-mail: scott@waitrose.com]

Aberdeen: Queen Street
Graham D.S. Deans MA BD MTh DMin 1978 2008 51 Osborne Place, Aberdeen AB25 2BX 01224 646429
[E-mail: graham.deans@btopenworld.com]

Aberdeen: Queen's Cross (H) (01224 644742)
Scott Rennie MA BD STM 1999 2009 1 St Swithin Street, Aberdeen AB10 6XH 01224 322549
[E-mail: scottmrennie@me.com]

Aberdeen: Rubislaw (H) (01224 645477)
Andrew G.N. Wilson MA BD DMin 1977 1987 45 Rubislaw Den South, Aberdeen AB15 4BD 01224 314878
[E-mail: agn.wilson@virgin.net]

Aberdeen: Ruthrieston West (H) See Aberdeen: Garthdee

Aberdeen: St Columba's Bridge of Don (H) (01224 825653)
Louis Kinsey BD DipMin 1991 151 Jesmond Avenue, Aberdeen AB22 8UG 01224 705337
[E-mail: louis@stcolumbaschurch.org.uk]

Aberdeen: St George's Tillydrone (H) (01224 482204)
James Weir BD 1991 2003 127 Clifton Road, Aberdeen AB24 4RH 01224 483976
[E-mail: rjimw@sky.com]

Aberdeen: St John's Church for Deaf People (H) (01224 494566)
John R. Osbeck BD 1979 1991 15 Deeside Crescent, Aberdeen AB15 7PT (Voice/Text) 01224 315595

Aberdeen: St Machar's Cathedral (H) (01224 485988)
Vacant 18 The Chanonry, Old Aberdeen AB24 1RQ 01224 483688

Aberdeen: St Mark's (H) (01224 640672)
Diane L. Hobson (Mrs) BA BD 2002 2010 65 Mile-end Avenue, Aberdeen AB15 5PU 01224 622470
[E-mail: dianehobson.rev@btinternet.com]

Aberdeen: St Mary's (H) (01224 487227)
Elsie J. Fortune (Mrs) BSc BD 2003 456 King Street, Aberdeen AB24 3DE 01224 633778
[E-mail: eric.fortune@lineone.net]

Aberdeen: St Nicholas Kincorth, South of
Edward C. McKenna BD DPS 1989 2002 The Manse, Kincorth Circle, Aberdeen AB12 5NX 01224 872820
[E-mail: eddiemckenna@uwclub.net]
Daniel Robertson BA BD (Assoc) 2009 2011 5 Bruce Walk, Nigg, Aberdeen AB12 3LX
[E-mail: dan_robertson100@hotmail.com]

Aberdeen: St Nicholas Uniting, Kirk of (H) (01224 643494)
B. Stephen C. Taylor BA BBS MA MDiv 1984 2005 12 Louisville Avenue, Aberdeen AB15 4TX 01224 314318
[E-mail: minister@kirk-of-st-nicholas.org.uk] 01224 649242 (Fax)

Aberdeen: St Stephen's (H) (01224 624443)
Maggie Whyte BD 2010 6 Belvidere Street, Aberdeen AB25 2QS 01224 635694
[E-mail: maggiewhyte@aol.com]

Aberdeen: South Holburn (H) (01224 211730)
George S. Cowie BSc BD 1991 2006 54 Woodstock Road, Aberdeen AB15 5JF 01224 315042
[E-mail: gscowie@aol.com]

Aberdeen: Summerhill (H) (Website: www.summerhillchurch.org.uk)
Michael R.R. Shewan MA BD CPS 1985 2010 36 Stronsay Drive, Aberdeen AB15 6JL 01224 324669
[E-mail: michaelshewan@btinternet.com]

Aberdeen: Torry St Fittick's (H) (01224 899183)
Iain C. Barclay 1976 1999 11 Devanha Gardens East, Aberdeen AB11 7UH 01224 588245
MBE TD MA BD MTh MPhil PhD [E-mail: iaincbarclay@gmail.com] 07882 885684 (Mbl)

Aberdeen: Woodside (H) (01224 277249)
Markus Auffermann DipTheol 1999 2006 322 Clifton Road, Aberdeen AB24 4HQ 01224 484562
[E-mail: mauffermann@yahoo.com]

Bucksburn Stoneywood (H) (01224 712411)

Nigel Parker BD MTh DMin	1994		25 Gilbert Road, Bucksburn, Aberdeen AB21 9AN [E-mail: revdr.n.parker@btinternet.com]	01224 712635

Cults (H)

Ewen J. Gilchrist BD DipMin DipComm	1982	2005	1 Cairnlee Terrace, Bieldside, Aberdeen AB15 9AE [E-mail: ewengilchrist@btconnect.com]	01224 861692

Dyce (H) (01224 771295)

Manson C. Merchant BD CPS	1992	2008	144 Victoria Street, Dyce, Aberdeen AB21 7BE [E-mail: mc.merchant@btinternet.com]	01224 722380

Kingswells

Dolly Purnell BD	2003	2004	Kingswells Manse, Lang Stracht, Aberdeen AB15 8PL [E-mail: revdollypurnell@btinternet.com]	01224 740229

Newhills (H) (Tel/Fax: 01224 716161)

Hugh M. Wallace MA BD	1980	2007	Newhills Manse, Bucksburn, Aberdeen AB21 9SS [E-mail: revhugh@hotmail.com]	01224 712655

Peterculter (H) (01224 735845)

John A. Ferguson BD DipMin DMin	1988	1999	7 Howie Lane, Peterculter AB14 0LJ [E-mail: john.ferguson525@btinternet.com]	01224 735041

Aitchison, James W. BD	1993	Chaplain: Army	84 Wakefords Park, Church Crookham, Fleet, Hampshire GU52 8EZ	
Alexander, William M. BD	1971 1998	(Berriedale and Dunbeath with Latheron)	110 Fairview Circle, Danestone, Aberdeen AB22 8YR	01224 703752
Beattie, Walter G. MA BD	1956 1995	(Arbroath: Old and Abbey)	126 Seafield Road, Aberdeen AB15 7YQ	01224 329259
Black, W. Graham MA BD	1983 1999	Urban Prayer Ministry	72 Linksview, Linksfield Road, Aberdeen AB24 5RG [E-mail: graham.black@virgin.net]	01224 492491
Campbell, W.M.M. BD CPS	1970 2003	(Hospital Chaplain)	43 Murray Terrace, Aberdeen AB11 7SA	07761 235815
Coutts, Fred MA BD	1973 1989	Hospital Chaplain	Ladebank, 1 Manse Place, Hatton, Peterhead AB42 0QU	01779 841320
Crawford, Michael S.M. LTh	1966 2002	(Aberdeen: St Mary's)	9 Craigton Avenue, Aberdeen AB15 7RP	01224 208341
Douglas, Andrew M. MA	1957 1995	(High Hilton)	219 Countesswells Road, Aberdeen AB15 7RD	01224 311932
Falconer, Alan D. MA BD DLitt	1972 2011	(Aberdeen: St Machar's Cathedral)	18 North Crescent Road, Ardrossan KA22 8NA [E-mail: alanfalconer@gmx.com]	01294 472991
Falconer, James B. BD	1982 1991	Hospital Chaplain	3 Brimmond Walk, Westhill AB32 6XH	01224 744621
Garden, Margaret J. (Miss) BD	1993 2009	(Cushnie and Tough)	26 Earns Heugh Circle, Cove Bay, Aberdeen AB12 3PY [E-mail: mj.garden@btinternet.com]	
Goldie, George D. ALCM	1953 1995	(Greyfriars)	27 Broomhill Avenue, Aberdeen AB10 6JL	01224 322503

Name			Charge	Address	Telephone
Gordon, Laurie Y.	1960	1995	(John Knox)	1 Alder Drive, Portlethen, Aberdeen AB12 4WA	01224 782703
Graham, A. David M. BA BD	1971	2005	(Aberdeen: Rosemount)	Elmhill House, 27 Shaw Crescent, Aberdeen AB25 3BT	01224 648041
Grainger, Harvey L. LTh	1975	2004	(Kingswells)	13 St Ronan's Crescent, Peterculter, Aberdeen AB14 0RL [E-mail: harveygrainger@tiscali.co.uk]	01224 739824 (Mbl) 07768 333216
Grashoff, Martin	1995	2011	Chaplain to UK Oil and Gas Industry	Chaplain's Office, Total E and P (UK) PLC, Loirston House, Wellington Road, Aberdeen AB12 3BH [E-mail: martin.grashoff@ukoilandgaschaplaincy.com]	01224 298532
Haddow, Angus BSc	1963	1999	(Methlick)	25 Lerwick Road, Aberdeen AB16 6RF	01224 696362
Hamilton, Helen (Miss) BD	1991	2003	(Glasgow: St James' Pollok)	The Cottage, West Tilbouries, Maryculter, Aberdeen AB12 5GD	01224 739632
Harley, Elspeth BA MTh	1991	2010	(Aberdeen: Middlefield)	8 Donmouth Road, Aberdeen AB23 8DT [E-mail: eharley@hotmail.co.uk]	01224 703017
Hutchison, A. Scott MA BD DD	1957	1991	(Hospital Chaplain)	Ashfield, Drumoak, Banchory AB31 5AG	01330 811309
Hutchison, Alison M. (Mrs) BD DipMin	1988	1988	Hospital Chaplain	Ashfield, Drumoak, Banchory AB31 5AG [E-mail: amhutch62@aol.com]	01330 811309
Hutchison, David S. BSc BD ThM	1991	1999	(Aberdeen: Torry St Fittick's)	51 Don Street, Aberdeen AB24 1UH	01224 276122
Johnstone, William MA BD	1963	2001	(University of Aberdeen)	9/5 Mount Alvernia, Edinburgh EH16 6AW	0131-664 3140
Kerr, Hugh F. MA BD	1968	2006	(Aberdeen: Ruthrieston South)	134C Great Western Road, Aberdeen AB10 6QE	01224 580091
Lundie, Ann V. DCS			(Deaconess)	20 Langdykes Drive, Cove, Aberdeen AB12 3HW [E-mail: ann.lundie@btopenworld.com]	01224 898416
McCallum, Moyra (Miss) MA BD DCS			(Deaconess)	176 Hilton Drive, Aberdeen AB24 4LT [E-mail: moymac@aol.com]	01224 486240
Maciver, Norman MA BD DMin	1976	2006	(Newhills)	4 Mundi Crescent, Newmachar, Aberdeen AB21 0LY [E-mail: norirene@aol.com]	01651 869442
Main, Alan TD MA BD STM PhD DD	1963	2001	(University of Aberdeen)	Kirkfield, Barthol Chapel, Inverurie AB51 8TD [E-mail: amain@talktalk.net]	01651 806773
Montgomerie, Jean B. (Miss) MA BD	1973	2005	(Forfar: St Margaret's)	12 St Ronan's Place, Peterculter, Aberdeen AB14 0QX [E-mail: revjeanb@tiscali.co.uk]	01224 732350
Phillippo, Michael MTh BSc BVetMed MRCVS	2003		(Auxiliary Minister)	25 Deeside Crescent, Aberdeen AB15 7PT [E-mail: phillippo@btinternet.com]	01224 318317
Richardson, Thomas C. LTh ThB	1971	2004	(Cults: West)	19 Kinkell Road, Aberdeen AB15 8HR [E-mail: thomas.richardson7@btinternet.com]	01224 315328
Rodgers, D. Mark BA BD MTh	1987	2003	Hospital Chaplain	152D Gray Street, Aberdeen AB10 6JW	01224 210810
Sefton, Henry R. MA BD STM PhD	1957	1992	(University of Aberdeen)	25 Albury Place, Aberdeen AB11 6TQ	01224 572305
Sheret, Brian S. MA BD DPhil	1982	2009	(Glasgow: Drumchapel Drumry St Mary's)	59 Airyhall Crescent, Aberdeen AB15 7QS	01224 323032
Stewart, James C. MA BD STM	1960	2000	(Aberdeen: Kirk of St Nicholas)	54 Murray Terrace, Aberdeen AB11 7SB	01224 587071
Swinton, John BD PhD	1999		University of Aberdeen	51 Newburgh Circle, Bridge of Don, Aberdeen AB22 8XA [E-mail: j.swinton@abdn.ac.uk]	01224 825637
Torrance, Iain R. TD DPhil DD DTheol LHD CorrFRSE	1982	2004	President: Princeton Theological Seminary	64 Mercer Street, Princeton, NJ 08542-0803, USA [E-mail: irt@ptsem.edu]	001 609 497 7800
Watson, John M. LTh	1989	2009	(Aberdeen: St Mark's)	20 Greystone Place, Newtonhill, Stonehaven AB39 3UL [E-mail: watson-john18@sky.com]	01569 730604 (Mbl) 07733 334380
Wilkie, William E. LTh	1978	2001	(Aberdeen: St Nicholas Kincorth, South of)	32 Broomfield Park, Portlethen, Aberdeen AB12 4XT	01224 782052

Wilson, Thomas F. BD	1984 1996	Education	55 Allison Close, Cove, Aberdeen AB12 3WG	01224 873501
Wood, James L.K.	1967 1995	(Ruthrieston West)	1 Glen Drive, Dyce, Aberdeen AB21 7EN	01224 722543

ABERDEEN ADDRESSES

Bridge of Don Oldmachar	Ashwood Park
Cove	Loirston Primary School, Loirston Avenue
Craigiebuckler	Springfield Road
Cults	Quarry Road, Cults
Dyce	Victoria Street, Dyce
Ferryhill	Fonthill Road x Polmuir Road
Garthdee	Ramsay Gardens
Gilcomston South	Union Street x Summer Street
High Hilton	Hilton Drive
Holburn West	Great Western Road
Kingswells	Old Skene Road, Kingswells
Mannofield	Great Western Road x Craigton Road
Mastrick	Greenfern Road
Middlefield	Manor Avenue
Midstocket	Mid Stocket Road
New Stockethill	
Northfield	Byron Crescent
Peterculter	Craigton Crescent
Queen Street	Queen Street
Queen's Cross	Albyn Place
Rubislaw	Queen's Gardens
Ruthrieston West	Broomhill Road
St Columba's	Braehead Way, Bridge of Don
St George's	Hayton Road, Tillydrone
St John's for the Deaf	Smithfield Road
St Machar's	The Chanonry
St Mark's	Rosemount Viaduct
St Mary's	King Street
St Nicholas Kincorth, South of	Kincorth Circle
St Nicholas Uniting, Kirk of	Union Street
St Stephen's	Powis Place
South Holburn	Holburn Street
Summerhill	Stronsay Drive
Torry St Fittick's	Walker Road
Woodside	Church Street, Woodside

(32) KINCARDINE AND DEESIDE

Meets in Birse and Feughside Church, Finzean, Banchory on the first Tuesday of September, October, November, December, March and May, and on the last Tuesday of June at 7pm.

Clerk:	**REV. HUGH CONKEY BSc BD**	**39 St Ternans Road, Newtonhill, Stonehaven AB39 3PF [E-mail: kincardinedeeside@cofscotland.org.uk]**	**01569 739297**

Aberluthnott linked with Laurencekirk (H)

Ronald Gall BSc BD	1985	2001	Aberdeen Road, Laurencekirk AB30 1AJ [E-mail: ronniegall@tiscali.co.uk]	01561 378838

Aboyne and Dinnet (H) (01339 886989) linked with Cromar (E-mail: aboynedinnet.cos@virgin.net)

Frank Ribbons MA BD DipEd	1985	2011	49 Charlton Crescent, Aboyne AB34 5GN [E-mail: frankribs@gmail.com]	01339 887267

Arbuthnott, Bervie and Kinneff
Dennis S. Rose LTh 1996 2010 10 Kirkburn, Inverbervie, Montrose DD10 0RT 01561 362560
[E-mail: dennis2327@aol.co.uk]

Banchory-Devenick and Maryculter/Cookney (01224 735983) (E-mail: thechurchoffice@tiscali.co.uk)
Heather M. Peacock BSc PhD BD 2009 The Manse, Kirkton of Maryculter, Aberdeen AB12 5FS 01224 730150
[E-mail: hmpeacock@btinternet.com]

Banchory-Ternan: East (H) (01330 820380) (E-mail: eastchurch@banchory.fsbusiness.co.uk)
Mary M. Haddow (Mrs) BD 2001 East Manse, Station Road, Banchory AB31 5YP 01330 822481
[E-mail: mary_haddow@btconnect.com]

Banchory-Ternan: West (H)
Antony Stephen MA BD 2001 2011 The Manse, 2 Wilson Road, Banchory AB31 5UY 01330 822811
[E-mail: tony@banchorywestchurch.com]

Birse and Feughside
Vacant The Manse, Finzean, Banchory AB31 6PB

Braemar and Crathie
Kenneth I. Mackenzie BD CPS 1990 2005 Manse, Crathie, Ballater AB35 5UL 01339 742208
[E-mail: crathiemanse@tiscali.co.uk]

Cromar See Aboyne and Dinnet

Drumoak (H)-Durris (H)
Vacant

Glenmuick (Ballater) (H)
Anthony Watts BD DipTechEd JP 1999 The Manse, Craigendarroch Walk, Ballater AB35 5ZB 01339 754014
[E-mail: tony.watts6@btinternet.com]

Laurencekirk See Aberluthnott

Mearns Coastal
Colin J. Dempster BD CertMin 1990 2010 The Manse, Kirkton, St Cyrus, Montrose DD10 0BW 01674 850880
[E-mail: coldcoast@btinternet.com]

Mid Deeside

Vacant			The Manse, Torphins, Banchory AB31 4GQ	

Newtonhill

Hugh Conkey BSc BD	1987	2001	39 St Ternans Road, Newtonhill, Stonehaven AB39 3PF [E-mail: hugh@conkey.plus.com]	01569 730143

Portlethen (H) (01224 782883)

Flora J. Munro (Mrs) BD DMin	1993	2004	18 Rowanbank Road, Portlethen, Aberdeen AB12 4NX [E-mail: floramunro@aol.co.uk]	01224 780211

Stonehaven: Dunnottar (H)

Rosslyn P. Duncan BD MTh	2007		Dunnottar Manse, Stonehaven AB39 3XL [E-mail: rpduncan@btinternet.com]	01569 762166

Stonehaven: Fetteresso (H) (01569 767689) (E-mail: fetteresso.office@btinternet.com)

Fyfe Blair BA BD DMin	1989	2009	11 South Lodge Drive, Stonehaven AB39 2PN [E-mail: fyfeblair@talktalk.net]	01569 762876

Stonehaven: South (H)

David J. Stewart BD MTh DipMin	2000		South Church Manse, Cameron Street, Stonehaven AB39 2HE [E-mail: brigodon@clara.co.uk]	01569 762576

West Mearns

Catherine A. Hepburn (Miss) BA BD	1982	2000	West Mearns Parish Church Manse, Fettercairn, Laurencekirk AB30 1UE [E-mail: cahepburn@btinternet.com]	01561 340203

Brown, J.W.S. BTh	1960 1995	(Cromar)	10 Forestside Road, Banchory AB31 5ZH [E-mail: iainisobel@aol.com]	01330 824353
Cameron, Ann J. (Mrs) CertCS DCE TEFL	2005	Auxiliary Minister	Currently resident in Qatar [E-mail: anncameron2@googlemail.com]	
Christie, Andrew C. LTh	1975 2000	(Banchory-Devenick and Maryculter/Cookney)	17 Broadstraik Close, Elrick, Aberdeen AB32 6JP	01224 746888
Forbes, John W.A. BD	1973 1999	(Edzell Lethnot with Fern, Careston and Menmuir with Glenesk)	Little Ennochie Steading, Finzean, Banchory AB31 6LX [E-mail: johnrose.bbbb@talktalk.net]	01330 850785
Kinniburgh, Elizabeth B.F. (Miss) MA BD	1970 1986	(Birse with Finzean with Strachan)	7 Huntly Cottages, Aboyne AB31 5HD	01339 886757
Lamb, A. Douglas MA	1964 2002	(Dalry: St Margaret's)	130 Denstrath Road, Edzell Woods, Brechin DD9 7XF [E-mail: lamb.edzell@talk21.com]	01356 648139

Massie, Robert W. LTh	1989	2007	(Monifieth: St Rule's)	50 Boswell Road, Portlethen, Aberdeen AB12 4BB [E-mail: robertmassie@btinternet.com]	
Smith, Albert E. BD	1983	2006	(Methlick)	42 Haulkerton Crescent, Laurencekirk AB30 1FB [E-mail: aesmith42@googlemail.com]	01561 376111
Taylor, Peter R. JP BD	1977	2001	(Torphins)	42 Beltie Road, Torphins, Banchory AB31 4JT [E-mail: ptaylor850@btinternet.com]	01339 882780
Tierney, John P. MA	1945	1985	(Peterhead West: Associate)	3 Queenshill Drive, Aboyne AB34 5DG	01339 886741
Wallace, William F. BDS BD	1968	2008	(Wick: Pulteneytown and Thrumster)	Lachan Cottage, 29 Station Road, Banchory AB31 5XX [E-mail: williamwallace39@talktalk.net]	01330 822259
Watt, William D. LTh	1978	1996	(Aboyne – Dinnet)	2 West Toll Crescent, Aboyne AB34 5GB [E-mail: wdwatt22@tiscali.co.uk]	01339 886943

(33) GORDON

Meets at various locations on the first Tuesday of February, March, April, May, September, October, November and December, and on the last Tuesday of June.

Clerk:	**MR GERALD MOORE**	**7 Allathan Park, Pitmedden, Ellon AB41 7PX** **[E-mail: gordon@cofscotland.org.uk]**	**01651 842526**

Barthol Chapel linked with Tarves				
Isabel C. Buchan (Mrs) BSc BD RE(PgCE)	1975	2006	8 Murray Avenue, Tarves, Ellon AB41 7LZ [E-mail: buchan.123@btinternet.com]	01651 851250
Belhelvie (H)				
Paul McKeown BSc PhD BD	2000	2005	Belhelvie Manse, Balmedie, Aberdeen AB23 8YR [E-mail: pmckeown1@btconnect.com]	01358 742227
Blairdaff and Chapel of Garioch				
D. Brian Dobby MA BA	1999	2008	The Manse, Chapel of Garioch, Inverurie AB51 5HE [E-mail: briandobby@googlemail.com]	01467 681619
Cluny (H) linked with Monymusk (H)				
G. Euan D. Glen BSc BD	1992		The Manse, 26 St Ninian's, Monymusk, Inverurie AB51 7HF [E-mail: euanglen@aol.com]	01467 651470

Culsalmond and Rayne linked with Daviot (H)				
Mary M. Cranfield (Miss) MA BD DMin	1989		The Manse, Daviot, Inverurie AB51 0HY [E-mail: marymc@ukgateway.net]	01467 671241
Cushnie and Tough (T) (H)				
Rosemary Legge (Mrs) BSc BD MTh	1992	2010	The Manse, Muir of Fowlis, Alford AB33 8JU [E-mail: cushnietough@aol.com]	01975 581239
Daviot See Culsalmond and Rayne				
Echt linked with Midmar (H)				
Alan Murray BSc BD PhD	2003		The Manse, Echt, Westhill AB32 7AB [E-mail: ladecottage@btinternet.com]	01330 860004
Ellon				
Stephen Emery BD DPS	2006		The Manse, 12 Union Street, Ellon AB41 9BA [E-mail: stephen.emery2@btinternet.com]	01358 720476
Fintray Kinellar Keithhall				
Ellen Larson Davidson BA MDiv		2007	20 Kinmohr Rise, Blackburn, Aberdeen AB21 0LJ [E-mail: larsondavidson@gmail.com]	01224 791350
Foveran				
W. Kenneth Pryde DA BD	1994	2009	The Manse, Foveran, Ellon AB41 6AP [E-mail: wkpryde@hotmail.com]	01358 789288
Howe Trinity				
John A. Cook MA BD	1986	2000	The Manse, 110 Main Street, Alford AB33 8AD [E-mail: john.cook2@homecall.co.uk]	01975 562282
Huntly Cairnie Glass				
Thomas R. Calder LLB BD WS	1994		The Manse, Queen Street, Huntly AB54 8EB [E-mail: cairniechurch@aol.com]	01466 792630
Insch-Leslie-Premnay-Oyne (H)				
Jane C. Taylor (Miss) BD DipMin	1990	2001	22 Western Road, Insch AB52 6JR [E-mail: jane.c.taylor@btinternet.com]	01464 820914
Inverurie: St Andrew's				
T. Graeme Longmuir OSJ MA BEd FASC	1976	2001	St Andrew's Manse, 1 Ury Dale, Inverurie AB51 3XW [E-mail: standrew@ukonline.co.uk]	01467 620468

Inverurie: West				
Ian B. Groves BD CPS	1989		West Manse, 1 Westburn Place, Inverurie AB51 5QS [E-mail: i.groves@inveruriewestchurch.org]	01467 620285
Kemnay				
John P. Renton BA LTh	1976	1990	Kemnay, Inverurie AB51 9ND [E-mail: johnrenton@btinternet.com]	01467 642219 (Tel/Fax)
Kintore (H)				
Alan Greig BSc BD	1977	1992	28 Oakhill Road, Kintore, Inverurie AB51 0FH [E-mail: greig@kincarr.free-online.co.uk]	01467 632219
Meldrum and Bourtie				
Alison Jaffrey (Mrs) MA BD FSAScot	1990	2010	The Manse, Urquhart Road, Oldmeldrum, Inverurie AB51 0EX [E-mail: alison.jaffrey@bigfoot.com]	01651 872250
Methlick				
Matthew C. Canlis BA MDiv MLitt	2007		The Manse, Manse Road, Methlick, Ellon AB41 7DG [E-mail: mattcanlis@googlemail.com]	01651 806215
Midmar (H) See Echt				
Monymusk See Cluny				
New Machar				
Douglas G. McNab BA BD	1999	2010	The New Manse, Newmachar, Aberdeen AB21 0RD [E-mail: dougmcnab@aol.com]	01651 862278
Noth				
Regine U. Cheyne (Mrs) MA BSc BD	1988	2010	Manse of Noth, Kennethmont, Huntly AB54 4NP	01464 831690
Skene (H)				
Vacant			The Manse, Kirkton of Skene, Skene AB32 6LX	01224 743277
Marion G. Stewart (Miss) DCS			Kirk Cottage, Kirkton of Skene, Skene AB32 6XE	01224 743407
Strathbogie Drumblade				
Neil I.M. MacGregor BD	1995		49 Deveron Park, Huntly AB54 8UZ	01466 792702
Tarves See Barthol Chapel				
Udny and Pitmedden				
Vacant			Manse Road, Udny Green, Udny, Ellon AB41 7RS	01651 842052

Upper Donside (H)				
Brian Dingwall BTh CQSW	1999 2006		The Manse, Lumsden, Huntly AB54 4GQ [E-mail: upperdonsideparishchurch@btinternet.com]	01464 861757

Andrew, John MA BD DipRE DipEd	1961 1995	(Teacher: Religious Education)	Cartar's Croft, Midmar, Inverurie AB51 7NJ	01330 833208
Bowie, Alfred LTh	1974 1998	(Alford with Keig with Tullynessle Forbes)	17 Stewart Road, Alford AB33 8UA	01975 563824
Buchan, Alexander MA BD PGCE	1975 1992	(North Ronaldsay with Sanday)	8 Murray Avenue, Tarves, Ellon AB41 7LZ [E-mail: revabuchan@bluebucket.org]	01651 851250
Craggs, Sheila (Mrs)	2001 2008	(Auxiliary Minister)	7 Morar Court, Ellon AB41 9GG	01358 723055
Craig, Anthony J.D. BD	1987 2009	(Glasgow: Maryhill)	4 Hightown, Collieston, Ellon AB41 8RS [E-mail: craig.glasgow@gmx.net]	01358 751247
Dryden, Ian MA DipEd	1988 2001	(New Machar)	16 Glenhome Gardens, Dyce, Aberdeen AB21 7FG	01224 722820
Hawthorn, Daniel MA BD DMin	1965 2004	(Belhelvie)	7 Crimond Drive, Ellon AB41 8BT [E-mail: donhawthorn@compuserve.com]	01358 723981
Jones, Robert A. LTh CA	1966 1997	(Marnoch)	13 Gordon Terrace, Inverurie AB51 4GT	01467 622691
Lyon, Andrew LTh	1971 2007	(Fraserburgh West with Rathen West)	Barmekyn, Keig, Alford AB33 8BH [E-mail: andrew@lyon60.orangehome.co.uk]	01975 562768
Macalister, Eleanor	1994 2006	(Ellon)	2 Crimond Drive, Ellon AB41 8BT [E-mail: macal1ster@aol.com]	01358 722711
Macallan, Gerald B.	1954 1992	(Kintore)	38 Thorngrove House, 500 Great Western Road, Aberdeen AB10 6PF	01224 316125
Mack, John C. JP	1985 2008	(Auxiliary Minister)	The Willows, Auchleven, Insch AB52 6QB	01464 820387
McLean, John MA BD	1967 2003	(Bathgate: Boghall)	16 Eastside Drive, Westhill AB32 6QN	01224 747701
McLeish, Robert S.	1970 2000	(Insch-Leslie-Premnay-Oyne)	19 Western Road, Insch AB52 6JR	01464 820749
Rodger, Matthew A. BD	1978 1999	(Ellon)	15 Meadowlands Drive, Westhill AB32 6EJ	01224 743184
Scott, Allan D. BD	1977 1989	(Culsalmond with Daviot with Rayne)	20 Barclay Road, Inverurie AB51 3QP	01467 625161
Stewart, George C. MA	1952 1995	(Drumblade with Huntly Strathbogie)	104 Scott Drive, Huntly AB54 8PF	01466 792503
Stoddart, A. Grainger	1975 2001	(Meldrum and Bourtie)	6 Mayfield Gardens, Insch AB52 6XL	01464 821124
Thomson, Iain U. MA BD	1970 2011	(Skene)	4 Keirhill Gardens, Westhill AB32 6AZ [E-mail: iainuthomson@googlemail.com]	

(34) BUCHAN

Meets at St Kane's Centre, New Deer, Turriff on the first Tuesday of February, March, May, September, October, November and December, and on the third Tuesday of June.

Clerk:	**MR GEORGE W. BERSTAN**	**Faithlie, Victoria Terrace, Turriff AB53 4EE** **[E-mail: buchan@cofscotland.org.uk]**	**01888 562392**

Aberdour linked with Pitsligo
Vacant — The Manse, 49 Pitsligo Street, Rosehearty, Fraserburgh AB43 7JL

Auchaber United linked with Auchterless
Vacant — The Manse, Auchterless, Turriff AB53 8BA — 01888 511217

Auchterless See Auchaber United

Banff linked with King Edward (E-mail: banffkirk@btconnect.com)
Vacant — 7 Colleonard Road, Banff AB45 1DZ

Crimond linked with Lonmay
Vacant — The Manse, Crimond, Fraserburgh AB43 8QJ — 01346 532431

Cruden (H)
Rodger Neilson JP BSc BD — 1972 — 1974 — Hatton, Peterhead AB42 0QQ — 01779 841229
[E-mail: minister@crudenchurch.org.uk]

Deer (H)
Sheila M. Kirk BA LLB BD — 2007 — 2010 — The Manse, Old Deer, Peterhead AB42 5JB — 01771 623582

Fordyce
Norman Nicoll BD — 2003 — 2010 — The Manse, 4 Seafield Terrace, Portsoy, Banff AB45 2QB — 01261 842272
[E-mail: fordycechurch@btinternet.com]

Fraserburgh: Old
Peter B. Park BD MCIBS — 1997 — 2007 — 4 Robbies Road, Fraserburgh AB43 7AF — 01346 515332
[E-mail: peterpark9@btinternet.com]

Fraserburgh: South (H) linked with Inverallochy and Rathen: East
Ronald F. Yule — 1982 — 15 Victoria Street, Fraserburgh AB43 9PJ — 01346 518244

Fraserburgh: West (H) linked with Rathen: West
Carol Anne Parker (Mrs) BEd BD — 2009 — 4 Kirkton Gardens, Fraserburgh AB43 8TU — 01346 513303
[E-mail: ca.parker76@btinternet.com]

Fyvie linked with Rothienorman
Robert J. Thorburn BD 1978 2004 The Manse, Fyvie, Turriff AB53 8RD 01651 891230
[E-mail: rjthorburn@aol.com]

Gardenstown
Donald N. Martin BD 1996 The Manse, Fernie Brae, Gardenstown, Banff AB45 3YL 01261 851256
[E-mail: ferniebrae@gmail.com]

Inverallochy and Rathen: East See Fraserburgh: South
King Edward See Banff

Longside
Robert A. Fowlie BD 2007 9 Anderson Drive, Longside, Peterhead AB42 4XG 01779 821224
[E-mail: bob.fowlie@googlemail.com]

Lonmay See Crimond

Macduff
Calum Stark LLB BD 2011 Sol-y-Mar, Bath Street, Macduff AB44 1SA 01261 832316
[E-mail: calumstark@yahoo.co.uk]

Marnoch
Paul van Sittert BA BD 1997 2007 Marnoch Manse, 53 South Street, Aberchirder, Huntly AB54 7TS 01466 781143
[E-mail: vansittert@btinternet.com]

Maud and Savoch linked with New Deer: St Kane's
Paul R. Read BSc MA(Th) 2000 2010 The Manse, New Deer, Turriff AB53 6TD 01771 644216
[E-mail: prr747@aol.com]

Monquhitter and New Byth linked with Turriff: St Andrew's
James Cook MA MDiv 1999 2002 Balmellie Road, Turriff AB53 4SP 01888 560304
[E-mail: jmscook9@aol.com]

New Deer: St Kane's See Maud and Savoch

New Pitsligo linked with Strichen and Tyrie
Vacant Kingsville, Strichen, Fraserburgh AB43 6SQ

Ordiquhill and Cornhill (H) linked with Whitehills
Vacant 6 Craigneen Place, Whitehills, Banff AB45 2NE

Peterhead: Old				
Pauline Thomson (Mrs) MA BD	2006		1 Hawthorn Road, Peterhead AB42 2DW [E-mail: paulinethomson1@hotmail.com]	01779 472618
Peterhead: St Andrew's (H)				
Abi T. Ngunga GTh LTh MDiv MTh PhD	2001	2011	1 Landale Road, Peterhead AB42 1QN [E-mail: abi.t.ngunga@gmail.com]	01779 238200
Peterhead: Trinity				
L. Paul McClenaghan BA	1973	1996	18 Landale Road, Peterhead AB42 1QP [E-mail: paul.mcclenaghan@gmail.com]	01779 472405
Pitsligo See Aberdour **Rathen: West** See Fraserburgh: West **Rothienorman** See Fyvie				
St Fergus				
Vacant				
Sandhaven				
Vacant				
Strichen and Tyrie See New Pitsligo **Turriff: St Andrew's** See Monquhitter and New Byth				
Turriff: St Ninian's and Forglen				
Vacant			4 Deveronside Drive, Turriff AB53 4SP	
Whitehills See Ordiquhill and Cornhill				

Blaikie, James BD	1972 1997	(Berwick-on-Tweed: St Andrew's Wallace Green and Lowick)	57 Glenugie View, Peterhead AB42 2BW	01779 490625
Fawkes, G.M. Allan BA BSc JP	1979 2000	(Lonmay with Rathen: West)	3 Northfield Gardens, Hatton, Peterhead AB42 0SW	01779 841814
McKay, Margaret (Mrs) MA BD MTh	1991 2003	(Auchaber United with Auchterless)	The Smithy, Knowes of Elrick, Aberchirder, Huntly AB54 7PN [E-mail: elricksmithy@yahoo.co.uk]	(Tel) 01466 780208 (Fax) 01466 780015
McMillan, William J. CA LTh BD	1969 2004	(Sandsting and Aithsting with Walls and Sandness)	7 Ardinn Drive, Turriff AB53 4PR [E-mail: revbillymcmillan@aol.com]	01888 560727

Macnee, Iain LTh BD MA PhD	1975 2011	(New Pitsligo with Strichen and Tyrie)	Wardend Cottage, Alvah, Banff AB45 3TR [E-mail: macneeiain4@googlemail.com]	01261 851647
Noble, George S. DipTh	1972 2000	(Carfin with Newarthill)	Craigowan, 3 Main Street, Inverallochy, Fraserburgh AB43 8XX	01346 582749
Ross, David S. MSc PhD BD	1978 2003	Prison Chaplain Service	3–5 Abbey Street, Old Deer, Peterhead AB42 5LN [E-mail: padsross@btinternet.com]	01771 623994
Taylor, William MA MEd	1984 1996	(Buckie: North)	23 York Street, Peterhead AB42 1SN [E-mail: william.taylor@globalnet.co.uk]	01779 481798

(35) MORAY

Meets at St Andrew's-Lhanbryd and Urquhart on the first Tuesday of February, March, May, September, October, November and December, and at the Moderator's church on the fourth Tuesday of June.

Clerk:	**REV. HUGH M.C. SMITH LTh**	**Mortlach Manse, Dufftown, Keith AB55 4AR** **[E-mail: moray@cofscotland.org.uk]** **[E-mail: clerk@moraypresbytery.plus.com]**	**01340 820538**
Depute Clerk:	**REV. GRAHAM W. CRAWFORD BSc BD STM**	**The Manse, Prospect Terrace, Lossiemouth IV31 6JS**	**01343 810676**

Aberlour (H)				
Shuna M. Dicks BSc BD	2010		The Manse, Mary Avenue, Aberlour AB38 9QU [E-mail: revshuna@minister.com]	01340 871687
Alves and Burghead linked with Kinloss and Findhorn				
Vacant			The Manse, 4 Manse Road, Kinloss, Forres IV36 3GH	01309 690931
Bellie linked with Speymouth				
Alison C. Mehigan BD DPS	2003		11 The Square, Fochabers IV32 7DG [E-mail: alisonc@mehigan-ug.fsnet.co.uk]	01343 820256
Margaret King MA DCS	2007		56 Murrayfield, Fochabers IV32 7EZ	01343 820937
Birnie and Pluscarden linked with Elgin High				
Vacant			Daisy Bank, 5 Forteath Avenue, Elgin IV30 1TQ	01343 542449
Buckie: North (H)				
Vacant			14 St Peter's Road, Buckie AB56 1DL	01542 831328
Buckie: South and West (H) linked with Enzie				
Alan Macgregor BA BD	1992	2010	Craigendarroch, 14 Cliff Terrace, Buckie AB56 1LX [E-mail: buckiesouwester@btconnect.com] [E-mail: enziekirk@btconnect.com]	01542 833775

Cullen and Deskford (E-mail: www.cullen-deskford-church.org.uk)
Douglas F. Stevenson BD DipMin 1991 2010 3 Seafield Place, Cullen, Buckie AB56 4UU 01542 841963
[E-mail: dstevenson655@btinternet.com]

Dallas linked with Forres: St Leonard's (H) linked with Rafford
Donald K. Prentice BSc BD 1989 2010 St Leonard's Manse, Nelson Road, Forres IV36 1DR 01309 672380

Duffus, Spynie and Hopeman (H)
Bruce B. Lawrie BD 1974 2001 The Manse, Duffus, Elgin IV30 5QP 01343 830276
[E-mail: blawrie@zetnet.co.uk]

Dyke linked with Edinkillie
John Macgregor BD 2001 2011 Manse of Dyke, Brodie, Forres IV36 2TD 01309 641239

Edinkillie See Dyke
Elgin: High See Birnie and Pluscarden

Elgin: St Giles' (H) and St Columba's South (01343 551501) (E-mail: julie@elginstgandcsth.plus.com)
(Office and Church Halls: Greyfriars Street, Elgin IV30 1LF)
Vacant 18 Reidhaven Street, Elgin IV30 1QH 01343 547208
Anne Attenburrow BSc MBChB (Aux) 2006 2008 4 Jock Inksons Brae, Elgin IV30 1QE 01343 552330

Enzie See Buckie: South and West

Findochty linked with Portknockie linked with Rathven
Vacant 20 Netherton Terrace, Findochty, Buckie AB56 4QD 01542 833484

Forres: St Laurence (H)
Barry J. Boyd LTh DPS 1993 12 Mackenzie Drive, Forres IV36 2JP 01309 672260
[E-mail: barryj.boydstlaurence@btinternet.com] 07778 731018 (Mbl)

Forres: St Leonard's See Dallas

Keith: North, Newmill, Boharm and Rothiemay (H) (01542 886390)
G. Hutton B. Steel MA BD 1982 2010 North Manse, Church Road, Keith AB55 5BR 01542 882559
[E-mail: hsteel57@btinternet.com]
Ian Cunningham DCS The Manse, Rothiemay, Huntly AB54 7NE 01466 711334
[E-mail: icunninghamdcs@btinternet.com]

Keith: St Rufus, Botriphnie and Grange (H)
Ranald S.R. Gauld MA LLB BD 1991 1995 Church Road, Keith AB55 5BR 01542 882799
[E-mail: rev_gauld@btinternet.com]
Kay Gauld (Mrs) BD STM PhD (Assoc) 1999 Church Road, Keith AB55 5BR 01542 882799
[E-mail: kay_gauld@btinternet.com]

Kinloss and Findhorn See Alves and Burghead

Knockando, Elchies and Archiestown (H) linked with Rothes
Robert J.M. Anderson BD 1993 2000 The Manse, Rothes, Aberlour AB38 7AF 01340 831381
[E-mail: robert@carmanse.freeserve.co.uk]

Lossiemouth: St Gerardine's High (H)
Thomas M. Bryson BD 1997 2002 The Manse, St Gerardine's Road, Lossiemouth IV31 6RA 01343 813146
[E-mail: thomas@bryson547.fsworld.co.uk]

Lossiemouth: St James'
Graham W. Crawford BSc BD STM 1991 2003 The Manse, Prospect Terrace, Lossiemouth IV31 6JS 01343 810676
[E-mail: pictishreiver@aol.com]

Mortlach and Cabrach (H)
Hugh M.C. Smith LTh 1973 1982 Mortlach Manse, Dufftown, Keith AB55 4AR 01340 820380
[E-mail: clerk@moraypresbytery.plus.com]

Pluscarden See Birnie
Portknockie See Findochty
Rafford See Dallas
Rathven See Findochty
Rothes See Knockando, Elchies and Archiestown

St Andrew's-Lhanbryd (H) and Urquhart
Andrew J. Robertson BD 2008 2010 39 St Andrews Road, Lhanbryde, Elgin IV30 8PU 01343 843995
[E-mail: ajr247@btinternet.com]

Speymouth See Bellie

Bain, Brian LTh	1980	2007	(Gask with Methven and Logiealmond)	Bayview, 13 Stewart Street, Portgordon, Buckie AB56 5QT	01542 831215
Davidson, A.A.B. MA BD	1960	1997	(Grange with Rothiemay)	11 Sutors Rise, Nairn IV12 5BU	
Douglas, Christina A. (Mrs)	1987	1993	(Inveraven and Glenlivet)	White Cottage, St Fillans, Crieff PH6 2ND	
Evans, John W. MA BD	1945	1984	(Elgin: High)	15 Weaver Place, Elgin IV30 1HB	01343 543607
Mathew, J. Gordon MA BD	1973	2011	(Buckie: North)	2 Mallard Drive, Montrose DD10 9ND	01674 671310

Morton, Alasdair J. MA BD DipEd FEIS	1960	2000	(Bowden with Newtown)	16 St Leonard's Road, Forres IV36 1DW [E-mail: alasgilmor@hotmail.co.uk]	01309 671719
Morton, Gillian M. (Mrs) MA BD PGCE	1983	1996	(Hospital Chaplain)	16 St Leonard's Road, Forres IV36 1DW [E-mail: alasgilmor@hotmail.co.uk]	01309 671719
Poole, Ann McColl (Mrs) DipEd ACE LTh	1983	2003	(Dyke with Edinkillie)	Kirkside Cottage, Dyke, Forres IV36 2TF	01309 641046
Rollo, George B. BD	1974	2010	(Elgin: St Giles' and St Columba's South)	'Struan', 13 Meadow View, Hopeman, Elgin IV30 5PL [E-mail: rollos@gmail.com]	01343 835226
Scotland, Ronald J. BD	1993	2003	(Birnie with Pluscarden)	7A Rose Avenue, Elgin IV30 1NX	01343 543086
Shaw, Duncan LTh CPS	1984	2011	(Alves and Burghead with Kinloss and Findhorn)	73 Woodside Drive, Forres IV36 0UF	
Wright, David L. MA BD	1957	1998	(Stornoway: St Columba)	84 Wyvis Drive, Nairn IV12 4TP	01667 451613
Thomson, James M. BA	1952	2000	(Elgin: St Giles' and St Columba's South: Associate)	48 Mayne Road, Elgin IV30 1PD	01343 547664
Whittaker, Mary	2011		Auxiliary Minister	11 Templand Road, Lhanbryde, Elgin IV30 8BR	
Whyte, David LTh	1993	2011	(Boat of Garten, Duthil and Kincardine)	1 Lemanfield Crescent, Garmouth, Fochabers IV32 7LS [E-mail: whytedj@btinternet.com]	01343 870667

(36) ABERNETHY

Meets at Boat of Garten on the first Tuesday of February, March, April, June, September, October, November and December.

Clerk: REV. JAMES A.I. MACEWAN MA BD — **The Manse, Nethy Bridge PH25 3DG** — **01479 821280**
[E-mail: abernethy@cofscotland.org.uk]

Abernethy (H) linked with Cromdale (H) and Advie
James A.I. MacEwan MA BD 1973 1980 The Manse, Nethy Bridge PH25 3DG 01479 821280
[E-mail: manse@nethybridge.freeserve.co.uk]

Alvie and Insh (T) (H) linked with Rothiemurchus and Aviemore (H)
Ron C. Whyte BD CPS 1990 2007 The Manse, 8 Dalfaber Park, Aviemore PH22 1QF 01479 810280
[E-mail: ron4xst@aol.com]

Boat of Garten (H), Duthil (H) and Kincardine
Vacant The Manse, Deshar Road, Boat of Garten PH24 3BN 01479 831252

Cromdale and Advie See Abernethy

Dulnain Bridge (H) linked with Grantown-on-Spey (H)
Morris Smith BD 1988 The Manse, Golf Course Road, Grantown-on-Spey PH26 3HY 01479 872084
[E-mail: mosmith.themanse@btinternet.com]

Grantown-on-Spey See Dulnain Bridge

Kingussie (H)
Helen Cook (Mrs) BD 1974 2003 The Manse, 18 Hillside Avenue, Kingussie PH21 1PA 01540 661311
[E-mail: revhcook@btinternet.com]

Laggan linked with Newtonmore (H)
Catherine A. Buchan (Mrs) MA MDiv 2002 2009 The Manse, Fort William Road, Newtonmore PH20 1DG 01540 673238
[E-mail: catherinebuchan567@btinternet.com]

Newtonmore See Laggan
Rothiemurchus and Aviemore (H) See Alvie and Insh

Tomintoul (H), Glenlivet and Inveraven
Vacant The Manse, Tomintoul, Ballindalloch AB37 9HA 01807 580254

Bardgett, Frank D. MA BD PhD	1987	2001	(Board of National Mission)	Tigh an Iasgair, Street of Kincardine, Boat of Garten PH24 3BY [E-mail: tigh@bardgett.plus.com]	01479 831751
Bjarnason, Sven S. CandTheol	1975	2011	(Tomintoul, Glenlivet and Inveraven)	14 Edward Street, Dunfermline KY12 0JW [E-mail: sven@bjarnason.org.uk]	01383 724625

(37) INVERNESS

Meets at Inverness, in Inverness: Trinity, on the first Tuesday of February, March, April, May, September, October, November and December, and at the Moderator's church on the fourth Tuesday of June.

Clerk: REV. ALASTAIR S. YOUNGER BScEcon ASCC 33 Duke's View, Slackbuie, Inverness IV2 6BB 01463 242873
[E-mail: inverness@cofscotland.org.uk]

Ardersier (H) linked with Petty
Alexander Whiteford LTh 1996 Ardersier, Inverness IV2 7SX 01667 462224
[E-mail: a.whiteford@ukonline.co.uk]

Auldearn and Dalmore linked with Nairn: St Ninian's				
Richard Reid BSc BD MTh	1991	2005	The Manse, Auldearn, Nairn IV12 5SX	01667 451675
Cawdor (H) linked with Croy and Dalcross (H)				
Janet S. Mathieson MA BD	2003		The Manse, Croy, Inverness IV2 5PH [E-mail: mathieson173@btinternet.com]	01667 493217
Croy and Dalcross See Cawdor				
Culloden: The Barn (H)				
James H. Robertson BSc BD	1975	1994	45 Oakdene Court, Culloden IV2 7XL [E-mail: revjimrculloden@aol.com]	01463 790504
Daviot and Dunlichity linked with Moy, Dalarossie and Tomatin				
Reginald F. Campbell BD DipChEd	1979	2003	The Manse, Daviot, Inverness IV2 5XL [E-mail: campbell578@talktalk.net]	01463 772242
Dores and Boleskine				
Vacant				
Inverness: Crown (H) (01463 238929)				
Peter H. Donald MA PhD BD	1991	1998	39 Southside Road, Inverness IV2 4XA [E-mail: pdonald7@aol.com]	01463 230537
Inverness: Dalneigh and Bona (GD) (H)				
Vacant			9 St Mungo Road, Inverness IV3 5AS	01463 232339
Inverness: East (H)				
Rev. Professor A.T.B. McGowan BD STM PhD	1979	2009	2 Victoria Drive, Inverness IV2 3QD [E-mail: ATBMcGowan@gmail.com]	01463 238770
Inverness: Hilton				
Duncan MacPherson LLB BD	1994		66 Culduthel Mains Crescent, Inverness IV2 6RG [E-mail: duncan@hiltonchurch.org.uk]	01463 231417

Inverness: Inshes (H)				
Alistair Malcolm BD DPS	1976	1992	48 Redwood Crescent, Milton of Leys, Inverness IV2 6HB [E-mail: ali.inshes@btinternet.com]	01463 772402
Inverness: Kinmylies (H)				
Peter M. Humphris BSc BD	1976	2001	2 Balnafettack Place, Inverness IV3 8TQ [E-mail: peter@humphris.co.uk]	01463 709893
Inverness: Ness Bank (T) (H)				
Fiona E. Smith (Mrs) LLB BD	2010		15 Ballifeary Road, Inverness IV3 5PJ [E-mail: fiona.denhead@btopenworld.com]	01463 234653
Inverness: Old High St Stephen's				
Peter W. Nimmo BD ThM	1996	2004	24 Damfield Road, Inverness IV2 3HU [E-mail: peternimmo@minister.com]	01463 250802
Inverness: St Columba (New Charge) (H)				
Vacant			20 Bramble Close, Inverness IV2 6BS	
Inverness: Trinity (H)				
Alistair Murray BD	1984	2004	60 Kenneth Street, Inverness IV3 5PZ [E-mail: a.murray111@btinternet.com]	01463 234756
Kilmorack and Erchless				
Edgar J. Ogston BSc BD	1976	2007	'Roselynn', Croyard Road, Beauly IV4 7DJ [E-mail: edgar.ogston@macfish.com]	01463 782260
Kiltarlity linked with Kirkhill				
Kobus Smit BA BTh MTh DLitt	1982	2010	Wardlaw Manse, Wardlaw Road, Kirkhill, Inverness IV5 7NZ [E-mail: kobus.smit1951@gmail.com]	01463 831662

Kirkhill See Kiltarlity
Moy, Dalarossie and Tomatin See Daviot and Dunlichity

Nairn: Old (H)				
Ian W.F. Hamilton BD LTh ALCM AVCM	1978	1986	3 Manse Road, Nairn IV12 4RN [E-mail: reviwfh@btinternet.com]	01667 452203

Nairn: St Ninian's (H) See Auldearn and Dalmore
Petty See Ardersier

Urquhart and Glenmoriston (H)

Hugh F. Watt BD DPS	1986	1996	Blairbeg, Drumnadrochit, Inverness IV3 6UG [E-mail: hw@tinyworld.co.uk]	01456 450231

Black, Archibald T. BSc	1964 1997	(Inverness: Ness Bank)	16 Elm Park, Inverness IV2 4WN		01463 230588
Brown, Derek G. BD DipMin DMin	1989 1994	Chaplain: NHS Highland	Cathedral Manse, Cnoc-an-Lobht, Dornoch IV25 3HN [E-mail: revsbrown@aol.com]		01862 810296
Buell, F. Bart BA MDiv	1980 1995	(Urquhart and Glenmoriston)	6 Towerhill Place, Cradlehall, Inverness IV2 5FN [E-mail: bart@tower22.freeserve.co.uk]		01463 794634
Chisholm, Archibald F. MA	1957 1997	(Braes of Rannoch with Foss and Rannoch)	32 Seabank Road, Nairn IV12 4EU		01667 452001
Christie, James LTh	1993 2003	(Dores and Boleskine)	20 Wester Inshes Crescent, Inverness IV2 5HL		01463 710534
Donn, Thomas M. MA	1932 1969	(Duthil)	Kingsmills Nursing Home, Inverness		
Frizzell, R. Stewart BD	1961 2000	(Wick: Old)	98 Boswell Road, Inverness IV2 3EW		01463 231907
Hunt, Trevor G. BA BD	1986 2011	(Evie with Firth with Rendall)	7 Woodville Court, Culduthel Avenue, Inverness IV2 6BX [E-mail: trevorghunt@yahoo.co.uk]	 (Mbl)	01463 250355 07753 423333
Jeffrey, Stewart D. BSc BD	1962 1997	(Banff with King Edward)	10 Grigor Drive, Inverness IV2 4LP [E-mail: stewart.jeffrey@talktalk.net]		01463 230085
Lacey, Eric R. BD	1971 1992	(Creich with Rosehall)	78 Laggan Road, Inverness IV2 4EW		01463 235006
Livesley, Anthony LTh	1979 1997	(Kiltearn)	87 Beech Avenue, Nairn IV12 5SX [E-mail: a.livesley@tesco.net]		01667 455126
Logan, Robert J.V. MA BD	1962 2001	(Abdie and Dunbog with Newburgh)	Lindores, 1 Murray Place, Smithton, Inverness IV2 7PX [E-mail: rjvlogan@btinternet.com]		01463 790226
Macdonald, Aonghas I. MA BD	1967 2007	(Inverness: East)	41 Castlehill Park, Inverness IV2 5GJ [E-mail: aonghas@ukonline.co.uk]		01463 792275
Mackenzie, Seoras L. BD	1996 1998	Chaplain: Army	3 Scots, Fort George, Ardersier, Inverness IV1 2TD		
Macritchie, Iain A.M. BSc BD STM PhD	1987 1998	Chaplain: Inverness Hospitals	7 Merlin Crescent, Inverness IV2 3TE		01463 235204
Mitchell, Joyce (Mrs) DCS	1994	(Deacon)	Sunnybank, Farr, Inverness IV2 6XG [E-mail: joyce@mitchell71.freeserve.co.uk]		01808 521285
Morrison, Hector BSc BD MTh	1981 1994	Lecturer: Highland Theological College	24 Oak Avenue, Inverness IV2 4NX		01463 238561
Rettie, James A. BTh	1981 1999	(Melness and Eriboll with Tongue)	2 Trantham Drive, Westhill, Inverness IV2 5QT		01463 798896
Robb, Rodney P.T.	1995 2004	(Stirling: St Mark's)	2A Mayfield Road, Inverness IV2 4AE		
Robertson, Fergus A. MA BD	1971 2010	(Inverness: Dalneigh and Bona)	16 Druid Temple Way, Inverness IV2 6UQ		01463 718462
Stirling, G. Alan S. MA	1960 1999	(Leochel Cushnie and Lynturk with Tough)	97 Lochlann Road, Culloden, Inverness IV2 7HJ		01463 798313
Turner, Fraser K. LTh	1994 2007	(Kiltarlity with Kirkhill)	[E-mail: fraseratq@yahoo.co.uk]		
Waugh, John L. LTh	1973 2002	(Ardclach with Auldearn and Dalmore)	58 Wyvis Drive, Nairn IV12 4TP [E-mail: jswaugh@care4free.net]	(Tel/Fax)	01667 456397
Wilson, Ian M.	1988 1993	(Cawdor with Croy and Dalcross)	17 Spires Crescent, Nairn IV12 5PZ		01667 452977

Younger, Alastair S. BScEcon ASCC	1969 2008	(Inverness: St Columba High)	33 Duke's View, Slackbuie, Inverness IV2 6BB [E-mail: younger873@btinternet.com]	01463 242873

INVERNESS ADDRESSES

Inverness			
Crown	Kingsmills Road x Midmills Road		
Dalneigh and Bona	St Mary's Avenue		
East	Academy Street x Margaret Street		
Hilton	Druid Road x Tomatin Road		
Inshes	Inshes Retail Park		
Kinmylies	Kinmylies Way		
Ness Bank	Ness Bank x Castle Road		
St Columba High	Bank Street x Fraser Street		
St Stephen's	Old Edinburgh Road x Southside Road		
The Old High	Church Street x Church Lane		
Trinity	Huntly Place x Upper Kessock Street		
Nairn			
Old	Academy Street x Seabank Road		
St Ninian's	High Street x Queen Street		

(38) LOCHABER

Meets at Caol, Fort William, in Kilmallie Church Hall at 6pm, on the first Tuesday of September and December, on the last Tuesday of October and on the fourth Tuesday of March. The June meeting is held at 6pm on the first Tuesday in the church of the incoming Moderator.

Clerk:	**MRS ELLA GILL**	**5 Camus Inas, Acharacle PH36 4JQ [E-mail: lochaber@cofscotland.org.uk]**	**01967 431834/431305**
Treasurer:	**MRS PAT WALKER**	**Tigh a' Chlann, Inverroy, Roy Bridge PH31 4AQ [E-mail: pw-15@tiscali.co.uk]**	**01397 712028**

Acharacle (H) linked with Ardnamurchan

Vacant			The Manse, Acharacle PH36 4JU	01967 431561

Ardgour and Kingairloch linked with Morvern linked with Strontian

Donald G.B. McCorkindale BD DipMin	1992	2011	The Manse, 2 The Meadows, Strontian, Acharacle PH36 4HZ [E-mail: donald.mccorkindale@live.com]	01967 402234

Ardnamurchan See Acharacle

Duror (H) linked with Glencoe: St Munda's (H) (T)

Vacant			The Manse, Ballachulish PH49 4JG	01855 811998

Fort Augustus linked with Glengarry				
Vacant			The Manse, Fort Augustus PH32 4BH	01320 366210
Fort William: Duncansburgh MacIntosh (H) linked with Kilmonivaig				
Donald A. MacQuarrie BSc BD	1979	1990	The Manse of Duncansburgh, The Parade, Fort William PH33 6BA [E-mail: pdmacq@ukgateway.net]	01397 702297
Glencoe: St Munda's See Duror				
Glengarry See Fort Augustus				
Kilmallie				
Richard T. Corbett BSc MSc PhD BD	1992	2005	Kilmallie Manse, Corpach, Fort William PH33 7JS [E-mail: richard.t.corbett@btinternet.com]	01397 772736
Kilmonivaig See Fort William: Duncansburgh MacIntosh				
Kinlochleven (H) linked with Nether Lochaber (H)				
Malcolm A. Kinnear MA BD PhD	2010		The Manse, Lochaber Road, Kinlochleven, Argyll PH50 4QW [E-mail: malcolmkinnear@live.co.uk]	01855 831227
Morvern See Ardgour				
Nether Lochaber See Kinlochleven				
North West Lochaber				
Vacant			Church of Scotland Manse, Mallaig PH41 4RG	01687 462816
Strontian See Ardgour				

Anderson, David M. MSc FCOptom	1984		Auxiliary Minister	'Mirlos', 1 Dumfries Place, Fort William PH33 6UQ	01397 703203
Beaton, Jamesina (Miss) DCS			(Deacon)	Farhills, Fort Augustus PH32 4DS	01320 366252
Burnside, William A.M. MA BD PGCE	1990		Teacher: Religious Education	The Manse, Ballachulish PH49 4JG	01855 811998
Carmichael, James A. LTh	1976	2006	(Ardgour with Strontian)	Linnhe View, 5 Clovulin, Ardgour, Fort William PH33 7AB	01855 841351
Grainger, Alison J. BD	1995		(Acharacle with Ardnamurchan)	c/o The Ministries Council, 121 George Street, Edinburgh EH2 4YN [E-mail: revajgrainger@btinternet.com]	0131-225 5722
Lamb, Alan H.W. BA MTh	1959	2005	(Associate Minister)	Smiddy House, Arisaig PH39 4NH [E-mail: h.a.lamb@handalamb.plus.com]	01687 450227

Rae, Peter C. BSc BD	1968 2000	(Beath and Cowdenbeath: North)	8 Wether Road, Great Cambourne, Cambridgeshire CB23 5DT	
Varwell, Adrian P.J. BA BD PhD	1983 2011	(Fort Augustus with Glengarry)	19 Enrick Close, Kilmore, Drumnadrochit, Inverness IV63 6TP	01456 459352
Winning, A. Ann MA DipEd BD	1984 2006	(Morvern)	'Westering', 13C Carnoch, Glencoe, Ballachulish PH49 4HQ [E-mail: annw@morvern13.fslife.co.uk]	01855 811929

LOCHABER Communion Sundays

Acharacle	1st Mar, Jun, Sep, Dec	Fort William Duncansburgh MacIntosh	1st Apr, Jun, Oct	Kinlochleven	1st Feb, Apr, Jun, Oct, Dec
Ardgour	1st Jun, Sep, Dec, Easter	Glencoe	1st Apr, Oct	Morvern	Easter, 1st Jul, 4th Sep, 1st Dec
Ardnamurchan	1st Apr, Aug, Dec	Glengarry	1st Jan, Apr, Jul, Oct	Nether Lochaber	1st Apr, Oct
Duror	2nd Jun, 3rd Nov	Kilmallie	3rd Mar, May, Sep, 1st Dec	North West Lochaber	1st May, Nov
Fort Augustus	1st Jan, Apr, Jul, Oct	Kilmonivaig	1st May, Nov	Strontian	1st Jun, Sep, Dec

(39) ROSS

Meets on the first Tuesday of September in the church of the incoming Moderator, and in Dingwall: Castle Street Church on the first Tuesday of October, November, December, February, March and May, and on the last Tuesday of June.

Clerk:	**MR RONALD W. GUNSTONE BSc**	**20 Bellfield Road, North Kessock, Inverness IV1 3XU** **[E-mail: ross@cofscotland.org.uk]**	**01463 731337**

Alness

Ronald Morrison BD	1996		27 Darroch Brae, Alness IV17 0SD [E-mail: ranald@rmorrison.plus.com]	01349 882238

Avoch linked with Fortrose and Rosemarkie

Alan T. McKean BD CertMin	1982	2010	5 Nessway, Fortrose IV10 8SS [E-mail: a.mckean2345@btinternet.com]	01381 621433

Contin (H) linked with Fodderty and Strathpeffer (H)

Vacant			The Manse, Contin, Strathpeffer IV14 9ES	01997 423296

Cromarty linked with Resolis and Urquhart

Vacant			The Manse, Culbokie, Dingwall IV7 8JN	01349 877452

Dingwall: Castle Street (H)
Bruce Ritchie BSc BD PhD 1977 2006 16 Achany Road, Dingwall IV15 9JB 01349 863167
[E-mail: brucezomba@hotmail.com]

Dingwall: St Clement's (H)
Russel Smith BD 1994 8 Castlehill Road, Dingwall IV15 9PB 01349 861011
[E-mail: russel@stclementschurch.fsnet.co.uk]

Fearn Abbey and Nigg linked with Tarbat
David V. Scott BTh 1994 2006 Church of Scotland Manse, Fearn, Tain IV20 1TN 01862 832626 (Tel/Fax)

Ferintosh
Andrew F. Graham BTh DPS 2001 2006 Ferintosh Manse, Leanaig Road, Conon Bridge, Dingwall IV7 8BE 01349 861275
[E-mail: afg1960@tiscali.co.uk]

Fodderty and Strathpeffer (H) See Contin
Fortrose and Rosemarkie See Avoch

Invergordon
Kenneth Donald Macleod BD CPS 1989 2000 The Manse, Cromlet Drive, Invergordon IV18 0BA 01349 852273
[E-mail: kd-macleod@tiscali.co.uk]

Killearnan (H) linked with Knockbain (H)
Iain Ramsden BTh 1999 The Church of Scotland Manse, Coldwell Road, Artafallie, North Kessock, Inverness IV1 3ZE 01463 731333
[E-mail: s4rev@cqm.co.uk]

Kilmuir and Logie Easter
Fraser M.C. Stewart BSc BD 1980 2011 Delny, Invergordon IV18 0NW 01862 842280
[E-mail: fraserstewart1955@hotmail.com]

Kiltearn (H)
Donald A. MacSween BD 1991 1998 The Manse, Swordale Road, Evanton, Dingwall IV16 9UZ 01349 830472
[E-mail: donaldmacsween@hotmail.com]

Knockbain See Killearnan

Lochbroom and Ullapool (GD)
Wilhelm Lectus Steenkamp BA BTh MTh DTh 1978 2009 The Manse, Garve Road, Ullapool IV26 2SX 01854 612050
[E-mail: lectusullapool@btinternet.com]

Resolis and Urquhart See Cromarty

Rosskeen
Robert Jones BSc BD 1990 Rosskeen Manse, Perrins Road, Alness IV17 0SX 01349 882265
[E-mail: rob2jones@btinternet.com]

Tain
Paul Gibson BA BD 2011 14 Kingsway Avenue, Tain IV19 1NJ 01862 894140
[E-mail: paulg1bson@talktalk.net]

Tarbat See Fearn Abbey and Nigg

Urray and Kilchrist
Scott Polworth LLB BD 2009 The Manse, Corrie Road, Muir of Ord IV6 7TL 01463 870259
[E-mail: scottpolworth@btinternet.com]

Name			Former charge	Address	Telephone
Bell, C.J. Grant DipTh	1983	2010	(Resolis and Urquhart)	Tikvah, 4 Tomich, Beauly IV4 7AS [E-mail: grantbell@hotmail.co.uk]	01463 783504 (Mbl) 07729 926381
Buchan, John BD MTh	1968	1993	(Fodderty and Strathpeffer)	'Faithlie', 45 Swanston Avenue, Inverness IV3 6QW	01463 713114
Dupar, Kenneth W. BA BD PhD	1965	1993	(Christ's College, Aberdeen)	The Old Manse, The Causeway, Cromarty IV11 8XJ	01381 600428
Forsyth, James LTh	1970	2000	(Fearn Abbey with Nigg Chapelhill)	Rhives Lodge, Golspie, Sutherland KW10 6DD	
Glass, Alexander OBE MA	1998	2009	(Auxiliary Minister)	Craigton, Tulloch Avenue, Dingwall IV15 9TU	01349 863258
Holroyd, Gordon BTh FPhS FSAScot	1959	1993	(Dingwall: St Clement's)	22 Stuarthill Drive, Maryburgh, Dingwall IV15 9HU	01349 863379
Horne, Douglas A. BD	1977	2009	(Tain)	151 Holm Farm Road, Culduthel, Inverness IV2 6BF [E-mail: douglas.horne@virgin.net]	01463 712677
Liddell, Margaret (Miss) BD DipTh	1987	1997	(Contin)	20 Wyvis Crescent, Conon Bridge, Dingwall IV7 8BZ [E-mail: margaretliddell@talktalk.net]	01349 865997
Mackinnon, R.M. LTh	1968	1995	(Kilmuir and Logie Easter)	27 Riverford Crescent, Conon Bridge, Dingwall IV7 8HL	01349 866293
McLean, Gordon LTh	1972	2008	(Contin)	Beinn Dhorain, Kinnettas Square, Strathpeffer IV14 9BD [E-mail: gmaclean@hotmail.co.uk]	01997 421380
MacLennan, Alasdair J. BD DCE	1978	2001	(Resolis and Urquhart)	Airdale, Seaforth Road, Muir of Ord IV6 7TA	01463 870704
Macleod, John MA	1959	1993	(Resolis and Urquhart)	'Benview', 19 Balvaird, Muir of Ord IV6 7RG [E-mail: sheilaandjohn@yahoo.co.uk]	01463 871286
McWilliam, Thomas M. MA BD	1964	2003	(Contin)	Flat 3, 13 Culduthel Road, Inverness IV2 4AG [E-mail: thomas.mcwilliam491@btinternet.com]	01463 718981
Niven, William W. BTh	1982	1995	(Alness)	4 Obsdale Park, Alness IV17 0TP	01349 882427
Rutherford, Ellen B. (Miss) MBE DCS			(Deaconess)	41 Duncanston, Conon Bridge, Dingwall IV7 8JB	01349 877439

Tallach, John MA MLitt 1970 2010 (Cromarty) 29 Firthview Drive, Inverness IV3 8NS 01463 418721
[E-mail: j.tallach@tiscali.co.uk]

(40) SUTHERLAND

Meets at Lairg on the first Tuesday of March, May, September, November and December, and on the first Tuesday of June at the Moderator's church.

Clerk: MRS MARY J. STOBO **Druim-an-Sgairnich, Ardgay IV24 3BG** **01863 766868**
[E-mail: sutherland@cofscotland.org.uk]

Altnaharra and Farr
Vacant The Manse, Bettyhill, Thurso KW14 7SS 01641 521208

Assynt and Stoer
Continued Vacancy Canisp Road, Lochinver, Lairg IV27 4LH 01571 844342

Clyne (H) linked with Kildonan and Loth Helmsdale (H)
Vacant Golf Road, Brora KW9 6QS 01408 621239

Creich See Kincardine Croick and Edderton

Dornoch Cathedral (H)
Susan M. Brown (Mrs) BD DipMin 1985 1998 Cnoc-an-Lobht, Dornoch IV25 3HN 01862 810296
[E-mail: revsbrown@aol.com]

Durness and Kinlochbervie
John T. Mann BSc BD 1990 1998 Manse Road, Kinlochbervie, Lairg IV27 4RG 01971 521287
[E-mail: jtmklb@aol.com]

Eddrachillis
John MacPherson BSc BD 1993 Church of Scotland Manse, Scourie, Lairg IV27 4TQ 01971 502431

Golspie
John B. Sterrett BA BD PhD 2007 The Manse, Fountain Road, Golspie KW10 6TH 01408 633295 (Tel/Fax)
[E-mail: johnbsterrett@yahoo.co.uk]

Kildonan and Loth Helmsdale (H) See Clyne

Kincardine Croick and Edderton linked with Creich linked with Rosehall

Anthony M. Jones BD DPS DipTheol CertMin FRSA	1994	2010	The Manse, Ardgay IV24 3BG [E-mail: revanthonymjones@amserve.com]	01863 766285

Lairg (H) linked with Rogart (H)

Vacant			The Manse, Lairg IV27 4EH	01549 402373

Melness and Tongue (H)

Stewart Goudie BSc BD	2010		St Andrew's Manse, Tongue, Lairg IV27 4XL [E-mail: Stewart@Goudie.me.uk]	01847 611230 (Tel/Fax) 07957 237757 (Mbl)

Rogart See Lairg
Rosehall See Kincardine Croick and Edderton

Archer, Nicholas D.C. BA BD	1971	1992	(Dores and Boleskine)	Hillview, Edderton, Tain IV19 4AJ	01862 821494
Chambers, John OBE BSc	1972	2009	(Inverness: Ness Bank)	Bannlagan Lodge, 4 Earls Cross Gardens, Dornoch IV25 3NR [E-mail: chambersdornoch@btinternet.com]	01862 811520
Goskirk, J.L. LTh	1968	2010	(Lairg with Rogart)	Rathvilly, Lairgmuir, Lairg IV27 4ED [E-mail: leslie_goskirk@sky.com]	01549 402569
McCree, Ian W. BD	1971	2011	(Clyne with Kildonan and Loth Helmsdale)	Tigh Ardachu, Mosshill, Brora KW9 6NG [E-mail: ian@mccree.f9.co.uk]	
Macdonald, Michael	2004		Auxiliary Minister	73 Firhill, Alness IV17 0RT [E-mail: mike_mary@hotmail.co.uk]	01349 884268
Muckart, Graeme W.M. MTh MSc FSAScot	1983	2009	(Kincardine Croick and Edderton)	Kildale, Clashmore, Dornoch IV25 3RG [E-mail: avqt18@dsl.pipex.com]	

(41) CAITHNESS

Meets alternately at Wick and Thurso on the first Tuesday of February, March, May, September, November and December, and the third Tuesday of June.

Clerk:	**REV. RONALD JOHNSTONE BD**	**2 Comlifoot Drive, Halkirk KW12 6ZA [E-mail: caithness@cofscotland.org.uk]**	**01847 839033**

Bower linked with Halkirk Westerdale linked with Watten

Alastair H. Gray MA BD	1978	2005	Station Road, Watten, Wick KW1 5YN [E-mail: alastair.h.gray@btinternet.com]	01955 621220

Canisbay linked with Dunnet linked with Keiss
Vacant | The Manse, Canisbay, Wick KW1 4YH | 01955 611756

Dunnet See Canisbay
Halkirk Westerdale See Bower
Keiss See Canisbay

Olrig linked with Thurso: St Peter's and St Andrew's (H)
Fanus Erasmus MA LTh MTh ThD 1978 2010 | The Manse, 40 Rose Street, Thurso KW14 8RF [E-mail: spacosminister@btinternet.com] | 01847 895186

The North Coast Parish
Vacant | Church of Scotland Manse, Reay, Thurso KW14 7RE | 01847 811441

The Parish of Latheron
Gordon Oliver BD 1979 2010 | Central Manse, Main Street, Lybster KW3 6BJ [E-mail: parish-of-latheron@btconnect.com] | 01593 721706

Thurso: St Peter's and St Andrew's See Olrig

Thurso: West (H)
Vacant | Thorkel Road, Thurso KW14 7LW | 01847 892663

Watten See Bower

Wick: Pulteneytown (H) and Thrumster
Vacant | The Manse, Coronation Street, Wick KW1 5LS | 01955 603166

Wick: St Fergus
John Nugent 1999 2011 | Mansefield, Miller Avenue, Wick KW1 4DF [E-mail: johnnugentis@mail2web.com] | 01955 602167

Craw, John DCS	1998 2009	(Deacon)	Liabost, 8 Proudfoot Road, Wick KW1 4PQ [E-mail: johncraw607@btinternet.com]	01955 603805 (Mbl) 07544 761653
Johnstone, Ronald BD	1977 2011	(Thurso: West)	2 Comlifoot Drive, Halkirk KW12 6ZA [E-mail: ronaldjohnstone@btinternet.com]	01847 839033
Mappin, Michael G. BA	1961 1998	(Bower with Watten)	Mundays, Banks Road, Watten, Wick KW1 5YL	01955 621720
Warner, Kenneth BD	1981 2008	(Halkirk and Westerdale)	Kilearnan, Clayock, Halkirk KW12 6UZ [E-mail: wrnrkenn@aol.com]	01847 831825

Warwick, Ivan C. TD MA BD	1980 2010	Development Officer and Community Minister	94 Willowbank, Wick KW1 4PE [E-mail: L70rev@btinternet.com]	(Mbl) 07787 535083

CAITHNESS Communion Sundays

Bower	1st Jul, Dec	North Coast	Mar, Easter, Jun, Sep, Dec	Watten	1st Jul, Dec
Canisbay	1st Jun, Nov	Olrig	last May, Nov	Wick	
Dunnet	last May, Nov	Thurso		Pulteneytown and Thrumster	1st Mar, Jun, Sep, Dec
Halkirk Westerdale	Apr, Jul, Oct	St Peter's and St Andrew's	Mar, Jun, Sep, Dec	St Fergus	Apr, Oct
Keiss	1st May, 3rd Nov	West	4th Mar, Jun, Nov		
Latheron	Apr, Jul, Sep, Nov				

(42) LOCHCARRON – SKYE

Meets in Kyle on the first Tuesday of each month, except January, May, July and August.

Clerk:	**REV. ALLAN J. MACARTHUR BD**	**High Barn, Croft Road, Lochcarron, Strathcarron IV54 8YA** **[E-mail: lochcarronskye@cofscotland.org.uk]** **[E-mail: a.macarthur@btinternet.com]**	**01520 722278 (Tel)** **01520 722674 (Fax)**

Applecross, Lochcarron and Torridon (GD)				
David Macleod	2008		The Manse, Colonel's Road, Lochcarron, Strathcarron IV54 8YG [E-mail: david.macleod@me.com]	01520 722829
Bracadale and Duirinish (GD)				
Geoffrey D. McKee BA	1997	2009	Duirinish Manse, Dunvegan, Isle of Skye IV55 8WQ [E-mail: geoff.mckee@btinternet.com]	01470 521457
Gairloch and Dundonnell				
Derek Morrison	1995	2000	Church of Scotland Manse, The Glebe, Gairloch IV21 2BT [E-mail: derekmorrison1@aol.com]	01445 712053 (Tel/Fax)
Glenelg and Kintail				
Roderick N. MacRae BTh	2001	2004	Church of Scotland Manse, Inverinate, Kyle IV40 8HE [E-mail: barvalous@msn.com]	01599 511245

Kilmuir and Stenscholl (GD)				
Ivor MacDonald BSc MSc BD	1993	2000	Staffin, Portree, Isle of Skye IV51 9JX [E-mail: ivormacdonald@btinternet.com]	01470 562759 (Tel/Fax)
Lochalsh				
John M. Macdonald	2002		The Church of Scotland Manse, Main Street, Kyle IV40 8DA [E-mail: john.macdonald53@btinternet.com]	01599 534294
Portree (GD)				
Sandor Fazakas BD MTh	1976	2007	Viewfield Road, Portree, Isle of Skye IV51 9ES [E-mail: fazakass52@yahoo.com]	01478 611868
Snizort (H) (GD)				
Robert L. Calhoun BBA MDiv DMin	1974	2009	The Manse, Kensaleyre, Snizort, Portree, Isle of Skye IV51 9XE [E-mail: drrc0911@yahoo.com]	01470 532453
Strath and Sleat (GD)				
Ben Johnstone MA BD DMin	1973	2003	The Manse, 6 Upper Breakish, Isle of Skye IV42 8PY [E-mail: benonskye@onetel.com]	01471 820063
John D. Urquhart BA BD (Part-Time: Gaelic Services)	1998	2003	The Manse, The Glebe, Kilmore, Teangue, Isle of Skye IV44 8RG [E-mail: ministear@hotmail.co.uk]	01471 844469

Beaton, Donald MA BD MTh	1961	2002	(Glenelg and Kintail)	Kilmaluag Croft, North Duntulm, Isle of Skye IV51 9UF	01470 552296
Kellas, David J. MA BD	1966	2004	(Kilfinan with Kyles)	Babhunn, Glenelg, Kyle IV40 8LA [E-mail: davidkellas@btinternet.com]	01599 522257
Macarthur, Allan J. BD	1973	1998	(Applecross, Lochcarron and Torridon)	High Barn, Croft Road, Lochcarron, Strathcarron IV54 8YA [E-mail: a.macarthur@btinternet.com]	(Tel) 01520 722278 (Fax) 01520 722674
McCulloch, Alen J.R. MA BD	1990	1995	Chaplain: Royal Navy	The Chaplaincy, HMS Drake, HMNB Devonport, Plymouth PL2 2BG [E-mail: aviljoen90@hotmail.com]	
Mackenzie, Hector M.	2008		Chaplain: Army	4 Scots and 2Bn REME, St Barbara Barracks, BFPO 38 [E-mail: mackenziehector@hotmail.com]	
Macleod, Donald LTh	1988	2000	(Snizort)	Burnside, Upper Galder, Glenelg, Kyle IV40 8JZ [E-mail: donaldpmacleod_7@btinternet.com]	01599 522265
Martin, George M. MA BD	1987	2005	(Applecross, Lochcarron and Torridon)	8(1) Buckingham Terrace, Edinburgh EH4 3AA	0131-343 3937

Murray, John W.	2003	Auxiliary Minister	1 Totescore, Kilmuir, Portree, Isle of Skye IV51 9YN [E-mail: jwm7@hotmail.co.uk]	01470 542297

LOCHCARRON – SKYE Communion Sundays

Applecross		Glenshiel	1st Jul	Plockton and Kyle	2nd May, 1st Oct
Arnisort	1st Sep	Kilmuir	1st Mar, Sep	Portree	Easter, Pentecost, Christmas, 2nd Mar, Aug, 1st Nov
Bracadale	3rd Mar, Sep	Kintail	3rd Apr, Jul	Sleat	Last May
Broadford	Last Feb	Kyleakin	Last Sep	Snizort	1st Jan, 4th Mar
Duirinish	3rd Jan, Easter, 3rd Sep	Lochalsh and Stromeferry	4th Jan, Jun, Sep, Christmas, Easter	Stenscholl	1st Jun, Dec
Dundonnell	4th Jun	Lochcarron and Shieldaig	Easter; communion held on a revolving basis when there is a fifth Sunday in the month	Strath	4th Jan
Elgol	1st Aug			Torridon and Kinlochewe	
Gairloch	3rd Jun, Nov				
Glenelg	2nd Jun, Nov				

In the Parish of Strath and Sleat, Easter communion is held on a revolving basis.

(43) UIST

Meets on the first Tuesday of February, March, September and November in Lochmaddy, and on the third Tuesday of June in Leverburgh.

Clerk:	**MR WILSON McKINLAY**	**Heatherburn Cottage, Rhughasnish, Isle of South Uist HS8 5PE** **[E-mail: uist@cofscotland.org.uk]**	**01870 610393**

Barra (GD)				
Vacant			Cuithir, Castlebay, Isle of Barra HS9 5XD	01871 810230
Benbecula (GD) (H)				
Andrew A. Downie BD BSc DipEd DipMin ThB	1994	2006	Church of Scotland Manse, Griminish, Isle of Benbecula HS7 5QA [E-mail: andownie@yahoo.co.uk]	01870 602180
Berneray and Lochmaddy (GD) (H)				
Donald Campbell MA BD DipTh	1997	2004	Church of Scotland Manse, Lochmaddy, Isle of North Uist HS6 5AA [E-mail: dc@hebrides.net]	01876 500414

Carinish (GD) (H)				
Iain Maciver BD	2007		Church of Scotland Manse, Clachan, Locheport, Lochmaddy, Isle of North Uist HS6 5HD [E-mail: iain.maciver@hebrides.net]	01876 580219
Kilmuir and Paible (GE)				
Vacant			Paible, Isle of North Uist HS6 5ED	01876 510310
Manish-Scarista (GD) (H)				
Murdo Smith MA BD	1988		Scarista, Isle of Harris HS3 3HX	01859 550200
South Uist (GD)				
Vacant			Daliburgh, Lochboisdale, Isle of South Uist HS8 5SS	01878 700265
Tarbert (GE) (H)				
Norman MacIver BD	1976	1988	The Manse, Manse Road, Tarbert, Isle of Harris HS3 3DF [E-mail: norman@n-cmaciver.freeserve.co.uk]	01859 502231

MacDonald, Angus J. BSc BD	1995 2001	(Lochmaddy and Trumisgarry)	7 Memorial Avenue, Stornoway, Isle of Lewis HS1 2QR	01851 706634
MacInnes, David MA BD	1966 1999	(Kilmuir and Paible)	9 Golf View Road, Kinmylies, Inverness IV3 8SZ	01463 717377
Macpherson, Kenneth J. BD	1988 2002	(Benbecula)	70 Baile na Cille, Balivanich, Isle of Benbecula HS7 5ND	01870 602751
Morrison, Donald John	2001	Auxiliary Minister	22 Kyles, Tarbert, Isle of Harris HS3 3BS	01859 502341
Petrie, Jackie G.	1989 2011	(South Uist)	Daliburgh, Lochboisdale, Isle of South Uist HS8 5SS [E-mail: jackiegpetrie@yahoo.com]	01878 700265
Smith, John M.	1956 1992	(Lochmaddy)	Hamersay, Clachan, Locheport, Lochmaddy, Isle of North Uist HS6 5HD	01876 580332

UIST Communion Sundays

Barra	2nd Mar, June, Sep, Easter, Advent	Carinish	4th Mar, Aug	South Uist	
Benbecula	2nd Mar, Sep	Kilmuir and Paible	1st Jun, 3rd Nov	Howmore	1st Jun
Berneray and Lochmaddy	4th Jun, last Oct	Manish-Scarista	3rd Apr, 1st Oct	Daliburgh	1st Sep
				Tarbert	2nd Mar, 3rd Sep

(44) LEWIS

Meets at Stornoway, in St Columba's Church Hall, on the first Tuesday of February, March, June, September and November. It also meets if required in April and December on dates to be decided.

Clerk:	**REV. THOMAS S. SINCLAIR MA LTh BD**		**An Caladh, East Tarbert, Tarbert, Isle of Harris HS3 3DB [E-mail: lewis@cofscotland.org.uk] [E-mail: presbytery@tsinclair.com]**	**01859 502849 07816 455820 (Mbl)**

Barvas (GD) (H)				
Paul Amed LTh DPS	1992	2008	Barvas, Isle of Lewis HS2 0QY [E-mail: paulamed@hebrides.net]	01851 840218
Carloway (GD) (H) (01851 643433)				
Stephen Macdonald BD MTh	2008		Church of Scotland Manse, Knock, Carloway, Isle of Lewis HS2 9AU [E-mail: smcarloway@live.co.uk]	01851 643255 07964 080494 (Mbl)
Cross Ness (GE) (H)				
Ian Murdo M. Macdonald DPA BD	2001		Cross Manse, Swainbost, Ness, Isle of Lewis HS2 0TB [E-mail: imacdonald375@btinternet.com]	01851 810375
Kinloch (GE) (H)				
Iain M. Campbell BD	2004	2008	Laxay, Lochs, Isle of Lewis HS2 9LA [E-mail: ianmstudy@aol.com]	01851 830218
Knock (GE) (H)				
J.R. Ross Macaskill BA MTh	2011		Knock Manse, Garrabost, Point, Isle of Lewis HS2 0PW [E-mail: afrobear@hotmail.co.uk]	01851 870368
Lochs-Crossbost (GD) (H)				
Vacant			Leurbost, Lochs, Isle of Lewis HS2 9NS	01851 860243
Lochs-in-Bernera (GD) (H) linked with Uig (GE) (H)				
Hugh Maurice Stewart DPA BD	2008		4 Seaview, Knock, Point, Isle of Lewis HS2 0PD (Temporary Manse) [E-mail: berneralwuig@btinternet.com]	01851 870691 07786 651796 (Mbl)

Stornoway: High (GD) (H)
Vacant — 1 Goathill Road, Stornoway, Isle of Lewis HS1 2NJ — 01851 703106

Stornoway: Martin's Memorial (H) (Church office: 01851 700820)
Thomas MacNeil MA BD — 2002 2006 — Matheson Road, Stornoway, Isle of Lewis HS1 2LR — 01851 704238
[E-mail: tommymacneil@hotmail.com]

Stornoway: St Columba (GD) (H) (Church office: 01851 701546)
Angus Morrison MA BD PhD — 1979 2000 — Lewis Street, Stornoway, Isle of Lewis HS1 2JF — 01851 703350
[E-mail: morrisonangus@btconnect.com]

Uig (GE) (H) See Lochs-in-Bernera

Jamieson, Esther M.M. (Mrs) BD	1984 2002	(Glasgow: Penilee St Andrew)	1 Redburn, Bayview, Stornoway, Isle of Lewis HS1 2UU [E-mail: iandejamieson@btinternet.com]	01851 704789 (Mbl) 07867 602963
Macdonald, James LTh CPS	1984 2001	(Knock)	Elim, 8A Lower Bayble, Point, Isle of Lewis HS2 0QA [E-mail: elim8a@hotmail.co.uk]	01851 870173
Maclean, Donald A. DCS		(Deacon)	8 Upper Barvas, Isle of Lewis HS2 0QX	01851 840454
MacLennan, Donald Angus	1975 2006	(Kinloch)	4 Kestrel Place, Inverness IV2 3YH [E-mail: maclennankinloch@btinternet.com]	01463 243750 (Mbl) 07799 668270
Macleod, William	1957 2006	(Uig)	54 Lower Barvas, Isle of Lewis HS2 0QY	01851 840217
Shadakshari, T.K. BTh BD MTh	1998 2006	Healthcare Chaplain	69 Plasterfield, Stornoway, Isle of Lewis HS1 2UR [E-mail: tk.shadakshari@nhs.net] [E-mail: shadaks2@yahoo.com]	01851 701727 (Mbl) 07403 697138
Sinclair, Thomas Suter MA LTh BD	1966 2004	(Stornoway: Martin's Memorial)	An Caladh, East Tarbert, Tarbert, Isle of Harris HS3 3DB [E-mail: lewis@cofscotland.org.uk] [E-mail: thomas@tsinclair.com]	01859 502849 (Mbl) 07816 455820

LEWIS Communion Sundays

Barvas	3rd Mar, Sep	Lochs-Crossbost	4th Mar, Sep	Stornoway	
Carloway	1st Mar, last Sep	Lochs-in-Bernera	1st Apr, 2nd Sep	St Columba	3rd Feb, last Aug
Cross Ness	2nd Mar, Oct	Stornoway		Uig	3rd Jun, 1st Sep
Kinloch	3rd Mar, 2nd Jun, 2nd Sep	High	3rd Feb, last Aug		
Knock	3rd Apr, 1st Nov	Martin's Memorial	3rd Feb, last Aug, 1st Dec, Easter		

(45) ORKNEY

Normally meets at Kirkwall, in the East Church King Street Halls, on the second Tuesday of September and February, and on the last Tuesday of November. The Presbytery meets in conference on the first Tuesday in May. One meeting is usually held outwith the King Street Halls.

Clerk: REV. JAMES WISHART BD			**Upper Westshore, Burray, Orkney KW17 2TE** **[E-mail: orkney@cofscotland.org.uk]** **[E-mail (personal): jwishart06@btinternet.com]**	**01856 731672**
Birsay, Harray and Sandwick				
Andrea E. Price (Mrs)	1997	2001	The Manse, North Biggings Road, Dounby, Orkney KW17 2HZ [E-mail: andrea@andreaneil.plus.com]	01856 771803
East Mainland				
Vacant			West Manse, Holm, Orkney KW17 2SB	01856 781422
Eday linked with Stronsay: Moncur Memorial (H)				
Jennifer D. (George) Graham (Mrs) BA MDiv PhD	2000	2005	Manse, Stronsay, Orkney KW17 2AF [E-mail: jennifergeorge@btinternet.com]	01857 616311
Evie (H) linked with Firth (H) linked with Rendall				
Vacant			Manse, Finstown, Orkney KW17 2EG	01856 761328
Firth (H) (01856 761117) See Evie				
Flotta linked with Hoy and Walls				
Vacant			South Isles Manse, Longhope, Stromness, Orkney KW16 3PG	01856 701325
Hoy and Walls See Flotta				
Kirkwall: East (H)				
Vacant			East Church Manse, Thoms Street, Kirkwall, Orkney KW15 1PF	01856 875469
Kirkwall: St Magnus Cathedral (H)				
G. Fraser H. Macnaughton MA BD	1982	2002	Berstane Road, Kirkwall, Orkney KW15 1NA [E-mail: fmacnaug@gotadsl.co.uk]	01856 873312
North Ronaldsay linked with Sanday (H)				
John L. McNab MA BD	1997	2002	The Manse, Sanday, Orkney KW17 2BW	01857 600429

Orphir (H) and Stenness (H)
Vacant — Stenness Manse, Stenness, Stromness, Orkney KW16 3HH — 01856 761331
(New charge formed by the union of Orphir and Stenness)

Papa Westray linked with Westray
Iain D. MacDonald BD — 1993 — The Manse, Hilldavale, Westray, Orkney KW17 2DW [E-mail: idmacdonald@btinternet.com] — 01857 677357 (Tel/Fax), 07710 443780 (Mbl)

Rendall See Evie

Rousay (Church centre: 01856 821271)
Continuing Vacancy

Sanday See North Ronaldsay

Shapinsay (50 per cent part-time)
Vacant

South Ronaldsay and Burray
Vacant — St Margaret's Manse, Church Road, St Margaret's Hope, Orkney KW17 2SR — 01856 831288

Stromness (H)
Vacant — 5 Manse Lane, Stromness, Orkney KW16 3AP — 01856 850203

Stronsay: Moncur Memorial See Eday
Westray See Papa Westray

Brown, R. Graeme BA BD	1961	1998	(Birsay with Rousay)	Bring Deeps, Orphir, Orkney KW17 2LX [E-mail: graeme_sibyl@btinternet.com]	(Tel/Fax) 01856 811707
Clark, Thomas L. BD	1985	2008	(Orphir with Stenness)	7 Headland Rise, Burghead, Elgin IV30 5HA [E-mail: toml.clark@btinternet.com]	01343 830144
Tait, Alexander	1967	1995	(Glasgow: St Enoch's Hogganfield)	Ingermas, Evie, Orkney KW17 2PH [E-mail: jen1957@hotmail.co.uk]	01856 751477
Wishart, James BD	1986	2009	(Deer)	Upper Westshore, Burray, Orkney KW17 2TE [E-mail: jwishart06@btinternet.com]	01856 731672

(46) SHETLAND

Meets at Lerwick on the first Tuesday of February, April, June, September, November and December.

Clerk: REV. CHARLES H.M. GREIG MA BD		**The Manse, Sandwick, Shetland ZE2 9HW** **[E-mail: shetland@cofscotland.org.uk]**	**01950 422468**

Name	Ordained	Inducted	Address	Telephone
Burra Isle linked with Tingwall				
Wilma A. Johnston MTheol MTh	2006	2008	The Manse, 25 Hogalee, East Voe, Scalloway, Shetland ZE1 0UU [E-mail: rev.wilmajohnston@btinternet.com]	01595 881157
Delting linked with Northmavine				
Vacant			The Manse, Grindwell, Brae, Shetland ZE2 9QJ	01806 522219
Robert M. MacGregor CMIOSH DipOSH RSP (Aux)	2004		Olna Cottage, Brae, Shetland ZE2 9QS [E-mail: revbobdelting@mypostoffice.co.uk]	01806 522604
Grace Russon (Mrs) (Aux)	2011		Marelda, Park Road, Sandwick, Shetland ZE2 9HP [E-mail: gracerusson@live.co.uk]	01950 431207
Dunrossness and St Ninian's inc. Fair Isle linked with Sandwick, Cunningsburgh and Quarff				
Charles H.M. Greig MA BD	1976	1997	The Manse, Sandwick, Shetland ZE2 9HW [E-mail: chm.greig@btopenworld.com]	01950 422468
Fetlar linked with Unst linked with Yell				
David Cooper BA MPhil (David Cooper is a minister of the Methodist Church)	1975	2008	Southerhouse, Gutcher, Yell, Shetland ZE2 9DF [E-mail: Reverenddavidcooper@googlemail.com]	01957 744258 (Tel/Fax)
Lerwick and Bressay				
Vacant			The Manse, 82 St Olaf Street, Lerwick, Shetland ZE1 0ES	01595 692125
Nesting and Lunnasting linked with Whalsay and Skerries				
Irene A. Charlton (Mrs) BTh	1994	1997	The Manse, Marrister, Symbister, Whalsay, Shetland ZE2 9AE [E-mail: irene.charlton@btinternet.com]	01806 566767
Richard M. Charlton (Aux)	2001		The Manse, Marrister, Symbister, Whalsay, Shetland ZE2 9AE [E-mail: revrm.charlton@btinternet.com]	01806 566767

Northmavine See Delting

Sandsting and Aithsting linked with Walls and Sandness
Vacant — The Manse, Happyhansel, Walls, Shetland ZE2 9PB — 01595 809709

Sandwick, Cunningsburgh and Quarff See Dunrossness and St Ninian's
Tingwall See Burra Isle
Unst See Fetlar
Walls and Sandness See Sandsting and Aithsting
Whalsay and Skerries See Nesting and Lunnasting
Yell See Fetlar

Name			Charge	Address	Tel
Kirkpatrick, Alice H. (Miss) MA BD FSAScot	1987	2000	(Northmavine)	4 Stendaal, Skellister, South Nesting, Shetland ZE2 9XA	
Knox, R. Alan MA LTh AInstAM	1965	2005	(Fetlar with Unst with Yell)	27 Killyvalley Road, Garvagh, Co. Londonderry, Northern Ireland BT51 5LX	02829 558925
Macintyre, Thomas MA BD	1972	2011	(Sandsting and Aithsting with Walls and Sandness)	'Lappideks', South Voxter, Cunningsburgh, Shetland ZE2 9HF [E-mail: the2macs.macintyre@btinternet.com]	01950 477549
Smith, Catherine (Mrs) DCS	1964	2003	(Presbytery Assistant)	21 Lingaro, Bixter, Shetland ZE2 9NN	01595 810207
Williamson, Magnus J.C.	1982	1999	(Fetlar with Yell)	Creekhaven, Houll Road, Scalloway, Shetland ZE1 0XA	01595 880023

(47) ENGLAND

Meets at London, in Crown Court Church, on the second Tuesday of March and December, and at St Columba's, Pont Street, on the second Tuesday of June and October.

Clerk: REV. PETER W. MILLS CB BD DD CPS — 43 Hempland Close, Corby NN18 8LR [E-mail: england@cofscotland.org.uk] — 01536 746429

Corby: St Andrew's (H)
Peter W. Mills CB BD DD CPS — 1984 — 2009 — 43 Hempland Close, Corby NN18 8LR [E-mail: pwmills@live.co.uk] — 01536 746429

Corby: St Ninian's (H) (01536 265245)
Vacant — The Manse, 46 Glyndebourne Gardens, Corby, Northants NN18 0PZ — 01536 352430

Guernsey: St Andrew's in the Grange (H)

Graeme W. Beebee BD	1993	2003	The Manse, Le Villocq, Castel, Guernsey GY5 7SB [E-mail: beehive@cwgsy.net]	01481 257345

Jersey: St Columba's (H)

Randolph Scott MA BD	1991	2006	18 Claremont Avenue, St Saviour, Jersey JE2 7SF [E-mail: rev.rs@hotmail.com]	01534 730659

Liverpool: St Andrew's

Continued Vacancy				
Session Clerk: Mr Robert Cottle				0151-524 1915

London: Crown Court (H) (020 7836 5643)

Philip L. Majcher BD	1982	2007	53 Sidmouth Street, London WC1H 8JX [E-mail: minister@crowncourtchurch.org.uk]	020 7278 5022
Timothy E.G. Fletcher BA FCMA (Aux)	1998		37 Harestone Valley Road, Caterham, Surrey CR3 6HN [E-mail: fletcherts@btinternet.com]	01883 340826

London: St Columba's (H) (020 7584 2321) linked with Newcastle: St Andrew's (H)

Vacant			29 Hollywood Road, Chelsea, London SW10 9HT	020 7376 5230
Dorothy Lunn (Aux)	2002	2002	14 Bellerby Drive, Ouston, Co. Durham DH2 1TW [E-mail: dorothylunn@hotmail.com]	0191-492 0647

Newcastle: St Andrew's See London: St Columba's

Bowie, A. Glen CBE BA BSc	1954	1984	(Principal Chaplain: RAF)	16 Weir Road, Hemingford Grey, Huntingdon PE18 9EH	01480 381425
Brown, Scott J. QHC BD RN	1993	1993	Chaplain of the Fleet: Royal Navy	Principal Church of Scotland and Free Churches Chaplain (Naval), and Director Naval Chaplaincy Service (Capability), Leach Building, Whale Island, Portsmouth PO2 8BY [E-mail: scott.brown943@mod.uk]	02392 625552 (Mbl) 07769 847876
Cairns, W. Alexander BD	1978	2006	(Corby: St Andrew's)	Kirkton House, Kirkton of Craig, Montrose DD10 9TB [E-mail: sandy.cairns@btinternet.com]	(Mbl) 07808 588045
Cameron, R. Neil	1975	1981	(Chaplain: Community)	[E-mail: neilandminacameron@yahoo.co.uk]	
Coulter, David G. BA BD MDA PhD CF	1989	1994	Chaplain: Army	8 Ashdown Terrace, Tidworth, Wilts SP9 7SQ [E-mail: padredgcoulter@yahoo.co.uk]	01980 842175
Craig, Gordon T. BD	1988		Principal Chaplain: RAF	40 Aiden Road, Quarrington, Sleaford, Lincs NG34 8UU [E-mail: gordon.craig705@mod.uk] [E-mail: principal@amporthouse.co.uk]	01529 300264
Cross, Brian F. MA	1961	1998	(Coalburn)	1474 High Road, Whetstone, London N20 9QD	020 8492 9313
Cumming, Alistair	2010		Auxiliary Minister: London: St Columba's	64 Prince George's Avenue, London SW20 8BH [E-mail: afcumming@hotmail.com]	020 8540 7365 (Mbl) 07534 943986

Name	Ord.	Appt.	Appointment	Address	Phone
Dalton, Mark BD DipMin	2002		Chaplain: RN	The Chaplaincy, HMS *Raleigh*, Torpoint, Cornwall PL11 2PD [E-mail: mark.dalton242@mod.uk]	01752 811282
Dowswell, James A.M.	1991	2001	(Lerwick and Bressay)	Mill House, High Street, Staplehurst, Tonbridge, Kent TN12 0AV [E-mail: jdowswell@btinternet.com]	01580 891271
Duncan, Denis M. BD PhD	1944	1986	(Editor: *The British Weekly*)	24 Caburn Court, Station Street, Lewes BN7 2DA [E-mail: denisduncan@dits.org.uk]	
Duncan, John C. BD MPhil	1987	2001	Chaplain: Army	3 Yorks, Battlesbury Barracks, Warminster BA12 9QT [E-mail: padrerhf@hotmail.com]	01985 223335 (Mbl) 07825 119227
Fields, James MA BD STM	1988	1997	School Chaplain	The Bungalow, The Ridgeway, Mill Hill, London NW7 1QX	020 8201 1397
Hood, Adam J.J. MA BD DPhil	1989		Lecturer	67A Farquhar Road, Edgbaston, Birmingham B15 2QP [E-mail: hooda@queens.ac.uk]	0121-452 2606
Kingston, David V.F. BD DipPTh	1993		Chaplain: Army	The Chaplain's Office, HQ Colchester Garrison, Melville Barracks, Colchester CO2 7UT [E-mail: d.v.f.k@btinternet.com]	01206 563638 (Mbl) 07802 417947
Langlands, Cameron H. BD MTh ThM PhD MInstLM	1995	2009	Pastoral and Spiritual Care Manager: Lancashire Teaching Hospitals NHS Trust	Department of Pastoral and Spiritual Care, Lancashire Teaching Hospitals NHS Foundation Trust, Royal Preston Hospital, Sharoe Green Lane, Fulwood, Preston PR2 9HT [E-mail: cameron.langlands@lthtr.nhs.uk]	01772 522350
Lugton, George L. MA BD	1955	1997	(Guernsey: St Andrew's in the Grange)	6 Clos de Beauvoir, Rue Cohu, Guernsey GY5 7TE	(Tel/Fax) 01481 254285
Macfarlane, Peter T. BA LTh	1970	1994	(Chaplain: Army)	4 rue de Rives, 37160 Abilly, France	
McIndoe, John H. MA BD STM DD	1966	2000	(London: St Columba's with Newcastle: St Andrew's	5 Dunlin, Westerlands Park, Glasgow G12 0FE [E-mail: johnandeve@mcindoe555.fsnet.co.uk]	0141-579 1366
MacLeod, C. Angus MA BD	1996		Chaplain: Army	HQ Scottish Div, Stirling FK7 7RR [E-mail: 959macle@armymail.mod.uk]	
MacLeod, Rory N. MA BD	1986	1992	Chaplain: Army	25 Redford Gardens, Edinburgh EH13 0AP	0131-441 6522
Mather, James	2010		Auxiliary Minister: University Chaplain	24 Ellison Road, Barnes, London SW13 0AD [E-mail: jsm.johnstonmather@btinternet.com]	(Home) 020 8876 6540 (Work) 020 7361 1670 (Mbl) 07836 715655
Middleton, Paul BMus BD ThM PhD	2000		University Lecturer	97B Whipcord Lane, Chester CH1	
Milloy, A. Miller DPE LTh DipTrMan	1979	1998	General Secretary: United Bible Societies	3 Lea Wood Road, Fleet, Hants GU51 5AL [E-mail: ammilloy@aol.com]	01252 628455
Munro, Alexander W. MA BD	1978		Chaplain and Teacher of Religious Studies	Columba House, 12 Alexandra Road, Southport PR9 0NB [E-mail: awmunro@tiscali.co.uk]	01704 543044
Pickles, Robert G.D.W. BD MPhil ThD	2003	2010	(Orwell and Portmoak)	Chadacres, 49 Rotton Park Road, Birmingham B16 0SG [E-mail: robert.pickles@btopenworld.com]	0121-454 4046
Rennie, Alistair McR. MA BD	1939	1986	(Kincardine Croick and Edderton)	Noble's Yard, St Mary's Gate, Wirksworth, Derbyshire DE4 4DQ [E-mail: alistairrennie@lineone.net]	01629 820289
Thomson, Steven BSc BD	2001	2004	Chaplain: Royal Navy	21 Kings Terrace, Southsea, Portsmouth PO5 3AR [E-mail: stevie.thomson1@ntlworld.com]	(Mbl) 07841 368797
Trevorrow, James A. LTh	1971	2003	(Glasgow: Cranhill)	12 Test Green, Corby, Northants NN17 2HA [E-mail: jimtrevorrow@compuserve.com]	01536 264018

Walker, R. Forbes BSc BD ThM	1987 2000	School Chaplain	2 Holmleigh, Priory Road, Ascot, Berks SL5 8EA [E-mail: revfw@gmail.com]	01344 883272
Wallace, Donald S.	1950 1980	(Chaplain: RAF)	7 Dellfield Close, Watford, Herts WD1 3BL	01923 223289
Ward, Michael J. BSc BD PhD MA PGCE	1983 2009	Training and Development Officer: Presbyterian Church of Wales	Apt 6, Bryn Hedd, Conwy Road, Penmaen-mawr, Gwynedd LL34 6BS [E-mail: revmw@btopenworld.com]	(Mbl) 07765 598816
Wood, Peter J. MA BD	1993	(College Lecturer)	97 Broad Street, Cambourne, Cambridgeshire CB23 6DH [E-mail: pejowood@tiscali.co.uk]	01954 715558

ENGLAND – Church Addresses

Corby
St Andrew's — Occupation Road
St Ninian's — Beanfield Avenue

Liverpool — The Western Rooms, Anglican Cathedral

London
Crown Court — Crown Court WC2
St Columba's — Pont Street SW1

Newcastle — Sandyford Road

(48) EUROPE

Clerk: REV. JOHN A. COWIE BSc BD — **Jan Willem Brouwersstraat 9, NL-1071 LH Amsterdam**
[E-mail: europe@cofscotland.org.uk]
[E-mail: j.cowie@chello.nl]
(Tel) 0031 20 672 2288
(Fax) 0031 842 221513

Amsterdam				
John A. Cowie BSc BD	1983	1989	Jan Willem Brouwersstraat 9, NL-1071 LH Amsterdam, The Netherlands [E-mail: minister@ercadam.nl]	(Tel) 0031 20 672 2288 (Fax) 0031 842 221513
Brussels (E-mail: secretary@churchofscotland.be)				
Andrew Gardner BSc BD PhD	1997	2004	23 Square des Nations, B-1000 Brussels, Belgium [E-mail: minister@churchofscotland.be]	0032 2 672 40 56
Budapest (Church telephone: 136 13730725)				
Aaron Stevens	2010		H-1143, Stefania ut 32, Budapest, Hungary [E-mail: revastevens@yahoo.co.uk]	(Mbl) 0036 70 615 5394

Colombo, Sri Lanka: St Andrew's Scots Kirk

John P.S. Purves MBE BSc BD	1978	2003	73 Galle Road, Colpetty, Colombo 3, Sri Lanka [E-mail: reverend@sltnet.lk]	0094 (11) 2386774

Costa del Sol

Vacant			Lux Mundi Centro Ecumenico, Calle Nueva 3, Fuengirola, E-29460 Malaga, Spain [E-mail: info@kirkojocks.eu]	0034 951 260 982

Geneva

Ian A. Manson BA BD	1989	2001	20 Ancienne Route, 1218 Grand Saconnex, Geneva, Switzerland [E-mail: cofsg@pingnet.ch] (Office)	0041 22 798 29 09 0041 22 788 08 31

Gibraltar

Ewen MacLean BA BD	1995	2009	St Andrew's Manse, 29 Scud Hill, Gibraltar [E-mail: scotskirk@gibraltar.gi]	00350 200 77040

Lausanne

Ian J.M. McDonald MA BD	1984	2010	26 Avenue de Rumine, CH-1005 Lausanne, Switzerland [E-mail: minister@scotskirklausanne.ch]	0041 21 323 98 28

Lisbon

Graham G. McGeoch MA BTh MTh	2009		Rua da Arriaga 13, 1200-625 Lisbon, Portugal [E-mail: cofslx@netcabo.pt]	00351 218 043 410

Malta

T. Douglas McRoberts BD CPS FRSA	1975	2009	La Romagnola, 15 Triq is-Seiqja, Misrah Kola, Attard ATD 1713, Malta (Tel/Fax) [E-mail: doug.mcroberts@btinternet.com] Church address: 210 Old Bakery Street, Valletta, Malta [E-mail: minister@saintandrewsmalta.com]	00356 214 15465

Paris

James M. Cowie BD	1977	2011	10 Rue Thimmonier, F-75009 Paris, France [E-mail: jimcowie@europe.com]	0033 1 48 78 47 94

Regensburg (University)

Rhona Dunphy (Mrs)	2005		Liskircherstrasse 9, D-93049 Regensburg, Germany [E-mail: rhona@dunphy.de]	(Mbl)	0049 (0) 176 83 10 69 67

Rome: St Andrew's

William B. McCulloch BD	1997	2002	Via XX Settembre 7, 00187 Rome, Italy [E-mail: revwbmcculloch@hotmail.com]	(Tel) (Fax)	0039 06 482 7627 0039 06 487 4370

Rotterdam (Church telephone: 0031 10 412 4779)

Robert A. Calvert BSc BD DMin	1983	1995	Church address: Schiedamse Vest 119–121, NL-2012 BH Rotterdam, The Netherlands Meeuwenstraat 4A, NL-3071 PE Rotterdam, The Netherlands [E-mail: scotsintchurch@cs.com]		0031 10 220 4199

Turin

Vacant			Via S. Pio V 17, 10125 Torino, Italy [E-mail: esc.torino@alice.it] Church address: Via Sant Anselmo 6, 10125 Turin, Italy		0039 011 650 5770 0039 011 650 9467

Warwick, Bermuda: Christ Church

Barry W. Dunsmore MA BD	1982	2009	Mailing address: PO Box PG88, Paget PG BX, Bermuda Church address: Christ Church, Middle Road, Warwick, Bermuda [E-mail: christchurch@logic.bm; Website: www.christchurch.bm] Manse address: The Manse, 6 Manse Road, Paget PG 01, Bermuda	(Office)	001 441 236 1882

Irene Bom (Auxiliary Minister: worship resourcing, children's and youth work)	2008		Bergpolderstraat 53A, NL-3038 KB Rotterdam, The Netherlands [E-mail: ibsalem@xs4all.nl]	0031 10 265 1703
James M. Brown MA BD	1982		Neustrasse 15, D-44787 Bochum, Germany [E-mail: j.brown56@gmx.de]	0049 234 133 65
Professor A.I.C. Heron BD DTheol	1975	1987	Priessnitzstrasse 10, D-91056 Erlangen, Germany [E-mail: arheron@gmx.de]	0049 9131 52443
Derek G. Lawson LLB BD	1998	2011	2 Rue Joseph Guillemot, F-87210 Oradour St Genest, France [E-mail: derek.lawson@sfr.fr]	00 33 5 55 68 53 03
Paraic Reamonn BA BD	1982		359B Route de Mandement, CH-1281 Russin, Switzerland [E-mail: paraic.reamonn@gmail.com]	0041 22 776 4834
James Sharp (Auxiliary Minister: training and education)	2005		102 Rue des Eaux-Vives, CH-1207 Geneva, Switzerland [E-mail: jimsharp@bluewin.ch]	0041 22 786 4847
(Turin) Alexander B. Cairns MA	1957	2009	Beechwood, Main Street, Sandhead, Stranraer DG9 9JG	
(Bermuda) T. Alan W. Garrity BSc BD MTh	1969	2008	17 Solomon's View, Dunlop, Kilmarnock KA3 4ES	01560 486879
(Rome) David F. Huie MA BD	1962	2001	15 Rosebank Gardens, Largs KA30 8TD [E-mail: david.huie@btopenworld.com]	01475 670733

(Brussels)	Charles C. McNeill OBE BD	1962	1991	17 All Saints Way, Beachamwell, Swaffham, Norfolk PE37 8BU	
(Brussels)	Thomas C. Pitkeathly MA CA BD	1984	2004	1 Lammermuir Court, Gullane EH31 2HU	01620 843373
(Rotterdam)	Joost Pot BSc (Auxiliary Minister)	1992	2004	[E-mail: joostpot@gmail.com]	
(Budapest)	Bertalan Tamas			Pozsonyi ut 34, Budapest H-1137, Hungary [E-mail: bertalantamas@hotmail.com]	0036 1 239 6315 (Mbl) 0036 30 638 6647

(49) JERUSALEM

Clerk: **MR J.G. MAXWELL**

Tabeetha School, PO Box 8170, Jaffa 61081, Israel **(Home) 00972 3 657 2003**
[E-mail: jmaxwell@churchofscotland.org.il] **(Mbl) 00972 52 374 0235**
[E-mail: jimmymaxwell27@yahoo.com]

Jerusalem: St Andrew's
George C. Shand MA BD 1981 2009 St Andrew's Scots Memorial Church, 1 David Remez Street, PO Box 8619, Jerusalem 91086, Israel (Tel) 00972 2 673 2401
[E-mail: stachjer@netvision.net.il]

Tiberias: St Andrew's
Colin D. Johnston MA BD 1986 2009 St Andrew's, Galilee, 1 Gdud Barak Street, PO Box 104, Tiberias 14100, Israel (Tel) 00972 4 671 0710
[E-mail: revcdj60@gmail.com]

SECTION 6

Additional Lists of Personnel

LIST A – AUXILIARY MINISTERS

NAME	ORD	ADDRESS	TEL	PR
Anderson, David M. MSc FCOptom	1984	'Mirlos', 1 Dumfries Place, Fort William PH33 6UQ	01397 703203	38
Attenburrow, Anne BSc MBChB	2006	4 Jock Inksons Brae, Elgin IV30 1QE	01343 552330	35
Binks, Mike	2007	5 Maxwell Drive, Newton Stewart DG8 6EL	01671 402201	9
Bom, Irene	2008	Bergpolderstraat 53A, NL-3038 KB Rotterdam, The Netherlands	0031 10 265 1703	48
Buck, Maxine	2007	Brownlee House, Mauldslie Road, Carluke ML8 5HW	01555 759063	17
Burroughs, Kirsty-Ann (Mrs) BA BD CertTheol DRM PhD	2007	Lorne and Lowland Manse, Castlehill, Campbeltown PA28 6AN	01586 552468	19
Cameron, Ann J. (Mrs) CertCS DCE TEFL	2005	Currently resident in Qatar		32
Campbell, Gordon MA BD CDipAF DipHSM MCMI MIHM AFRIN ARSGS FRGS FSAScot	2001	2 Falkland Place, Kingoodie, Invergowrie, Dundee DD2 5DY	01382 561383	29
Charlton, Richard M.	2001	The Manse, Marrister, Symbister, Whalsay, Shetland ZE2 9AE	01806 566767	46
Cumming, Alistair	2010	64 Prince George's Avenue, London SW20 8BH	020 8540 7365 (Mbl) 07534 943986	47
Dick, Roddy S.	2010	27 Easter Crescent, Wishaw ML2 8XB	01698 383453	17
Don, Andrew MBA	2006	5 Eskdale Court, Penicuik EH26 8HT	01968 675766	3
Fletcher, Timothy E.G. BA FCMA	1998	37 Hareston Valley Road, Caterham, Surrey CR3 6HN	01883 340826	47
Forrest, Kenneth P. CBE BSc PhD	2006	5 Carruth Road, Bridge of Weir PA11 3HQ	01505 612651	14
Griffiths, Ruth I. (Mrs)	2004	Kirkwood, Mathieson Lane, Innellan, Dunoon PA23 7TA	01369 830145	19
Hood, Catriona A.	2006	'Elyside', Dalintober, Campbeltown PA28 6EB	01586 551490	19
Howie, Marion L.K. (Mrs) MA ARCS	1992	51 High Road, Stevenston KA20 3DY	01294 466571	12
Jackson, Nancy	2009	Cygnet House, Holmfarm Road, Catrine, Mauchline KA5 6TA	01290 550511	10
Kay, Elizabeth (Miss) DipYCS	1993	1 Kintail Walk, Inchture, Perth PH14 9RY	01828 686029	29
Kemp, Tina MA	2005	12 Oaktree Gardens, Dumbarton G82 1EU	01389 730477	18
Landale, William S.	2005	Green Hope Guest House, Green Hope, Duns TD11 3SG	01361 890242	5
Lunn, Dorothy	2002	14 Bellerby Drive, Ouston, Co. Durham DH2 1TW	0191-492 0647	47
Macdonald, Michael	2004	73 Firhill, Alness IV17 0RT	01349 884268	40
MacDougall, Lorna A. (Miss) MA	2003	34 Millar Place, Carron, Falkirk FK2 8QB	01324 552739	22
MacGregor, Robert M. CMIOSH DipOSH RSP	2004	Olna Cottage, Brae, Shetland ZE2 9QS	01806 522604	46
Manson, Eileen (Mrs) DipCE	1994	1 Cambridge Avenue, Gourock PA19 1XT	01475 632401	14
Mather, James	2010	24 Ellison Road, Barnes, London SW13 0AD	(Home) 020 8876 6540 (Work) 020 7361 1670 (Mbl) 07836 715655	47
Moore, Douglas T.	2003	9 Midton Avenue, Prestwick KA9 1PU	01292 671352	10
Morrison, Donald John	2001	22 Kyles, Tarbert, Isle of Harris HS3 3BS	01859 502341	43
Murray, John W.	2003	1 Totescore, Kilmuir, Portree, Isle of Skye IV51 9YN	01470 542297	42
O'Donnell, Barbara	2007	Ashbank, 258 Main Street, Alexandria G83 0NU	01389 752356	18
Paterson, Andrew E. JP	1994	6 The Willows, Kelty KY4 0FQ	01383 830998	24
Perry, Marion (Mrs)	2009	0/2, 75 Earl Street, Glasgow G14 0DG	07563 180662	16

Ramage, Alistair E. MA BA ADB CertEd	1996	16 Claremont Gardens, Milngavie, Glasgow G62 6PG	0141-956 2897	18
Riddell, Thomas S. BSc CEng FIChemE	1993	4 The Maltings, Linlithgow EH49 6DS	01506 843251	2
Robson, Brenda (Dr)	2005	2 Baird Road, Ratho, Newbridge EH28 8RA	0131-333 2746	1
Russon, Grace (Mrs)	2011	Marelda, Park Road, Sandwick, Shetland ZE2 9HP	01950 431207	46
Sharp, James	2005	102 Rue des Eaux-Vives, CH-1207 Geneva, Switzerland	0041 22 786 4847	48
Shearer, Anne BA DipEd	2010	10 Colsnaur, Menstrie FK11 7HG	01259 769176	23
Sutherland, David A.	2001	6 Cromarty Drive, Dundee DD2 2UQ	01382 621473	29
Vivers, Katherine A.	2004	Blacket House, Eaglesfield, Lockerbie DG11 3AA	01461 500412	7
Walker, Linda	2008	18 Valeview Terrace, Glasgow G42 9LA	0141-649 1340	16
Wandrum, David	1993	5 Cawder View, Carrickstone Meadows, Cumbernauld, Glasgow G68 0BN	01236 723288	22
Whittaker, Mary	2011	11 Templand Road, Lhanbryde, Elgin IV30 8BR		35
Wilkie, Robert	2011	24 Huntingtower Road, Perth PH1 2JS	01738 628301	28
Zambonini, James LIADip	1997	100 Old Manse Road, Netherton, Wishaw ML2 0EP	01698 350889	17

AUXILIARY MINISTERS: RETIRED

NAME	ORD	ADDRESS	TEL	PR
Birch, James PgDip FRSA FIOC	2001	1 Kirkhill Grove, Cambuslang, Glasgow G72 8EH	0141-583 1722	16
Brown, Elizabeth (Mrs) JP RGN	1996	8 Viewlands Place, Perth PH1 1BS	01738 552391	28
Cloggie, June (Mrs)	1997	11A Tulipan Crescent, Callander FK17 8AR	01877 331021	23
Craggs, Sheila (Mrs)	2001	7 Morar Court, Ellon AB41 9GG	01358 723055	33
Cruickshank, Alistair A.B. MA	1991	Thistle Cottage, 2A Chapel Place, Dollar FK14 7DW	01259 742549	23
Ferguson, Archibald M. MSc PhD CEng FRINA	1989	The Whins, 2 Barrowfield, Station Road, Cardross, Dumbarton G82 5NL	01389 841517	18
Glass, Alexander OBE MA	1998	Craigton, Tulloch Avenue, Dingwall IV15 9TU	01349 863258	39
Harrison, Cameron	2006	Woodfield House, Priormuir, St Andrews KY16 8LP	01334 478067	26
Jenkinson, John J. JP LTCL ALCM DipEd DipSen	1991	8 Rosehall Terrace, Falkirk FK1 1PY	01324 625498	22
McAlpine, John BSc	1988	Braeside, 201 Bonkle Road, Newmains, Wishaw ML2 9AA	01698 384610	17
MacDonald, Kenneth MA BA	2001	5 Henderland Road, Bearsden, Glasgow G61 1AH	0141-943 1103	16
MacFadyen, Anne M. (Mrs) BSc BD FSAScot	1995	295 Mearns Road, Glasgow G77 5LT	0141-639 3605	16
Mack, Elizabeth A. (Miss) DipPEd	1994	24 Roberts Crescent, Dumfries DG2 7RS	01387 264847	8
Mack, John C. JP	1985	The Willows, Auchleven, Insch AB52 6QB	01464 820387	33
Mailer, Colin	1996	Innis Chonain, Back Row, Polmont, Falkirk FK2 0RD	01324 712401	22
Munro, Mary (Mrs) BA	1993	14 Auchneel Crescent, Stranraer DG9 0JH	01776 702305	9
Paterson, Maureen (Mrs) BSc	1992	91 Dalmahoy Crescent, Kirkcaldy KY2 6TA	01592 262300	25
Phillippo, Michael MTh BSc BVetMed MRCVS	2003	25 Deeside Crescent, Aberdeen AB15 7PT	01224 318317	31
Pot, Joost BSc	1992	[E-mail: joostpot@gmail.com]		48
Shaw, Catherine A.M. MA	1998	40 Merrygreen Place, Stewarton, Kilmarnock KA3 5EP	01560 483352	11
Thomas, Shirley A. (Mrs) DipSocSci AMIA	2000	14 Kirkgait, Letham, Forfar DD8 2XQ	01307 818084	30

Watson, Jean S. (Miss) MA	1993	29 Strachan Crescent, Dollar FK14 7HL	01259 742872	23
Wilson, Mary D. (Mrs) RGN SCM DTM	1990	Berbice, The Terrace, Bridge of Tilt, Blair Atholl, Pitlochry PH18 5SZ	01796 481619	27

LIST B – CHAPLAINS TO HM FORCES

NAME	ORD	COM	BCH	ADDRESS
Abeledo, Benjamin J.A. BTh DipTh PTh	1991	1999	A	HQ4 Mech Bde, Catterick Garrison, North Yorks DL9 3JS
Aitchison, James W. BD	1993		A	HQ101 Log Bde, Buller Barracks, Aldershot, Hants GU11 2BY
Almond, David M. BD			ACF	West Lowland Bn
Anderson, David P. BSc BD	2002	2007	A	3 Scots, Fort George, Ardersier, Inverness IV1 2TD
Andrews, J. Edward MA BD DipCG FSAScot			TA	Glasgow and Lanark Bn
Barclay, Iain C. MBE TD MA BD MTh MPhil PhD			ACF	Black Watch Bn
Barclay, Iain C. MBE TD MA BD MTh MPhil PhD			OC	Aberdeen Universities Officer Training Corps
Berry, Geoff T. BD BSc	2009		OC	2 Scots
Blakey, Stephen A. BSc BD			TA	6 Bn The Royal Regiment of Scotland
Brown, Scott J. QHC BD RN	1993		RN	Principal Chaplain, MP 1.2, Leach Building, Whale Island, Portsmouth, Hants PO2 8BY
Bryson, Thomas M. BD			ACF	2 Bn The Highlanders
Campbell, Roderick D.M. TD BD FSAScot			ACF	Argyll and Sutherland Highlanders Bn
Connolly, Daniel BD DipTheol DipMin	1983		A	36 Engr Regt, Invicta Barracks, Maidstone ME14 2NA
Coulter, David G. BA BD MDA PhD CF	1989	1994	A	AFCC, Amport House, Amport, Andover, Hants SP11 8BG
Craig, Gordon T. BD DipMin	1988		RAF	Armed Forces Chaplaincy Centre, Amport House, Amport, Andover, Hants SP11 8BG
Dalton, Mark BD DipMin	2002		RN	The Chaplaincy, HMS *Raleigh*, Torpoint, Cornwall PL11 2PD
Davidson Kelly, Thomas A. MA BD FSAScot			OC	Army Personnel Centre, Glasgow
Duncan, John C. BD MPhil	1987	2001	A	3 Yorks, Battlesbury Barracks, Warminster BA12 9OT
Forsyth, Alexander R. TD BA MTh			TA	25 (Highland) Field Ambulance (V)
Frail, Nicola BLE MBA MDiv			TA	225 (Highland) Field Ambulance
Francis, James BD PhD	2002	2009	A	2 Royal Anglian, Trenchard Barracks, BFPO 23
Gardner, Neil N. MA BD	1991		OC	Edinburgh University Officer Training Corps
Kennon, Stanley BA BD	1992	2000	RN	The Chaplaincy, HMS *Drake*, HMMB Devonport, Plymouth PL2 2BG
Kingston, David V.F. BD DipPTh	1993		A	The Chaplain's Office, HQ Colchester Garrison, Melville Barracks, Colchester CO2 7UT
Kinsey, Louis BD DipMin			TA	205 (Scottish) Field Hospital (V)

Lancaster, Craig MA BD	2004	2011	RAF	RAF Cranwell, Sleaford NG34 8HB
London, Dale BTh FSAScot	2011		A	39 Morrison Street, Kirriemuir DD8 5DB
McCulloch, Alen J.R. MA BD	1990	1995	RN	The Chaplaincy, Defiance Building, HMMB Devonport, Plymouth PL2 2BG
McDonald, Ross J. BA BD ThM			RNR	HMS *Dalriada*, Greenock
MacKay, Stewart A.			A	HQ Coy, 5 Scots, BFPO 792
MacKenzie, Hector M.	2008		A	4 Scots and 2 Bn REME, St Barbara Barracks, BFPO 38
Mackenzie, Seoras L. BD	1996	1998	A	3 Scots, Fort George, Ardersier, Inverness IV1 2TD
MacLean, Marjory A. LLB BD PhD			RNR	HMS *Scotia*, Rosyth
MacLeod, C. Angus MA BD	1996		A	HQ Scottish Div, Stirling FK7 7RR
MacLeod, Rory N. MA BD	1986	1992	A	1 Scots, Dreghorn Barracks, Edinburgh EH13 9QW
MacPherson, Duncan J. BSc BD	1993	2002	A	RMA Sandhurst, Camberley, Surrey GU15 4PQ
Mathieson, Angus R. MA BD			OC	Resident Battalion, Dreghorn and Glencorse Barracks
Munro, Sheila BD	1995	2003	RAF	RAF Halton, Aylesbury, Bucks HP22 5PG
Rowe, Christopher BA BD	2008		TA	32 (Scottish) Signal Regiment
Shackleton, Scott J.S. BA BD PhD	1993	2010	RN	45 Commando Group Royal Marines, RM *Condor*, Arbroath DD11 3SJ
Stewart, Fraser M.C. BSc BD	1980		ACF	1 Bn The Highlanders
Sutherland, Iain A. BSc BD			TA	2 Bn The Highlanders
Thom, David J. BD			TA	105 Regiment Royal Artillery (V)
Thom, David J. BD			TA	Cumbria ACF
Thomson, Steven BSc BD	2001	2004	RN	The Chaplaincy, Lancelot Building, HMMB, Portsmouth, Hants PO1 3NT
Thornthwaite, Anthony P. MTh			TA	Resident Battalion, Redford Barracks and The Castle
Walker, James B. MA BD DPhil			OC	Tayforth Universities Officer Training Corps
Warwick, Ivan C. MA BD TD			TA	1 Bn The Highlanders
Watson, Karen K. BD MTh	1997		OC	Edinburgh Garrison
Whiteford, Alexander LTh			OC	Resident Battalion, Fort George

LIST C – HOSPITAL CHAPLAINS

NHS LOTHIAN

Head of Service and Lead Chaplain (Acute)
Alexander W. Young 0131-242 1990/1
Lead Chaplain (Community, Mental Health and Primary Care)
John McMahon 0131-537 6734

ACUTE HOSPITALS
(Spiritual Care Office: 0131-242 1990)

The Royal Infirmary of Edinburgh
51 Little France Crescent, Edinburgh EH16 4SA (0131-536 1000)

Alexander W. Young	0131-242 1990/1
Anne Mulligan	0131-242 1996
Ian Telfer	0131-242 1997

Liberton Hospital
113 Lasswade Road, Edinburgh EH16 6UB (0131-536 7800)

Anne Mulligan	0131-242 1996
Ian Telfer	0131-242 1997

The Western General Hospital
Crewe Road South, Edinburgh EH4 2XU (0131-537 1000)

Alistair Ridland	0131-537 1400
Liz Markey	0131-537 1401

The Royal Victoria Hospital
13 Craigleith Road, Edinburgh EH4 2DN (0131-537 5000)

Alistair Ridland	0131-537 1400
Liz Markey	0131-537 1401

The Royal Hospital for Sick Children
9 Sciennes Road, Edinburgh EH9 1LF (0131-536 0000)

Caroline Upton	0131-536 0144

St John's Hospital
Howden Road West, Livingston EH54 6PP (01506 523000)

Georgina Nelson	01506 522188

PRIMARY CARE, COMMUNITY AND MENTAL HEALTH SERVICES
(Spiritual Care Office: 0131-537 6516)

The Royal Edinburgh Hospital
Morningside Place, Edinburgh EH10 5HF (0131-537 6000)

John McMahon	0131-537 6734
Lynne MacMurchie	0131-537 6368
Maxwell Reay	0131-537 6366

Edinburgh Community Mental Health (Community Office 0131-220 5159)

Lynne MacMurchie	0131-537 6368
Maxwell Reay	0131-537 6366

St John's Hospital
Howden Road West, Livingston EH54 6PP (01506 523000)

Joe Gierasik	01506 522187

Edenhall Hospital
Edenhall Road, Musselburgh EH21 7TZ (0131-536 8000)
Anne Jones 0131-537 6516

For further information and full details of all e-mail/telephone contacts, see www.nhslothian.scot.nhs.uk

HOSPICES

MARIE CURIE HOSPICE, EDINBURGH			
ST COLUMBA'S HOSPICE	Rev. Michael Paterson		

HOSPITALS

CORSTORPHINE	Rev. J. William Hill	33/9 Murrayfield Road, Edinburgh EH12 6EP	
EASTERN GENERAL	Rev. John Tait	52 Pilrig Street, Edinburgh EH6 5AS	0131-554 1842
LINLITHGOW ST MICHAEL'S	Rev. Dr Georgina Nelson	Chaplain's Office, St John's Hospital, Livingston	01506 522188
BELHAVEN	Rev. Laurence H. Twaddle	The Manse, Belhaven Road, Dunbar EH42 1NH	01368 863098
EDENHALL	Rev. Anne M. Jones	7 North Elphinstone Farm, Tranent EH33 2ND	01875 614442
HERDMANFLAT	Rev. Anne M. Jones	7 North Elphinstone Farm, Tranent EH33 2ND	01875 614442
LOANHEAD	Mrs Susan Duncan	35 Kilmaurs Road, Edinburgh EH16 5DB	0131-667 2995
ROODLANDS	Rev. Anne M. Jones	7 North Elphinstone Farm, Tranent EH33 2ND	01875 614442
ROSSLYNLEE	Rev. John W. Fraser	North Manse, Penicuik EH26 8AG	01968 672213

BORDERS

MELROSE – BORDERS GENERAL HOSPITAL	Rev. J. Ronald Dick	Chaplaincy Centre, Borders General Hospital, Melrose TD6 9BS	01896 826564
HUNTLYBURN			
HAY LODGE, PEEBLES	Rev. James H. Wallace	Innerleithen Road, Peebles EH45 8BD	01721 721749
KNOLL	Post vacant		
KELSO	Rev. Robin McHaffie	Kirk Yetholm, Kelso TD5 8RD	01573 420308

DUMFRIES AND GALLOWAY

Hospital	Chaplain	Address	Telephone
DUMFRIES AND GALLOWAY ROYAL INFIRMARY [01387 241625]	Rev. Alexander E. Strachan		
THOMAS HOPE, LANGHOLM	Post vacant		
LOCHMABEN	Rev. Jack Brown	The Manse, Barrashead, Lochmaben, Lockerbie DG11 1QF	01387 810066
MOFFAT			
NEW ANNAN	Rev. Mairi C. Byers	Meadowbank, Plumdon Road, Annan DG12 6SJ	01461 206512
CASTLE DOUGLAS	Rev. Robert Malloch	1 Castle View, Castle Douglas DG7 1BG	01556 502171
DUMFRIES AND GALLOWAY ROYAL INFIRMARY			
KIRKCUDBRIGHT	Rev. Douglas R. Irving	6 Bourtree Avenue, Kirkcudbright DG6 4AU	01557 330489
THORNHILL			
NEWTON STEWART			
STRANRAER: GALLOWAY COMMUNITY			

AYRSHIRE AND ARRAN

Hospital	Chaplain	Address	Telephone
AYRSHIRE AND ARRAN PRIMARY CARE [01292 513023]			
AILSA HOSPITAL, AYR	Rev. Sheila Mitchell	Chaplaincy Centre, Dalmellington Road, Ayr KA6 6AB	01292 610555
AYR HOSPITAL/BIGGART HOSPITAL	Rev. Paul Russell		
AYRSHIRE AND ARRAN ACUTE HOSPITALS [01563 521133]			
CROSSHOUSE HOSPITAL KILMARNOCK	Rev. Alex Welsh	8 Greenside Avenue, Prestwick KA9 2HB	01292 475341
	Rev. Judith Huggett	4 Westmoor Crescent, Kilmarnock KA1 1TX	
STATE CARE AND OCCUPATIONAL HEALTH	Rev. Roderick H. McNidder	6 Hollow Park, Alloway, Ayr KA7 4SR	01292 442554
EAST AYRSHIRE COMMUNITY	Rev. John Paterson	33 Barrhill Road, Cumnock KA18 1PJ	01290 420769
WAR MEMORIAL, ARRAN	Rev. Elizabeth Watson	The Manse, Whiting Bay, Isle of Arran KA27 8RE	01770 700289
LADY MARGARET, MILLPORT			

LANARKSHIRE

Hospital	Chaplain	Address	Telephone
LADY HOME	Rev. Susan G. Cowell	3 Gavel Lane, Regency Gardens, Lanark ML11 9FB	01555 665509
LOCKHART	Rev. Alison Meikle	2 Kaimhill Court, Lanark ML11 9HU	01555 662600
CLELAND	Rev. John Jackson	The Manse, Bellside Road, Cleland, Motherwell ML1 5NP	01698 860260
KELLO			

ROADMEETINGS			
WISHAW GENERAL	Rev. James S.G. Hastie	Chalmers Manse, Quarry Road, Larkhall ML9 1HH	01698 882238
	Rev. J. Allardyce	6 Kelso Crescent, Wishaw ML2 7HD	01698 372657
	Rev. Sharon Colvin	48 Dunrobin Road, Airdrie ML6 8LR	01236 763154
	Rev. Mhorag MacDonald	350 Kirk Road, Wishaw ML2 8LH	01698 381305
STRATHCLYDE	Rev. David W. Doyle	19 Orchard Street, Motherwell ML1 3JE	01698 263472
HAIRMYRES	Rev. John Brewster	21 Turnberry Place, East Kilbride, Glasgow G75 8TB	01355 242564
	Rev. Dr John McPake	30 Eden Grove, East Kilbride, Glasgow G75 8XY	01355 234196
	Rev. James S.G. Hastie	Chalmers Manse, Quarry Road, Larkhall ML9 1HH	01698 882238
KIRKLANDS			
STONEHOUSE	Rev. Paul G.R. Grant	4 Hamilton Way, Stonehouse, Larkhall ML9 3PU	01698 792947
UDSTON			
COATHILL			
MONKLANDS GENERAL	Rev. James Munton	2 Moorcroft Drive, Airdrie ML6 8ES	01236 754848
	Rev. James Grier	14 Love Drive, Bellshill ML4 1BY	01698 742545
	Rev. Kay Gilchrist	48 Dunrobin Road, Airdrie ML6 8LR	01236 760154
WESTER MOFFAT	Rev. James Munton	2 Moorcroft Drive, Airdrie ML6 8ES	01263 754848
HARTWOODHILL	Rev. Derek Pope	35 Birrens Road, Motherwell ML1 3NS	01698 266716
HATTONLEA	Rev. Agnes Moore	16 Croftpark Street, Bellshill ML4 1EY	01698 842877

GREATER GLASGOW AND CLYDE

Head of Chaplaincy and Spiritual Care	Rev. Blair Robertson	SGH, Govan Road, Glasgow G51 4TF	0141-201 2156
GLASGOW ROYAL INFIRMARY (GRI)	Mrs Sandra Bell	Chaplaincy Centre, GRI, Castle Street, Glasgow G4 0SF	0141-211 4661
	Ms Helen Bunce	Chaplaincy Centre, GRI, Castle Street, Glasgow G4 0SF	0141-211 4661
WESTERN INFIRMARY (WI)	Rev. Keith Saunders	Chaplaincy Centre, WI, Dumbarton Road, Glasgow G11 6NT	0141-211 2812
GARTNAVEL GENERAL HOSPITAL (GGH)	Rev. Keith Saunders	Chaplaincy Centre, GGH, Great Western Road, Glasgow G12 0YN	0141-211 3026
GARTNAVEL ROYAL HOSPITAL (GRH)	Rev. Dr Kevin Franz	Chaplain's Office, GRH, Great Western Road, Glasgow G12 0XH	0141-211 3686
	Ms Anne MacDonald	Chaplain's Office, Leverndale Hospital, 510 Crookston Road, Glasgow G53 7TU	0141-211 6695
SOUTHERN GENERAL HOSPITAL (SGH)	Rev. Blair Robertson	Chaplaincy Centre, SGH, Govan Road, Glasgow G51 4TF	0141-201 2156
	Rev. Ann Purdie	Chaplaincy Centre, SGH, Govan Road, Glasgow G51 4TF	0141-201 2357
VICTORIA INFIRMARY (VI)	Rev. Ishaku Bitrus	Chaplaincy Centre, VI, Langside Road, Glasgow G42 9TY	0141-201 5164
YORKHILL AND QUEEN MOTHER'S	Rev. Alistair Bull	Chaplain's Office, RHSC, Dalnair Street, Glasgow G3 8SJ	0141-201 0595
LEVERNDALE	Rev. Alasdair MacDonald	Chaplain's Office, Leverndale Hospital, 510 Crookston Road, Glasgow G53 7TU	0141-211 6695
	Ms Anne MacDonald	Chaplain's Office, Leverndale Hospital, 510 Crookston Road, Glasgow G53 7TU	0141-211 6695

DRUMCHAPEL	Post vacant	c/o Chaplaincy Centre, GGH, Great Western Road, Glasgow G12 0YN	0141-211 3026
RUTHERGLEN	Ms Anne MacDonald	Chaplain's Office, Leverndale Hospital, 510 Crookston Road, Glasgow G53 7TU	0141-211 6695
PRINCE AND PRINCESS OF WALES HOSPICE	Rev. Leslie Edge	71 Carlton Place, Glasgow G5 9TD	0141-429 5599
FOURHILLS		c/o Chaplaincy, Gartnavel Royal Hospital	0141-211 3686
HUNTERS HILL MARIE CURIE CENTRE	Miss Dawn Allan	1 Belmont Road, Glasgow G21 3AY	0141-531 1346
INVERCLYDE ROYAL HOSPITAL (IRH)	Mrs Joyce Nicol	Chaplain's Office, IRH, Larkfield Road, Greenock PA16 0XN	01475 504759
DYKEBAR		c/o Chaplaincy Centre, RAH, Paisley PA2 9PN	0141-314 9561
ROYAL ALEXANDRA	Rev. Carol Campbell	Chaplaincy Centre, RAH, Paisley PA2 9PN	0141-314 9561
RAVENSCRAIG		c/o Chaplaincy Centre, RAH, Paisley PA2 9PN	0141-314 9561
DUMBARTON JOINT	Rev. Daniel Cheyne	217 Glasgow Road, Dumbarton G82 1EE	01389 763075
ERSKINE	Rev. Janet P.H. MacMahon (Mrs)	14 Hillfoot Drive, Bearsden, Glasgow G61 3QQ [E-mail: janet.macmahon@erskine.org.uk]	0141-942 8611
VALE OF LEVEN GENERAL	Rev. Ian Miller	1 Glebe Gardens, Bonhill, Alexandria G83 9HB	01389 753039
VALE OF LEVEN GERIATRIC	Rev. Frederick Booth	Achnashie Coach House, Clynder, Helensburgh G84 0QD	01436 831858

FORTH VALLEY

Head of Spiritual Care	Rev. Margery Collin	Forth Valley Royal Hospital, Larbert FK5 4WR	01324 566071
FORTH VALLEY ROYAL	Rev. Robert MacLeod		01324 566073
	Rev. Kenneth G. Russell		01324 566072
	Rev. Helen Christie		01324 813786
MENTAL HEALTH UNITS	Rev. Timothy Njuguna		07824 460903
BO'NESS	Mr Frank Hartley	49 Argyll Place, Kilsyth, Glasgow G65 0PY	01236 824135
FALKIRK COMMUNITY	Rev. Helen Christie	5 Watson Place, Dennyloanhead, Bonnybridge FK4 2BG	01324 813786
BANNOCKBURN	Rev. James Landels	Allan Manse, Bogend Road, Bannockburn, Stirling FK7 8NP	01786 814692
CLACKMANNAN COUNTY	Rev. Robert MacLeod	Forth Valley Royal Hospital, Larbert FK5 4WR	01324 566073
STIRLING COMMUNITY	Rev. Kenneth G. Russell	Forth Valley Royal Hospital, Larbert FK5 4WR	01324 566072

FIFE

QUEEN MARGARET HOSPITAL, DUNFERMLINE [01383 674136]	Mr Mark Evans DCS	Queen Margaret Hospital, Whitefield Road, Dunfermline KY12 0SU [E-mail: mark.evans59@nhs.net]	01383 674136
VICTORIA HOSPITAL, KIRKCALDY [01592 643355]			
LYNEBANK	Mr Allan Grant	6 Normandy Place, Rosyth, Dunfermline KY11 2HJ	01383 428760

CAMERON	Rev. James L. Templeton	Innerleven Manse, McDonald Street, Methil, Leven KY8 3AJ	01333 426310
GLENROTHES	Rev. Ian D. Gordon	2 Somerville Way, Forester's Grove, Glenrothes KY7 5GE	01592 742487
RANDOLPH WEMYSS	Rev. Elizabeth Cranfield	9 Chemiss Road, Methilhill, Leven KY8 2BS	01592 713142
ADAMSON, CUPAR	Rev. Lynn Brady	2 Guthrie Court, Cupar Road, Newburgh, Cupar KY14 6HA	01337 842228
NETHERLEA, NEWPORT	Rev. James Connolly	5 Westwater Place, Newport-on-Tay DD6 8NS	01382 542626
STRATHEDEN, CUPAR	Mr Allan Grant	6 Normandy Place, Rosyth, Dunfermline KY11 2HJ	01383 428760
ST ANDREWS COMMUNITY	Rev. James Connolly	5 Westwater Place, Newport-on-Tay DD6 8NS	01382 542626

TAYSIDE

Head of Spiritual Care	Rev. Gillian Munro	Royal Dundee Liff Hospital, Dundee DD2 5NF	01382 423116
Bereavement Co-ordinator	Rev. John M. Birrell	Perth Royal Infirmary, Perth PH1 1NX	01738 473850
DUNDEE NINEWELLS HOSPITAL	Mr David Gordon	Chaplain's Office, Ninewells Hospital, Dundee DD1 9SY	01382 632755
[01382 660111]	Rev. Anne Findlay	Chaplain's Office, Ninewells Hospital, Dundee DD1 9SY	01382 632755
PERTH ROYAL INFIRMARY	Rev. Anne Findlay	Chaplain's Office, Perth Royal Infirmary	01738 473896
	Mrs Sarah Lawson	Chaplain's Office, Perth Royal Infirmary	01738 473896
ABERFELDY COMMUNITY	Rev. Anne Brennan	The Manse, Balnaskeag, Kenmore, Aberfeldy PH15 2HB	01887 830218
BLAIRGOWRIE COMMUNITY	Rev. Alan Gibbon	61 Fifth Avenue, Glasgow G12 0AR	0141-334 1351
PITLOCHRY COMMUNITY	Post vacant		
CRIEFF COMMUNITY	Rev. James W. MacDonald	8 Strathearn Terrace, Crieff PH7 3AQ	01764 653907
MACMILLAN HOSPICE	Rev. Anne Findlay	Chaplain's Office, Perth Royal Infirmary	01738 473896
	Mrs Sarah Lawson	Chaplain's Office, Perth Royal Infirmary	01738 473896
ST MARGARET'S COMMUNITY	Rev. Anne Findlay	Chaplain's Office, Perth Royal Infirmary	01738 473896
	Mrs Sarah Lawson	Chaplain's Office, Perth Royal Infirmary	01738 473896
ASHLUDIE	Rev. David Jamieson	Panmure Manse, 8A Albert Street, Monifieth DD5 4JS	01382 532772
DUNDEE, ROYAL LIFF	Miss Jane Martin	16 Wentworth Road, Dundee DD2 3SD	01382 813786
STRATHMARTINE	Miss Jane Martin	16 Wentworth Road, Dundee DD2 3SD	01382 813786
ARBROATH INFIRMARY	Rev. Alasdair G. Graham	1 Charles Avenue, Arbroath DD11 2EZ	01241 872244
ANGUS, DUNDEE AND PERTH MENTAL HEALTHCARE	Rev. Rona Phillips	Spiritual Care Department, Dundee	01382 423110

GRAMPIAN

Head of Spiritual Care:
Rev. Fred Coutts, Chaplains' Office, Aberdeen Royal Infirmary, Foresterhill, Aberdeen AB25 2ZN 01224 553166

1. ACUTE SECTOR
ABERDEEN ROYAL INFIRMARY, ABERDEEN MATERNITY HOSPITAL
Chaplains' Office, Aberdeen Royal Infirmary, Foresterhill, Aberdeen AB25 2ZN 01224 553316
Rev. Fred Coutts
Rev. Sylvia Spencer

Rev. Alison M. Hutchison
Rev. Mark Rodgers
Mrs Trudy Noble (Assistant Chaplain)

ROYAL ABERDEEN CHILDREN'S HOSPITAL
Chaplain's Office, Royal Aberdeen Children's Hospital, Westburn Drive, Aberdeen AB25 2ZG — 01224 554905
Rev. James Falconer

ROXBURGHE HOUSE
Chaplain's Office, Roxburghe House, Ashgrove Road, Aberdeen AB25 2ZH — 01224 557077
Rev. Sylvia Spencer

WOODEND HOSPITAL
Chaplain's Office, Woodend Hospital, Eday Road, Aberdeen AB15 6XS — 01224 556788
Rev. Muriel Knox
Rev. John Duthie (Assistant Chaplain)

DR GRAY'S HOSPITAL, ELGIN
Rev. Thomas Bryson, The Manse, St Gerardine's Road, Lossiemouth IV31 6RA — 01343 813146
Rev. Andrew Willis, Deanshaugh Croft, Mulben, Keith AB55 6YJ — 01542 860240
Rev. Norma Milne, 26 Green Road, Huntly AB54 8BE — 01466 793841
Rev. David Young, 15 Mannachie Rise, Forres IV36 2US — 01309 672849

THE OAKS, ELGIN
Rev. Stuart Macdonald, 55 Forsyth Street, Hopeman, Elgin IV30 2SY — 01343 831175

2. MENTAL HEALTH
ROYAL CORNHILL HOSPITAL, WOODLANDS
Chaplain's Office, Royal Cornhill Hospital, Cornhill Road, Aberdeen AB25 2ZH — 01224 557293
Rev. Jim Simpson
Miss Pamela Adam (Assistant Chaplain)
Mr Donald Meston (Assistant Chaplain)

3. COMMUNITY HOSPITALS

ABOYNE	Rev. Alison M. Hutchison	Ashfield, Drumoak, Banchory AB31 5AG	01330 811309
GLEN O'DEE, BANCHORY	Rev. Alison M. Hutchison	Ashfield, Drumoak, Banchory AB31 5AG	01330 811309
CAMPBELL, PORTSOY	Rev. Alan Macgregor	7 Colleonard Road, Banff AB45 1DZ	01261 812107
CHALMERS, BANFF	Rev. Alan Macgregor	7 Colleonard Road, Banff AB45 1DZ	01261 812107
FLEMING, ABERLOUR	Rev. Andrew Willis	Deanshaugh Croft, Mulben, Keith AB55 6YJ	01542 860240

FRASERBURGH	Rev. James Newell	39 Grattan Place, Fraserburgh AB43 9SD	01346 514905
INVERURIE	Rev. Ian B. Groves	1 Westburn Place, Inverurie AB51 5QS	01467 620285
INSCH	Rev. Jane C. Taylor	22 Western Road, Insch AB52 6JR	01464 820914
JUBILEE, HUNTLY	Rev. Norma Milne	26 Green Road, Huntly AB54 8BE	01466 793841
KINCARDINE COMMUNITY, STONEHAVEN	Rev. Elizabeth Campbell	3 Ramsay Road, Stonehaven AB39 2HJ	
LEANCHOIL, FORRES	Rev. David Young	15 Mannachie Rise, Forres IV36 2US	01309 672284
MUIRTON	Rev. Andrew Willis	Deanshaugh Croft, Mulben, Keith AB55 6YJ	01542 860240
PETERHEAD COMMUNITY	Rev. David S. Ross	3–5 Abbey Street, Deer, Peterhead AB42 5LN	01771 623994
SEAFIELD, BUCKIE	Rev. Andrew Willis	Deanshaugh Croft, Mulben, Keith AB55 6YJ	01542 860240
STEPHEN, DUFFTOWN	Rev. Hugh M.C. Smith	The Manse, Church Street, Dufftown, Keith AB55 4AR	01340 820380
TURNER, KEITH	Rev. Kay Gauld	The Manse, Church Road, Keith AB55 5BR	01542 882799
TURRIFF	Mrs Margaret Robb	Chrislovan, Keithhall, Invervrie AB51 0LN	
UGIE, PETERHEAD	Mrs Sena Allen	Berea Cottage, Kirk Street, Peterhead AB42 1RY	01779 477327

HIGHLAND

THE RAIGMORE HOSPITAL [01463 704000]	Rev. Derek Brown	Cathedral Manse, Dornoch IV25 3HV	
IAN CHARLES	Rev. Morris Smith	Golf Course Road, Grantown-on-Spey PH26 3HY	01479 872084
ST VINCENT	Rev. Helen Cook	The Manse, West Terrace, Kingussie PH21 1HA	01340 661311
NEW CRAIGS	Rev. Dr Iain Macritchie		01463 704000
NAIRN TOWN AND COUNTY	Rev. Ian Hamilton	3 Manse Road, Nairn IV12 4RN	01667 452203
BELFORD AND BELHAVEN	Rev. Donald A. MacQuarrie	Manse of Duncansburgh, Fort William PH33 6BA	01397 702297
GLENCOE			
ROSS MEMORIAL, DINGWALL	Rev. Russel Smith	8 Castlehill Road, Dingwall IV15 9PB	01349 861011
INVERGORDON COUNTY	Rev. Kenneth D. Macleod	The Manse, Cromlet Drive, Invergordon IV18 0BA	01349 852273
LAWSON MEMORIAL	Rev. Eric Paterson	Free Church Manse, Golspie KW10 6TT	01408 633529
MIGDALE	Rev. Kenneth Hunter	Free Church Manse, Gower Street, Brora KW9 6PU	01408 621271
CAITHNESS GENERAL	Mr John Craw	'Craiglockhart', Latheronwheel, Latheron KW5 6DW	01593 741779
DUNBAR	Rev. Alastair H. Gray	The Manse, Station Road, Watten, Wick KW1 5YN	01955 621220
BROADFORD MACKINNON MEMORIAL	Rev. Dr Ben Johnstone	The Shiants, 5 Upper Breakish, Breakish, Isle of Skye IV42 8PY	01471 822538
PORTREE	Rev. Donald G. MacDonald	Free Church Manse, 3 Sluggans, Portree, Isle of Skye IV51 9LY	01478 613256
CAMPBELTOWN			
LOCHGILPHEAD	Mrs Margaret Sinclair	2 Quarry Park, Furnace, Inveraray PA32 8XW	01499 500633
ISLAY	Post vacant		
DUNOON	Rev. Ruth Griffiths	Kirkwood, Mathieson Lane, Innellan, Dunoon PA23 7TA	01369 830145
ROTHESAY	Mr Raymond Deans	60 Ardmory Road, Rothesay PA20 0PG	01700 504893
LORN AND THE ISLANDS DISTRICT GENERAL	Rev. William Gray	Liogh, Glengallan Road, Oban PA34	01631 567500

WESTERN ISLES HEALTH BOARD

UIST AND BARRA HOSPITAL WESTERN ISLES, STORNOWAY	Rev. T.K. Shadakshari	69 Plasterfield, Stornoway, Isle of Lewis HS1 2UR	01851 701727

ORKNEY HEALTH BOARD

BALFOUR AND EASTBANK	Mrs Marion Dicken	6 Claymore Brae, Kirkwall KW15 1UQ	01856 879509

LIST D – FULL-TIME INDUSTRIAL CHAPLAINS

EDINBURGH (Edinburgh City Mission Appointment)	Mr John Hopper	26 Mulberry Drive, Dunfermline KY11 5BZ	01383 737189
EDINBURGH AND CENTRAL	Mr Paul Wilson	121 George Street, Edinburgh EH2 4YN	(Mbl) 07908 102437
WEST OF SCOTLAND	Rev. Gordon Armstrong	52 Balgonie Avenue, Paisley PA2 9LP	0141-587 3124
UK OIL AND GAS INDUSTRY	Rev. Martin Grashoff	Total E and P (UK) Ltd, Loirston House, Wellington Road, Aberdeen AB12 3BH	01224 298538
ABERDEEN CITY CENTRE (part-time)	Mrs Cate Adams	The Citadel, 28 Castle Street, Aberdeen AB11 5BG	01224 597373
NATIONAL DIRECTOR	Rev. Iain McFadzean	Church of Scotland Offices, 121 George Street, Edinburgh EH2 4YN	0131-225 5722
EASTERN AREA	Rev. Allan F. Webster	65 Clepington Road, Dundee DD4 7BQ	01382 458764

LIST E – PRISON CHAPLAINS

ADVISER TO SCOTTISH PRISON SERVICE (NATIONAL)	Rev. William Taylor	SPS HQ, Calton House, Edinburgh EH12 9HW	0131-244 8640
ABERDEEN CRAIGINCHES	Rev. Dr David Ross	HM Prison, Aberdeen AB11 8FN	01224 238300
	Rev. Louis Kinsey	HM Prison, Aberdeen AB11 8FN	01224 238300
	Rev. Iain Barclay	HM Prison, Aberdeen AB11 8FN	01224 238300
ADDIEWELL	Rev. Robert Craig	HM Prison, Addiewell, West Calder EH55 8QA	01506 874500
CORNTON VALE	Rev. Alexander Wark	HM Prison, Cornton Vale, Stirling FK9 5NU	01786 832591
DUMFRIES	Rev. Neil Campbell	HM Prison, Dumfries DG2 9AX	01387 261218
EDINBURGH: SAUGHTON	Rev. Colin Reed	Chaplaincy Centre, HMP Edinburgh EH11 3LN	0131-444 3115
	Rev. Robert Akroyd	HM Prison, Edinburgh EH11 3LN	0131-444 3115
	Rev. Chris Currie	HM Prison, Edinburgh EH11 3LN	0131-444 3115
GLASGOW: BARLINNIE	Rev. Martin Forrest	HM Prison, Barlinnie, Glasgow G33 2QX	0141-770 2059
	Rev. Ian McInnes	HM Prison, Barlinnie, Glasgow G33 2QX	0141-770 2059
	Rev. Douglas Clark	HM Prison, Barlinnie, Glasgow G33 2QX	0141-770 2059
	Rev. Alexander Wilson	HM Prison, Barlinnie, Glasgow G33 2QX	0141-770 2059
	Rev. Jonathan Keefe	HM Prison, Barlinnie, Glasgow G33 2QX	0141-770 2059
GLENOCHIL	Rev. Graham Bell	HM Prison, Glenochil FK10 3AD	01259 760471
	Rev. Elizabeth Kenny	HM Prison, Glenochil FK10 3AD	01259 760471
GREENOCK	Rev. James Munro	80 Bardrainney Avenue, Port Glasgow PA14 6UD	01475 701213
INVERNESS	Rev. Alexander Shaw	HM Prison, Inverness IV2 3HN	01463 229000
	Rev. Christopher Smart	HM Prison, Inverness IV2 3HN	01463 229000
	Rev. Peter Donald	39 Southside Road, Inverness IV2 4XA	01463 230537
KILMARNOCK	Rev. Andrew Black	HMP Bowhouse, Mauchline Road, Kilmarnock KA1 5AA	01563 548928
	Rev. Nigel Johns	HMP Bowhouse, Mauchline Road, Kilmarnock KA1 5AA	01563 548928
	Rev. Colin Cuthbert	HMP Bowhouse, Mauchline Road, Kilmarnock KA1 5AA	01563 548928

OPEN ESTATE: CASTLE HUNTLY AND NORANSIDE	Rev. Anne E. Stewart	Open Estate Chaplaincy, HMP Castle Huntly, Longforgan, Dundee DD2 5HL	01382 319388
PERTH	Rev. Graham Matthews	Chaplaincy Centre, HMP Perth PH2 8AT	01738 622293
	Mrs Deirdre Yellowlees	Chaplaincy Centre, HMP Perth PH2 8AT	01738 622293
PETERHEAD	Rev. Dr David Ross	HM Prison, Peterhead AB42 6YY	01779 479101
POLMONT	Rev. Donald H. Scott	Chaplaincy Centre, HMYOI Polmont, Falkirk FK2 0AB	01324 711558
	Mr Craig Bryan	Chaplaincy Centre, HMYOI Polmont, Falkirk FK2 0AB	01324 711558
SHOTTS	Ms Dorothy Russell	Chaplaincy Centre, HMP Shotts ML7 4LE	01501 824071

LIST F – UNIVERSITY CHAPLAINS

ABERDEEN	Easter Smart MDiv DMin	01224 488396
ABERTAY, DUNDEE	Leslie M. Barrett BD FRICS	01382 308447
CALEDONIAN	Euan Dodds	0141-558 7451
CAMBRIDGE	Vacant	
DUNDEE	Fiona C. Douglas MBE MA BD PhD	01382 384157
EDINBURGH	Richard Frazer (Honorary)	0131-650 2595
GLASGOW	Stuart D. MacQuarrie JP BD BSc	0141-330 5419
HERIOT-WATT	Alistair P. Donald MA PhD BD	0131-451 4508
NAPIER	John Smith (Honorary)	0131-447 8724
OXFORD	Carla Grosch-Miller (U.R.C. and C. of S.)	01865 554358
PAISLEY	Morris M. Dutch BD BA	0141-571 4059
ROBERT GORDON	Daniel French	01224 262000 (ext 3506)
ST ANDREWS		01334 462866
STIRLING	Gillian Weighton BD STM (Honorary)	01786 832753
STRATHCLYDE	Marjory Macaskill LLB BD	0141-553 4144

LIST G – THE DIACONATE

NAME	COM	APP	ADDRESS	TEL	PRES
Anderson, Janet (Miss) DCS	1979	2006	Creagard, 31 Lower Breakish, Isle of Skye IV42 8QA [E-mail: jaskye31@tiscali.co.uk]	01471 822403	38
Beaton, Margaret (Miss) DCS	1989	1988	64 Gardenside Grove, Carmyle, Glasgow G32 8EZ [E-mail: margaret@churchhouse.plus.com]	0141-646 2297 (Mbl) 07796 642382	16
Bell, Sandra (Mrs)	2001	2004	62 Loganswell Road, Thornliebank, Glasgow G46 8AX	0141-638 5884	16
Black, Linda (Miss) BSc DCS	1993	2004	148 Rowan Road, Abronhill, Cumbernauld, Glasgow G67 3DA [E-mail: lnan@blueyonder.co.uk]	01236 786265	22
Buchanan, Marion (Mrs) MA DCS	1983	2006	16 Almond Drive, East Kilbride, Glasgow G74 2HX		16
Burns, Marjory (Mrs) DCS	1997	1998	22 Kirklee Road, Mossend, Bellshill ML4 2QN [E-mail: mburns8070@aol.co.uk]	01698 292685 (Mbl) 07792 843922	17
Carson, Christine (Miss) MA DCS	2006		36 Upper Wellhead, Limekilns, Dunfermline KY11 3JQ	01383 873131 (Mbl) 07919 137294	24
Cathcart, John Paul (Mr) DCS	2000		9 Glen More, East Kilbride, Glasgow G74 2AP [E-mail: paulcathcart@msn.com]	01355 243970 (Mbl) 07708 396074	16
Corrie, Margaret (Miss) DCS	1989	1998	44 Sunnyside Street, Camelon, Falkirk FK1 4BH	01324 670656	22
Crawford, Morag (Miss) MSc DCS	1977	1998	118 Wester Drylaw Place, Edinburgh EH4 2TG [E-mail: morag.crawford.dcs@blueyonder.co.uk]	(Tel/Fax) 0131-332 2253 (Mbl) 07970 982563	24
Crocker, Elizabeth (Mrs) DCS DipComEd	1985	2003	77C Craigcrook Road, Edinburgh EH4 3PH	0131-332 0227	1
Cunningham, Ian (Mr) DCS	1994	2002	The Manse, Rothiemay, Huntly AB54 7NE	01466 711334	35
Cuthbertson, Valerie (Miss) DipTMus DCS	2003		105 Bellshill Road, Motherwell ML1 3SJ [E-mail: v.cuthbertson333@btinternet.com]	01698 259001	22
Deans, Raymond (Mr) DCS	1994	2003	60 Ardmory Road, Rothesay, Isle of Bute PA20 0PG [E-mail: r.deans93@btinternet.com]	01700 504893	19
Dunnett, Linda (Mrs)	1976	2000	5 Fincastle Place, Cowie, Stirling FK7 7DS [E-mail: lindadunnett@sky.com]	01786 818413	23
Evans, Mark (Mr) BSc RGN DCS	1988	2006	13 Easter Drylaw Drive, Edinburgh EH4 2QA [E-mail: mark.evans59@nhs.net]	0131-343 3089 (Office) 01383 674136	24
Forrest, Janice (Mrs)	1990		38 Lochview Drive, Glasgow G33 1QF	0141-770 9611	16
Gargrave, Mary (Mrs) DCS	1989	2002	The Manse, 90 Mount Annan Drive, Glasgow G44 4RZ [E-mail: mary.gargrave@btinternet.com]	0141-561 4681	16
Getliffe, Dorothy (Mrs) DCS BA BD	2006		3 Woodview Terrace, Hamilton ML3 9DP [E-mail: DGetliffe@aol.com]	01698 423504	17
Gordon, Margaret (Mrs) DCS	1998	2001	92 Lanark Road West, Currie EH14 5LA	0131-449 2554	1
Gray, Greta (Miss) DCS	1992	1998	67 Crags Avenue, Paisley PA2 6SG	0141-884 6178	14
Hamilton, James (Mr) DCS	1997	2000	6 Beckfield Gate, Glasgow G33 1SW [E-mail: j.hamilton111@btinternet.com]	0141-558 3195	16

Name			Address		Telephone	
Hamilton, Karen (Mrs) DCS	1995	2009	6 Beckfield Gate, Glasgow G33 1SW		0141-558 3195	17
			[E-mail: k.hamilton6@btinternet.com]	(Mbl)	07970 872859	
King, Margaret (Miss) DCS	2002		56 Murrayfield, Fochabers IV32 7EZ		01343 820937	35
Love, Joanna (Ms) BSc DCS	2006		92 Everard Drive, Glasgow G21 1XQ		0141-563 5859	16
Lyall, Ann (Miss) DCS	1980	2011	17 Mercat Loan, Biggar ML12 6DG		01899 220625	13
			[E-mail: ann.lyall@btinternet.com]			
MacDonald, Anne (Miss) BA	1980	2002	502 Castle Gait, Paisley PA1 2PA		0141-840 1875	16
McKay, Kenneth (Mr) DCS	1996	1998	11F Balgowan Road, Letham, Perth PH1 2JG		01738 621169	28
			[E-mail: deakendan@gmail.com]	(Mbl)	07843 883042	
MacKinnon, Ronald (Mr) DCS	1996	2004	12 Mossywood Court, McGregor Avenue, Airdrie ML6 7DY		01236 763389	22
McLellan, Margaret (Mrs)	1986	2000	18 Broom Road East, Newton Mearns, Glasgow G77 5SD		0141-639 6853	16
McPheat, Elspeth (Miss)	1985	2001	11/5 New Orchardfield, Edinburgh EH6 5ET		0131-554 4143	1
Mulligan, Anne MA DCS	1974	1986	27A Craigour Avenue, Edinburgh EH17 7NH		0131-664 3426	1
			[E-mail: mulliganne@aol.com]	(Office)	0131-242 1996	
Munro, Patricia (Ms) BSc DCS	1986	2002	82 Balbedie Avenue, Lochore, Lochgelly KY5 8HP		01592 869240	24
			[E-mail: pat_munro@btinternet.com]	(Mbl)	07814 836314	
Nicholson, David (Mr) DCS	1994	1993	2D Doonside, Kildrum, Cumbernauld, Glasgow G67 2HX		01236 732260	22
			[E-mail: deacdave@btinternet.com]	(Mbl)	07703 332270	
Nicol, Joyce (Mrs) BA DCS	1974	1998	93 Brisbane Street, Greenock PA16 8NY		01475 723235	14
				(Mbl)	07957 642709	
Ogilvie, Colin (Mr) DCS	1998	2003	32 Upper Bourtree Court, Glasgow G73 4HT		0141-569 2725	16
Philip, Elizabeth (Mrs) DCS MA BA PGCSE			12 Torvean Place, Dunfermline KY11 4YY		01383 721054	24
Porter, Jean (Mrs) DCS	2006		3 Cochrie Place, Tullibody, Alloa FK10 2RR	(Mbl)	07729 316321	23
			[E-mail: jeanjeanniet@aol.com]			
Rennie, Agnes M. (Miss) DCS	1974	1979	3/1 Craigmillar Court, Edinburgh EH16 4AD		0131-661 8475	1
Ross, Duncan (Mr) DCS	1996	2006	28 Fulbar Crescent, Paisley PA2 9AS		01505 812304	14
			[E-mail: ssornacnud@hotmail.com]			
Rycroft-Sadi, Pauline (Mrs) DCS	2003	2006	6 Ashville Terrace, Edinburgh EH6 8DD		0131-554 6564	1
				(Mbl)	07759 436303	
Steele, Marilynn J. (Mrs) BD DCS	1999	1999	2 Northfield Gardens, Prestonpans EH32 9LQ		01875 811497	1
Steven, Gordon BD DCS	1997	2004	51 Nantwich Drive, Edinburgh EH7 6RB		0131-669 2054	3
				(Mbl)	07904 385256	
Stewart, Marion (Miss) DCS	1991	1994	Kirk Cottage, Kirkton of Skene, Westhill, Skene AB32 6XE		01224 743407	33
Thomson, Jacqueline (Mrs) DCS MTh	2004	2004	1 Barron Terrace, Leven KY8 4DL		01333 301115	24
			[E-mail: churchdeacon@blueyonder.co.uk]	(Mbl)	07713 637054	
Urquhart, Barbara (Mrs) DCS	1986	2006	9 Standalane, Kilmaurs, Kilmarnock KA3 2NB		01563 538289	11
			[E-mail: barbaraurquhart@uko2.co.uk]			
Wallace, Sheila (Mrs)			Mayfield Salisbury Church, 18 West Mayfield, Edinburgh EH9 1TQ	(Mbl)	07733 243046	1
Wilson, Glenda (Mrs) DCS	1990	2006	Glenmorven, 74 Alexander Street, Dunoon PA23 7BB		01369 700848	19
Wilson, Muriel (Miss) MA BD DCS	1997	2001	28 Bellevue Crescent, Ayr KA7 2DR		01292 264939	10
			[E-mail: muriel.wilson4@btinternet.com]			

Wishart, William (Mr) DCS	1994	2004	10 Stanely Drive, Paisley PA2 6HE [E-mail: bill@saintninians.co.uk]	0141-884 4177 (Mbl) 07846 555654	14
Wright, Lynda (Miss) BEd DCS	1979	1992	Key Cottage, High Street, Falkland, Cupar KY15 7BU	01337 857705	26

THE DIACONATE (Retired List)

NAME	COM	ADDRESS	TEL	PRES
Allan, Jean (Mrs) DCS	1989	12C Hindmarsh Avenue, Dundee DD3 7LW	01382 827299	29
Bayes, Muriel C. (Mrs) DCS	1963	Flat 6, Carleton Court, 10 Fenwick Road, Glasgow G46 4AN	0141-633 0865	16
Beaton, Jamesina (Miss) DCS	1953	Farhills, Fort Augustus PH32 4DS	01320 366252	38
Buchanan, John (Mr) DCS	2010	19 Gillespie Crescent, Edinburgh EH10 4HZ	0131-229 0794	3
Cameron, Margaret (Miss) DCS	1961	2 Rowans Gate, Paisley PA2 6RD	0141-840 2479	14
Copland, Agnes M. (Mrs) MBE DCS	1950	Altnacraig House, Lyle Road, Greenock PA16 7XT		14
Craw, John (Mr) DCS	1998	Liabost, 8 Proudfoot Road, Wick KW1 4PQ	01955 603805 (Mbl) 07544 761653	41
Cunningham, Alison W. (Miss) DCS	1961	23 Strathblane Road, Milngavie, Glasgow G62 8DL	0141-563 9232	18
Drummond, Rhoda (Miss) DCS	1960	Flat K, 23 Grange Loan, Edinburgh EH9 2ER	0131-668 3631	1
Erskine, Morag (Miss) DCS	1979	111 Mains Drive, Park Mains, Erskine PA8 7JJ	0141-812 6096	14
Flockhart, Andrew (Mr) DCS	1988	Flat 0/1, 8 Hardie Avenue, Rutherglen, Glasgow G73 3AS	0141-569 0716	16
Gordon, Fiona S. (Mrs) MA DCS	1958	Machrie, 3 Cupar Road, Cuparmuir, Cupar KY15 5RH [E-mail: machrie@madasafish.com]	01334 652341	26
Gray, Catherine (Miss) DCS	1969	10C Eastern View, Gourock PA19 1RJ	01475 637479	14
Gray, Christine M. (Mrs) DCS	1969	11 Woodside Avenue, Thornliebank, Glasgow G46 7HR	0141-571 1008	16
Howden, Margaret (Miss) DCS	1954	38 Munro Street, Kirkcaldy KY1 1PY	01592 205913	25
Hughes, Helen (Miss) DCS	1977	2/2, 43 Burnbank Terrace, Glasgow G20 6UQ	0141-333 9459	16
Hutchison, Alan E.W. (Mr) DCS	1988	132 Lochbridge Road, North Berwick EH39 4DR	01620 894077	3
Johnston, Mary (Miss) DCS	1988	19 Lounsdale Drive, Paisley PA2 9ED	0141-849 1615	14
King, Chris (Mrs) DCS	2002	28 Kilnford, Dundonald, Kilmarnock KA2 9ET [E-mail: chrisking99@tiscali.co.uk]	01563 851197	10
Lundie, Ann V. (Miss) DCS	1972	20 Langdykes Drive, Cove, Aberdeen AB12 3HW	01224 898416	31
McBain, Margaret (Miss) DCS	1974	33 Quarry Road, Paisley PA2 7RD	0141-884 2920	14
McCallum, Moyra (Miss) MA BD DCS	1965	176 Hilton Drive, Aberdeen AB24 4LT [E-mail: moymac@aol.com]	01224 486240	31
McCully, M. Isobel (Miss) DCS	1974	10 Broadstone Avenue, Port Glasgow PA14 5BB	01475 742240	14
MacLean, Donald A. (Mr) DCS	1988	8 Upper Barvas, Isle of Lewis HS2 0QX	01851 840454	44
McNaughton, Janette (Miss) DCS	1982	4 Dunellan Avenue, Moodiesburn, Glasgow G69 0GB	01236 870180	22
MacPherson, James B. (Mr) DCS	1988	104 Cartside Street, Glasgow G42 9TQ	0141-616 6468	16

MacQuien, Duncan (Mr) DCS	1988	35 Criffel Road, Mount Vernon, Glasgow G32 9JE	0141-575 1137	14
Martin, Jane (Miss) DCS	1979	16 Wentworth Road, Dundee DD2 3SD [E-mail: janimar@aol.com]	01382 813786	29
Merrilees, Ann (Miss) DCS	1994	23 Cuthill Brae, Willow Wood Residential Park, West Calder EH55 8QE [E-mail: ann@merrilees.freeserve.co.uk]	01501 762909	2
Miller, Elsie M. (Miss) DCS	1974	30 Swinton Avenue, Rowanbank, Baillieston, Glasgow G69 6JR	0141-771 0857	22
Mitchell, Joyce (Mrs) DCS	1994	Sunnybank, Farr, Inverness IV2 6XG [E-mail: joyce@mitchell71.freeserve.co.uk]	01808 521285	37
Morrison, Jean (Dr) DCS	1964	45 Corslet Road, Currie EH14 5LZ [E-mail: jean.morrison@blueyonder.co.uk]	0131-449 6859	1
Moyes, Sheila (Miss) DCS	1957	158 Pilton Avenue, Edinburgh EH5 2JZ	0131-551 1731	1
Palmer, Christine (Ms) DCS	2003	39 Fortingall Place, Perth PH1 2NF	01738 587488	28
Ramsay, Katherine (Miss) MA DCS	1958	25 Homeroyal House, 2 Chalmers Crescent, Edinburgh EH9 1TP	0131-667 4791	1
Ronald, Norma A. (Miss) MBE DCS	1961	2B Saughton Road North, Edinburgh EH12 7HG	0131-334 8736	1
Rose, Lewis (Mr) DCS	1993	5 Lyndhurst Avenue, Dundee DD2 3HR [E-mail: scimnorth@uk.uumail.com]	01382 622167 (Mbl) 07899 790466	29
Rutherford, Ellen B. (Miss) MBE DCS	1962	41 Duncanston, Conon Bridge, Dingwall IV7 8JB	01349 877439	39
Smith, Catherine (Mrs) DCS	1964	21 Lingaro, Bixter, Shetland ZE2 9NN	01595 810207	46
Smith, Lillian (Miss) MA DCS	1977	6 Fintry Mains, Dundee DD4 9HF	01382 500052	29
Stuart, Anne (Miss) DCS	1966	1 Murrell Terrace, Burntisland KY3 0XH	01383 860049	24
Tait, Agnes (Mrs) DCS	1995	10 Carnoustie Crescent, Greenhills, East Kilbride, Glasgow G75 8TE	01389 873196	17
Teague, Yvonne (Mrs) DCS	1965	46 Craigcrook Avenue, Edinburgh EH4 3PX	0131-336 3113	1
Thom, Helen (Miss) BA DipEd MA DCS	1959	84 Great King Street, Edinburgh EH3 6QU	0131-556 5687	1
Thomson, Phyllis (Miss) DCS	2003	63 Caroline Park, Mid Calder, Livingston EH53 0SJ	01506 883207	2
Trimble, Robert DCS	1988	5 Templar Rise, Livingston EH54 6PJ	01506 412504	2
Webster, Elspeth H. (Miss) DCS	1950	82 Broomhill Avenue, Burntisland KY3 0BP	01592 873616	25

THE DIACONATE (Supplementary List)

Gilroy, Lorraine (Mrs) DCS	1988	5 Bluebell Drive, Cheverel Court, Bedward CO12 0GE	02476 366031
Guthrie, Jennifer M. (Miss) DCS		14 Eskview Terrace, Ferryden, Montrose DD10 9RD	01674 674413
Harris, Judith (Mrs) DCS	1993	243 Western Avenue, Sandfields, Port Talbot, West Glamorgan SA12 7NF	01639 884855
Hood, Katrina (Mrs) DCS	1988	67C Farquhar Road, Edgbaston, Birmingham B18 2QP	
Hudson, Sandra (Mrs) DCS	1982	10 Albany Drive, Rutherglen, Glasgow G73 3QN	

McIntosh, Kay (Mrs) DCS	2008	4 Jacklin Green, Livingston EH54 8PZ [E-mail: deaconess@backedge.co.uk]	01506 495472
Muir, Alison M. (Mrs) DCS	1969	77 Arthur Street, Dunfermline KY12 0JJ	
Ramsden, Christine (Miss) DCS	1978	2 Wykeham Close, Bassett, Southampton SO16 7LZ	
Walker, Wikje (Mrs) DCS	1970	24 Brodie's Yard, Queen Street, Coupar Angus PH13 9RA	01828 628251
Wallace, Catherine (Mrs) DCS		5 Strathearn Terrace, Perth PH2 0LS	01738 621709

LIST H – MINISTERS HAVING RESIGNED MEMBERSHIP OF PRESBYTERY

(in Terms of Act III 1992)

(Resignation of Presbytery membership does not imply the lack of a practising certificate. Some of those listed do have practising certificates; others do not.)

NAME	ORD	ADDRESS	TEL	PRES
Anderson, Kenneth G. MA BD	1967	8 School Road, Arbroath DD11 2LT	01241 874825	30
Bailey, W. Grahame MA BD	1939	148 Craiglea Drive, Edinburgh EH10 5PU	0131-447 1663	1
Barbour, Robin A.S. KCVO MC MA BD STM DD	1954	Old Fincastle, Pitlochry PH16 5RJ	01796 473209	27
Bartholomew, Julia (Mrs) BSc BD	2002	Kippenhill, Dunning, Perth PH2 0RA	01764 684929	28
Beck, John C. BD	1975	43A Balvenie Street, Dufftown, Keith AB55 4AS		35
Brown, Alastair BD	1986	52 Henderson Drive, Kintore, Inverurie AB51 0FB	01467 632787	32
Brown, Joseph MA	1954	The Orchard, Hermitage Lane, Shedden Park Road, Kelso TD5 7AN	01573 223481	6
Caie, Albert LTh	1983	34 Ringwell Gardens, Stonehouse, Larkhall ML9 3QW	01698 792187	32
Campbell, J. Ewen R. MA BD	1967	20 St Margaret's Road, North Berwick EH39 4PJ	01620 893814	25
Coghill, Andrew W.F. BD DPS	1993			
Cooper, George MA BD	1943	8 Leighton Square, Alyth, Blairgowrie PH11 8AQ	01828 633746	1
Craig, Eric MA BD BA	1959	5 West Relugas Road, Edinburgh EH9 2PW	0131-667 8210	1
Craig, Gordon W. MBE MA BD	1972	1 Beley Bridge, Dunino, St Andrews KY16 8LT	01334 880285	26
Crawford, S.G. Victor	1980	Crofton, 65 Main Road, East Wemyss, Kirkcaldy KY1 4RL	01592 712325	25
Cumming, David P.L. MA	1957	Shillong, Tarbat Ness Road, Portmahomack, Tain IV20 1YA	01862 871794	19
Currie, Gordon C.M. MA BD	1975	43 Deanburn Park, Linlithgow EH49 6HA	01506 842759	2
Davidson, John F. BSc DipEdTech	1970	49 Craigmill Gardens, Carnoustie DD7 6HX [E-mail: davidson900@btinternet.com]	01241 854566	30
Davies, Gareth W. BA BD	1979	Pitadro House, Fordell Gardens, Dunfermline KY11 7EY	01383 417634	24
Doherty, Arthur James DipTh	1957	1 Murdiston Avenue, Callander FK17 8AY		23
Donaldson, Colin V.	1982	3A Playfair Terrace, St Andrews KY16 9HX	01334 472889	3
Drake, Wendy F. (Mrs) BD	1978	21 William Black Place, South Queensferry EH30 9QR [E-mail: revwdrake@hotmail.co.uk]	0131-331 1520	1

Name	Ord.	Address	Tel.	Pres.
Drummond, R. Hugh	1953	19 Winton Park, Edinburgh EH10 7EX [E-mail: hughdrummond1@activemail.co.uk]	0131-445 3634	1
Ferguson, Ronald MA BD ThM	1972	Vinbreck, Orphir, Orkney KW17 2RE [E-mail: ronbluebrazil@aol.com]	01856 811353	45
Finlayson, Duncan MA	1943	Flat 3, Nicholson Court, Kinnettas Road, Strathpeffer IV14 9BG	01997 420014	39
Gordon, Alasdair B. BD LLB EdD	1970	31 Binghill Park, Milltimber, Aberdeen AB13 0EE [E-mail: alasdairbgordon@hotmail.com]	01224 732464	31
Greig, James C.G. MA BD STM	1955	Block 2, Flat 2, Station Lofts, Strathblane, Glasgow G63 9BD [E-mail: james.greig12@btinternet.com]	01360 771915	16
Grubb, George D.W. BA BD BPhil DMin	1962	10 Wellhead Close, South Queensferry EH30 9WA	0131-331 2072	1
Hamilton, David S.M. MA BD STM	1958	49 Paddocks Lane, Cheltenham GL50 4NU	01242 254917	47
Hosie, James MA BD MTh	1959	Hilbre, Baycrofts, Strachur, Cairndow, Argyll PA27 8BY	01369 860634	19
Howie, William MA BD STM	1964	26 Morgan Road, Aberdeen AB16 5JY	01224 483669	31
Hurst, Frederick R. MA	1965	Flat 6, 21 Bulldale Place, Glasgow G14 0NE	0141-959 2604	40
Lambie, Andrew E. BD	1957	1 Mercat Loan, Biggar ML12 6DG	01899 221352	13
Levison, Mary I. (Mrs) BA BD DD	1978	Chamberlain Nursing Home, 7–9 Chamberlain Road, Edinburgh EH10 4DJ		1
Lindsay, W. Douglas BD CPS	1978	3 Drummond Place, Calderwood, East Kilbride, Glasgow G74 3AD	01355 234169	16
Lynn, Joyce (Mrs) MIPM BD	1995	Simbister, Sanday, Orkney KW17 2BA	01857 600289	
McDonald, William J.G. DD	1953	7 Blacket Place, Edinburgh EH9 1RN	0131-667 2100	1
Macfarlane, Alwyn J.C. MA	1951	Flat 12, Homeburn House, 177 Fenwick Road, Giffnock, Glasgow G46 6JD	0141-620 3235	1
MacFarlane, Donald MA	1940	Free Presbyterian Care Home, Ness Walk, Inverness IV3 5NE	01463 234679	37
McGillivray, A. Gordon MA BD STM	1951	36 Larchfield Neuk, Balerno EH14 7NL		1
Mackenzie, J.A.R. MA	1947	West Lodge, Inverness Road, Nairn IV12 4SD	01667 452827	26
McKenzie, Mary O. (Miss)	1976	4 Dunellan Avenue, Moodiesburn, Glasgow G69 0GB	01236 870180	16
Mackie, John F. BD	1979	1A Halls Close, Weldon, Corby, Northants NN17 3HH		40
Mackinnon, Thomas J.R. LTh DipMin	1996	4 Flashadder, Arnisort, Portree, Isle of Skye IV51 9PT	01470 582377	39
Mair, John BSc	1965	21 Kenilworth Avenue, Helensburgh G84 7JR	01436 671744	18
Millar, John L. MA BD	1981	17 Whittingehame Court, 1350 Great Western Road, Glasgow G12 0BH	0141-339 4098	38
Miller, Irene B. (Mrs) MA BD	1984	5 Braeside Park, Aberfeldy PH15 2DT	01887 829396	27
Morton, Andrew Q. MA BSc BD FRSE	1949	Sunnyside, 4A Manse Street, Aberdour, Burntisland KY3 0TY		18
Munro, John P.L. MA BD PhD	1977	5 Marchmont Crescent, Edinburgh EH9 1HN [E-mail: jplmunro@yahoo.co.uk]	0131-623 0198	1
O'Leary, Thomas BD	1983	1 Carter's Place, Irvine KA12 0BU	01294 313274	11
Ramsay, Alan MA	1967	12 Riverside Grove, Lochyside, Fort William PH33 7NY		38
Reid, Janette G. (Miss) BD	1991	c/o Glasgow Presbytery Office, 260 Bath Street, Glasgow G2 4JP		16
Reid, William M. MA BD	1966	10 Rue Rossini, F-75009 Paris, France		48
Ritchie, Garden W.M.	1961	23 Croft Road, Kelso TD5 7EP	01573 224419	6
Scott, J.A. Miller MA BD FSAScot DD	1949	St Martins, 6 Trinity Place, St Andrews KY16 8SG	01334 479518	26

NAME	ORD	ADDRESS	TEL	PRES
Duncan Shaw of Chapelverna *Bundesverdienstkreuz* PhD ThDr Drhc	1951	4 Sydney Terrace, Edinburgh EH7 6SL		19
Shaw, D.W.D. BA BD LLB WS DD	1960	4/13 Succoth Court, Edinburgh EH12 6BZ	0131-337 2130	26
Smith, Ralph C.P. MA STM	1960	2A Waverley Road, Eskbank, Dalkeith EH22 3DJ [E-mail: rcpsmith@waitrose.com]	0131-663 1234	1
Speed, David K. LTh	1969	153 West Princes Street, Helensburgh G84 8EZ	01436 674493	16
Spowart, Mary G. (Mrs) BD	1978	Aldersyde, St Abbs Road, Coldingham, Eyemouth TD14 5NR	01890 771697	26
Strachan, Ian M. MA BD	1959	'Cardenwell', Glen Drive, Dyce, Aberdeen AB21 7EN	01224 772028	31
Taylor, David J. MA BD	1982	32 Croft an Righ, Inverkeithing KY11 1PF	01383 413227	24
Thomson, Gilbert L. BA	1965	3 Fortharfield, Freuchie, Cupar KY15 7JJ	01337 857431	25
Todd, James F. BD CPS	1984	21 Harrow Terrace, Wick KW1 5BS	01955 605320	41
Weatherhead, James L. CBE MA LLB DD	1960	59 Brechin Road, Kirriemuir DD8 4DE	01575 572237	30
Webster, John G. BSc	1964	Plane Tree, King's Cross, Brodick, Isle of Arran KA27 8RG	01770 700747	16
Westmarland, Colin A.	1971	PO Box 5, Cospicua, CSPOI, Malta	00356 216 923552	48
Wilkie, George D. OBE BL	1948	2/37 Barnton Avenue West, Edinburgh EH4 6EB	0131-339 3973	1

LIST I – MINISTERS HOLDING PRACTISING CERTIFICATES (under Act II, as amended by Act VIII 2000)

Not all Presbyteries have stated whether or not some of those listed have taken a seat in Presbytery. There is still some variation in practice.

NAME	ORD	ADDRESS	TEL	PRES
Abeledo, Benjamin J.A. BTh DipTh PTh	1991	HQ4 Mech Bde, Catterick Garrison, North Yorks DL9 3JS		23
Alexander, Helen J.R.	1981	3/18 Fisher Street, Fullarton 5063, Australia	0061 8837 97536	1
Anderson, David MA BD	1975	Rowan Cottage, Aberlour Gardens, Aberlour AB38 9LD	01340 871906	35
Anderson, Kenneth G. MA BD	1967	8 School Road, Arbroath DD11 2LT	01241 874825	30
Arbuthnott, Joan E. (Mrs) MA BD	1993	139/1 New Street, Musselburgh EH21 6DH	0131-665 6736	3
Barbour, Robin A.S. KCVO MC MA BD STM DD	1954	Old Fincastle, Pitlochry PH16 5RJ	01796 473209	27
Barclay, Neil W. BSc BEd BD	1986	4 Gibsongray Street, Falkirk FK2 7LN	01324 874681	22
Barron, Jane L. (Mrs) BA DipEd BD	1999	Riverdog Cottage, 37 Queen Street, Newport-on-Tay DD6 8BD		26
Bartholomew, Julia (Mrs) BSc BD	2002	Kippenhill, Dunning, Perth PH2 0RA	01764 684929	28

Name	Year	Address	Telephone	Presbytery
Beattie, Warren R. BSc BD MSc PhD	1991	Director for Mission Research, OMF International, 2 Cluny Road, Singapore 259570 [E-mail: beattiewarren@omf.net]	0065 6319 4550	1
Bell, Ruth	2009	Flat 2/2, 22 Caledonia Street, Clydebank G81 4ER		18
Biddle, Lindsay		30 Ralston Avenue, Glasgow G52 3NA [E-mail: lindsaybiddle@hotmail.com]	0141-883 7405	
Birrell, John M. MA LLB BD	1974	'Hiddlehame', 5 Hewat Place, Perth PH1 2UD [E-mail: john.birrell@nhs.net]	01738 625694	28
Black, James S. BD DPS	1976	7 Breck Terrace, Penicuik EH26 0RJ [E-mail: jsb.black@btopenworld.com]	01968 677559	3
Blane, Quintin A. BSc BD MSc	1979	18D Kirkhill Road, Penicuik EH26 8HZ [E-mail: quintin@qab.org.uk]	01968 670017	3
Bonar, Sandy F. LTh	1988	7 Westbank Court, Westbank Terrace, Macmerry, Tranent EH33 1QS [E-mail: sandy.bonar@btinternet.com]	01875 615165	3
Bowman, Norman McG. MA BD	1940	Abbotsford Nursing Home, 98 Eglinton Road, Ardrossan KA22 8NN		12
Boyd, Ian R. MA BD PhD	1989	33 Castleton Drive, Newton Mearns, Glasgow G77 3LE		
Brown, Robert F. MA BD ThM	1971	55 Hilton Drive, Aberdeen AB24 4NJ [E-mail: Bjacob546@aol.com]	01224 491451	31
Caie, Albert LTh	1983	34 Ringwell Gardens, Stonehouse, Larkhall ML9 3QW	01698 792187	17
Carvalho, Jose R. BD	2002	c/o The Ministries Council, 121 George Street, Edinburgh EH2 4YN (Mr Carvalho is currently living in Brazil)	0131-225 5722	28
Coltart, Ian O. CA BD	1988	25 Bothwell Gardens, Dunbar EH42 1PZ	01368 860064	3
Coogan, J. Melvyn LTh	1992	19 Glen Grove, Largs KA30 8QQ		12
Davidson, John F. BSc DipEdTech	1970	49 Craigmill Gardens, Carnoustie DD7 6HX [E-mail: davidson900@btinternet.com]	01241 854566	30
Davidson, Mark R. MA BD STM	2005	20 Kinmohr Rise, Blackburn, Aberdeen AB21 0LJ	01224 791350	33
Dickson, Graham T. MA BD	1985	19/4 Stead's Place, Edinburgh EH6 5DY [E-mail: gtd22@blueyonder.co.uk]	0131-476 0187	1
Donaldson, Colin V.	1982	3A Playfair Terrace, St Andrews KY16 9HX	01334 472889	3
Drake, Wendy F. (Mrs) BD	1978	21 William Black Place, South Queensferry EH30 9QR [E-mail: revwdrake@hotmail.co.uk]	0131-331 1520	1
Drummond, Professor Norman W. MA BD FRSE	1976	c/o Columba 1400 Ltd, Staffin, Isle of Skye IV51 9JY	01478 611400	42
Ellis, David W. GIMechE GIProdE	1962	4 Wester Tarsappie, Rhynd Road, Perth PH2 8PT	01738 449618	16
Ferguson, Ronald MA BD ThM	1972	Vinbreck, Orphir, Orkney KW17 2RE [E-mail: ronbluebrazil@aol.com]	01856 811353	45
Fleming, Thomas G.	1961			22
Flockhart, D. Ross OBE BA BD DUniv	1955	Longwood, Humbie EH36 5PN [E-mail: rossflock@ednet.co.uk]	01875 833208	3
Fowler, Richard C.A. BSc MSc BD	1978	4 Gardentown, Whalsay, Shetland ZE2 9AB	01806 566538	46
Fraser, Ian M. MA BD PhD	1946	Ferndale, Gargunnock, Stirling FK8 3BW	01786 860612	23
Frew, John M. MA BD	1946	17 The Furrows, Walton-on-Thames KT12 3JQ		16

Gow, Neil BSc MEd BD	1996	Hillhead Lodge, Portknockie, Buckie AB56 4PB	01542 840625	35
Groenewald, Jonanda BA BD MTh DD	1999	8 Manse Court, East Calder, Livingston EH53 0HF [E-mail: jonandagroenewald@yahoo.com]	01506 884585	2
Grubb, George D.W. BA BD BPhil DMin	1962	10 Wellhead Close, South Queensferry EH30 9WA	0131-331 2072	1
Henderson, Frances M. BA BD	2006	Stoneyburn Farm, Crawford, Biggar ML12 6RH [E-mail: frances.henderson@tiscali.co.uk]	01864 502387	3
Hendrie, Yvonne (Mrs) MA BD	1995	The Manse, 3 Barns Terrace, Maybole KA19 7EP	01655 883710	
Hibbert, Frederick W. BD	1986	4 Cemydd Terrace, Senghemydd, Caerphilly, Mid Glamorgan CF83 4HL	02920 831653	47
Homewood, Ivor Maxwell MSc BD	1997	An der Fliebwiese 26, D-14052 Berlin, Germany	0049 (30) 3048722	48
Hosie, James MA BD MTh	1959	Hilbre, Baycrofts, Strachur, Cairndow PA27 8BY	01369 860634	19
Jenkinson, John J. JP LTCL ALCM DipEd DipSen (Aux)	1991	8 Rosehall Terrace, Falkirk FK1 1PY	01324 625498	22
Johnstone, Donald B.	1969	22 Glenhove Road, Cumbernauld, Glasgow G67 2JZ	01236 612479	22
Johnstone, Robert MTheol	1973	59 Cliffburn Road, Arbroath DD11 5BA	01241 439292	30
Kenny, Celia G. BA MTh	1995	37 Grosvenor Road, Rathgar, Dublin 6, Ireland		5
Lawrie, Robert M. BD MSc DipMin LLCM(TD) MCMI	1994	18/1 John's Place, Edinburgh EH6 7EN [E-mail: robert.lawrie@ed.ac.uk]	0131-554 9765	1
Liddiard, F.G.B. MA	1957	34 Trinity Fields Crescent, Brechin DD9 6YF	01356 622966	30
Lindsay, W. Douglas BD CPS	1978	3 Drummond Place, Calderwood, East Kilbride, Glasgow G74 3AD	01355 234169	16
Logan, Thomas M. LTh	1971	3 Duncan Court, Kilmarnock KA3 7TF	01563 524398	11
Lyall, David BSc BD STM PhD	1965	16 Brian Crescent, Tunbridge Wells, Kent TN4 0AP	01892 670323	47
Macaskill, Donald MA BD PhD	1994			
McDonald, Ross J. BA BD ThM	1998	HMS Dalriada, Navy Buildings, Eldon Street, Greenock PA16 7SL	(Mbl) 07952 558767	16
McGillivray, A. Gordon MA BD STM	1951	36 Larchfield Neuk, Balerno EH14 7NL		1
McKean, Martin J. BD DipMin	1984	56 Kingsknowe Drive, Edinburgh EH14 2JX	0131-466 1157	1
MacPherson, Gordon C.	1963	203 Capelrig Road, Patterton, Newton Mearns, Glasgow G77 6ND	0141-616 2107	16
McPherson, William BD DipEd	1993	83 Laburnum Avenue, Port Seton, Prestonpans EH32 0UD	01875 812252	22
Mailer, Colin (Aux)	1996	Innis Chonain, Back Row, Polmont, Falkirk FK2 0RD	01324 712401	22
Main, Arthur W.A. BD	1954	13/3 Eildon Terrace, Edinburgh EH3 5NL	0131-556 1344	16
Masson, John D. MA BD PhD BSc	1984	2 Beechgrove, Craw Hall, Brampton CA8 1TS [E-mail: jmasson96@btinternet.com]	ex-directory	7
Mill, J. Stuart	1976	100 West Princes Street, Helensburgh G84 8XD		18
Millar, Peter W. MA BD PhD	1971	6/5 Ettrickdale Place, Edinburgh EH3 5JN [E-mail: ionacottage@hotmail.com]	0131-557 0517	1
Miller, Irene B. (Mrs) MA BD	1984	5 Braeside Park, Aberfeldy PH15 2DT	01887 829396	27
Moodie, Alastair R. MA BD	1978	5 Buckingham Terrace, Glasgow G12 8EB		16
Morton, Andrew Q. MA BSc BD FRSE	1949	Sunnyside, 4A Manse Street, Aberdour, Burntisland KY3 0TY		18
Munro, John P.L. MA BD PhD	1977	5 Marchmont Crescent, Edinburgh EH9 1HN [E-mail: jplmunro@yahoo.co.uk]	0131-623 0198	1

Name	Year	Address	Telephone	
Newell, Alison M. (Mrs) BD	1986	1A Inverleith Terrace, Edinburgh EH3 5NS [E-mail: alinewell@aol.com]	0131-556 3505	1
Newell, J. Philip MA BD PhD	1982	1A Inverleith Terrace, Edinburgh EH3 5NS	0131-556 3505	1
Notman, John R. BSc BD	1990	5 Dovecote Road, Bromsgrove, Worcs B61 7BN		47
Ostler, John H. MA LTh	1975	5 Osborne Terrace, Port Seton, Prestonpans EH32 0BZ	01875 814358	3
Owen, Catherine W. MTh	1984	10 Waverley Park, Kirkintilloch, Glasgow G66 2BP	0141-776 0407	16
Penman, Iain D. BD	1977	33/5 Carnbee Avenue, Edinburgh EH16 6GA [E-mail: iainpenmanklm@aol.com]	0131-664 0673 (Mbl) 07931 993427	1
Provan, Iain W. MA BA PhD	1991	Regent College, 5800 University Boulevard, Vancouver BC V6T 2E4, Canada	001 604 224 3245	1
Roy, Alistair A. MA BD	1955	1 Broaddykes Close, Kingswells, Aberdeen AB15 8UF	01224 743310	31
Sawers, Hugh BA	1968	2 Rosemount Meadows, Castlepark, Bothwell, Glasgow G71 8EL	01698 853960	17
Scott, J.A. Miller MA BD FSAScot DD	1949	St Martins, 6 Trinity Place, St Andrews KY16 8SG	01334 479518	26
Scouller, Hugh BSc BD	1985	11 Kirk View, Haddington EH41 4AN [E-mail: h.scouller@btinternet.com]		3
Shaw, D.W.D. BA BD LLB WS DD	1960	4/13 Succoth Court, Edinburgh EH12 6BZ	0131-337 2130	26
Stewart, Margaret L. (Mrs) BSc MB ChB BD	1985	28 Inch Crescent, Bathgate EH48 1EU	01506 653428	2
Storrar, William F. MA BD PhD	1984	Director, Centre of Theological Enquiry, 50 Stockton Street, Princeton, NJ 08540, USA		1
Strachan, David G. BD DPS	1978	1 Deeside Park, Aberdeen AB15 7PQ	01224 324101	31
Strachan, Ian M. MA BD	1959	'Cardenwell', Glen Drive, Dyce, Aberdeen AB21 7EN	01224 772028	31
Thomas, W. Colville ChLJ BTh BPhil DPS DSc	1964	11 Muirfield Crescent, Gullane EH31 2HN	01620 842415	3
Todd, James F. BD CPS	1984	21 Harrow Terrace, Wick KW1 5BS	01955 605320	41
Tollick, Frank BSc DipEd	1958	3 Bellhouse Road, Aberdour, Burntisland KY3 0TL	01383 860559	24
Turnbull, Julian S. BSc BD MSc CEng MBCS	1980	25 Hamilton Road, Gullane EH31 2HP [E-mail: jules-turnbull@zetnet.co.uk]	01620 842958	3
Walker, Donald K. BD	1979	St Columba's Presbyterian Church, Mutare, Zimbabwe [E-mail: donaldandjudithwalker@googlemail.com]		32
Weatherhead, James L. CBE MA LLB DD	1960	59 Brechin Road, Kirriemuir DD8 4DE	01575 572237	30
Weir, Mary K. (Mrs) BD PhD	1968	1249 Millar Road RR1, SITEH-46, BC V0N 1G0, Canada	001 604 947 0636	1
Whitton, John P.	1977	115 Sycamore Road, Farnborough, Hants GU14 6RE	01252 674488	47
Yarwood, Derek				48

LIST J – PRESBYTERY/PARISH WORKERS (PPWs)

Associate Ministers and Deacons employed by the Ministries Council and placed in charges appear under the name of the charge.

It has not proved easy to compile a fully comprehensive and accurate list of these valued workers. We offer apologies where there are errors or omissions.

Where a year is given, this indicates when the appointment referred to was made.

NAME	APP	ADDRESS	APPOINTMENT	TEL
Anderson, Christopher	2008	14 Edmonstone Drive, Danderhall, Dalkeith EH22 1QQ	Newton and Loanhead	0131-663 0819
Atkin, Clare BEd	2009	38 Alford Drive, Glenrothes KY6 2HH [E-mail: clare@stninians.co.uk]	Glenrothes: St Ninian's	01592 565624 07783 685376 (Mbl)
Baker, Paula (Mrs)	2007	Kernow, 18 Main Street, Buckpool, Buckie AB56 1XQ [E-mail: mikepaulabaker@aol.com]	Moray Presbytery: Children's Ministry Training and Development	01542 832662
Barrowcliffe, Donna		8 Milncroft Place, Glasgow G33 3PA	Glasgow: Ruchazie	
Bauer, Alex (Ms)	2001			07903 120226 (Mbl)
Beautyman, Paul H. (Rev.) MA BD	2009	59 Alexander Street, Dunoon PA23 7BB [E-mail: paul.beautyman@ dunoongrammar.argyll-bute.sch.uk]	Argyll Presbytery: Team Leader: Youth Education Ministries	
Beggs, Stuart	2009	4 Trondra Place, Glasgow G34 9AX	Glasgow: Lochwood	07793 039656 (Mbl)
Blackwood, Katrina	2009	21 Forest Avenue, Aberdeen AB15 4TU [E-mail: beanie.blackwood@btinternet.com]	Aberdeen: Torry St Fittick's	
Blair, Fiona DCS	2010	5 Gilbertfield Place, Irvine KA12 0EY	Irvine: St Andrew's: Parish Assistant	
Bruce, Nicola (Mrs)	2009	9 Monktonhall Terrace, Musselburgh EH21 6ER [E-mail: overhills@hotmail.com]	Lothian Presbytery: Tranent Cluster	07711 223100 (Mbl)
Bruce, Stuart	2009		Glasgow: Govanhill Trinity	
Campbell, Alasdair BA	2000	3 Gellatly Road, Dunfermline KY11 4BH [E-mail: adcam@talktalk.net]	Dunfermline Presbytery: Dalgety/Forth Churches Group: Parish Assistant	01383 726238
Campbell, Neil	2010	36 Clovis Duveau Drive, Dundee DD2 5JB [E-mail: neilcampbell98@btinternet.com]	Dundee: Douglas and Mid Craigie: Youth and Young Adult Development Worker	07877 983150 (Mbl)
Chaba, Sumtende MSc PgDipCE	2008	61 Anderson Avenue, Aberdeen AB24 4LR [E-mail: astiras@yahoo.com]	Aberdeen: Middlefield	01224 682310
Collard, John K. (Rev.) MA BD	2003	1 Nelson Terrace, East Kilbride, Glasgow G74 2EY [E-mail: jkcollard@blueyonder.co.uk]	Glasgow Presbytery Congregational Facilitator	01355 520093 07762 567813 (Mbl)
Cowie, Marjorie (Miss)	2002	35 Balbirnie Avenue, Markinch, Glenrothes KY7 6BS	Glenrothes: St Margaret's: Parish Assistant	01592 758402

Name	Year	Address	Appointment	Telephone
Crossan, Morag	2010		Dalmellington with Patna and Waterside: Youth and Children's Worker	
Crumlin, Melodie (Mrs)	2000	St Luke's and St Andrew's Church, 17 Bain Street, Glasgow G40 2JZ	PEEK (Possibilities for East End Kids): Project Development Manager	0141-552 5757
Dale-Pimentil, Sheila (Mrs)	1999/2007	3 Golf Road, Lundin Links, Leven KY8 6BB	Kennoway, Windygates and Balgonie: St Kenneth's: Parish Assistant	01333 329618
Dyer, Eildon BSc MSc RGN DNCert	2008	Ruchazie Parish Church, 4 Elibank Street, Glasgow G33 3QN [E-mail: eildon@ruchazie.eclipse.co.uk]	Glasgow: Ruchazie Interim Project Manager	0141-774 2759 07776 201270 (Mbl)
Faubert, Ellen	2009	School of Divinity, King's College, Aberdeen AB25 3UE [E-mail: ellen.faubert@abdn.ac.uk]	Aberdeen: Northfield	07531 682695 (Mbl)
Finch, John		71 Maxwell Avenue, Westerton, Bearsden, Glasgow G61 1NZ [E-mail: johnfinch10@ntlworld.com]		0141-587 7390 07715 119263 (Mbl)
Finegan, Sarah (Mrs) BA	2007	261 Main Street, East Calder, Livingston EH53 0ED	Kirknewton and East Calder: Youth Worker	01506 882628
Forbes, Farquhar	2006/2008	The Heights, Inverarnie, Inverness IV2 6XA [E-mail: f.forbes@live.com]	Inverness: Inshes: Congregational Development Worker	07749 539981 (Mbl)
Groenewald, Johannes (Rev.)	2009		Falkirk: Camelon: Associate Minister	
Guy, Helen (Miss)		24D Cattofield Place, Aberdeen AB25 3QL [E-mail: helenjguy@googlemail.com]	Aberdeen: St George's Tillydrone	01224 488686
Haringman, Paul BA MSc	2010	11 Tower Gardens, Westhill, Inverness IV2 5DQ [E-mail: paul.haringman@barnchurch.org.uk]	Inverness: Culloden: The Barn	01463 795428 (Home) 01463 798946 (Work)
Harper, Kirsty (Mrs) BA	2009	Richmond Craigmillar Church, 227–229 Niddrie Mains Road, Edinburgh EH16 4AR [E-mail: k-harper@richmondshope.org.uk]		0131-661 6561 (Work) 0131-258 5162 (Home)
Harvey, P. Ruth (Rev.)	2007	Croslands, Beacon Street, Penrith, Cumbria CA11 7TZ [E-mail: ruthharvey@phonecoop.coop]	Annandale and Eskdale Presbytery: Congregational Facilitator (p/t)	01768 840749 07882 259631 (Mbl)
Hercus, Heidi	2008	Findon Cottage, Main Street, North Kessock, Inverness IV1 3XN [E-mail: jonseyi@hotmail.com]	Inverness: Trinity	07949 628877 (Mbl)
Higham, Oliver	2009	25 Hawthornhill Road, Dumbarton G82 4JD	Paisley: Linwood	
Hunter, Jean (Mrs)	2006	The Manse, Shiskine, Isle of Arran KA27 8EP [E-mail: j.hunter744@btinternet.com]	Brodick with Corrie with Lochranza: Parish Assistant	01770 860380
Hutchison, John BA	2001	30/4 West Pilton Gardens, Edinburgh EH4 4EG	Edinburgh: The Old Kirk: Parish Assistant	0131-538 1622

Hutchison, Moira	2010	9 Craigenbay Road, Lenzie, Glasgow G66 5JN	Glasgow Presbytery Good Neighbour Network Co-ordinator	
Johnston, Heather	2009	11 Eden Drive, Mossneuk, East Kilbride, Glasgow G75 8XX	East Kilbride: Mossneuk and East Kilbride: Westwood	07894 538340 (Mbl)
Johnstone, Christine	2009	4 Ramsay Avenue, Johnstone PA5 0EU	East Kilbride: Claremount and South Parishes	01505 324087
Jones, Helen (Miss)	2007	36 Sydney Place, Lockerbie DG11 2JB [E-mail: aandeyouth@gmail.com]	Annandale and Eskdale Presbytery: Youth Worker	01576 202863 07789 631822 (Mbl)
Keenan, Deborah	2009	104 Tillycairn Road, The Glen, Glasgow G33 5EH	Glasgow: Easterhouse St George's and St Peter's	07928 116142 (Mbl)
MacChoille, Stiubhart MA	2009	61 Don Street, Aberdeen AB24 2RX [E-mail: smacchoille@fsmail.net]	Aberdeen	01224 481359 07951 846262 (Mbl)
McEwan, Craig	2010	Tarquah, Glasgow Road, Dumfries DG2 9DE	Dumfries: Northwest: Parish Assistant	01387 249964
McIver, Ian	2009	68 York Street, Peterhead AB42 1SP	Aberdeen City Centre Parish Grouping: Community Development and Outreach Worker	01779 479162
Mackenzie, Norman	2009	41 Kilmailing Road, Glasgow G44 5UH [E-mail: mackenzie799@btinternet.com]	Larkhall: Chalmers	0141-637 5958
McKinnon, Laura	2009	28 Daisy Street, Glasgow G42 8JL [E-mail: lmckinnon334@googlemail.com]	Glasgow: Govanhill Trinity	0141-237 4838
MacRae, Christopher LLB	2009	24 Ringwell Gardens, Stonehouse, Larkhall ML9 3QW (Home) 260 Bath Street, Glasgow G2 4JP (Office) [E-mail: strategy@presbyteryofglasgow.org.uk]	Presbytery of Glasgow Strategy Officer	0141-332 6606 (Office) 07786 965030 (Mbl)
Montgomery, Rilza (Ms)	2009	71 Glendinning Crescent, Edinburgh EH16 6DN	Edinburgh: Muirhouse St Andrew's	0131-440 4442
Myles, Alan	2009	1 Honeygreen Road, Dundee DD4 8BG	Dundee: Mains Parish Church	07773 895303 (Mbl)
Naismith, Kenneth	2010	Seafield Cottage, Swiney, Lybster, Wick KW3 6BT [E-mail: kencaitheast@btinternet.com]	Caithness Presbytery: East Grouping: Parish Assistant	07787 764105 (Mbl)
Notman, Alison	2008	68 George Drive, Loanhead EH20 9DW [E-mail: alison_notman@yahoo.co.uk]	Loanhead and Gilmerton	
Orr, Gillian	2009	'Zippity Do Da', Loch Alvie, Aviemore PH22 1QB	Presbytery of Abernethy	01479 811699
Philip, Darren	2009	29 Traprain Terrace, Haddington EH41 3QE [E-mail: darphilip@aol.com]	Livingston Ecumenical Parish: Youth and Children's Worker	01620 823743 07861 455121 (Mbl)
Pimentil, Sheila Dale (Mrs)		3 Golf Road, Lundin Links, Leven KY8 6BB	Kennoway, Windygates and Balgonie: St Kenneth's	01333 329618
Ramsay, Sheila BA	2008	18 Morrison Quadrant, Clydebank G81 2SZ		07794 508544 (Mbl)
Reford, Susan (Miss)	2001	32 Jedburgh Street, Blantyre, Glasgow G72 0SU [E-mail: susan.reford@btopenworld.com]	Glasgow: Springburn and Tron St Mary's	01698 820122
Robertson, Douglas	2009	5 Aspen Drive, Glasgow G21 4EG	Glasgow: Robroyston (New Charge Development)	07825 397018 (Mbl)

Ross, Duncan DCS	2009	28 Fulbar Crescent, Paisley PA2 9AS	Paisley: St Columba Foxbar and Greenock: Old West Kirk	01505 812304
Ross, Keith W. (Rev.) MA BD	2007	Easter Bavelaw House, Pentland Hills Regional Park EH14 7JS	Hamilton Presbytery: Congregational Development Officer	07855 163449 (Mbl)
Scott, Blair	2009	Flat 0/1, 48 Murano Street, Glasgow G20 7RU [E-mail: blair.d.scott@btinternet.com]	East Kilbride: Westwood Parish Church	07584 635812 (Mbl)
Scoular, Iain W.	2010	'The Wee Hoose', Ecclesmachan Road, Uphall, Broxburn EH42 6JP [E-mail: iain@iwsconsultants.com]	Bathgate: St John's Parish Assistant	01506 855794 07717 131596 (Mbl)
Smith, David	2003	66 Hendry Road, Kirkcaldy KY2 5DB [E-mail: dave@tibal.org.uk]	Lochgelly and Benarty: Children's and Young People's Development Worker	01592 641823 07553 386137 (Mbl)
Stark, Jennifer	2010	South Leith Parish Halls, 6 Henderson Street, Edinburgh EH6 6BS	Presbytery of Edinburgh: Leader: Outreach Project	0131-554 2578
Stewart, Gregor	2010	30 Cairnhill Road, Newtonhill, Stonehaven AB39 3NF	Montrose and Area Churches: Youth and Children's Worker	
Stewart, Peter	2009	5 Craigievar Crescent, Glasgow G33 5DN [E-mail: pete@clanstewart.co.uk]	Glasgow: Barlanark Greyfriars	07855 424633 (Mbl)
Stirling, Diane (Miss)	2009	29 Kaimes Court, Livingston Village EH54 7DB [E-mail: parish.assistant@yahoo.co.uk]	Polbeth Harwood with West Kirk of Calder: Parish Assistant	01506 426887
Thomas, Jason	2009	4 Dairsie Court, Glasgow G44 3JF	Glasgow: St James' Pollok	
Thomson, Andrew (Rev.)	2010	3 Laurel Wynd, Cambuslang, Glasgow G72 7BH	Glasgow: Govan and Linthouse: Pastoral Assistant	0141-641 2936
Thomson, John D. (Rev.) BD	2007	3 Tottenham Court, Hill Street, Dysart, Kirkcaldy KY1 2XY [E-mail: j.thomson10@sky.com]	Kennoway, Windygates and Balgonie: St Kenneth's: Parish Assistant	01592 655313
Vint, Allan S. (Rev.) BSc BD MTh	2008	St Ninian's Church, Allan Crescent, Dunfermline KY11 4HE [E-mail: allan@vint.co.uk]	Dunfermline Presbytery: Mission Development Officer	07795 483070 (Mbl)
Wellstood, Keith	2009	47 Carrington Terrace, Crieff PH7 4DZ	Perth: Riverside	07963 766782 (Mbl)
White, Ian	2009	4 Gilchrist Walk, Lesmahagow, Lanark ML11 0FQ	Craigneuk and Belhaven with Wishaw: Old	
Willis, Mags	2008	1 Union Place, Dundee DD2 1AA	Dundee: Chalmers Ardler	07513 415835 (Mbl)
Wyllie, John	2007	51 Seafar Drive, Kelty KY4 0JX	Cowdenbeath: Trinity: Pastoral Assistant	01383 839200
Young, Neil James	2001	Holmlea, Main Street, Banton, Kilsyth, Glasgow G65 0QY [E-mail: neil.young@bigfoot.com]	Glasgow: St Paul's: Youth Worker	0141-770 8559 07748 808488 (Mbl)

LIST K – OVERSEAS LOCATIONS

PRESBYTERY OF EUROPE

AMSTERDAM	The English Reformed Church, The Begijnhof (off the Spui). Service each Sunday at 10:30am. [Website: www.ercadam.nl]
BERMUDA	Christ Church Warwick, Middle Road, Warwick, Bermuda. Postal address: PO Box PG 88, Paget PGBX, Bermuda. Sunday services: 8am and 11am. [Website: www.christchurch.bm]
BOCHUM	English-speaking Christian congregation – ECC Bochum: Pauluskirche, Grabenstraße 9, D-44787 Bochum. Service each Sunday at 12:30pm. [Website: www.ecc-bochum.de]
BRUSSELS	St Andrew's Church, Chaussée de Vleurgat 181 (off Ave. Louise). Service each Sunday at 11:00am. [E-mail: st-andrews@welcome.to; Website: www.churchofscotland.be]
BUDAPEST	St Columba's Scottish Mission, Vorosmarty utca 51, H-1064 Budapest, Hungary. (Church Tel) 0036 1 343 8479 Service in English and Sunday School each Sunday at 11:00am. The General Synod of the Reformed Church in Hungary, 1440 Budapest, PF5, Hungary. [E-mail: zsinat.kulugy@zsinatiiroda.hu] (Tel/Fax) 0036 1 460 0708
COLOMBO	St Andrew's Scots Kirk, 73 Galle Road, Colombo 3, Sri Lanka. Service each Sunday at 9:30am. [Website: www.internationalchurchcolombo.info]
COSTA DEL SOL	Services at Lux Mundi Ecumenical Centre, Calle Nueva 7, Fuengirola. Service each Sunday at 10:30am.
GENEVA	[E-mail: cofsg@pingnet.ch; Website: www.churchofscotlandgeneva.com] The Calvin Auditoire, Place de la Taconnerie (beside Cathedral of St Pierre). Service each Sunday at 11:00am.
GIBRALTAR	St Andrew's Church, Governor's Parade. Service each Sunday at 10:30am. [Website: www.scotskirkgibraltar.com]
LAUSANNE	26 Avenue de Rumine, CH-1005 Lausanne, Switzerland. Service each Sunday at 10:30am. [E-mail: scotskirklausanne@bluewin.ch; Website: www.scotskirklausanne.ch]

LISBON
St Andrew's Church, Rua da Arriaga 13–15, Lisbon, Portugal. Service each Sunday at 11:00am.
[Website: www.standrewslisbon.com.sapo.pt]

MALTA
St Andrew's Church, 210 Old Bakery Street, Valletta. Service each Sunday at 10:30am.
[Website: www.standrewsmalta.com]

PARIS
[E-mail: scotskirk@wanadoo.fr; Website: www.scotskirkparis.com]
The Scots Kirk, 17 Rue Bayard, F-75008 Paris (Metro: Roosevelt)
Service each Sunday at 11am.

REGENSBURG
English-language congregation: Alumneum, Am Olberg 2, D-93047 Regensburg, Germany.
Sunday service: second Sunday 10:30am; fourth Sunday 6pm.
[Website: www.esg-regensburg.de]

ROME
Via XX Settembre 7, 00187 Rome, Italy. Service each Sunday at 11:00am. (Fax) 0039 06 487 4370
[Website: www.presbyterianchurchrome.org]

ROTTERDAM
[E-mail: scotsintchurch@cs.com; Website: www.scotsintchurch.com]
The Scots Kirk, Schiedamsevest 121, Rotterdam. Service each Sunday at 10:30am. (Tel/Fax) 0031 10 220 4199
Informal service at 9:15am. (Tel) 0031 10 412 4779

TURIN
English-speaking congregation of the Waldensian Church in co-operation with the Church of Scotland.
Via Principe Tommaso 1, 10125 Torino. Service each Sunday at 10:30am.
[Website: www.torinovaldese.orglesc]

AFRICA AND THE CARIBBEAN

MALAWI

Church of Central Africa Presbyterian
Synod of Blantyre
Dr Ruth Shakespeare (2011) — Mulanje Mission Hospital, PO Box 45, Mulanje, Malawi — (Tel) 00265 999 360 381 (Fax) 00265 1 467 022

Synod of Livingstonia
Miss Helen Scott (2000, held previous appointment) — CCAP Girls' Secondary School, PO Box 2, Ekwendeni, Malawi — (Tel) 00265 1929 1932

	Synod of Nkhoma		
	Dr David Morton (2009)	Nkhoma Hospital, PO Box 48, Nkhoma, Malawi [E-mail: kuluva2@gmail.com]	
	Mr Rob Jones (2010)	Nkhoma Hospital, PO Box 48, Nkhoma, Malawi [E-mail: robertjones1@gmail.com]	
ZAMBIA	**United Church of Zambia**		
	Mr Keith and Mrs Ida Waddell (Ecum) (2008)	Mwandi UCZ Mission, PO Box 60693, Livingstonia, Zambia [E-mail: keith_ida2002@yahoo.co.uk]	(Tel) 00260 977 328 767
	Ms Jenny Featherstone (Ecum) (2007)	Mindolo Ecumenical Foundation, PO Box 21493, Kitwe, Zambia [E-mail: jenny.featherstone@googlemail.com]	
	Mr Glen Lund (2010)	UCZ Theological College, PO Box 20429, Kitwe, Zambia [E-mail: redhair.community@googlemail.com]	
TRINIDAD	Rev. Garwell Bacchas	Church of Scotland Greyfriars St Ann's, 50 Frederick Street, Port of Spain, Trinidad [E-mail: greyfriars@tstt.net.tt]	(Tel) 001 868 627 9312

ASIA

BANGLADESH	**Church of Bangladesh**		
	Mr James Pender (Ecum) (2004)	Development Consultant, CBSDP – Rajshani [E-mail: penderjs@gmail.com] [E-mail: ohenepender@yahoo.co.uk]	
	Mr David Hall (Ecum) (2005)	c/o St Thomas' Church, 54 Johnston Road, Dhaka 1100, Bangladesh [E-mail: dhall.dhaka@gmail.com]	
	Pat Jamieson (Ecum) (2010)	c/o St Thomas' Church, 54 Johnston Road, Dhaka 1100, Bangladesh	
CHINA	Amity Foundation: Overseas Co-ordination Office, 13/F Ultragrace Building, 5 Jordan Road, Kowloon, Hong Kong [E-mail: amityhk@pacific.net.hk]		

Nanjing Union Theological Seminary: 17 Pa Jian Yin Xiang, Nanjing 210029, China

China Christian Council: 219 Jiujrang Road, Shanghai 200003, PR China
[E-mail: tspmcco@online.sh.cn]

MIDDLE EAST

ISRAEL

[Note: **Church Services are held in St Andrew's Scots Memorial Church, Jerusalem, each Sunday at 10am, and at St Andrew's, Galilee each Sunday at 6pm**]

Jerusalem

Rev. George Shand (2009) — St Andrew's, Jerusalem, 1 David Remez Street, PO Box 8619, Jerusalem 91086, Israel
(Tel: 00 972 2 673 2401; Fax: 00 972 2 673 1711)
[E-mail: stachjer@netvision.net.il]
[Website: www.scotsguesthouse.com]

Mr James Laing (2009) — St Andrew's, Jerusalem, 1 David Remez Street, PO Box 8619, Jerusalem 91086, Israel
(Tel: 00 972 2 673 2401; Fax: 00 972 2 673 1711; Mobile: 00 972 50 202 3773)
[E-mail: jlaing@churchofscotland.org.il]
[Website: www.scotsguesthouse.com]

Tiberias

Rev. Colin D. Johnston (2009) — St Andrew's, Galilee, 1 Gdud Barak Street, PO Box 104, Tiberias 14100, Israel
(Tel: 00 972 4 671 0710; Fax: 00 972 4 671 0711)
[E-mail: revcdj60@gmail.com]
[Website: www.scotshotels.co.il]

Jaffa

Mr Anthony Short (2006) — Tabeetha School, 21 Yefet Street, PO Box 8170, Jaffa 61081, Israel
(Tel: 00 972 3 682 1581; Fax: 00 972 3 681 9357; Mobile: 00 972 54 757 2104)
[E-mail: principal@tabeethaschool.org]
[Website: www.tabeethaschool.com]

Mr James Maxwell (2009) — Tabeetha School, 21 Yefet Street, PO Box 8170, Jaffa 61081, Israel
(Tel: 00 972 3 682 1581; Fax: 00 972 3 681 9357)
[E-mail: jmaxwell@churchofscotland.org.il]
[Website: www.tabeethaschool.com]

LIST L – OVERSEAS RESIGNED AND RETIRED MISSION PARTNERS (ten or more years' service)

NAME	APP	RET	AREA	ADDRESS
Aitken, Faith (Mrs)	1957	1968	Nigeria	High West, Urlar Road, Aberfeldy PH15 2ET
	1987	1990	Zambia	
Anderson, Karen (Mrs)	1992	2006	Israel	23 Allanpark Street, Largs KA30 9AG
Anderson, Kathleen (Mrs)	1955	1968	Pakistan	1A Elms Avenue, Great Shelford, Cambridge CB2 5LN
Archibald, Mary L. (Miss)	1964	1982	Nigeria/Ghana	490 Low Main Street, Wishaw ML2 7PL
Barbour, Edith R. (Miss)	1952	1983	North India	13/11 Pratik Nagar, Yerwada, Pune 411006, Maharashta, India
Baxter, Mrs Ray	1954	1969	Malawi	138 Braid Road, Edinburgh EH10 6JB
Berkeley, Dr John	1967	1977	Bhutan	Drumbeg, Coylumbridge, Aviemore PH22 1QU
and Dr Muriel	1995	1998	Yemen	
Boyle, Lexa (Miss)	1959	1992	Aden/Yemen/Sudan	7 Maxwell Grove, Glasgow G41 5JP
Bone, Mr David and Mrs Isobel	1977	1988	Malawi	315 Blackness Road, Dundee DD2 1SH
Bone, Elizabeth (Mrs)	1950	1964	Malawi	2A Elm Street, Dundee DD2 2AY
	1980	1984	Malawi	
Brodie, Rev. Jim	1955	1974	North India	25A Keptie Road, Arbroath DD11 3ED
	1996	1998	Nepal	
Brown, Janet H. (Miss)	1967	1980	Pakistan	6 Baxter Park Terrace, Dundee DD4 6NL
Burnett, Dr Fiona	1988	1998	Zambia	The Glenholm Centre, Broughton, Biggar ML12 6JF
Burnett, Dr Robin	1964	1967	Nigeria	79 Bank Street, Irvine KA12 0LL
and Mrs Storm	1968	1977	South Africa	
Burt, M.R.C. (Miss)	1940	1975	Kenya	22 The Loaning, Chirnside, Duns TD11 3YE
Byers, Rev. Alan and Rev. Mairi	1960	1971	Ghana	Meadowbank, Plumdon Road, Annan DG12 6SJ
Campbell, George H.	1957	1971	Livingstonia	20 Woodlands Grove, Kilmarnock KA3 1TZ
Coltart, Rev. Ian O.	1967	1985	North India	The Manse, Arbirlot, Arbroath DD11 2NX
Conacher, Marion (Miss)	1963	1993	India	41 Magdalene Drive, Edinburgh EH15 3BG
Cooper, Rev. George	1966	1986	Kenya	8 Leighton Square, Alyth, Blairgowrie PH11 8AQ
Crosbie, Ann R. (Miss)	1955	1967	Nigeria	21 Fieldhead Square, Glasgow G43 IHL
Dawson, Miss Anne	1976	2000	Malawi	31 Colville Gardens, Alloa FK10 1DU
Dick, Dr James and Mrs Anne	1954	1957	North India	1 Tummel Place, Comrie, Crieff PH6 2PG
	1957	1968	Nepal	
Dodman, Rev. Roy				
and Mrs Jane	1983	2006	Jamaica	PO Box 64, Stony Hill, Kingston 9, Jamaica
Dougall, Ian C.	1960	1990	Kenya	60B Craigmillar Park, Edinburgh EH16 5PU
Drever, Dr Bryan	1962	1982	Aden/Yemen/Pakistan	188 Addison Road, King's Head, Birmingham
Duncan, Mr David				
and Mrs Allison	1952	1969	Nigeria	7 Newhailes Avenue, Musselburgh EH21 6DW
Duncan, Rev. Graham	1977	1987	South Africa	56 Daphne Road, Maroelana, 0081 Pretoria, South Africa
and Mrs Sandra	1998	2006		

Name	From	To	Country	Address
Dunlop, Mr Walter T. and Mrs Jennifer	1979	1994	Malawi/Israel	50 Oxgangs Road, Edinburgh EH13 9DR
Fauchelle, Mrs Margaret	1991	1999	Zambia, Malawi, Zimbabwe	Flat 3, 22 North Avenue, Devonport, Auckland 1309, New Zealand
Ferguson, Mr John K.P.	1977	1989	Pakistan	15 Ashgrove, Craigshill, Livingston EH54 5JQ
Finlay, Carol (Ms)	1990	2001	Malawi	96 Broomfield Crescent, Edinburgh EH12 7LX
Fischbacher, Dr Colin M. and Mrs Sally	1986	1998	Malawi	11 Barclay Square, Gosforth, Newcastle-upon-Tyne NE3 2JB
Foster, Joyce (Miss) BSc	1968	1972	Kenya	99 Sixth Street, Newtongrange EH22 4LA
	1972	1981	Malawi	
Fowler, Rev. Margaret	1988	2007	Jamaica	PO Box 3097, Negril, Westmorland, Jamaica
Fucella, Rev. Mike and Mrs Jane	1990	2006	Thailand	95/5 Sathorn SOI 9, Pikul, Sathorn Road, Yannawa, Sathorn, Bangkok 10120, Thailand
Gaston, Dr Andrew and Mrs Felicity	1997	2008	Malawi	26 Bradford Close, Eggbuckland, Plymouth, Devon PL6 5SW
Irvine, Mr Clive and Mrs Su	1984	1999	Nepal	McGregor Flat, 92 Blackford Avenue, Edinburgh EH9 3ES
Irvine, Elsabe (Mrs)	1951	1987	Malawi	60 Thirlestane Road, Edinburgh EH9 1AR
Karam, Ishbel (Mrs)	1968	1985	Pakistan	Hillsgarth, Baltasound, Unst, Shetland ZE2 9DY
King, Mrs Betty	1955	1971	North India	23 Main Street, Newstead, Melrose TD6 9DX
Knowles, Dr John K. and Mrs Heather	1976	1992	Malawi	Trollopes Hill, Monton Combe, Bath BA2 7HX
Laidlay, Mrs Una	1961	1968	Yemen	Isles View, 5 Bell's Road, Lerwick, Shetland ZE1 0QB
	1968	1971	Pakistan	
	1971	1978	Yemen	
Liddell, Margaret (Miss)	1964	1980	Zambia	20 Wyvis Crescent, Conon Bridge, Dingwall IV7 8BZ
Logie, Robina (Mrs)	1950	1960	North India	23 Stonefield Drive, Inverurie AB51 9DZ
McCulloch, Lesley (Mrs)	1982	1992	Malawi/Pakistan	316 North Jones Street, Port Angeles, WA 98362-4218, USA
McCutcheon, Agnes W.F. (Miss)	1957	1989	India	10A Hugh Murray Grove, Cambuslang, Glasgow G72 7NG
MacDonald, Dr Alistair and Mrs Freda	1949	1962	Nigeria	10 Millside, Morpeth, Northumberland NE61 1PN
McDougall, Rev. John N.	1935	1960	West Pakistan	Everill Orr Home, Allendale Road, Mount Albert, Auckland 3, New Zealand
McGoff, A.W. (Miss)	1954	1974	Kolhapur	6 Mossvale Walk, Craigend, Glasgow G33 5PF
MacGregor, Rev. Margaret	1959	1994	India	Gordon Flat, 16 Learmonth Court, Edinburgh EH4 1PB
McKenzie, Rev. Robert P.	1936	1951	India	23 Foulis Crescent, Edinburgh EH14 5BN
McKenzie, Rev. W.M.	1958	1974	Zambia	Troqueer Road, Dumfries DG2 7DF
MacKinnon, E.L. (Miss)	1952	1972	Nigeria	
McMahon, Mrs Jessie	1959	1976	North India	7 Ridgepark Drive, Lanark ML11 7PG
Macrae, Rev. Norman	1943	1960	Nigeria	49 Lixmount Avenue, Edinburgh EH5 3EW
Malley, Beryl Stevenson (Miss)	1982	1992	Malawi	272/2 Craigcrook Road, Edinburgh EH4 7TF
Marshall, Rev. Fred J.	1946	1992	Bermuda	Flat 3, 31 Oswald Road, Edinburgh EH9 2HT
Millar, Rev. Margaret R.M.	1967	1996	Malawi/Zambia	The Manse, Taynuilt, Argyll PA35 1HW
Millar, Rev. Peter	1976	1989	South India	6/5 Ettrickdale Place, Edinburgh EH3 5JN
Moir, Rev. Ian and Mrs Elsie	1962	1973	South Africa	28/6 Comely Bank Avenue, Edinburgh EH4 1EL

Name			Area	Address
Moore, Rev. J. Wilfred	1943	1957	Ghana	31 Lennox Gardens, Linlithgow EH49 7PZ
Morrice, Mrs Margaret	1971	1998	Buenos Aires/Kenya	104 Baron's Hill Avenue, Linlithgow EH49 7JG
Morton, Rev. Alasdair J. and Mrs Gillian M.	1960	1973	Zambia	St Leonard's, 16 St Leonard's Road, Forres IV36 1DW
Munro, Harriet (Miss)	1959	1969	Malawi	26 The Forge, Braidpark Drive, Glasgow G46 6LB
Murray, Rev. Douglas and Mrs Sheila	1994	2004	Switzerland	Flat 9, 4 Bonnington Gait, Edinburgh EH6 5NZ
Murray, Mr Ian and Mrs Isabel	1962	2000	Pakistan	17 Piershill Terrace, Edinburgh EH8 7EY
Musgrave, Rev. Clarence W.	1966	1980	Zambia	4 Ravelston Heights, Edinburgh EH4 3LX
and Mrs Joan	2000	2006	Jerusalem	
Musk, Mrs Lily	1959	1959	Malawi	1 Tulloch Place, St Andrews KY16 8XJ
	1959	1974	Zambia	
Nelson, Rev. John and Mrs Anne	1947	1952	Pakistan	7 Manse Road, Roslin EH25 9LF
	1952	1959	North India	
	1970	1973	North India	
Nicholson, Rev. Thomas S.	1981	1995	Taiwan	Todholes, Greenlaw, Duns TD10 6XD
Nicol, Catherine (Miss)	1960	2000	Pakistan	St Columba Christian Girls' RTC, Barah Patthar, Sialkot 2, Pakistan
Nutter, Margaret (Miss)	1966	1979	Pakistan	Kilmorich, 14 Balloch Road, Balloch, Alexandria G83 8SR
Pacitti, Rev. Stephen A.	1977	1996	Taiwan	157 Nithsdale Road, Pollokshields, Glasgow G41 5RD
Pattison, Rev. Kenneth and Mrs Susan	1966	1977	Malawi	2 Castle Way, St Madoes, Glencarse, Perth PH2 7NY
Philip, Mrs Margaret	1951	1968	Nigeria	Penlan, Holm Farm Road, Catrine, Mauchline KA5 6TA
Philpot, Rev. David	1981	1995	WCC Geneva	2/27 Pentland Drive, Edinburgh EH10 6PX
Reid, Dr Ann	1988	1996	Ghana	19 Cloughwood Crescent, Shevington, Lancs WN6 8EP
Reid, Margaret I. (Miss)	1964	1982	Malawi	26A Angle Park Terrace, Edinburgh EH11 2JT
Rennie, Rev. Alistair M.	1939	1976	Malawi	Noble's Yard, St Mary's Gate, Wirksworth, Derbyshire DE4 4DQ
Ritchie, Ishbel M. (Miss)	1955	1996	Eastern Himalaya	8 Ross Street, Dunfermline KY12 0AN
Ritchie, Rev. J.M.	1974	1977	Yemen	46 St James' Gardens, Penicuik EH26 9DU
Ritchie, Mary Scott (Miss)	1968	1991	Malawi/Zambia/Israel	Afton Villa, 1 Afton Bridgend, New Cumnock KA18 4AX
Ross, Rev. Prof. Kenneth and Mrs Hester	1988	1998	Malawi	35 Madeira Street, Edinburgh EH6 4AJ
Rough, Mary E. (Miss)	1966	1987	Blantyre	6 Glebe Street, Dumfries DG1 2LF
Roy, Rev. Alan J.	1960	1972	Zambia	14 Comerton Place, Drumoig, St Andrews KY16 0NQ
Russell, M.M. (Miss)	1946	1969	Nigeria	14 Hozier Street, Carluke ML8 5DW
Samuel, Lynda (Mrs)	1974	1990	Madras	28 Braehead, Methven Walk, Dundee DD2 3FJ [E-mail: rasam42@onetel.com]
Shepherd, Dr Clyne	1956	1968	Nigeria	10 Kingsknowe Road South, Edinburgh EH14 2JE
Smith, Mr Harry	1959	1967	Nigeria	31 Woodville Crescent, Sunderland SR4 8RE
and Mrs Margaret	1968	1970	Malawi	
Smith, M.L. (Miss)	1956	1973	Madras	6 Fintry Mains, Dundee DD4 9HF
Sneddon, Mr Sandy and Mrs Marie	1986	2003	Pakistan	84 Greenend Gardens, Edinburgh EH17 7QH
Steedman, Martha (Mrs) (née Hamilton)	1955	1966	North India	Muir of Blebo, Blebo Craigs, Cupar KY15 5TZ

Stewart, Marion G. (Miss)	1976	1989	Malawi/Israel	Kirk Cottage, Kirkton of Skene, Westhill, Skene AB32 6XX
Stiven, Rev. Iain	1959	1969	Pakistan	7 Gloucester Place, Edinburgh EH3 6EE
Stone, W. Vernon MA BD	1949	1966	Zambia	36 Woodrow Court, Port Glasgow Road, Kilmacolm PA13 4QA
Taylor, Rev. A.T.H.	1938	1972	Nigeria/Jamaica	4 The Pleasance, Strathkinness, St Andrews KY16 9SD
Tennant, Frances (Miss)	1965	1977	Pakistan	101 St John's Road, Edinburgh EH12 6NN
Wallace, A. Dorothy (Miss)	1953	1991	North India	Amberley, Mill Lane, Nethy Bridge PH25 3DR
Walker, Rev. Donald and Mrs Judith	1981	1994	Zambia	2 Wilson Road, Banchory AB31 3UY
Westmarland, Rev. Colin	1975	2001	Malta	PO Box 5, Cospicua, CSPOI, Malta
Wilkie, Rev. James L.	1959	1976	Zambia	7 Comely Bank Avenue, Edinburgh EH4 1EW
Wilkinson, Dr Alison	1992	2007	Kenya	5 Birch Avenue, Stirling FK8 2PL
Wilkinson, Rev. John	1946	1975	Kenya	70 Craigleith Hill Gardens, Edinburgh EH4 2JH
Wilson, Irene (Ms)	1993	2004	Israel	
Wilson, Rev. Mark	1953	1978	Nagpur	37 Kings Avenue, Longniddry EH32 0QN

LIST M – PARISH ASSISTANTS AND PROJECT WORKERS

Those who in previous years would have been named here are now included in List J – Presbytery/Parish Workers.

LIST N – READERS

1. EDINBURGH

Christie, Gillian L. (Mrs)	45 Allan Park Drive, Edinburgh EH16 1LW	0131-443 4472
Davies, Ruth (Mrs) (attached to Liberton)	4 Hawkhead Grove, Edinburgh EH16 6LS	0131-664 3608
Farrant, Yvonne (Mrs)	Flat 7, 14 Duddingston Mills, Edinburgh EH8 7NF [E-mail: yfarrant@charis.org.uk]	0131-661 0672
Farrell, William J.	50 Ulster Crescent, Edinburgh EH8 7JS [E-mail: w.farrell@btinternet.com]	0131-661 1026
Farrow, Edmund	14 Brunswick Terrace, Edinburgh EH7 5PG [E-mail: efsc18422@blueyonder.co.uk]	0131-558 8210
Johnston, Alan	8/19 Constitution Street, Edinburgh EH6 7BT [E-mail: alancj@cairnassoc.wanadoo.co.uk]	0131-554 1326

Kerrigan, Herbert A. MA LLB QC	Airdene, 20 Edinburgh Road, Dalkeith EH22 1JY [E-mail: kerriganqc@btconnect.com]	0131-660 3007
Macfarlane, Helen (Mrs)	5/5 Moat Drive, Edinburgh EH14 1NU [E-mail: helen@butterflytrust.org.uk]	0131-444 1709
McKenzie, Janet	80C Colinton Road, Edinburgh EH14 1DD [E-mail: jintymck@talktalk.net]	0131-444 2054
McPherson, Alistair	77 Bonaly Wester, Edinburgh EH13 0RQ [E-mail: amjhmcpherson@blueyonder.co.uk]	0131-478 5384
Pearce, Martin	4 Corbiehill Avenue, Edinburgh EH4 5DR [E-mail: martin.j.pearce@blueyonder.co.uk]	0131-336 4864
Scouller, Alastair	3 Oxford Terrace, Edinburgh EH4 1PX [E-mail: scouller@globalnet.co.uk]	0131-332 9581
Sherriffs, Irene (Mrs)	22/2 West Mill Bank, Edinburgh EH13 0QT	0131-466 9530
Wyllie, Anne (Miss)	46 Jordan Lane, Edinburgh EH10 4QX	0131-447 9035
2. WEST LOTHIAN		
Beatson, David	'Schiefer Hof', Keepscaith Farm, Longridge, Bathgate EH47 9AL [E-mail: ireneagape@tiscali.co.uk]	01501 740494
Coyle, Charlotte (Mrs)	28 The Avenue, Whitburn EH47 0DA	01501 740687
Elliott, Sarah (Miss)	105 Seafield, Bathgate EH47 7AW [E-mail: sarah.elliott6@btopenworld.com]	01506 654950
Galloway, Brenda (Miss)	16 Barons Hill Court, Linlithgow EH49 7SP	01506 842028
Middleton, Alex	36 Fivestanks Place, Broxburn EH52 6BJ [E-mail: alex.middleton@btinternet.com]	01506 852645
Salmon, Jeanie (Mrs)	81 Croftfoot Drive, Fauldhouse, Bathgate EH47 9EH [E-mail: jeaniesalmon@aol.com]	01501 772468
Scoular, Iain W.	'The Wee Hoose', Ecclesmachan Road, Uphall, Broxburn EH52 6JP [E-mail: iain@iwsconsultants.com]	01506 855794
Wilkie, David	53 Goschen Place, Broxburn EH52 5JH [E-mail: david-fmu_09@tiscali.co.uk]	01506 854777
3. LOTHIAN		
Cannon, S. Christopher MA	Briarwood, Winterfield Place, Belhaven, Dunbar EH42 1QQ	01368 864991
Evans, W. John IEng MIIE(Elec)	Waterlily Cottage, 10 Fenton Steading, North Berwick EH39 5AF [E-mail: jevans7is@hotmail.com]	01620 842990
Gibson, C.B. Stewart	27 King's Avenue, Longniddry EH32 0QN [E-mail: stewartgibson27@tiscali.co.uk]	01875 853464
Hogg, David MA	82 Eskhill, Penicuik EH26 8DQ [E-mail: david@hoggdavid.wanadoo.co.uk]	01968 676350
Johnston, June E. (Ms) BSc MEd BD	49 Braeside Road South, Gorebridge EH23 4DL [E-mail: johnston330@btinternet.com]	01875 823086
Millan, Mary (Mrs)	33 Polton Vale, Loanhead EH20 9DF [E-mail: marymillan@fsmail.net]	0131-440 1624

Trevor, A. Hugh MA MTh	29A Fidra Road, North Berwick EH39 4NE [E-mail: htrevor@talktalk.net]	01620 894924
Yeoman, Edward T.N. FSAScot	75 Newhailes Crescent, Musselburgh EH21 6EF [E-mail: edwardyeoman6@aol.com]	0131-653 2291
4. MELROSE AND PEEBLES		
Butcher, John W.	'Sandal', 13 Ormiston Grove, Melrose TD6 9SR	01896 822339
Cashman, Margaret D. (Mrs)	38 Abbotsford Road, Galashiels TD1 3HR	01896 752711
Selkirk, Frances (Mrs)	2 The Glebe, Ashkirk, Selkirk TD7 4PJ	01750 32204
5. DUNS		
Deans, M. (Mrs) BA (Reader Emeritus)	10 The Granary, Love Lane, Berwick-upon-Tweed TD15 1AR	01289 307699
Elphinston, Enid (Mrs)	The Hollies, Woodlands, Foulden, Berwick-upon-Tweed TD15 1UH	01289 386359
Landale, Alison (Mrs)	Green Hope, Duns TD11 3SG	01361 890242
Taylor, Christine (Mrs)	Rowardennan, Main Street, Gavinton, Duns TD11 3QT	01361 882994
6. JEDBURGH		
Findlay, Elizabeth (Mrs)	2 Hendersons Court, Kelso TD5 7BG [E-mail: elizabeth@findlay8124.fsworld.co.uk]	01573 226641
Knox, Dagmar (Mrs)	3 Stichill Road, Ednam, Kelso TD5 7QQ [E-mail: dagmar@knox-riding.wanadoo.co.uk]	01573 224883
Thomson, Robert R. (retired)	34/36 Fisher Avenue, Hawick TD9 9NB	01450 373851
7. ANNANDALE AND ESKDALE		
Boncey, David	Redbrae, Beattock, Moffat DG10 9RF [E-mail: david.boncey613@btinternet.com]	01683 300613
Brown, Martin J.	Lochhouse Farm, Beattock, Moffat DG10 9SG [E-mail: martin@lochhousefarm.com]	01683 300451
Brown, S. Jeffrey BA	Skara Brae, 8 Ballplay Road, Moffat DG10 9JU [E-mail: sjbrown@btinternet.com]	01683 220475
Chisholm, Dennis A.G. MA BSc	Moss-side, Hightae, Lockerbie DG11 1JR	01387 811803
Dodds, Alan	Trinco, Battlehill, Annan DG12 6SN [E-mail: alanandjen46@talktalk.net]	01461 201235
Jackson, Susan (Mrs)	48 Springbells Road, Annan DG12 6LQ [E-mail: shjackson@supanet.com]	01461 204159
Morton, Andrew A. BSc	19 Sherwood Park, Lockerbie DG11 2DX [E-mail: andrew.a.morton@btinternet.com]	01576 203164
Saville, Hilda A. (Mrs)	32 Crosslaw Burn, Moffat DG10 9LP [E-mail: qjhnic@sky.com]	01683 222854

8. DUMFRIES AND KIRKCUDBRIGHT		
Carroll, J. Scott	17 Downs Place, Heathhall, Dumfries DG1 3RF	01387 265350
Corson, Gwen (Mrs)	7 Sunnybrae, Borgue, Kirkcudbright DG6 4SJ	01557 870328
Ogilvie, D.W. MA FSAScot	Lingerwood, 2 Nelson Street, Dumfries DG2 9AY	01387 264267
Paterson, Ronald M. (Dr)	Mirkwood, Ringford, Castle Douglas DG7 2AL	01557 820202
Piggins, Janette (Mrs)	Cleugh Wood, Dalbeattie DG5 4PF	01387 780655
Wallace, Mhairi (Mrs)	The Manse, Twynholm, Kirkcudbright DG6 4NY	01557 860381
9. WIGTOWN AND STRANRAER		
Connery, Graham	Skellies Knowe, West Ervie, Stranraer DG9	01776 854277
Harvey, Joyce (Mrs)	4A Allanfield Place, Newton Stewart DG8 6BS	01671 403693
McQuistan, Robert	Old School House, Carsluith, Newton Stewart DG8 7DT	01671 820327
Williams, Roy	120 Belmont Road, Stranraer DG9 7BG	
10. AYR		
Anderson, James (Dr) BVMS PhD DVM FRCPath FIBiol MRCVS	67 Henrietta Street, Girvan KA26 9AN	01465 710059
Black, Sandra (Mrs)	5 Doon Place, Troon KA10 7EQ	01292 220075
Jamieson, Iain	2 Whinfield Avenue, Prestwick KA9 2BH	01242 476898
Morrison, James	27 Monkton Road, Prestwick KA9 1AP	01292 479313
Murphy, Ian	56 Lamont Crescent, Cumnock KA18 3DU	01290 423675
Riome, Elizabeth (Mrs)	Monkwood Mains, Minishant, Maybole KA19 8EY	01292 443440
11. IRVINE AND KILMARNOCK		
Bircham, James	8 Holmlea Place, Kilmarnock KA1 1UU	01563 532287
Cooper, Fraser	5 Balgray Way, Irvine KA11 1RP	01294 211235
Crosbie, Shona (Mrs)	4 Campbell Street, Darvel KA17 0PA	01560 322229
Dempster, Ann (Mrs)	20 Graham Place, Kilmarnock KA3 7SD	01563 529361
Findlay, Elizabeth (Mrs) (Reader Emeritus)	19 Keith Place, Kilmarnock KA3 7NS	01563 528084
Gillespie, Janice (Miss)	12 Jeffrey Avenue, Kilmarnock KA1 4EB	01563 540009
Hamilton, Margaret A. (Mrs)	59 South Hamilton Street, Kilmarnock KA1 2DT	01563 534431
Jamieson, John BSc(Hons) DEP AFBPSS	22 Moorfield Avenue, Kilmarnock KA1 1TS	01563 534065
Lightbody, Hunter B. (Reader Emeritus)	36 Rannoch Place, Irvine KA12 9NQ	01294 273955
McAllister, Anne C. (Mrs)	39 Bowes Rigg, Stewarton KA3 5EN	01560 483191
McGeever, Gerard	23 Kinloch Avenue, Stewarton, Kilmarnock KA3 3HQ	01560 484331
McLean, Donald	1 Four Acres Drive, Kilmaurs, Kilmarnock KA3 2ND	01563 381475
MacTaggart, Elspeth (Miss)	21 Scargie Road, Kilmarnock KA3 1QR	01563 527713
Mills, Catherine (Mrs)	59 Crossdene Road, Crosshouse, Kilmarnock KA2 0JU	01563 535305
Raleigh, Gavin	21 Landsborough Drive, Kilmarnock KA3 1RY	01563 520836
Robertson, William	1 Archers Avenue, Irvine KA11 2GB	01294 203577
Scott, William BA DipEd	6 Elgin Avenue, Stewarton, Kilmarnock KA3 3HJ	01560 484273
Whitelaw, David	9 Kirkhill, Kilwinning KA13 6NB	01294 551695
Wilson, Robert L.S. MA BD (Reader Emeritus)	57 West Woodstock Street, Kilmarnock KA1 2JH	01563 526658

12. ARDROSSAN

Barclay, Elizabeth (Mrs)	2 Jacks Road, Saltcoats KA21 5NT	01294 471855
Currie, Archie BD	55 Central Avenue, Kilbirnie KA25 6JP [E-mail: archiecurrie@yahoo.co.uk]	01505 681474
Hunter, Jean C.Q. (Mrs) BD	The Manse, Lamlash, Brodick, Isle of Arran KA27 8LE	01770 860380
McCool, Robert	17 McGregor Avenue, Stevenston KA20 4BA	01294 466548
Mackay, Brenda H. (Mrs)	19 Eglinton Square, Ardrossan KA22 8LN [E-mail: bremac82@aol.com]	01294 464491
Nimmo, M. (Mrs)	12 Muirfield Place, Kilwinning KA13 6NL [E-mail: margtmcmn@aol.com]	01294 553718
Ross, Magnus BA MEd	39 Beachway, Largs KA30 8QH [E-mail: m.b.ross@btinternet.com]	01475 689572
Smith, N. (Mrs)	5 Kames Street, Millport, Isle of Cumbrae KA28 0BN [E-mail: nsasmith@fsmail.net]	01475 530747

13. LANARK

Grant, Alan	25 Moss-side Avenue, Carluke ML8 5UG [E-mail: amgrant25@aol.com]	01555 771419
Love, William	30 Barmore Avenue, Carluke ML8 4PE [E-mail: janbill30@tiscali.co.uk]	01555 751243

14. GREENOCK AND PAISLEY

Banks, Russell	18 Aboyne Drive, Paisley PA2 7SJ [E-mail: margaret.banks2@ntlworld.com]	0141-884 6925
Boag, Jennifer (Miss)	11 Madeira Street, Greenock PA16 7UJ [E-mail: jenniferboag@hotmail.com]	01475 720125
Campbell, Tom BA DipCPC	3 Grahamston Place, Paisley PA2 7BY [E-mail: tomcam38@googlemail.com]	0141-840 2273
Davey, Charles L.	16 Divert Road, Gourock PA19 1DT [E-mail: charles.davey@talktalk.net]	01475 631544
Geddes, Elizabeth (Mrs)	40 Hazelwood Road, Bridge of Weir PA11 3DT [E-mail: geddes_liz@hotmail.com]	01505 612639
Glenny, John C.	49 Cloch Road, Gourock PA19 1AT [E-mail: jacklizg@aol.com]	01475 636415
Hood, Eleanor (Mrs)	12 Clochoderick Avenue, Kilbarchan, Johnstone PA10 2AY [E-mail: eleanor.hood.kilbarchan@ntlworld.com]	01505 704208
McFarlan, Elizabeth (Miss)	20 Fauldswood Crescent, Paisley PA2 9PA [E-mail: elizabeth.mcfarlan@ntlworld.com]	01505 358411
McHugh, Jack	'Earlshaugh', Earl Place, Bridge of Weir PA11 3HA [E-mail: jackmchugh@tiscali.co.uk]	01505 612789
Marshall, Leon M.	'Glenisla', Gryffe Road, Kilmacolm PA13 4BA [E-mail: lm@stevenson-kyles.co.uk]	01505 872417

Maxwell, Margaret (Mrs) BD	2 Grants Avenue, Paisley PA2 6AZ [E-mail: sandra1.maxwell@virgin.net]	0141-884 3710
Munro, Irene (Mrs)	80 Bardrainney Avenue, Port Glasgow PA14 6HA [E-mail: irenemunro906@hotmail.com]	01475 701213
Noonan, Pam (Mrs)	18 Woodburn Place, Houston, Johnstone PA6 7NA [E-mail: pam.noonan@btinternet.com]	01505 326254
Orry, Geoff	'Rhu Ellan', 4 Seaforth Crescent, Barrhead, Glasgow G78 1PL [E-mail: geoff.orry@googlemail.com]	0141-881 9748
Shaw, Ian	The Grove, 8 Commercial Road, Barrhead, Glasgow G78 1AJ	0141-881 2038
16. GLASGOW		
Armstrong, John (Reader Emeritus)	44 Eckford Street, Glasgow G32 7AJ	
Birchall, Edwin R. (Reader Emeritus)	11 Sunnybank Grove, Clarkston, Glasgow G76 7SU	0141-638 4332
Bremner, David	Greenhill Lodge, 1 Old Humbie Road, Glasgow G77 5DF	0141-639 1742
Callander, Thomas M.S.	31 Dalkeith Avenue, Bishopbriggs, Glasgow G64 2HQ	0141-563 6955
Campbell, Jack T. BD BEd	40 Kenmure Avenue, Bishopbriggs, Glasgow G64 2DE	0141-563 5837
Clark, J. Michael (Reader Emeritus)	1/2, 7 Grantully Drive, Glasgow G12 0DP	
Dickson, Hector M.K.	'Gwito', 61 Whitton Drive, Giffnock, Glasgow G46 6EF	0141-637 0080
Findlay, William (Reader Emeritus)	36 Firpark Road, Bishopbriggs, Glasgow G64 1SP	
Fullarton, Andrew	225 Aros Drive, Glasgow G52 1TJ	0141-883 9518
Galbraith, Iain B.	Beechwood, Overton Road, Alexandria G83 0LJ	01389 753563
Gibson, James N. (Reader Emeritus)	44 Ayton Road, Glasgow G41 5HN	0141-423 8290
Grant, George	44 Brownside Road, Cambuslang, Glasgow G72 8NJ	0141-560 0059
Grieve, Lesley	23 Hertford Avenue, Glasgow G12 0LG	0141-576 1376
Horner, David J.	20 Ledi Road, Glasgow G43 2AJ	0141-637 7369
Hunt, Roland BSc PhD CertEd	4 Flora Gardens, Bishopbriggs, Glasgow G64 1DS	0141-563 3257 (Evenings and weekends) 0141-563 3257
Joansson, Todd	1/2, 18 Eglinton Court, Glasgow G5 9NE	0141-429 6733
Kilpatrick, Mrs Joan	39 Brent Road, Regent's Park, Glasgow G46 8JG	0141-621 1809
McChlery, Stuart	The Manse, Cheapside Street, Eaglesham, Glasgow G76 0NS	01355 303495
MacColl, Duncan M. (Reader Emeritus)	14 Mosspark Avenue, Glasgow G52 1JX	
McColl, John	53 Aberfoyle Street, Glasgow G31 3RP	0141-554 9881 (Mbl) 07757 303195
McFarlane, Robert	25 Avenel Road, Glasgow G13 2PB	0141-954 5540
McInally, Gordon	10 Melville Gardens, Bishopbriggs, Glasgow G64 3DF	0141-563 2685
Mackenzie, Norman	Flat 3/2, 41 Kilmailing Road, Glasgow G44 5UH	(Mbl) 07780 733710
McLaughlin, Cathy (Mrs)	8 Lamlash Place, Glasgow G33 3XH	0141-774 2483
McLellan, Duncan (Reader Emeritus)	138 King's Park Avenue, Glasgow G44 4HS	
MacLeod, John	2 Shuna Place, Newton Mearns, Glasgow G77 6TN	0141-639 6862
Maxwell, David	248 Old Castle Road, Glasgow G44 5EZ	0141-569 6379
Montgomery, Hamish (Reader Emeritus)	13 Avon Avenue, Bearsden, Glasgow G61 2PS	
Nairne, Mrs Elizabeth (Reader Emeritus)	229 Southbrae Drive, Glasgow G13 1TT	
Phillips, John B.	2/3, 30 Handel Place, Glasgow G5 0TP [E-mail: johnphillips@fish.co.uk]	0141-429 7716

Robertson, Adam	423 Amulree Street, Glasgow G32 7SS	0141-573 6662
Roy, Mrs Shona	81 Busby Road, Clarkston, Glasgow G76 8BD	0141-644 3713
Stead, Mrs Mary	9A Carrick Drive, Mount Vernon, Glasgow G32 0RW	0141-764 1016
Stewart, James	45 Airthrey Avenue, Glasgow G14 9LY	0141-959 5814
Stuart, Alex	107 Baldorran Crescent, Cumbernauld, Glasgow G68 9EX	01236 727710
Sturrock, Roger	36 Thomson Drive, Glasgow G61 3PA	0141-942 7412
Tindall, Margaret (Mrs)	23 Ashcroft Avenue, Lennoxtown, Glasgow G65 7EN [E-mail: margarettindall@aol.com]	01360 310911
Webster, James	65 Fruin Avenue, Newton Mearns, Glasgow G77 6HG	0141-639 0035
Williamson, John G. (Reader Emeritus)	34 King Edward Road, Glasgow G13 1QW	
Wilson, George A.	46 Maxwell Drive, Garrowhill, Baillieston, Glasgow G69 6LS	0141-771 3862
17. HAMILTON		
Allan, A.J.	9 Thornwood Road, Strathaven ML10 6UR	(Mbl) 07793 243336
Beattie, Richard	4 Bent Road, Hamilton ML3 6QB	01698 420086
Bell, Sheena	2 Langdale, East Kilbride, Glasgow G74 4RP	01355 248217
Chirnside, Peter	141 Kyle Park Drive, Uddingston, Glasgow G71 7DB	01698 813769
Clemenson, Anne	25 Dempsey Road, Lochview, Bellshill ML4 2UF [E-mail: aclemenson@msn.com]	01698 291019
Cruickshanks, William	63 Progress Drive, Caldercruix, Airdrie ML6 7PU	01236 843352
Haggarty, Frank	46 Glen Road, Caldercruix, Airdrie ML6 7PZ	01236 842182
Hastings, William Paul	186 Glen More, East Kilbride, Glasgow G74 2AN	01355 521228
Hawthorne, William G. MBE	172 Main Street, Plains, Airdrie ML6 7JH	01236 842230
Hewitt, Samuel	3 Corrie Court, Earnock, Hamilton ML3 9XE	01698 457403
Hislop, Eric	1 Castlegait, Strathaven ML10 6FF	01357 520003
Jardine, Lynette	32 Powburn Crescent, Uddingston, Glasgow G71 7SS	01698 812204
Keir, Dickson	46 Brackenhill Drive, Hamilton ML3 8AY	01698 457351
Leckie, Elizabeth	41 Church Street, Larkhall ML9 1EZ	01698 308933
McCart, Frances	19 White Cart Tower, East Kilbride, Glasgow G74 2EE	01355 246939
McCleary, Isaac	719 Coatbridge Road, Bargeddie, Glasgow G69 7PH	0141-236 0158
McIlroy, Stuart	17 Dentdale, Stewartfield, East Kilbride, Glasgow G74 4LP	01355 247958
MacMillan, Georgina	1 Darngaber Gardens, Quarter, Hamilton ML3 7XX	01698 424040
Murphy, Jim	10 Hillview Crescent, Bellshill ML4 1NX	01698 740185
Queen, Leslie	60 Loch Assynt, East Kilbride, Glasgow G74 2DW	01355 233932
Preston, J. Steven	24 Glen Prosen, East Kilbride, Glasgow G74 3TA	01355 237359
Robertson, Rowan	68 Townhead Road, Coatbridge ML5 2HU	01236 425703
Smith, Alexander (Reader Emeritus)	6 Coronation Street, Wishaw ML2 8LF	01698 385797
Stevenson, Thomas	34 Castle Wynd, Quarter, Hamilton ML3 7XD	01698 282263
White, Ian	21 Muirhead, Stonehouse, Larkhall ML9 3HG	01698 792772
Wilson, William (Reader Emeritus)	115 Chatelherault Crescent, Low Waters Estate, Hamilton ML3 9PL	01698 421856

18. DUMBARTON		
Brown, Ivan	28 Millig Street, Helensburgh G84 9PN	01436 678734
Foster, Peter	The Forge, Colgrain Steading, Colgrain, Cardross, Dumbarton G82 5JL	01389 849200
Giles, Donald (Dr)	Levern House, Stuckenduff, Shandon, Helensburgh G84 8NW	01436 820565
Harold, Sandy	The Laurels, Risk Street, Clydebank G81 3LW	0141-952 3673
Hart, R.J.M. BSc	7 Kidston Drive, Helensburgh G84 8QA	01436 672039
McCutcheon, John	Flat 2/6 Parkview, Milton Brae, Milton, Dumbarton G82 2TT	01389 739034
Nutter, Margaret (Miss)	14 Balloch Road, Balloch, Alexandria G83 8SR	01436 754505
Rettie, Sara (Mrs)	86 Dennistoun Crescent, Helensburgh G84 7JF	01436 677984
Robertson, Ishbell (Miss)	81 Bonhill Road, Dumbarton G82 2DU	01389 763436
19. ARGYLL		
Binner, Aileen (Mrs)	'Ailand', Connel, Oban PA37 1QX	01631 710264
Challis, John O.	Bay Villa, Strachur, Cairndow PA27 8DE	01369 860436
Goodison, Michael	Dalriada Cottage, Bridge of Awe, Taynuilt PA35 1HT [E-mail: dalriada@btinternet.com]	01866 822479
Holden, Robert	Orsay, West Bank Road, Ardrishaig, Lochgilphead PA30 8HG	01546 603211
Logue, David	3 Braeface, Tayvallich, Lochgilphead PA31 8PN	01546 870647
McLellan, James A.	West Drimvore, Lochgilphead PA31 8SU [E-mail: james.mclellan@argyll-bute.gov.uk]	01546 606403
Mitchell, James S.	4 Main Street, Port Charlotte, Isle of Islay PA48 7TX	01496 850650
Morrison, John L.	Tigh na Barnashaig, Tayvallich, Lochgilphead PA31 8PN	01546 870637
Ramsay, Matthew M.	Portnastorm, Carradale, Campbeltown PA28 6SB [E-mail: portnastorm@tiscali.co.uk]	01583 431381
Sinclair, Margaret (Mrs)	2 Quarry Place, Furnace, Inveraray PA32 8XW [E-mail: margaret_sinclair@btinternet.com]	01499 500633
Stather, Angela (Mrs)	9 Gartness Cottages, Ballygrant, Isle of Islay PA45 7QN	01496 840527
Stewart, Agnes (Mrs)	Creagdhu Mansions, New Quay Street, Campbeltown PA28 6BB	01586 552805
Thornhill, Christopher R.	4 Ardfern Cottages, Ardfern, Lochgilphead PA31 9QN	01852 500674
Waddell, Martin	2 Kilbrandon Cottages, Balvicar, Isle of Seil, Oban PA34 4RA	01852 300395
Zielinski, Jennifer C. (Mrs)	26 Cromwell Street, Dunoon PA23 7AX	01369 706136
22. FALKIRK		
Brown, Kathryn (Mrs)	1 Callendar Park Walk, Callendar Grange, Falkirk FK1 1TA	01324 617352
Duncan, Lorna (Mrs) BA	Richmond, 28 Solway Drive, Head of Muir, Denny FK6 5NS	01324 813020
MacDonald, Monica (Mrs)	32 Reilly Gardens, High Bonnybridge, Bonnybridge FK4 2BB	01324 874807
McDonald, Rhona	3 Carron View, Maddiston, Falkirk FK2 0NF	01324 870752
Mathers, S. (Mrs)	10 Ercall Road, Brightons, Falkirk FK2 0RS	01324 872253
Sarle, Andrew BSc BD	114 High Station Road, Falkirk FK1 5LN	01324 621648
Stewart, Arthur MA	51 Bonnymuir Crescent, Bonnybridge FK4 1GD	01324 812667
Struthers, I.	7 McVean Place, Bonnybridge FK4 1QZ [E-mail: ivar.struthers@btinternet.com]	01324 841145

23. STIRLING		
Durie, Alastair (Dr)	25 Forth Place, Stirling FK8 1UD	01786 451029
Grier, Hunter	17 Station Road, Bannockburn, Stirling FK7 8LG	01786 815192
Mack, Lynne (Mrs)	36 Middleton, Menstrie FK11 7HD	01259 761465
Ross, Alastair	7 Elm Court, Doune FK16 6JG	01786 841648
Tilly, Patricia (Mrs)	4 Innerdownie Place, Dollar FK14 7BY	01259 742094
Weir, Andrew (Dr)	16 The Oaks, Killearn, Glasgow G63 9SF	01360 550779
24. DUNFERMLINE		
Adams, William	24 Foulford Street, Cowdenbeath KY4 0EQ	01383 510540
Arnott, Robert G.K.	25 Sealstrand, Dalgety Bay, Dunfermline KY11 5GH	01383 822293
Blane, David	10 Ordnance Road, Crombie, Dunfermline KY12 8JZ	01383 873002
Conway, Bernard	4 Centre Street, Kelty KY4 0DU	01383 830442
McCaffery, Joyce (Mrs)	79 Union Street, Cowdenbeath KY4 9SA	01383 515775
McDonald, Elizabeth (Mrs)	Parleyhill, Culross, Dunfermline KY12 8JD	01383 880231
Meiklejohn, Barry	40 Lilac Grove, Dunfermline KY11 8AP	01383 731550
Mitchell, Ian G. QC	17 Carlingnose Point, North Queensferry, Inverkeithing KY11 1ER	01383 416240
25. KIRKCALDY		
Biernat, Ian	2 Formonthills Road, Glenrothes KY6 3BX [E-mail: ian.biernat@virgin.net]	01592 741487
26. ST ANDREWS		
Elder, Morag Anne (Ms)	5 Provost Road, Tayport DD6 9JE	01382 552218
Grant, Allan	6 Normandy Place, Rosyth KY11 2HJ [E-mail: allan75@btinternet.com]	01383 428760
King, C.M. (Mrs)	8 Bankwell Road, Anstruther KY10 3DA	01333 310017
Kinnis, W.K.B. (Dr) (Reader Emeritus)	4 Dempster Court, St Andrews KY16 9EU	01334 476959
Smith, Elspeth (Mrs)	Whinstead, Dalgairn, Cupar KY15 4PH	01334 653269
27. DUNKELD AND MEIGLE		
Carr, Graham	St Helens, Meigle Road, Alyth PH11 8EU	01828 632474
Ewart, Ellen (Mrs)	Cara Beag, Essendy Road, Blairgowrie PH10 6QU	01250 876897
Howat, David	Lilybank Cottage, Newton Street, Blairgowrie PH10 6HZ	01250 874715
Steele, Grace (Miss)	12A Farragon Drive, Aberfeldy PH15 2BQ	01887 820025
Templeton, Elizabeth (Mrs)	Milton of Pitgur Farmhouse, Dalcapon, Pitlochry PH9 0ND	01796 482232
Theaker, Philip	5 Altamount Road, Blairgowrie PH10 6QL	01250 871162

28. PERTH

Archibald, Michael	Wychwood, Culdeesland Road, Methven, Perth PH1 3QE [E-mail: michael.archibald@googlemail.com]	01738 840996
Begg, James	8 Park Village, Turretbank Road, Crieff PH7 4JN [E-mail: Bjimmy37@aol.com]	01764 655907
Brown, Gordon	Nowell, Fossoway, Kinross KY13 0UW [E-mail: brown.nowell@hotmail.co.uk]	01577 840248
Brown, Stanley	14 Buchan Drive, Perth PH1 1NQ	01738 628818
Coulter, Hamish	95 Cedar Drive, Perth PH1 1RW [E-mail: hamish@hamlynperth.co.uk]	01738 636761
Davidson, Andrew	95 Needless Road, Perth PH2 0LD [E-mail: a.r.davidson.91@cantab.net]	01738 620839
Laing, John	10 Graybank Road, Perth PH2 0GZ [E-mail: laing_middlechurch@hotmail.com]	01738 623888
Livingstone, Alan	Meadowside, Lawmuir, Methven, Perth PH1 3SZ [E-mail: livingstone24@btinternet.com]	01738 840682
Michie, Margaret (Mrs)	3 Loch Leven Court, Wester Balgedie, Kinross KY13 9NE [E-mail: margaretmichie@btinternet.com]	01592 840602
Moore, Susan H. (Mrs)	Hoolie Hoose, Dunira, Crieff PH6 2JZ [E-mail: s.hardmanmoore@ed.ac.uk]	01764 670010
Ogilvie, Brian	67 Whitecraigs, Kinnesswood, Kinross KY13 9JN [E-mail: brianj.ogilvie1@btopenworld.com]	01592 840823
Thorburn, Susan (Mrs) MTh	3 Daleally Cottages, St Madoes Road, Errol, Perth PH2 7TJ [E-mail: s_thor2@yahoo.com]	
Yellowlees, Deirdre (Mrs)	Ringmill House, Gannochy Farm, Perth PH2 7JH [E-mail: d.yellowlees@btinternet.com]	01738 633773

29. DUNDEE

Bell, Stephen (Dr)	10 Victoria Street, Newport-on-Tay DD6 8DJ [E-mail: stephen.bell@dundeepresbytery.org.uk]	01382 542315
Brown, Isobel (Mrs)	10 School Wynd, Muirhead, Dundee DD2 5LW	01382 580545
Brown, Janet (Miss)	G2, 6 Baxter Park Terrace, Dundee DD4 6NL [E-mail: janet.brown@dundeepresbytery.org.uk]	01382 453066
Rodgers, Mary (Mrs)	12 Balmerino Road, Dundee DD4 8RN	01382 500291
Simpson, Webster	51 Wemyss Crescent, Monifieth, Dundee DD5 4RA	01382 535218
Webster, Charles A.	16 Bath Street, Broughty Ferry, Dundee DD5 2BY [E-mail: charles.webster@dundeepresbytery.org.uk]	01382 739520
Woodley, Alan G. (Dr)	67 Marlee Road, Broughty Ferry, Dundee DD5 3UT [E-mail: alan.woodley@dundeepresbytery.org.uk]	01382 739820
Xenophontos-Hellen, Tim	23 Ancrum Drive, Dundee DD2 2JG [E-mail: tim.xenophontos-hellen@dundeepresbytery.org.uk]	01382 630355

30. ANGUS		
Anderson, Gordon	33 Grampian View, Ferryden, Montrose DD10 9SU	01674 674915
Beedie, A.W.	62 Newton Crescent, Arbroath DD11 3JZ	01241 875001
Davidson, P.I.	24 Kinnaird Place, Brechin DD9 7HF	
Edwards, Dougal	25 Mackenzie Street, Carnoustie DD7 6HD	01241 852666
Gray, Ian	'The Mallards', 15 Rossie Island Road, Montrose DD10 9NH	01674 677126
Gray, Linda (Mrs)	8 Inchgarth Street, Forfar DD8 3LY	01307 464039
Ironside, Colin (Emeritus)	21 Tailyour Crescent, Montrose DD10 9BL	01674 673959
Nicol, Douglas C.	Edenbank, 16 New Road, Forfar DD8 2AE	01307 463264
Stevens, Peter J. BSc BA	7 Union Street, Montrose DD10 8PZ [E-mail: peterstevens@montrose56.freeserve.co.uk]	01674 673710
Thompson, Anne	22 Braehead Drive, Carnoustie DD7 7SX	01241 852084
Wheat, M.	16A South Esk Street, Montrose DD10 8BJ	01674 676083
31. ABERDEEN		
Anderson, William	1 Farepark Circle, Westhill, Skene AB32 6WJ	01224 740017
Gray, Peter PhD	165 Countesswells Road, Aberdeen AB15 7RA	01224 318172
Morgan, Richard	73A Bon-Accord Street, Aberdeen AB11 6ED	01224 210270
Sinton, George P. FIMLS (Emeritus)	12 North Donside Road, Bridge of Don, Aberdeen AB23 8PA	01224 702273
32. KINCARDINE AND DEESIDE		
Broere, Teresa (Mrs)	3 Balnastraid Cottages, Dinnet, Aboyne AB34 5NE [E-mail: dirk.broere@talktalk.net]	01339 880058
Coles, Stephen	43 Mearns Walk, Laurencekirk AB30 1FA [E-mail: steve@sbcco.com]	01561 378400
McCafferty, W. John	Lynwood, Cammachmore, Stonehaven AB39 3NR [E-mail: wjmccafferty@yahoo.co.uk]	01569 730281
McLuckie, John	7 Monaltrie Close, Ballater AB35 5PT [E-mail: johnemcluckie@btinternet.com]	01339 755489
Middleton, Robbie (Capt.)	7 St Ternan's Road, Newtonhill, Stonehaven AB39 3PF [E-mail: randjmiddleton@tiscali.co.uk]	01569 730852
Platt, David	2 St Michael's Road, Newtonhill, Stonehaven AB39 3RW [E-mail: daveplatt01@btinternet.com]	01569 730465
Simpson, Elizabeth (Mrs)	33 Golf Road, Ballater AB35 5RE [E-mail: connemara33@yahoo.com]	01339 755597
33. GORDON		
Bichard, Susanna (Mrs)	Beechlee, Haddo Lane, Tarves, Ellon AB41 7JZ	01651 851343
Doak, Alan B.	17 Chievres Place, Ellon AB41 9WH [E-mail: AlanbDoak@aol.com]	01358 721819
Findlay, Patricia (Mrs)	Douglas View, Tullynessle, Alford AB33 8QR	01975 562379

Mitchell, Jean (Mrs)	6 Cowgate, Oldmeldrum, Inverurie AB51 0EN	01651 872745
Robb, Margaret (Mrs)	Chrislouan, Keithhall, Inverurie AB51 0LN	01651 882310
Robertson, James Y.	1 Nicol Road, Kintore, Inverurie AB51 0QA	01467 633001
34. BUCHAN		
Allen, Sena (Mrs)	88 Kirk Street, Peterhead AB42 1RY [E-mail: sama@allen159.fsnet.co.uk]	01779 477327
Armitage, Rosaline (Mrs)	Whitecairn, Blackhills, Peterhead AB42 3LR [E-mail: r.r.armitage@btinternet.com]	01779 477267
Brown, Lillian (Mrs)	45 Main Street, Aberchirder, Huntly AB54 7ST	01466 780330
Davidson, James	19 Great Stuart Street, Peterhead AB42 1JX [E-mail: jimdavidson156@googlemail.com]	01779 470242
Forsyth, Alicia (Mrs)	Rothie Inn Farm, Rothienorman, Inverurie AB51 8YH [E-mail: a.forsyth@btinternet.com]	01651 821359
Givan, James	Zimra, Longmanhill, Banff AB45 3RP [E-mail: jim.givan@btinternet.com]	01261 833318
Higgins, Scott	St Ninian's, Manse Terrace, Turriff AB53 4BA [E-mail: mhairiandscott@btinternet.com]	01888 569103
Lumsden, Vera (Mrs)	8 Queen's Crescent, Portsoy, Banff AB45 2PX [E-mail: ivsd@lumsden77.freeserve.co.uk]	01261 842712
McColl, John	East Cairnchina, Lonmay, Fraserburgh AB43 8RH [E-mail: info@solomonsfolly.co.uk]	01346 532558
Macnee, Anthea (Mrs)	Wardend Cottage, Alvah, Banff AB45 3TR [E-mail: macneeiain4@googlemail.com]	01261 851647
Mair, Dorothy (Miss)	15 The Quay, Newburgh, Ellon AB41 6DA [E-mail: dorothymair2@aol.com]	01358 788832 (Mbl) 07505 051305
Michie, William	34 Seafield Street, Whitehills, Banff AB45 2NR [E-mail: b.michie@talktalk.net]	01261 861439
Noble, John	44 Henderson Park, Peterhead AB42 2WR [E-mail: john_m_noble@hotmail.co.uk]	01779 472522
Ogston, Norman	Rowandale, 6 Rectory Road, Turriff AB53 4SU [E-mail: norman.ogston@gmail.com]	01888 560342
Simpson, Andrew C.	10 Wood Street, Banff AB45 1JX [E-mail: andy.louise1@btinternet.com]	01261 812538
Smith, Ian M.G. MA	Chomriach, 2 Hill Street, Cruden Bay, Peterhead AB42 0HF	01779 812698
Smith, Jenny (Mrs)	5 Seatown Place, Cairnbulg, Fraserburgh AB43 8WP [E-mail: jennyfsmith@hotmail.com]	(Mbl) 07842 209291
Sneddon, Richard	100 West Road, Peterhead AB42 2AQ [E-mail: richard.sneddon@btinternet.com]	01779 480803
Stewart, William	Denend, Strichen AB43 6RN [E-mail: clan@wmsjas.freeserve.co.uk]	01771 637256
Williams, Paul	20 Soy Burn Gardens, Portsoy AB45 2QG [E-mail: paul.williams447@virgin.net]	01261 842338

Yule, Joseph	5 Staffa Street, Peterhead AB42 1NF [E-mail: josephyule@ifb.co.uk]	01779 476400
35. MORAY		
Benson, F. Stewart	8 Springfield Court, Forres IV36 3WY	01309 671525
Forbes, Jean (Mrs)	Greenmoss, Drybridge, Buckie AB56 5JB	01542 831646
36. ABERNETHY		
Bardgett, Alison (Mrs)	Tigh an Iasgair, Street of Kincardine, Boat of Garten PH24 3BY [E-mail: tigh@bardgett.plus.com]	01479 831751
Duncanson, Mary (Mrs)	Glenelg, 72B High Street, Kingussie PH21 1HZ [E-mail: mary1105@hotmail.co.uk]	01540 662075
37. INVERNESS		
Archer, Morven (Mrs)	42 Firth View Drive, Inverness IV3 8QE	01463 237840
Barry, Dennis	50 Holm Park, Inverness IV2 4XU	01463 225883
Cazaly, Leonard	9 Moray Park, Culloden, Inverness IV2 4SX	01463 794469
Cook, Arnett D.	128 Laurel Avenue, Inverness IV3 5RS	01463 242586
Ogston, Jean (Mrs)	Roselynn, Croyard Road, Beauly IV4 7DJ	01463 782260
Robertson, Hendry	'Park House', 51 Glenurquhart Road, Inverness IV3 5PB	01463 231858
Robertson, Stewart J.H.	27 Towerhill Drive, Inverness IV2 5FD	01463 793144
Roden, Vivien (Mrs)	15 Oldmill Road, Tomatin, Inverness IV13 7YW	01808 511355
Todd, Ian	9 Leanach Gardens, Inverness IV2 5DD	01463 791161
38. LOCHABER		
Chalkley, Andrew BSc	2 Telford Place, Claggan, Fort William PH33 6QG	01397 700271
Fraser, John A. BA	26 Clunes Avenue, Caol, Fort William PH33 7BJ [E-mail: john.afraser@btopenworld.com]	01397 703467
Maitland, John	St Monance, Ardgour, Fort William PH33 7AA	01855 841267
Muirhead, Morag (Mrs)	6 Dumbarton Road, Fort William PH33 6UU [E-mail: mowgli49@aol.com]	01397 703643
Walker, Eric	Tigh a' Chlann, Inverroy, Roy Bridge PH31 4AQ [E-mail: line15@btinternet.com]	01397 712028
Walker, Pat (Mrs)	Tigh a' Chlann, Inverroy, Roy Bridge PH31 4AQ [E-mail: pw-15@tiscali.co.uk]	01397 712028
39. ROSS		
Finlayson, Michael R.	Amberlea, Evanton, Dingwall IV16 9UY	01349 830598
Greer, Kathleen (Mrs) MEd	17 Duthac Wynd, Tain IV19 1LP [E-mail: greer2@talktalk.net]	01862 892065

Gunstone, Ronald W.	20 Bellfield Road, North Kessock, Inverness IV1 3XU [E-mail: ronald.gunstone@virgin.net]	01463 731337
Jamieson, Patricia A. (Mrs)	7 Craig Avenue, Tain IV19 1JP [E-mail: hapijam179@yahoo.co.uk]	01862 893154
McAlpine, James	5 Cromlet Park, Invergordon IV18 0RN [E-mail: jmca1@tinyworld.co.uk]	01349 852801
McCreadie, Frederick	Highfield, Highfield Park, Conon Bridge, Dingwall IV7 8AP	01349 862171
Riddell, Keith	2 Station Cottages, Fearn, Tain IV20 1RR [E-mail: riddell293@btinternet.com]	01862 832867
40. SUTHERLAND		
Bruce, Dorothy (Mrs) (Reader Emeritus)	Eastwood, Altass, Rosehall, by Lairg IV27 4EU	01549 441285
Innes, Derek	Hill Cottage, Lairg Muir, Lairg IV27 4ED	01549 402215
Stobo, Mary (Mrs)	Druim-an-Sgairnich, Ardgay IV24 3BG	01863 766868
Weidner, Karl	St Vincent Road, Tain IV19 1JR	01862 894202
41. CAITHNESS		
Duncan, Esme (Miss)	Avalon, Upper Warse, Canisbay, Wick KW1 4YD [E-mail: esmeduncan@btinternet.com]	01955 611455
Rennie, Lyall	The Manse, Canisbay, Wick KW1 4YH [E-mail: lyall.rennie@btinternet.com]	01955 611756
Stewart, Heather (Mrs)	Burnthill, Thrumster, Wick KW1 5AX [E-mail: heatherburnthill@btopenworld.com]	01955 651717
42. LOCHCARRON – SKYE		
Lamont, John H.	Aultbea, Ross-shire [E-mail: john.lamont@saipem-sa.com]	
Mackenzie, Hector	9 Fairburn, Gairloch IV21 2DB	01445 712433
Macrae, D.E.	Nethania, 52 Strath, Gairloch IV21 2DB [E-mail: Dmgair@aol.com]	01445 712235
Ross, R. Ian	St Conal's, Inverinate, Kyle IV40 8HB	01599 511371
43. UIST		
Browning, Margaret	1 Middlequarter, Sollas, Lochmaddy, Isle of North Uist HS6	01876 560392
MacAulay, John	Flodabay, Isle of Harris HS3 3HA	01859 530340
MacNab, Ann (Mrs)	Druim Skilivat, Scolpaig, Lochmaddy, Isle of North Uist HS6 5DH	01876 510701
MacSween, John	5 Scott Road, Tarbert, Isle of Harris HS3 3DL	01859 502338
Taylor, Hamish	Tigh na Tobair, Flodabay, Isle of Harris HS3 3HA	01859 530310
44. LEWIS		
Macleod, Donald	14 Balmerino Drive, Stornoway, Isle of Lewis HS1 2TD [E-mail: donaldmacleod25@btinternet.com]	01851 704516

Macmillan, Iain	34 Scotland Street, Stornoway, Isle of Lewis HS1 2JR [E-mail: member@brocair.fsnet.co.uk]	01851 704826
Murray, Angus	4 Ceann Chilleagraidh, Stornoway, Isle of Lewis HS1 2UJ	01851 703550
45. ORKNEY		
Fidler, David G.	34 Guardhouse Park, Stromness, Orkney KW16 3DP [E-mail: dvdfid@aol.com]	01856 850575
Prentice, Martin	Cott of Howe, Cairston, Stromness, Orkney KW16 3JU [E-mail: mwm.prentice@virgin.net]	01856 851139
Robertson, Johan (Mrs)	Old Manse, Eday, Orkney KW17 2AA	01857 622251
Steer, John	Beckington, Hillside Road, Stromness, Orkney KW16 3AH	01856 850815
46. SHETLAND		
Christie, William C. (Reader Emeritus)	11 Fullaburn, Bressay, Shetland ZE2 9ET	01595 820244
Greig, Diane (Mrs) MA	The Manse, Sandwick, Shetland ZE2 9HW	01950 422468
Harrison, Christine (Mrs) BA	Gerdavatn, Baltasound, Unst, Shetland ZE2 9DY	01957 711578
Laidlay, Una (Mrs) (Reader Emeritus)	5 Bells Road, Lerwick, Shetland ZE1 0QB	01595 695147
Smith, M. Beryl (Mrs) DCE MSc	Vakterlee, Cumliewick, Sandwick, Shetland ZE2 9HH	01950 431280
47. ENGLAND		
Dick, R.G.	Duneagle, Church Road, Sparkford, Somerset	01963 40475
Green, Peter (Dr)	Samburu Cottage, Russells Green Road, Ninfield, East Sussex	01424 892033
Mackay, Donald (Reader Emeritus)	90 Hallgarth Street, Elvet, Durham DH1 3AS	0191-383 2110
Menzies, Rena (Mrs)	49 Elizabeth Avenue, St Brelade's, Jersey JE3 8GR	01534 741095
48. EUROPE		
Ross, David	Urb. El Campanario, EDF Granada, Esc. 14, Baja B, Ctra Cadiz N-340, Km 168, 29680 Estepona, Malaga, Spain [E-mail: rosselcampanario@yahoo.co.uk]	(Tel/Fax) 0034 952 88 26 34

LIST O – REPRESENTATIVES ON COUNCIL EDUCATION COMMITTEES

COUNCIL	NAME	ADDRESS	TEL
ABERDEEN CITY	Mr Peter Campbell	12 Station Road East, Aberdeen AB14 0PT	01224 734245
ABERDEENSHIRE	Mr Alexander Corner	4 Bain Road, Mintlaw, Peterhead AB42 5EW [E-mail: sandycorner@hotmail.com]	01771 622562
ANGUS	Mr David Adams	Glebe House, Farnell, by Brechin DD9 6UH	01674 820227
ARGYLL and BUTE	Mr William Dalby	Kwimona, Ardentinny, Dunoon PA23 8TR [E-mail: wmdalby@aol.com]	01369 810291
BORDERS	Mr Graeme Donald	1 Upper Loan Park, Lauder TD2 6TR [E-mail: graeme.donald@btopenwoprld.com]	01578 722422
CLACKMANNAN	Rev. Mairi Lovett	The Manse, 7 Long Row, Menstrie FK11 7BA [E-mail: mairi@kanyo.co.uk]	01259 761461
DUMFRIES and GALLOWAY	Mr Robert McQuistan	Kirkdale Schoolhouse, Carsluith, Newton Stewart DG8 7DT [E-mail: mcquistan@quista.net]	01387 722165
DUNDEE	Rev. James L. Wilson	53 Old Craigie Road, Dundee DD4 7JD [E-mail: R3VJW@aol.com]	01382 459249
EAST AYRSHIRE			
EAST DUNBARTONSHIRE	Mrs Barbara Jarvie	18 Cannerton Crescent, Milton of Campsie, Glasgow G66 8DR [E-mail: bj@bjarvie.fsnet.co.uk]	01360 319729
EAST LOTHIAN	Mrs Marjorie K. Goldsmith	20 St Lawrence, Haddington EH41 3RL	01620 823249
EAST RENFREWSHIRE	Rev. Maureen Leitch	14 Maxton Avenue, Barrhead, Glasgow G78 1DY [E-mail: maureen.leitch@ntlworld.com]	0141-881 1462
EDINBURGH CITY	Mr A. Craig Duncan	2 East Barnton Gardens, Edinburgh EH4 6AR [E-mail: acraigduncan@btinternet.com]	0131-336 4432
EDINBURGH SCRUTINY PANEL	Dr J. Mitchell Manson	17 Huntingdon Place, Edinburgh EH7 4AX [E-mail: MitchellManson@aol.com]	0131-557 1933
FALKIRK	Mrs Margaret Coutts	34 Pirleyhill Gardens, Falkirk FK1 5NB [E-mail: margaret.coutts1@tiscali.co.uk]	01324 628732
FIFE	Rev. Andrew J. Philip	12 Torvean Place, Dunfermline KY11 4YY [E-mail: andrewphilip@minister.com]	01383 721054
GLASGOW CITY	Rev. Graham R.G. Cartlidge	54 Mansewood Road, Eastwood, Glasgow G43 1TL [E-mail: g.cartlidge@ntlworld.com]	0141-649 0463
GLASGOW CITY SCRUTINY PANEL	Rev. David A. Keddie	21 Ilay Road, Bearsden, Glasgow G61 1QG [E-mail: revked@hotmail.com]	0141-942 5173
HIGHLAND	Rev. Alexander Glass	Craigton, Tulloch Avenue, Dingwall IV15 9TU	01349 863258
INVERCLYDE	Rev. Andrew T. MacLean	St Andrew's Manse, Barr's Brae, Port Glasgow PA14 5QA [E-mail: standrews.pg@me.com]	01475 741486

MIDLOTHIAN	Mr Paul Hayes	Kingsway Management Services Ltd, 127 Deanburn, Penicuik EH26 0JA [E-mail: paul.hayes@basilicon.com]	
MORAY	Rev. Shuna M. Dicks	The Manse, Mary Avenue, Aberlour AB38 9QU [E-mail: revshuna@minister.com]	01340 871687
NORTH AYRSHIRE	Mr Gordon McConnell	9 Old Woodwynd Road, Kilwinning KA13 7DN	01294 466849
NORTH LANARKSHIRE	Mr John William Maddock	137 Manse Road, Motherwell ML1 2PS [E-mail: john@maddockfamily.plus.com]	01698 251137
ORKNEY			
PERTH and KINROSS			
RENFREWSHIRE	Rev. Robin N. Allison	282 Main Road, Elderslie PA5 9EF [E-mail: revrobin@sky.com]	01505 321767
SHETLAND	Rev. Tom Macintyre	The Rock, Whiteness, Shetland ZE2 9LJ [E-mail: the2macs.macintyre@btinternet.com]	
SOUTH AYRSHIRE	Rev. David R. Gemmell	58 Monument Road, Ayr KA7 2UB [E-mail: drgemmell@hotmail.com]	01292 262580
SOUTH LANARKSHIRE	Rev. Sarah L. Ross	22 Lea Rig, Forth, Lanark ML11 8EA [E-mail: rev_sross@btinternet.com]	01555 812832
STIRLING	Mrs Joan Kerr	36 Strathallan Court, Bridge of Allan, Stirling FK9 4BW	01786 834939
WEST DUNBARTONSHIRE	Miss Sheila Rennie	128 Dumbuie Avenue, Dumbarton G82 2JW [E-mail: sheila_rennie@tiscali.co.uk]	01389 763246
WEST LOTHIAN	Rev. W. Richard Houston	29 Philip Avenue, Linlithgow EH49 7BH [E-mail: wrichardhouston@blueyonder.co.uk]	01506 202246
WESTERN ISLES	Dr Neil Galbraith	Four Winds, 1 Churchill Drive, Stornoway, Isle of Lewis HS1 2NP [E-mail: n.galbraith@tiscali.net]	01851 702209

LIST P – RETIRED LAY AGENTS

Falconer, Alexander J.	84 Bridge Street, Dollar FK14 7DQ [E-mail: falconer@falconer59.freeserve.co.uk]
Forrester, Arthur A.	158 Lee Crescent North, Bridge of Don, Aberdeen AB22 8FR
Scott, John W.	15 Manor Court, Forfar DD8 1BR

LIST Q – MINISTERS ORDAINED FOR SIXTY YEARS AND UPWARDS

Until 1992, the *Year Book* contained each year a list of those ministers who had been ordained 'for fifty years and upwards'. For a number of reasons, that list was thereafter discontinued. The current Editor was encouraged to reinstate such a list, and the edition for 2002 included the names of those ordained for sixty years and upwards. With ministers, no less than the rest of society, living longer, it was felt reasonable to proceed on that basis. Correspondence made it clear that this list was welcomed, and it has been included in an appropriately revised form each year since then. Again this year, an updated version is offered following the best enquiries that could be made. The date of ordination is given in full where it is known.

1932	14 August	Thomas Mackenzie Donn (Duthil)
1938	29 June	George Alestair Alison Bennett (Strathkinness)
1939	12 November	Alexander McRae Houston (Tibbermore)
	10 December	Wellesley Grahame Bailey (Ladykirk with Whitsome)
	22 December	Alistair McRae Rennie (Kincardine Croick and Edderton)
1940	24 February	James Johnstone Turnbull (Arbirlot with Colliston)
	29 May	Norman McGathan Bowman (Edinburgh: St Mary's)
	21 August	Donald MacFarlane (Inverness: East)
1941	3 July	Donald William MacKenzie (Auchterarder: The Barony)
1942	15 April	Frank Haughton (Kirkintilloch: St Mary's)
	5 July	Norman Christopher Macrae (Loanhead)
	24 December	James Bews (Dundee: Craigiebank)
1943	11 May	Leon David Levison (Ormiston with Pencaitland)
	2 June	Duncan Finlayson (Morvern)
	3 September	George Cooper (Delting with Nesting and Lunnasting)
1944	21 June	Denis Macdonald Duncan (Editor: *The British Weekly*)
	10 November	Alexander Spence (Elgin: St Giles': Associate)
1945	24 January	Thomas Morton (Rutherglen: Stonelaw)
	4 February	James Shirra (St Martin's with Scone: New)

	5 May	Robert Stockbridge Whiteford (Shapinsay)
	27 June	Ian Arthur Girdwood Easton (University of Strathclyde)
	1 August	John Walter Evans (Elgin: High)
	4 September	John Paul Tierney (Peterhead West: Associate)
1946	11 April	James Martin (Glasgow: High Carntyne)
	19 May	John McClymont Frew (Glasgow: Dennistoun)
	23 June	Ian Masson Fraser (Selly Oak Colleges)
	18 September	John Wilkinson (Kikuyu)
	3 October	John Henry Whyte (Gourock: Ashton)
	13 November	Ian Bruce Doyle (Department of National Mission)
1947	22 June	James Alexander Robertson Mackenzie (Largo: St David's)
	27 November	William Duncan Crombie (Glasgow: Calton New with Glasgow: St Andrew's)
1948	31 March	Gilbert Mollison Mowat (Dundee: Albany-Butterburn)
	20 April	Andrew Kerr (Kilbarchan: West)
	6 July	Alexander Chestnut (Greenock: St Mark's Greenbank)
	8 September	David Stuart Forsyth (Belhelvie)
	6 October	George Davidson Wilkie (Kirkcaldy: Viewforth)
1949	5 January	Andrew Queen Morton (Culross and Torryburn)
	14 February	Hamish Norman Mackenzie McIntosh (Fintry)
	12 June	Alexander Francis Grimstone (Glasgow: Calton Parkhead)
	26 June	Robert Ferguson (Glasgow: North Kelvinside)
	17 July	Walter Vernon Stone (Langbank)
	1 September	John Anderson Macnaughton (Glasgow: Hyndland)
	22 November	John Alexander Miller Scott (Jerusalem)
	18 December	James McMichael Orr (Aberfoyle with Port of Menteith)
1950	9 July	Alexander Craig Barr (Glasgow: St Nicholas' Cardonald)
	10 July	Kenneth MacVicar (Kenmore with Lawers with Fortingall and Glenlyon)
	26 July	Alexander Hamilton Lawson (Clydebank: Kilbowie)
	27 August	Robert Govan Clarkson (Dundee: Strathmartine)
	5 September	James McLaren Ritchie (Coalsnaughton)
	28 December	Donald Stewart Wallace (Chaplain: RAF)

1951	28 January	William Henry Greenway Bristow (Chaplain: Army)
	30 March	William John Macintyre (Crail with Kingsbarns)
	5 June	Malcolm Nicholson Henry (Perth: Craigie)
	12 June	Donald John Barker McAlister (North Berwick: Blackadder)
	27 June	John Clark Scroggie (Mains)
	26 July	Duncan Shaw (Edinburgh: Craigentinny St Christopher's)
	9 September	Alwyn James Cecil Macfarlane (Glasgow: Newlands South)
	1 October	William James Morris (Glasgow: Cathedral)
	24 October	Thomas Dick (Dunkeld)
	6 November	Alexander Gordon McGillivray (Edinburgh: Presbytery Clerk)
	15 November	Andrew Whittingham Rae (Annan: St Andrew's Greenknowe Erskine)
	20 November	Donald Iain McMillan (Bearsden: South)
	28 November	James Pringle Fraser (Strathaven: Avendale Old and Drumclog)

LIST R – DECEASED MINISTERS

The Editor has been made aware of the following ministers who have died since the publication of the previous volume of the *Year Book*.

Allan, Alexander George	(Glasgow: Candlish Polmadie)
Anderson, Colin MacEwen	(Inverness: St Stephen's with The Old High)
Benson, James William	(Balquhidder)
Black, William	(Durness and Kinlochbervie)
Bruce, Lilian Margaret (Miss)	(Daviot and Dunlichity with Moy, Dalarossie and Tomatin)
Capstick, Dwin	(Jura)
Charlton, George Wilson	(Fort Augustus with Glengarry)
Collie, Joyce Philip (Miss)	(Corgarff Strathdon with Glenbuchat Towie)
Dean, John McBride	(Hamilton: Gilmour and Whitehill)
Donald, Thomas Wilson	(Bowden with Lilliesleaf)
Erskine, Austin Urquhart	(Anwoth and Girthon with Borgue)
Fox, George Dudley Andrew	(Kelso: Old)
Handley, John	(Motherwell: Clason Memorial)
Higgins, George Kerr	(Oban: St Columba's Argyll Square)
Jolly, Andrew John	Chaplain to UK Oil and Gas Industry
Lithgow, Thomas	(Banchory-Devenick with Maryculter)
Longmuir, William Macgregor	(Bedrule with Denholm with Minto)
Low, Nan (Mrs)	Neilston
Lyon, David Henry Scott	(Board of World Mission and Unity)
McAreavey, William	(Glasgow: Kelvin Stevenson Memorial)
McAulay, Alick Hugh	(Bellie with Speymouth)
Mackie, Steven Gabriel	(The University of St Andrews)
Macleod, Allan MacInnes	(Gordon: St Michael's with Legerwood with Westruther)

Miller, Harry Galbraith	(Iona and Ross of Mull)
Morton, Robert Colin Maxwell	(Jerusalem)
Murison, William George	(Department of World Mission)
Philip, David Stuart	(Gibraltar)
Philp, Connie (Miss)	(Arbuthnott with Bervie)
Porter, Richard	(Glasgow: Govanhill)
Preston, Thomas	Breich Valley
Robertson, Thomas Parker	(Dundee: Broughty Ferry St James')
Scobie, Andrew John	Cardross
Scott, John	(Aberdour: St Fillan's)
Shaw, Wallace Allen	(Glenrothes: St Margaret's)
Skinner, Donald McLean	(Edinburgh: Gilmerton)
Smith, William Ewing	(Livingston: Old)
Spence, Charles Keith Omond	(Craigrownie)
Stiven, Ian Kay	(Strachur and Strathlachlan)
Taylor, Alan Hunter Stuart	(Brydekirk with Hoddam)
Thomson, George Fullerton Monteath	(Associate: Dollar)
Thomson, Peter George	(Irvine: Fullarton)
Williamson, Thomas	(Dyke with Edinkillie)
Wilson, William Stewart	(Kirkcudbright)
Wylie, William Andrew	(Industrial Chaplain)

SECTION 7

Legal Names and Scottish Charity Numbers for Individual Congregations (Congregations in Scotland only)

EXPLANATORY NOTE:
All documents, as defined in the Charities References in Documents (Scotland) Regulations 2007, must specify the Charity Number, Legal Name of the congregation, any other name by which the congregation is commonly known and the fact that it is a Charity.

For more information, please refer to the Law Department circular on the Regulations on the Church of Scotland website.

SCOTTISH CHARITY NUMBER	NEW LEGAL NAME
1.	**Presbytery of Edinburgh**
SC018012	Balerno Church of Scotland
SC001554	Edinburgh Currie Kirk (Church of Scotland)
SC010971	Dalmeny Parish Church of Scotland
SC018321	Albany Deaf Church, Edinburgh (Church of Scotland)
SC014757	Edinburgh Barclay Viewforth Church of Scotland
SC008756	Blackhall St Columba's Church of Scotland, Edinburgh
SC011625	Bristo Memorial Church of Scotland, Craigmillar, Edinburgh
SC012642	Edinburgh: Broughton St Mary's Parish Church (Church of Scotland)
SC015251	Canongate Parish Church of Scotland, Edinburgh
SC004783	Carrick Knowe Parish Church of Scotland, Edinburgh
SC010313	Colinton Parish Church of Scotland, Edinburgh
SC015982	Colinton Mains Parish Church of Scotland, Edinburgh
SC014719	Edinburgh: Corstorphine Craigsbank Parish Church (Church of Scotland)
SC016009	Corstorphine Old Parish Church, Church of Scotland, Edinburgh
SC006300	Edinburgh: Corstorphine St Anne's Parish Church (Church of Scotland)
SC016557	Edinburgh: Corstorphine St Ninian's Parish Church (Church of Scotland)
SC003466	Edinburgh: Craigentinny St Christopher's Parish Church of Scotland
SC010545	Craiglockhart Parish Church, Edinburgh (Church of Scotland)
SC017061	Craigmillar Park Church of Scotland, Edinburgh
SC003430	Cramond Kirk, Edinburgh (Church of Scotland)
SC009470	Davidsons Mains Parish Church of Scotland, Edinburgh
SC001692	Dean Parish Church, Edinburgh – The Church of Scotland
SC005744	Drylaw Parish Church of Scotland, Edinburgh
SC016610	Duddingston Kirk (Church of Scotland), Edinburgh
SC015967	Fairmilehead Parish Church of Scotland, Edinburgh
SC009146	Edinburgh: Gorgie Dalry Church of Scotland
SC011985	Granton Parish Church of Scotland, Edinburgh
SC011325	Edinburgh Greenbank Parish Church of Scotland
SC009749	Edinburgh Greenside Church of Scotland
SC003761	Edinburgh: Greyfriars Tolbooth and Highland Kirk (Church of Scotland)
SC003565	St Giles' Cathedral, Edinburgh (Church of Scotland)
SC012562	Holy Trinity Church of Scotland, Edinburgh
SC000052	Holyrood Abbey Parish Church of Scotland, Edinburgh
SC015442	Inverleith Church of Scotland, Edinburgh
SC005197	Edinburgh Juniper Green Parish Church of Scotland
SC004950	Kaimes: Lockhart Memorial Church of Scotland, Edinburgh
SC014430	Kirk o' Field Parish Church, Edinburgh (Church of Scotland)
SC004932	Edinburgh Leith North Parish Church of Scotland
SC004695	South Leith Parish Church of Scotland, Edinburgh
SC012680	Leith St Andrew's Church of Scotland, Edinburgh
SC008572	Edinburgh: Leith St Serf's Parish Church of Scotland
SC008710	Wardie Parish Church of Scotland, Edinburgh
SC011602	Edinburgh: Liberton Kirk (Church of Scotland)
SC008891	Liberton Northfield Parish Church of Scotland, Edinburgh
SC000896	London Road Church of Scotland, Edinburgh
SC009338	Marchmont St Giles Parish Church of Scotland, Edinburgh
SC000785	Mayfield Salisbury Parish (Edinburgh) Church of Scotland
SC034396	Morningside Parish Church of Scotland, Edinburgh
SC015552	Edinburgh: Morningside United Church
SC000871	Muirhouse Parish Church of Scotland, Edinburgh
SC005198	Edinburgh Murrayfield Parish Church of Scotland
SC000963	New Restalrig Church of Scotland, Edinburgh
SC019117	Newhaven Church of Scotland, Edinburgh
SC006457	The Old Kirk of Edinburgh (Church of Scotland)
SC004291	Edinburgh: Palmerston Place Church of Scotland
SC007277	Edinburgh: Pilrig St Paul's Church of Scotland
SC004183	Polwarth Parish Church, Edinburgh (Church of Scotland)
SC002328	Edinburgh: Portobello Old Parish Church of Scotland
SC007372	Edinburgh: Portobello St James' Parish Church of Scotland
SC011728	St Philip's Church of Scotland: Edinburgh
SC014499	Priestfield Parish Church of Scotland, Edinburgh
SC014027	Church of Scotland, Reid Memorial Church, Edinburgh
SC009035	Richmond Craigmillar Parish Church of Scotland, Edinburgh
SC030896	Slateford Longstone Parish Church of Scotland, Edinburgh
SC002748	Edinburgh: St Andrew's Clermiston Church of Scotland
SC009379	St Catherine's Argyle Parish Church of Scotland Edinburgh
SC010592	St Cuthberts Parish Church of Scotland, Edinburgh
SC004746	St Davids Broomhouse Church of Scotland, Edinburgh
SC008990	St Andrew's and St George's West Church of Scotland, Edinburgh
SC030819	St John's Oxgangs Church of Scotland: Edinburgh
SC004779	St Margaret's Church of Scotland: Edinburgh
SC013918	St Martins Church of Scotland, Portobello, Edinburgh
SC009038	St Michaels Parish Church of Scotland, Edinburgh
SC007068	Edinburgh: St Nicholas' Sighthill Parish Church of Scotland
SC004487	St Stephen's Comely Bank Church of Scotland, Edinburgh
SC010004	Stenhouse St Aidan's Parish Church of Scotland: Edinburgh
SC002499	Stockbridge Parish Church of Scotland, Edinburgh

SC009274 Tron Kirk (Gilmerton and Moredun), Edinburgh, Church of Scotland
SC013924 Kirkliston Parish Church of Scotland
SC002329 Queensferry Parish Church of Scotland
SC001169 Ratho Church of Scotland

2. Presbytery of West Lothian

SC013100 Abercorn Parish Church of Scotland
SC000791 Armadale Parish Church of Scotland
SC007454 Avonbridge Parish Church of Scotland
SC001881 Boghall Parish Church of Scotland, Bathgate
SC007418 Bathgate High Parish Church of Scotland
SC016755 St John's Parish Church of Scotland, Bathgate
SC024154 Blackburn and Seafield Parish Church of Scotland
SC006811 Blackridge Parish Church of Scotland
SC000800 Breich Valley Parish Church of Scotland
SC017180 Broxburn Parish Church of Scotland
SC016313 Fauldhouse St Andrews Parish Church of Scotland
SC007601 Harthill St Andrew's Parish Church of Scotland
SC013461 Kirk of Calder Parish (Church of Scotland)
SC006973 Kirknewton & East Calder Parish Church of Scotland
SC016185 St Michaels Parish Church of Scotland: Linlithgow
SC011348 St Ninians Craigmailen Parish Church of Scotland, Linlithgow
SC011826 Livingston Old Parish Church of Scotland
SC026230 Pardovan, Kingscavil and Winchburgh Parish Church of Scotland
SC017373 Polbeth Harwood Parish Church of Scotland
SC006336 Strathbrock Parish Church of Scotland, Uphall
SC021516 Torphichen Parish Church of Scotland
SC024255 Uphall South Parish Church of Scotland
SC004703 West Kirk of Calder (Church of Scotland)
SC003362 Brucefield Parish Church of Scotland, Whitburn
SC001053 Whitburn South Parish Church of Scotland

3. Presbytery of Lothian

SC004580 Aberlady Parish Church (Church of Scotland)
SC009401 Athelstaneford Parish Church (Church of Scotland)
SC007231 Belhaven Parish Church (Church of Scotland)
SC032180 Bilston Parish Church (Church of Scotland)
SC003230 Bolton and Saltoun Parish Church (Church of Scotland)
SC003482 Bonnyrigg Parish Church (Church of Scotland)
SC004630 Cockenzie and Port Seton: Chalmers Memorial Parish Church (Church of Scotland)
SC007052 Cockenzie and Port Seton: Old Parish Church (Church of Scotland)
SC013139 Cockpen and Carrington Parish Church (Church of Scotland)
SC006926 Tyne Valley Parish (Church of Scotland)
SC008958 Dalkeith: St John's and King's Park Parish Church (Church of Scotland)
SC014158 Dalkeith: St Nicholas Buccleuch Parish Church (Church of Scotland)
SC004533 Dirleton Parish Church (Church of Scotland)
SC000455 Dunbar Parish Church (Church of Scotland)
SC014299 Dunglass Parish Church (Church of Scotland)
SC014972 Garvald and Morham Parish Church (Church of Scotland)
SC005996 Gladsmuir Parish Church (Church of Scotland)
SC030433 Glencorse Parish Church (Church of Scotland)
SC004673 Gorebridge Parish Church (Church of Scotland)
SC005237 Gullane Parish Church (Church of Scotland)
SC010614 Haddington: St Mary's Parish Church (Church of Scotland)
SC022183 Haddington: West Parish Church (Church of Scotland)
SC014364 Howgate Parish Church (Church of Scotland)
SC016765 Humbie Parish Church (Church of Scotland)
SC015878 Lasswade and Rosewell Parish Church (Church of Scotland)
SC014420 Loanhead Parish Church (Church of Scotland)
SC016556 Longniddry Parish Church (Church of Scotland)
SC004722 Musselburgh: Northesk Parish Church (Church of Scotland)
SC000129 Musselburgh: St Andrew's High Parish Church (Church of Scotland)
SC001726 Musselburgh: St Clement's and St Ninian's Parish Church (Church of Scotland)
SC013559 Musselburgh: St Michael's Inveresk Parish Church (Church of Scotland)
SC035087 Newbattle Parish Church (Church of Scotland)
SC030879 Newton Parish Church (Church of Scotland)
SC004761 Abbey Church, North Berwick, Church of Scotland
SC006421 St Andrew Blackadder, Church of Scotland, North Berwick
SC014810 Ormiston Parish Church (Church of Scotland)
SC004871 Pencaitland Parish Church (Church of Scotland)
SC010902 Penicuik: North Parish Church (Church of Scotland)
SC005838 Penicuik: St Mungo's Parish Church (Church of Scotland)
SC011871 Penicuik: South Parish Church (Church of Scotland)
SC031191 Prestonpans: Prestongrange Parish Church (Church of Scotland)
SC005457 Roslin Parish Church (Church of Scotland)
SC008667 Spott Parish Church (Church of Scotland)
SC017423 Tranent Parish Church (Church of Scotland)
SC012277 Traprain Parish Church (Church of Scotland)
SC000494 Whitekirk and Tyninghame Parish Church (Church of Scotland)
SC015414 Yester Parish Church (Church of Scotland)

4. Presbytery of Melrose and Peebles

SC010768 Ashkirk Parish Church of Scotland
SC006480 Bowden and Melrose Church of Scotland
SC030062 Broughton, Glenholm and Kilbucho Church of Scotland
SC016990 Caddonfoot Parish Church of Scotland
SC001340 Carlops Parish Church of Scotland
SC009892 Channelkirk and Lauder Church of Scotland
SC003895 Earlston Parish Church of Scotland
SC010081 Eddleston Parish Church of Scotland
SC010389 Old Parish and St Paul's Church of Scotland: Galashiels
SC001386 Galashiels Trinity Church of Scotland
SC034662 Ettrick and Yarrow Parish (Church of Scotland)
SC000281 St John's Church of Scotland: Galashiels
SC001100 Innerleithen, Traquair and Walkerburn Parish Church of Scotland
SC021456 Lyne & Manor Church of Scotland
SC013481 Maxton and Mertoun Parish Church of Scotland
SC000575 Newtown Church of Scotland

SC013316 Peebles Old Parish Church of Scotland
SC009159 Church of Scotland St Andrews Leckie Parish: Peebles
SC010210 St Boswells Parish Church of Scotland
SC000228 Stow St Mary of Wedale & Heriot Church of Scotland
SC004728 Skirling Church of Scotland
SC001866 Stobo and Drumelzier Church of Scotland
SC013564 Tweedsmuir Kirk Church of Scotland
SC003938 St Andrews Parish Church of Scotland: West Linton
SC018087 Kirkurd and Newlands Parish Church of Scotland
SC014883 Selkirk Parish Church of Scotland

5. Presbytery of Duns

SC001208 Church of Scotland: Ayton and Burnmouth Parish Church
SC000867 St Andrew's Wallace Green and Lowick Church of Scotland, Berwick-upon-Tweed
SC000246 Bonkyl & Preston Church of Scotland
SC006722 Chirnside Church of Scotland
SC009185 The Church of Scotland, Coldingham Priory
SC001456 Coldstream Parish Church of Scotland
SC005161 Duns Parish Church of Scotland
SC000031 Eccles Parish Church of Scotland
SC007567 Edrom & Allanton Church of Scotland
SC006499 The Church of Scotland, Eyemouth Parish Church
SC002789 Fogo & Swinton Church of Scotland
SC024535 Church of Scotland: Foulden and Mordington Parish Church
SC022349 Gordon St Michael's Church of Scotland
SC016400 Church of Scotland: Grantshouse, Houndwood and Reston Parish Church
SC013136 Greenlaw Parish, Church of Scotland
SC002216 Hutton, Fishwick and Paxton Church of Scotland
SC010680 Langton and Lammermuir Kirk, Church of Scotland
SC009995 Ladykirk Parish Church (Church of Scotland)
SC004582 Legerwood Parish, Church of Scotland
SC005115 Leitholm Parish Church (Church of Scotland)
SC004903 Westruther Parish, Church of Scotland
SC001611 Whitsome Church (Church of Scotland)

6. Presbytery of Jedburgh

SC016457 Ale & Teviot United Church of Scotland
SC004550 Cavers and Kirkton Parish Church (Church of Scotland)
SC004517 Hawick Burnfoot Church of Scotland
SC005574 St Mary's & Old Parish Church of Scotland, Hawick
SC005191 Teviot and Roberton Church of Scotland
SC013892 Trinity Parish Church, Hawick (Church of Scotland)
SC017381 Wilton Parish Church of Scotland
SC012830 Hobkirk & Southdean Parish Church of Scotland
SC004530 Jedburgh Old and Trinity Parish Church of Scotland
SC000958 Kelso Country Churches (Church of Scotland)
SC014039 Kelso North and Ednam Parish Church of Scotland
SC010009 Kelso Old & Sprouston Parish Church of Scotland
SC003023 Linton, Morebattle, Hownam and Yetholm Parish Church of Scotland
SC010593 Oxnam Parish Church of Scotland
SC034629 Ruberslaw Parish Church of Scotland
SC006917 Teviothead Parish Church of Scotland

7. Presbytery of Annandale and Eskdale

SC010555 Annan Old Parish Church of Scotland
SC010891 St Andrews Parish Church of Scotland, Annan
SC013947 Applegarth, Sibbaldbie & Johnstone Church of Scotland
SC012516 Brydekirk Parish Church of Scotland
SC000717 Canonbie Parish Church of Scotland
SC006344 Dalton Parish Church of Scotland
SC004542 Dornock Parish Church of Scotland
SC016747 Gretna Old, Gretna St Andrew's, Half Morton and Kirkpatrick Fleming Parish Church of Scotland
SC022170 Hightae Parish Church of Scotland
SC005701 Kirkpatrick Juxta Church of Scotland
SC011946 Langholm, Eskdalemuir, Ewes and Westerkirk Church of Scotland
SC006519 Liddesdale Parish Church of Scotland
SC004644 Lochmaben Church of Scotland
SC007116 Lockerbie Dryfesdale, Hutton and Corrie Church of Scotland
SC000722 Hoddom, Kirtle-Eaglesfield and Middlebie Church of Scotland
SC012236 St Andrews Church of Scotland, Moffat
SC001060 St Mungo Parish Church of Scotland, Lockerbie
SC013190 Tundergarth Church of Scotland
SC007536 Wamphray Church of Scotland

8. Presbytery of Dumfries and Kirkcudbright

SC016850 Auchencairn & Rerrick Church of Scotland
SC016053 Balmaclellan & Kells Church of Scotland
SC000498 Balmaghie Church of Scotland
SC004450 Borgue Parish Church of Scotland
SC003844 Buittle & Kelton Church of Scotland
SC008648 Caerlaverock Parish Church of Scotland
SC015242 Carsphairn Church of Scotland
SC011037 Castle Douglas Parish Church of Scotland
SC005624 Closeburn Parish Church of Scotland
SC009384 Colvend Southwick & Kirkbean Church of Scotland
SC007152 Corsock & Kirkpatrick Durham Church of Scotland
SC014901 Crossmichael & Parton Church of Scotland
SC002443 Dalbeattie Parish Church of Scotland
SC013121 Dalry Kirkcudbrightshire Church of Scotland
SC010748 Dumfries Northwest Church of Scotland
SC006404 St George's Church of Scotland, Dumfries
SC009432 St Mary's-Greyfriars' Parish Church, Dumfries (Church of Scotland)
SC016201 St Michael's & South Church of Scotland, Dumfries
SC000973 Troqueer Parish Church of Scotland, Dumfries
SC016060 Dunscore Parish Church of Scotland
SC014783 Durisdeer Church of Scotland
SC000961 Gatehouse of Fleet Parish Church of Scotland
SC014663 Glencairn & Moniaive Parish Church of Scotland
SC033058 Irongray Lochrutton & Terregles Parish Church of Scotland
SC014150 Kirkconnel Parish Church of Scotland
SC005883 Kirkcudbright Parish Church of Scotland
SC002286 Kirkgunzeon Church of Scotland
SC010508 Kirkmahoe Parish Church of Scotland
SC030785 Kirkmichael Tinwald & Torthorwald Church of Scotland
SC014590 Lochend and New Abbey Church of Scotland
SC015925 Maxwelltown West Church of Scotland, Dumfries
SC015087 Penpont Keir & Tynron Church of Scotland
SC015399 Cummertrees, Mouswald and Ruthwell Church of Scotland

SC000845	St Bride's Parish Church of Scotland: Sanquhar
SC004475	Tarff & Twynholm Church of Scotland
SC012722	Thornhill Parish Church of Scotland
SC014465	Urr Parish Church of Scotland
9.	**Presbytery of Wigtown and Stranraer**
SC003122	Ervie-Kirkcolm Church of Scotland
SC001705	Glasserton and the Isle of Whithorn Church of Scotland
SC007375	Inch Church of Scotland
SC007136	Kirkcowan Parish Church (Church of Scotland)
SC001946	Kirkinner Church of Scotland
SC010150	Kirkmabreck Church of Scotland
SC007708	Kirkmaiden Parish Church (Church of Scotland)
SC009412	Leswalt Parish Church (Church of Scotland)
SC003300	Mochrum Church of Scotland
SC006014	Monigaff Church of Scotland
SC006316	New Luce Church of Scotland
SC005302	Old Luce Church of Scotland
SC031847	Parish of Penninghame (Church of Scotland)
SC015452	Portpatrick Parish Church (Church of Scotland)
SC010621	Sorbie Parish Church of Scotland
SC007346	Stoneykirk Parish Church (Church of Scotland)
SC017312	High Kirk of Stranraer (Church of Scotland)
SC002247	Stranraer: St Ninian's Parish Church (Church of Scotland)
SC009905	Town Kirk of Stranraer (Church of Scotland)
SC016881	Whithorn: St Ninian's Priory Church of Scotland
SC014552	Wigtown Parish Church (Church of Scotland)
10.	**Presbytery of Ayr**
SC012456	Alloway Parish Church of Scotland
SC013225	Annbank Parish Church of Scotland
SC008536	Ballantrae Parish Church of Scotland
SC006707	Auchinleck Parish Church of Scotland
SC001792	Castlehill Parish Church of Scotland: Ayr
SC031474	Dalmellington Parish Church of Scotland
SC001994	Ayr: Newton Wallacetown Church of Scotland
SC001757	St Andrew's Parish Church of Scotland: Ayr
SC009336	St James' Parish Church of Scotland: Ayr
SC016860	St Leonard's Parish Church of Scotland: Ayr
SC015366	Barr Parish Church of Scotland
SC013689	Catrine Parish Church of Scotland
SC005283	Coylton Parish Church (Church of Scotland)
SC002633	Craigie Parish Church of Scotland: Kilmarnock
SC017520	Crosshill Parish Church (Church of Scotland)
SC012591	Dailly Parish Church of Scotland
SC013503	Dalrymple Parish Church (Church of Scotland)
SC008482	Dundonald Church of Scotland
SC008226	Fisherton Church of Scotland
SC007347	Girvan: North Parish Church of Scotland
SC010381	Girvan South Parish Church of Scotland
SC031952	Kirkmichael Parish Church of Scotland: Maybole
SC000213	Kirkoswald Parish Church of Scotland
SC007714	Mauchline Parish Church of Scotland
SC014055	Lugar Parish Church of Scotland
SC004906	St Quivox Parish Church: Ayr (Church of Scotland)
SC014794	New Cumnock Parish Church (Church of Scotland)
SC010606	Muirkirk Parish Church of Scotland
SC003164	Maybole Parish Church of Scotland
SC034504	Church of Scotland Cumnock Trinity Church
SC000130	Ochiltree Parish Church of Scotland
SC006025	Old Cumnock Old Church of Scotland
SC001940	Kingcase Parish Church of Scotland: Prestwick
SC011750	St Nicholas Parish Church of Scotland: Prestwick
SC007403	Prestwick South Church of Scotland
SC004271	Monkton & Prestwick North Parish Church of Scotland
SC014381	St Colmon (Arnsheen Barrhill and Colmonell) Church of Scotland
SC015899	Sorn Parish Church of Scotland
SC035601	Stair Parish Church (Church of Scotland)
SC013366	Straiton (St Cuthbert's) Parish Church of Scotland: Maybole
SC014767	Tarbolton Parish Church of Scotland
SC030714	Drongan: The Schaw Kirk (Church of Scotland)
SC007246	Troon Old Parish Church of Scotland
SC003477	Portland Parish Church of Scotland: Troon
SC015019	Troon St Meddan's Parish Church of Scotland
SC016648	The Auld Kirk of Ayr Church of Scotland
SC008562	Patna Waterside Parish Church of Scotland
SC002144	Symington Parish Church of Scotland
SC014338	Ayr St Columba Church of Scotland
11.	**Presbytery of Irvine and Kilmarnock**
SC011414	Crosshouse Parish Church (Church of Scotland)
SC012014	Darvel Parish Church of Scotland
SC008684	Dreghorn & Springside Parish Church of Scotland
SC000447	Dunlop Church of Scotland
SC010062	Fenwick Parish Church (Church of Scotland)
SC010370	Galston Parish Church of Scotland
SC001084	Hurlford Church of Scotland
SC005491	Girdle Toll Church of Scotland, Irvine New Town
SC008725	Fullarton Parish Church (Church of Scotland), Irvine
SC002299	Mure Parish Church of Scotland, Irvine
SC008345	Irvine Old Parish Church of Scotland
SC002469	Relief Church of Scotland, Irvine
SC010167	St Andrews Church of Scotland: Irvine
SC008154	Kilmarnock: Henderson Parish Church of Scotland
SC031334	Kilmarnock: New Laigh Kirk (Church of Scotland)
SC008405	Old High Kirk of Kilmarnock (Church of Scotland)
SC006040	Kilmarnock Riccarton Church of Scotland
SC029057	Kilmarnock: Shortlees Parish Church of Scotland
SC006345	St Andrew's and St Marnock's Parish Church of Scotland, Kilmarnock
SC033107	St Johns Parish Church of Scotland – Onthank: Kilmarnock
SC001324	St Kentigern's Parish Church of Scotland: Kilmarnock
SC012430	Kilmarnock: St Ninian's Bellfield Church of Scotland
SC009036	St Maurs Glencairn Church of Scotland, Kilmaurs
SC013880	Loudoun Church of Scotland, Newmilns
SC015890	John Knox Parish Church of Scotland, Stewarton
SC013595	St Columba's Parish Church of Scotland, Stewarton

12. Presbytery of Ardrossan

SC004736 Ardrossan Park Parish Church of Scotland
SC002350 Ardrossan Barony St John's Church of Scotland
SC004660 Beith High Parish Church of Scotland
SC005680 Beith Trinity Church of Scotland
SC012017 Brodick Church of Scotland
SC005030 Corrie Parish Church of Scotland
SC004919 Cumbrae Parish Church of Scotland
SC013170 Dalry St Margaret's Parish Church of Scotland
SC006882 Dalry Trinity Church of Scotland
SC017304 Fairlie Parish Church of Scotland
SC016024 Kilbirnie Auld Kirk (Church of Scotland)
SC013750 St Columbas Parish Church of Scotland: Kilbirnie
SC023602 Kilmory Parish Church of Scotland
SC016499 Kilwinning Mansefield Trinity Church of Scotland
SC001856 Kilwinning Old Parish Church of Scotland
SC015072 Lamlash Church of Scotland
SC002782 Largs Clark Memorial Church of Scotland
SC002294 The Church of Scotland, Largs: St Columba's Parish Church
SC009048 Largs St John's Church of Scotland
SC009377 Lochranza & Pirnmill Church of Scotland
SC023003 Saltcoats New Trinity Parish Church of Scotland
SC003299 Saltcoats North Parish Church of Scotland
SC002905 Saltcoats St Cuthberts Parish Church of Scotland
SC005323 Shiskine Church of Scotland
SC015397 Stevenston Ardeer Parish Church of Scotland
SC009848 Stevenston High Church of Scotland
SC000452 Stevenston Livingstone Parish Church of Scotland
SC013464 West Kilbride Parish Church of Scotland
SC014005 Whiting Bay & Kildonan Church of Scotland

13. Presbytery of Lanark

SC000333 Biggar Parish Church of Scotland
SC000603 Blackmount Parish Church (Church of Scotland)
SC017001 Cairngryffe Parish Church (Church of Scotland)
SC026539 Kirkton Parish Church, Carluke (Church of Scotland)
SC013968 St Andrews Parish Church of Scotland: Carluke
SC004066 St Johns Church of Scotland: Carluke
SC016360 Carnwath Parish Church of Scotland
SC028124 Carstairs & Carstairs Junction Church of Scotland
SC016493 Coalburn Parish Church (Church of Scotland)
SC014659 Crossford Church of Scotland
SC018252 Culter Parish Church (Church of Scotland)
SC003080 Forth St Paul's Parish Church (Church of Scotland)
SC017506 Glencaple Parish Church (Church of Scotland)
SC011211 Kirkfieldbank Parish Church (Church of Scotland)
SC014451 Kirkmuirhill Parish Church (Church of Scotland)
SC016504 Greyfriars Parish Church, Lanark (Church of Scotland)
SC011368 St Nicholas Parish Church, Lanark (Church of Scotland)
SC013217 Law Parish Church (Church of Scotland)
SC006516 Lesmahagow Abbeygreen (Church of Scotland)
SC017014 Lesmahagow Old Parish Church (Church of Scotland)
SC016304 Libberton & Quothquan Parish Church (Church of Scotland)
SC034654 Lowther Parish Church (Church of Scotland)
SC009095 Symington Parish Church (Church of Scotland)
SC001718 The Douglas Valley Church (Church of Scotland)

14. Presbytery of Greenock and Paisley

SC015730 Arthurlie Parish Church of Scotland Barrhead
SC016467 Barrhead Bourock Parish Church of Scotland
SC007776 Barrhead South and Levern Church of Scotland
SC006109 Bishopton Parish Church (Church of Scotland)
SC002293 Freeland Church of Scotland, Bridge of Weir
SC003766 Church of Scotland, St Machar's Ranfurly Church, Bridge of Weir
SC008214 Caldwell Parish Church of Scotland
SC015701 Elderslie Kirk (Church of Scotland)
SC017177 Erskine Parish Church of Scotland
SC007324 Old Gourock and Ashton Parish Church of Scotland
SC006412 St Johns Church of Scotland: Gourock
SC010818 Greenock: Lyle Community Kirk (Church of Scotland)
SC037023 Greenock East End Parish Church of Scotland
SC008357 Greenock The Mount Kirk (Church of Scotland)
SC004855 Old West Kirk, Greenock (Church of Scotland)
SC016711 St Margarets Church of Scotland: Greenock
SC008059 St Ninians Parish Church of Scotland: Greenock
SC001043 Wellpark Mid Kirk of Greenock (Church of Scotland)
SC005106 Greenock Westburn Church of Scotland
SC012822 Houston and Killellan Kirk (Church of Scotland)
SC003487 Howwood Parish Church of Scotland
SC011778 Inchinnan Parish Church (Church of Scotland)
SC001079 Inverkip Church of Scotland
SC009588 Johnstone High Parish Church of Scotland
SC011696 St Andrews Trinity Parish Church of Scotland Johnstone
SC011747 St Pauls Church of Scotland: Johnstone
SC012123 Kilbarchan East Church of Scotland
SC017140 Kilbarchan West Church of Scotland
SC009291 Kilmacolm Old Kirk (Church of Scotland)
SC007992 St Columba Church of Scotland Kilmacolm
SC015085 Langbank Church of Scotland
SC020972 Linwood Parish Church of Scotland
SC014518 Lochwinnoch Parish Church of Scotland
SC035155 Neilston Parish Church of Scotland
SC007633 Paisley Abbey (Church of Scotland)
SC006718 Paisley: Glenburn Parish Church of Scotland
SC006437 Paisley: Stow Brae Kirk (Church of Scotland)
SC012648 Lylesland Parish Church of Scotland, Paisley
SC011798 Paisley: Martyrs Sandyford Church of Scotland
SC005362 Oakshaw Trinity Church, Paisley
SC007484 Sherwood Greenlaw Parish Church of Scotland, Paisley
SC005770 St Columba Foxbar Church of Scotland, Paisley
SC000949 St James's Paisley (Church of Scotland)
SC000558 St Luke's Church of Scotland: Paisley
SC011210 St Marks Church of Scotland (Oldhall): Paisley
SC004753 St Ninians Church of Scotland: Paisley

SC012650 Paisley Wallneuk North Church of Scotland
SC005421 Church of Scotland Port Glasgow: Hamilton Bardrainney Church
SC009018 Port Glasgow: St Andrew's Church of Scotland
SC002410 St Martins Church of Scotland: Port Glasgow
SC006605 Renfrew North Parish Church of Scotland
SC004411 Renfrew Old Parish Church of Scotland
SC003785 Renfrew Trinity (Church of Scotland)
SC003309 Skelmorlie and Wemyss Bay Parish Church of Scotland

16. Presbytery of Glasgow

SC017638 Banton Parish Church of Scotland
SC012329 Kenmure Parish Church of Scotland
SC005642 Springfield Cambridge Church of Scotland, Bishopbriggs
SC003290 Broom Parish Church of Scotland
SC006633 Burnside Blairbeth Church of Scotland
SC016612 Busby Parish Church of Scotland
SC015193 Cadder Parish Church of Scotland
SC006638 Flemington Hallside Parish Church of Scotland
SC000061 Cambuslang Parish Church of Scotland
SC023596 St Andrews Parish Church of Scotland Cambuslang: Glasgow
SC011456 Trinity St Pauls Church of Scotland, Cambuslang
SC000835 Campsie Parish Church of Scotland
SC006752 Chryston Church of Scotland
SC006377 Eaglesham Parish Church of Scotland
SC001077 Fernhill & Cathkin Church of Scotland
SC007541 Gartcosh Parish Church of Scotland
SC009774 Orchardhill Parish Church of Scotland, Giffnock
SC007807 Giffnock South Parish Church of Scotland
SC002965 Giffnock Park Church of Scotland
SC014631 Anderston Kelvingrove Church of Scotland, Glasgow
SC002220 Glasgow: Mure Memorial Church of Scotland
SC005625 Baillieston St Andrews Church of Scotland, Glasgow
SC000885 Balshagray Victoria Park Parish Church of Scotland, Glasgow
SC025730 Barlanark Greyfriars Parish Church of Scotland, Glasgow
SC006410 Blawarthill Parish Church of Scotland, Glasgow
SC012535 Bridgeton St Francis in the East Church of Scotland, Glasgow
SC007820 Broomhill Church of Scotland, Glasgow
SC006958 Calton Parkhead Parish Church of Scotland, Glasgow
SC010265 Cardonald Parish Church of Scotland, Glasgow
SC011224 Carmunnock Parish Church of Scotland, Glasgow
SC000532 Carmyle Church of Scotland, Glasgow
SC030150 Carnwadric Church of Scotland, Glasgow
SC015309 Castlemilk East Parish Church of Scotland, Glasgow
SC009813 Castlemilk West Church of Scotland, Glasgow
SC002727 Cathcart Old Parish Church of Scotland, Glasgow
SC033802 Cathcart Trinity Church of Scotland, Glasgow
SC013966 Glasgow Cathedral (Church of Scotland)
SC012939 Colston Milton Parish Church of Scotland, Glasgow
SC005709 Colston Wellpark Parish Church of Scotland, Glasgow
SC009874 Cranhill Parish Church of Scotland, Glasgow
SC009761 Croftfoot Parish Church of Scotland, Glasgow
SC008824 Glasgow Dennistoun New Parish Church of Scotland
SC022128 Drumchapel St Andrews Parish Church of Scotland, Glasgow
SC008954 St Marks Parish Church of Scotland, Glasgow
SC004642 Glasgow Shettleston New Church of Scotland
SC003021 St Georges & St Peters Parish Church of Scotland: Easterhouse, Glasgow
SC000277 Eastwood Parish Church of Scotland, Glasgow
SC030168 Gairbraid Parish Church of Scotland, Glasgow
SC016862 Garthamlock & Craigend East Parish Church of Scotland, Glasgow
SC002214 Gorbals Parish Church of Scotland, Glasgow
SC004153 Glasgow Govan and Linthouse Parish Church of Scotland
SC012752 Govanhill Trinity Parish Church of Scotland, Glasgow
SC006729 High Carntyne Church of Scotland, Glasgow
SC002614 Hillington Park Church of Scotland, Glasgow
SC007798 St Christophers Church of Scotland: Glasgow
SC002398 Hyndland Parish Church of Scotland, Glasgow
SC009841 Ibrox Parish Church of Scotland, Glasgow
SC027651 John Ross Memorial Church for Deaf People, Glasgow (Church of Scotland)
SC015683 Jordanhill Parish Church of Scotland, Glasgow
SC014414 Kelvin – Stevenson Memorial Parish Church of Scotland, Glasgow
SC006629 Kelvinside Hillhead Parish Church of Scotland, Glasgow
SC008980 Kenmuir Mount Vernon Church of Scotland, Glasgow
SC017040 Kings Park Church of Scotland, Glasgow
SC014895 Kinning Park Parish Church of Scotland, Glasgow
SC007757 Knightswood St Margarets Parish Church of Scotland, Glasgow
SC007055 Langside Parish Church of Scotland, Glasgow
SC015778 Lansdowne Church of Scotland, Glasgow
SC002161 Lochwood Parish Church of Scotland, Glasgow
SC002102 Maryhill Parish Church of Scotland, Glasgow
SC004016 Merrylea Parish Church of Scotland Newlands, Glasgow
SC013281 Mosspark Church of Scotland, Glasgow
SC010138 Glasgow: Clincarthill Church of Scotland
SC000042 Newlands South Church of Scotland, Glasgow
SC008315 Partick South Church of Scotland, Glasgow
SC007632 Partick Trinity Church of Scotland, Glasgow
SC022874 Penilee St Andrew Church of Scotland, Glasgow
SC006683 Pollokshaws Parish Church of Scotland, Glasgow
SC013690 Pollokshields Church of Scotland, Glasgow
SC003241 Possilpark Parish Church of Scotland, Glasgow
SC015858 Priesthill & Nitshill Church of Scotland, Glasgow
SC001575 Queens Park Parish Church of Scotland, Glasgow
SC011423 Renfield St Stephens Parish Church of Scotland, Glasgow
SC032401 Robroyston Church of Scotland, Glasgow
SC003149 Ruchazie Parish Church of Scotland, Glasgow
SC014538 Glasgow: Ruchill Kelvinside Parish Church of Scotland
SC002155 Sandyford Henderson Memorial Church of Scotland, Glasgow
SC009460 Sandyhills Church of Scotland, Glasgow
SC030418 Scotstoun Parish Church of Scotland, Glasgow

SC012969 Shawlands Parish Church of Scotland, Glasgow
SC015155 Sherbrooke St Gilberts Church of Scotland, Glasgow
SC004642 Glasgow Shettleston New Church of Scotland
SC001070 Shettleston Old Parish Church of Scotland, Glasgow
SC010899 South Carntyne Church of Scotland, Glasgow
SC005196 South Shawlands Church of Scotland, Glasgow
SC004397 Springburn Parish Church of Scotland, Glasgow
SC009600 St Andrews East Parish Church, Glasgow (Church of Scotland)
SC006342 St Columbas Gaelic Church of Scotland, Glasgow
SC017297 St Davids Parish Church of Scotland: Glasgow
SC004918 St Enoch's – Hogganfield Parish Church of Scotland, Glasgow
SC004931 St Georges Tron Church of Scotland, Glasgow
SC013313 St James Pollok Parish Church of Scotland: Glasgow
SC012920 St Johns Renfield Church of Scotland, Glasgow
SC032738 Gallowgate Parish Church of Scotland, Glasgow
SC005764 St Margarets Tollcross Church of Scotland: Glasgow
SC011527 St Nicholas Parish Church of Scotland, Cardonald, Glasgow
SC016306 St Pauls Church of Scotland: Provanmill, Glasgow
SC015459 St Rollox Church of Scotland: Glasgow
SC015579 Temple Anniesland Parish Church of Scotland, Glasgow
SC009399 Toryglen Church of Scotland, Glasgow
SC009578 Trinity Possil & Henry Drummond Church of Scotland, Glasgow
SC017015 Tron St Marys Parish Church of Scotland, Glasgow
SC004821 Victoria Tollcross Church of Scotland, Glasgow
SC008840 Glasgow Wallacewell Church of Scotland New Charge
SC000289 Wellington Church of Scotland, Glasgow
SC030362 Whiteinch Church of Scotland, Glasgow
SC017408 Yoker Parish Church of Scotland, Glasgow
SC002834 Glenboig Parish Church of Scotland
SC011453 Greenbank Parish Church of Scotland
SC009866 Kilsyth Anderson Church of Scotland
SC009912 Kilsyth Burns & Old Parish Church of Scotland
SC002424 Kirkintilloch Hillhead Church of Scotland
SC008735 St Columba Parish Church of Scotland, Kirkintilloch
SC007427 St Davids Memorial Park Church of Scotland, Kirkintilloch
SC007260 St Marys Parish Church of Scotland, Kirkintilloch
SC008935 Lenzie Old Parish Church of Scotland
SC015287 Lenzie Union Church of Scotland
SC017317 Maxwell Mearns Church of Scotland
SC007125 Mearns Kirk (Church of Scotland)
SC014735 Milton of Campsie Parish Church of Scotland
SC015303 Netherlee Church of Scotland
SC004219 Newton Mearns Parish Church of Scotland
SC006856 Rutherglen Old Parish Church of Scotland
SC013558 Stonelaw Parish Church of Scotland, Rutherglen
SC007585 Rutherglen West and Wardlawhill Parish Church of Scotland
SC003155 Stamperland Parish Church of Scotland, Clarkston
SC014212 Stepps Parish Church of Scotland, Stepps
SC008426 Thornliebank Parish Church of Scotland
SC016058 Torrance Parish Church of Scotland
SC011672 Twechar Church of Scotland
SC009939 Williamwood Parish Church of Scotland

17. Presbytery of Hamilton

SC016464 Airdrie Broomknoll Parish Church of Scotland
SC011239 Airdrie Clarkston Parish Church of Scotland
SC014555 Airdrie Flowerhill Parish Church of Scotland
SC024357 Airdrie High Parish Church of Scotland
SC004083 Airdrie Jackson Parish Church of Scotland
SC011674 Airdrie New Monkland Parish Church of Scotland
SC002900 Airdrie St Columbas Parish Church of Scotland
SC004209 Bargeddie Parish Church of Scotland
SC012556 Bellshill Macdonald Memorial Parish Church of Scotland
SC006007 Bellshill Orbiston Parish Church of Scotland
SC008340 Bellshill West Parish Church of Scotland
SC005955 Blantyre St Andrew's Parish Church of Scotland
SC004084 Blantyre Livingstone Memorial Parish Church of Scotland
SC018492 Blantyre Old Parish Church of Scotland
SC012944 The New Wellwynd Parish Church of Scotland Airdrie
SC009819 Bothwell Parish Church of Scotland
SC015831 Calderbank Parish Church of Scotland
SC030492 Caldercruix and Longriggend Parish Church of Scotland
SC036085 Carfin Parish Church of Scotland
SC008486 Chapelhall Parish Church of Scotland
SC011817 Chapelton Parish Church of Scotland
SC017084 Cleland Parish Church of Scotland
SC009704 Coatbridge Blairhill Dundyvan Parish Church of Scotland
SC006854 Coatbridge Calder Parish Church of Scotland
SC016362 Coatbridge Middle Parish Church of Scotland
SC013521 Coatbridge New St Andrew's Parish Church of Scotland
SC010236 Coatbridge Old Monkland Parish Church of Scotland
SC008809 Coatbridge Townhead Parish Church of Scotland
SC016156 Dalserf Parish Church of Scotland
SC007396 East Kilbride Claremont Parish Church of Scotland
SC030300 East Kilbride Greenhills Parish Church of Scotland
SC016751 East Kilbride Moncreiff Parish Church of Scotland
SC000609 East Kilbride Old Parish Church of Scotland
SC008332 East Kilbride South Parish Church of Scotland
SC000250 East Kilbride West Kirk Church of Scotland
SC001857 East Kilbride Westwood Parish Church of Scotland
SC014716 Glassford Parish Church of Scotland
SC012692 East Kilbride Mossneuk Parish Church of Scotland
SC018154 Greengairs Parish Church of Scotland
SC015042 Hamilton Burnbank Parish Church of Scotland
SC006611 Cadzow Parish Church of Scotland, Hamilton
SC011571 Hamilton Gilmour & Whitehill Parish Church of Scotland
SC005376 Hamilton Hillhouse Parish Church of Scotland

SC014508 Hamilton North Parish Church of Scotland
SC010855 Hamilton Old Parish Church of Scotland
SC007145 Hamilton St Andrew's Parish Church of Scotland
SC008779 Hamilton St John's Parish Church of Scotland
SC022166 Hamilton South Parish Church of Scotland
SC007051 Hamilton Trinity Parish Church of Scotland
SC008451 Hamilton West Parish Church of Scotland
SC012888 Holytown Parish Church of Scotland
SC013309 Chalmers Parish Church of Scotland Larkhall
SC002870 St Machan's Parish Church of Scotland Larkhall
SC008611 Trinity Parish Church of Scotland, Larkhall
SC034242 Church of Scotland Stewartfield New Charge Development East Kilbride
SC008810 Motherwell Crosshill Parish Church of Scotland
SC016821 Motherwell North Parish Church of Scotland
SC008601 Motherwell South Parish Church of Scotland
SC010924 Motherwell St Margaret's Parish Church of Scotland
SC012233 Motherwell St Marys Parish Church of Scotland
SC005427 Newarthill Parish Church of Scotland
SC006540 Bonkle Parish Church of Scotland
SC001381 Newmains Coltness Memorial Parish Church of Scotland
SC004688 New Stevenston Wrangholm Parish Church of Scotland
SC007360 Overtown Parish Church of Scotland
SC009689 Quarter Parish Church of Scotland
SC015503 Motherwell Dalziel St Andrew's Parish Church of Scotland
SC013269 Kirk o' Shotts Parish Church of Scotland
SC003239 Stonehouse St Ninian's Parish Church of Scotland
SC001956 Strathaven Avendale Old and Drumclog Memorial Parish Church of Scotland
SC015591 Strathaven East Parish Church of Scotland
SC001020 Strathaven Rankin Parish Church of Scotland
SC010039 Uddingston Burnhead Parish Church of Scotland
SC006538 Shotts Calderhead – Erskine Parish Church of Scotland
SC009991 Uddingston Viewpark Parish Church of Scotland
SC013037 Wishaw: Cambusnethan North Parish Church of Scotland
SC011532 Wishaw Cambusnethan Old and Morningside Parish Church of Scotland
SC013841 Wishaw Craigneuk and Belhaven Church of Scotland
SC011253 Wishaw Old Parish Church of Scotland
SC012529 Wishaw St Marks Parish Church of Scotland
SC016893 Uddingston Old Parish Church of Scotland
SC010775 South Wishaw Parish Church of Scotland

18. Presbytery of Dumbarton

SC001268 Alexandria Parish Church of Scotland
SC008929 Arrochar Parish Church of Scotland
SC006355 Baldernock Parish Church of Scotland
SC037739 Bearsden: Baljaffray Parish Church of Scotland
SC009748 Killermont Parish Church (Church of Scotland) Bearsden
SC012997 New Kilpatrick Parish Church of Scotland
SC009082 The Church of Scotland Bearsden Cross Church
SC004489 Westerton Fairlie Memorial Parish Church of Scotland, Bearsden
SC000886 Bonhill Church of Scotland
SC003494 Cardross Parish Church of Scotland
SC004596 Abbotsford, Church of Scotland, Clydebank
SC005108 Faifley Parish Church of Scotland, Clydebank
SC015005 Kilbowie St Andrews Church of Scotland, Clydebank
SC013242 Radnor Park Church of Scotland, Clydebank
SC003077 St Cuthberts Parish Church of Scotland: Clydebank
SC001725 Craigrownie Parish Church of Scotland
SC013599 Dalmuir Barclay Church of Scotland
SC002937 Riverside Parish Church of Scotland, Dumbarton
SC006235 St Andrews Church of Scotland: Dumbarton
SC010474 West Kirk, Dumbarton (Church of Scotland)
SC008854 Duntocher Trinity Parish Church of Scotland
SC016699 Garelochhead Parish Church of Scotland
SC007801 Park Church of Scotland, Helensburgh
SC014837 St Columba Church of Scotland, Helensburgh
SC012053 West Kirk of Helensburgh (Church of Scotland)
SC012346 Jamestown Parish Church of Scotland
SC002145 Kilmaronock Gartocharn Church of Scotland
SC017192 Luss Parish Church of Scotland
SC009913 Cairns Church of Scotland, Milngavie
SC003870 St Lukes Church of Scotland: Milngavie
SC002737 St Pauls Parish Church of Scotland: Milngavie
SC011630 Old Kilpatrick Bowling Parish Church of Scotland
SC014833 Renton Trinity Parish Church of Scotland
SC010086 Rhu and Shandon Parish Church of Scotland
SC001510 Rosneath St Modans Church of Scotland

19. Presbytery of Argyll

SC015795 Appin Parish Church (Church of Scotland)
SC000680 Ardchattan (Church of Scotland)
SC010713 Ardrishaig Parish Church (Church of Scotland)
SC002493 Campbeltown: Highland Parish Church of Scotland
SC011686 Campbeltown: Lorne and Lowland Church of Scotland
SC035582 Coll Parish Church (Church of Scotland)
SC031271 Colonsay & Oronsay Church of Scotland
SC006738 Connel Parish Church of Scotland
SC003718 Craignish Parish Church of Scotland
SC016097 Cumlodden, Lochfyneside and Lochgair (Church of Scotland)
SC003216 Dunoon: St John's Church (Church of Scotland)
SC017524 Dunoon: The High Kirk (Church of Scotland)
SC002567 Gigha & Cara Church (Church of Scotland)
SC002121 Glassary, Kilmartin & Ford Parish Church of Scotland
SC016665 Glenaray & Inveraray Parish Church (Church of Scotland)
SC003179 Glenorchy & Innishael Church of Scotland
SC013247 Innellan Church (Church of Scotland)
SC036399 Iona Parish Church (Church of Scotland)
SC002925 Jura Parish Church of Scotland
SC009853 Kilarrow Parish Church of Scotland
SC006941 Kilberry Parish Church (Church of Scotland)
SC017005 Kilbrandon & Kilchattan Parish Church (Church of Scotland)
SC006948 Kilcalmonell Parish Church (Church of Scotland)
SC013203 Kilchoman Parish Church (Church of Scotland)
SC009417 Kilchrenan & Dalavich Parish Church (Church of Scotland)

SC006032 Kildalton & Oa Parish Church (Church of Scotland)
SC003483 Kilfinan Parish Church (Church of Scotland)
SC013473 Kilfinichen & Kilvickeon & the Ross of Mull Church of Scotland
SC016020 Killean & Kilchenzie Parish Church (Church of Scotland)
SC015317 Kilmeny Parish Church of Scotland
SC021449 Kilmodan & Colintraive Parish Church of Scotland
SC011171 Kilmore & Oban Church of Scotland
SC001694 Kilmun: St Munn's Church (Church of Scotland)
SC025506 Kilninian & Kilmore Church of Scotland
SC002458 Kilninver & Kilmelford Parish Church of Scotland
SC001976 Kirn Parish Church (Church of Scotland)
SC014928 Kyles Parish Church (Church of Scotland)
SC030972 Lismore Parish Church (Church of Scotland)
SC016311 Lochgilphead Church of Scotland
SC006458 Lochgoilhead & Kilmorich Church (Church of Scotland)
SC013377 Muckairn Parish Church (Church of Scotland)
SC001002 North Knapdale Parish Church of Scotland
SC004086 Portnahaven Parish Church of Scotland
SC006420 Rothesay: Trinity Church (Church of Scotland)
SC002609 Saddell & Carradale Church (Church of Scotland)
SC026099 Salen and Ulva Church of Scotland
SC006657 Sandbank Church (Church of Scotland)
SC004280 Skipness: St Brendan's Church (Church of Scotland)
SC010782 South Knapdale Parish Church (Church of Scotland)
SC005484 Southend Parish Church (Church of Scotland)
SC001767 Strachur & Strathlachlan Church (Church of Scotland)
SC004088 Strathfillan Parish Church of Scotland
SC003410 Strone & Ardentinny Church (Church of Scotland)
SC002622 Tarbert, Argyll, Church of Scotland
SC030563 The United Church of Bute (Church of Scotland)
SC000878 Tiree Parish Church of Scotland
SC002878 Tobermory Parish Church of Scotland
SC003909 Torosay & Kinlochspelvie Church of Scotland
SC015531 Toward Church (Church of Scotland)

22. Presbytery of Falkirk

SC029326 Cumbernauld Abronhill Church of Scotland
SC011038 Airth Parish Church of Scotland
SC008191 Bo'ness Old Kirk (Church of Scotland)
SC015225 Bonnybridge St Helen's Parish Church of Scotland
SC001385 Brightons Parish Church of Scotland
SC014816 Camelon Parish Church, Church of Scotland
SC011839 Cumbernauld: Condorrat Parish Church of Scotland
SC000877 Cumbernauld Old Parish Church of Scotland
SC016255 Denny Old Parish Church of Scotland
SC007072 Denny Westpark Church of Scotland
SC002943 Dunipace Parish Church of Scotland
SC000652 Falkirk Old & St Modan's Parish Church of Scotland
SC000775 Grangemouth Abbotsgrange Church of Scotland
SC014536 Haggs Parish Church of Scotland
SC004564 Cumbernauld Kildrum Parish Church of Scotland
SC001603 Grangemouth, Kirk of the Holy Rood, Church of Scotland
SC006456 Larbert East Church of Scotland
SC000445 Larbert Old Church of Scotland
SC012251 Larbert West Parish Church of Scotland
SC007383 Laurieston Parish Church of Scotland
SC003421 Polmont Old Parish Church of Scotland
SC008787 Redding & Westquarter Church of Scotland
SC013602 Slamannan Parish Church of Scotland
SC005066 St Andrews West Church of Scotland, Falkirk
SC002263 Stenhouse & Carron Parish Church of Scotland: Stenhousemuir
SC013114 Grangemouth Zetland Parish Church of Scotland
SC036366 St Mungo's Church of Scotland, Cumbernauld
SC007546 The Church of Scotland Falkirk Erskine Parish Church
SC002512 Blackbraes & Shieldhill Parish Church of Scotland
SC007665 St James Church of Scotland, Falkirk
SC016991 Grahamston United Church
SC011448 St Andrew's Church of Scotland, Bo'ness
SC007571 Muiravonside Parish Church of Scotland
SC009754 Bothkennar & Carronshore Parish Church (Church of Scotland)
SC007811 Carriden Parish Church of Scotland
SC004142 Bainsford Parish Church of Scotland, Falkirk

23. Presbytery of Stirling

SC001308 Aberfoyle Parish Church of Scotland
SC007821 St Mungo's Parish Church of Scotland, Alloa
SC007605 Alloa Ludgate Church of Scotland
SC000006 Alva Parish Church of Scotland
SC005335 Balfron Church of Scotland
SC012316 Balquhidder Parish Church of Scotland
SC002953 Allan Church of Scotland, Bannockburn
SC011345 Bannockburn Ladywell Church of Scotland
SC015171 Bridge of Allan Parish Church of Scotland
SC012927 Buchanan Parish Church of Scotland
SC000833 Buchlyvie Church of Scotland
SC000396 Callander Kirk Church of Scotland
SC019113 Cambusbarron Parish Church of Scotland Bruce Memorial
SC002324 Clackmannan Parish Church of Scotland
SC016296 Cowie and Plean Church of Scotland
SC009713 Dollar Parish Church of Scotland
SC004824 Drymen Church of Scotland
SC004454 Dunblane Cathedral Church of Scotland
SC005185 Dunblane: St Blane's Church of Scotland
SC028465 Fallin Parish Church of Scotland
SC012537 Fintry Church of Scotland
SC012154 Gargunnock Parish Church of Scotland
SC009788 Gartmore Parish Church of Scotland
SC003028 Glendevon Parish Church of Scotland
SC012140 Killearn Kirk (Church of Scotland)
SC010198 Killin & Ardeonaig Parish Church of Scotland
SC012031 Kilmadock Parish Church of Scotland, Doune
SC000802 Kincardine in Menteith Church of Scotland, Blair Drummond
SC004286 Kippen Parish Church of Scotland
SC014031 Lecropt Kirk Parish Church of Scotland
SC001298 Logie Kirk Stirling (Church of Scotland)
SC004778 Menstrie Parish Church of Scotland
SC009418 Muckhart Parish Church of Scotland
SC028719 Norrieston Parish Church of Scotland
SC001864 Port of Menteith Church of Scotland
SC018155 Sauchie and Coalsnaughton Parish Church of Scotland
SC001414 Allan Park South Church of Scotland, Stirling

SC011473 Church of the Holy Rude, Stirling (Church of Scotland)
SC011795 Stirling North Parish Church of Scotland
SC013444 St Columba's Church of Scotland Stirling
SC005432 St Marks Parish Church of Scotland: Stirling
SC016320 St Ninians Old Parish Church of Scotland, Stirling
SC007533 Viewfield Erskine Church of Scotland, Stirling
SC007261 Strathblane Parish Church of Scotland
SC016570 Tillicoultry Parish Church of Scotland
SC005918 St Serfs Church of Scotland, Tullibody

24. Presbytery of Dunfermline

SC005851 St Fillans Church of Scotland: Aberdour
SC031695 Beath and Cowdenbeath North Church of Scotland
SC012892 Cairneyhill Parish Church of Scotland
SC010676 Carnock and Oakley Church of Scotland
SC003799 Cowdenbeath Trinity Church of Scotland
SC015149 Culross & Torryburn Church of Scotland
SC020926 Dalgety Parish Church of Scotland
SC016883 The Abbey Church of Dunfermline (Church of Scotland)
SC035690 Dunfermline East Church of Scotland
SC011659 Dunfermline Gillespie Memorial Church of Scotland
SC013226 Dunfermline North Parish Church of Scotland
SC007302 St Andrew's Erskine Church of Scotland, Dunfermline
SC007799 Dunfermline St Leonard's Parish Church of Scotland
SC007080 Dunfermline St Margaret's Parish Church of Scotland
SC007453 St Ninians Church of Scotland: Dunfermline
SC008085 Dunfermline Townhill & Kingseat Parish Church of Scotland
SC000968 Inverkeithing Parish Church of Scotland
SC011004 Kelty Church of Scotland
SC002435 Limekilns Church of Scotland
SC032353 Lochgelly and Benarty St Serf's Parish Church of Scotland
SC007414 North Queensferry Church of Scotland
SC013620 Rosyth Parish Church of Scotland
SC013688 Saline & Blairingone Parish Church of Scotland
SC002951 Tulliallan & Kincardine Parish Church of Scotland

25. Presbytery of Kirkcaldy

SC031143 Auchterderran: St Fothads Parish Church of Scotland
SC025310 Auchtertool Kirk (Church of Scotland)
SC009495 Buckhaven and Wemyss Parish Church of Scotland
SC016418 Burntisland Parish Church of Scotland
SC008991 Dysart Kirk (Church of Scotland)
SC007397 Glenrothes Christ's Kirk (Church of Scotland)
SC016386 St Columba's Parish Church of Scotland, Glenrothes
SC009845 St Margaret's Parish Church of Scotland: Glenrothes
SC002472 St Ninian's Parish Church of Scotland: Glenrothes
SC009342 Innerleven East Parish Church of Scotland: Methil
SC016733 Kennoway, Windygates and Balgonie: St Kenneth's Church of Scotland
SC007848 Kinghorn Parish Church of Scotland
SC012030 Kinglassie Parish Church of Scotland
SC002586 Abbotshall Parish Church of Scotland, Kirkcaldy
SC012039 Linktown Church of Scotland, Kirkcaldy
SC002858 Pathhead Parish Church of Scotland, Kirkcaldy
SC031064 St Bryce Kirk, Church of Scotland, Kirkcaldy
SC005628 Bennochy Parish Church of Scotland, Kirkcaldy
SC012756 Templehall Parish Church of Scotland, Kirkcaldy
SC015807 Torbain Parish Church of Scotland, Kirkcaldy
SC004264 Viewforth Parish Church of Scotland, Kirkcaldy
SC014025 Trinity Church of Scotland, Leslie
SC031969 Leven Parish Church of Scotland
SC005820 Markinch Parish Church of Scotland
SC009581 Methil Parish Church of Scotland
SC007949 Methilhill and Denbeath Parish Church of Scotland
SC003417 Thornton Parish Church of Scotland

26. Presbytery of St Andrews

SC004848 Abdie & Dunbog Parish Church of Scotland
SC012986 Anstruther Parish Church of Scotland
SC005402 Auchtermuchty Parish Church of Scotland
SC002542 Balmerino Parish Church of Scotland
SC001108 Boarhills and Dunino Parish Church of Scotland
SC005565 Cameron Parish Church (Church of Scotland)
SC016744 Carnbee Church of Scotland
SC000181 Cellardyke Parish Church of Scotland
SC017442 Ceres, Kemback & Springfield Church of Scotland
SC001601 Crail Parish Church of Scotland
SC001907 Creich, Flisk and Kilmany Church of Scotland
SC013123 Cupar Old & St Michael of Tarvit Parish Church (of Scotland)
SC015721 Cupar St John's and Dairsie United Parish Church of Scotland
SC015226 Edenshead and Strathmiglo Church of Scotland
SC003163 Elie, Kilconquhar and Colinsburgh Church of Scotland
SC012247 Falkland Parish Church of Scotland
SC016622 Freuchie Parish Church of Scotland
SC005381 Howe of Fife Parish Church (Church of Scotland)
SC002653 Kilrenny Parish Church of Scotland
SC012192 Kingsbarns Parish Church of Scotland
SC003465 Largo & Newburn Parish Church of Scotland
SC013075 Largo St David's Church of Scotland
SC009474 Largoward Church of Scotland
SC015677 Leuchars: St Athernase Church of Scotland
SC015182 Monimail Parish (Church of Scotland)
SC004607 Newburgh Parish Church of Scotland
SC006758 Newport-on-Tay Church of Scotland
SC015271 Pittenweem Church of Scotland
SC017173 The Parish Church of the Holy Trinity, St Andrews (Church of Scotland)
SC014934 Hope Park and Martyrs' Parish Church St Andrews (Church of Scotland)
SC013586 St Andrews: St Leonard's Parish Church of Scotland Congregation
SC005556 St Monans Church of Scotland
SC014710 Strathkinness Parish Church of Scotland
SC008659 Tayport Parish Church of Scotland
SC006447 Wormit Parish Church of Scotland

27. Presbytery of Dunkeld and Meigle

SC007899 Aberfeldy Parish Church of Scotland
SC028023 Amulree and Strathbraan Parish Church of Scotland

SC001465 Dull and Weem Parish Church of Scotland
SC000540 Alyth Parish Church of Scotland
SC000098 Ardler Kettins & Meigle Parish Church of Scotland
SC004358 Bendochy Parish Church of Scotland
SC014438 Coupar Angus Abbey Church of Scotland
SC013516 Blair Atholl and Struan Church of Scotland
SC001984 Tenandry Parish Church of Scotland
SC033757 Blairgowrie Parish Church of Scotland
SC011351 Braes of Rannoch Church of Scotland
SC006570 Foss and Rannoch Church of Scotland
SC001957 Caputh and Clunie Church of Scotland
SC009251 Kinclaven Church of Scotland
SC009867 Dunkeld Parish Church of Scotland
SC003310 Fortingall & Glenlyon Church of Scotland
SC006260 Kenmore and Lawers Church of Scotland
SC004275 Grantully Logierait & Strathtay Church of Scotland
SC008021 Kirkmichael Straloch & Glenshee Church of Scotland
SC000323 Rattray Parish Church of Scotland
SC008361 Pitlochry Church of Scotland

28. Presbytery of Perth

SC000586 Abernethy and Dron and Arngask Church of Scotland
SC005203 Almondbank Tibbermore Parish Church of Scotland
SC000139 Ardoch Parish Church of Scotland
SC001688 Auchterarder Parish Church of Scotland
SC010247 Auchtergaven and Moneydie Parish Church of Scotland
SC005594 Blackford Parish Church of Scotland
SC007283 Cargill Burrelton Parish Church of Scotland
SC003168 Cleish Parish Church of Scotland
SC009031 Collace Church of Scotland
SC001878 Comrie Parish Church of Scotland
SC004304 Crieff Parish Church of Scotland
SC009638 Dunbarney and Forgandenny Parish Church (Church of Scotland)
SC010311 St Fillans Dundurn Parish Church of Scotland
SC015895 Errol Parish Church of Scotland
SC013157 Fossoway St Serf's & Devonside Parish Church of Scotland
SC002209 Fowlis Wester, Madderty and Monzie Parish Church of Scotland
SC009632 Gask Parish Church of Scotland
SC010838 Kilspindie & Rait Parish Church of Scotland
SC012555 Kinross Parish Church of Scotland
SC010807 Methven and Logiealmond Church of Scotland
SC004984 Muthill Parish Church of Scotland
SC015523 Orwell and Portmoak Parish Church of Scotland
SC001330 Perth: Craigie and Moncreiffe Church of Scotland
SC007509 Kinnoull Parish Church of Scotland, Perth
SC002467 Perth: Letham St Mark's Church of Scotland
SC013014 Perth North, Church of Scotland
SC011113 Perth Riverside Church of Scotland
SC017132 St John's Kirk of Perth (Church of Scotland)
SC002919 Perth St Leonard's-in-the-Fields Church of Scotland
SC016829 Perth: St Matthew's Church of Scotland
SC010629 Redgorton and Stanley Parish Church – Church of Scotland
SC007094 Scone New Church of Scotland
SC014964 St Madoes and Kinfauns Church of Scotland, Glencarse
SC030799 The Church of Scotland: The Stewartry of Strathearn
SC000004 Trinity Gask and Kinkell Church (Church of Scotland)
SC002844 Scone Old Parish Church of Scotland
SC002000 St Martin's Church of Scotland, Perth

29. Presbytery of Dundee

SC007847 Abernyte Parish Church of Scotland
SC016717 Auchterhouse Parish Church of Scotland
SC017449 Dundee: Balgay Parish Church of Scotland
SC007031 Broughty Ferry New Kirk (Church of Scotland)
SC003677 Dundee: Camperdown Parish Church of Scotland
SC021763 Chalmers-Ardler Parish Church of Scotland, Dundee
SC012089 Dundee: Coldside Parish Church of Scotland
SC016701 Dundee: Craigiebank Parish Church of Scotland
SC005707 Dundee: Downfield South Church of Scotland
SC010030 Dundee Douglas and Mid Craigie Church of Scotland
SC033313 Dundee Lochee Parish Church of Scotland
SC017136 Dundee: West Church of Scotland
SC002792 Fowlis & Liff Parish Church of Scotland
SC009839 Inchture & Kinnaird Parish Church of Scotland
SC009454 Invergowrie Parish Church of Scotland
SC009115 Dundee: Logie & St John's (Cross) Church of Scotland
SC012230 Longforgan Parish Church of Scotland
SC001085 Lundie and Muirhead Parish Church of Scotland
SC013884 Dundee: Mains Parish Church of Scotland
SC020742 Fintry Parish Church of Scotland, Dundee
SC013162 Dundee: Meadowside St Paul's Church of Scotland
SC004496 Dundee: Menzieshill Parish Church of Scotland
SC012137 Monikie & Newbigging and Murroes & Tealing Church of Scotland
SC011775 Dundee: St Andrew's Parish Church of Scotland
SC000723 St David's High Kirk Dundee (Church of Scotland)
SC005210 St James Church of Scotland: Broughty Ferry
SC000088 St Luke's and Queen Street Church of Scotland: Broughty Ferry
SC011017 Barnhill St Margaret's Parish Church of Scotland
SC002198 Dundee Parish Church (St Mary's) Church of Scotland
SC003714 St Stephen's & West Parish Church of Scotland: Broughty Ferry
SC000384 Stobswell Parish Church of Scotland: Dundee
SC018015 Strathmartine Church of Scotland: Dundee
SC011021 Dundee: Trinity Parish Church of Scotland
SC000316 Dundee: Whitfield Parish Church of Scotland
SC014314 The Steeple Church: Dundee (Church of Scotland)
SC008965 Monifieth Parish Church of Scotland

30. Presbytery of Angus

SC018944 Aberlemno Parish Church of Scotland
SC002545 Barry Parish Church of Scotland
SC008630 Brechin Gardner Memorial Church of Scotland
SC015146 Carnoustie Church of Scotland
SC001293 Colliston Church of Scotland
SC007997 Farnell Parish Church of Scotland

SC000572 Dun and Hillside Church of Scotland
SC013105 Edzell Lethnot Glenesk Church of Scotland
SC009017 Inchbrayock Parish Church of Scotland
SC031461 The Isla Parishes Church of Scotland
SC013352 Newtyle Church of Scotland
SC017413 Arbirlot Parish Church of Scotland
SC006482 Arbroath West Kirk Church of Scotland
SC011361 Arbroath Knox's Parish Church of Scotland
SC005478 Arbroath: St Andrew's Church of Scotland
SC017424 Carmyllie Parish Church of Scotland
SC004594 Carnoustie Panbride Church of Scotland
SC003833 Dunnichen, Letham and Kirkden Church of Scotland
SC016937 Eassie and Nevay Church of Scotland
SC004921 Forfar East and Old Parish Church of Scotland
SC002417 Forfar Lowson Memorial Parish Church of Scotland
SC010332 Brechin Cathedral Church of Scotland
SC005085 Friockheim and Kinnell Parish Church of Scotland
SC017785 Inverkeilor and Lunan Church of Scotland
SC004395 Kirriemuir St Andrew's Parish Church of Scotland
SC015123 The Glens and Kirriemuir Old Parish Church of Scotland
SC009016 Montrose Melville South Church of Scotland
SC009934 Montrose: Old and St Andrew's Church of Scotland
SC003049 Arbroath St Vigeans Church of Scotland
SC006317 Oathlaw Tannadice Church of Scotland
SC001506 Forfar St Margaret's Church of Scotland
SC013052 Arbroath Old and Abbey Church of Scotland
SC011205 Glamis, Inverarity and Kinnettles Parish Church of Scotland
SC017327 Guthrie and Rescobie Church of Scotland
SC003236 Fern, Careston and Menmuir Church of Scotland

31. Presbytery of Aberdeen

SC025324 Aberdeen Bridge of Don Oldmachar Church of Scotland
SC032413 Cove Church of Scotland, Aberdeen
SC017158 Craigiebuckler Church of Scotland, Aberdeen
SC010756 Aberdeen Ferryhill Parish Church of Scotland
SC022497 Garthdee Parish Church of Scotland, Aberdeen
SC013916 Gilcomston South Church of Scotland, Aberdeen
SC003789 High Hilton Church of Scotland, Aberdeen
SC013318 Holburn West Church of Scotland, Aberdeen
SC001680 Mannofield Church of Scotland, Aberdeen
SC013459 Mastrick Parish Church of Scotland, Aberdeen
SC010643 Midstocket Parish Church of Scotland, Aberdeen
SC034441 Northfield Parish Church of Scotland, Aberdeen
SC014117 Queen Street Church of Scotland Aberdeen
SC002019 Queens Cross Church of Scotland Aberdeen
SC015841 Rubislaw Parish Church of Scotland, Aberdeen
SC013020 Ruthrieston West Church of Scotland, Aberdeen
SC017516 Aberdeen South Holburn Church of Scotland
SC027440 Aberdeen Bridge of Don St Columba's Church of Scotland
SC015451 Aberdeen St Marks Church of Scotland
SC018173 St Mary's Church of Scotland: Aberdeen
SC016043 South St Nicholas & Kincorth Church of Scotland, Aberdeen
SC014120 The Church of Scotland – Aberdeen: St Stephens Church
SC030587 New Stockethill Church of Scotland, Aberdeen
SC007076 Summerhill Parish Church of Scotland, Aberdeen
SC001966 Woodside Parish Church of Scotland, Aberdeen
SC017404 Bucksburn Stoneywood Parish Church of Scotland
SC017517 Cults Parish Church of Scotland
SC011204 Newhills Parish Church of Scotland
SC001452 Peterculter Parish Church of Scotland
SC009020 Torry St Fitticks Parish Church of Scotland, Aberdeen
SC006865 Kingswells Church of Scotland
SC031403 Middlefield Parish Church of Scotland, Aberdeen
SC016950 Dyce Parish Church of Scotland
SC024795 St Georges Tillydrone Church of Scotland, Aberdeen
SC008157 St Machar's Cathedral, Aberdeen, Church of Scotland
SC021283 St John's Church for Deaf People in the North of Scotland, Church of Scotland
SC008689 Kirk of St Nicholas Uniting

32. Presbytery of Kincardine and Deeside

SC016449 Aberluthnott Church of Scotland
SC014112 Aboyne-Dinnet Parish Church of Scotland
SC009239 Arbuthnott, Bervie and Kinneff (Church of Scotland)
SC011251 Banchory-Ternan East Church of Scotland
SC003306 Banchory-Ternan West Parish Church of Scotland
SC013648 Banchory Devenick & Maryculter-Cookney Parish Church of Scotland
SC018517 Birse & Feughside Church of Scotland
SC012075 Braemar and Crathie Parish, The Church of Scotland
SC015856 Parish of Cromar Church of Scotland
SC033779 Drumoak-Durris Church of Scotland
SC005522 Glenmuick (Ballater) Parish Church of Scotland
SC007436 Kinneff Church of Scotland
SC014830 Laurencekirk Church of Scotland
SC011997 Mearns Coastal Parish Church of Scotland
SC012967 Mid Deeside Parish, Church of Scotland
SC005679 Newtonhill Parish Church (Church of Scotland)
SC007420 Portlethen Parish Church of Scotland
SC013165 Stonehaven Dunnottar Church of Scotland
SC011191 Stonehaven Fetteresso Church of Scotland
SC016565 Stonehaven South Church of Scotland
SC016193 West Mearns Parish Church of Scotland

33. Presbytery of Gordon

SC010960 Barthol Chapel Church of Scotland
SC016387 Belhelvie Church of Scotland
SC000935 Insch-Leslie-Premnay-Oyne Church of Scotland
SC004050 Blairdaff and Chapel of Garioch Church of Scotland
SC003429 Cluny Church of Scotland
SC010911 Culsalmond and Rayne Church of Scotland
SC030817 Cushnie and Tough Parish Church of Scotland
SC003254 Daviot Parish Church of Scotland
SC003215 Echt Parish Church of Scotland
SC008819 Ellon Parish Church of Scotland
SC003115 Fintray Kinellar Keithhall Church of Scotland
SC011701 Foveran Church of Scotland
SC007979 Howe Trinity Parish Church of Scotland
SC001405 Huntly Cairnie Glass Church of Scotland
SC008791 St Andrews Parish Church of Scotland Inverurie

SC016907 Inverurie West Church of Scotland
SC014790 Kemnay Parish Church of Scotland
SC001406 Kintore Parish Church of Scotland
SC015960 Meldrum & Bourtie Parish Church of Scotland
SC016542 Methlick Parish Church of Scotland
SC009556 Midmar Parish Church of Scotland
SC004525 Monymusk Parish Church of Scotland
SC024017 Newmachar Parish Church of Scotland
SC007582 Parish of Noth Church of Scotland
SC009462 Skene Parish Church of Scotland
SC017161 Tarves Parish Church of Scotland
SC006056 Udny & Pitmedden Church of Scotland
SC014679 Upper Donside Parish Church of Scotland
SC000534 Strathbogie Drumblade Church of Scotland Huntly

34. Presbytery of Buchan

SC007197 Aberdour Church of Scotland
SC017101 Auchaber United Parish Church of Scotland
SC009168 Auchterless Parish Church of Scotland
SC015501 Banff Parish Church of Scotland
SC006889 Crimond Parish Church of Scotland
SC006408 Cruden Parish Church of Scotland
SC012985 Deer Parish Church of Scotland
SC000522 Fordyce Parish Church of Scotland
SC013119 Fraserburgh Old Church of Scotland
SC005714 Fraserburgh South Church of Scotland
SC016334 Fraserburgh West Parish Church of Scotland
SC001475 Fyvie Church of Scotland
SC012282 Gardenstown Church of Scotland
SC000375 Inverallochy & Rathen East Parish Church of Scotland
SC015077 King Edward Parish Church of Scotland
SC008873 Longside Parish Church of Scotland
SC008813 Lonmay Parish Church of Scotland
SC015786 Macduff Parish Church of Scotland
SC009773 Maud & Savoch Church of Scotland
SC010291 Monquhitter & New Byth Parish Church of Scotland
SC007917 New Deer St Kane's Church of Scotland
SC001107 Marnoch Church of Scotland
SC014620 New Pitsligo Parish Church of Scotland
SC001971 Ordiquhill & Cornhill Church of Scotland
SC011147 Peterhead Old Parish Church of Scotland
SC010841 Peterhead St Andrews Church of Scotland
SC009990 Peterhead Trinity Parish Church of Scotland
SC005498 Pitsligo Parish Church of Scotland
SC015604 Rathen West Parish Church of Scotland
SC032016 Rothienorman Parish Church of Scotland
SC000710 St Fergus Parish Church of Scotland
SC024874 Sandhaven Parish Church of Scotland
SC007273 Strichen and Tyrie Parish Church of Scotland
SC015620 St Andrews Parish Church of Scotland, Turriff
SC007470 Turriff St Ninians and Forglen Parish Church of Scotland
SC002085 Whitehills Parish Church of Scotland

35. Presbytery of Moray

SC001336 Aberlour Parish Church of Scotland
SC010330 Alves & Burghead Parish Church of Scotland
SC005310 Bellie Parish Church of Scotland
SC016720 Birnie and Pluscarden Church of Scotland
SC001235 Buckie North Church of Scotland
SC005608 Buckie South & West Church of Scotland
SC011231 Cullen & Deskford Church of Scotland
SC015881 St Michael's Parish Church of Scotland, Dallas
SC004853 Duffus Spynie & Hopeman Church of Scotland
SC000585 Dyke Parish Church of Scotland
SC009986 Edinkillie Church of Scotland
SC005240 Elgin High Church of Scotland
SC015164 St Giles & St Columbas Church of Scotland, Elgin
SC015093 Enzie Parish Church of Scotland
SC010045 Findochty Parish Church of Scotland
SC000711 St Laurence Parish Church of Scotland, Forres
SC005094 St Leonard's Church of Scotland, Forres
SC033804 Keith North Newmill Boharm & Rothiemay Church of Scotland
SC031791 Kirk of Keith: St Rufus, Botriphnie and Grange (Church of Scotland)
SC014557 Kinloss & Findhorn Parish Church of Scotland
SC014428 Knockando Elchies & Archiestown Parish Church of Scotland
SC009793 St Gerardine's High Church of Scotland, Lossiemouth
SC000880 St James Church of Scotland: Lossiemouth
SC010193 Mortlach and Cabrach Church of Scotland
SC014485 Portknockie Parish Church of Scotland
SC022567 Rafford Parish Church of Scotland
SC015906 Rathven Parish Church of Scotland
SC016116 Rothes Parish Church of Scotland
SC007113 Speymouth Parish Church of Scotland
SC008850 St Andrews Lhanbryd & Urquhart Parish Church of Scotland, Elgin

36. Presbytery of Abernethy

SC003652 Abernethy Church of Scotland
SC002884 Cromdale & Advie Church of Scotland
SC010001 Grantown-on-Spey Church of Scotland
SC014015 Dulnain Bridge Church of Scotland
SC021546 Kingussie Church of Scotland
SC003282 Rothiemurchus & Aviemore Church of Scotland
SC001802 Tomintoul, Glenlivet and Inveravon Church of Scotland
SC000043 Alvie and Insh Church of Scotland
SC008346 Boat of Garten, Duthil and Kincardine Church of Scotland
SC008016 Laggan Church of Scotland
SC005490 Newtonmore Church of Scotland

37. Presbytery of Inverness

SC015446 Ardersier Parish Church of Scotland
SC026653 Auldearn & Dalmore Parish Church of Scotland
SC001695 Cawdor Parish Church (Church of Scotland)
SC013601 Croy & Dalcross Parish Church (Church of Scotland)
SC000662 The Barn, Church of Scotland, Culloden
SC003301 Daviot & Dunlichity Church of Scotland
SC013579 Dores & Boleskine Church of Scotland
SC018159 Crown Church, Inverness (Church of Scotland)
SC011773 Dalneigh & Bona Parish Church of Scotland, Inverness
SC016866 East Church of Scotland Inverness
SC016775 Hilton Parish Church of Scotland, Inverness
SC005553 Inshes Church of Scotland, Inverness
SC010870 Ness Bank Church of Scotland, Inverness
SC035073 Old High St Stephen's Church of Scotland, Inverness
SC008109 Inverness: St Columba Church of Scotland New Charge
SC015432 Inverness Trinity Church of Scotland
SC008121 Kilmorack & Erchless Church of Scotland
SC014918 Kiltarlity Church of Scotland
SC020888 Kinmylies Church of Scotland, Inverness

SC003866 Kirkhill Church of Scotland
SC015653 Moy Dalarossie & Tomatin Church of Scotland
SC000947 Nairn Old Parish Church of Scotland
SC015361 St Ninians Church of Scotland, Nairn
SC004952 Petty Church of Scotland
SC016627 Urquhart & Glenmoriston Church of Scotland

38. Presbytery of Lochaber

SC002916 Acharacle Parish Church of Scotland
SC008222 Ardgour and Kingairloch Parish Church of Scotland
SC030394 Ardnamurchan Parish Church of Scotland
SC021584 North West Lochaber Church of Scotland
SC018259 Duror Parish Church of Scotland
SC022635 Fort Augustus Parish Church of Scotland
SC013279 Fort William Duncansburgh MacIntosh Parish Church of Scotland
SC005211 Glencoe St Munda's Parish Church of Scotland
SC023413 Glengarry Parish Church of Scotland
SC005687 Kilmallie Parish Church of Scotland
SC014745 Kilmonivaig Parish Church of Scotland
SC030288 Kinlochleven Parish Church of Scotland
SC015532 Morvern Parish Church of Scotland
SC006700 Nether Lochaber Parish Church of Scotland
SC008982 Strontian Parish Church of Scotland

39. Presbytery of Ross

SC015227 Alness Parish Church of Scotland
SC003921 Avoch Parish Church of Scotland
SC011897 Contin Parish Church of Scotland
SC006666 Cromarty Parish Church of Scotland
SC001167 Dingwall Castle Street Church of Scotland
SC001056 Dingwall St Clements Parish Church of Scotland
SC009309 Fearn Abbey & Nigg Church of Scotland
SC012675 Ferintosh Parish Church of Scotland
SC003499 Fodderty & Strathpeffer Parish Church of Scotland
SC004472 Fortrose & Rosemarkie Parish Church of Scotland
SC010964 Invergordon Church of Scotland
SC010319 Killearnan Parish Church of Scotland
SC013375 Kilmuir & Logie Easter Church of Scotland
SC009180 Kiltearn Parish Church of Scotland
SC014467 Knockbain Parish Church of Scotland
SC015631 Lochbroom & Ullapool Church of Scotland
SC013643 Resolis & Urquhart Church of Scotland
SC010093 Rosskeen Parish Church of Scotland
SC012425 Tain Parish Church of Scotland
SC021420 Tarbat Parish Church of Scotland
SC009902 Urray & Kilchrist Church of Scotland

40. Presbytery of Sutherland

SC016038 Altnaharra & Farr Church of Scotland
SC010171 Assynt & Stoer Parish Church of Scotland
SC004973 Clyne Church of Scotland
SC003840 Creich Parish Church of Scotland
SC000315 Dornoch Cathedral (Church of Scotland)
SC005079 Durness & Kinlochbervie Church of Scotland
SC007326 Eddrachillis Parish Church of Scotland
SC004560 Golspie (St Andrews) Church of Scotland
SC004056 Kildonan & Loth Helmsdale Church of Scotland
SC016877 Kincardine Croick & Edderton Church of Scotland
SC020871 Lairg Church of Scotland
SC014066 Melness & Tongue Church of Scotland
SC010035 Rogart Church of Scotland
SC017558 Rosehall Church of Scotland

41. Presbytery of Caithness

SC001363 Bower Church of Scotland
SC032164 Canisbay Parish Church of Scotland
SC030261 Dunnet Church of Scotland
SC008544 Halkirk & Westerdale Church of Scotland
SC010874 Keiss Parish Church of Scotland
SC034424 The Parish of Latheron Church of Scotland
SC010296 Olrig Church of Scotland
SC001815 North Coast Parish Church of Scotland
SC016691 Thurso St Peter's & St Andrew's Church of Scotland
SC007248 Thurso West Church of Scotland
SC003365 Watten Church of Scotland
SC013840 Wick St Fergus Church of Scotland
SC001291 Pulteneytown & Thrumster Church of Scotland

42. Presbytery of Lochcarron – Skye

SC032334 Applecross, Lochcarron and Torridon Church of Scotland
SC022592 Bracadale and Duirinish Church of Scotland
SC015448 Gairloch and Dundonnell Church of Scotland
SC017510 Glenelg and Kintail Church of Scotland
SC014072 Kilmuir and Stenscholl Church of Scotland
SC016505 Lochalsh Church of Scotland
SC000416 Portree Church of Scotland
SC030117 Snizort Church of Scotland
SC001285 Strath and Sleat Church of Scotland

43. Presbytery of Uist

SC003980 Barra Church of Scotland
SC002191 Benbecula Church of Scotland
SC016358 Berneray and Lochmaddy Church of Scotland
SC016461 Carinish Church of Scotland
SC030955 Kilmuir and Paible Church of Scotland
SC001770 Manish-Scarista Church of Scotland
SC031790 South Uist Church of Scotland
SC004787 Tarbert Church of Scotland

44. Presbytery of Lewis

SC006563 Barvas Church of Scotland
SC032250 Carloway Church of Scotland
SC000991 Cross Ness Church of Scotland
SC008004 Kinloch Church of Scotland
SC014492 Knock Church of Scotland
SC024236 Lochs Crossbost Parish Church of Scotland
SC008746 Lochs-in-Bernera Church of Scotland
SC010164 Stornoway High Church of Scotland
SC000753 Martins Memorial Church of Scotland, Stornoway
SC006777 St Columba Old Parish Church of Scotland, Stornoway
SC007879 Uig Parish Church of Scotland

45. Presbytery of Orkney

SC035048 Birsay Harray & Sandwick Church of Scotland
SC019770 East Mainland Church of Scotland
SC005404 Eday Church of Scotland
SC005062 Evie Church of Scotland
SC013330 Firth Church of Scotland
SC016203 Flotta Parish Church of Scotland
SC023194 Hoy & Walls Parish Church of Scotland
SC018002 Kirkwall East Church, Church of Scotland
SC005322 Kirkwall St Magnus Cathedral (Church of Scotland)
SC030098 North Ronaldsay Parish Church of Scotland

SC016221 Orphir Church of Scotland
SC013661 Papa Westray Church of Scotland
SC016806 Rendall Church of Scotland
SC001078 Rousay Church of Scotland
SC000271 Sanday Church of Scotland
SC006097 Shapinsay Church of Scotland
SC003298 South Ronaldsay & Burray Church of Scotland
SC008306 Stenness Church of Scotland
SC003099 Stromness Church of Scotland
SC006572 Moncur Memorial Church of Scotland, Stronsay
SC025053 Westray Parish Church of Scotland

46. Presbytery of Shetland

SC030483 Burra Church of Scotland
SC029873 Delting Parish Church (Church of Scotland)
SC015253 Dunrossness and St Ninian's Parish Church (incl. Fair Isle) (Church of Scotland)
SC038365 Fetlar Church of Scotland
SC017535 Lerwick and Bressay Parish Church (Church of Scotland)
SC031996 Nesting and Lunnasting Church of Scotland
SC002341 Northmavine Parish Church of Scotland
SC012345 Sandsting and Aithsting Parish Church of Scotland
SC014545 Sandwick, Cunningsburgh and Quarff Church of Scotland
SC030748 St Paul's Church of Scotland Walls: Shetland
SC032982 Tingwall Parish Church of Scotland
SC007954 Unst Church of Scotland
SC000293 Whalsay and Skerries Parish Church of Scotland
SC020628 Yell Parish Church of Scotland

SECTION 8

Church Buildings: Ordnance Survey National Grid References

NOTE:
The placing of symbols denoting churches may vary according to the edition of published maps. The references which follow should be sufficiently accurate to allow church buildings to be located. The correction of any errors will always be welcomed, and appropriate details should be sent to the Editor of the *Year Book*.

The Churches are listed in the order in which they appear in the Presbytery Lists in the *Year Book*.

1. Presbytery of Edinburgh
Albany Deaf Church of Edinburgh, at Greenside NT263745
Balerno, NT163664
Barclay Viewforth, NT249726
Blackhall St Columba's, NT219747
Bristo Memorial Craigmillar, NT287716
Broughton St Mary's, NT256748
Canongate, NT265738
Carrick Knowe, NT203721
Colinton, NT216692
Colinton Mains, NT233692
Corstorphine Craigsbank, NT191730
Corstorphine Old, NT201728
Corstorphine St Anne's, NT204730
Corstorphine St Ninian's, NT198730
Craigentinny St Christopher's, NT292748
Craiglockhart, NT224705
Craigmillar Park, NT269714
Cramond, NT190768
Currie, NT183676
Dalmeny, NT144775
Davidson's Mains, NT207752
Dean, NT238742
Drylaw, NT221754
Duddingston, NT284726
Fairmilehead, NT248683
Gorgie Dalry, NT231724
Granton, NT237766
Greenbank, NT243702
Greenside, NT263745
Greyfriars Tolbooth and Highland, NT256734
High (St Giles'), NT257736
Holyrood Abbey, NT274744
Holy Trinity, NT201700
Inverleith, NT243759
Juniper Green, NT199687
Kaimes Lockhart Memorial, NT277684
Kirkliston, NT125744
Kirk o' Field, NT263732
Leith North, NT263765
Leith St Andrew's, NT273757
Leith St Serf's, NT248761
Leith South, NT271761
Leith Wardie, NT246768
Liberton, NT275695
Liberton Northfield, NT280699
London Road, NT268745
Marchmont St Giles', NT256718
Mayfield Salisbury, NT266717
Morningside, NT246707
Morningside United, NT245719
Muirhouse St Andrew's, NT215763
Murrayfield, NT227733
Newhaven, NT254769
New Restalrig, NT284742
Old Kirk, NT220760
Palmerston Place, NT241734
Pilrig St Paul's, NT266752
Polwarth, NT236719
Portobello Old, NT309738
Portobello St James', NT303738
Portobello St Philip's Joppa, NT313736
Priestfield, NT271721
Queensferry, NT130782
Ratho, NT138710
Reid Memorial, NT261710
Richmond Craigmillar, NT296717
St Andrew's and St George's West, NT255741
St Andrew's Clermiston, NT201746
St Catherine's Argyle, NT257721
St Cuthbert's, NT248736
St David's Broomhouse, NT203714
St John's Oxgangs, NT237687
St Margaret's, NT284745
St Martin's, NT305726
St Michael's, NT234722
St Nicholas' Sighthill, NT194707
St Stephen's Comely Bank, NT241748
Slateford Longstone, NT213707
Stenhouse St Aidan's, NT218716
Stockbridge, NT247748
The Tron Kirk (Gilmerton and Moredun):
Gilmerton, NT293686
Moredun, NT294697

2. Presbytery of West Lothian
Abercorn, NT082792
Armadale, NS935684
Avonbridge, NS910730
Bathgate: Boghall, NS996686
Bathgate: High, NS976691
Bathgate: St John's, NS977687
Blackburn and Seafield, NS991655
Blackridge, NS897671
Breich Valley, NS968622
Broxburn, NT085723
Fauldhouse: St Andrew's, NS931607
Harthill: St Andrew's, NS896643
Kirknewton and East Calder:
Kirknewton, NT106670
East Calder, NT086678
Kirk of Calder, NT074673
Linlithgow: St Michael's, NT002773
Linlithgow: St Ninian's Craigmailen, NS994771
Livingston Ecumenical Church:
Carmondean, Knightsridge, Craigshill (St Columba's), NT063681
Ladywell (St Paul's), NT054682
Dedridge and Murieston: Lanthorn Centre, Dedridge, NT060663
Livingston: Old, NT037669
Deans, NT021686
Pardovan, Kingscavil and Winchburgh:
Kingscavil, NT030764
Winchburgh, NT087750
Polbeth Harwood, NT030641
Strathbrock, NT060722
Ecclesmachan, NT059737
Torphichen, NS969725
Uphall: South, NT061718
West Kirk of Calder, NT014629
Whitburn: Brucefield, NS948650
Whitburn: South, NS947646

3. Presbytery of Lothian
Aberlady, NT462799
Athelstaneford, NT533774
Belhaven, NT668787
Bilston, NT262647
Bolton and Saltoun:
Bolton, NT507701
Saltoun, NT474678
Bonnyrigg, NT307654
Cockenzie and Port Seton: Chalmers Memorial, NT403757
Cockenzie and Port Seton: Old, NT401758
Cockpen and Carrington, NT319642
Dalkeith: St John's and King's Park, NT330670

Dalkeith: St Nicholas' Buccleuch, NT333674
Dirleton, NT513842
Dunbar, NT682786
Dunglass:
Cockburnspath, NT774711
Innerwick, NT721739
Oldhamstocks, NT738707
Garvald and Morham:
Garvald, NT591709
Morham, NT557726
Gladsmuir, NT457733
Glencorse, NT247627
Gorebridge, NT343619
Gullane, NT483827
Haddington: St Mary's, NT519736
Haddington: West, NT512739
Howgate, NT248580
Humbie, NT461637
Lasswade and Rosewell:
Lasswade, NT305661
Rosewell, NT288624
Loanhead, NT278654
Longniddry, NT442763
Musselburgh: Northesk, NT340727
Musselburgh: St Andrew's High, NT345727
Musselburgh: St Clement's and St Ninian's, NT360727
Wallyford, NT368722
Musselburgh: St Michael's Inveresk, NT344721
St John's, Whitecraig, NT351701
Newbattle, NT331661:
Newtongrange, NT334643
Easthouses, NT348652
Newton, NT315693
North Berwick: Abbey, NT551853
North Berwick: St Andrew Blackadder, NT553853
Ormiston, NT414693
Pencaitland, NT443690
Penicuik: North, NT234603
Penicuik: St Mungo's, NT237599
Penicuik: South, NT236595
Prestonpans: Prestongrange, NT388746
Roslin, NT270631
Spott, NT673755
Tranent, NT403734
Traprain:
Prestonkirk, NT592778
Stenton, NT622743
Whittingehame, NT603737
Tyne Valley Parish:
Borthwick, NT369596
Cranston, Crichton and Ford, NT386656
Fala and Soutra, NT438609
Whitekirk and Tyninghame, NT596815
Yester, NT535681

4. Presbytery of Melrose and Peebles
Ashkirk, NT466220
Bowden and Melrose:
Bowden, NT554301
Melrose, NT544344
Broughton, Glenholm and Kilbucho, NT114357
Caddonfoot, NT451348
Carlops, NT161559
Channelkirk and Lauder:
Channelkirk, NT482545
Lauder, NT531475
Earlston, NT581388
Eddleston, NT244472
Ettrick and Yarrow:
Ettrick, NT259145
Yarrow, NT356278
Kirkhope, NT390244
Galashiels: Old and St Paul's, NT492358
Galashiels: St John's, NT509357
Galashiels: Trinity, NT491363
Innerleithen, Traquair and Walkerburn:
Innerleithen, NT332369
Traquair, NT320335
Kirkurd and Newlands, NT162467
Lyne and Manor:
Lyne, NT192405
Manor, NT220380
Maxton and Mertoun:
Maxton, NT610303
Mertoun, NT615318
Newtown, NT581316
Peebles: Old, NT250404
Peebles: St Andrew's Leckie, NT253404
St Boswells, NT594310
Selkirk, NT472287
Skirling, NT075390
Stobo and Drumelzier:
Stobo, NT183377
Drumelzier, NT135343
Stow: St Mary of Wedale and Heriot:
Stow: St Mary of Wedale, NT459444
Heriot, NT390526
Tweedsmuir, NT101245
West Linton: St Andrew's, NT149516

5. Presbytery of Duns
Ayton and Burnmouth:
Ayton, NT927609
Burnmouth, NT956610
Berwick-upon-Tweed: St Andrew's Wallace Green and Lowick, NT999532
Bonkyl and Preston, NT808596
Chirnside, NT869561
Coldingham and St Abb's, NT904659
Coldstream, NT843398
Duns, NT786539
Eccles, NT764413
Edrom: Allanton, NT826558
Eyemouth, NT943640
Fogo and Swinton:
Fogo, NT773492
Swinton, NT838477
Foulden and Mordington, NT931558
Gordon: St Michael's, NT645432
Grantshouse and Houndwood and Reston:
Reston, NT878621
Grantshouse congregation meets in village hall
Greenlaw, NT712462
Hutton and Fishwick and Paxton:
Hutton and Fishwick, NT907540
Paxton, NT934532
Ladykirk, NT889477
Langton and Lammermuir:
Cranshaws, NT692619
Langton, NT767523
Longformacus, NT694573
Legerwood, NT594434
Leitholm, NT791441
Westruther, NT633500
Whitsome, NT861504

6. Presbytery of Jedburgh
Ale and Teviot United:
Ancrum, NT627246
Crailing, NT682250
Lilliesleaf, NT539253

Cavers and Kirkton:
Cavers, NT538159
Kirkton, NT541140
Hawick: Burnfoot, NT510162
Hawick: St Mary's and Old, NT502143
Hawick: Teviot and Roberton:
Hawick: Teviot, NT501144
Roberton, NT432142
Hawick: Trinity, NT505147
Hawick: Wilton, NT502153
Hobkirk and Southdean:
Hobkirk, NT587109
Southdean, NT624109
Jedburgh: Old and Trinity, NT651203
Kelso Country Churches:
Makerstoun, NT669331
Roxburgh, NT700307
Smailholm, NT649364
Stichill, NT711383
Kelso North and Ednam:
Kelso: North, NT725343
Ednam, NT737372
Kelso: Old and Sprouston:
Kelso: Old, NT725343
Sprouston, NT757353
Linton, Morebattle, Hownam and Yetholm:
Linton, NT773262
Hoselaw, NT802318
Morebattle, NT772250
Hownam, NT778193
Yetholm, NT826281
Oxnam, NT701190
Ruberslaw:
Bedrule, NT599179
Denholm, NT569186
Minto, NT567201
Teviothead, NT403052

7. Presbytery of Annandale and Eskdale
Annan: Old, NY197666
Annan: St Andrew's, NY193665
Applegarth, Sibbaldbie and Johnstone, NY104843
Brydekirk, NY183705
Canonbie United, NY395763
Dalton, NY114740
Dornock, NY231660
Gretna: Old, Gretna: St Andrew's, Half Morton and Kirkpatrick Fleming:
Gretna: Old, NY319680
Gretna: St Andrew's, NY317670
Kirkpatrick Fleming, NY277701
Hightae, NY090793
Hoddom, Kirtle-Eaglesfield and Middlebie:
Eaglesfield, NY233743
Middlebie, NY214762
Kirkpatrick Juxta, NT083009
Langholm Eskdalemuir Ewes and Westerkirk:
Langholm, NY362844
Eskdalemuir, NY253979
Ewes, NY369908
Westerkirk, NY312903
Liddesdale:
Castleton, NY482877
Saughtree, NY562968
Lochmaben, NY084823
Lockerbie: Dryfesdale, Hutton and Corrie
Hutton and Corrie, NY171908
Lockerbie: Dryfesdale, NY135818
Moffat: St Andrew's, NT084051
St Mungo, NY143771
The Border Kirk, NY402561
Tundergarth, NY175808
Wamphray, NY131965

8. Presbytery of Dumfries and Kirkcudbright
Auchencairn and Rerrick, NX799512
Balmaclellan and Kells:
Balmaclellan, NX651791
Kells, NX632784
Balmaghie, NX722663
Borgue, NX629483
Buittle and Kelton, NX758603
Caerlaverock, NX996688
Carsphairn, NX563932
Castle Douglas, NX765622
Closeburn, NX904923
Colvend, Southwick and Kirkbean:
Colvend, NX862541
Southwick, NX927573
Kirkbean, NX980592
Corsock and Kirkpatrick Durham:
Corsock, NX762760
Kirkpatrick Durham, NX786699
Crossmichael and Parton:
Crossmichael, NX729670
Parton, NX697699
Cummertrees, Mouswald and Ruthwell, NY101683
Dalbeattie, NX831611
Dalry, NX618813
Dumfries: Maxwelltown West, NX967760
Dumfries: North West, NX958774
Dumfries: St George's, NX971764
Dumfries: St Mary's-Greyfriars, NX975763
Dumfries: St Michael's and South, NX975757
Dumfries: Troqueer, NX975751
Dunscore, NX867843
Durisdeer, NS894038
Gatehouse of Fleet, NX602566
Glencairn and Moniaive:
Glencairn, NX809904
Moniaive, NX777910
Irongray, Lochrutton and Terregles:
Irongray, NX915794
Terregles, NX931771
Kirkconnel, NS728123
Kirkcudbright, NX683509
Kirkgunzeon, NX866667
Kirkmahoe, NX974815:
Dalswinton, NX942850
Kirkmichael, Tinwald and Torthorwald:
Kirkmichael, NY005884
Tinwald, NY003816
Torthorwald, NY035783
Lochend and New Abbey, NX965660
Penpont, Keir and Tynron, NX849944
Sanquhar: St Bride's, NS779102
Tarff and Twynholm, NX664542
Thornhill, NX883957
Urr, NX817658

9. Presbytery of Wigtown and Stranraer
Ervie Kirkcolm, NX026687
Glasserton and Isle of Whithorn:
Glasserton, NX421381
Isle of Whithorn, NX478363
Inch, NX101603
Kirkcowan, NX327610
Kirkinner, NX423514
Kirkmabreck, NX477585
Kirkmaiden, NX125369:
Drummore, NX135366
Leswalt, NX020638

Mochrum, NX347463
Monigaff, NX410666
New Luce, NX175645
Old Luce, NX197574
Penninghame, NX410654
Portpatrick, NX002544
Sorbie, NX468463
Stoneykirk:
  Sandhead, NX097500
  Ardwell, NX101457
Stranraer: High Kirk, NX057609
Stranraer: St Ninian's, NX060607
Stranraer: Town Kirk, NX064606
Whithorn: St Ninian's Priory, NX444403
Wigtown, NX436555

10. Presbytery of Ayr
Alloway, NS332180
Annbank, NS407243
Auchinleck, NS552216
Ayr: Auld Kirk of Ayr, NS339219
Ayr: Castlehill, NS347203
Ayr: Newton Wallacetown, NS339224
Ayr: St Andrew's, NS338213
Ayr: St Columba, NS337209
Ayr: St James', NS342232
Ayr: St Leonard's, NS338204
Ayr: St Quivox:
  Auchincruive, NS375241
  Dalmilling, NS363229
Ballantrae, NX083825:
  Glenapp, NX075746
Barr, NX275941
Catrine, NS528260
Coylton, NS422198
Craigie, NS427323
Crosshill, NS327068
Dailly, NS271016
Dalmellington, NS481061:
  Bellsbank, NS480046
Dalrymple, NS358144
Drongan: The Schaw Kirk, NS441185
Dundonald, NS366343
Fisherton, NS275175
Girvan: North (Old and St Andrew's), NX187982
Girvan: South, NX183977
Kirkmichael, NS345090
Kirkoswald, NS240073
Lugar, NS591213
Mauchline, NS498272
Maybole, worshipping in Maybole Baptist Church, NS299099
Monkton and Prestwick: North, NS353263
Muirkirk, NS701278
New Cumnock, NS617135
Ochiltree, NS504212
Old Cumnock: Old, NS568202
Old Cumnock: Trinity, NS567200:
  Netherthird, NS578187
Patna: Waterside, NS412106
Prestwick: Kingcase, NS348243
Prestwick: St Nicholas', NS351256
Prestwick: South, NS351259
St Colmon (Arnsheen Barrhill and Colmonell):
  Colmonell, NX144857
  Barrhill congregation meets in community centre
Sorn, NS550268
Stair, NS439236
Straiton: St Cuthbert's, NS381049
Symington, NS384314
Tarbolton, NS430272
Troon: Old, NS321309
Troon: Portland, NS323308
Troon: St Meddan's, NS323309

11. Presbytery of Irvine and Kilmarnock
Caldwell, NS435552
Crosshouse, NS395384
Darvel, NS563375
Dreghorn and Springside, NS352383
Dunlop, NS405494
Fenwick, NS465435
Galston, NS500367
Hurlford, NS454372
Irvine: Fullarton, NS316389
Irvine: Girdle Toll, NS341409
Irvine: Mure, NS319390
Irvine: Old, NS322387
Irvine: Relief Bourtreehill, NS344392
Irvine: St Andrew's, NS325399
Kilmarnock: Henderson, NS431380
Kilmarnock: New Laigh, NS428379
Kilmarnock: Old High Kirk, NS430382
Kilmarnock: Riccarton, NS428364
Kilmarnock: St Andrew's and St Marnock's, NS427377
Kilmarnock: St John's Onthank, NS433399
Kilmarnock: St Kentigern's, NS442388
Kilmarnock: St Ninian's Bellfield, NS435359
Kilmarnock: Shortlees, NS428353
Kilmaurs: St Maur's Glencairn, NS415408
Newmilns: Loudoun, NS537373
Stewarton: John Knox, NS421460
Stewarton: St Columba's, NS419457
Ayrshire Mission to the Deaf, Kilmarnock, NS430377

12. Presbytery of Ardrossan
Ardrossan: Barony St John's, NS231420
Ardrossan: Park, NS233436
Beith: High, NS350539
Beith: Trinity, NS351544
Brodick, NS012359
Corrie, NS024437
Cumbrae, NS160550
Dalry: St Margaret's, NS291496
Dalry: Trinity, NS292494
Fairlie, NS209556
Kilbirnie: Auld Kirk, NS315536
Kilbirnie: St Columba's, NS314546
Kilmory, NR963218
Kilwinning: Mansefield Trinity, NS290432
Kilwinning: Old, NS303433
Lamlash, NS026309
Largs: Clark Memorial, NS202593
Largs: St Columba's, NS203596
Largs: St John's, NS201593
Lochranza and Pirnmill:
  Lochranza, NR937503
  Pirnmill, NR874447
Saltcoats: New Trinity, NS246414
Saltcoats: North, NS252423
Saltcoats: St Cuthbert's, NS244418
Shiskine, NR910295
Stevenston: Ardeer, NS269411
Stevenston: High, NS266422
Stevenston: Livingston, NS268416
West Kilbride, NS207484
Whiting Bay and Kildonan, NS047273

13. Presbytery of Lanark
Biggar, NT040379
Black Mount, NT101464
Cairngryffe, NS923384

Carluke: Kirkton, NS844503
Carluke: St Andrew's, NS844508
Carluke: St John's, NS847503
Carnwath, NS976465:
  Auchengray, NS995540
  Tarbrax, NT025549
Carstairs and Carstairs Junction (The United Church):
  Carstairs, NS938461
  Carstairs Junction, NS954450
Coalburn, NS813345
Crossford, NS827466
Culter, NT027342
Forth: St Paul's, NS942538
Glencaple, NS930234
Kirkfieldbank, NS866438
Kirkmuirhill, NS799429
Lanark: Greyfriars, NS880437
Lanark: St Nicholas', NS881437
Law, NS821527
Lesmahagow: Abbeygreen, NS813402
Lesmahagow: Old, NS814399
Libberton and Quothquan, NS992428
Lowther, NS885148
Symington, NS999352
The Douglas Valley Church:
  Douglas, NS835310
  Douglas Water and Rigside, NS873347

14. Presbytery of Greenock and Paisley
Barrhead: Arthurlie, NS501588
Barrhead: Bourock, NS499589
Barrhead: South and Levern, NS503589
Bishopton, NS445721
Bridge of Weir: Freeland, NS387656
Bridge of Weir: St Machar's Ranfurly, NS392653
Elderslie Kirk, NS441631
Erskine, NS466707
Gourock: Old Gourock and Ashton, NS243775
Gourock: St John's, NS241778
Greenock: Ardgowan, NS271768
Greenock: East End
Greenock: Finnart St Paul's, NS265774
Greenock: Mount Kirk, NS271759
Greenock: Old West Kirk, NS273772
Greenock: St Margaret's, NS255764
Greenock: St Ninian's, NS242755
Greenock: Wellpark Mid Kirk, NS279762
Greenock: Westburn, NS273763
Houston and Killellan, NS410671
Howwood, NS396603
Inchinnan, NS479689
Inverkip, NS207720
Johnstone: High, NS426630
Johnstone: St Andrew's Trinity, NS434623
Johnstone: St Paul's, NS424626
Kilbarchan: East, NS403633
Kilbarchan: West, NS401632
Kilmacolm: Old, NS358700
Kilmacolm: St Columba, NS358697
Langbank, NS380734
Linwood, NS432645
Lochwinnoch, NS353587
Neilston, NS480574
Paisley: Abbey, NS486640
Paisley: Glenburn, NS473617
Paisley: Lylesland, NS488626
Paisley: Martyrs' Sandyford:
  Martyrs', NS474639
  Sandyford, NS493657
Paisley: Oakshaw Trinity, NS480641
Paisley: St Columba Foxbar, NS458622
Paisley: St James', NS477644
Paisley: St Luke's, NS482632
Paisley: St Mark's Oldhall, NS511640
Paisley: St Ninian's Ferguslie, NS464644
Paisley: Sherwood Greenlaw, NS492642
Paisley: Stow Brae Kirk, NS483634
Paisley: Wallneuk North, NS486643
Port Glasgow: Hamilton Bardrainney, NS337733
Port Glasgow: St Andrew's, NS319745
Port Glasgow: St Martin's, NS306747
Renfrew: North, NS508678
Renfrew: Old, NS509676
Renfrew: Trinity, NS505674
Skelmorlie and Wemyss Bay, NS192681

16. Presbytery of Glasgow
Banton, NS752788
Bishopbriggs: Kenmure, NS604698
Bishopbriggs: Springfield, NS615702
Broom, NS554563
Burnside Blairbeth:
  Burnside, NS622601
  Blairbeth, NS616603
Busby, NS577563
Cadder, NS616723
Cambuslang: Flemington Hallside, NS663595
Cambuslang Parish, NS646600
Campsie, NS629777
Chryston, NS688702:
  Moodiesburn, NS699708
Eaglesham, NS574519
Fernhill and Cathkin, NS624594
Gartcosh, NS698682
Giffnock: Orchardhill, NS563587
Giffnock: South, NS559582
Giffnock: The Park, NS559593
Glenboig, NS723687
Greenbank, NS574568
Kilsyth: Anderson, NS717782
Kilsyth: Burns and Old, NS716778
Kirkintilloch: Hillhead, NS663730
Kirkintilloch: St Columba's, NS664733
Kirkintilloch: St David's Memorial Park, NS653736
Kirkintilloch: St Mary's, NS654739
Lenzie: Old, NS655720
Lenzie: Union, NS654722
Maxwell Mearns Castle, NS553553
Mearns, NS543551
Milton of Campsie, NS652768
Netherlee, NS577590
Newton Mearns, NS537557
Rutherglen: Old, NS613617
Rutherglen: Stonelaw, NS617612
Rutherglen: West and Wardlawhill, NS609618
Stamperland, NS576581
Stepps, NS657686
Thornliebank, NS546588
Torrance, NS620744
Twechar, NS700753
Williamwood, NS566576
Glasgow: Anderston Kelvingrove, NS577655
Glasgow: Baillieston Mure Memorial, NS673643
Glasgow: Baillieston St Andrew's, NS681639
Glasgow: Balshagray Victoria Park, NS549671
Glasgow: Barlanark Greyfriars, NS667649
Glasgow: Blawarthill, NS522683
Glasgow: Bridgeton St Francis in the East, NS611639
Glasgow: Broomhill, NS549674
Glasgow: Calton Parkhead, NS624638
Glasgow: Cardonald, NS526639
Glasgow: Carmunnock, NS599575

Glasgow: Carmyle, NS649618
Glasgow: Carnwadric, NS544599
Glasgow: Castlemilk East, NS607593
Glasgow: Castlemilk West, NS596594
Glasgow: Cathcart Old, NS587606
Glasgow: Cathcart Trinity, NS582604
Glasgow: Cathedral (High or St Mungo's), NS603656
Glasgow: Clincarthill, NS586613
Glasgow: Colston Milton, NS592697
Glasgow: Colston Wellpark, NS606692
Glasgow: Cranhill, NS643658
Glasgow: Croftfoot, NS603602
Glasgow: Dennistoun New, NS613652
Glasgow: Drumchapel Drumry St Mary's, NS515709
Glasgow: Drumchapel St Andrew's, NS523707
Glasgow: Drumchapel St Mark's, NS521719
Glasgow: Easterhouse St George's and St Peter's, NS678657
Glasgow: Eastwood, NS558607
Glasgow: Gairbraid, NS568688
Glasgow: Gallowgate:
David Street, NS614646
Bain Square, NS602646
Glasgow: Gardner Street, NS558667
Glasgow: Garthamlock and Craigend East, NS658667
Glasgow: Gorbals, NS587641
Glasgow: Govan and Linthouse, NS555658
Glasgow: Govanhill Trinity, NS587627
Glasgow: High Carntyne, NS636653
Glasgow: Hillington Park, NS534639
Glasgow: Househillwood St Christopher's, NS534616
Glasgow: Hyndland, NS559675
Glasgow: Ibrox, NS560642
Glasgow: John Ross Memorial Church for Deaf People, NS588644
Glasgow: Jordanhill, NS544682
Glasgow: Kelvin Stevenson Memorial, NS576673
Glasgow: Kelvinside Hillhead, NS567673
Glasgow: Kenmuir Mount Vernon, NS655626
Glasgow: King's Park, NS601608
Glasgow: Kinning Park, NS570648
Glasgow: Knightswood St Margaret's, NS536694
Glasgow: Langside, NS582614
Glasgow: Lansdowne, NS576669
Glasgow: Lochwood, NS685663
Glasgow: Martyrs', The, NS597657
Glasgow: Maryhill, NS563695
Glasgow: Merrylea, NS575603
Glasgow: Mosspark, NS544633
Glasgow: Newlands South, NS573611
Glasgow: Partick South, NS559665
Glasgow: Partick Trinity, NS563668
Glasgow: Penilee St Andrew, NS518647
Glasgow: Pollokshaws, NS561612
Glasgow: Pollokshields, NS577635
Glasgow: Possilpark, NS592677
Glasgow: Priesthill and Nitshill:
Priesthill, NS531607
Nitshill, NS522603
Glasgow: Queen's Park, NS579625
Glasgow: Renfield St Stephen's, NS582659
Glasgow: Robroyston, NS638688
Glasgow: Ruchazie, NS643662
Glasgow: Ruchill Kelvinside, NS573683
Glasgow: St Andrew's East, NS619656
Glasgow: St Columba, NS583657
Glasgow: St David's Knightswood, NS528689
Glasgow: St Enoch's Hogganfield, NS629660
Glasgow: St George's Tron, NS590655
Glasgow: St James' (Pollok), NS530626
Glasgow: St John's Renfield, NS558683
Glasgow: St Margaret's Tollcross Park, NS637631
Glasgow: St Nicholas' Cardonald, NS524646
Glasgow: St Paul's, NS631671
Glasgow: St Rollox, NS603668
Glasgow: Sandyford Henderson Memorial, NS570659
Glasgow: Sandyhills, NS658638
Glasgow: Scotstoun, NS533676
Glasgow: Shawlands, NS572621
Glasgow: Sherbrooke St Gilbert's, NS561636
Glasgow: Shettleston New, NS647642
Glasgow: Shettleston Old, NS649639
Glasgow: South Carntyne, NS630652
Glasgow: South Shawlands, NS569615
Glasgow: Springburn, NS607677
Glasgow: Temple Anniesland, NS547689
Glasgow: Toryglen, NS602615
Glasgow: Trinity Possil and Henry Drummond, NS593687
Glasgow: Tron St Mary's, NS618676
Glasgow: Victoria Tollcross, NS642632
Glasgow: Wallacewell, NS621690
Glasgow: Wellington, NS570667
Glasgow: Whiteinch, NS540668
Glasgow: Yoker, NS511689

17. Presbytery of Hamilton

Airdrie: Broomknoll, NS761653
Airdrie: Clarkston, NS783661
Airdrie: Flowerhill, NS765655
Airdrie: High, NS760658
Airdrie: Jackson, NS782647
Airdrie: New Monkland, NS753678
Airdrie: St Columba's, NS766665
Airdrie: The New Wellwynd, NS759654
Bargeddie, NS692648
Bellshill: Macdonald Memorial, NS738602
Bellshill: Orbiston, NS729593
Bellshill: West, NS727603
Blantyre: Livingstone Memorial, NS687577
Blantyre: Old, NS679565
Blantyre: St Andrew's, NS693573
Bothwell, NS705586
Calderbank, NS770631
Caldercruix and Longriggend, NS819677
Carfin, NS772584
Chapelhall, NS783627
Chapelton, NS685485
Cleland, NS797581
Coatbridge: Blairhill Dundyvan, NS726650
Coatbridge: Calder, NS738639
Coatbridge: Middle, NS723646
Coatbridge: Old Monkland, NS718633
Coatbridge: New St Andrew's, NS733653
Coatbridge: Townhead, NS718664
Dalserf, NS800507:
Ashgill, NS783503
East Kilbride: Claremont, NS653543
East Kilbride: Greenhills, NS616525
East Kilbride: Moncreiff, NS647555
East Kilbride: Mossneuk, NS607532
East Kilbride: Old, NS635545
East Kilbride: South, NS633537
East Kilbride: Stewartfield, meets in a community centre at NS643561
East Kilbride: West, NS634547
East Kilbride: Westwood, NS618537
Glasford, NS726470
Greengairs, NS783705
Hamilton: Burnbank, NS699562
Hamilton: Cadzow, NS723550
Hamilton: Gilmour and Whitehill, NS704563
Hamilton: Hillhouse, NS696554
Hamilton: North, NS719558

Hamilton: Old, NS723555
Hamilton: St Andrew's, NS723551
Hamilton: St John's, NS724553
Hamilton: South, NS717538
Hamilton: Trinity, NS711543
Hamilton: West, NS712558
Holytown, NS773608
Kirk o' Shotts, NS843629
Larkhall: Chalmers, NS763499
Larkhall: St Machan's, NS763511
Larkhall: Trinity, NS762513
Motherwell: Crosshill, NS756566
Motherwell: Dalziel St Andrew's, NS752571
Motherwell: North, NS741577
Motherwell: St Margaret's, NS769549
Motherwell: St Mary's, NS750566
Motherwell: South, NS757560
Newarthill, NS781597
Newmains: Bonkle, NS837571
Newmains: Coltness Memorial, NS819557
New Stevenston: Wrangholm Kirk, NS760596
Overtown, NS801527
Quarter, NS722512
Shotts: Calderhead Erskine, NS877600:
Allanton, NS850578
Stonehouse: St Ninian's, NS752467
Strathaven: Avendale Old and Drumclog: Avendale Old, NS701443:
Drumclog, NS640389
Strathaven: East, NS702446
Strathaven: Rankin, NS701446
Uddingston: Burnhead, NS717614
Uddingston: Old, NS696603
Uddingston: Viewpark, NS702616
Wishaw: Cambusnethan North, NS808554
Wishaw: Cambusnethan Old, NS806553
Wishaw: Craigneuk and Belhaven, NS773561
Wishaw: Old, NS796552
Wishaw: St Mark's, NS801566
Wishaw: South Wishaw, NS797548

18. Presbytery of Dumbarton
Alexandria, NS387817
Arrochar, NM296037
Baldernock, NS577751
Bearsden: Baljaffray, NS534736
Bearsden: Cross, NS542722
Bearsden: Killermont, NS557713
Bearsden: New Kilpatrick, NS543723
Bearsden: Westerton Fairlie Memorial, NS543706
Bonhill, NS395796
Cardross, NS345775
Clydebank: Abbotsford, NS498703
Clydebank: Faifley, NS502732
Clydebank: Kilbowie St Andrew's, NS499712
Clydebank: Radnor Park, NS495713
Clydebank: St Cuthbert's, NS511704
Craigrownie, NS224811
Dalmuir: Barclay, NS479715
Dumbarton: Riverside, NS398752
Dumbarton: St Andrew's, NS407764
Dumbarton: West Kirk, NS390755
Duntocher, NS494727
Garelochhead, NS239912
Helensburgh: Park, NS300823
Helensburgh: St Columba, NS297825
Helensburgh: The West Kirk, NS295825
Jamestown, NS397813
Kilmaronock and Gartocharn:
Kilmaronock, NS452875
Gartocharn, NS428864
Luss, NS361929
Milngavie: Cairns, NS556748
Milngavie: St Luke's, NS543747
Milngavie: St Paul's, NS557745
Old Kilpatrick Bowling, NS463731
Renton: Trinity, NS390780
Rhu and Shandon, NS267841
Rosneath: St Modan's, NS255832

19. Presbytery of Argyll
Appin, NM938459
Ardchattan, NM944360:
Benderloch, NM905384
Ardrishaig, NR854852
Campbeltown: Highland, NR720201
Campbeltown: Lorne and Lowland, NR718206
Coll, NM223573
Colonsay and Oronsay, NR390941
Connel, NM914343
Craignish, NM805042
Cumlodden, Lochfyneside and Lochgair:
Cumlodden, NS015997
Lochfyneside, NR979962
Lochgair, NR922905
Dunoon: St John's, NS172769
Dunoon: The High Kirk, NS174765
Gigha and Cara, NR648489
Glassary, Kilmartin and Ford:
Glassary, NR859935
Kilmartin, NR834988
Ford, NM869037
Glenaray and Inveraray, NN095085
Glenorchy and Innishael, NN168275
Innellan, NS151707
Iona, NM285243
Jura, NR527677
Kilarrow, NR312596
Kilberry, NR741620
Kilbrandon and Kilchattan:
Kilbrandon, NM758155
Kilchattan, NM743104
Kilcalmonell, NR763561
Kilchoman, NR257596
Kilchrenan and Dalavich:
Kilchrenan, NN037229
Dalavich, NM968124
Kildalton and Oa, NR368450
Kilfinan, NR934789
Kilfinichen and Kilvickeon and the Ross of Mull:
Kilfinichen and Kilvickeon, NM383218
The Ross of Mull, NM316232
Killean and Kilchenzie, NR681418
Kilmeny, NR390657
Kilmodan and Colintraive:
Kilmodan, NR995842
Colintraive, NS045735
Kilmore and Oban:
Kilmore, NM872258
Oban: Old, NM861296
Corran Esplanade, NM856306
Kilmun (St Munn's), NS166821
Kilninian and Kilmore, NM432517
Kilninver and Kilmelford:
Kilninver, NM825217
Kilmelford, NM849130
Kirn, NS184783
Kyles, NR973713
Lismore, NM861435
Lochgilphead, NR863882
Lochgoilhead and Kilmorich:
Lochgoilhead, NN198015

Kilmorich, NN181108
Muckairn, NN005310
North Knapdale, Kilmichael Inverlussa, NR776859:
Bellanoch, NR797923
Tayvallich, NR742871
Portnahaven, NR168523
Rothesay: Trinity, NS089645
Saddell and Carradale, NR796376
Salen and Ulva, NM573431
Sandbank, NS163803
Skipness, NR902579
South Knapdale, NR781775
Southend, NR698094
Strachur and Strathlachlan:
Strachur, NN096014
Strathlachlan, NS022958
Strathfillan, Crianlarich, NN387252:
Bridge of Orchy, NN297395
Strone and Ardentinny:
Strone, NS193806
Ardentinny, NS188876
Tarbert, NR863686
The United Church of Bute, NS086637
Tiree:
Heylipol, NL964432
Kirkapol, NM041468
Tobermory, NM504554
Torosay and Kinlochspelvie, NM721367
Toward, NS135679:
Inverchaolain, NS091753

22. Presbytery of Falkirk
Airth, NS898878
Blackbraes and Shieldhill, NS899769
Bo'ness: Old, NS994813
Bo'ness: St Andrew's, NT007813
Bonnybridge: St Helen's, NS821804
Bothkennar and Carronshore, NS903834
Brightons, NS928778
Carriden, NT019812:
Blackness, NT053798
Cumbernauld: Abronhill, NS781758
Cumbernauld: Condorrat, NS732730
Cumbernauld: Kildrum, NS767747
Cumbernauld: Old, NS764760
Cumbernauld: St Mungo's, NS757745
Denny: Dunipace, NS807833
Denny: Old, NS812828
Denny: Westpark, NS809828
Falkirk: Bainsford, NS887814
Falkirk: Camelon, NS873804
Falkirk: Erskine, NS884798
Falkirk: Grahamston United, NS889807
Falkirk: Laurieston, NS913794
Falkirk: Old and St Modan's, NS887800
Falkirk: St Andrew's West, NS887801
Falkirk: St James', NS893806
Grangemouth: Abbotsgrange, NS928817
Grangemouth: Kirk of the Holy Rood, NS931805
Grangemouth: Zetland, NS931818
Haggs, NS791793
Larbert: East, NS871829
Larbert: Old, NS856822
Larbert: West, NS863827
Muiravonside, NS956770
Polmont: Old, NS937793
Redding and Westquarter, NS921786
Slamannan, NS856734:
Limerigg, NS857707
Stenhouse and Carron, NS876831

23. Presbytery of Stirling
Aberfoyle, NN514013
Alloa: Ludgate, NS884927
Alloa: St Mungo's, NS883926
Alva, NS882970
Balfron, NS547893
Balquhidder, NN536209
Bannockburn: Allan, NS810903
Bannockburn: Ladywell, NS803907
Bridge of Allan, NS791974
Buchanan, NS443903
Buchlyvie, NS577939
Callander, NN629077:
Trossachs, NN515066
Cambusbarron: The Bruce Memorial, NS778924
Clackmannan, NS910918
Cowie and Plean:
Cowie, NS837892
Plean, NS836867
Dollar, NS964980
Drymen, NS474881
Dunblane: Cathedral, NN782014
Dunblane: St Blane's, NN783014
Fallin, NS844913
Fintry, NS627862
Gargunnock, NS707943
Gartmore, NS521971
Glendevon, NN979051
Killearn, NS523861
Killin and Ardeonaig, NN573332:
Morenish, NN607356
Kilmadock, NN727016
Kincardine-in-Menteith, NS719988
Kippen, NS650948
Lecropt, NS781979
Logie, NS818968
Menstrie, NS849969
Muckhart, NO001010
Norrieston, NN670001
Port of Menteith, NN583012
Sauchie and Coalsnaughton, NS897945
Stirling: Allan Park South, NS795933
Stirling: Church of the Holy Rude, NS792937
Stirling: North, NS802920
Stirling: St Columba's, NS796930
Stirling: St Mark's, NS791948
Stirling: St Ninian's Old, NS795916
Stirling: Viewfield, NS795938
Strathblane, NS557797
Tillicoultry, NS923968
Tullibody: St Serf's, NS860954

24. Presbytery of Dunfermline
Aberdour: St Fillan's, NT193855
Beath and Cowdenbeath: North, NT166925
Cairneyhill, NT052863
Carnock and Oakley:
Carnock, NT043890
Oakley, NT025890
Cowdenbeath: Trinity:
Cowdenbeath, NT157908
Crossgates, NT145893
Culross and Torryburn:
Culross, NS989863
Torryburn, NT027861
Valleyfield, NT003866
Dalgety, NT155836
Dunfermline: Abbey, NT090873
Dunfermline: Gillespie Memorial, NT090876
Dunfermline: North, NT086879
Dunfermline: St Andrew's Erskine, NT107884

Dunfermline: St Leonard's, NT096869
Dunfermline: St Margaret's, NT114878
Dunfermline: St Ninian's, NT113868
Dunfermline: St Paul's East, NT109886
Dunfermline: Townhill and Kingseat:
  Townhill, NT106894
  Kingseat, NT126904
Inverkeithing, NT131830
Kelty, NT144942
Limekilns, NT078833
Lochgelly and Benarty: St Serf's:
  Lochgelly, NT186933
  Ballingry, NT173977
North Queensferry, NT132808
Rosyth, NT114839
Saline and Blairingone, NT023924
Tulliallan and Kincardine, NS933879

25. Presbytery of Kirkcaldy
Auchterderran: St Fothad's, NT214960
Auchtertool, NT207902
Buckhaven and Wemyss:
  Buckhaven, NT358981
  Wemyss, NT336968
  West Wemyss, NT328949
Burntisland, NT234857
Dysart, NT302931
Glenrothes: Christ's Kirk, NO275023
Glenrothes: St Columba's, NO270009
Glenrothes: St Margaret's, NO285002
Glenrothes: St Ninian's, NO257007
Innerleven: East, NO372003
Kennoway, Windygates and Balgonie: St Kenneth's:
  Kennoway, NO350027
  Windygates, NO345006
Kinghorn, NT272869
Kinglassie, NT227985
Kirkcaldy: Abbotshall, NT274913
Kirkcaldy: Bennochy, NT275925
Kirkcaldy: Linktown, NT278910
Kirkcaldy: Pathhead, NT291928
Kirkcaldy: St Bryce Kirk, NT280917 and NT279917
Kirkcaldy: Templehall, NT265934
Kirkcaldy: Torbain, NT259939
Kirkcaldy: Viewforth, NT294936
Leslie: Trinity, NO247015
Leven, NO383009
Markinch, NO297019
Methil, NT370994
Methilhill and Denbeath, NT357999
Thornton, NT289976

26. Presbytery of St Andrews
Abdie and Dunbog, NO257167
Anstruther, NO567037
Auchtermuchty, NO238117
Balmerino, NO368245:
  Gauldry, NO379239
Boarhills and Dunino:
  Boarhills, NO562137
  Dunino, NO541109
Cameron, NO484116
Carnbee, NO532065
Cellardyke, NO574037
Ceres, Kemback and Springfield:
  Ceres, NO399117
  Kemback, NO419151
  Springfield, NO342119
Crail, NO613080
Creich, Flisk and Kilmany:
  Creich, NO328200
  Kilmany, NO388217
Cupar: Old and St Michael of Tarvit,
  NO373143
Cupar: St John's and Dairsie United:
  Cupar: St John's, NO373147
  Dairsie, NO413173
Edenshead and Strathmiglo, NO217103
Elie, Kilconquhar and Colinsburgh:
  Elie, NO491001
  Kilconquhar, NO485020
  Colinsburgh, NO475034
Falkland, NO252074
Freuchie, NO283067
Howe of Fife:
  Collessie, NO287133
  Cults, NO347099
  Kettle, NO310083
  Ladybank, NO302102
Kilrenny, NO575049
Kingsbarns, NO593121
Largo and Newburn, NO423035
Largo: St David's, NO419026
Largoward, NO469077
Leuchars: St Athernase, NO455214
Monimail, NO303142
Newburgh, NO240183
Newport-on-Tay, NO422280
Pittenweem, NO549026
St Andrews: Holy Trinity, NO509167
St Andrews: Hope Park and Martyrs', NO505167
St Andrews: St Leonard's, NO502164
St Monans, NO523014
Strathkinness, NO460163
Tayport, NO458286
Wormit, NO403267

27. Presbytery of Dunkeld and Meigle
Aberfeldy, NN854491
Alyth, NO243488
Amulree and Strathbraan, NN899366
Ardler, Kettins and Meigle:
  Kettins, NO238390
  Meigle, NO287446
Bendochy, NO218415
Blair Atholl, NN874654:
  Struan, NN808654
Blairgowrie, NO177454
Braes of Rannoch, NN507566
Caputh and Clunie:
  Caputh, NO088401
  Clunie, NO109440
Coupar Angus: Abbey, NO223398
Dull and Weem, NN844497
Dunkeld: Cathedral, NO024426:
  Little Dunkeld, NO028423
  Dowally, NO001480
Fortingall and Glenlyon:
  Fortingall, NN742471
  Glenlyon, NN588475
Foss and Rannoch:
  Foss, NN790581
  Rannoch, NN663585
Grantully, Logierait and Strathtay:
  Logierait, NN967520
  Strathtay, NN908532
Kenmore and Lawers, NN772454
Kinclaven, NO151385
Kirkmichael, Straloch and Glenshee:
  Kirkmichael, NO081601
  Glenshee, NO109702
  Netherton Bridge, NO143522

Pitlochry, NO940582
Rattray, NO190457
Tenandry, NN911615

28. Presbytery of Perth
Abernethy and Dron and Arngask:
Abernethy, NO190164
Arngask (Glenfarg), NO133104
Almondbank and Tibbermore, NO065264
Ardoch, NO839098
Auchterarder, NN948129
Auchtergaven and Moneydie, NO061347
Blackford, NN899092
Cargill Burrelton, NO202377
Cleish, NT095981
Collace, NO197320
Comrie, NN770221
Crieff, NN867219
Dunbarney and Forgandenny:
Dunbarney, NO130185
Forgandenny, NO087183
Dundurn, NN697241
Errol, NO253230
Fossoway: St Serf's and Devonside, NO033001
Fowlis Wester, Madderty and Monzie:
Fowlis Wester, NN928241
Madderty, NN947217
Monzie, NN879250
Gask, NO003203
Kilspindie and Rait, NO220258
Kinross, NO118023
Methven and Logiealmond, NO026260
Muthill, NN868171
Orwell and Portmoak:
Orwell, NO121051
Portmoak, NO183019
Perth: Craigie and Moncreiffe:
Craigie, NO110228
Moncreiffe, NO113218
Perth: Kinnoull, NO123235
Perth: Letham St Mark's, NO095243
Perth: North, NO116237
Perth: Riverside, NO110256
Perth: St John the Baptist's, NO119235
Perth: St Leonard's-in-the-Fields and Trinity, NO117232
Perth: St Matthew's, NO121235
Redgorton and Stanley, NO110329
St Madoes and Kinfauns, NO197212
Scone and St Martin's:
Scone, NO136262
St David's Stormontfield, NO108298
St Martin's, NO154304
The Stewartry of Strathearn:
Aberdalgie and Dupplin, NO079203
Aberuthven, NN979155
Forteviot, NO052175
Dunning, NO020147
Trinity Gask and Kinkell, NN963183

29. Presbytery of Dundee
Abernyte, NO267311
Auchterhouse, NO342381
Dundee: Balgay, NO385309
Dundee: Barnhill St Margaret's, NO478316
Dundee: Broughty Ferry New Kirk, NO464309
Dundee: Broughty Ferry St James', NO460307
Dundee: Broughty Ferry St Luke's and Queen Street, NO457312
Dundee: Broughty Ferry St Stephen's and West, NO458309
Dundee: Camperdown, NO363320
Dundee: Chalmers Ardler, NO377333
Dundee: Coldside, NO403316
Dundee: Craigiebank, NO429315
Dundee: Douglas and Mid Craigie, NO444322
Dundee: Downfield South, NO389336
Dundee: Dundee St Mary's, NO401301
Dundee: Fintry, NO423334
Dundee: Lochee, NO377318
Dundee: Logie and St John's Cross, NO386299
Dundee: Mains, NO403337
Dundee: Meadowside St Paul's, NO402300
Dundee: Menzieshill, NO362312
Dundee: St Andrew's, NO404307
Dundee: St David's High Kirk:
St David's North, NO391318
High Kirk, NO394313
Dundee: Steeple, NO402301
Dundee: Stobswell, NO411315
Dundee: Strathmartine, NO384343
Dundee: Trinity, NO410310
Dundee: West, NO395297
Dundee: Whitfield, NO435334
Fowlis and Liff:
Fowlis, NO322334
Liff, NO333328
Inchture and Kinnaird:
Inchture, NO281288
Kinnaird, NO243287
Invergowrie, NO346304
Longforgan, NO309300
Lundie and Muirhead:
Lundie, NO291366
Muirhead, NO342345
Monifieth:
Panmure, NO500327
St Rule's, NO495323
South, NO493324
Monikie and Newbigging and Murroes and Tealing:
Monikie, NO518388
Murroes, NO461351
Newbigging, NO498362

30. Presbytery of Angus
Aberlemno, NO523555
Arbirlot, NO602406
Arbroath: Knox's, NO638414
Arbroath: Old and Abbey, NO644413
Arbroath: St Andrew's, NO643414
Arbroath: St Vigean's, NO638429
Arbroath: West Kirk, NO636410
Barry, NO541346
Brechin: Cathedral, NO595601:
Stracathro, NO617657
Brechin: Gardner Memorial, NO601602
Carmyllie, NO549426
Carnoustie, NO559346
Carnoustie: Panbride, NO570347:
Panbride, NO572358
Colliston, NO604453
Dun and Hillside:
Dun, NO664600
Hillside, NO709609
Dunnichen, Letham and Kirkden:
Dunnichen, NO510488
Letham, NO528488
Eassie and Nevay, NO333450
Edzell Lethnot Glenesk:
Edzell Lethnot, NO599693

Glenesk, NO497795
Farnell, NO627554
Fern Careston Menmuir:
Fern, NO484616
Careston, NO528603
Forfar: East and Old, NO457506
Forfar: Lowson Memorial, NO465509
Forfar: St Margaret's, NO454505
Friockheim Kinnell, NO592497
Glamis, Inverarity and Kinnettles:
Glamis, NO386469
Inverarity, NO453443
Guthrie and Rescobie:
Guthrie, NO568505
Rescobie, NO509521
Inchbrayock, NO714567
Inverkeilor and Lunan, NO664496
Kirriemuir: St Andrew's, NO386535
Montrose: Melville South, NO713575
Montrose: Old and St Andrew's, NO715578
Newtyle, NO296413
Oathlaw Tannadice, NO475581
The Glens and Kirriemuir: Old:
Kirriemuir Old, NO386539
Cortachy, NO396597
Glen Prosen, NO328657
Memus, NO427590
The Isla Parishes:
Airlie, NO313515
Glenisla, NO215604
Kilry, NO246538
Kingoldrum, NO333550
Ruthven, NO286489

31. Presbytery of Aberdeen
Aberdeen: Bridge of Don Oldmachar, NJ928121
Aberdeen: Cove, meets in Loirston Primary School
Aberdeen: Craigiebuckler, NJ907053
Aberdeen: Ferryhill, NJ937051
Aberdeen: Garthdee, NJ918034
Aberdeen: Gilcomston South, NJ935058
Aberdeen: High Hilton, NJ923078
Aberdeen: Holburn West, NJ926052
Aberdeen: Mannofield, NJ917045
Aberdeen: Mastrick, NJ902073
Aberdeen: Middlefield, NJ911088
Aberdeen: Midstocket, NJ919066
Aberdeen: New Stockethill, meets in community centre
Aberdeen: Northfield, NJ903085
Aberdeen: Queen Street, NJ943064
Aberdeen: Queen's Cross, NJ925058
Aberdeen: Rubislaw, NJ924058
Aberdeen: Ruthrieston West, NJ924042
Aberdeen: St Columba's Bridge of Don, NJ935104
Aberdeen: St George's Tillydrone, NJ931090
Aberdeen: St John's Church for Deaf People, NJ923087
Aberdeen: St Machar's Cathedral, NJ939088
Aberdeen: St Mark's, NJ937063
Aberdeen: St Mary's, NJ943081
Aberdeen: St Nicholas Kincorth, South of, NJ934033
Aberdeen: St Nicholas Uniting, Kirk of, NJ941063
Aberdeen: St Stephen's, NJ936074
Aberdeen: South Holburn, NJ930042
Aberdeen: Summerhill, NJ904063
Aberdeen: Torry St Fittick's, NJ947050
Aberdeen: Woodside, NJ924088
Bucksburn Stoneywood, NJ897096
Cults, NJ886026
Dyce, NJ887130
Kingswells, NJ869063
Newhills, NJ876095
Peterculter, NJ841007

32. Presbytery of Kincardine and Deeside
Aberluthnott, NO687656:
Luthermuir, NO655685
Aboyne and Dinnet, NO525983
Arbuthnott, Bervie and Kinneff:
Arbuthnott, NO801746
Bervie, NO830727
Banchory-Devenick and Maryculter/Cookney:
Banchory-Devenick, NJ907024
Maryculter/Cookney, NO857993
Banchory-Ternan: East, NO707958
Banchory-Ternan: West, NO693957
Birse and Feughside, NO605925
Braemar and Crathie:
Braemar, NO150913
Crathie, NO265949
Cromar:
Coldstone, NJ436043
Coull, NJ512024
Tarland, NJ485047
Drumoak-Durris:
Drumoak, NO792993
Durris, NO772965
Glenmuick (Ballater), NO369957
Glengairn, NJ300012
Laurencekirk, NO718717
Mearns Coastal:
Johnshaven, NO798672
St Cyrus, NO750648
Mid Deeside:
Kincardine O'Neil, NO594997
Torphins, NJ626021
Newtonhill, NO911934
Portlethen, NO924966
Stonehaven: Dunnottar, NO863853
Stonehaven: Fetteresso, NO869864
Stonehaven: South, NO872857
West Mearns:
Fettercairn, NO651735
Fordoun, NO726784
Glenbervie, NO766807

33. Presbytery of Gordon
Barthol Chapel, NJ814339
Belhelvie, NJ957184
Blairdaff and Chapel of Garioch:
Blairdaff, NJ704173
Chapel of Garioch, NJ716242
Cluny, NJ685124
Culsalmond and Rayne, NJ698302
Cushnie and Tough:
Cushnie, NJ530108
Tough, NJ616129
Daviot, NJ750283
Echt, NJ739057
Ellon, NJ959304:
Slains, NK042290
Fintray Kinellar Keithhall:
Fintray, NJ841166
Keithhall, NJ803210
Foveran, NJ999253
Howe Trinity, NJ582157
Huntly Cairnie Glass, NJ530398
Insch-Leslie-Premnay-Oyne, NJ631283
Inverurie: St Andrew's, NJ777211
Inverurie: West, NJ774215

Kemnay, NJ737162
Kintore, NJ793163
Meldrum and Bourtie:
Meldrum, NJ813273
Bourtie, NJ804248
Methlick, NJ858372
Midmar, NJ699065
Monymusk, NJ684152
New Machar, NJ887194
Noth, NJ497272
Skene, NJ803077:
Westhill, NJ833072
Strathbogie Drumblade:
Strathbogie, NJ531399
Drumblade, NJ588402
Tarves, NJ868312
Udny and Pitmedden:
Udny, NJ880264
Pitmedden, NJ893274
Upper Donside:
Strathdon, NJ355127
Towie, NJ440129
Lumsden, NJ475220

34. Presbytery of Buchan
Aberdour, NJ885634
Auchaber United, NJ632411
Auchterless, NJ713415
Banff, NJ689638
Crimond, NK054568
Cruden, NK071366
Deer, NJ979477:
Fetterangus, NJ987508
Fordyce, NJ554637:
Portsoy, NJ587659
Fraserburgh: Old, NJ998671
Fraserburgh: South, NJ998666
Fraserburgh: West, NJ994667
Fyvie, NJ768377
Gardenstown, NJ801648
Inverallochy and Rathen: East, NK043651
King Edward, NJ716579
Longside, NK037473
Lonmay, NK038602
Macduff, NJ701643
Marnoch, NJ628527
Maud and Savoch, NJ927478
Monquhitter and New Byth, NJ803506
New Deer: St Kane's, NJ886469
New Pitsligo, NJ880562
Ordiquhill and Cornhill, NJ587583
Peterhead: Old, NK131462
Peterhead: St Andrew's, NK131465
Peterhead: Trinity, NK132463:
Boddam, NK133423
Pitsligo, NJ929673
Rathen: West, NK000609
Rothienorman, NJ723357
St Fergus, NK093519
Sandhaven, NJ963675
Strichen and Tyrie:
Strichen, NJ945554
Tyrie, NJ930631
Turriff: St Andrew's, NJ729497
Turriff: St Ninian's and Forglen, NJ723500
Whitehills, NJ655653

35. Presbytery of Moray
Aberlour, NJ264428:
Craigellachie, NJ290451
Alves and Burghead:
Alves, NJ125616
Burghead, NJ114688
Bellie, NJ345588
Birnie and Pluscarden:
Birnie, NJ207587
Pluscarden, NJ149573
Buckie: North, NJ427657
Buckie: South and West, NJ426654
Cullen and Deskford, NJ507664
Dallas, NJ122518
Duffus, Spynie and Hopeman:
Duffus, NJ168687
Spynie, NJ183642
Hopeman, NJ144693
Dyke, NH990584
Edinkillie, NJ020466
Elgin: High, NJ215627
Elgin: St Giles' and St Columba's South:
St Giles', NJ217628
St Columba's South, NJ219623
Enzie, NJ397643
Findochty, NJ464682
Forres: St Laurence, NJ035588
Forres: St Leonard's, NJ038591
Keith: North, Newmill, Boharm and Rothiemay:
Keith: North, NJ433507
Newmill, NJ439527
Boharm, NJ355505
Rothiemay, NJ547483
Keith: St Rufus, Botriphnie and Grange:
Keith: St Rufus, NJ430508
Botriphnie, NJ375441
Grange, NJ481515
Kinloss and Findhorn:
Kinloss, NJ063617
Findhorn, NJ042642
Knockando, Elchies and Archiestown, NJ186429
Lossiemouth: St Gerardine's High, NJ233706
Lossiemouth: St James', NJ235707
Mortlach and Cabrach:
Mortlach, NJ324393
Lower Cabrach, NJ382313
Portknockie, NJ488684
Rafford, NJ061564
Rathven, NJ444657
Rothes, NJ278492
St Andrew's-Lhanbryd and Urquhart, NJ256622
Speymouth, NJ337607

36. Presbytery of Abernethy
Abernethy, NJ007218:
Nethy Bridge, NJ003203
Alvie and Insh:
Alvie, NH864093
Insh, NH837053
Boat of Garten, Duthil and Kincardine:
Boat of Garten, NH941190
Duthil, NH908225
Kincardine, NH938155
Cromdale and Advie:
Cromdale, NJ067289
Advie, NJ127343
Dulnain Bridge, NH998249
Grantown-on-Spey, NJ032281
Kingussie, NH761007
Laggan, NN615943
Newtonmore, NN715993
Rothiemurchus and Aviemore:
Rothiemurchus, NH903108
Aviemore, NH896130

Tomintoul, Glenlivet and Inveraven:
Tomintoul, NJ169185
Inveraven, NJ183376

37. Presbytery of Inverness
Ardersier, NH781553
Auldearn and Dalmore, NH919556
Cawdor, NH844499
Croy and Dalcross, NH797498
Culloden: The Barn, NH719461
Daviot and Dunlichity:
Daviot, NH722394
Dunlichity, NH660330
Dores and Boleskine:
Dores, NH601350
Boleskine, NH507183
Inverness: Crown, NH671452
Inverness: Dalneigh and Bona:
Dalneigh, NH655450
Bona, NH595377
Inverness: East, NH666455
Inverness: Hilton, NH674436
Inverness: Inshes, NH688441
Inverness: Kinmylies, NH646446
Inverness: Ness Bank, NH665448
Inverness: Old High St Stephen's:
Old High, NH665455
St Stephen's, NH670447
Inverness: St Columba High, NH665453
Inverness: Trinity, NH661458
Kilmorack and Erchless:
Beauly, NH525465
Struy, NH402402
Cannich, NH336318
Kiltarlity, NH513413
Kirkhill, NH553454
Moy, Dalarossie and Tomatin:
Moy, NH772342
Dalarossie, NH767242
Tomatin, NH803290
Nairn: Old, NH879564
Nairn: St Ninian's, NH883563
Petty, NH767502
Urquhart and Glenmoriston, NH509294

38. Presbytery of Lochaber
Acharacle, NM674683
Ardgour, NN011642:
Kingairloch, NM862526
Ardnamurchan, NM488638
Duror, NM993553
Fort Augustus, NH377090
Fort William: Duncansburgh MacIntosh, NN104741
Glencoe: St Munda's, NN083578
Glengarry, NH304012:
Tomdoun, NH154011
Kilmallie, Achnacarry, NN181873:
Caol, NN106762
Corpach, NN092770
Kilmonivaig, NN212819
Kinlochleven, NN187621
Morvern, NM672452
Nether Lochaber, NN031614
North West Lochaber:
Arisaig, NM661866
Canna, NG277054
Eigg, NM481855
Mallaig: St Columba, NM676967
Strontian, NM817617

39. Presbytery of Ross
Alness, NH647693
Avoch, NH701552
Contin, NH457557:
Kinlochluichart, NH317622
Cromarty, NH786674
Dingwall: Castle Street, NH552588
Dingwall: St Clement's, NH548589
Fearn Abbey and Nigg:
Fearn Abbey, NH837773
Nigg, NH825736
Ferintosh, NH543556
Fodderty and Strathpeffer, NH482580
Fortrose and Rosemarkie:
Fortrose, NH728568
Rosemarkie, NH737576
Invergordon, NH707687
Killearnan, NH577494
Kilmuir and Logie Easter:
Kilmuir, NH758732
Logie Easter, NH779757
Kiltearn, NH607662
Knockbain, NH647530:
Kessock, NH655479
Lochbroom and Ullapool:
Lochbroom, NH177848
Ullapool, NH130942
Resolis and Urquhart, meets in Findon Hall, Culbokie
Rosskeen, NH658697
Tain, NH780820
Tarbat, NH917846
Urray and Kilchrist:
Urray, NH509524
Muir of Ord, NH528507

40. Presbytery of Sutherland
Altnaharra and Farr:
Altnaharra, NC568355
Farr, NC708622
Strathnaver, NC694439
Assynt and Stoer, NC093225
Clyne, NC905044
Creich, NH611917
Dornoch Cathedral, NH797897
Durness and Kinlochbervie:
Durness, NC404669
Kinlochbervie, NC221564
Eddrachillis, NC151443
Golspie, NC837003
Kildonan and Loth Helmsdale, ND025154
Kincardine Croick and Edderton:
Ardgay, NH595910
Croick, NH457915
Edderton, NH710847
Lairg, NC583065
Melness and Tongue:
Melness, NC586634
Tongue, NC591570
Rogart, Pitfure, NC715038:
St Callan's, NC739035
Rosehall, NC484013

41. Presbytery of Caithness
Bower, ND238622
Canisbay, ND343728
Dunnet, ND220712
Halkirk and Westerdale, ND131594
Keiss, ND348611
Olrig, ND191682
The North Coast Parish:
Halladale, NC893558

Reay, NC967648
Strathy, NC843653
The Parish of Latheron:
Lybster, ND248361
Dunbeath, ND157295
Thurso: St Peter's and St Andrew's, ND115683
Thurso: West, ND114681
Watten, ND243547
Wick: Pulteneytown and Thrumster:
Pulteneytown, ND365504
Thrumster, ND333447
Wick: St Fergus, ND362512

42. Presbytery of Lochcarron – Skye
Applecross, Lochcarron and Torridon:
Applecross, NG711417
Lochcarron, NG893391
Shieldaig, NG816542
Torridon, NG864572
Bracadale and Duirinish:
Bracadale, NG355387
Duirinish, NG251479
Gairloch and Dundonnell:
Gairloch, NG807756
Aultbea, NG875886
Dundonnell, NH019919
Glenelg and Kintail:
Glenelg, NG813193
Kintail, NG930213
Kilmuir and Stenscholl:
Kilmuir, NG389694
Stenscholl, NG489673
Lochalsh, NG761277:
Kirkton, NG829272
Plockton, NG801331
Stromeferry, NG863346
Portree, NG482436
Snizort, NG420517:
Arnisort, NG348532
Uig, NG398642
Strath and Sleat:
Broadford, NG642235
Elgol, NG523143
Isleornsay, NG699128
Kilmore, NG657069
Kyleakin, NG751263

43. Presbytery of Uist
Barra, NF670034
Benbecula, NF800519
Berneray and Lochmaddy:
Berneray, NF920819
Lochmaddy, NF918684
Carinish, NF811637
Kilmuir and Paible:
Kilmuir, NF727703
Sollas, NF802744
Manish-Scarista:
Manish, NG102892
Scaristabeg, NG007927
Leverburgh, NG020868
South Uist:
Daliburgh, NF754214
Howmore, NF758364
Tarbert, NG159998

44. Presbytery of Lewis
Barvas, NB360494
Carloway, NB206424
Cross Ness, NB506619
Kinloch:
Laxay, NB323220
Lemreway, NB380118
Knock, NB522336
Lochs-Crossbost, NB382255
Lochs-in-Bernera, NB159366
Stornoway: High, NB427330
Stornoway: Martin's Memorial, NB424327
Stornoway: St Columba, NB426330
Uig, NB087347

45. Presbytery of Orkney
Birsay, Harray and Sandwick, HY314179
East Mainland, HY503019
Eday, HY562328
Evie, HY368255
Firth, HY359138
Flotta, ND366931
Hoy and Walls, ND312908
Kirkwall: East, HY451110
Kirkwall: St Magnus Cathedral, HY449108
North Ronaldsay, congregation meets in community school, HY758532
Orphir, HY343059
Papa Westray, HY496516
Rendall, HY393206
Rousay, HY442278
Sanday, HY659408
Shapinsay, HY497173
South Ronaldsay and Burray, St Margaret's Hope, ND449934:
St Peter's Eastside, ND472908
Stenness, HY311125
Stromness, HY254090
Stronsay: Moncur Memorial, HY654252
Westray, HY457462

46. Presbytery of Shetland
Burra Isle, HU371330
Delting, Brae, HU359673:
Togon, HU404637
Mossbank, HU451753
Muckle Roe, HU342647
Dunrossness and St Ninian's:
Bigton, HU384213
Boddam, HU391151
Fair Isle, HZ206706
Fetlar, HU607905
Lerwick and Bressay:
Lerwick, HU478411
Gulberwick, HU443389
Bressay, HU493410
Nesting and Lunnasting:
Nesting, HU487578
Lunna, HU486690
Northmavine, Hillswick, HU282771:
North Roe, HU365895
Ollaberry, HU366806
Sandsting and Aithsting, HU345556
Sandwick, Cunningsburgh and Quarff:
Sandwick, HU432237
Cunningsburgh, HU430293
Quarff, HU429358
Tingwall:
Scalloway, HU401395
Veensgarth, HU419437
Weisdale, HU394526
Unst, Baltasound, HP614088:
Uyeasound, HP601011
Walls and Sandness:
Walls, HU240493

Mid Walls, HU220502
Sandness, HU195571
Papa Stour, HU177600
Foula, HT969378
Whalsay and Skerries:
Whalsay, HU555654
Skerries, HU680717
Yell:
Cullivoe, HP544021
Hamnavoe, HU494804
Mid Yell, HU515907
Sellafirth, HU517985

SECTION 9

Congregational Statistics 2010

CHURCH OF SCOTLAND
Comparative Statistics: 1970–2010

	2010	*2000*	*1990*	*1980*	*1970*
Communicants	445,646	607,714	786,787	953,933	1,154,211
Elders	36,519	43,661	46,651	48,669	49,807

NOTES ON CONGREGATIONAL STATISTICS

Com Number of communicants at 31 December 2010.

Eld Number of elders at 31 December 2010.

G Membership of the Guild including Young Woman's Group and others as recorded on the 2010 annual return submitted to the Guild Office.

In 10 Ordinary General Income for 2010. Ordinary General Income consists of members' offerings, contributions from congregational organisations, regular fund-raising events, income from investments, deposits and so on. This figure does not include extraordinary or special income, or income from special collections and fund-raising for other charities.

M&M Final amount allocated to congregations after allowing for Presbytery-approved amendments up to 31 December 2010, but before deducting stipend endowments and normal allowances given for stipend purposes in a vacancy.

–18 This figure shows 'the number of children and young people aged 17 years and under who are involved in the life of the congregation'.

(NB: Figures may not be available for new charges created or for congregations which have entered into readjustment late in 2010 or during 2011. Figures might also not be available for congregations which failed to submit the appropriate schedule.)

Congregation	Com	Eld	G	In 10	M&M	-18
1. Edinburgh						
Albany Deaf Church of Edinburgh	116	7	–	–	–	–
Balerno	708	61	47	114,081	71,569	60
Barclay Viewforth	333	34	–	144,997	99,970	39
Blackhall St Columba's	962	84	31	180,204	99,816	76
Bristo Memorial Craigmillar	113	5	15	50,451	19,928	64
Broughton St Mary's	243	30	–	71,988	41,865	75
Canongate	374	44	–	84,031	59,825	12
Carrick Knowe	444	52	73	58,917	37,294	219
Colinton	931	78	–	226,535	118,073	278
Colinton Mains	182	13	–	53,996	30,345	60
Corstorphine Craigsbank	553	31	–	95,030	57,278	54
Corstorphine Old	488	53	57	86,724	91,074	49
Corstorphine St Anne's	413	54	59	109,155	54,008	220
Corstorphine St Ninian's	816	74	50	160,444	89,513	55
Craigentinny St Christopher's	104	12	–	28,632	18,328	15
Craiglockhart	500	58	33	197,923	89,482	90
Craigmillar Park	246	15	24	84,306	55,772	21
Cramond	1,113	98	13	216,318	148,842	82
Currie	648	54	89	159,829	83,955	70
Dalmeny	113	13	–	15,791	18,373	8
Queensferry	685	51	56	85,010	48,946	116
Davidson's Mains	712	50	50	186,276	110,376	150
Dean	210	25	–	–	38,390	23
Drylaw	136	12	–	20,708	11,334	7
Duddingston	855	60	46	–	65,732	262
Fairmilehead	703	55	39	85,605	59,999	510
Gilmerton	–	–	–	–	–	15
Gorgie	232	30	–	86,701	52,838	47
Granton	275	18	–	–	30,938	34
Greenbank	871	92	47	249,027	134,792	70
Greenside	181	29	–	–	36,797	30
Greyfriars Tolbooth and Highland Kirk	358	41	14	–	70,942	20
High (St Giles')	529	39	–	278,065	133,584	5
Holyrood Abbey	222	24	–	140,348	80,861	92
Holy Trinity	234	29	–	121,733	58,449	41
Inverleith	304	33	–	69,127	53,993	15
Juniper Green	366	31	–	94,671	57,929	40
Kaimes Lockhart Memorial	42	6	–	–	11,470	3
Liberton	762	80	54	189,481	96,121	85
Kirkliston	305	34	50	88,582	49,159	25
Kirk o' Field	155	18	–	32,840	28,814	1
Leith North	324	44	–	57,261	58,556	157
Leith St Andrew's	353	31	–	85,608	59,053	172
Leith St Serf's	280	28	19	68,965	49,091	8
Leith South	460	69	–	120,407	67,004	120
Leith Wardie	555	68	30	139,736	72,742	103

Congregation	Com	Eld	G	In 10	M&M	–18
Liberton Northfield	263	12	26	46,682	33,437	25
London Road	281	32	24	51,939	31,289	10
Marchmont St Giles'	243	37	30	79,218	52,681	32
Mayfield Salisbury	597	65	–	236,030	139,919	55
Morningside	645	95	27	–	109,602	23
Morningside United	240	44	–	94,139	–	27
Muirhouse St Andrew's	54	8	–	12,163	473	76
Murrayfield	508	60	–	154,821	84,444	70
Newhaven	229	20	44	83,641	47,397	126
New Restalrig	183	14	16	–	62,442	38
Old Kirk	118	11	–	18,367	17,435	14
Palmerston Place	428	37	–	154,687	94,062	110
Pilrig St Paul's	273	19	28	41,838	35,424	31
Polwarth	227	27	17	61,921	56,417	67
Portobello Old	321	48	37	69,847	42,623	83
Portobello St James'	346	26	–	46,765	33,763	14
Portobello St Philip's Joppa	588	53	71	153,984	84,005	186
Priestfield	179	19	20	61,790	43,544	20
Ratho	208	19	12	45,138	27,264	20
Reid Memorial	331	21	–	90,559	59,665	20
Richmond Craigmillar	102	8	–	12,324	7,653	12
St Andrew's and St George's West	412	56	–	–	125,799	20
St Andrew's Clermiston	259	15	–	47,403	31,557	96
St Catherine's Argyle	274	28	–	148,235	77,074	185
St Colm's	115	14	25	–	21,519	19
St Cuthbert's	366	54	–	146,974	105,129	14
St David's Broomhouse	158	13	–	32,792	22,006	65
St John's Oxgangs	218	21	34	–	21,994	9
St Margaret's	387	35	19	48,517	33,577	89
St Martin's	102	11	–	19,622	4,300	55
St Michael's	366	29	–	–	32,816	13
St Nicholas' Sighthill	401	30	17	–	32,245	20
St Stephen's Comely Bank	385	19	–	141,180	62,351	105
Slateford Longstone	269	20	40	51,191	29,039	31
Stenhouse St Aidan's	94	10	–	26,271	18,576	4
Stockbridge	296	26	–	–	62,597	31
Tron Moredun	111	17	–	–	5,249	22
2. West Lothian						
Abercorn	75	10	8	12,111	12,218	2
Pardovan, Kingscavil and Winchburgh	279	29	13	59,827	28,060	60
Armadale	566	43	29	64,046	43,053	213
Avonbridge	95	8	–	14,188	6,545	4
Torphichen	264	19	–	42,301	24,356	56
Bathgate: Boghall	266	29	24	65,569	37,505	69
Bathgate: High	489	38	32	76,663	58,985	62
Bathgate: St John's	375	23	35	53,353	34,263	115
Blackburn and Seafield	445	29	–	73,167	35,176	90

Congregation	Com	Eld	G	In 10	M&M	–18
Blackridge	87	6	–	21,010	10,594	–
Harthill: St Andrew's	223	13	36	62,391	38,792	70
Breich Valley	217	11	27	29,989	20,990	4
Broxburn	410	34	44	76,414	40,635	178
Fauldhouse: St Andrew's	226	11	–	41,340	30,025	10
Kirknewton and East Calder	346	38	29	100,437	60,299	79
Kirk of Calder	612	47	28	76,692	45,605	60
Linlithgow: St Michael's	1,428	108	59	301,494	151,172	366
Linlithgow: St Ninian's Craigmailen	461	44	63	67,281	44,202	109
Livingston Ecumenical Parish	713	49	–	–	–	197
Livingston: Old	406	38	22	75,419	53,006	53
Polbeth Harwood	193	29	–	22,744	18,557	12
West Kirk of Calder	271	25	31	43,498	32,033	17
Strathbrock	337	39	22	93,714	64,138	101
Uphall: South	211	25	–	–	31,554	70
Whitburn: Brucefield	279	19	16	66,845	50,083	240
Whitburn: South	396	31	37	59,806	43,157	103
3. Lothian						
Aberlady	259	30	–	–	21,082	30
Gullane	404	33	32	67,024	37,022	24
Athelstaneford	210	16	–	24,851	11,134	16
Whitekirk and Tyninghame	150	14	–	–	24,011	–
Belhaven	686	36	58	72,459	41,011	50
Spott	110	7	–	10,963	6,198	6
Bilston	102	5	18	12,081	2,846	3
Glencorse	319	15	–	25,082	15,788	4
Roslin	263	9	–	29,133	18,566	12
Bolton and Saltoun	155	20	12	25,882	15,274	17
Humbie	84	9	–	17,787	10,343	6
Yester	200	18	12	23,549	14,541	–
Bonnyrigg	744	69	46	101,828	60,870	38
Cockenzie and Port Seton: Chalmers Memorial	222	37	34	–	42,954	25
Cockenzie and Port Seton: Old	419	14	12	42,375	19,593	30
Cockpen and Carrington	242	23	47	24,076	15,051	32
Lasswade and Rosewell	371	24	–	25,860	21,166	6
Dalkeith: St John's and King's Park	538	45	24	117,761	46,902	70
Dalkeith: St Nicholas' Buccleuch	405	29	–	57,553	28,329	10
Dirleton	233	17	–	31,535	30,163	10
North Berwick: Abbey	324	30	49	74,532	37,469	34
Dunbar	594	25	39	79,927	58,479	60
Dunglass	325	15	14	18,575	20,034	–
Garvald and Morham	44	10	–	–	8,174	15
Haddington: West	490	29	39	59,897	38,310	–
Gladsmuir	190	14	–	–	15,537	5
Longniddry	397	42	36	80,825	44,227	25
Gorebridge	442	17	–	85,541	48,972	50
Haddington: St Mary's	565	60	–	–	77,053	45

Congregation	Com	Eld	G	In 10	M&M	–18
Howgate	53	3	–	15,574	8,167	11
Penicuik: South	163	11	–	71,441	52,138	43
Loanhead	348	26	39	59,831	33,217	40
Musselburgh: Northesk	360	33	46	66,187	37,678	105
Musselburgh: St Andrew's High	334	33	26	50,689	33,863	12
Musselburgh: St Clement's and St Ninian's	246	25	9	33,945	19,904	–
Musselburgh: St Michael's Inveresk	449	40	20	–	39,970	20
Newbattle	536	32	24	61,292	40,480	240
Newton	145	9	14	11,111	11,103	–
North Berwick: St Andrew Blackadder	645	36	33	116,789	67,702	108
Ormiston	190	12	27	–	20,397	1
Pencaitland	260	11	–	–	32,382	30
Penicuik: North	586	37	–	90,332	51,892	92
Penicuik: St Mungo's	395	25	26	72,182	37,281	16
Prestonpans: Prestongrange	350	36	19	43,002	33,823	45
Tranent	254	16	28	53,337	28,740	34
Traprain	465	32	28	55,163	42,932	42
Tyne Valley Parish	375	35	–	66,977	47,169	40
4. Melrose and Peebles						
Ashkirk	60	5	9	9,890	3,273	11
Selkirk	530	18	–	64,820	41,599	13
Bowden and Melrose	929	51	38	116,032	82,366	39
Broughton, Glenholm and Kilbucho	160	12	28	17,407	10,413	–
Skirling	80	8	–	8,384	4,545	7
Stobo and Drumelzier	92	11	–	14,190	8,795	–
Tweedsmuir	40	6	–	8,553	3,327	7
Caddonfoot	218	14	–	–	6,904	13
Galashiels: Trinity	814	50	45	52,529	45,110	15
Carlops	64	13	–	19,769	5,984	–
Kirkurd and Newlands	108	11	20	16,765	11,680	–
West Linton: St Andrew's	230	17	–	36,576	18,560	–
Channelkirk and Lauder	447	31	30	56,640	30,220	16
Earlston	442	16	13	43,142	32,080	14
Eddleston	113	7	9	14,772	5,718	26
Peebles: Old	568	47	–	–	53,489	50
Ettrick and Yarrow	200	16	–	34,811	23,999	11
Galashiels: Old and St Paul's	301	22	31	62,133	39,234	35
Galashiels: St John's	243	14	–	56,494	27,136	96
Innerleithen, Traquair and Walkerburn	424	34	39	52,926	42,536	80
Lyne and Manor	115	11	–	27,213	15,949	12
Maxton and Mertoun	141	11	–	15,188	13,753	13
Newtown	156	11	–	11,638	6,375	–
St Boswells	241	29	29	36,709	23,415	40
Peebles: St Andrew's Leckie	643	33	–	96,267	55,390	53
Stow: St Mary of Wedale and Heriot	183	13	–	35,106	21,365	25

Congregation	Com	Eld	G	In 10	M&M	-18
5. Duns						
Ayton and Burnmouth	176	11	–	17,030	9,274	14
Foulden and Mordington	85	11	–	5,810	6,399	–
Grantshouse and Houndwood and Reston	108	9	14	9,571	9,432	3
Berwick-upon-Tweed: St Andrew's Wallace Green and Lowick	416	27	33	53,125	40,159	12
Bonkyl and Preston	82	6	–	7,585	4,950	–
Chirnside	176	9	19	22,997	15,689	–
Edrom: Allanton	74	7	–	5,824	4,724	4
Coldingham and St Abb's	88	8	–	34,416	19,950	3
Eyemouth	187	25	42	37,210	24,178	–
Coldstream	393	27	–	39,889	23,775	11
Eccles	73	11	16	8,217	5,899	3
Duns	520	26	40	50,324	32,750	22
Fogo and Swinton	121	4	–	9,115	8,175	–
Ladykirk	27	6	8	8,532	6,359	–
Leitholm	80	8	–	14,914	4,478	–
Whitsome	40	3	–	2,327	3,649	–
Gordon: St Michael's	69	7	–	–	7,265	7
Greenlaw	120	8	13	17,162	11,716	6
Legerwood	66	7	–	9,155	3,725	8
Westruther	43	7	16	6,809	3,366	14
Hutton and Fishwick and Paxton	64	8	11	12,609	6,786	2
Langton and Lammermuir Kirk	166	17	25	42,899	29,936	1
6. Jedburgh						
Ale and Teviot United	458	33	17	–	43,021	15
Cavers and Kirkton	137	10	–	10,537	8,677	–
Hawick: Trinity	798	29	54	45,560	26,740	22
Hawick: Burnfoot	115	15	11	–	15,646	126
Hawick: St Mary's and Old	519	26	33	40,167	25,117	114
Hawick: Teviot and Roberton	325	9	8	51,149	34,718	20
Hawick: Wilton	395	27	30	51,303	29,605	80
Teviothead	75	4	6	6,533	3,644	–
Hobkirk and Southdean	177	12	19	13,850	15,457	15
Ruberslaw	278	18	16	32,468	20,645	19
Jedburgh: Old and Trinity	738	20	41	84,887	46,171	3
Kelso Country Churches	220	21	17	24,626	31,185	–
Kelso: Old and Sprouston	578	37	–	51,564	33,102	8
Kelso: North and Ednam	1,242	78	46	123,231	68,246	95
Linton, Morebattle, Hownam and Yetholm	454	25	41	69,760	40,869	35
Oxnam	123	10	–	12,617	4,005	12
7. Annandale and Eskdale						
Annan: Old	392	43	43	71,316	44,882	37
Dornock	145	12	–	–	6,749	14
Annan: St Andrew's	704	45	69	64,327	37,672	105
Brydekirk	60	5	–	6,036	3,081	–

Congregation	Com	Eld	G	In 10	M&M	–18
Applegarth, Sibbaldbie and Johnstone	180	9	12	9,341	10,439	–
Lochmaben	500	23	43	60,437	31,385	19
Canonbie United	123	13	–	28,250	–	21
Liddesdale	150	13	23	37,210	25,835	4
Dalton	108	9	–	–	8,084	–
Hightae	86	5	13	10,504	5,678	22
St Mungo	87	12	13	12,457	9,117	–
Gretna: Old, Gretna: St Andrew's Half Morton and Kirkpatrick Fleming	382	25	29	–	24,742	50
Hoddam	60	4	–	7,333	6,629	–
Kirtle-Eaglesfield	81	10	16	11,921	6,598	–
Middlebie	83	10	13	7,520	4,588	–
Waterbeck	–	–	–	–	1,948	–
Kirkpatrick Juxta	153	10	–	14,012	9,258	3
Moffat: St Andrew's	454	39	28	69,842	48,819	45
Wamphray	55	7	–	9,235	2,590	7
Langholm Eskdalemuir Ewes and Westerkirk	524	31	52	50,573	34,814	34
Lockerbie: Dryfesdale, Hutton and Corrie	844	48	35	62,468	37,762	30
The Border Kirk	346	43	38	68,215	34,351	25
Tundergarth	51	8	9	9,771	3,180	–
8. Dumfries and Kirkcudbright						
Auchencairn and Rerrick	80	8	–	10,379	6,428	2
Buittle and Kelton	173	16	11	20,206	17,968	–
Balmaclellan and Kells	78	7	17	19,768	14,599	5
Carsphairn	99	10	–	10,403	4,574	6
Dalry	162	12	17	14,363	7,195	2
Balmaghie	91	7	8	11,510	8,443	–
Tarff and Twynholm	173	16	27	–	17,863	3
Borgue	48	5	10	4,854	4,049	5
Gatehouse of Fleet	292	22	22	–	30,731	13
Caerlaverock	155	10	–	9,925	5,978	8
Dumfries: St Mary's-Greyfriars	666	38	36	69,841	47,017	8
Castle Douglas	419	28	14	61,112	35,683	6
Closeburn	227	14	–	24,132	16,248	17
Colvend, Southwick and Kirkbean	303	21	23	78,107	48,425	–
Corsock and Kirkpatrick Durham	98	15	19	19,478	14,230	7
Crossmichael and Parton	168	11	16	–	12,288	12
Cummertrees	46	4	–	3,556	4,134	–
Mouswald	70	7	–	–	6,803	–
Ruthwell	92	6	12	–	8,691	–
Dalbeattie	585	38	45	55,631	32,737	28
Urr	204	11	–	–	12,563	9
Dumfries: Maxwelltown West	645	51	51	87,742	49,341	123
Dumfries: Northwest	461	23	17	34,822	31,740	62
Dumfries: St George's	553	49	36	108,507	56,799	65
Dumfries: St Michael's and South	879	48	34	77,300	53,672	122
Dumfries: Troqueer	288	28	34	96,461	60,299	49

Congregation	Com	Eld	G	In 10	M&M	–18
Dunscore	251	25	13	33,977	20,724	24
Glencairn and Moniaive	190	17	–	38,841	18,283	16
Durisdeer	156	6	19	24,019	14,207	8
Penpont, Keir and Tynron	173	9	–	19,818	19,671	30
Thornhill	218	12	15	24,945	18,479	–
Irongray, Lochrutton and Terregles	299	23	18	–	29,966	–
Kirkconnel	301	8	–	–	27,439	9
Kirkcudbright	589	24	–	63,908	50,809	60
Kirkgunzeon	55	7	–	8,348	2,903	1
Lochend and New Abbey	221	16	14	24,245	15,317	8
Kirkmahoe	339	17	12	–	16,534	9
Kirkmichael, Tinwald and Torthorwald	489	42	27	44,804	42,739	17
Sanquhar: St Bride's	456	27	20	44,189	24,313	34
9. Wigtown and Stranraer						
Ervie Kirkcolm	233	16	–	23,280	13,780	35
Leswalt	300	15	–	27,617	16,717	14
Glasserton and Isle of Whithorn	114	7	–	16,680	11,890	–
Whithorn: St Ninian's Priory	329	9	18	37,062	17,745	36
Inch	251	16	11	13,529	12,850	24
Stranraer: Town Kirk	584	46	–	80,407	53,185	64
Kirkcowan	145	10	–	28,293	18,945	–
Wigtown	198	15	13	34,014	21,730	17
Kirkinner	154	6	14	10,883	8,852	–
Sorbie	142	9	–	14,018	10,121	–
Kirkmabreck	158	12	18	17,036	11,416	10
Monigaff	376	26	–	34,116	22,757	12
Kirkmaiden	214	18	14	22,419	17,174	8
Stoneykirk	344	21	12	35,526	23,237	10
Mochrum	277	21	29	–	16,370	10
New Luce	98	8	–	10,201	6,827	8
Old Luce	153	19	30	32,980	23,401	30
Penninghame	483	23	28	66,798	41,105	18
Portpatrick	234	9	26	27,111	13,530	15
Stranraer: St Ninian's	418	20	22	42,679	25,399	25
Stranraer: High Kirk	593	41	28	–	44,176	60
10. Ayr						
Alloway	1,206	109	21	211,981	118,942	425
Annbank	284	20	22	39,028	23,430	7
Tarbolton	480	30	26	41,700	30,575	12
Auchinleck	353	19	35	–	25,764	24
Catrine	136	14	25	26,486	13,164	1
Ayr: Auld Kirk of Ayr	575	63	41	83,456	52,455	–
Ayr: Castlehill	653	41	52	98,119	58,628	210
Ayr: Newton Wallacetown	497	56	68	120,314	90,586	212
Ayr: St Andrew's	439	31	9	66,780	48,373	80
Ayr: St Columba	1,377	106	62	238,384	113,168	135

Congregation	Com	Eld	G	In 10	M&M	–18
Ayr: St James'	429	43	51	68,898	37,512	124
Ayr: St Leonard's	568	55	33	105,446	45,894	34
Dalrymple	253	17	–	26,997	14,454	–
Ayr: St Quivox	295	26	18	44,918	32,086	7
Ballantrae	252	21	38	32,916	26,812	19
St Colmon (Arnsheen Barrhill and Colmonell)	256	12	–	20,384	18,071	6
Barr	72	4	–	5,302	3,721	–
Dailly	159	10	13	14,036	11,832	5
Girvan: South	317	20	31	31,816	18,878	7
Coylton	324	–	–	44,938	16,593	–
Drongan: The Schaw Kirk	234	21	19	–	13,904	95
Craigie	124	9	–	12,244	7,768	12
Symington	357	21	24	52,901	32,047	10
Crosshill	189	14	22	18,484	11,480	12
Maybole	389	25	28	51,544	35,046	18
Dalmellington	277	29	61	–	28,516	90
Patna: Waterside	154	–	–	–	15,643	–
Dundonald	497	45	57	–	48,933	97
Fisherton	131	9	9	13,375	8,813	–
Kirkoswald	242	14	10	32,036	18,050	12
Girvan: North (Old and St Andrew's)	756	56	–	65,189	47,507	58
Kirkmichael	224	–	24	20,710	11,742	–
Straiton: St Cuthbert's	165	10	14	16,468	11,577	11
Lugar	166	11	15	13,742	9,143	26
Old Cumnock: Old	381	16	36	60,732	37,329	38
Mauchline	476	25	58	80,196	46,602	31
Sorn	156	14	14	22,984	13,511	10
Monkton and Prestwick: North	434	36	44	95,692	60,660	36
Muirkirk	192	16	–	26,994	18,273	6
Old Cumnock: Trinity	381	22	40	58,716	32,815	21
New Cumnock	522	35	41	80,796	35,507	78
Ochiltree	264	22	20	34,096	19,378	18
Stair	215	–	15	31,257	16,829	–
Prestwick: Kingcase	720	81	70	114,849	83,377	221
Prestwick: St Nicholas'	713	70	69	107,408	64,576	190
Prestwick: South	321	37	42	84,171	47,561	85
Troon: Old	1,023	–	–	128,843	77,576	–
Troon: Portland	636	51	32	119,256	72,409	34
Troon: St Meddan's	975	106	49	171,457	96,619	54
11. Irvine and Kilmarnock						
Caldwell	234	17	–	71,150	36,359	26
Dunlop	408	45	26	62,495	34,693	34
Crosshouse	317	28	20	–	25,675	22
Darvel	404	30	41	37,947	25,140	15
Dreghorn and Springside	582	55	33	70,605	45,266	40
Fenwick	351	18	28	66,592	40,583	25
Galston	703	62	67	100,348	69,879	97

Congregation	Com	Eld	G	In 10	M&M	–18
Hurlford	430	22	33	60,360	36,403	18
Irvine: Fullarton	435	44	50	105,005	59,879	165
Irvine: Girdle Toll	182	19	25	–	21,787	112
Irvine: Mure	385	28	24	70,409	46,736	64
Irvine: Old	454	27	20	–	53,061	9
Irvine: Relief Bourtreehill	248	23	33	48,591	29,266	12
Irvine: St Andrew's	290	17	23	–	35,244	–
Kilmarnock: Henderson	523	58	51	106,572	68,859	16
Kilmarnock: Laigh West High	1,228	87	87	155,228	110,919	159
Kilmarnock: Old High Kirk	166	13	15	33,182	28,343	13
Kilmarnock: Riccarton	296	30	23	66,707	40,238	69
Kilmarnock: St Andrew's and St Marnock's	1,015	85	55	169,979	98,145	487
Kilmarnock: St John's Onthank	268	22	25	38,131	28,807	109
Kilmarnock: St Kentigern's	289	25	–	52,330	33,548	146
Kilmarnock: St Ninian's Bellfield	211	14	18	30,585	18,620	26
Kilmarnock: Shortlees	101	9	–	23,647	16,947	–
Kilmaurs: St Maur's Glencairn	328	18	24	47,349	29,459	25
Newmilns: Loudoun	312	5	–	–	48,355	33
Stewarton: John Knox	277	36	22	79,392	42,061	45
Stewarton: St Columba's	474	42	33	74,312	45,290	36
12. Ardrossan						
Ardrossan: Barony St John's	289	29	31	50,073	27,433	12
Ardrossan: Park	426	40	44	61,978	36,032	150
Beith: High	698	66	21	70,084	36,071	21
Beith: Trinity	231	–	18	48,360	35,168	–
Brodick	149	18	–	53,352	25,034	52
Corrie	64	6	–	21,169	8,391	5
Lochranza and Pirnmill	66	10	9	20,838	9,488	9
Shiskine	69	10	14	28,023	10,498	17
Cumbrae	279	27	52	48,546	32,123	70
Dalry: St Margaret's	732	58	34	114,046	63,003	125
Dalry: Trinity	227	16	42	87,194	45,780	40
Fairlie	251	29	41	74,066	42,247	25
Kilbirnie: Auld Kirk	379	41	15	48,908	27,221	12
Kilbirnie: St Columba's	578	35	25	56,589	38,680	56
Kilmory	42	8	–	13,502	4,622	7
Lamlash	114	15	24	31,294	19,230	11
Kilwinning: Mansefield Trinity	305	19	38	41,896	20,721	–
Kilwinning: Old	639	44	56	102,557	59,129	26
Largs: Clark Memorial	868	93	47	148,639	89,323	53
Largs: St Columba's	432	45	58	85,130	57,993	30
Largs: St John's	838	45	89	154,326	90,970	79
Saltcoats: New Trinity	281	45	18	51,362	37,284	13
Saltcoats: North	327	28	37	53,110	35,042	86
Saltcoats: St Cuthbert's	372	32	15	84,724	53,919	120
Stevenston: Ardeer	286	28	30	41,289	26,346	122
Stevenston: Livingstone	343	41	31	55,980	29,335	14

Congregation	Com	Eld	G	In 10	M&M	–18
Stevenston: High	259	22	39	–	52,332	25
West Kilbride	779	56	47	130,718	82,759	45
Whiting Bay and Kildonan	105	8	–	50,440	24,794	22
13. Lanark						
Biggar	598	32	40	91,320	47,542	30
Black Mount	68	9	15	12,682	8,801	–
Culter	87	7	–	8,691	5,228	–
Libberton and Quothquan	86	13	–	15,050	3,879	12
Cairngryffe	171	14	21	23,437	20,302	15
Symington	210	20	17	32,451	21,021	9
Carluke: Kirkton	803	–	22	110,464	63,849	–
Carluke: St Andrew's	301	13	22	50,272	29,653	44
Carluke: St John's	762	41	35	94,300	49,491	41
Carnwath	294	–	22	39,259	27,188	–
Carstairs and Carstairs Junction	296	27	28	56,137	25,424	90
Coalburn	144	7	20	18,567	8,236	15
Lesmahagow: Old	462	25	25	70,323	38,940	42
Crossford	182	9	–	11,691	17,117	18
Kirkfieldbank	89	9	18	15,990	9,629	–
Forth: St Paul's	368	27	51	72,025	33,056	30
Glencaple	192	11	24	22,423	18,783	9
Lowther	36	4	–	4,510	2,533	–
Kirkmuirhill	317	–	48	116,022	69,914	–
Lanark: Greyfriars	610	41	41	89,798	51,425	185
Lanark: St Nicholas'	546	50	32	–	55,411	105
Law	174	–	34	–	20,698	–
Lesmahagow: Abbeygreen	227	16	–	103,190	45,679	179
The Douglas Valley Church	368	38	41	56,167	26,968	10
14. Greenock and Paisley						
Barrhead: Arthurlie	271	31	32	79,047	54,047	50
Barrhead: Bourock	464	42	50	93,728	52,981	259
Barrhead: South and Levern	414	32	21	83,807	46,402	150
Bishopton	675	52	–	107,084	58,096	126
Bridge of Weir: Freeland	414	55	–	102,040	65,011	70
Bridge of Weir: St Machar's Ranfurly	443	45	30	103,162	56,360	25
Elderslie Kirk	539	60	60	123,763	67,068	213
Erskine	330	32	81	106,096	57,420	250
Gourock: Old Gourock and Ashton	767	59	33	–	79,031	230
Gourock: St John's	599	69	16	110,301	59,586	330
Greenock: Ardgowan	337	43	34	–	49,982	200
Greenock: East End	57	–	–	12,189	–	9
Greenock: Finnart St Paul's	264	24	–	61,670	41,654	–
Greenock: Mount Kirk	323	38	–	59,913	42,413	160
Greenock: Old West Kirk	347	27	–	71,484	48,961	8
Greenock: St Margaret's	161	22	14	23,032	14,178	12
Greenock: St Ninian's	228	22	–	24,769	15,212	93

Congregation	Com	Eld	G	In 10	M&M	–18
Greenock: Wellpark Mid Kirk	596	43	24	–	56,953	80
Greenock: Westburn	890	104	45	121,516	90,087	186
Houston and Killellan	690	61	69	151,511	87,824	250
Howwood	201	11	24	49,849	29,825	20
Inchinnan	369	38	29	50,886	42,939	120
Inverkip	405	26	29	52,559	34,594	24
Johnstone: High	250	32	44	89,544	52,355	120
Johnstone: St Andrew's Trinity	239	30	34	44,424	33,018	117
Johnstone: St Paul's	474	78	–	78,028	48,476	133
Kilbarchan: East	366	41	29	74,195	44,489	70
Kilbarchan: West	437	48	30	90,531	62,732	46
Kilmacolm: Old	504	51	–	120,976	68,671	40
Kilmacolm: St Columba	546	34	16	96,064	62,439	42
Langbank	145	13	–	32,156	20,082	17
Linwood	418	31	20	–	38,623	15
Lochwinnoch	154	15	–	–	27,063	185
Neilston	621	43	20	–	56,096	–
Paisley: Abbey	747	46	–	–	87,338	126
Paisley: Castlehead	224	25	16	36,596	31,220	12
Paisley: Glenburn	261	19	–	–	27,687	33
Paisley: Laigh Kirk	367	52	59	72,251	53,707	44
Paisley: Lylesland	394	52	37	97,266	49,426	45
Paisley: Martyrs' Sandyford	612	75	21	122,807	54,255	105
Paisley: Oakshaw Trinity	571	96	47	135,000	–	37
Paisley: St Columba Foxbar	205	28	22	32,627	22,786	140
Paisley: St James'	358	32	–	68,596	35,159	9
Paisley: St Luke's	252	29	–	–	35,491	13
Paisley: St Mark's Oldhall	556	45	79	108,926	65,918	62
Paisley: St Ninian's Ferguslie	54	–	–	11,210	–	–
Paisley: Sherwood Greenlaw	662	85	45	123,107	75,266	200
Paisley: Wallneuk North	427	39	–	57,544	46,257	10
Port Glasgow: Hamilton Bardrainney	210	19	18	39,561	26,059	6
Port Glasgow: St Andrew's	582	62	40	–	45,722	370
Port Glasgow: St Martin's	174	18	–	–	11,234	29
Renfrew: North	616	68	33	103,831	65,584	135
Renfrew: Old	497	30	38	73,913	47,145	184
Renfrew: Trinity	326	31	36	75,808	52,306	17
Skelmorlie and Wemyss Bay	373	34	–	83,477	45,082	24
16. Glasgow						
Banton	76	10	–	19,410	9,019	10
Twechar	70	12	–	17,775	7,088	12
Bishopbriggs: Kenmure	288	31	51	86,275	50,484	140
Bishopbriggs: Springfield	695	44	97	118,511	65,032	150
Broom	625	59	36	138,344	83,096	44
Burnside Blairbeth	659	51	97	283,302	135,380	226
Busby	298	41	30	69,755	38,095	50
Cadder	812	84	59	143,358	88,106	200

Congregation	Com	Eld	G	In 10	M&M	–18
Cambuslang: Flemington Hallside	308	15	25	46,574	23,341	40
Cambuslang Parish Church	860	72	45	163,611	114,436	146
Campsie	177	16	17	58,719	34,396	90
Chryston	629	35	18	204,509	94,962	89
Eaglesham	603	50	69	125,170	68,314	100
Fernhill and Cathkin	293	25	37	50,220	28,417	64
Gartcosh	134	9	–	18,934	10,396	80
Glenboig	122	8	12	–	6,645	7
Giffnock: Orchardhill	465	55	23	147,059	91,757	263
Giffnock: South	786	92	53	–	104,510	80
Giffnock: The Park	283	26	–	69,039	41,844	90
Greenbank	959	78	52	226,751	115,173	260
Kilsyth: Anderson	365	21	40	73,240	55,226	120
Kilsyth: Burns and Old	434	31	45	65,532	50,226	81
Kirkintilloch: Hillhead	115	9	13	15,918	8,241	30
Kirkintilloch: St Columba's	493	45	47	87,296	52,997	90
Kirkintilloch: St David's Memorial Park	669	55	33	–	75,267	153
Kirkintilloch: St Mary's	752	58	57	138,777	81,974	–
Lenzie: Old	476	43	–	115,269	63,077	29
Lenzie: Union	726	71	79	177,799	92,534	258
Maxwell Mearns Castle	280	34	–	153,078	87,941	86
Mearns	851	54	–	–	103,338	65
Milton of Campsie	353	37	56	79,003	37,774	108
Netherlee	753	75	40	195,718	108,913	297
Newton Mearns	577	51	20	116,814	70,682	124
Rutherglen: Old	346	29	–	61,537	34,998	32
Rutherglen: Stonelaw	388	44	33	137,750	71,257	48
Rutherglen: West and Wardlawhill	522	51	59	102,451	64,786	23
Stamperland	392	31	24	67,426	43,371	236
Stepps	354	27	–	–	32,587	120
Thornliebank	187	11	42	49,743	31,669	40
Torrance	311	13	–	96,051	43,418	125
Williamwood	457	72	37	125,701	72,586	329
Glasgow: Anderston Kelvingrove	65	10	12	12,958	15,777	18
Glasgow: Baillieston Mure Memorial	473	29	95	94,377	50,858	205
Glasgow: Baillieston St Andrew's	340	24	41	60,668	39,818	162
Glasgow: Balshagray Victoria Park	229	35	22	86,936	59,939	62
Glasgow: Barlanark Greyfriars	125	21	15	43,663	23,219	212
Glasgow: Blawarthill	182	23	35	–	17,711	117
Glasgow: Bridgeton St Francis in the East	92	17	11	37,093	21,001	8
Glasgow: Broomhill	542	60	49	144,669	80,754	268
Glasgow: Calton Parkhead	89	12	–	19,336	12,006	58
Glasgow: Cardonald	426	43	67	121,926	72,147	264
Glasgow: Carmunnock	323	27	33	54,075	36,217	20
Glasgow: Carmyle	104	6	16	29,978	13,886	20
Glasgow: Kenmuir Mount Vernon	139	10	28	56,519	34,976	80
Glasgow: Carnwadric	146	16	21	37,006	18,834	50
Glasgow: Castlemilk East	132	9	7	20,282	19,259	–

Congregation	Com	Eld	G	In 10	M&M	–18
Glasgow: Castlemilk West	94	18	–	23,544	13,164	30
Glasgow: Cathcart Old	268	47	45	93,389	56,770	541
Glasgow: Cathcart Trinity	492	56	59	121,576	108,087	96
Glasgow: Cathedral (High or St Mungo's)	371	59	–	94,092	62,223	15
Glasgow: Clincarthill	315	33	55	107,802	79,608	128
Glasgow: Colston Milton	90	–	–	–	15,275	–
Glasgow: Colston Wellpark	108	13	–	23,677	22,703	82
Glasgow: Cranhill	41	7	–	–	3,285	63
Glasgow: Croftfoot	295	45	37	–	47,572	64
Glasgow: Dennistoun New	314	37	27	84,189	57,938	97
Glasgow: Drumchapel Drumry St Mary's	55	12	–	6,583	2,433	15
Glasgow: Drumchapel St Andrew's	180	43	–	44,518	35,032	20
Glasgow: Drumchapel St Mark's	71	–	–	10,542	1,664	–
Glasgow: Easterhouse St George's and St Peter's	59	10	–	–	159	50
Glasgow: Eastwood	270	38	30	77,421	54,733	60
Glasgow: Gairbraid	180	15	15	30,774	20,549	15
Glasgow: Gallowgate	80	15	7	25,391	11,815	66
Glasgow: Gardner Street	37	–	–	–	23,927	2
Glasgow: Garthamlock and Craigend East	87	14	–	–	2,805	85
Glasgow: Gorbals	90	15	–	26,082	15,881	16
Glasgow: Govan Old	266	56	43	–	46,632	127
Glasgow: Govanhill Trinity	92	16	–	–	16,883	5
Glasgow: High Carntyne	306	27	65	59,815	46,280	103
Glasgow: Hillington Park	312	36	37	72,446	42,001	155
Glasgow: Househillwood St Christopher's	124	–	15	12,126	9,310	–
Glasgow: Hyndland	262	34	32	94,022	62,429	30
Glasgow: Ibrox	155	20	24	50,089	29,879	91
Glasgow: John Ross Memorial (for Deaf People)	59	6	–	–	–	–
Glasgow: Jordanhill	439	73	30	180,412	104,212	135
Glasgow: Kelvin Stevenson Memorial	142	26	21	37,321	26,996	103
Glasgow: Kelvinside Hillhead	169	27	–	72,516	45,335	102
Glasgow: King's Park	712	77	42	160,129	85,177	169
Glasgow: Kinning Park	138	14	14	32,344	21,629	10
Glasgow: Knightswood St Margaret's	257	29	33	51,845	36,530	96
Glasgow: Langside	195	44	20	66,863	42,638	25
Glasgow: Lansdowne	89	12	–	8,448	6,855	5
Glasgow: Lochwood	68	2	8	–	6,041	81
Glasgow: Martyrs', The	55	4	–	11,783	14,192	75
Glasgow: Maryhill	172	18	18	36,663	23,181	114
Glasgow: Merrylea	350	–	38	86,630	52,527	185
Glasgow: Mosspark	158	32	39	51,546	35,258	66
Glasgow: Newlands South	532	68	24	166,706	97,127	30
Glasgow: Partick South	161	23	–	–	37,986	130
Glasgow: Partick Trinity	183	–	–	78,666	34,433	–
Glasgow: Penilee St Andrew's	133	23	–	42,224	22,792	136
Glasgow: Pollokshaws	151	21	26	41,478	24,930	54
Glasgow: Pollokshields	228	35	37	–	62,748	27
Glasgow: Possilpark	167	21	17	26,264	18,245	11

Congregation	Com	Eld	G	In 10	M&M	–18
Glasgow: Priesthill and Nitshill	115	17	–	34,056	21,323	8
Glasgow: Queen's Park	208	26	34	95,449	50,292	–
Glasgow: Renfield St Stephen's	160	–	40	–	48,014	–
Glasgow: Robroyston	67	–	–	23,715	–	–
Glasgow: Ruchazie	60	10	–	5,501	6,930	87
Glasgow: Ruchill Kelvinside	117	21	14	71,481	56,512	27
Glasgow: St Andrew's East	77	18	22	35,014	20,714	40
Glasgow: St Columba	136	–	12	31,382	26,266	–
Glasgow: St David's Knightswood	349	30	37	91,255	58,285	26
Glasgow: St Enoch's Hogganfield	157	14	30	32,752	21,715	8
Glasgow: St George's Tron	396	27	–	25,078	119,072	68
Glasgow: St James' (Pollok)	151	25	20	49,385	32,455	62
Glasgow: St John's Renfield	376	46	–	159,818	88,463	220
Glasgow: St Margaret's Tollcross Park	132	5	–	–	17,222	14
Glasgow: St Nicholas' Cardonald	312	30	11	56,629	36,591	327
Glasgow: St Paul's	63	6	–	13,075	4,061	112
Glasgow: St Rollox	103	12	–	39,093	16,396	30
Glasgow: Sandyford Henderson Memorial	214	23	16	203,901	76,698	50
Glasgow: Sandyhills	313	29	51	–	41,993	32
Glasgow: Scotstoun	200	11	–	60,679	46,727	25
Glasgow: Shawlands	305	25	32	98,931	61,307	55
Glasgow: Sherbrooke St Gilbert's	381	53	–	130,446	73,770	140
Glasgow: Shettleston New	246	35	33	72,520	46,124	84
Glasgow: Shettleston Old	225	26	19	52,656	24,104	50
Glasgow: South Carntyne	69	8	–	29,094	16,850	33
Glasgow: South Shawlands	192	29	–	72,370	41,866	127
Glasgow: Springburn	243	34	27	67,315	45,867	130
Glasgow: Temple Anniesland	342	28	59	93,774	58,793	90
Glasgow: Toryglen	108	13	–	17,829	11,217	10
Glasgow: Trinity Possil and Henry Drummond	93	7	–	56,650	35,162	16
Glasgow: Tron St Mary's	132	19	–	40,642	23,770	196
Glasgow: Victoria Tollcross	124	14	18	–	13,974	105
Glasgow: Wallacewell	126	–	–	–	16,931	–
Glasgow: Wellington	239	24	–	87,702	56,074	30
Glasgow: Whiteinch	43	7	–	–	24,451	130
Glasgow: Yoker	97	11	–	22,219	19,161	7
17. Hamilton						
Airdrie: Broomknoll	284	34	34	51,926	37,873	156
Calderbank	125	9	19	20,293	12,316	2
Airdrie: Clarkston	374	35	22	59,256	34,838	206
Airdrie: Flowerhill	636	38	18	115,059	73,047	285
Airdrie: High	345	33	–	62,012	35,606	138
Airdrie: Jackson	340	51	21	78,881	37,634	235
Airdrie: New Monkland	314	23	20	56,221	24,990	121
Greengairs	134	7	–	21,713	12,769	–
Airdrie: St Columba's	234	6	–	–	11,879	57
Airdrie: The New Wellwynd	722	85	–	129,337	63,493	196

Congregation	Com	Eld	G	In 10	M&M	–18
Bargeddie	130	9	–	–	38,256	13
Bellshill: Macdonald Memorial	265	19	20	43,816	26,245	12
Bellshill: Orbiston	212	17	14	15,521	8,676	3
Bellshill: West	573	55	35	71,620	38,823	30
Blantyre: Livingstone Memorial	262	25	22	59,201	32,306	140
Blantyre: Old	318	17	33	63,144	31,545	31
Blantyre: St Andrew's	250	24	25	60,621	37,684	55
Bothwell	498	52	41	106,898	64,434	134
Caldercruix and Longriggend	223	–	–	38,476	32,257	–
Carfin	43	5	–	7,122	3,973	5
Newarthill	402	28	21	51,051	31,559	159
Chapelhall	273	25	39	42,879	25,356	73
Chapelton	181	14	20	–	16,480	27
Strathaven: Rankin	549	60	43	78,701	47,771	163
Cleland	199	16	–	30,700	15,352	–
Coatbridge: Blairhill Dundyvan	300	24	30	63,512	35,437	149
Coatbridge: Calder	354	26	33	49,773	34,883	78
Coatbridge: Middle	376	37	31	61,201	27,655	164
Coatbridge: St Andrew's	787	74	31	119,584	74,883	233
Coatbridge: Old Monkland	292	20	21	45,139	34,972	75
Coatbridge: Townhead	169	17	32	50,190	29,324	111
Dalserf	229	21	23	78,042	50,316	60
East Kilbride: Claremont	681	73	29	–	60,948	230
East Kilbride: Greenhills	176	15	33	32,475	19,018	322
East Kilbride: Moncreiff	727	66	60	115,160	66,978	250
East Kilbride: Mossneuk	261	17	–	35,214	25,901	220
East Kilbride: Old	703	65	44	111,038	56,746	122
East Kilbride: South	352	43	34	79,433	54,041	15
East Kilbride: Stewartfield	–	–	–	14,466	–	–
East Kilbride: West	451	38	52	62,204	40,136	–
East Kilbride: Westwood	591	48	113	83,180	46,627	142
Glasford	127	8	24	20,476	11,770	–
Strathaven: East	280	31	46	53,901	28,415	44
Hamilton: Burnbank	87	10	–	25,047	15,904	6
Hamilton: North	124	29	21	36,477	21,221	12
Hamilton: Cadzow	533	61	63	130,498	64,658	140
Hamilton: Gilmour and Whitehill	155	27	–	30,253	20,696	95
Hamilton: Hillhouse	391	52	33	73,878	32,747	44
Hamilton: Old	500	55	30	–	71,687	103
Hamilton: St Andrew's	207	34	28	58,779	37,285	129
Hamilton: St John's	522	63	59	117,106	67,276	256
Hamilton: South	258	30	32	53,917	32,207	34
Quarter	102	13	24	26,480	12,643	18
Hamilton: Trinity	304	28	–	56,780	23,900	102
Hamilton: West	294	26	–	75,772	41,770	24
Holytown	189	20	30	47,749	26,138	72
New Stevenston: Wrangholm Kirk	111	12	19	50,918	22,229	58
Kirk o' Shotts	170	11	11	28,352	18,777	20

Congregation	Com	Eld	G	In 10	M&M	–18
Larkhall: Chalmers	128	12	30	–	20,203	9
Larkhall: St Machan's	470	50	40	104,577	59,302	101
Larkhall: Trinity	205	19	30	49,253	29,540	127
Motherwell: Crosshill	465	55	60	85,270	45,768	35
Motherwell: Dalziel St Andrew's	543	67	49	135,421	75,196	200
Motherwell: North	205	23	–	50,071	29,977	180
Motherwell: St Margaret's	357	19	19	–	23,785	22
Motherwell: St Mary's	876	101	72	120,867	65,187	265
Motherwell: South	444	71	113	110,589	63,316	35
Newmains: Bonkle	149	20	–	37,400	21,785	18
Newmains: Coltness Memorial	221	28	20	–	36,079	76
Overtown	283	29	50	46,692	25,982	217
Shotts: Calderhead Erskine	499	35	34	–	47,539	16
Stonehouse: St Ninian's	372	36	30	81,035	46,100	50
Strathaven: Avendale Old and Drumclog	649	55	56	–	76,129	62
Strathaven: West	198	19	21	32,602	24,751	32
Uddingston: Burnhead	262	20	11	46,156	17,419	71
Uddingston: Old	654	69	60	125,803	69,892	125
Uddingston: Viewpark	444	63	38	95,685	49,195	220
Wishaw: Cambusnethan North	501	34	–	77,264	47,214	150
Wishaw: Cambusnethan Old and Morningside	501	42	26	76,873	44,980	210
Wishaw: Craigneuk and Belhaven	169	29	27	42,803	30,350	24
Wishaw: Old	276	37	–	42,641	28,890	75
Wishaw: St Mark's	392	35	30	70,923	44,448	125
Wishaw: South Wishaw	513	42	40	93,393	57,603	86
18. Dumbarton						
Alexandria	342	40	22	71,093	42,953	40
Arrochar	65	11	17	19,449	8,753	56
Luss	107	15	20	32,799	16,362	640
Baldernock	194	19	–	37,708	25,747	15
Bearsden: Baljaffray	354	32	61	72,690	38,377	57
Bearsden: Cross	934	103	41	177,106	102,720	85
Bearsden: Killermont	662	63	62	154,626	85,039	200
Bearsden: New Kilpatrick	1,577	137	124	–	156,061	140
Bearsden: Westerton Fairlie Memorial	429	42	44	89,661	45,874	83
Bonhill	863	52	–	67,629	48,902	3
Cardross	419	–	27	92,324	55,407	–
Clydebank: Abbotsford	296	18	–	50,275	34,171	46
Clydebank: Faifley	209	15	38	–	20,860	27
Clydebank: Kilbowie St Andrew's	282	18	26	46,811	29,077	91
Clydebank: Radnor Park	198	23	35	48,856	31,448	–
Clydebank: St Cuthbert's	126	15	24	17,312	15,272	10
Duntocher	266	32	26	47,985	35,329	–
Craigrownie	210	22	30	35,830	26,951	12
Rosneath: St Modan's	142	13	27	27,682	16,856	7
Dalmuir: Barclay	245	16	18	42,288	26,601	35
Dumbarton: Riverside	560	73	70	105,277	62,809	25

Congregation	Com	Eld	G	In 10	M&M	-18
Dumbarton: St Andrew's	139	27	–	33,440	18,943	6
Dumbarton: West Kirk	299	38	13	–	30,316	5
Garelochhead	177	14	–	59,888	32,672	55
Helensburgh: Park	422	40	20	76,298	45,464	25
Helensburgh: St Columba	519	50	29	93,274	56,516	43
Helensburgh: The West Kirk	563	54	39	146,317	71,690	45
Jamestown	356	23	20	–	35,060	12
Kilmaronock Gartocharn	263	–	–	23,159	19,195	–
Renton: Trinity	257	21	–	–	19,797	–
Milngavie: Cairns	519	45	–	159,367	76,263	23
Milngavie: St Luke's	395	36	28	77,342	40,804	50
Milngavie: St Paul's	1,014	89	93	221,762	117,575	126
Old Kilpatrick Bowling	286	22	28	42,701	38,203	103
Rhu and Shandon	281	27	41	–	51,362	12
19. Argyll						
Appin	89	14	20	11,472	9,325	20
Lismore	55	5	10	14,015	6,269	8
Ardchattan	124	–	8	23,256	11,404	–
Ardrishaig	151	22	26	33,226	22,474	21
South Knapdale	37	6	–	13,322	3,092	–
Campbeltown: Highland	430	30	25	55,588	34,304	12
Campbeltown: Lorne and Lowland	871	74	56	85,456	48,083	74
Coll	15	3	–	4,065	1,118	–
Connel	132	23	14	43,066	26,203	4
Colonsay and Oronsay	12	2	–	–	4,544	–
Craignish	50	7	–	8,862	5,346	–
Kilbrandon and Kilchattan	89	–	–	28,607	13,084	–
Kilninver and Kilmelford	62	5	–	–	5,837	12
Cumlodden, Lochfyneside and Lochgair	94	14	17	20,645	11,989	4
Dunoon: St John's	222	27	45	41,763	29,810	15
Sandbank	144	14	–	–	11,632	–
Dunoon: The High Kirk	351	35	39	–	34,546	514
Innellan	101	12	–	21,712	14,041	4
Toward	91	12	–	14,258	11,153	52
Gigha and Cara	36	7	–	8,202	4,447	14
Glassary, Kilmartin and Ford	110	15	–	19,745	15,868	6
North Knapdale	63	9	–	26,218	22,916	3
Glenaray and Inveraray	117	19	–	26,301	15,289	12
Glenorchy and Innishael	67	9	–	15,039	4,101	3
Strathfillan	44	5	–	8,665	4,375	3
Iona	19	7	–	4,768	3,095	5
Kilfinichen and Kilvickeon and the Ross of Mull	32	6	–	10,295	5,025	14
Jura	45	8	–	10,064	6,557	4
Kilarrow	81	12	–	26,013	20,585	20
Kildalton and Oa	110	17	–	40,385	18,939	22
Kilberry	10	2	–	1,690	559	–
Tarbert (Loch Fyne)	157	18	20	38,739	20,054	9

Congregation	Com	Eld	G	In 10	M&M	–18
Kilcalmonell	53	11	13	10,220	3,153	7
Killean and Kilchenzie	165	10	21	20,720	21,900	17
Kilchoman	88	10	–	13,953	18,233	7
Kilmeny	33	5	–	10,898	4,370	–
Portnahaven	22	5	12	4,789	1,903	–
Kilchrenan and Dalavich	27	5	7	8,240	8,452	–
Muckairn	135	19	11	28,615	12,600	18
Kilfinan	29	5	–	4,524	2,145	–
Kilmodan and Colintraive	112	12	–	18,001	10,812	15
Kyles	151	17	25	27,488	15,958	2
Kilmore and Oban	558	47	46	–	58,781	48
Kilmun (St Munn's)	100	9	21	16,703	10,121	–
Strone and Ardentinny	117	11	16	26,792	17,441	5
Kirn	325	29	–	72,309	41,074	26
Lochgilphead	217	–	21	31,358	18,499	–
Lochgoilhead and Kilmorich	93	11	–	25,166	19,659	1
Mull, Isle of, Kilninian and Kilmore	27	–	–	9,937	6,374	–
Salen and Ulva	38	–	–	10,565	5,224	–
Tobermory	68	–	–	16,444	10,939	–
Torosay and Kinlochspelvie	26	–	–	6,711	2,602	–
Rothesay: Trinity	411	34	28	55,884	36,422	51
Saddell and Carradale	207	14	27	–	18,611	8
Skipness	26	–	–	6,296	3,050	–
Southend	247	13	16	–	22,226	15
Strachur and Strachlachlan	98	17	19	30,715	25,067	8
The United Church of Bute	590	48	47	69,686	52,414	64
Tiree	93	14	20	27,885	12,654	5
22. Falkirk						
Airth	151	6	20	–	23,669	42
Blackbraes and Shieldhill	172	17	18	29,445	14,246	15
Muiravonside	201	21	–	35,705	21,452	10
Bo'ness: Old	413	38	22	66,182	39,683	53
Bo'ness: St Andrew's	521	27	–	85,801	45,558	110
Bonnybridge: St Helen's	351	20	28	56,490	32,579	40
Bothkennar and Carronshore	254	28	–	33,642	19,922	19
Brightons	701	40	60	–	75,404	246
Carriden	472	37	22	44,524	32,080	9
Cumbernauld: Abronhill	273	27	36	47,591	40,880	175
Cumbernauld: Condorrat	414	29	32	71,270	41,738	105
Cumbernauld: Kildrum	335	40	–	49,213	30,872	241
Cumbernauld: Old	388	44	–	66,344	45,675	115
Cumbernauld: St Mungo's	293	25	–	34,739	26,973	37
Denny: Dunipace	373	33	14	68,627	36,271	82
Denny: Old	427	42	26	–	40,485	100
Denny: Westpark	562	34	40	77,797	52,552	120
Falkirk: Bainsford	259	13	–	35,172	21,590	93
Falkirk: Camelon	346	–	25	76,104	51,649	–

Congregation	Com	Eld	G	In 10	M&M	–18
Falkirk: Erskine	435	42	34	80,944	45,162	35
Falkirk: Grahamston United	377	39	39	64,156	–	–
Falkirk: Laurieston	229	22	30	–	21,319	18
Redding and Westquarter	170	13	32	29,034	16,292	11
Falkirk: Old and St Modan's	518	58	27	–	67,182	105
Falkirk: St Andrew's West	530	37	–	108,157	62,211	85
Falkirk: St James'	249	18	9	39,061	19,504	51
Grangemouth: Abbotsgrange	572	60	29	57,515	46,013	121
Grangemouth: Kirk of the Holy Rood	512	49	–	61,874	39,299	53
Grangemouth: Zetland	815	67	68	107,807	68,471	201
Haggs	272	28	17	38,941	25,427	75
Larbert: East	667	49	50	105,123	57,745	219
Larbert: Old	489	35	18	94,738	55,059	250
Larbert: West	449	42	41	77,831	48,442	120
Polmont: Old	409	31	70	–	50,771	111
Slamannan	242	–	–	–	19,987	–
Stenhouse and Carron	417	39	25	–	43,907	12
23. Stirling						
Aberfoyle	120	10	28	–	14,096	19
Port of Menteith	61	9	–	14,009	5,340	3
Alloa: Ludgate	344	24	34	79,787	51,874	20
Alloa: St Mungo's	403	40	49	57,637	39,432	14
Alva	559	55	37	68,413	45,413	60
Balfron	164	–	24	–	42,947	–
Fintry	122	12	24	17,318	12,051	6
Balquhidder	82	3	–	15,162	15,672	6
Killin and Ardeonaig	110	8	9	21,365	16,382	12
Bannockburn: Allan	430	31	–	58,517	39,023	35
Bannockburn: Ladywell	422	22	–	–	19,856	10
Bridge of Allan	761	54	44	125,245	77,907	75
Buchanan	96	7	–	22,422	13,777	11
Drymen	264	22	–	63,265	34,714	38
Buchlyvie	222	15	16	24,669	17,911	9
Gartmore	70	8	–	16,174	13,320	7
Callander	625	45	47	110,300	73,774	76
Cambusbarron: The Bruce Memorial	342	21	–	–	26,114	57
Clackmannan	454	32	39	67,624	47,349	41
Cowie and Plean	212	10	8	–	15,963	–
Fallin	255	8	–	31,397	21,271	56
Dollar	431	36	57	86,403	61,075	19
Glendevon	43	3	–	5,761	2,455	–
Muckhart	123	7	–	20,791	9,128	10
Dunblane: Cathedral	923	88	58	237,658	123,420	333
Dunblane: St Blane's	370	41	28	98,294	58,283	28
Gargunnock	158	14	–	23,123	16,066	14
Kilmadock	96	10	–	11,885	7,784	–
Kincardine-in-Menteith	78	8	–	12,312	7,440	20

Congregation	Com	Eld	G	In 10	M&M	-18
Killearn	433	36	37	82,639	54,710	26
Kippen	263	19	21	31,439	24,628	–
Norrieston	127	12	14	16,007	12,175	2
Lecropt	222	16	–	52,848	26,757	28
Logie	568	58	38	87,830	57,093	36
Menstrie	383	28	25	63,230	41,187	18
Sauchie and Coalsnaughton	720	34	13	54,516	40,936	10
Stirling: Allan Park South	201	41	–	39,290	28,010	21
Stirling: Church of the Holy Rude	198	28	–	47,350	29,579	–
Stirling: Viewfield Erskine	368	20	33	40,952	33,452	18
Stirling: North	502	36	25	74,895	41,395	58
Stirling: St Columba's	533	59	–	96,821	58,811	23
Stirling: St Mark's	234	9	–	29,472	20,966	6
Stirling: St Ninian's Old	744	51	–	80,933	49,543	65
Strathblane	192	25	43	78,749	43,836	12
Tillicoultry	746	65	40	89,881	56,149	90
Tullibody: St Serf's	431	17	25	–	40,903	60
24. Dunfermline						
Aberdour: St Fillan's	406	28	–	74,592	47,285	76
Beath and Cowdenbeath: North	223	22	17	54,335	28,035	24
Cairneyhill	110	17	–	24,278	13,438	12
Limekilns	306	50	–	58,743	45,170	15
Carnock and Oakley	214	21	17	49,838	32,581	14
Cowdenbeath: Trinity	410	28	14	61,639	34,720	110
Culross and Torryburn	258	20	–	50,877	29,416	19
Dalgety	576	36	29	102,807	69,005	86
Dunfermline: Abbey	670	76	–	129,672	79,522	200
Dunfermline: Gillespie Memorial	314	73	20	106,634	67,507	40
Dunfermline: North	192	15	–	–	21,647	7
Dunfermline: St Andrew's Erskine	200	27	25	39,648	26,878	20
Dunfermline: St Leonard's	386	40	29	68,680	41,008	44
Dunfermline: St Margaret's	385	51	21	64,715	32,480	–
Dunfermline: St Ninian's	280	27	37	41,508	24,136	64
Dunfermline: St Paul's East	–	–	–	9,593	–	45
Dunfermline: Townhill and Kingseat	358	32	32	66,479	38,115	30
Inverkeithing	343	36	–	53,814	37,428	101
North Queensferry	65	8	–	19,888	9,627	24
Kelty	314	31	44	67,877	41,587	8
Lochgelly and Benarty: St Serf's	465	43	–	56,660	41,298	22
Rosyth	260	25	–	34,791	22,896	35
Saline and Blairingone	158	14	16	37,687	31,796	19
Tulliallan and Kincardine	484	32	47	51,517	34,724	12
25. Kirkcaldy						
Auchterderran: St Fothad's	287	25	12	35,568	27,381	15
Kinglassie	161	12	–	–	12,449	9
Auchtertool	72	7	–	9,674	3,683	8

Congregation	Com	Eld	G	In 10	M&M	-18
Kirkcaldy: Linktown	300	37	35	55,401	34,856	30
Buckhaven and Wemyss	301	32	30	48,313	33,046	14
Burntisland	488	39	20	49,164	44,732	25
Dysart	326	33	17	52,614	31,092	24
Glenrothes: Christ's Kirk	263	20	43	42,425	26,014	12
Glenrothes: St Columba's	523	33	9	56,573	33,131	31
Glenrothes: St Margaret's	327	27	42	61,911	36,890	65
Glenrothes: St Ninian's	281	40	14	61,770	37,231	16
Innerleven: East	114	7	12	–	15,104	65
Kennoway, Windygates and Balgonie: St Kenneth's	668	47	72	73,519	49,307	40
Kinghorn	386	25	–	72,182	45,334	52
Kirkcaldy: Abbotshall	562	48	–	77,273	47,982	14
Kirkcaldy: Bennochy	530	56	62	–	20,270	4
Kirkcaldy: Pathhead	432	38	47	84,514	51,445	107
Kirkcaldy: St Bryce Kirk	553	31	37	100,842	60,794	53
Kirkcaldy: Templehall	225	17	19	44,107	26,455	10
Kirkcaldy: Torbain	244	31	22	41,494	24,196	130
Kirkcaldy: Viewforth	253	10	–	25,697	18,961	5
Thornton	177	7	–	17,333	12,834	5
Leslie: Trinity	231	20	22	34,596	21,231	5
Leven	628	39	38	108,552	62,539	10
Markinch	555	35	31	87,191	47,062	40
Methil	273	24	23	22,578	19,264	44
Methilhill and Denbeath	220	21	38	28,012	67,932	10
26. St Andrews						
Abdie and Dunbog	171	18	–	17,575	13,784	18
Newburgh	246	12	–	19,158	14,147	21
Anstruther	234	24	–	56,835	25,933	15
Cellardyke	279	22	49	49,971	24,416	8
Kilrenny	122	14	20	28,743	17,698	22
Auchtermuchty	297	–	21	42,652	19,832	10
Edenshead and Strathmiglo	181	12	–	–	16,577	6
Balmerino	135	11	16	–	16,138	9
Wormit	282	20	33	37,650	17,601	11
Boarhills and Dunino	161	9	–	17,424	13,241	1
St Andrews: Martyrs'	241	–	–	24,095	24,693	–
Cameron	97	12	13	19,620	11,283	21
St Andrews: St Leonard's	575	42	27	–	69,947	24
Carnbee	108	–	18	14,920	10,873	–
Pittenweem	293	16	20	25,888	21,752	16
Ceres, Kemback and Springfield	444	39	30	51,811	70,541	10
Crail	410	30	43	40,542	36,229	50
Kingsbarns	88	10	–	–	10,368	–
Creich, Flisk and Kilmany	115	13	17	18,425	13,615	11
Monimail	97	13	–	21,510	13,859	8
Cupar: Old and St Michael of Tarvit	625	48	28	–	66,692	181
Cupar: St John's and Dairsie United	816	51	42	73,918	55,147	38

Congregation	Com	Eld	G	In 10	M&M	–18
Elie Kilconquhar and Colinsburgh	541	47	67	96,061	62,714	10
Falkland	281	16	–	33,617	22,804	5
Freuchie	213	13	23	21,108	14,560	14
Howe of Fife	545	30	–	46,888	36,227	36
Largo and Newburn	277	23	–	–	24,167	15
Largo: St David's	180	21	46	35,421	17,611	18
Largoward	85	6	–	15,899	4,175	11
St Monans	287	14	41	–	36,198	70
Leuchars: St Athernase	474	29	37	58,849	39,478	16
Newport-on-Tay	389	–	–	–	44,874	–
St Andrews: Holy Trinity	486	41	48	–	59,970	45
St Andrews: Hope Park	765	69	40	100,528	73,448	10
Strathkinness	111	13	–	18,507	11,523	–
Tayport	437	36	26	41,046	31,802	20
27. Dunkeld and Meigle						
Aberfeldy	212	10	16	–	27,221	193
Amulree and Strathbraan	22	3	–	–	3,462	–
Dull and Weem	109	10	16	17,672	12,896	16
Alyth	743	34	38	64,801	47,787	27
Ardler, Kettins and Meigle	430	27	44	43,118	34,049	20
Bendochy	91	14	–	22,609	11,917	1
Coupar Angus: Abbey	313	19	14	37,404	27,243	7
Blair Atholl and Struan	158	19	15	18,788	20,372	7
Tenandry	57	11	–	20,700	12,000	5
Blairgowrie	949	50	46	105,715	57,827	33
Braes of Rannoch	30	6	–	12,280	8,236	–
Foss and Rannoch	103	13	18	17,927	15,294	9
Caputh and Clunie	170	17	19	19,771	18,818	–
Kinclaven	153	14	11	21,954	11,644	1
Dunkeld	405	31	20	94,504	59,441	50
Fortingall and Glenlyon	49	10	–	19,862	13,454	6
Kenmore and Lawers	90	8	23	28,515	20,704	24
Grantully, Logierait and Strathtay	145	11	13	31,208	24,772	12
Kirkmichael, Straloch and Glenshee	113	5	–	14,942	9,668	7
Rattray	390	17	28	33,439	21,444	5
Pitlochry	418	34	27	105,588	48,111	15
28. Perth						
Abernethy and Dron and Arngask	335	30	21	36,050	36,808	25
Almondbank Tibbermore	304	22	39	–	25,106	10
Methven and Logiealmond	310	18	2	–	19,525	–
Ardoch	179	15	28	23,192	22,596	24
Blackford	113	17	–	27,387	9,801	37
Auchterarder	609	27	49	89,689	55,014	70
Auchtergaven and Moneydie	505	22	37	41,944	27,591	113
Cargill Burrelton	295	12	20	29,197	27,675	1
Collace	122	8	20	18,964	10,576	9

Congregation	Com	Eld	G	In 10	M&M	–18
Cleish	246	19	19	51,670	35,590	12
Fossoway: St Serf's and Devonside	259	22	–	37,859	24,359	46
Comrie	454	27	26	94,530	40,152	–
Dundurn	63	8	–	14,624	9,376	–
Crieff	851	54	37	114,741	63,290	100
Dunbarney and Forgandenny	611	35	14	75,093	46,165	29
Errol	305	17	17	38,993	22,186	22
Kilspindie and Rait	68	7	–	10,500	7,276	–
Fowlis Wester, Madderty and Monzie	320	38	12	48,826	24,836	16
Gask	129	12	15	17,607	16,018	4
Kinross	684	40	41	97,103	48,028	212
Muthill	281	24	19	–	26,915	15
Trinity Gask and Kinkell	54	4	–	8,119	3,285	–
Orwell and Portmoak	483	39	26	55,859	49,013	7
Perth: Craigie and Moncreiffe	773	40	44	–	48,587	31
Perth: Kinnoull	462	38	26	–	42,416	45
Perth: Letham St Mark's	564	10	29	–	48,805	80
Perth: North	1,160	87	28	210,084	107,743	50
Perth: Riverside	69	–	–	–	–	65
Perth: St John's Kirk of Perth	543	34	–	88,324	61,319	–
Perth: St Leonard's-in-the-Fields	517	51	–	93,094	61,441	12
Perth: St Matthew's	812	55	32	110,325	61,761	41
Redgorton and Stanley	379	27	34	46,865	25,957	55
St Madoes and Kinfauns	338	29	29	48,423	21,862	56
St Martin's	179	5	15	9,536	6,257	2
Scone: New	479	38	53	70,492	37,637	7
Scone: Old	587	37	33	–	40,992	101
The Stewartry of Strathearn	454	32	–	64,908	45,928	18
29. Dundee						
Abernyte	90	10	–	17,486	9,195	11
Inchture and Kinnaird	212	29	–	33,877	18,664	12
Longforgan	202	20	26	–	22,317	22
Auchterhouse	151	15	18	21,433	16,091	15
Monikie and Newbigging and Murroes and Tealing	574	34	24	–	40,244	14
Dundee: Balgay	456	38	24	81,558	47,753	58
Dundee: Barnhill St Margaret's	801	58	64	155,981	70,454	40
Dundee: Broughty Ferry New Kirk	880	64	53	117,368	74,468	35
Dundee: Broughty Ferry St James'	265	13	27	–	30,543	59
Dundee: Broughty Ferry St Luke's and Queen Street	471	55	39	75,078	50,057	–
Dundee: Broughty Ferry St Stephen's and West	350	26	–	46,986	21,706	28
Dundee: Camperdown	168	16	8	28,347	18,764	8
Dundee: Chalmers Ardler	233	22	37	81,655	43,060	105
Dundee: Clepington and Fairmuir	382	24	–	41,980	34,915	46
Dundee: Craigiebank	231	12	–	34,057	30,238	73
Dundee: Douglas and Mid Craigie	170	15	19	41,342	21,047	60
Dundee: Downfield South	321	32	31	78,614	42,237	170
Dundee: Dundee (St Mary's)	592	56	31	93,240	57,624	15

Congregation	Com	Eld	G	In 10	M&M	–18
Dundee: Fintry Parish Church	112	9	–	53,014	27,823	28
Dundee: Lochee	625	38	33	71,481	46,222	213
Dundee: Logie and St John's Cross	338	18	29	–	70,987	60
Dundee: Mains	132	9	–	21,855	9,158	40
Dundee: Meadowside St Paul's	537	–	31	73,317	44,162	–
Dundee: Menzieshill	291	15	–	–	21,254	130
Dundee: St Andrew's	589	65	31	–	58,763	26
Dundee: St David's High Kirk	344	49	35	56,839	37,084	72
Dundee: Steeple	334	36	–	133,441	76,451	35
Dundee: Stobswell	494	43	–	71,464	46,506	4
Dundee: Strathmartine	347	25	27	68,887	37,589	5
Dundee: Trinity	563	40	34	48,134	36,002	66
Dundee: West	347	25	25	77,927	44,822	4
Dundee: Whitfield	40	8	–	13,415	3,924	130
Fowlis and Liff	151	14	15	–	26,696	33
Lundie and Muirhead	330	31	–	41,476	25,004	46
Invergowrie	427	50	56	64,468	38,867	94
Monifieth	1,240	76	61	148,669	86,590	72
30. Angus						
Aberlemno	194	9	–	13,893	11,643	25
Guthrie and Rescobie	224	11	14	20,146	14,189	11
Arbirlot	193	12	–	21,442	13,248	9
Carmyllie	123	12	9	–	17,137	–
Arbroath: Knox's	337	26	36	36,954	29,432	–
Arbroath: St Vigeans	588	44	–	68,313	44,633	4
Arbroath: Old and Abbey	585	40	34	101,677	63,441	60
Arbroath: St Andrew's	660	65	32	145,137	71,386	100
Arbroath: West Kirk	903	80	59	97,312	53,044	–
Barry	223	14	14	25,121	15,500	4
Carnoustie	418	26	24	69,439	44,724	40
Brechin: Cathedral	815	43	18	–	46,140	9
Brechin: Gardner Memorial	511	23	9	54,129	31,663	10
Farnell	113	11	–	7,006	9,022	1
Carnoustie: Panbride	740	33	–	55,981	39,038	53
Colliston	189	9	10	18,697	11,827	8
Friockheim Kinnell	210	17	21	17,916	11,800	8
Inverkeilor and Lunan	191	8	22	22,167	15,353	10
Dun and Hillside	451	52	39	57,656	33,497	47
Dunnichen, Letham and Kirkden	339	18	28	35,146	27,645	14
Eassie and Nevay	51	5	–	6,673	6,465	–
Newtyle	282	15	52	31,019	18,378	24
Edzell Lethnot Glenesk	363	21	31	37,187	34,297	2
Fern Careston Menmuir	104	8	–	11,423	14,414	10
Forfar: East and Old	1,133	43	41	78,588	54,187	45
Forfar: Lowson Memorial	940	40	24	86,725	44,648	140
Forfar: St Margaret's	829	29	25	–	47,566	105
Glamis, Inverarity and Kinnettles	396	22	–	35,152	35,450	51

Congregation	Com	Eld	G	In 10	M&M	–18
Inchbrayock	202	11	–	36,167	26,920	12
Montrose: Melville South	309	16	–	34,134	21,485	9
Kirriemuir: St Andrew's	355	28	43	45,671	39,740	12
Oathlaw Tannadice	176	9	–	19,379	17,134	15
Montrose: Old and St Andrew's	823	50	36	92,725	71,173	47
The Glens and Kirriemuir: Old	1,111	77	38	–	95,292	50
The Isla Parishes	259	22	21	29,763	26,623	20
31. Aberdeen						
Aberdeen: Bridge of Don Oldmachar	260	7	–	–	40,720	20
Aberdeen: Cove	79	5	–	18,384	3,564	29
Aberdeen: Craigiebuckler	809	76	55	–	66,607	140
Aberdeen: Ferryhill	427	57	31	86,278	50,214	32
Aberdeen: Garthdee	250	15	12	29,732	14,437	10
Aberdeen: Ruthrieston West	378	31	23	79,236	37,544	8
Aberdeen: Gilcomston South	382	27	–	169,640	96,699	59
Aberdeen: High Hilton	495	34	34	–	81,592	60
Aberdeen: Holburn West	469	49	27	110,003	58,549	38
Aberdeen: Mannofield	1,313	122	65	–	102,231	209
Aberdeen: Mastrick	331	18	19	38,974	30,561	–
Aberdeen: Middlefield	149	8	–	13,030	1,482	9
Aberdeen: Midstocket	654	58	45	111,095	71,535	26
Aberdeen: New Stockethill	–	–	–	28,454	–	–
Aberdeen: Northfield	272	12	15	23,972	15,314	60
Aberdeen: Queen Street	768	55	47	75,074	63,197	48
Aberdeen: Queen's Cross	468	52	29	139,096	89,414	90
Aberdeen: Rubislaw	614	81	50	146,445	79,373	105
Aberdeen: St Columba's Bridge of Don	339	23	–	–	55,703	40
Aberdeen: St George's Tillydrone	115	12	17	14,812	7,341	24
Aberdeen: St John's Church for Deaf People	96	3	–	–	–	–
Aberdeen: St Machar's Cathedral	621	51	–	–	65,999	15
Aberdeen: St Mark's	453	40	25	93,714	56,525	31
Aberdeen: St Mary's	459	43	14	62,849	33,878	108
Aberdeen: St Nicholas Kincorth, South of	389	28	27	63,963	36,742	40
Aberdeen: St Nicholas Uniting, Kirk of	429	44	17	–	–	5
Aberdeen: St Stephen's	196	20	12	–	39,490	47
Aberdeen: South Holburn	685	57	78	90,317	68,960	74
Aberdeen: Summerhill	145	21	–	26,760	18,098	5
Aberdeen: Torry St Fittick's	449	26	25	58,097	31,987	–
Aberdeen: Woodside	303	27	24	43,926	30,244	–
Bucksburn Stoneywood	499	–	22	–	30,772	–
Cults	825	68	42	146,576	79,650	33
Dyce	1,181	73	41	–	51,103	230
Kingswells	420	31	23	54,846	29,026	25
Newhills	493	43	62	111,197	67,606	20
Peterculter	641	49	–	96,364	55,234	158

Congregation	Com	Eld	G	In 10	M&M	–18
32. Kincardine and Deeside						
Aberluthnott	214	7	14	14,452	11,976	4
Laurencekirk	475	10	34	32,444	21,312	16
Aboyne and Dinnet	354	12	28	–	41,167	–
Cromar	246	14	–	–	16,176	–
Arbuthnott, Bervie and Kinneff	715	39	25	71,604	46,063	27
Banchory-Devenick and Maryculter/Cookney	212	29	10	36,887	36,708	8
Banchory-Ternan: East	603	45	26	112,989	59,601	35
Banchory-Ternan: West	588	36	32	115,544	65,432	56
Birse and Feughside	241	24	17	37,690	30,596	18
Braemar and Crathie	245	37	20	88,665	44,206	17
Drumoak-Durris	436	25	38	73,594	44,806	45
Glenmuick (Ballater)	315	24	23	–	31,124	–
Mearns Coastal	284	18	23	25,443	23,374	5
Mid Deeside	729	39	27	47,376	48,152	20
Newtonhill	371	12	16	–	21,401	105
Portlethen	474	17	–	59,695	46,160	167
Stonehaven: Dunnottar	793	28	30	–	45,242	18
Stonehaven: Fetteresso	865	37	42	146,492	95,699	132
Stonehaven: South	290	19	10	48,456	26,427	21
West Mearns	522	21	41	43,852	35,156	24
33. Gordon						
Barthol Chapel	100	11	7	–	2,972	23
Tarves	419	25	35	31,545	25,663	12
Belhelvie	385	37	21	–	44,769	59
Blairdaff and Chapel of Garioch	409	34	16	–	30,485	19
Cluny	203	11	7	26,412	14,174	12
Monymusk	122	6	–	16,860	9,867	15
Culsalmond and Rayne	191	8	–	11,398	8,243	25
Daviot	146	9	–	12,484	11,933	8
Cushnie and Tough	287	16	9	25,873	21,163	11
Echt	254	8	–	17,232	15,749	10
Midmar	153	7	–	13,673	10,309	5
Ellon	1,651	94	–	144,142	83,557	204
Fintray Kinellar Keithhall	219	20	11	–	23,791	10
Foveran	337	15	–	56,961	19,414	47
Howe Trinity	632	25	43	48,218	31,915	27
Huntly Cairnie Glass	706	15	23	42,331	30,745	11
Insch-Leslie-Premnay-Oyne	521	33	27	–	29,377	20
Inverurie: St Andrew's	1,091	38	39	–	63,565	230
Inverurie: West	734	59	33	–	49,702	56
Kemnay	602	46	–	60,011	37,761	132
Kintore	749	50	24	–	66,783	82
Meldrum and Bourtie	476	36	38	67,858	47,296	30
Methlick	355	24	24	48,621	30,812	40
New Machar	484	22	20	52,893	39,781	38
Noth	316	14	–	28,445	17,488	11

Congregation	Com	Eld	G	In 10	M&M	–18
Skene	1,421	97	52	133,192	80,946	175
Strathbogie Drumblade	569	44	31	72,549	38,266	44
Udny and Pitmedden	452	26	17	60,531	36,635	17
Upper Donside	413	21	–	37,495	29,000	55
34. Buchan						
Aberdour	134	10	12	10,750	5,951	12
Pitsligo	98	10	–	–	9,064	–
Sandhaven	74	7	–	24,342	3,485	50
Auchaber United	169	14	11	14,016	13,244	1
Auchterless	191	19	16	17,408	14,130	7
Banff	685	30	29	62,017	52,016	160
King Edward	157	17	15	–	13,949	9
Crimond	220	11	–	19,529	11,962	–
Lonmay	117	13	15	9,710	9,148	52
Cruden	439	26	26	46,173	33,917	21
Deer	790	35	19	47,671	40,682	12
Fordyce	445	23	40	52,450	44,113	17
Fraserburgh: Old	656	64	79	118,278	68,876	231
Fraserburgh: South	309	21	–	–	22,272	18
Inverallochy and Rathen: East	92	11	–	15,049	5,113	6
Fraserburgh: West	567	48	–	58,634	38,519	122
Rathen: West	105	10	–	11,680	3,813	7
Fyvie	355	24	29	36,794	27,290	–
Rothienorman	146	11	12	12,087	7,869	10
Gardenstown	68	9	33	56,402	30,932	59
Longside	531	29	–	58,471	35,709	107
Macduff	701	39	51	84,216	53,656	156
Marnoch	430	14	16	30,517	24,160	20
Maud and Savoch	224	14	21	–	15,584	10
New Deer: St Kane's	406	22	18	53,318	30,457	66
Monquhitter and New Byth	351	22	12	26,890	21,458	11
Turriff: St Andrew's	546	31	15	42,673	26,665	63
New Pitsligo	318	8	–	20,802	15,538	27
Strichen and Tyrie	556	20	26	41,790	29,488	51
Ordiquhill and Cornhill	145	10	12	8,998	8,017	15
Whitehills	297	23	30	32,272	22,100	3
Peterhead: Old	424	27	27	62,438	39,722	38
Peterhead: St Andrew's	513	35	34	52,263	32,694	18
Peterhead: Trinity	332	26	25	148,891	71,671	8
St Fergus	185	13	15	–	5,272	12
Turriff: St Ninian's and Forglen	875	36	40	76,241	49,089	100
35. Moray						
Aberlour	317	24	28	41,344	28,551	38
Alves and Burghead	155	17	37	25,245	15,109	13
Kinloss and Findhorn	94	13	9	18,654	12,331	–
Bellie	315	21	35	46,862	34,413	94

Congregation	Com	Eld	G	In 10	M&M	–18
Speymouth	205	9	12	21,200	11,225	18
Birnie and Pluscarden	288	29	41	–	22,329	10
Elgin: High	595	44	–	67,480	42,014	51
Buckie: North	439	34	61	63,050	35,506	18
Buckie: South and West	305	–	35	–	24,086	–
Enzie	91	–	14	–	9,580	–
Cullen and Deskford	364	27	27	41,530	30,059	–
Dallas	60	7	12	10,865	8,491	10
Forres: St Leonard's	242	14	42	52,198	37,456	25
Rafford	78	–	–	11,381	5,696	–
Duffus, Spynie and Hopeman	319	29	18	42,585	30,235	21
Dyke	139	12	12	23,298	11,611	21
Edinkillie	91	13	–	9,088	11,785	1
Elgin: St Giles' and St Columba's South	1,109	100	46	132,888	91,333	165
Findochty	49	8	10	14,202	14,006	2
Portknockie	77	9	25	24,337	14,205	37
Rathven	97	14	21	15,034	12,023	8
Forres: St Laurence	437	29	32	75,036	49,145	11
Keith: North, Newmill, Boharm and Rothiemay	632	54	23	55,651	66,633	13
Keith: St Rufus, Botriphnie and Grange	1,034	67	30	91,715	48,251	128
Knockando, Elchies and Archiestown	252	16	11	27,336	20,633	16
Rothes	318	16	18	39,694	20,707	18
Lossiemouth: St Gerardine's High	381	18	26	46,578	34,453	8
Lossiemouth: St James'	339	–	41	51,264	28,053	–
Mortlach and Cabrach	383	16	14	27,878	20,111	22
St Andrew's-Lhanbryd and Urquhart	479	47	26	–	41,313	40
36. Abernethy						
Abernethy	149	12	–	–	25,806	82
Cromdale and Advie	84	2	–	14,711	11,230	–
Alvie and Insh	66	7	–	30,685	17,000	28
Rothiemurchus and Aviemore	90	8	–	19,893	11,675	25
Boat of Garten, Duthil and Kincardine	157	18	30	24,508	21,594	10
Dulnain Bridge	33	5	–	11,372	9,580	–
Grantown-on-Spey	228	17	17	44,308	24,137	20
Kingussie	111	15	–	26,123	15,258	7
Laggan	40	7	–	14,972	7,607	5
Newtonmore	86	13	–	31,007	17,165	15
Tomintoul, Glenlivet and Inveraven	161	11	–	30,847	19,678	10
37. Inverness						
Ardersier	60	11	–	17,363	10,081	16
Petty	69	12	14	19,449	10,799	7
Auldearn and Dalmore	71	5	11	14,644	7,711	9
Nairn: St Ninian's	249	15	29	44,458	27,374	20
Cawdor	166	18	–	29,896	21,241	8
Croy and Dalcross	55	11	12	14,926	7,398	7
Culloden: The Barn	355	23	24	90,100	47,959	120

Congregation	Com	Eld	G	In 10	M&M	–18
Daviot and Dunlichity	63	11	9	17,978	10,541	8
Moy, Dalarossie and Tomatin	33	5	11	8,751	9,181	12
Dores and Boleskine	73	9	–	18,763	11,134	5
Inverness: Crown	604	54	48	133,107	78,319	193
Inverness: Dalneigh and Bona	272	26	24	86,792	56,787	95
Inverness: East	294	37	–	121,653	75,658	53
Inverness: Hilton	311	8	22	85,230	40,660	95
Inverness: Inshes	221	20	–	136,925	64,819	71
Inverness: Kinmylies	108	12	–	60,254	19,549	30
Inverness: Ness Bank	608	65	33	127,673	66,426	142
Inverness: Old High St Stephen's	492	57	–	119,080	71,419	48
Inverness: St Columba High	142	–	16	36,681	25,132	13
Inverness: Trinity	268	27	20	75,621	47,831	72
Kilmorack and Erchless	127	13	26	46,869	24,755	30
Kiltarlity	54	8	–	21,792	12,473	–
Kirkhill	80	10	15	21,355	6,899	14
Nairn: Old	807	52	28	114,163	66,381	62
Urquhart and Glenmoriston	131	7	–	54,127	34,167	40
38. Lochaber						
Acharacle	43	6	–	13,728	10,254	7
Ardnamurchan	18	5	–	7,711	3,371	10
Ardgour	53	7	14	12,529	7,696	3
Morvern	44	6	10	–	6,107	7
Strontian	30	5	–	10,964	3,281	12
Duror	43	7	12	14,643	5,491	10
Glencoe: St Munda's	56	7	12	12,622	8,669	6
Fort Augustus	70	8	11	22,881	14,644	5
Glengarry	31	3	10	11,164	8,146	10
Fort William: Duncansburgh MacIntosh	426	36	25	88,331	59,171	70
Kilmonivaig	77	8	12	21,782	18,072	12
Kilmallie	141	14	30	46,684	31,317	12
Kinlochleven	63	8	19	21,219	10,647	23
Nether Lochaber	50	10	–	15,346	9,952	14
North West Lochaber	108	11	19	37,257	21,639	25
39. Ross						
Alness	95	8	–	34,743	22,307	21
Avoch	27	6	–	14,042	9,653	12
Fortrose and Rosemarkie	105	14	–	40,901	27,027	8
Contin	58	12	–	18,086	17,540	34
Cromarty	49	7	–	16,251	2,648	15
Dingwall: Castle Street	138	22	28	56,957	27,139	15
Dingwall: St Clement's	240	28	29	56,926	33,556	30
Fearn Abbey and Nigg	96	11	–	29,034	20,291	2
Tarbat	59	9	–	13,175	10,401	2
Ferintosh	181	22	28	44,016	29,387	38
Fodderty and Strathpeffer	127	16	–	31,410	19,184	30

Congregation	Com	Eld	G	In 10	M&M	–18
Invergordon	162	12	–	55,447	29,495	28
Killearnan	138	18	–	37,665	25,870	18
Knockbain	57	9	–	18,877	14,556	–
Kilmuir and Logie Easter	71	9	23	22,917	18,377	12
Kiltearn	69	7	–	47,884	17,612	32
Lochbroom and Ullapool	43	6	10	34,645	19,049	7
Resolis and Urquhart	72	5	–	39,280	17,547	11
Rosskeen	133	12	18	57,275	30,688	70
Tain	132	12	19	58,807	39,452	20
Urray and Kilchrist	83	12	17	45,407	26,198	117
40. Sutherland						
Altnaharra and Farr	24	–	–	14,595	6,770	–
Assynt and Stoer	11	1	–	5,601	7,897	10
Clyne	75	9	–	23,772	12,627	5
Kildonan and Loth Helmsdale	32	6	–	5,339	4,619	7
Dornoch Cathedral	338	34	52	124,949	69,753	61
Durness and Kinlochbervie	19	2	–	–	12,143	4
Eddrachillis	12	2	–	14,235	8,002	2
Golspie	79	–	11	–	22,094	–
Kincardine Croick and Edderton	71	13	12	22,966	18,302	19
Creich	28	–	11	17,240	12,449	–
Rosehall	20	3	–	10,918	4,639	8
Lairg	54	–	17	–	14,300	–
Rogart	25	–	9	15,003	9,154	–
Melness and Tongue	44	–	–	17,509	11,905	9
41. Caithness						
Bower	35	7	12	11,602	5,714	9
Halkirk Westerdale	59	7	12	15,032	10,501	9
Watten	41	4	–	10,333	9,073	12
Canisbay	45	7	18	–	5,559	16
Dunnet	18	3	8	–	3,301	–
Keiss	28	1	10	9,962	3,557	3
Olrig	51	3	7	11,641	5,119	12
Thurso: St Peter's and St Andrew's	208	18	35	–	35,765	–
The North Coast Parish	55	14	30	22,911	12,189	8
The Parish of Latheron	71	14	13	20,993	18,856	26
Thurso: West	230	29	33	46,159	47,034	12
Wick: Pulteneytown and Thrumster	242	17	26	51,087	30,313	46
Wick: St Fergus	272	33	36	67,785	51,031	14
42. Lochcarron – Skye						
Applecross, Lochcarron and Torridon	88	5	18	41,863	23,478	37
Bracadale and Duirinish	71	8	14	28,871	17,431	15
Gairloch and Dundonnell	83	5	–	64,966	44,186	25
Glenelg and Kintail	54	7	–	30,767	20,199	34
Kilmuir and Stenscholl	75	9	–	38,665	27,414	30

Congregation	Com	Eld	G	In 10	M&M	-18
Lochalsh	82	8	20	43,674	26,629	25
Portree	82	7	–	58,902	32,826	16
Snizort	58	5	–	41,344	23,989	8
Strath and Sleat	191	14	12	99,995	59,193	65
43. Uist						
Barra	39	5	–	18,754	6,125	41
Benbecula	68	11	8	37,624	22,074	53
Berneray and Lochmaddy	56	4	14	34,998	21,936	11
Carinish	71	7	14	65,952	28,135	10
Kilmuir and Paible	27	4	–	31,071	21,959	20
Manish-Scarista	42	4	–	43,478	21,295	22
South Uist	57	12	–	22,292	18,624	22
Tarbert	139	15	–	82,651	48,979	63
44. Lewis						
Barvas	88	7	–	68,250	43,597	–
Carloway	46	5	–	34,122	16,182	35
Cross Ness	75	8	–	56,557	27,059	44
Kinloch	47	10	–	34,863	18,480	26
Knock	49	2	–	40,862	27,446	1
Lochs-Crossbost	26	5	–	28,194	11,872	18
Lochs-in-Bernera	27	3	–	19,409	11,550	15
Uig	34	5	–	29,317	15,838	15
Stornoway: High	258	16	–	139,154	74,741	85
Stornoway: Martin's Memorial	230	12	12	128,305	38,902	90
Stornoway: St Columba	116	17	42	104,136	45,916	93
45. Orkney						
Birsay, Harray and Sandwick	334	28	34	–	27,335	12
East Mainland	248	20	22	31,727	21,793	14
Eday	10	3	–	–	1,064	–
Stronsay: Moncur Memorial	82	8	–	12,726	8,018	17
Evie	35	–	–	5,067	7,019	–
Firth	109	8	13	25,810	14,242	40
Rendall	45	4	–	7,643	6,402	20
Flotta	24	7	–	3,305	1,594	–
Hoy and Walls	57	11	13	7,272	1,991	–
Kirkwall: East	417	35	40	70,871	42,962	41
Kirkwall: St Magnus Cathedral	601	53	22	53,415	40,958	–
North Ronaldsay	12	2	–	844	1,187	–
Sanday	77	10	12	7,682	6,469	–
Orphir	113	10	17	12,613	9,958	10
Stenness	77	5	–	6,031	7,933	–
Papa Westray	9	5	–	3,963	2,467	4
Westray	78	18	24	–	12,490	35
Rousay	20	2	–	2,011	3,469	–
Shapinsay	54	8	–	6,591	3,717	–

Congregation	Com	Eld	G	In 10	M&M	–18
South Ronaldsay and Burray	147	11	11	17,249	12,872	16
Stromness	342	25	24	–	34,941	10
46. Shetland						
Burra Isle	38	6	19	8,385	3,360	13
Tingwall	152	18	10	28,102	20,435	–
Delting	85	8	–	16,217	9,967	20
Northmavine	70	9	–	–	6,324	10
Dunrossness and St Ninian's	62	16	–	17,305	11,550	58
Sandwick, Cunningsburgh and Quarff	88	10	20	22,812	16,240	47
Fetlar	17	5	–	1,269	872	–
Unst	118	9	18	19,779	11,545	–
Yell	112	13	16	12,318	9,092	–
Lerwick and Bressay	433	33	8	67,895	52,858	60
Nesting and Lunnasting	35	5	16	5,785	6,863	–
Whalsay and Skerries	207	17	20	27,191	15,492	20
Sandsting and Aithsting	44	9	–	7,658	2,884	15
Walls and Sandness	37	10	–	8,221	3,280	10
47. England						
Corby: St Andrew's	285	17	29	49,858	26,947	9
Corby: St Ninian's	236	18	–	39,724	28,886	3
Guernsey: St Andrew's in the Grange	207	23	–	54,662	35,417	28
Jersey: St Columba's	127	17	–	67,545	36,340	21
Liverpool: St Andrew's	35	4	–	22,093	9,886	8
London: Crown Court	255	29	7	–	51,306	15
London: St Columba's	1,018	50	–	–	145,117	128
Newcastle: St Andrew's	97	20	–	–	5,200	28

INDEX OF MINISTERS

NOTE: Ministers who are members of a Presbytery are designated 'A' if holding a parochial appointment in that Presbytery, or 'B' if otherwise qualifying for membership.

'A-1, A-2' etc. indicate the numerical order of congregations in the Presbyteries of Edinburgh, Glasgow and Hamilton.

Also included are:

(1) Ministers who have resigned their seat in Presbytery (List 6-H)
(2) Ministers who hold a Practising Certificate (List 6-I)
(3) Ministers serving overseas (List 6-K)
(4) Auxiliary Ministers (List 6-A)
(5) Ministers ordained for sixty years and upwards (List 6-Q)
(6) Ministers who have died since the publication of the last *Year Book* (List 6-R)

NB *For a list of the Diaconate, see List 6-G.*

INDEX OF PARISHES AND PLACES

NOTE: Numbers on the right of the column refer to the Presbytery in which the district lies. Names in brackets are given for ease of identification. They may refer to the name of the parish, which may be different from that of the district, or they distinguish places with the same name, or they indicate the first named charge in a union.

INDEX OF DISCONTINUED PARISH AND CONGREGATIONAL NAMES

The following index updates and corrects the 'Index of Discontinued Parish and Congregational Names' printed in the previous edition of the *Year Book*. As before, it lists the parishes of the Church of Scotland and the congregations of the United Presbyterian Church (and its constituent denominations), the Free Church (1843–1900) and the United Free Church (1900–29) whose names have completely disappeared, largely as a consequence of union.

It should be noted, as has been stressed in previous years, that this index is *not* intended to be 'a comprehensive guide to readjustment in the Church of Scotland'; that would require a considerably larger number of pages. Despite the annual reiteration of this statement, the editor's attention continues to be drawn to the omission from the list of this or that now-vanished congregation whose name does not in fact fall within the criteria for inclusion given below.

The specific purpose of this index is to assist those who are trying to identify the present-day successor of some former parish or congregation whose name is now wholly out of use and which can therefore no longer be easily traced. Where the former name has not disappeared completely, and the whereabouts of the former parish or congregation may therefore be easily established by reference to the name of some existing parish, the former name has not been included in this index. The following examples will illustrate some of the criteria used to determine whether a name should be included or not:

- Where all the former congregations in a town have been united into one, as in the case of Melrose or Selkirk, the names of these former congregations have not been included; but in the case of towns with more than one congregation, such as Galashiels or Hawick, the names of the various constituent congregations are listed.
- The same principle applies in the case of discrete areas of cities. For example, as Dundee: Lochee and Glasgow: Dennistoun New are now the only congregations in Lochee and Dennistoun respectively, there is no need to list Dundee: Lochee St Ninian's, Glasgow: Dennistoun South and any other congregations which had Lochee or Dennistoun in their names.
- Where a prefix such as North, Old, Little, Mid or the like has been lost but the substantive part of the name has been retained, the former name has not been included: it is assumed that someone searching for Little Dalton or Mid Yell will have no difficulty in connecting these with Dalton or Yell.
- Where the present name of a united congregation includes the names of some or all of its constituent parts, these former names do not appear in the list: thus, neither Glasgow: Anderston nor Glasgow: Kelvingrove appears, since both names are easily traceable to Glasgow: Anderston Kelvingrove.

Two other criteria for inclusion or exclusion may also be mentioned:

- Some parishes and congregations have disappeared, and their names have been lost, as a consequence of suppression, dissolution or secession. The names of rural parishes in this category have been included, together with the names of their Presbyteries to assist with identification, but those in towns and cities have not been included, as there will clearly be no difficulty in establishing the general location of the parish or congregation in question.
- Since 1929, a small number of rural parishes have adopted a new name (for example, Whitehills, formerly Boyndie). The former names of these parishes have been included, but it would have been too unwieldy to include either the vast numbers of such changes of name in towns and cities, especially those which occurred at the time of the 1900 and 1929 unions, or the very many older names of pre-Reformation parishes which were abandoned in earlier centuries (however fascinating a list of such long-vanished names as Fothmuref, Kinbathock and Toskertoun might have been).

In this index, the following abbreviations have been used:

C of S	Church of Scotland
FC	Free Church
R	Relief Church
RP	Reformed Presbyterian Church
UF	United Free Church
UP	United Presbyterian Church
US	United Secession Church

Name no longer used	Present name of parish
Abbey St Bathan's	Langton and Lammermuir Kirk
Abbotrule	charge suppressed: Presbytery of Jedburgh
Aberargie	charge dissolved: Presbytery of Perth
Aberchirder	Marnoch
Aberdalgie	The Stewartry of Strathearn
Aberdeen: Beechgrove	Aberdeen: Midstocket
Aberdeen: Belmont Street	Aberdeen: St Mark's
Aberdeen: Carden Place	Aberdeen: Queen's Cross
Aberdeen: Causewayend	Aberdeen: St Stephen's
Aberdeen: East	Aberdeen: St Mark's
Aberdeen: Gallowgate	Aberdeen: St Mary's
Aberdeen: Greyfriars	Aberdeen: Queen Street
Aberdeen: Hilton	Aberdeen: Woodside
Aberdeen: Holburn Central	Aberdeen: South Holburn
Aberdeen: John Knox Gerrard Street	Aberdeen: Queen Street
Aberdeen: John Knox's (Mounthooly)	Aberdeen: Queen Street
Aberdeen: King Street	Aberdeen: Queen Street
Aberdeen: Melville	Aberdeen: Queen's Cross
Aberdeen: Nelson Street	Aberdeen: Queen Street
Aberdeen: North	Aberdeen: Queen Street
Aberdeen: North of St Andrew	Aberdeen: Queen Street
Aberdeen: Pittodrie	Aberdeen: St Mary's
Aberdeen: Powis	Aberdeen: St Stephen's
Aberdeen: Ruthrieston (C of S)	Aberdeen: South Holburn
Aberdeen: Ruthrieston (FC)	Aberdeen: Ruthrieston West
Aberdeen: South (C of S)	Aberdeen: South of St Nicholas, Kincorth
Aberdeen: South (FC)	Aberdeen: St Mark's
Aberdeen: St Andrew's	Aberdeen: Queen Street
Aberdeen: St Columba's	Aberdeen: High Hilton
Aberdeen: St Mary's	Aberdeen: St Machar's Cathedral
Aberdeen: St Ninian's	Aberdeen: Midstocket
Aberdeen: Trinity (C of S)	Aberdeen: Kirk of St Nicholas Uniting
Aberdeen: Trinity (FC)	Aberdeen: St Mark's
Aberuthven	The Stewartry of Strathearn
Abington	Glencaple
Addiewell	Breich Valley
Afton	New Cumnock
Airdrie: West	Airdrie: New Wellwynd
Airlie	The Isla Parishes
Aldbar	Aberlemno
Aldcambus	Dunglass
Alford	Howe Trinity
Alloa: Chalmers	Alloa: Ludgate
Alloa: Melville	Alloa: Ludgate
Alloa: North	Alloa: Ludgate
Alloa: St Andrew's	Alloa: Ludgate
Alloa: West	Alloa: Ludgate
Altries	charge dissolved: Presbytery of Kincardine and Deeside
Altyre	Rafford
Alvah	Banff
Ancrum	Ale and Teviot United
Annan: Erskine	Annan: St Andrew's
Annan: Greenknowe	Annan: St Andrew's
Anwoth	Gatehouse of Fleet
Arbroath: East	Arbroath: St Andrew's
Arbroath: Erskine	Arbroath: West Kirk
Arbroath: High Street	Arbroath: St Andrew's
Arbroath: Hopemount	Arbroath: St Andrew's

Name no longer used	Present name of parish
Arbroath: Ladyloan	Arbroath: West Kirk
Arbroath: Princes Street	Arbroath: West Kirk
Arbroath: St Columba's	Arbroath: West Kirk
Arbroath: St Margaret's	Arbroath: West Kirk
Arbroath: St Ninian's	Arbroath: St Andrew's
Arbroath: St Paul's	Arbroath: St Andrew's
Ardallie	Deer
Ardclach	charge dissolved: Presbytery of Inverness
Ardwell	Stoneykirk
Arisaig	North West Lochaber
Ascog	The United Church of Bute
Auchindoir	Upper Donside
Auchmithie	Arbroath: St Vigean's
Auldcathie	Dalmeny
Aultbea	Gairloch and Dundonnell
Ayr: Cathcart	Ayr: St Columba
Ayr: Darlington New	Ayr: Auld Kirk of Ayr
Ayr: Darlington Place	Ayr: Auld Kirk of Ayr
Ayr: Lochside	Ayr: St Quivox
Ayr: Martyrs'	Ayr: Auld Kirk of Ayr
Ayr: Sandgate	Ayr: St Columba
Ayr: St John's	Ayr: Auld Kirk of Ayr
Ayr: Trinity	Ayr: St Columba
Ayr: Wallacetown North	Ayr: Newton Wallacetown
Ayr: Wallacetown South	Ayr: Auld Kirk of Ayr
Back	charge dissolved: Presbytery of Lewis
Badcall	Eddrachillis
Balbeggie	Collace
Balfour	charge dissolved: Presbytery of Dundee
Balgedie	Orwell and Portmoak
Baliasta	Unst
Ballachulish	Nether Lochaber
Ballater	Glenmuick
Ballingry	Lochgelly and Benarty: St Serf's
Balmacolm	Howe of Fife
Balmullo	charge dissolved: Presbytery of St Andrews
Balnacross	Tarff and Twynholm
Baltasound	Unst
Banchory-Ternan: North	Banchory-Ternan: West
Banchory-Ternan: South	Banchory-Ternan: West
Bandry	Luss
Bara	Garvald and Morham
Bargrennan	Penninghame
Barnweil	Tarbolton
Barrhead: Westbourne	Barrhead: Arthurlie
Barrock	Dunnet
Bearsden: North	Bearsden: Cross
Bearsden: South	Bearsden: Cross
Bedrule	Ruberslaw
Beith: Hamilfield	Beith: Trinity
Beith: Head Street	Beith: Trinity
Beith: Mitchell Street	Beith: Trinity
Belkirk	Liddesdale
Benholm	Mearns Coastal
Benvie	Fowlis and Liff
Berriedale	The Parish of Latheron
Binny	Linlithgow: St Michael's
Blackburn	Fintray Kinellar Keithhall

Name no longer used	Present name of parish
Blackhill	Longside
Blairlogie	congregation seceded: Presbytery of Stirling
Blanefield	Strathblane
Blantyre: Anderson	Blantyre: St Andrew's
Blantyre: Burleigh Memorial	Blantyre: St Andrew's
Blantyre: Stonefield	Blantyre: St Andrew's
Blyth Bridge	Kirkurd and Newlands
Boddam	Peterhead: Trinity
Bonhill: North	Alexandria
Borthwick	Tyne Valley Parish
Bothwell: Park	Uddingston: Viewpark
Bourtreebush	Newtonhill
Bow of Fife	Monimail
Bowmore	Kilarrow
Boyndie	Whitehills
Brachollie	Petty
Braco	Ardoch
Braehead	Forth
Brechin: East	Brechin: Gardner Memorial
Brechin: Maison Dieu	Brechin: Cathedral
Brechin: St Columba's	Brechin: Gardner Memorial
Brechin: West	Brechin: Gardner Memorial
Breich	Breich Valley
Bridge of Teith	Kilmadock
Brora	Clyne
Bruan	The Parish of Latheron
Buccleuch	Ettrick and Yarrow
Burnhead	Penpont, Keir and Tynron
Cairnryan	charge dissolved: Presbytery of Wigtown and Stranraer
Cambuslang: Old	Cambuslang
Cambuslang: Rosebank	Cambuslang
Cambuslang: St Andrew's	Cambuslang
Cambuslang: St Paul's	Cambuslang
Cambuslang: Trinity	Cambuslang
Cambuslang: West	Cambuslang
Cambusmichael	St Martin's
Campbeltown: Longrow	Campbeltown: Lorne and Lowland
Campsail	Rosneath: St Modan's
Canna	North West Lochaber
Carbuddo	Guthrie and Rescobie
Cardenden	Auchterderran: St Fothad's
Carlisle	The Border Kirk
Carmichael	Cairngryffe
Carnoch	Contin
Carnousie	Turriff: St Ninian's and Forglen
Carnoustie: St Stephen's	Carnoustie
Carrbridge	Boat of Garten, Duthil and Kincardine
Carruthers	Hoddom, Kirtle-Eaglesfield and Middlebie
Castle Kennedy	Inch
Castleton	Liddesdale
Caterline	Arbuthnott, Bervie and Kinneff
Chapelknowe	congregation seceded: Presbytery of Annandale and Eskdale
Clatt	Noth
Clayshant	Stoneykirk
Climpy	charge dissolved: Presbytery of Lanark
Clola	Deer
Clousta	Sandsting and Aithsting
Clova	The Glens and Kirriemuir: Old

Name no longer used	Present name of parish
Clydebank: Bank Street	Clydebank: St Cuthbert's
Clydebank: Boquhanran	Clydebank: Kilbowie St Andrew's
Clydebank: Hamilton Memorial	Clydebank: St Cuthbert's
Clydebank: Linnvale	Clydebank: St Cuthbert's
Clydebank: St James'	Clydebank: Abbotsford
Clydebank: Union	Clydebank: Kilbowie St Andrew's
Clydebank: West	Clydebank: Abbotsford
Coatbridge: Clifton	Coatbridge: New St Andrew's
Coatbridge: Cliftonhill	Coatbridge: New St Andrew's
Coatbridge: Coatdyke	Coatbridge: New St Andrew's
Coatbridge: Coats	Coatbridge: New St Andrew's
Coatbridge: Dunbeth	Coatbridge: New St Andrew's
Coatbridge: Gartsherrie	Coatbridge: New St Andrew's
Coatbridge: Garturk	Coatbridge: Calder
Coatbridge: Maxwell	Coatbridge: New St Andrew's
Coatbridge: Trinity	Coatbridge: New St Andrew's
Coatbridge: Whifflet	Coatbridge: Calder
Cobbinshaw	charge dissolved: Presbytery of West Lothian
Cockburnspath	Dunglass
Coigach	charge dissolved: Presbytery of Lochcarron – Skye
Coldstone	Cromar
Collessie	Howe of Fife
Corgarff	Upper Donside
Cortachy	The Glens and Kirriemuir: Old
Coull	Cromar
Covington	Cairngryffe
Cowdenbeath: Cairns	Cowdenbeath: Trinity
Cowdenbeath: Guthrie Memorial	Beath and Cowdenbeath: North
Cowdenbeath: West	Cowdenbeath: Trinity
Craggan	Tomintoul, Glenlivet and Inveraven
Craig	Inchbrayock
Craigdam	Tarves
Craigend	Perth: Craigie and Moncreiffe
Crailing	Ale and Teviot United
Cranshaws	Langton and Lammermuir Kirk
Cranstoun	Tyne Valley Parish
Crawford	Glencaple
Crawfordjohn	Glencaple
Cray	Kirkmichael, Straloch and Glenshee
Creetown	Kirkmabreck
Crichton	Tyne Valley Parish
Crofthead	Fauldhouse St Andrew's
Crombie	Culross and Torryburn
Crossgates	Cowdenbeath: Trinity
Cruggleton	Sorbie
Cuikston	Farnell
Culbin	Dyke
Cullicudden	Resolis and Urquhart
Cults	Howe of Fife
Cumbernauld: Baird	Cumbernauld: Old
Cumbernauld: Bridgend	Cumbernauld: Old
Cumbernauld: St Andrew's	Cumbernauld: Old
Dalgarno	Closeburn
Dalguise	Dunkeld
Daliburgh	South Uist
Dalkeith: Buccleuch Street	Dalkeith: St Nicholas Buccleuch
Dalkeith: West (C of S)	Dalkeith: St Nicholas Buccleuch
Dalkeith: West (UP)	Dalkeith: St John's and King's Park

Name no longer used	Present name of parish
Dundee: Tay Square	Dundee: Meadowside St Paul's
Dundee: Victoria Street	Dundee: Stobswell
Dundee: Wallacetown	Dundee: Trinity
Dundee: Wishart Memorial	Dundee: Steeple
Dundurcas	charge suppressed: Presbytery of Moray
Duneaton	Glencaple
Dunfermline: Chalmers Street	Dunfermline: St Andrew's Erskine
Dunfermline: Maygate	Dunfermline: Gillespie Memorial
Dunfermline: Queen Anne Street	Dunfermline: St Andrew's Erskine
Dungree	Kirkpatrick Juxta
Duninald	Inchbrayock
Dunlappie	Brechin: Cathedral
Dunning	The Stewartry of Strathearn
Dunoon: Gaelic	Dunoon: St John's
Dunoon: Old	Dunoon: The High Kirk
Dunoon: St Cuthbert's	Dunoon: The High Kirk
Dunrod	Kirkcudbright
Dunsyre	Black Mount
Dupplin	The Stewartry of Strathearn
Ecclefechan	Hoddom, Kirtle-Eaglesfield and Middlebie
Ecclesjohn	Dun and Hillside
Ecclesmachan	Strathbrock
Ecclesmoghriodan	Abernethy and Dron and Arngask
Eckford	Ale and Teviot United
Edgerston	Jedburgh: Old and Trinity
Edinburgh: Abbey	Edinburgh: Greenside
Edinburgh: Abbeyhill	Edinburgh: Holyrood Abbey
Edinburgh: Arthur Street	Edinburgh: Kirk o' Field
Edinburgh: Barony	Edinburgh: Greenside
Edinburgh: Belford	Edinburgh: Palmerston Place
Edinburgh: Braid	Edinburgh: Morningside
Edinburgh: Bruntsfield	Edinburgh: Barclay Viewforth
Edinburgh: Buccleuch	Edinburgh: Kirk o' Field
Edinburgh: Cairns Memorial	Edinburgh: Gorgie Dalry
Edinburgh: Candlish	Edinburgh: Polwarth
Edinburgh: Canongate (FC, UP)	Edinburgh: Holy Trinity
Edinburgh: Chalmers	Edinburgh: Barclay Viewforth
Edinburgh: Charteris Memorial	Edinburgh: Kirk o' Field
Edinburgh: Cluny	Edinburgh: Morningside
Edinburgh: College	Edinburgh: Muirhouse St Andrew's
Edinburgh: College Street	Edinburgh: Muirhouse St Andrew's
Edinburgh: Cowgate (FC)	Edinburgh: Muirhouse St Andrew's
Edinburgh: Cowgate (R)	Edinburgh: Barclay Viewforth
Edinburgh: Cowgate (US)	Edinburgh: Mayfield Salisbury
Edinburgh: Davidson	Edinburgh: Stockbridge
Edinburgh: Dean (FC)	Edinburgh: Palmerston Place
Edinburgh: Dean Street	Edinburgh: Stockbridge
Edinburgh: Fountainhall Road	Edinburgh: Mayfield Salisbury
Edinburgh: Grange (C of S)	Edinburgh: Marchmont St Giles
Edinburgh: Grange (FC)	Edinburgh: St Catherine's Argyle
Edinburgh: Guthrie Memorial	Edinburgh: Greenside
Edinburgh: Haymarket	Edinburgh: Gorgie Dalry
Edinburgh: Henderson (C of S)	Edinburgh: Craigmillar Park
Edinburgh: Henderson (UP)	Edinburgh: Richmond Craigmillar
Edinburgh: Hillside	Edinburgh: Greenside
Edinburgh: Holyrood	Edinburgh: Holyrood Abbey
Edinburgh: Hope Park	Edinburgh: Mayfield Salisbury
Edinburgh: Hopetoun	Edinburgh: Greenside

Name no longer used	Present name of parish
Elgin: South Street	Elgin: St Giles and St Columba's South
Ellem	Langton and Lammermuir Kirk
Elsrickle	Black Mount
Eshaness	Northmavine
Essie	Noth
Essil	Speymouth
Ethie	Inverkeilor and Lunan
Ettiltoun	Liddesdale
Ewes Durris	Langholm Eskdalemuir Ewes and Westerkirk
Fala	Tyne Valley Parish
Falkirk: Graham's Road	Falkirk: Grahamston United
Farnua	Kirkhill
Fergushill	Kilwinning: Mansefield Trinity
Ferryden	Inchbrayock
Fetterangus	Deer
Fettercairn	West Mearns
Fetternear	Blairdaff and Chapel of Garioch
Finzean	Birse and Feughside
Fochabers	Bellie
Forbes	Howe Trinity
Ford	Tyne Valley Parish
Fordoun	West Mearns
Forfar: South	Forfar: St Margaret's
Forfar: St James'	Forfar: St Margaret's
Forfar: West	Forfar: St Margaret's
Forgan	Newport-on-Tay
Forgue	Auchaber United
Forres: Castlehill	Forres: St Leonard's
Forres: High	Forres: St Leonard's
Forteviot	The Stewartry of Strathearn
Forvie	Ellon
Foula	Walls and Sandness
Galashiels: East	Galashiels: Trinity
Galashiels: Ladhope	Galashiels: Trinity
Galashiels: South	Galashiels: Trinity
Galashiels: St Aidan's	Galashiels: Trinity
Galashiels: St Andrew's	Galashiels: Trinity
Galashiels: St Columba's	Galashiels: Trinity
Galashiels: St Cuthbert's	Galashiels: Trinity
Galashiels: St Mark's	Galashiels: Trinity
Galashiels: St Ninian's	Galashiels: Trinity
Galtway	Kirkcudbright
Gamrie	charge dissolved: Presbytery of Buchan
Garmouth	Speymouth
Gartly	Noth
Garvell	Kirkmichael, Tinwald and Torthorwald
Garvock	Mearns Coastal
Gauldry	Balmerino
Gelston	Buittle and Kelton
Giffnock: Orchard Park	Giffnock: The Park
Girthon	Gatehouse of Fleet
Girvan: Chalmers	Girvan: North (Old and St Andrew's)
Girvan: Trinity	Girvan: North (Old and St Andrew's)
Glasgow: Abbotsford	Glasgow: Gorbals
Glasgow: Albert Drive	Glasgow: Pollokshields
Glasgow: Auldfield	Glasgow: Pollokshaws
Glasgow: Baillieston Old	Glasgow: Baillieston St Andrew's
Glasgow: Baillieston Rhinsdale	Glasgow: Baillieston St Andrew's

Name no longer used	Present name of parish
Glasgow: Hall Memorial	Rutherglen: Old
Glasgow: Hamilton Crescent	Glasgow: Partick South
Glasgow: Highlanders' Memorial	Glasgow: Knightswood St Margaret's
Glasgow: Hyndland (UF)	Glasgow: St John's Renfield
Glasgow: John Knox's	Glasgow: Gorbals
Glasgow: Johnston	Glasgow: Springburn
Glasgow: Jordanvale	Glasgow: Whiteinch
Glasgow: Kelvinhaugh	Glasgow: Anderston Kelvingrove
Glasgow: Kelvinside Botanic Gardens	Glasgow: Kelvinside Hillhead
Glasgow: Kelvinside Old	Glasgow: Kelvin Stevenson Memorial
Glasgow: Kingston	Glasgow: Carnwadric
Glasgow: Lancefield	Glasgow: Anderston Kelvingrove
Glasgow: Langside Avenue	Glasgow: Shawlands
Glasgow: Langside Hill	Glasgow: Clincarthill
Glasgow: Langside Old	Glasgow: Langside
Glasgow: Laurieston (C of S)	Glasgow: Gorbals
Glasgow: Laurieston (FC)	Glasgow: Carnwadric
Glasgow: London Road	Glasgow: Bridgeton St Francis in the East
Glasgow: Lyon Street	Glasgow: Renfield St Stephen's
Glasgow: Macgregor Memorial	Glasgow: Govan and Linthouse
Glasgow: Macmillan	Glasgow: Gallowgate
Glasgow: Milton	Glasgow: Renfield St Stephen's
Glasgow: Mount Florida	Glasgow: Clincarthill
Glasgow: Netherton St Matthew's	Glasgow: Knightswood St Margaret's
Glasgow: New Cathcart	Glasgow: Cathcart Trinity
Glasgow: Newhall	Glasgow: Bridgeton St Francis in the East
Glasgow: Newton Place	Glasgow: Partick South
Glasgow: Nithsdale	Glasgow: Queen's Park
Glasgow: North Kelvinside	Glasgow: Ruchill Kelvinside
Glasgow: Old Partick	Glasgow: Partick Trinity
Glasgow: Paisley Road	Glasgow: Kinning Park
Glasgow: Partick Anderson	Glasgow: Partick South
Glasgow: Partick East	Glasgow: Partick Trinity
Glasgow: Partick High	Glasgow: Partick South
Glasgow: Phoenix Park	Glasgow: Springburn
Glasgow: Plantation	Glasgow: Kinning Park
Glasgow: Pollok St Aidan's	Glasgow: St James' Pollok
Glasgow: Pollok Street	Glasgow: Kinning Park
Glasgow: Polmadie	Glasgow: Govanhill Trinity
Glasgow: Queen's Cross	Glasgow: Ruchill Kelvinside
Glasgow: Renfield (C of S)	Glasgow: Renfield St Stephen's
Glasgow: Renfield (FC)	Glasgow: St John's Renfield
Glasgow: Renfield Street	Glasgow: Renfield St Stephen's
Glasgow: Renwick	Glasgow: Gorbals
Glasgow: Robertson Memorial	Glasgow: The Martyrs'
Glasgow: Rockcliffe	Rutherglen: Old
Glasgow: Rockvilla	Glasgow: Possilpark
Glasgow: Rose Street	Glasgow: Langside
Glasgow: Rutherford	Glasgow: Dennistoun New
Glasgow: Shamrock Street	Glasgow: Renfield St Stephen's
Glasgow: Shawholm	Glasgow: Pollokshaws
Glasgow: Shawlands Cross	Glasgow: Shawlands
Glasgow: Shawlands Old	Glasgow: Shawlands
Glasgow: Sighthill	Glasgow: Springburn
Glasgow: Somerville	Glasgow: Springburn
Glasgow: Springbank	Glasgow: Lansdowne
Glasgow: St Andrew's (C of S)	Glasgow: Gallowgate
Glasgow: St Andrew's (FC)	Glasgow: St Andrew's East

Name no longer used	Present name of parish
Glasgow: St Clement's	Glasgow: Bridgeton St Francis in the East
Glasgow: St Columba Gaelic	Glasgow: Govan and Linthouse
Glasgow: St Cuthbert's	Glasgow: Ruchill Kelvinside
Glasgow: St Enoch's (C of S)	Glasgow: St Enoch's Hogganfield
Glasgow: St Enoch's (FC)	Glasgow: Anderston Kelvingrove
Glasgow: St George's (C of S)	Glasgow: St George's Tron
Glasgow: St George's (FC)	Glasgow: Anderston Kelvingrove
Glasgow: St George's Road	Glasgow: Renfield St Stephen's
Glasgow: St James' (C of S)	Glasgow: St James' Pollok
Glasgow: St James' (FC)	Glasgow: Gallowgate
Glasgow: St John's (C of S)	Glasgow: Gallowgate
Glasgow: St John's (FC)	Glasgow: St John's Renfield
Glasgow: St Kenneth's	Glasgow: Govan and Linthouse
Glasgow: St Kiaran's	Glasgow: Govan and Linthouse
Glasgow: St Luke's	Glasgow: Gallowgate
Glasgow: St Mark's	Glasgow: Anderston Kelvingrove
Glasgow: St Mary's Partick	Glasgow: Partick South
Glasgow: St Matthew's (C of S)	Glasgow: Renfield St Stephen's
Glasgow: St Matthew's (FC)	Glasgow: Knightswood St Margaret's
Glasgow: St Ninian's	Glasgow: Gorbals
Glasgow: St Peter's	Glasgow: Anderston Kelvingrove
Glasgow: St Thomas'	Glasgow: Gallowgate
Glasgow: Steven Memorial	Glasgow: Ibrox
Glasgow: Strathbungo	Glasgow: Queen's Park
Glasgow: Summerfield	Rutherglen: Old
Glasgow: Summertown	Glasgow: Govan and Linthouse
Glasgow: Sydney Place	Glasgow: Dennistoun New
Glasgow: The Park	Giffnock: The Park
Glasgow: Titwood	Glasgow: Pollokshields
Glasgow: Tradeston	Glasgow: Gorbals
Glasgow: Trinity	Glasgow: Gallowgate
Glasgow: Trinity Duke Street	Glasgow: Dennistoun New
Glasgow: Tron St Anne's	Glasgow: St George's Tron
Glasgow: Union	Glasgow: Carnwadric
Glasgow: Victoria	Glasgow: Queen's Park
Glasgow: Wellfield	Glasgow: Springburn
Glasgow: Wellpark	Glasgow: Dennistoun New
Glasgow: West Scotland Street	Glasgow: Kinning Park
Glasgow: White Memorial	Glasgow: Kinning Park
Glasgow: Whitehill	Glasgow: Dennistoun New
Glasgow: Whitevale (FC)	Glasgow: Gallowgate
Glasgow: Whitevale (UP)	Glasgow: Dennistoun New
Glasgow: Wilton	Glasgow: Kelvin Stevenson Memorial
Glasgow: Woodlands	Glasgow: Wellington
Glasgow: Woodside	Glasgow: Lansdowne
Glasgow: Wynd (C of S)	Glasgow: Gallowgate
Glasgow: Wynd (FC)	Glasgow: Gorbals
Glasgow: Young Street	Glasgow: Dennistoun New
Glen Convinth	Kiltarlity
Glen Ussie	Fodderty and Strathpeffer
Glenapp	Ballantrae
Glenbervie	West Mearns
Glenbuchat	Upper Donside
Glenbuck	Muirkirk
Glencaple	Caerlaverock
Glendoick	St Madoes and Kinfauns
Glenfarg	Abernethy and Dron and Arngask
Glengairn	Glenmuick

Name no longer used	Present name of parish
Glengarnock	Kilbirnie: Auld Kirk
Glenisla	The Isla Parishes
Glenluce	Old Luce
Glenmoriston (FC)	Fort Augustus
Glenprosen	The Glens and Kirriemuir: Old
Glenrinnes	Mortlach and Cabrach
Glenshiel	Glenelg and Kintail
Glentanar	Aboyne and Dinnet
Gogar	Edinburgh: Corstorphine Old
Gordon	Monquhitter and New Byth
Graemsay	Stromness
Grangemouth: Dundas	Grangemouth: Abbotsgrange
Grangemouth: Grange	Grangemouth: Zetland
Grangemouth: Kerse	Grangemouth: Abbotsgrange
Grangemouth: Old	Grangemouth: Zetland
Greenloaning	Ardoch
Greenock: Ardgowan	Greenock: Lyle Community Kirk
Greenock: Augustine	Greenock: East End
Greenock: Cartsburn	Greenock: East End
Greenock: Cartsdyke	Greenock: East End
Greenock: Crawfordsburn	Greenock: East End
Greenock: Finnart	Greenock: Lyle Community Kirk
Greenock: Gaelic	Greenock: Westburn
Greenock: Greenbank	Greenock: Westburn
Greenock: Martyrs'	Greenock: Westburn
Greenock: Middle	Greenock: Westburn
Greenock: Mount Park	Greenock: Mount Kirk
Greenock: Mount Pleasant	Greenock: Mount Kirk
Greenock: North (C of S)	Greenock: Lyle Community Kirk
Greenock: North (FC)	Greenock: Westburn
Greenock: Old West	Greenock: Lyle Community Kirk
Greenock: Sir Michael Street	Greenock: Lyle Community Kirk
Greenock: South	Greenock: Mount Kirk
Greenock: South Park	Greenock: Mount Kirk
Greenock: St Andrew's	Greenock: Lyle Community Kirk
Greenock: St Columba's Gaelic	Greenock: Lyle Community Kirk
Greenock: St George's	Greenock: Westburn
Greenock: St Luke's	Greenock: Westburn
Greenock: St Mark's	Greenock: Westburn
Greenock: St Paul's	Greenock: Lyle Community Kirk
Greenock: St Thomas'	Greenock: Westburn
Greenock: The Old Kirk	Greenock: Westburn
Greenock: The Union Church	Greenock: Lyle Community Kirk
Greenock: Trinity	Greenock: Lyle Community Kirk
Greenock: Union Street	Greenock: Lyle Community Kirk
Greenock: West	Greenock: Westburn
Gress	Stornoway: St Columba
Guardbridge	Leuchars: St Athernase
Haddington: St John's	Haddington: West
Hamilton: Auchingramont North	Hamilton: North
Hamilton: Avon Street	Hamilton: St Andrew's
Hamilton: Brandon	Hamilton: St Andrew's
Hamilton: Saffronhall Assoc. Anti-Burgher	Hamilton: North
Hardgate	Urr
Hassendean	Ruberslaw
Hawick: East Bank	Hawick: Trinity
Hawick: Orrock	Hawick: St Mary's and Old
Hawick: St Andrew's	Hawick: Trinity

Name no longer used	Present name of parish
Kilchousland	Campbeltown: Highland
Kilcolmkill (Kintyre)	Southend
Kilcolmkill (Lochaber)	Morvern
Kildrummy	Upper Donside
Kilkerran	Campbeltown: Highland
Kilkivan	Campbeltown: Highland
Killintag	Morvern
Kilmacolm: St James'	Kilmacolm: St Columba
Kilmahew	Cardross
Kilmahog	Callander
Kilmarnock: Grange	Kilmarnock: New Laigh Kirk
Kilmarnock: High (C of S)	Kilmarnock: Old High Kirk
Kilmarnock: High (FC)	Kilmarnock: New Laigh Kirk
Kilmarnock: Howard	Kilmarnock: St Andrew's and St Marnock's
Kilmarnock: King Street	Kilmarnock: St Andrew's and St Marnock's
Kilmarnock: Portland Road	Kilmarnock: St Andrew's and St Marnock's
Kilmarrow	Killean and Kilchenzie
Kilmichael (Inverness)	Urquhart and Glenmoriston
Kilmichael (Kintyre)	Campbeltown: Highland
Kilmoir	Brechin: Cathedral
Kilmore	Urquhart and Glenmoriston
Kilmoveonaig	Blair Atholl and Struan
Kilmun: St Andrew's	Strone and Ardentinny
Kilpheder	South Uist
Kilry	The Isla Parishes
Kilwinning: Abbey	Kilwinning: Old
Kilwinning: Erskine	Kilwinning: Old
Kinairney	Midmar
Kincardine O'Neil	Mid Deeside
Kincraig	Alvie and Insh
Kinedar	Lossiemouth: St Gerardine's High
Kingarth	The United Church of Bute
Kingoldrum	The Isla Parishes
Kininmonth	charge dissolved: Presbytery of Buchan
Kinkell	Fintray Kinellar Keithhall
Kinloch	Caputh and Clunie
Kinlochewe	Applecross, Lochcarron and Torridon
Kinlochluichart	Contin
Kinlochrannoch	Foss and Rannoch
Kinneil	Bo'ness: Old
Kinnettas	Fodderty and Strathpeffer
Kinnoir	Huntly Cairnie Glass
Kinrossie	Collace
Kirkandrews	Borgue
Kirkapol	Tiree
Kirkcaldy: Abbotsrood	Kirkcaldy: Bennochy
Kirkcaldy: Bethelfield	Kirkcaldy: Linktown
Kirkcaldy: Dunnikier	Kirkcaldy: Bennochy
Kirkcaldy: Gallatown	Kirkcaldy: Viewforth
Kirkcaldy: Invertiel	Kirkcaldy: Linktown
Kirkcaldy: Old	Kirkcaldy: St Bryce Kirk
Kirkcaldy: Raith	Kirkcaldy: Abbotshall
Kirkcaldy: Sinclairtown	Kirkcaldy: Viewforth
Kirkcaldy: St Andrew's	Kirkcaldy: Bennochy
Kirkcaldy: St Brycedale	Kirkcaldy: St Bryce Kirk
Kirkcaldy: St John's	Kirkcaldy: Bennochy
Kirkcaldy: Victoria Road	Kirkcaldy: Bennochy
Kirkchrist	Tarff and Twynholm

Name no longer used	Present name of parish
Paisley: South	Paisley: St Luke's
Paisley: St Andrew's	Paisley: Stow Brae Kirk
Paisley: St George's	Paisley: Stow Brae Kirk
Paisley: St John's	Paisley: Oakshaw Trinity
Paisley: Thread Street	Paisley: Martyrs' Sandyford
Papa Stour	Walls and Sandness
Park	Kinloch
Pathhead	Ormiston
Pathstruie	The Stewartry of Strathearn
Pearston	Dreghorn and Springside
Peebles: West	Peebles: St Andrew's Leckie
Pennersaughs	Hoddom, Kirtle-Eaglesfield and Middlebie
Pentland	Lasswade and Rosewell
Persie	Kirkmichael, Straloch and Glenshee
Perth: Bridgend	Perth: St Matthew's
Perth: East	Perth: St Leonard's-in-the-Fields
Perth: Knox's	Perth: St Leonard's-in-the-Fields
Perth: Middle	Perth: St Matthew's
Perth: St Andrew's	Perth: Riverside
Perth: St Columba's	Perth: North
Perth: St Leonard's	Perth: North
Perth: St Stephen's	Perth: Riverside
Perth: West	Perth: St Matthew's
Perth: Wilson	Perth: St Matthew's
Perth: York Place	Perth: St Leonard's-in-the-Fields
Peterhead: Charlotte Street	Peterhead: Trinity
Peterhead: East	Peterhead: St Andrew's
Peterhead: South	Peterhead: St Andrew's
Peterhead: St Peter's	Peterhead: Trinity
Peterhead: West Associate	Peterhead: Trinity
Pettinain	Cairngryffe
Pitcairn (C of S)	Redgorton and Stanley
Pitcairn (UF)	Almondbank Tibbermore
Pitlessie	Howe of Fife
Pitroddie	St Madoes and Kinfauns
Plockton	Lochalsh
Polmont South	Brightons
Polwarth	Langton and Lammermuir Kirk
Poolewe	Gairloch and Dundonnell
Port Bannatyne	The United Church of Bute
Port Ellen	Kildalton and Oa
Port Glasgow: Clune Park	Port Glasgow: St Andrew's
Port Glasgow: Newark	Port Glasgow: St Andrew's
Port Glasgow: Old	Port Glasgow: St Andrew's
Port Glasgow: Princes Street	Port Glasgow: St Andrew's
Port Glasgow: West	Port Glasgow: St Andrew's
Port Sonachan	Glenorchy and Inishail
Port William	Mochrum
Portobello: Regent Street	Edinburgh: Portobello Old
Portobello: Windsor Place	Edinburgh: Portobello Old
Portsoy	Fordyce
Prestonkirk	Traprain
Prinlaws	Leslie: Trinity
Quarrier's Mount Zion	Kilmacolm: St Columba
Raasay	Portree
Rathillet	Creich, Flisk and Kilmany
Rathmuriel	Noth
Reay	The North Coast Parish

Name no longer used	Present name of parish
Soutra	Tyne Valley Parish
Spittal (Caithness)	Halkirk Westerdale
Spittal (Duns)	charge dissolved: Presbytery of Duns
Springfield	Gretna, Half Morton and Kirkpatrick Fleming
St Andrew's (Orkney)	East Mainland
St Cyrus	Mearns Coastal
St Ola	Kirkwall: St Magnus Cathedral
Stenton	Traprain
Stewartfield	Deer
Stewarton: Cairns	Stewarton: St Columba's
Stewarton: Laigh	Stewarton: St Columba's
Stichill	Kelso Country Churches
Stirling: Craigs	Stirling: St Columba's
Stirling: North (FC)	Stirling: St Columba's
Stobhill	Gorebridge
Stockbridge	Dunglass
Stonehaven: North	Stonehaven: South
Stoneyburn	Breich Valley
Stornoway: James Street	Stornoway: Martin's Memorial
Stracathro	Brechin: Cathedral
Strachan	Birse and Feughside
Stranraer: Bellevilla	Stranraer: St Ninian's
Stranraer: Bridge Street	Stranraer: St Ninian's
Stranraer: Ivy Place	Stranraer: Town Kirk
Stranraer: Old	Stranraer: Town Kirk
Stranraer: St Andrew's	Stranraer: Town Kirk
Stranraer: St Margaret's	Stranraer: High
Stranraer: St Mark's	Stranraer: Town Kirk
Strathaven: West	Strathaven: Avendale Old and Drumclog
Strathconon	Contin
Strathdeveron	Mortlach and Cabrach
Strathdon	Upper Donside
Stratherrick	Dores and Boleskine
Strathgarve	Contin
Strathglass	Kilmorack and Erchless
Strathmartine (C of S)	Dundee: Mains
Strathy	The North Coast Parish
Strowan	Comrie
Suddie	Knockbain
Tarfside	Edzell Lethnot Glenesk
Tarland	Cromar
Tarvit	Cupar: Old and St Michael of Tarvit
Temple	Gorebridge
Thankerton	Cairngryffe
The Bass	North Berwick: St Andrew Blackadder
Tighnabruaich	Kyles
Tongland	Tarff and Twynholm
Torphins	Mid Deeside
Torrance	East Kilbride: Old
Towie	Upper Donside
Trailflat	Kirkmichael, Tinwald and Torthorwald
Trailtrow	Cummertrees, Mouswald and Ruthwell
Trefontaine	Langton and Lammermuir Kirk
Trossachs	Callander
Trumisgarry	Berneray and Lochmaddy
Tullibole	Fossoway: St Serf's and Devonside
Tullich	Glenmuick
Tullichetil	Comrie

Name no longer used	Present name of parish
Tullynessle	Howe Trinity
Tummel	Foss and Rannoch
Tushielaw	Ettrick and Yarrow
Uddingston: Aitkenhead	Uddingston: Viewpark
Uddingston: Chalmers	Uddingston: Old
Uddingston: Trinity	Uddingston: Old
Uig	Snizort
Uphall: North	Strathbrock
Uyeasound	Unst
Walston	Black Mount
Wandel	Glencaple
Wanlockhead	Lowther
Waterbeck	charge dissolved: Presbytery of Annandale and Eskdale
Waternish	Bracadale and Duirinish
Wauchope	Langholm Eskdalemuir Ewes and Westerkirk
Waulkmill	Insch-Leslie-Premnay-Oyne
Weisdale	Tingwall
Wheelkirk	Liddesdale
Whitehill	New Pitsligo
Whiteness	Tingwall
Whittingehame	Traprain
Wick: Bridge Street	Wick: St Fergus
Wick: Central	Wick: Pulteneytown and Thrumster
Wick: Martyrs'	Wick: Pulteneytown and Thrumster
Wick: Old	Wick: St Fergus
Wick: St Andrew's	Wick: Pulteneytown and Thrumster
Wilkieston	Edinburgh: Ratho
Wilsontown	Forth
Wishaw: Chalmers	Wishaw: South Wishaw
Wishaw: Thornlie	Wishaw: South Wishaw
Wiston	Glencaple
Wolfhill	Cargill Burrelton
Wolflee	Hobkirk and Southdean
Woomet	Newton
Ythan Wells	Auchaber United

INDEX OF SUBJECTS

INDEX OF ADVERTISERS